ADOLESCENCE

Robert S. Feldman
University of Massachusetts at Amherst

PEARSON

Prentice
Hall

Upper Saddle River, New Jersey 07458

Library of Congress Cataloging-in-Publication Data

Feldman, Robert S. (Robert Stephen)
  Adolescence / Robert S. Feldman.
    p. cm.
  ISBN-13: 978-0-13-175061-6
  ISBN-10: 0-13-175061-5
  1. Adolescent psychology.   2. Adolescence.   I. Title.
  BF724.F4185 2008
  155.5—dc22
          2007034427

To My Family

Executive Editor: *Jeff Marshall*
Editorial Director: *Leah Jewell*
Editorial Assistant: *Aaron Talwar*
Sr. Marketing Manager: *Jeanette Koskinas*
Marketing Assistant: *Laura Kennedy*
Assoc. Managing Editor: *Maureen Richardson*
Production Liaison: *Fran Russello*
Permissions Coordinator: *Michael Farmer*
Senior Operations Supervisor: *Sherry Lewis*
Senior Art Director: *Nancy Wells*
Interior Design: *Kenny Beck*

Cover Design: *Kenny Beck*
Cover Illustration/Photo: *Shutterstock*
Director, Image Resource Center: *Melinda Patelli*
Manager, Rights and Permissions: *Zina Arabia*
Manager, Visual Research: *Beth Brenzel*
Manager, Cover Visual Research & Permissions: *Karen Sanatar*
Image Permission Coordinator: *Kathy Gavilanes*
Photo Researcher: *Toni Michaels*
Composition/Full-Service Project Management: *John Shannon/Pine Tree Composition*
Printer/Binder: *Quebecor/World Color*

Credits and acknowledgments borrowed from other sources and reproduced, with permission, in this textbook appear on appropriate page within text or on pages 523–524.

Microsoft® and Windows® are registered trademarks of the Microsoft Corporation in the U.S.A. and other countries. Screen shots and icons reprinted with permission from the Microsoft Corporation. This book is not sponsored or endorsed by or affiliated with the Microsoft Corporation.

Pearson Prentice Hall™ is a trademark of Pearson Education, Inc.
Pearson® is a registered trademark of Pearson plc
Prentice Hall® is a registered trademark of Pearson Education, Inc.

Pearson Education LTD., London
Pearson Education Singapore, Pte. Ltd
Pearson Education, Canada, Ltd
Pearson Education—Japan
Pearson Education Australia PTY, Limited

Pearson Education North Asia Ltd
Pearson Educación de Mexico, S.A. de C.V.
Pearson Education Malaysia, Pte. Ltd
Pearson Education, Upper Saddle River, New Jersey

10 9 8 7 6 5 4 3
ISBN (10): 0-13-175061-5
ISBN (13): 978-0-13-175061-6

Brief Contents

Contents

Preface

When the typical adult hears hear the word "adolescence," a variety of images come to mind. They might include a parent and teenager engaged in an angry interchange ... a teenage boy dressed in black, with piercing and tattoos scattered across his body ... two teenagers engaged in a rushed and furtive sexual encounter ... a group of boys smoking marijuana in the front seat of a car.

Probably no other period of the lifespan so easily evokes such strong—and often negative—images. Most adults view adolescence as a period of great stress, extraordinary peer pressure, and engagement in risky and unthinking behaviors.

Yet the reality of adolescence is quite different. As we will see throughout this book, adolescence is a time of growth, of change, and more-often-than-not socially positive behavior—despite the negative stereotypes of the period. It is a time when teenagers often find their first romance, think harder and more deeply about issues than they ever did (or could) earlier in their lives, and experience a new-found freedom that is exhilarating to experience and to observe. It is a time of rapid and exciting changes, changes that affect individuals for the rest of their lives.

This book is designed to capture the physical, cognitive, social, and personality development of this period as individuals move from childhood into adulthood. It is meant to provide an accurate, broad, and comprehensive introduction to the field of adolescent development. Not only does it cover basic theories and research findings, but it places them in the context of how the information can be applied to readers' lives.

The book is intended to excite readers about the field of adolescence, to draw them into its way of looking at the world, and to shape their understanding of the significant developmental issues that characterize this period. By presenting the useful, practical information that will help readers make life decisions about relationships, education, and careers—the very stuff of adolescence—the book is intended to keep enthusiasm about the discipline alive long after students' formal introduction to the field has ended.

The Goals of the Book

Adolescence seeks to accomplish the following primary goals:

- First and foremost, the book is designed to provide a broad, balanced overview of the field of adolescence. It introduces readers to the theories, research, and applications that constitute the discipline, examining both the traditional areas of the field as well as more recent innovations.

The text pays particular attention to the applications developed by adolescent specialists. While not slighting theoretical material, the text emphasizes what we know about development across adolescence, rather than focusing on unanswered questions. It demonstrates how this knowledge may be applied to real-world problems.

In short, the book highlights the interrelationships among theory, research, and application, accentuating the scope and diversity of the field. It also illustrates how adolescent scientists use theory, research, and applications to help solve significant social problems.

- The second major goal of the text is to explicitly tie adolescent development to students' lives. Findings from the study of adolescent development have a significant degree of relevance to students, and this text illustrates how these findings can be applied in a meaningful, practical sense. Applications are presented in a contemporaneous framework, including current news items, timely world events, and contemporary adolescent issues that draw readers into the field. Numerous descriptive scenarios and vignettes reflect everyday situations in people's lives, explaining how they relate to the field. In addition, numerous first-person quotes are used, primarily derived from adolescents' blogs posted on the Web.

- The third goal of this book is to highlight both the commonalities and diversity of today's multicultural society. The book incorporates material relevant to diversity throughout every chapter, as well as having a full chapter devoted to culture and diversity. In addition, every chapter has at least one "Adolescent Diversity" section. These features explicitly consider how cultural factors relevant to development both unite and diversify our contemporary, global society.

- The text's fourth goal is to increase students' critical thinking, not only about specific adolescent developmental issues but about the scientific method general. The objective is to make readers think analytically about the nature of evidence and to evaluate information that they will encounter in their future lives more effectively.

- Finally, the fifth goal of the text is one that underlies the other four: making the field of adolescence engaging, accessible, and interesting to students. Because all of us are involved in our own developmental paths—and many, if not most, of the readers will be adolescents themselves—readers are tied in very personal ways to the content areas covered by the book. *Adolescence,* then, is meant to engage and nurture this interest, planting a seed that will develop and flourish.

Content and Features

In order to accomplish these goals, *Adolescence* is divided into five broad parts: Introduction, Key Developmental Transitions, Relationships, Society, and Challenges of Adolescence.

Each chapter with a part contains a number of specific features. They include:

- **Chapter-opening prologues.** Each chapter begins with a short vignette describing an individual or situation that is relevant to the basic issues being addressed in the chapter. The Prologue is designed to bring home the relevance of the subject matter to readers' lives, as well as beginning to frame the key issues of the chapter. For example, the chapter on physical development begins with the story of an adolescent who is cut from an athletic team, the chapter on culture talks about students involved in an interfaith exchange program, and the chapter on work and leisure presents two students involved in multitasking, online activities.

- **Think About This** sections. These opening sections will orient readers to the topics to be covered, bridging the opening prologue with the remainder of the chapter. They also provide orienting questions that serve as advance organizers for the material.

- **Adolescent Voices.** Each chapter contains several first-person anonymous quotes that will be used to begin major sections. These quotes (kept anonymous to protect the privacy of the authors) are derived from actual adolescents' blogs on the Web and add a real-world flavor to the material.

- **Transitions.** Each chapter includes a box presenting contemporary research and applications on issues involving significant issues or turning-points relating to adolescence. Topics include an examination of school transitions, the consequences of self-esteem, making informed sexual choices, and bullying. In order to facilitate critical thinking, every box ends with questions designed to provoke analytic and critical thinking.

- **Adolescent Diversity** sections. Every chapter has at least one "Adolescent Diversity" section, in addition to other material on diversity incorporated into the chapter. These sections highlight issues relevant to the multicultural society in which we live. They cover a broad swath of diversity, including gender, race, ethnicity, and sexual orientation.

- **Becoming an Informed Consumer of Adolescent Science.** Every chapter contains information on specific uses that can be derived from research conducted by adolescent investigators. Specific topics include increasing humane behavior in adolescents, promoting emotional competence, and avoiding unwanted pregnancy.

- **Career Choices.** Chapters include a box discussing a career working with adolescents that is relevant to the chapter content. For example, the chapter on schooling presents an interview with a special educator, and the chapter on adolescent problems discusses the work of a drug abuse counselor.

- **Review & Apply sections.** Three short recaps of the chapters' main points are interspersed throughout each chapter. These questions are followed by questions designed to provoke critical thinking.

- **Running Glossary.** Key terms are defined in the margins of the page on which the term is presented, as well as in an end-of-book Glossary.

- **End-of-chapter material.** Each chapter includes a numbered summary and a list of key terms and concepts. This material is designed to help students study effectively and to retain the information in the chapter.

- **Epilogue.** Each chapter ends with an epilogue that incorporates critical thinking questions relating to the prologue at the opening of the chapter. The end-of-chapter thought-provoking questions in the epilogue provide a way of tying the chapter together and illustrate how the concepts addressed in the chapter apply to the real-world situation described in the prologue.

All of these features are designed to support the goal of writing a book that not only provides a contemporary, thorough, and accurate guide to adolescence, but is thought-provoking and engaging. My hope is that after students have read this introduction to the theories, research, and applications of the study of adolescence, they will be as excited about the field as I am.

Ancillaries

Adolescence, first edition, is accompanied by a superb set of teaching and learning materials.

Print and Media Supplements for the Instructor

- **Test Item File with Test Gen Software.** Authored by Tim Killian, University of Arkansas, this diligently prepared set of test questions includes a balance of definitional, applied, and conceptual questions designed to better measure student comprehension of important concepts. Together with the compatible TestGen software, the Test Item File helps to ensure that all text topics are covered, and take student learning to the next level. The Test Item File is available as a print item and the TestGen as a CD ROM software package. Both are also availbale for download on the Prentice Hall Instructor's Resource Center via *www.prenhall.com.*

- **Instructor's Manual.** The IRM includes learning objectives, key terms and concepts, self-contained lecture suggestions and classroom activities for each chapter, supplemental reading suggestions, and a list of multi-media resources. The IRM is available for download on the Prentice Hall Instructor's Resource Center via *www.prenhall.com.*

- **PowerPoint Lecture slides.** The PPT slides feature prominent figures and illustrations from the text as well as lecture slides to facilitate classroom instruction. The PPTs are available for download on the Prentice Hall Instructor's Resource Center via *www.prenhall.com.*

- **Virtual Child Software.** The Virtual Child is an interactive, web-based simulation that allows students to act as a parent and raise their own "child." By making decisions about specific scenarios, students can raise their children from birth to age 17 and learn first-hand how their own decisions and other parenting-actions affect their child over time. At each age, student are given feedback about the various milestones their child has attained; key stages of the child's development will include personalized feedback. As in real life, certain "unplanned" events may occur randomly. Access codes are needed for the Virtual Child, and can be obtained by purchase via the Prentice Hall or Pearson website. Existing users can login to the site at http://www.prenhall.com/virtualchild.

Video Resources for Instructors

Prentice Hall is proud to present you with the following video packages, available exclusively to qualified adopters of *Adolescence.*

- **Prentice Hall Lecture Launcher Video for Developmental Psychology.** Adopters can receive this new video that includes short clips covering all major topics in introductory psychology. The videos have been carefully selected from the Films for Humanities and Sciences library and edited to provide brief and compelling video content for enhancing your lectures. Contact your local representative for a full list of video clips on this tape.

Print and Media Supplements for the Student

- **MyAdolescenceKit.** This online study tool allows students to review each chapter's material, take practice tests, research topics for course projects, and interact with The Virtual Child. MyAdolescenceKit for the text includes chapter overview, summary, online flashcards, Research Navigator, self tests with multiple choice, true/false, and essay questions, and the Virtual Child program.

- **CouseSmart WebBook.** This new Pearson Choice offers students an online subscription to Adolescence, First Edition online at a 50% savings. With the CourseSmart WebBook, students can search the text, make notes online, print out reading assignments that incorporate lecture notes, and bookmark important passages. Ask your Pearson representative for details, or visit www.coursesmart.com.

- **Observations in Developmental Psychology.** These videos bring to life key concepts discussed in the narrative of the text. Students get to view each video twice: once with an introduction to the concept being illustrated and again with commentary describing what is taking place at crucial points in the video. Whether your course has an observation component or not, these videos provide your students the opportunity to see children in action. The videos can be accessed by purchasing the supplementary CD-ROM on mypearsonstore.com.

Supplementary Texts

Contact your representative to package any of these supplementary texts with *Adolescence,* First Edition.

- Current Directions in Developmental Psychology. Readings from the Association for Psychological Science (APS). This new and exciting reader includes over 20 articles that have been carefully selected for the undergraduate audience, and taken from the very accessible Current Directions in Psychological Science Journal. These timely, cutting-edge articles allow intructors to bring their students real-world perspective about today's most current and pressing issues in psychology. Discounted when packaged with this text for college adoptions.

- **Twenty Studies That Revolutionized Child Psychology by Wallace E. Dixon, Jr.** Presenting the seminal research studies that have shaped modern developmental psychology, this brief text provides an overview of the environment that gave rise to each study, its experimental design, its findings, and its impact on current thinking in the discipline.

- **Human Development in Multicultural Context: A Book of Readings.** Written by Michele A. Paludi, this compilation of readings highlights cultural influences in developmental psychology.

- **The Psychology Major: Careers and Strategies for Success.** Written by Eric Landrum (Idaho State University), Stephen Davis (Emporia State University), and Terri Landrum (Idaho State University), this 160-page paperback provides valuable information on career options available to psychology majors, tips for improving academic performance, and a guide to the APA style of research reporting.

Acknowledgments

I am grateful to the following reviewers who provided a wealth of comments, constructive criticism, and encouragement.

Many others deserve a great deal of thanks. I am indebted to the many people who provided me with a superb education, first at Wesleyan University and later at the University of Wisconsin. Specifically, Karl Scheibe played a pivotal role in my undergraduate education, and the late Vernon Allen acted as mentor and guide through my graduate years. It was in graduate school that I learned about development, being exposed to such experts as Ross Parke, John Balling, Joel Levin, Herb Klausmeier, and many others. My education continued when I became a professor. I am especially grateful to my colleagues at the University of Massachusetts, who make the university such a wonderful place in which to teach and do research.

Several people played central roles in the development of this book. Edward Murphy brought a keen intelligence and editorial eye to the manuscript, and John Bickford provided superb research support. Most of all, John Graiff was essential in juggling and coordinating the multiple aspects of writing a book, and I am very grateful for the substantial role he played.

I am also grateful to the superb Prentice Hall team that was instrumental in the inception and development of this book. Jeff Marshall, Executive Editor, provided good ideas, encouragement, and a great sense of publishing insight. Thanks also go to Jennifer Gilliland, who provided the impetus for this project, and to Leah Jewell, who stood behind it. On the production end of things, John Shannon, project manager, managed the production of the book, and Aaron Talwar, photo editor, helped in giving the book its beautiful look. Finally, I'd like to thank marketing manager Jeanette Koskinas, on whose skills I'm counting. I would like to than the reviewers of this edition: Jerome Dusek, Syracuse University; Katina Oaks, Wingate University; Dr. Olive Poliks, Aurora University; Dawn Lewis, Prince George's Community College; Jack A. Palmer, University of Louisiana at Monroe; Linda M. Symanski, Kean University; Dale Fryxell, Chaminade University; Christian Mueller, The University of Memphis; Gwendolyn Scott, University of Houston-Downtown; Stephen Burgess, SWOSU; Lee Shumow, Northern Illinois University; Sharon E. Paulson, Ball State University; Rob Weisskirch, California State University; Maureen Smith, San Jose State University; Nancy Darling, Oberlin College; Lonna M. Murphy, Iowa State University; Shirley Theriot, University of Texas at Arlington; James Sullivan, Florida State University; Susan McClure, Westmoreland County Community College; Kathy Frost, University of Texas; Allison D. Boroda, Texas Tech University; Patti Tolar, University of Houston; Wendy Post, University of Missouri-St. Louis; Bethann Bierer, Metropolitan State College of Denver; Melanie A. Reap, Winona State University; Christopher Daddis, The Ohio State University; W. Jared DuPree, Kansas State University; Mark Durm, Athens State University; Janet Gebelt, Westfield State College; Christine Ohannessian, University of Delaware; Laura Duvall, Heartland Community College; Sherry Ginn, Wingate University; Mellisa Wines, Mohawk Valley Community College; Leilani Brown, University of Hawai'i at Manoa; Valerie A. O'Krentk, California State University-Fullerton; Christopher Barry, University of Southern Mississippi; Jerilyn Thorman, Oklahoma State University; Jennifer Leszczynski, Eastern Connecticut State University; and Diane Finley, Prince George's Community College. I also wish to acknowledge the members of my family, who play such a pivotal role in my life. My brother, Michael, my sisters-in-law and brother-in-law, my nieces and nephews, all make up an important part of my life. In addition, I am always indebted to the older generation of my family, who led the way in a manner I can only hope to emulate. I will always be obligated to Harry Brochstein, Ethel Radler, and the late Mary Vorwerk. Most of all, the list is headed by my father, the late Saul Feldman, and my mother, Leah Brochstein.

In the end, it is my immediate family who deserve the greatest thanks. My terrific children and grandchild (Jonathan, his wife, Leigh, their wonderful son Alex, and Joshua and Sarah), not only are nice, smart, and good-looking, but my pride and joy. And ultimately my wife, Katherine Vorwerk, provides the love and grounding that makes everything worthwhile. I thank them, with all my love.

ROBERT S. FELDMAN
University of Massachusetts at Amherst

About the Author

Robert S. Feldman is Professor of Psychology and Associate Dean of the College of Social and Behavioral Sciences at the University of Massachusetts at Amherst. Feldman, who is winner of the College Distinguished Teacher award, has also taught courses at Mount Holyoke College, Wesleyan University, and Virginia Commonwealth University.

Feldman initiated the Minority Mentoring Program at University of Massachusetts and teaches classes ranging in size from 10 to nearly 500 students. He also has served as a Hewlett Teaching Fellow and Senior Online Teaching Fellow, and he frequently gives talks on the use of technology in teaching. He initiated distance learning courses in psychology at the University of Massachusetts.

A Fellow of the American Psychological Association and the American Psychological Society, he received a B.A. with High Honors from Wesleyan University and an M.S. and Ph.D. from the University of Wisconsin-Madison. He is a winner of a Fulbright Senior Research Scholar and Lecturer award, and has written more than 100 books, book chapters, and scientific articles. His books include *Development of Nonverbal Behavior in Children, Child Development, Development Across the Life Span, Understanding Psychology,* and *P.O.W.E.R. Learning: Strategies for Success in College and Life,* and they have been translated into a number of languages, including Spanish, French, Portuguese, Dutch, Chinese, and Japanese. His research interests include honesty and deception and the use of nonverbal behavior in impression management, and it has been supported by grants from the National Institute of Mental Health and the National Institute on Disabilities and Rehabilitation Research.

Feldman's spare time is most often devoted to traveling, cooking, and earnest, if not entirely expert, piano playing. He has three children and one grandchild, and he lives with his wife Katherine, who is also a psychologist, overlooking the Holyoke mountain range in Amherst, Massachusetts.

ADOLESCENCE

Introduction to Adolescence

CHAPTER OUTLINE

DEFINING ADOLESCENCE: THE SCOPE OF THE FIELD

Topical areas of adolescence
The link between age and topics
Adolescents today

THE STUDY OF ADOLESCENCE: PAST, PRESENT, AND FUTURE

The roots of the study of adolescence
Adolescent science emerges in the 20th century
The scientific method and the study of adolescence
Measuring change during adolescence
Today's perspectives on adolescence

KEY QUESTIONS: MAJOR THEMES OF THE STUDY OF ADOLESCENCE

What are the key transitions and tasks of adolescence?
What are the effects of cohort membership on adolescents?
How does developmental change occur during adolescence?
What is the relative influence of nature and nurture on adolescent development?
How can sound social policy be developed that can improve the lives of adolescents?
The future of adolescence

PROLOGUE: An Adolescent Quartet

IT IS NO small feat to earn a 95 average at the Humanities Preparatory Academy in Greenwich Village and to graduate at the top of a class of 158. It is almost unheard of to pull it off in two years.

It certainly does not help if, like 18-year-old Elizabeth Murray, you did your homework in the littered Bronx hallways and stairwells where you usually slept because your mother had died of AIDS and your drug-addicted father was suffering from the same disease.

■ ■ ■

Carly, a freshman at Benjamin Franklin High School, a school for gifted kids, says she has no interest in politics or social issues. "It's probably because of my mom— she's racked my brain with statistics and feminism and the environment," she says. "I'm like, 'Well, what do you want me to do?'" Since her parents split when she was 3, Carly has lived mainly in Louisiana with her mother. . . . So what *is* she passionate about? "My friends."

■ ■ ■

Trevor is the third of four sons of Richard Kelson, 56, a retired truck driver, and his wife, JoAnn, 46, a medical tape transcriber. The family lives in a four-bedroom home across from Hunter Junior High School, where Trevor is in ninth grade. He spent the summer volunteering in a leadership-training program at the Sugar House Boys and Girls Club in Salt Lake City. "I guess it gives you a good feeling to help somebody else," he says. In off-hours, he plays Nintendo with pal Andy Muhlestein, 15. "When we don't have anything else to do, and we're tired of playing videos," he says, "we sit around and talk about girls."

■ ■ ■

At 16, Purva Chawla holds good rankings in school and loves competing in drama and elocution contests. The New Delhi student is "head girl" of her school and plays for a table tennis team. Recently, she won a public-speaking contest. . . . Even with all her extracurricular activities, she still makes it home for dinner with her parents and goes out to the movies with them twice a week. "I talk with them very freely about what's happening with my friends, boyfriends, whatever," she says. (Kennedy, 1999, p. A18; Fields-Meyer, 1995, pp. 52, 53; Kantrowitz & Springen, 2005, p. 50) ■

th!nk ABOUT THIS

EACH OF THESE FOUR ADOLESCENTS IS very different. At the same time, though, they share some fundamental characteristics of passing through the same period of life, attending school, relying on friends and family, and perhaps most importantly, facing a set of challenges that will set them on the course to adulthood and influence them for the rest of their lives.

Adolescence is a period of transitions and challenges. No longer children, yet not yet adults, adolescents live in a period of considerable physical growth and psychological change, making it one of the most intense and critical periods of life. Adolescents also comprise the largest age group in the world in terms of population, making up almost 20% of the world's population (Richter, 2006).

In seeking to understand adolescence, specialists in the field ask a variety of questions. Some are broad and far-reaching: How do adolescents develop physically? How does their understanding of the world grow and change over time? How do their personalities and social world develop over the course of adolescence?

Other questions are more focused. For example, consider the range of approaches that specialists in the study of adolescence might take to understanding the adolescents profiled in the chapter Prologue:

- Adolescent researchers who investigate behavior at the level of biological processes might ask how changes in hormonal levels might affect the level of emotionality of the four adolescents.

- Specialists in adolescence who study the impact of the social environment might look at how Elizabeth Murray was able to flourish despite living in such an impoverished environment that she was forced to do her homework and sleep in littered hallways.

- For specialists who investigate how thought processes develop during adolescence, the school performance of the four adolescents might be examined to see in what ways their thinking became more sophisticated over the time period.

- Other researchers on adolescence who focus on physical growth might consider the differences between the boys' and the girls' rates of growth.

- Adolescent experts who specialize in family relationships might look at how Carly's life with a single parent affected her development.

- Specialists in adolescents' social world might look at how Trevor interacted with his friends and how his newfound interest in girls affected his personal interactions.

Although their interests are broad, all these specialists in adolescence share an underlying concern: How do youth grow and change during the course of adolescence? Taking many differing approaches, and employing a variety of methods, adolescent specialists examine the joint effects on adolescents' behavior of the mixture of their biological inheritance from their parents with the environment in which they live. Furthermore, they all share the concern of improving the lives of adolescents and hope that their work will inform and support the efforts of professionals whose lives are devoted to working directly with adolescents. Practitioners in fields ranging from education

Specialists in adolescence share an underlying concern: How do youth grow and change during the course of adolescence?

to health care to social work draw on the findings of adolescent researchers, using their results to advance the welfare of adolescents.

In this chapter we orient ourselves to the study of adolescence. We begin by looking at the various topical areas that adolescent specialists study, as well as painting a portrait of adolescents in the 21st century. We then turn to the background of the field, examining its historical roots and development. We focus on the major perspectives of the field, showing the widely different approaches that are used to understand adolescence. Finally, we look at major themes in the study of adolescence, considering some of the key questions that drive specialists' study. ■

After reading this chapter,

YOU WILL BE ABLE TO
ANSWER THESE QUESTIONS:

- What are the major topics and issues that researchers on adolescence study today?
- How did the study of adolescence begin, and how has it developed historically?
- What are some modern perspectives on adolescence?

- **What transitions and tasks are adolescents engaged in during the period?**
- **How do nature and nurture interact during adolescence?**

Defining Adolescence: The Scope of the Field

I guess this is part of being an adolescent. It's all about trying to find yourself (no emo jokes intended). I am currently on a massive journey—no, hunt—doing just that. I wish I saw everything a lot clearer so this would be easier to sort through.

■ ■ ■

One part of being an adolescent is negotiating the transition from being a child, most of the features of whose life are determined by parents, to being an adult, who is responsible for him- or herself. When you're a child, you don't have to take responsibility for the really big decisions. Your parents may put you in charge of feeding the dog or cleaning your room, but they will typically not allow you to decide whether to drop out of school, or to train full-time to be an Olympic athlete, or to stow away on a ship bound for South America (as I once tried to do. I didn't get very far.)

■ ■ ■

i'm lost between being an adolescent and an adult. i'm lost between college and graduate school. i'm lost between wanting to be young and knowing how important it is to appear like an adult. i'm lost between professions and grad degrees. i'm lost between wanting life to be religiously meaningful and not wanting to think about anything that maybe doesn't even exist. i'm lost between hook ups and marriage. i'm lost between work and play.

As these comments from Internet blogs suggest, there are many ways of looking at adolescence. It is a period of time that encompasses a variety of transitions and challenges. It is also a period that evokes a range of images: an angry, defiant 15-year-old teenage girl arguing with her parents . . . a 12-year-old boy who has grown three inches in the last 2 months and whose voice has just begun to change . . . a 20-year-old college sophomore beginning the first term of college.

Adolescence is the developmental stage that lies between childhood and adulthood. Although the definition of the field is straightforward, the simplicity is somewhat misleading because adolescence covers a period of the life span that brings significant changes on the biological, cognitive, personality, and social levels—more rapid and profound changes than those that occur in any other period of life except infancy.

Furthermore, adolescence is getting longer. Biological and social changes occurring over the last 100 years have extended adolescence to a degree that the founding fathers—and mothers—of the formal field of adolescence might not even recognize today. In the past century, children have begun to mature physically earlier than ever before in human history, often as early as the age of 9 or 10. At the same time, social changes have extended the time that individuals remain dependent on their parents, and work and marriage have been delayed for many people until well into their 20s.

Consequently, it is difficult to pinpoint the beginning and end of adolescence. We'll use a rough approximation of the period, which begins around the age of 10 and extends until about the age of 20. In addition, largely for purposes of convenience, we also can think of adolescence as encompassing the teenage years. And some researchers go further, dividing adolescence into the periods of *early adolescence* (covering the ages of 10 to 13), *middle adolescence* (14 through 17), and *late adolescence* (18 through 22).

These age ranges are in many ways arbitrary. Because the three categories roughly coincide with U.S. school-based changes (elementary/middle school, high school, and college), for

adolescence the developmental stage that lies between childhood and adulthood

adolescents outside the United States—for whom schooling might be divided in very different ways—the ages for each category might well be different.

It's also important to keep in mind that the study of adolescence takes a scientific approach. Like members of other scientific disciplines, researchers in adolescence test their assumptions about the nature and course of adolescence by applying scientific methods. They develop theories about adolescence, and they use methodical, scientific techniques to systematically validate the accuracy of their assumptions.

As adolescent specialists focus on the ways people change and grow during adolescence, they also consider stability in adolescents' lives. They ask in which areas and in what ways adolescents show change and growth and when and how their behavior reveals consistency and continuity with prior behavior.

Finally, although the study of adolescence focuses by definition on one age period, the process of development persists throughout every part of people's lives, beginning with the moment of conception and continuing until death. Adolescent specialists assume that in some ways people continue to grow and change right up to the end of their lives, whereas in other respects their behavior remains stable. Furthermore, despite their focus on growth during adolescence, they believe that no particular, single period of life governs all development. Instead, they have concluded that every period of life contains the potential for both growth and decline in abilities, and that individuals maintain the capacity for substantial growth and change throughout their lives.

Topical Areas of Adolescence

Chronological age is hardly the only way to conceptualize adolescence. Depending on the research interests of a particular specialist on adolescence, the focus might be on physical development, cognitive development, or social development.

Physical Development. Extraordinary changes take place in the human body during adolescence. The biological changes that occur at the start of adolescence, collectively known as *puberty,* alter the body both in terms of appearance (such as the growth of breasts in girls, the lowering of boys' voices, and the increase in height and weight for both boys and girls) and internal functioning. Ultimately, these biological changes lead to sexual maturation and the ability to have children.

Specialists on *physical development* focus on how the body's biological makeup—the brain, nervous system, muscles, senses, and reproductive system—operates and changes during adolescence. For example, one specialist in physical development might examine the effects of hormonal changes on adolescents, while another might look at obesity and wellness during the period. A focus on physical development might lead a specialist to consider the onset of adolescence to be when physical maturation begins at puberty, and the end of adolescence to be when an individual is capable of sexual reproduction.

Cognitive Development. Children start adolescence thinking concretely. They understand the world in terms of what *is,* rather than what *might* or *could* be. They see the world from an egocentric perspective, with relatively little appreciation for the fact that others see things from perspectives different from their own.

By the time they finish adolescence, though, they are thinking abstractly. They are able to reason about hypothetical questions, make sophisticated decisions, and think more critically about the world around them.

Adolescent specialists who focus on *cognitive development* seek to understand how growth and change in intellectual capabilities influence an adolescent's behavior. Specialists in cognitive development might examine how information is processed during adolescence or how decision-making changes during the course of the period. A specialist who focuses on cognitive development might view adolescence as starting at the point when more sophisticated cognitive abilities emerge and as ending when thinking has reached the most advanced levels of which an individual is capable.

Social and Personality Development.   At the start of adolescence, children are dependent on their parents and families. At the end, they are leading independent, self-sufficient lives, typically starting jobs in the workplace and having deep-seated relationships with others their own age. They develop an understanding of who they are as individuals and how they fit into society. They have rights and privileges—drivers licenses, voter registration cards, and marriage certificates—that allow them to participate fully in society.

Adolescent specialists who are interested in such transitions focus on social and personality development. *Personality development* is the study of stability and change in the enduring characteristics that differentiate one person from another. *Social development* is the way in which adolescents' interactions with others and their social relationships grow, change, and remain stable over the period.

A specialist in personality development might look at how adolescents change in their moral behavior, whereas a specialist in social development might ask how adolescents' relationships with their parents change over the course of adolescence. Specialists in adolescence who take a social perspective might look at adolescence as beginning when schooling begins for one's adult professional life and ending when an individual actually enters a profession. (The major approaches are summarized in Table 1-1).

TABLE 1-1 Approaches to Adolescent Development		
Orientation	**Defining Characteristics**	**Examples of Questions Asked***
Physical Development	Examines how brain, nervous system, muscles, sensory capabilities, and needs for food, drink, and sleep affect behavior	How do people grow and change through adolescence? (1) What are the physical consequences of risk taking? (3) What are the consequences of teen pregnancy? (9) What are the best ways to deal with stress? (13) What is adolescent abuse? (14)
Cognitive Development	Examines intellectual abilities, including learning, memory, problem solving, and intelligence	How does culture influence how adolescents learn? (3) Are there racial differences in IQ? (3) How do teachers' expectations influence adolescent students? (10) Are adolescents more capable of multitasking than adults? (11)
Personality and Social Development	Examines enduring characteristics that differentiate one person from another and how interactions with others and social relationships grow and change over the life span	What are some consequences of self-esteem? (5) What is the downside to being popular? (7) Is there a link between work and character? (11) What are the roots of prejudice? (12) What are some reasons for juvenile delinquency? (14)

*Numbers in parentheses indicate in which chapter the question is addressed.

The Link between Age and Topics

Each of the broad topical areas of adolescence—physical, cognitive, and social and personality development—plays a role throughout adolescence. The fact that there is so much change during adolescence has meant that experts studying the same general topic, such as physical development, might do so at particular stages of adolescence. For instance, some experts focus on physical development only during early adolescence, while others focus on physical development during late adolescence. Similarly, some might specialize in social development during middle adolescence, whereas others look at social relationships toward the end of late adolescence.

Adolescent DIVERSITY

How Culture, Ethnicity, and Race Influence Adolescent Development

WHEN ADWOA HASWANa was 12 years old, she was blindfolded and held down by her parents. An older woman, who actually had rather limited knowledge of female anatomy, used a knife to perform a female circumcision. The circumcision—to which Adwoa had been looking forward with a combination of excitement and trepidation—consisted of the removal of her clitoris, resulting in a permanent inability to experience sexual pleasure. Adwoa joined the estimated 80 million other women, mostly living in Africa and Asia, who have undergone what is considered an important rite of passage for females in many cultures.

Is the practice of female circumcision, which results not only in severe pain but frequently in health problems, sterility, and sometimes death, a horrific practice that is morally and socially wrong? Or should it be viewed as a cultural and religious practice that has been part of various cultures for centuries, one that needs to be respected?

Specialists in adolescence must address questions like this as they consider how culture affects adolescent development. Sometimes the questions are quite specific, whereas other times they are broader, such as how a culture's orientation toward individualism affects adolescent behavior. In addition, researchers must take into account finer ethnic, racial, socioeconomic, and gender differences if they are to achieve an understanding of how people change and grow throughout adolescence. If these specialists succeed in doing so, not only can they achieve a better understanding of adolescence, but they may also be able to derive more successful applications for improving the social conditions of adolescence.

Efforts to understand how diversity affects adolescent development have been hindered by difficulties in finding an appropriate vocabulary. For example, members of the research community—as well as society at large—have sometimes used terms such as *race* and *ethnic group* in inappropriate ways. *Race* is a biological concept, which should be employed only to refer to classifications based on physical and structural characteristics of species. In contrast, *ethnic group* and *ethnicity* are broader terms, referring to cultural background, nationality, religion, and language.

The concept of race has proved particularly problematic. Although it formally refers to biological factors, race has taken on a substantially wider range of meanings—many of them inappropriate—that include everything from skin color to religion to culture. Moreover, the concept of race is exceedingly imprecise; depending on how it is defined, there are between 3 and 300 races, and no race is biologically pure. Furthermore, the fact that 99.9% of the genetic makeup of all humans is identical makes the question of race seem comparatively insignificant (Angier, 2000; Bamshad & Olson, 2003; Carpenter, 2000).

In addition, there is little agreement about which names best reflect different races and ethnic groups. Should the term *African American*—which has geographical and cultural implications—be preferred over *black*, which focuses primarily on skin color? Is *Native American* preferable to *Indian*? Is *Hispanic* more appropriate than *Latino*? And how can researchers accurately describe adolescents with multiethnic backgrounds? The choice of category has important implications for the validity and usefulness of research. The choice even has political implications. For example, the decision to permit people to identify themselves as "multiracial" on U.S. government forms and in the 2000 U.S. Census was highly controversial (Perlmann & Waters, 2002).

As the proportion of minorities in U.S. society continues to increase, it becomes crucial to take the complex issues associated with human diversity into account to fully understand development. In fact, it is only by looking for similarities and differences among various ethnic, cultural, and racial groups that adolescent researchers can distinguish principles of development that are universal from ones that are culturally determined. In the years ahead, then, it is likely that adolescent specialists will move from a discipline that primarily focuses on adolescents with North American and European backgrounds to one that encompasses the development of adolescents around the globe (Olson et al., 2003; Bamshad et al., 2003; Quintana, 2004).

Adolescents Today

More adolescents are alive today than at any other point in history, and, in many ways, they face an increasingly complex and demanding world. For many adolescents living in the United States, lower family stability due to high divorce rates, the challenges and temptations of alcohol

In order to understand growth and change during the course of adolescence, researchers need to take into account cultural, ethnic, racial and socioeconomic factors.

and drugs, pressures to succeed afterward in school and the world of work, and many other sources of stress make adolescence a difficult time.

Adolescents also face a set of negative stereotypes held by society at large. From TV shows like *My So-Called Life* to books like *Don't Take it Personally: A Parent's Guide to Surviving Adolescence,* the portrayal of adolescence is often negative (Davis, 2004).

Adolescents living in other cultures face their own set of challenges. They may have more limited economic opportunities, without the potential for economic mobility that is more characteristic of the United States. If they are female, they may have far fewer educational opportunities, as encouragement for girls to attend school is minimal even today in many cultures.

Despite such challenges, many, if not most, adolescents pass through the period with relatively few problems. Although they face the normal stress inherent in living life in any period of the life span, for many adolescents the period is one of relative tranquility (Nicholas & Good, 2004).

Furthermore, most adolescents see themselves in a positive light. For example, one large, 10-country cross-cultural study found that three quarters of adolescents held a favorable self-image, viewing themselves in positive terms. Moreover, the majority held an optimistic view of the future (Offer et al., 1988; Mallan & Pearce, 2003).

Consequently, although many adolescents face difficulties during the period, more pass through adolescence relatively happily, with harmonious relations with their parents, teachers, and peers. It is certainly a challenging period, but most adolescents have sufficient resources to meet the challenges (Nicholas & Good, 2004).

As we consider adolescence throughout this book, it is important to keep in mind that we are primarily discussing broad generalizations. No two adolescents are alike; all are individuals, with personal hopes, dreams, skills, and abilities. Adolescents do not make up a homogeneous group, but rather reflect substantial individual differences.

Furthermore, it is likely that the heterogeneity of adolescence will increase on dimensions ranging from race to socioeconomic status. For example, the number of nonwhites is projected to increase substantially over the first half of the 21st century at the same time the white population declines (see Figure 1-1).

In sum, as the diversity of the United States increases, adolescents themselves will be more diverse, and the challenges that they face will increase. But as you'll see throughout the remainder of this book, the period of adolescence is both fascinating and central to who people are and who they become.

▶ **FIGURE 1-1**

U.S. population projections show a decline in the proportion of whites over the next five decades as the diversity of the country increases.

(*Source:* U.S. Census Bureau, 2004, "U.S. Interim Projections by Age, Sex, Race, and Hispanic origin," http://www.census .gov/ipc/www/usinterimproj/, Internet release date: March 18, 2004.)

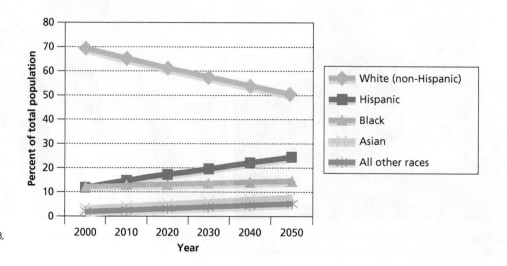

Review and Apply

Review

1. The simplicity of defining *adolescence* conceals the complexity of the period, the changes that adolescents experience, and the exact age ranges that are included within the period.

2. Adolescent specialists focus on physical, cognitive, and social and personality development, all of which involve rapid and profound changes.

3. Adolescent researchers consider a variety of topics and adolescents of different ages, resulting in a discipline with considerable breadth.

4. Despite a popular stereotype as a stressful period, adolescence is in fact relatively calm and adolescents comparatively happy and hopeful.

Apply

1. Which adolescent developmental changes—physical, cognitive, or social and personality— do you think are most responsible for the view of adolescence as a stormy period? Why?

2. How do you think the increase in diversity will affect the normal concerns of adolescence? Will multiculturalism decrease or increase the difficulties of being an adolescent?

The Study of Adolescence: Past, Present, and Future

Sometimes, I feel like as though I'm trying too hard to prove myself to the world. . . . I have this urge to constantly impress people with either intellect or maturity. . . . Why? It's hard to just let go . . . after so long of people looking down on me because I can't do anything right, nor perform "well," I just can't help but show really what I'm capable of . . . and sometimes, it becomes so fake and untrue. . . . I'm not like that . . . really . . . or not? I can't help but wish that I had more recognition for the stuff that I really love to do . . . even if I sucked at it and not be the top, I'd still like some praise. . . . Let's hope someone up there finally will give me the wings that (I think) are very much overdue. . . .

Few have characterized adolescence as an easy time of life, and this adolescent blogger certainly illustrates that point. Adolescents sometimes see themselves as having arrived at a unique period of life beset by demands that they may perceive as impossible to fulfill adequately.

Outside observers, too, have regarded adolescence as an exceptional period. As we see next, adolescence has been a focus of interest for centuries.

The Roots of the Study of Adolescence

As long ago as the time of the ancient Greeks, the period of adolescence was of special interest. For example, the philosophers Plato and Aristotle saw adolescence as a period in which it was possible to reason effectively for the first time. Plato, for instance, thought that children's time was best spent in athletic and musical activities, in part because that was all they could understand. On the other hand, he argued that adolescents should focus on math and science, which they were newly capable of understanding.

Aristotle saw adolescents as having the ability to make rational, logical choices, and he viewed them as capable of making reasonable decisions. But he also viewed adolescents as lacking maturity in some ways, judging them egocentric and as bearers of a belief that they knew more than they actually did.

Later philosophers, and society in general, took a different view of adolescents. For example, according to Philippe Ariès, who studied paintings and other forms of art, prior to 1600 adolescents in medieval Europe were not given any special status. Instead, they were viewed as miniature, although somewhat imperfect, adults. They were dressed in adult clothing and treated the same as adults in every significant way. Adolescence was not seen as a stage qualitatively different from adulthood (Ariès, 1962; Acocella, 2003; Hutton, 2004).

In the 17th century, a more progressive view of adolescence was promoted by the French philosopher Jean-Jacques Rousseau. Arguing against the conception that adolescents were simply miniature adults, he suggested that the ability to reason gradually emerged during adolescence. Especially during the early teenage years, adolescents needed to have their curiosity encouraged to produce more sophisticated thinking. During later stages of adolescence, from around ages 15 to 20, he saw youth as losing their innate selfishness and egocentrism and becoming more interested in others and their well-being.

The details of Rousseau's views are less important than his speculation that adolescence was divided into different stages. Rejecting the earlier view that adolescents were simply miniature adults, he revitalized the view of adolescence as a unique period of the life span.

But the speculations of the early philosophers were just that—speculations. Their views were based on philosophical reasoning and arguments, and not on anything approaching careful and systematic observation of adolescence. It was not until the 20th century that the study of adolescence moved beyond speculation and emerged as a scientific discipline.

Adolescent Science Emerges in the 20th Century

If there's a date that's central to the field of adolescence, it's 1904. In that year, psychologist G. Stanley Hall published a two-volume book called, aptly, *Adolescence.* It marked the beginning of the scientific study of the field of adolescence.

Hall argued that development during adolescence, which he saw lasting from ages 12 to 23, was largely the result of inherited, genetic factors. Hall was strongly influenced by the work of Charles Darwin, whose theory of evolution held that humans evolve through a process of natural selection. Darwin believed that understanding the development of individuals within a species could help identify how the species itself had developed.

Based on Darwin's work, Hall suggested adolescence was a period of *sturm und drang*—a German phrase meaning "storm and stress." He saw adolescence as analogous to the period of human evolution in which people acted in a savage, uncontrolled manner, before they became more civilized.

Hall's **storm and stress view** was that adolescence could be characterized in a fundamental way as a period of extraordinary turbulence, filled with mood swings and upheaval. One minute an adolescent could be relaxed, cheery, and cooperative, but just a short time later could be tense, angry, and rebellious. Similarly, an adolescent might act loving and affectionate, but only a few moments later be cold, remote, and unfeeling. Because in Hall's view these mood swings were genetically based, he believed that little could be done to prevent them. Furthermore, he argued that adolescents were susceptible to them until they reached adulthood.

Hall's views had considerable impact on the field of adolescence. His systematic theorizing about adolescence was an impetus for decades of work on the nature of adolescence. Further-

storm and stress view psychologist G. Stanley Hall's theory that adolescence could be characterized in a fundamental way as a period of extraordinary turbulence, filled with mood swings and upheaval

more, his views on the genetic origins of adolescence and the importance of biological factors in leading to adolescent behavior have caused him to be called the father of the scientific study of adolescence.

At the same time, subsequent research has shown that Hall's view of adolescence as a period of persistent storm and stress was overdrawn. As we'll see in future chapters, although there are periods of storminess in relations between adolescents and their parents and other adults, for the majority of youth and most of the time, interactions are quite tranquil. However, Hall's influence was so great that his view held sway not only over the field of adolescence, but in popular thinking as well. Even today, conventional wisdom holds that adolescence is a time of turmoil—an example of how conventional wisdom can be entirely wrong.

Despite Hall's overestimation of the degree of adolescent storm and stress, he remains a pivotal figure in the formal study of science. His views influenced the field for the next century, and his theorizing led to a significant amount of research. Furthermore, his perspective that the behavior of adolescents was largely influenced by biological factors has been supported by contemporary research on *neuroscience,* a field that focuses on the way that the brain, nervous system, and body structures affect behavior.

Furthermore, Hall's work paved the way for the development of **adolescent science,** a research-based approach to the study of adolescence. Rather than relying on mere intuition, Hall pioneered the use of questionnaires to illuminate adolescents' thinking and behavior. His use of research-based methods began a trend of looking at adolescence in a more objective manner, leading to substantial advances.

G. Stanley Hall, a central figure in the study of adolescence, believed adolescence was a period of storm and stress.

The Scientific Method and the Study of Adolescence

As the 20th century progressed, the study of adolescence was increasingly characterized by the use of the scientific method. The **scientific method** is the process of posing and answering questions using careful, controlled techniques that include systematic, orderly observation and the collection of data. As shown in Figure 1-2, the scientific method involves three major steps: (a) identifying questions of interest, (b) formulating an explanation, and (c) carrying out research that either lends support to the explanation or refutes it.

What is the advantage of using the scientific method when one's own experiences and common sense might seem to provide reasonable answers to questions? After all, we've all been adolescents and thus have personal experience with that phase of life.

One important reason for preferring the scientific method is that our own experience is limited. Most of us—even experts such as Hall—encounter only a relatively small number of people and situations, and drawing suppositions from that restricted sample may lead us to the wrong conclusion.

Similarly, although common sense may seem helpful, it turns out that common sense often makes contradictory predictions. For example, common sense tells us that "birds of a feather flock together." But it also says that "opposites attract." You see the problem: Because common sense is often contradictory, we can't rely on it to provide objective answers to questions. That's why adolescent researchers insist on using the controlled techniques of the scientific method, focusing on particular procedures to measure change across the period.

Measuring Change during Adolescence

How people grow and change through adolescence is central to the work of adolescent specialists. Consequently, one of the thorniest research issues they face concerns the measurement

adolescent science a research-based approach to the study of adolescence that evolved from the work of psychologist G. Stanley Hall

scientific method the process of posing and answering questions using careful, controlled techniques that include systematic, orderly observation and the collection of data

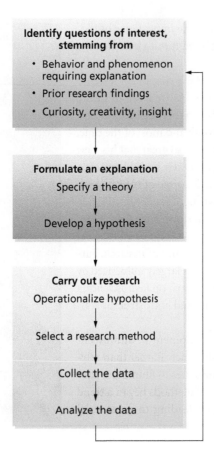

Identify questions of interest, stemming from

- Behavior and phenomenon requiring explanation
- Prior research findings
- Curiosity, creativity, insight

Formulate an explanation

Specify a theory

Develop a hypothesis

Carry out research

Operationalize hypothesis

Select a research method

Collect the data

Analyze the data

▶ **FIGURE 1-2**

Used by developmental scientists, and every other scientific discipline, the scientific method uses the processes of identifying, asking, and answering questions to help understand the world and unlock its secrets.

of change and differences over the period. To solve this problem, researchers have developed three major research strategies: longitudinal research, cross-sectional research, and sequential research.

Longitudinal Studies: Measuring Individual Change over Time. If you were interested in learning how an adolescent's moral development changes between the ages of 13 and 17, the most direct approach would be to take a group of 13-year-olds and follow them until age 17, testing them periodically.

Such a strategy illustrates longitudinal research. In **longitudinal research,** the behavior of one or more study participants is measured as they age. Longitudinal research measures change over time. By following many individuals over time, researchers can understand the general course of change across some period of life.

Longitudinal studies can provide a wealth of information about change over time. However, they have several drawbacks. For one thing, they require a tremendous investment of time because researchers must wait for participants to become older before they complete their studies. Furthermore, participants often quit the study, dropping out, moving away, becoming ill, or even dying as the research proceeds.

Finally, participants who are observed or tested repeatedly may become "test-wise" and perform better each time they are assessed as they become more familiar with the procedure. Consequently, despite the benefits of longitudinal research, particularly its ability to look at change within individuals, adolescent researchers often turn to other methods in conducting research. The alternative they choose most often is the cross-sectional study.

Cross-Sectional Studies: Measuring Different Ages at the Same Time. Suppose again that you want to consider how adolescents' moral development, their sense of right and wrong, changes from ages 13 to 17. Instead of using a longitudinal approach and following the same children over several years, we might conduct the study by simultaneously looking at three groups of adolescents: 13-year-olds, 15-year-olds, and 17-year-olds, perhaps presenting each group with the same problem and then seeing how they respond to it and explain their choices.

Such an approach typifies cross-sectional research. In **cross-sectional research,** adolescents of different ages are compared at the same point in time. Cross-sectional studies provide information about differences in development between different age groups.

Cross-sectional research is considerably more economical in terms of time than longitudinal research: Participants are tested at just one point in time. Because they are not repeatedly tested, there would be no chance that they would become test-wise, and problems of participant attrition would not occur. Why, then, would anyone choose to use any procedure but cross-sectional research?

The answer is that cross-sectional research brings its own set of difficulties Recall that every person belongs to a particular *cohort,* the group of people born at around the same time in the same place. If we find that adolescents of different ages vary along some dimension, it may be

longitudinal research   research in which the behavior of one or more study participants is measured as they age

cross-sectional research   research in which adolescents of different ages are compared at the same point in time

due to differences in cohort membership, not age per se. Furthermore, cross-sectional studies may suffer from *selective dropout,* in which participants in some age groups are more likely to quit participating in a study than others. For example, younger adolescents might be more receptive to a request by a researcher to participate in a study, whereas older ones, feeling busier, might be less inclined to participate. The results of such a study would be questionable (Miller, 1998).

Finally, cross-sectional studies have an additional, and more basic, disadvantage: They are unable to inform us about *changes* in individuals or groups. If longitudinal studies are like videos taken of a person at various ages, cross-sectional studies are like snapshots of entirely different groups. Although we can establish differences related to age, we cannot fully determine if such differences are related to change over time.

Sequential Studies: Combining Longitudinal and Cross-Sectional Studies.   Because both longitudinal and cr\oss-sectional studies have drawbacks, researchers have turned to some compromise techniques. Among the most frequently employed are sequential studies, which are essentially a combination of longitudinal and cross-sectional studies.

In **sequential studies,** researchers examine a number of different age groups at several points in time. For instance, an investigator interested in children's moral behavior might begin a sequential study by examining the behavior of groups of 13-year-olds, 15-year-olds, and 17-year-olds at the time the study begins. (This is no different from the way a cross-sectional study would be done.)

However, the study wouldn't stop there, but would continue for the next several years. During this period, each of the research participants would be tested every two years. Thus, the 13-year-olds would be tested at ages 13, 15, and 17; the 15-year-olds at ages 15, 17, and 19; and the 17-year-olds at ages 17, 19, and 21. Such an approach combines the advantages of longitudinal and cross-sectional research, and it permits developmental researchers to tease out the consequences of age *change* versus age *difference.*

The major research techniques for studying development across adolescence are summarized in Figure 1-3.

sequential studies   an approach in which researchers examine a number of different age groups at several points in time

Today's Perspectives on Adolescence

The early work on adolescence has led to the development of several broad perspectives on the period. We'll consider five major perspectives: the psychodynamic, behavioral, cognitive, contextual, and evolutionary perspectives. These diverse outlooks emphasize somewhat different aspects of development that steer inquiry in particular directions. Just as we can use multiple maps to find our way around a region—for example, one map might show the roadways and another might focus on key landmarks—the various developmental perspectives provide us with different views of child and adolescent behavior. And just as maps must continually be revised, each perspective continues to evolve and change, as befits a growing and dynamic discipline.

The Psychodynamic Perspective: Focusing on Internal Forces.   When Marisol was 6 months old, she was involved in a bloody automobile accident—or so her parents tell her, because she has no conscious

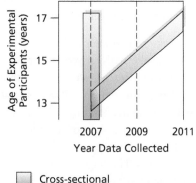

◄ **FIGURE 1-3**

Research Techniques for Studying Development   In a *cross-sectional study,* 13-, 15-, and 17-year-olds are compared at a similar point in time (in 2007). In *longitudinal research,* a set of participants who are 13 years old in 2007 are studied when they are 15 years old (in 2009) and when they are 17 years old (in 2011). Finally, a *sequential study* combines cross-sectional and longitudinal techniques; here, a group of 13-year-olds would be compared initially in 2007 with 15- and 17-year-olds, but would also be studied later, when they themselves were 15 and 17 years old. Although the graph does not illustrate this, researchers carrying out this sequential study might also choose to retest the children who were 15 and 17 in 2007 for the next 2 years. What advantages do the three kinds of studies offer?

According to the psychodynamic perspective, childhood traumas can have lingering effects on adolescents' behavior, even if specific events are not consciously recalled.

recollection of it. Now, however, at age 17, she is having a particularly difficult adolescence, having problems getting along with her parents. A family therapist from whom she and her parents are seeking treatment is trying to determine whether her current problems are a result of that early accident.

Looking for such a link might seem a bit far-fetched, but to proponents of the **psychodynamic perspective,** the search is not so improbable. Advocates of the psychodynamic perspective believe that behavior is motivated by inner forces, memories, and conflicts of which a person has little awareness or control. The inner forces, which may stem from one's childhood, continually influence behavior throughout the life span.

Freud's Psychoanalytic Theory. The psychodynamic perspective is most closely associated with Sigmund Freud and his psychoanalytic theory. Freud, who lived from 1856 to 1939, was a Viennese physician whose revolutionary ideas ultimately had a profound effect not just on the fields of psychology and psychiatry but on Western thought in general, and even on the rest of culture (Masling & Bornstein, 1996).

Freud's **psychoanalytic theory** suggests that unconscious forces act to determine personality and behavior. To Freud, the *unconscious* is a part of the personality about which a person is unaware. It contains infantile wishes, desires, demands, and needs that are hidden, because of their disturbing nature, from conscious awareness. Freud suggested that the unconscious is responsible for a good part of our everyday behavior.

According to Freud, everyone's personality has three aspects: id, ego, and superego. The *id* is the raw, unorganized, inborn part of personality that is present at birth. It represents primitive drives related to hunger, sex, aggression, and irrational impulses. The *ego* is the part of personality that is rational and reasonable. The ego acts as a buffer between the real world outside us and the primitive id. Finally, Freud proposed that the *superego* represents a person's conscience, incorporating distinctions between right and wrong. It develops around age 5 or 6 and is learned from an individual's parents, teachers, and other significant figures.

In addition to providing an account of the various parts of the personality, Freud also suggests the ways in which personality develops during childhood and adolescence. He argues that **psychosexual development** occurs as children and adolescents pass through a series of stages, in which pleasure, or gratification, is focused on a particular biological function and body part. He suggested that pleasure shifts from the mouth (the *oral stage*) to the anus (the *anal stage*) and eventually to the genitals (the *phallic stage* and the *genital stage*).

Erikson's Psychosocial Theory. Psychoanalyst Erik Erikson, who lived from 1902 to 1994, provides an alternative psychodynamic view in his theory of psychosocial development, which emphasizes our social interaction with other people. In Erikson's view, society and culture both challenge and shape us. **Psychosocial development** encompasses changes in our interactions with and understandings of one another, as well as in our knowledge and understanding of ourselves as members of society (Erikson, 1963; Côté, 2005).

Erikson's theory suggests that developmental change occurs throughout our lives in eight distinct stages. The stages emerge in a fixed pattern and are similar for all people. Erikson argues that each stage presents a crisis or conflict that the individual must resolve. Although no crisis is ever fully resolved, making life increasingly complicated, the individual must at least address the crisis of each stage sufficiently to deal with demands made during the next stage of development.

Unlike Freud, who regarded development as relatively complete by adolescence, Erikson suggested that growth and change continue throughout the life span. For instance, he suggested that during middle adulthood, people pass through the *generativity-versus-stagnation stage,* in which

psychodynamic perspective   the approach that states behavior is motivated by inner forces, memories, and conflicts that are generally beyond people's awareness and control

psychoanalytic theory   the theory proposed by Freud that suggests that unconscious forces act to determine personality and behavior

psychosexual development   according to Freud, a series of stages that children pass through in which pleasure, or gratification, is focused on a particular biological function and body part

psychosocial development   the approach that encompasses changes in our interactions with and understandings of one another as well as in our knowledge and understanding of ourselves as members of society

their contributions to family, community, and society can produce either positive feelings about the continuity of life or a sense of stagnation and disappointment about what they are passing on to future generations (De St. Aubin, McAdams, & Kim, 2004).

Assessing the Psychodynamic Perspective. It is hard for us to grasp the full significance of psychodynamic theories, represented by Freud's psychoanalytic theory and Erikson's theory of psychosocial development. Freud's introduction of the notion that unconscious influences affect behavior was a monumental accomplishment, and the fact that it seems at all reasonable to us shows how extensively the idea of the unconscious has pervaded thinking in Western cultures. In fact, work by contemporary researchers studying memory and learning suggests that we carry with us memories of which we are not consciously aware that have a significant impact on our behavior.

Some of the most basic principles of psychoanalytic theory have been called into question, however, because they have not been validated by subsequent research. In particular, the notion that people pass through stages in childhood and adolescence that determine their adult personalities has little definitive research support. Furthermore, the theory is vague and hard to test in a rigorous manner. In sum, although the psychodynamic perspective provides reasonably good descriptions of past behavior, its predictions of future behavior are imprecise (Whitbourne et al., 1992; Zauszniewski & Martin, 1999; De St. Aubin & McAdams, 2004).

The Behavioral Perspective: Focusing on External Forces.

When Eve Sheehan was 3, a large brown dog bit her, and she needed dozens of stitches and several operations. From the time she was bitten and continuing into adolescence, she broke into a sweat whenever she saw a dog and in fact never enjoyed being around any pet.

To a specialist using the behavioral perspective, the explanation for Eve's behavior is straightforward: She has a learned fear of dogs. Rather than looking inside the organism at unconscious processes, the **behavioral perspective** suggests that the keys to understanding development are observable behavior and outside stimuli in the environment. If we know the stimuli, we can predict the behavior.

Behavioral theories reject the notion that people universally pass through a series of stages. Instead, people are assumed to be affected by the environmental stimuli to which they happen to be exposed. Developmental patterns, then, are personal, reflecting a particular set of environmental stimuli, and behavior is the result of continuing exposure to specific factors in the environment. Furthermore, developmental change is viewed in quantitative, rather than qualitative, terms. For instance, behavioral theories hold that advances in problem-solving capabilities as adolescents age are largely a result of greater mental *capacities* rather than of changes in the *kind* of thinking that adolescents are able to bring to bear on a problem.

One of the primary forms of learning is *operant conditioning,* a form of learning in which a voluntary response is strengthened or weakened by its association with positive or negative consequences. In operant conditioning, which was formulated and championed by psychologist B. F. Skinner (1904–1990), individuals learn to act deliberately on their environments to bring about desired consequences. In a sense, then, adolescents *operate* on their environments to bring about a desired state of affairs. Whether or not adolescents will seek to repeat a behavior depends on whether it is followed by reinforcement. *Reinforcement* is the process by which a stimulus is provided that increases the probability that a preceding behavior will be repeated.

Another important type of learning is social-cognitive learning, in which a person learns by observing the behavior of another person, called a *model.* Rather than learning being a matter of trial and error, as it is with operant conditioning, social-cognitive learning theory suggests that behavior is learned through observation. Social-cognitive learning theory holds that when we see the behavior of a model being rewarded, we are likely to imitate that behavior (Bandura, 1994, 2002).

behavioral perspective the approach that suggests that the keys to understanding development are observable behavior and outside stimuli in the environment

Assessing the Behavioral Perspective. Work using the behavioral perspective has made significant contributions, ranging from creating techniques for educating adolescents with mental retardation to identifying procedures for curbing aggression. At the same time, there are controversies regarding the behavioral perspective. For example, operant conditioning considers learning in terms of external stimuli and responses, in which the only important factors are the observable features of the environment. In such an analysis, adolescents and other organisms are "black boxes"; nothing that occurs inside the box is understood—or much cared about, for that matter.

To social learning theorists, such an analysis is an oversimplification. They argue that what makes people different from rats and pigeons is mental activity, in the form of thoughts and expectations. A full understanding of adolescents' development, they maintain, cannot occur without moving beyond external stimuli and responses.

The Cognitive Perspective: Examining the Roots of Understanding.

When 4-year-old Jake is asked why it sometimes rains, he answers, "So the flowers can grow." When his 11-year-old sister Lila is asked the same question, she responds, "Because of evaporation from the surface of the earth." And when their adolescent cousin Ajima, who is studying meteorology in her high school science class, considers the same question, her extended answer includes a discussion of cumulonimbus clouds, the Coriolis effect, and synoptic charts.

To a developmental theorist using the cognitive perspective, the difference in the sophistication of the answers is evidence of a different degree of knowledge and understanding, or cognition. The **cognitive perspective** focuses on the processes that allow people to know, understand, and think about the world.

cognitive perspective the approach that focuses on the processes that allow people to know, understand, and think about the world

As we'll discuss more fully in Chapter 3, the cognitive perspective emphasizes how people internally represent and think about the world. By using this perspective, researchers hope to understand how adolescents process information and how their ways of thinking and understanding affect their behavior. They also seek to learn how cognitive abilities change as adolescents develop, the degree to which cognitive development represents quantitative and qualitative growth in intellectual abilities, and the ways in which different cognitive abilities are related to one another.

Jean Piaget's stage theory of cognitive development had a major influence in our understanding of how adolescents think.

Piaget's Theory of Cognitive Development. According to Jean Piaget, arguably the most influential of cognitive theorists, all people pass in a fixed sequence through a series of universal stages of cognitive development. He suggested that not only does the quantity of information increase in each stage, but that the quality of knowledge and understanding changes as well. His focus was on the change in cognition that occurs as children and adolescents move from one stage to the next (Piaget, 1952, 1962, 1983).

Piaget suggested that human thinking is arranged into *schemes,* organized mental patterns that represent behaviors and actions. In infants, such schemes represent concrete behavior—a scheme for sucking, for reaching, and for each separate behavior. In adolescents, the schemes become more sophisticated and abstract, such as the set of skills involved in driving a car or playing an interactive video game. Schemes are like intellectual computer software that directs and determines how data from the world are looked at and dealt with.

Piaget profoundly influenced our understanding of cognitive development, and he is a significant figure in adolescent development. However, the specifics of his theory, particularly in terms of change in cognitive capabilities over time, have been called into question. For instance, some cognitive skills clearly emerge earlier than Piaget suggested. Furthermore, the universality of Piaget's stages has been disputed. A growing amount of evidence suggests that the emergence of particular cognitive skills occurs according to a different timetable in non-Western cultures. And in every culture, some people never seem to reach Piaget's highest level of cognitive sophistication—formal, logical thought. Finally, many developmental researchers argue that growth is considerably more continuous than Piaget's stage approach suggests (McDonald & Stuart-Hamilton, 2003; Rogoff & Chavajay, 1995).

Information Processing Approaches. Information processing approaches have become an important alternative to Piagetian approaches. **Information processing approaches** to cognitive development seek to identify the ways individuals take in, use, and store information.

Information processing approaches grew out of developments in the electronic processing of information, particularly as carried out by computers. Information processing researchers assume that even complex behavior such as learning, remembering, categorizing, and thinking can be broken down into a series of individual, specific steps. As adolescents develop, they are assumed to employ increasingly sophisticated strategies that allow them to process information more efficiently.

In stark contrast to Piaget's view that thinking undergoes qualitative advances with increasing age, information processing approaches assume that development is marked more by quantitative advances. Our capacity to handle information changes with age, as does our processing speed and efficiency. Furthermore, information processing approaches suggest that as adolescents age, they are better able to control the nature of processing, and that they can change the strategies they choose for processing information.

Although information processing approaches have become a central part of our understanding of cognitive development, they are limited in scope. For example, information processing approaches have paid little attention to behavior such as creativity, in which the most profound ideas often are developed in a seemingly nonlogical, nonlinear manner.

Cognitive Neuroscience Approaches. **Cognitive neuroscience approaches** look at adolescent development by focusing on brain processes. Like other cognitive perspectives, cognitive neuroscience approaches consider internal, mental processes, but they focus specifically on the neurological activity that underlies thinking, problem solving, and other cognitive behavior (Dahl, 2004).

Cognitive neuroscientists seek to identify actual locations and functions within the brain that are related to different types of cognitive activity, rather than simply assuming that there are hypothetical or theoretical cognitive structures related to thinking. For example, using sophisticated brain scanning techniques, cognitive neuroscientists have demonstrated that thinking about the meaning of a word activates different areas of the brain than thinking about how the word sounds when spoken.

Cognitive neuroscience approaches are also on the forefront of research that has identified specific genes associated with disorders ranging from physical problems such as breast cancer to psychological disorders such as schizophrenia. Identifying the genes that make one vulnerable to such disorders is the first step in genetic engineering in which gene therapy can reduce symptoms or even prevent the disorder from occurring.

Although cognitive neuroscience approaches represent something of a new frontier, critics of the approach have suggested that it sometimes provides a better *description* of developmental phenomena than *explanation* of them. Still, such work not only offers important clues to appropriate treatments for disorders but ultimately it can lead to a full understanding of a range of developmental phenomena.

The Contextual Perspective: Taking a Broad Approach to Adolescent Development.

Although adolescent specialists often consider the course of development in terms of physical, cognitive, and personality and social factors by themselves, such a categorization has one serious drawback: In the real world, none of these broad influences occurs in isolation from any other. Instead, there is a constant, ongoing interaction between the different types of influence.

information processing approaches the model that seeks to identify the ways individuals take in, use, and store information

cognitive neuroscience approaches the approach that examines cognitive development by examining lens of brain processes

The **contextual perspective** considers the relationship between individuals and their physical, cognitive, personality, and social worlds. It suggests that an adolescent's unique development cannot be properly viewed without seeing the adolescent enmeshed within a complex social and cultural context. We'll consider two major theories that fall into this category, Bronfenbrenner's bioecological approach and Vygotsky's sociocultural theory.

The Bioecological Approach to Development. Psychologist Urie Bronfenbrenner (1989, 2000, 2002) has proposed the **bioecological approach,** which suggests that five levels of the environment simultaneously influence individuals. Bronfenbrenner suggested that we cannot fully understand development without considering how a person is influenced by each of these levels (illustrated in Figure 1-4).

- The *microsystem* is the everyday, immediate environment in which adolescents lead their daily lives. Parents, friends, and teachers all are influences that are part of the microsystem. But adolescents are not just passive recipients of these influences. Instead, they actively help construct the microsystem, shaping the immediate world in which they live.

- The *mesosystem* provides connections between the various aspects of the microsystem. Like links in a chain, the mesosystem binds adolescents to parents, students to teachers, employees to bosses, friends to friends. It acknowledges the direct and indirect influences that bind us to one another, such as those that affect an adolescent who has a bad day at school and then is short-tempered with her parents at home.

- The *exosystem* represents broader influences, encompassing societal institutions such as local government, the community, schools, places of worship, and the local media. Each of these larger institutions of society can have an immediate, and major, impact on personal development, and each affects how the microsystem and mesosystem operate. For example, the quality of a school will affect an adolescent's cognitive development and potentially can have long-term consequences.

contextual perspective   the approach that considers the relationship between individuals and their physical, cognitive, personality, and social worlds

bioecological approach   the perspective suggesting that different levels of the environment simultaneously influence individuals

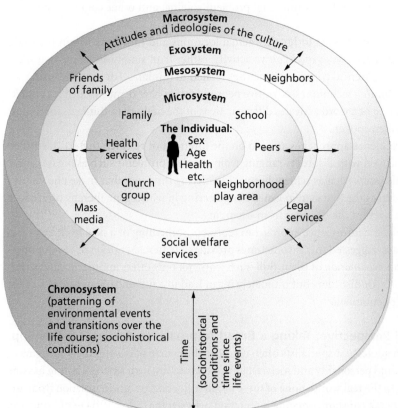

► **FIGURE 1-4**
Urie Bronfenbrenner's bioecological approach to development presents five levels of the environment that simultaneously influence individuals: the macrosystem, exosystem, mesosytem, microsystem, and chryosystem.
(*Source:* Bronfenbrenner, 1989)

- The *macrosystem* represents the larger cultural influences on an individual. Society in general, types of governments, religious and political value systems, and other broad, encompassing factors are parts of the macrosystem. For example, the value a culture or society places on education or the family will affect the values of the people who live in that society. Adolescents are part of both a broader culture (such as Western culture) as well as being influenced by their membership in a particular subculture (for instance, being part of Mexican American subculture).

- Finally, the *chronosystem* underlies each of the previous systems. It involves the way the passage of time, including historical events (such as the terrorist attacks in September of 2001 or Hurricane Katrina) and more gradual historical changes (such as changes in the number of women who work outside the home) affect adolescent development.

The bioecological approach emphasizes the *interconnectedness of the influences on development.* Because the various levels are related to one another, a change in one part of the system affects other parts of the system. For instance, a parent's loss of a job (involving the mesosystem) has an impact on an adolescent's microsystem.

Conversely, changes on one environmental level may make little difference if other levels are not also changed. For instance, improving the school environment may have a negligible effect on academic performance if adolescents receive little support for academic success at home. Similarly, the bioecological approach illustrates that the influences among different family members are multidirectional. Parents don't just influence their adolescent child's behavior—the adolescent also influences the parents' behavior.

Finally, the bioecological approach stresses the importance of broad cultural factors that affect development. Consider, for instance, whether you agree that adolescents should be taught that their classmates' assistance is indispensable to getting good grades in school or that they should definitely plan to continue their fathers' business or that adolescents should follow their parents' advice in determining their career plans. If you have been raised in the most widespread North American culture, you would likely disagree with all three statements because they violate the premises of *individualism,* the dominant Western philosophy that emphasizes personal identity, uniqueness, freedom, and the worth of the individual.

By contrast, if you were raised in a traditional Asian culture, it is considerably more likely that you will agree with the three statements. Why? The statements reflect the value orientation known as collectivism. *Collectivism* is the notion that the well-being of the group is more

The contextual perspective pays particular attention to the social world of adolescents.

Evolutionary perspectives focus on the unfolding of innate, genetically-determined behavior and how it affects later development.

important than that of the individual. Adolescents raised in collectivistic cultures tend to emphasize the welfare of the groups to which they belong, sometimes even at the expense of their own personal well-being.

The individualism–collectivism spectrum is one of several dimensions along which cultures differ, and it illustrates differences in the cultural contexts in which adolescents operate. Such broad cultural values play an important role in shaping the ways adolescents view the world and behave (Sedikides, Gaertner, & Toguchi, 2003; Leung, 2005).

Vygotsky's Sociocultural Theory. To Russian developmentalist Lev Semenovich Vygotsky, a full understanding of development is impossible without taking into account the culture in which adolescents develop. Vygotsky's **sociocultural theory** emphasizes how cognitive development proceeds as a result of social interactions between members of a culture (Vygotsky, 1978, 1926/1997; Winsler, 2003; Edwards, 2005).

Vygotsky argued that adolescents' understanding of the world is acquired through their problem-solving interactions with adults and others. As they interact and cooperate with others, they learn what is important in their society and, at the same time, advance cognitively in their world knowledge. Consequently, to understand the course of adolescent development, we must consider what is meaningful to members of a given culture.

More than most other theories, sociocultural theory emphasizes that development is a *reciprocal transaction* between the people in an adolescent's environment and the adolescent. Vygotsky believed that people and settings influence the adolescent, who in turn influences the people and settings. For example, adolescents raised with their extended family nearby will grow up with a different sense of family life than adolescents whose relatives live a considerable distance away. Those relatives, too, are affected by that situation and that adolescent, depending on how close and frequent the contact is with the adolescent.

Sociocultural theory has become increasingly influential. The reason is the growing acknowledgment of the central importance of cultural factors in development. Adolescents do not develop in a cultural vacuum. Instead, their attention is directed by society to certain areas, and as a consequence, they develop particular kinds of skills that are an outcome of their cultural environment. Vygotsky was one of the first developmentalists to recognize and acknowledge the importance of culture, and—as today's society becomes increasingly multicultural—sociocultural theory is helping us to understand the rich and varied influences that shape development (Edwards, 2005; Matusov & Hayes, 2000; Reis, Collins, & Berscheid, 2000).

Evolutionary Perspectives: Our Ancestors' Contributions to Behavior.

One increasingly influential approach is the evolutionary perspective, the final perspective that we will consider. The **evolutionary perspective** seeks to identify behavior that is the result of our genetic inheritance from our ancestors. It focuses on how genetic and environmental factors combine to influence behavior (Blasi & Bjorklund, 2003; Buss & Kern, 2003; Bjorklund, & Ellis 2005).

Evolutionary approaches grew out of the groundbreaking work of Charles Darwin. In 1859, Darwin argued in his book, *On the Origin of Species,* that a process of natural selection creates traits in a species that are adaptive to its environment. Using Darwin's arguments, evolutionary approaches contend that our genetic inheritance not only determines such physical traits as skin and eye color, but certain personality traits and social behaviors as well. For instance, some evolutionary developmentalists suggest that behaviors such as shyness and jealousy are produced in part by genetic causes, presumably because they helped in increasing the survival rates of humans' ancient relatives (Plomin & McClearn, 1993; Buss, 2003).

The evolutionary perspective draws heavily on the field of *ethology,* which examines the ways in which our biological makeup influences our behavior. A primary proponent of ethology was

sociocultural theory the approach that emphasizes how cognitive development proceeds as a result of social interactions between members of a culture

evolutionary perspective the approach that seeks to identify behavior that is the result of our genetic inheritance from our ancestors

Konrad Lorenz (1903–1989), who discovered that newborn geese are genetically preprogrammed to become attached to the first moving object they see after birth. His work, which demonstrated the importance of biological determinants in influencing behavior patterns, ultimately led developmentalists to consider the ways in which human behavior might reflect inborn genetic patterns.

The evolutionary perspective encompasses one of the fastest-growing areas within the field of lifespan development—behavioral genetics. *Behavioral genetics* studies the effects of heredity on behavior. Behavioral geneticists seek to understand how we might inherit certain behavioral traits and how the environment influences whether we actually display such traits. It also considers how genetic factors may produce psychological disorders such as schizophrenia (Gottlieb, 2003; Eley, Lichtenstein, & Moffitt, 2003; Li, 2003; Bjorklund, 2005).

Why "Which Perspective Is Right?" Is the Wrong Question.   We have considered five major perspectives: psychodynamic, behavioral, cognitive, contextual, and evolutionary (summarized in Table 1-2). It would be natural to wonder which of them provides the most accurate account of adolescence.

For several reasons, this is not an entirely appropriate question. For one thing, each perspective emphasizes a somewhat different aspect of development. For instance, the psychodynamic approach emphasizes emotions, motivational conflicts, and unconscious determinants of behavior. In contrast, behavioral perspectives emphasize overt behavior, paying far more attention to what adolescents *do* than to what goes on inside their heads, which is deemed largely irrelevant. The cognitive and humanistic perspectives take quite the opposite tack, looking more at what adolescents *think* than at what they do. Finally, the evolutionary perspective focuses on how inherited biological factors underlie development.

TABLE 1-2   Major Perspectives on Adolescent Development

Perspective	Key Ideas About Human Behavior and Development	Major Proponents	Example: How perspective might explain obesity in an adolescent
Psychodynamic	Behavior throughout life is motivated by inner, unconscious forces, stemming from childhood, over which we have little control.	Sigmund Freud, Erik Erikson	This view might suggest that an adolescent who is overweight has a fixation in the oral stage of development.
Behavioral	Development can be understood through studying observable behavior and environmental stimuli.	John B. Watson, B. F. Skinner, Albert Bandura	In this perspective, an adolescent who is overweight might be seen as not being rewarded for good nutritional and exercise habits.
Cognitive	Emphasis is on how changes or growth in the ways people know, understand, and think about the world affect behavior.	Jean Piaget	This view might suggest that an adolescent who is overweight hasn't learned effective ways to stay at a healthy weight and doesn't value good nutrition.
Contextual	Behavior is determined by the relationship between individuals and their physical, cognitive, personality, social, and physical worlds.	Lev Vygotsky, Urie Bronfenbrenner	In this perspective an adolescent may become overweight because of a family environment in which food and meals are unusually important and intertwined with family rituals.
Evolutionary	Behavior is the result of genetic inheritance from our ancestors; traits and behavior that are adaptive for promoting the survival of our species have been inherited through natural se-	Konrad Lorenz; influenced by early work of Charles Darwin	This view might suggest that an adolescent might have a genetic tendency toward obesity because extra fat helped his or her ancestors to survive in times of famine.

For example, an adolescent specialist using the psychodynamic approach might consider how the terrorist attacks on the World Trade Center and Pentagon might affect adolescents, unconsciously, years later. A cognitive approach might focus on how adolescents perceived and came to interpret and understand the attacks, while a contextual approach might consider what personality and social factors led the perpetrators to adopt terrorist tactics.

Clearly, each perspective is based on its own premises and focuses on different aspects of development. Furthermore, the same phenomenon can be looked at from a number of perspectives simultaneously. In fact, some adolescent specialists use an *eclectic* approach, drawing on more than one perspective at a single time, because each of the various theoretical perspectives provide different views of adolescence. Considering them together paints a fuller portrait of the myriad ways human beings change and grow over the course of their lives.

BECOMING AN INFORMED CONSUMER OF ADOLESCENT SCIENCE

Evaluating the Truths—and Myths—of Adolescence

It's important for all adolescents to have high self-esteem, so every effort should be made to boost their self-esteem.

■ ■ ■

Adolescents are very different from adults in their behaviors, values, attitudes, and so forth, and these differences commonly cause significant disruptions in parent–adolescent relationships.

■ ■ ■

Adolescents who don't have any close friends are likely to become criminal, antisocial, or mentally ill later in life.

■ ■ ■

As a wealthy country with a well-educated population, the United States has a low rate of teenage pregnancy.

■ ■ ■

Adolescents who experience much good fortune—such as being accepted to a prestigious school, winning an athletic championship, or being awarded a large scholarship—lead happier lives than those who experience more misfortune.

Do the preceding statements seem correct to you?

In fact, each of them is wrong, representing a common myth about adolescence. As you learn more and more of what social scientists have to tell us about adolescence, you'll probably notice a recurring theme: The scientific study of adolescence is based on research. Why do scientists bother conducting research on questions that have commonsense answers?

It is true that research sometimes just confirms our intuitions. But most of the time, we perceive a research finding to be "just common sense" only after the fact; if we were asked to predict the finding ahead of time, we usually wouldn't find it so obvious! And sometimes "common sense" actually leads us to the wrong prediction—many myths and misconceptions about adolescence are widely believed to be true.

It is only through the use of systematic research built on the scientific perspectives we have been discussing that we know which seemingly obvious "facts" about adolescence are accurate. For instance, consider each of the myths listed earlier (and dispelled in Table 1-3). How many of these myths did you personally believe? Do you find the reality surprising?

TABLE 1-3	Dispelling the Myths of Adolescence	
Myth	**Reality**	**Discussed in Chapter**
Myth #1: It's important for all adolescents to have high self-esteem, so every effort should be made to boost their self-esteem.	Although high self-esteem is certainly associated with positive outcomes, we can't say for sure that one causes the other. There is no evidence that artificially inflating a person's self-esteem will automatically produce these positive outcomes, and more importantly, there can be a significant downside to exaggerated self-esteem.	Chapter 5
Myth #2: Adolescents are very different from adults in their behaviors, values, attitudes, and so forth, and these differences commonly cause significant disruptions in parent–adolescent relationships.	This is the myth of the generation gap. Actually, although adolescence may be a period of increased tension between parents and children, these relationships usually remain strong and positive.	Chapter 6
Myth #3: Adolescents who don't have any close friends are likely to become criminal, antisocial, or mentally ill later in life.	There is no evidence that adolescents who lack close friendships are at risk of any severe negative outcomes.	Chapter 8
Myth #4: As a wealthy country with a well-educated population, the United States has a low rate of teenage pregnancy.	The rate of teenage pregnancy is two to ten times higher in the United States than it is in other industrialized countries.	Chapter 9
Myth #5: Adolescents who experience much good fortune—such as being accepted to a prestigious school, winning an athletic championship, or being awarded a large scholarship—lead happier lives than those who experience more misfortune.	Although incidents of good or bad fortune can cause short-term changes in mood, adolescents tend to return eventually to their baseline level of happiness. Happiness seems to remain relatively stable throughout life.	Chapter 13

Keep in mind that the point of presenting these myths is to illustrate how easily we can be convinced of erroneous information that sounds plausible. That's why it's important for scientists to conduct controlled, systematic research as a way to separate the truth of adolescence from the myths.

But how can we differentiate the truth from plausible-sounding myths? The following approaches may help:

- Consider the source of the advice. Information from established, respected organizations such as the Society for Research in Child Development, the American Medical Association, the American Psychological Association, and the American Academy of Pediatrics is likely to be the result of years of study, and its accuracy is probably high.

- Evaluate the credentials of the person providing the information. Material coming from established, acknowledged researchers and experts in a field is likely to be more accurate than that coming from a person whose credentials are obscure.

- Understand the difference between anecdotal evidence and scientific evidence. Anecdotal evidence is based on one or two instances of a phenomenon, haphazardly discovered or encountered; scientific evidence is based on careful, systematic procedures.

- Keep cultural context in mind. Although an assertion may be valid in some contexts, it may not be true in all.

- Finally, don't assume that because many people believe something, it is necessarily true. Scientific evaluation has often proved that some of the most basic assumptions about adolescent problems and the effectiveness of various techniques for dealing with them are invalid. For instance, consider DARE, the Drug Abuse Resistance Education antidrug program that is used in about half of the middle and high schools in the United States. DARE is designed to prevent the spread of drugs through lectures and question-and-answer sessions run by police officers. Careful evaluation, however, finds no evidence that the program is effective in reducing drug use (Lyman et al., 1999; West & O'Neal, 2005).

In short, the key to evaluating information relating to adolescence is to maintain a healthy dose of skepticism. No source of information is invariably, unfailingly accurate, but material derived from scientific research findings is sure to be more accurate than what comes from intuition or "common sense." By thinking critically about information regarding adolescents, you'll be in a better position to determine the very real contributions made by adolescent scientists in understanding how adolescents change and grow over the course of one of the most critical periods of the life span.

Review and Apply

Review

1. G. Stanley Hall originated the scientific study of adolescence, but his "storm and stress" view of the period is exaggerated.

2. The scientific method consists of (a) identifying questions of interest, (b) formulating an explanation, and (c) carrying out research that supports or refutes it.

3. Adolescent researchers use longitudinal studies, cross-sectional studies, and sequential studies to examine change and development during the period.

4. Modern perspectives on adolescence include the psychodynamic perspective, the behavioral perspective, the cognitive perspective, the contextual perspective, and evolutionary perspectives.

5. No single perspective is correct or entirely sufficient; all have something to say about some aspect of adolescent development, and each is incomplete alone.

Apply

1. Do you think that Bronfenbrenner's five levels of the environment (microsystem, mesosystem, exosystem, macrosystem, and chronosystem) exert different amounts of influence as adolescents age and pass through different stages of development?

2. Why would many otherwise aware and skeptical adults persistently believe myths about adolescence instead of the truth? Is there any way to change this?

Key Questions: Major Themes of the Study of Adolescence

I know things change as life goes on, people go their separate ways, and you go off into different paths of your life. But I can't handle it. I can't handle growing up. I can't handle changing. I ... sit here looking at pictures of friends from middle school and high school, realizing that I don't even talk to one of them on a regular basis. Of all the friends I've had in the first 18 years of my life, it's like they are gone. Completely out of my life. I see Myspaces and Facebooks and Away messages, but that's it. No interaction, no conversations,

TABLE 1-4 The Major Questions of Adolescence
What are the key transitions and tasks of adolescence?
How can we identify the most important of the "firsts" that occur during adolescence and understand how these transitions play out?
What are the effects of cohort membership on adolescents?
How do we determine the consequences of cohort (a group of people born at around the same time in the same place) on adolescent development?
How does developmental change occur during adolescence?
Does adolescent development largely reflect continuous change (in which developmental is gradual and progressive) or discontinuous change (changes occurring in distinct, qualitatively different development)?
What is the relative influence of nature and nurture on development?
How and to what degree is adolescent development a reflection of maturation (the predetermined unfolding of genetic information) versus a reflection of environmental influences?
How can sound social policy be developed that can improve the lives of adolescents?
What is the most effective type of social policy (national, state, or local governmental actions designed to improve the welfare of citizens)?

nothing. I'm not saying that I don't like my friends now. I love them to death. It just scares me. Are they all of a sudden gonna disappear one day too? . . . I don't have the slightest clue as to what my future will be.

For adolescents, the changes that occur in their lives can be overwhelming. For adolescent specialists, too, whose job is to characterize the nature of these changes and examine how they affect adolescents, the range and variation in adolescent experience is daunting, raising a number of issues and questions. What are the best ways to think about the changes that an adolescent experiences from the beginning to the end of adolescence? How important is chronological age? Is there a clear timetable for development? How can one begin to find common threads and patterns?

These questions have been debated since adolescence first became established as a field with the publication of G. Stanley Hall's *Adolescence* in 1904, though a fascination with the nature and course of adolescence can be traced back to the ancient Greeks. Let's look at some of the key questions, which are summarized in Table 1-4.

What are the Key Transitions and Tasks of Adolescence?

Reaching puberty. Entering high school. Getting a job for the first time. Leaving home. Entering college. Leaving adolescence and becoming an adult.

Each of these events represents an important transition for adolescents. Some occur at one point in time (there's a particular day that an adolescent begins high school), and others are more gradual and occur over an extended period of time (such as puberty or—as we consider in the accompanying *Transitions* box—the end of adolescence and the start of adulthood). Consequently, one of the key questions asked by specialists in adolescence is how to identify the most

Transitions

From Adolescence to Emerging Adulthood

There's no graduation ceremony that marks the end of adolescence and the start of adulthood. It's a transition that occurs gradually and, according to a growing number of adolescent specialists, marks a period that can affect the course of life in significant ways (Arnett & Tanner, 2006).

According to psychologist Jeffrey Jensen Arnett (2000, 2004), the period of around ages 18 to 25 can be characterized as *emerging adulthood*. Emerging adults have not fully left adolescence, but at the same time they are not yet independent adults. Instead, they are somewhere in between. They believe that they have outgrown many of the earlier struggles of adolescence, and they are feeling responsible for themselves. However, they are still closely tied to their parents and families.

Because of changes in society, emerging adults are no longer expected to be holding down jobs, to be married, or to be involved in parenting, unlike in earlier historical eras. In fact, there is a relative lack of expectations about what emerging adults should be doing—a fact that permits a significant degree of freedom and allows them the opportunity for exploration and experimentation. On the other hand, such freedom can be difficult, because it forces emerging adults to determine largely on their own what it is they want from life and how to achieve their goals.

More specifically, Arnett suggested that emerging adulthood has several characteristics (Munsey, 2006):

- **Identity exploration and self-focus.** Emerging adults feel a renewed motivation to determine who they are and what they want out of life. They are very much focused on themselves, rather than others.

- **Instability.** Emerging adults haven't yet settled down into adult roles. Even their physical home is unstable: They move frequently, leaving (and returning) to their childhood homes and living temporarily in residence halls and apartments.

- **Feeling "in between."** Emerging adults report feeling like they have grown out of adolescence, but are not yet adults. This "in-between" status produces a degree of uncertainty, but it is coupled with significant freedom.

- **Optimism.** Most emerging adults are optimistic about their future. They expect that they will establish strong, lasting relationships, and that their jobs will be rewarding and fulfilling.

Of course, not every emerging adult exhibits all these characteristics, and certainly not all to the same degree. In fact, there is a significant degree of heterogeneity within the group relating to personality and to demographic, socioeconomic, and cultural factors. Certainly, in cultures in which adolescents take on adult jobs earlier than in Western societies, emerging adulthood may begin earlier or may not even be a significant phase of life. Similarly, in ethnic minority groups within the United States, where adult responsibilities may be given to adolescents earlier for economic and cultural reasons, emerging adulthood may be a quite different phenomenon (Phinney, 2006).

It is too early to tell if emerging adulthood will become an established period signifying the transition between adolescence and adulthood. What is clear is that the study of adolescence is continuing to evolve and—through the research conducted by adolescent scientists—is painting an increasingly full and accurate account of adolescence.

What are some of the effects of the freedom from expectations during emerging adolescence? If, as some economists think, financial prosperity declines in the future, what effects will economic limits have on this group?

- Do you think that recent social changes justify considering emerging adulthood a separate period that is distinct from both adolescence and adulthood? If so, is it likely to continue being a distinct period of development? Why or why not?

important of the many "firsts" that occur during adolescence and coming to understand how these transitions play out.

The transitions that adolescents encounter are significant because they offer the opportunity to engage in what psychologists refer to as developmental tasks. *Developmental tasks* are the activities and achievements that society and culture say are typical for normal development at a particular stage of life. For example, the developmental tasks of infancy include learning to walk and talk.

In some respects, the developmental tasks of adolescence occur across a broader variety of domains—physical, cognitive, and social—than in earlier stages of life. In a classic enumeration that has proven surprisingly enduring, psychologist Robert Havighurst (1972) suggested that the primary developmental tasks of adolescence include the following:

In early adolescence:

- Achieving new and more mature relations with peers of both sexes
- Achieving a gender-appropriate role
- Accepting one's physique and using the body effectively
- Achieving emotional independence from parents and other adults

In late adolescence:

- Preparing for marriage and family life
- Preparing for an economic career
- Acquiring a set of values and an ethical system as a guide to behavior
- Desiring and achieving socially responsible behavior

This list is not exhaustive; other tasks might reasonably be thought of as central to adolescence. Furthermore, adolescent specialists may argue that certain tasks that do appear are less crucial than others or that the division of tasks into early and late adolescence is not fully accurate. Still, the list is useful because it provides a broad overview of the major developmental tasks in which youth are engaged during adolescence. Furthermore, adolescent specialists continue to seek to identify the major tasks of adolescence.

What are the Effects of Cohort Membership on Adolescents?

Matthew, born in 1947, is a baby boomer; he was born soon after the end of World War II, when an enormous bulge in the birthrate occurred as soldiers returned to the United States from overseas. He was an adolescent at the height of the Civil Rights movement and the beginning of protests against the Vietnam War. His mother, Ronnie, was born in 1922; she is part of the generation that passed its teenage years in the shadow of the depression. Matthew's daughter, Kiela, was born in 1988. Her adolescence, which occurred at the start of the 21st century, has been marked by relative prosperity and the lingering war in Iraq.

These people are in part products of the social times in which they live. Each belongs to a particular **cohort,** a group of people born at around the same time in the same place. Such major social events as wars, economic upturns and depressions, famines, and epidemics (like the one due to the AIDS virus) work similar influences on members of a particular cohort.

Cohort effects provide an example of *history-graded influences,* which are biological and environmental influences associated with a particular historical moment. For instance, adolescents who lived in New Orleans, Louisiana, in the summer of 2005 shared both biological and environmental challenges due to Hurricane Katrina, which devastated their city.

In contrast, *age-graded influences* are biological and environmental influences that are similar for individuals in a particular age group, regardless of when or where they are raised. For example, biological events such as puberty and menopause are universal events that occur at relatively the same time throughout all societies. Similarly, a sociocultural event such as entry into formal education can be considered a normative age-graded influence because it occurs in most cultures around age six.

Development is also affected by *sociocultural-graded influences,* the social and cultural factors present at a particular time for a particular individual, depending on such variables as ethnicity, social class, and subcultural membership. For example, sociocultural-graded influences will be considerably different for adolescents who are white and affluent than for adolescents who are members of a minority group and living in poverty (Rose et al., 2003).

Finally, *nonnormative life events* are specific, atypical events that occur in a particular person's life at a time when such events do not happen to most adolescents. For example, an

cohort   a group of people born around the same time in the same place

adolescent whose parents die in a car crash when she is 16 years old has experienced a significant nonnormative life event.

How Does Developmental Change Occur during Adolescence?

One important issue challenging adolescent specialists is whether development proceeds in a continuous or discontinuous fashion. In **continuous change**, development is gradual, with achievements at one level building on those of previous levels. Continuous change is quantitative; the basic underlying developmental processes that drive change remain the same over the course of the life span. Continuous change, then, produces changes that are a matter of degree, not of kind. Changes in height during adolescence, for example, are continuous (despite the fact that they occur in spurts). Similarly, some theorists suggest that changes in adolescents' thinking capabilities are also continuous, showing gradual quantitative improvements rather than developing entirely new cognitive processing capabilities.

In contrast, **discontinuous change** occurs in distinct steps or stages. Each stage brings about behavior that is assumed to be qualitatively different from behavior at earlier stages. Consider the example of cognitive development. We'll see in Chapter 3 that some cognitive developmentalists suggest that thinking changes in fundamental ways as adolescents develop and that such development is a matter of not just quantitative change but qualitative change as well.

What is the Relative Influence of Nature and Nurture on Adolescent Development?

One of the enduring questions involves how much of people's behavior is due to their genetically determined nature and how much is due to nurture, the influences of the physical and social environment in which an adolescent is raised. This issue, which has deep philosophical and historical roots, has dominated much of the work on adolescence.

In this context, *nature* refers to traits, abilities, and capacities that are inherited from one's parents. It encompasses any factor that is produced by the predetermined unfolding of genetic information—a process known as **maturation.** These genetic, inherited influences are at work as we move from the one-cell organism that is created at the moment of conception to the billions of cells that make up a fully formed human.

Nature influences whether our eyes are blue or brown, whether we have thick hair throughout life or eventually go bald, and how good we are at athletics. Nature allows our brains to develop in such a way that we can read the words on this page.

In contrast, *nurture* refers to the environmental influences that shape behavior. Some of these influences may be biological, such as the impact of a pregnant mother's use of cocaine on her unborn child or the amounts and kinds of food available to adolescents. Other environmental influences are more social, such as the ways parents discipline their children and the effects of peer pressure on an adolescent. Finally, some influences are a result of larger, societal-level factors, such as the socioeconomic circumstances in which people find themselves living.

If our traits and behavior were determined solely by either nature or nurture, there would probably be little debate regarding the issue. However, for most critical behaviors, this is hardly the case. Take, for instance, one of the most controversial arenas: intelligence. The question of whether intelligence is determined primarily by inherited, genetic factors—nature—or is shaped by environmental factors—nurture—has caused lively and often bitter arguments. Largely because of its social implications, the issue has spilled out of the scientific arena and into the realm of politics and social policy.

The question of how much of a given behavior is due to nature and how much to nurture is challenging. Ultimately, we should consider the two sides of the nature–nurture issue as op-

continuous change   gradual development in which achievements at one level build on those of previous levels

discontinuous change   development that occurs in distinct steps or stages, with each stage bringing about behavior that is assumed to be qualitatively different from behavior at earlier stages

maturation   the predetermined unfolding of genetic information

posite ends of a continuum, with particular behaviors falling somewhere between the two ends. We can say something similar about the other controversies that we have considered. For instance, continuous versus discontinuous development is not an either–or proposition; some forms of development fall toward the continuous end of the continuum, while others lie closer to the discontinuous end. In short, few statements about development involve either–or absolutes.

How Can Sound Social Policy Be Developed That Can Improve the Lives of Adolescents?

It may be a cliché to state that the future of the world rests on the shoulders of youth, but it is no less true. The success of future generations depends on how well younger generations can cope with the myriad world problems that older generations have created.

Society, then, needs to promote the welfare of adolescents, and it can do so through the development of sound social policy. **Social policy** is national, state, or local governmental actions designed to improve the welfare of citizens. It includes laws meant to protect adolescents, as well as governmental support of programs designed to help adolescents achieve their potential or avoid difficulties that might negatively impact their lives (Lerner et al., 2005; Mannes, Roehlkepartain, & Benson, 2005).

For example, young adolescents are prohibited from working more than a certain number of hours per week and are allowed to work only in certain jobs, under the assumption that too much work or dangerous work will put them at risk. Similarly, governmental programs designed to reduce the incidence of teenage pregnancy have been established to improve the welfare of adolescents.

Despite the importance of adolescence, in some significant ways social policy has been skewed in favor of generations other than adolescence. Probably the best example of *generational inequality*, in which certain generations are favored at the expense of other generations, are the Social Security and Medicare programs. Social Security and Medicare are financed by payroll taxes paid by younger workers. No one doubts the importance of the two programs, but one can conclude that social policy is favoring one generation over the other.

The answer to such inequality is not to reduce benefits to older generations but to support programs designed to benefit all generations. Adolescents, in particular, have not received the same share of social policy support that older generations or, for that matter, infants and children, have (for example, the Head Start program). It's critical that social policies be designed to aggressively support adolescents.

But it's also critical that such social policy be based on sound research and data. Politicians need to develop policies that are *empirically based*, meaning that a particular approach or program designed to solve a problem has been tested and shown to be effective before being implemented on a wide-scale basis. Some specialists on adolescence focus on public policy, as exemplified in the *Career Choices* box.

The Future of Adolescence

In this chapter, we've examined the foundations of the field of adolescence, along with the key issues and questions that underlie the discipline. But what lies ahead? Several trends appear likely to emerge:

- As researchers on adolescence continues to amass data, the field will become increasingly specialized. New areas of study and fresh perspectives will emerge.

- The explosion in information about genes and the genetic foundations of behavior will influence all spheres of adolescent science. Adolescent specialists increasingly will link work

social policy a national, state, or local governmental response designed to improve the welfare of citizens

CAREER CHOICES

Public Policy Specialist

Name: Steve Manchester

Education: BS, political science, and M.S. in secondary school administration, Eastern Michigan University, Ypsilanti, Michigan

Position: Public Policy Specialist

Home: Lansing, Michigan

A S GOVERNMENTAL agencies seek to determine how to use their limited funds to best improve the social conditions of adolescents, they increasingly involve the expertise of public policy analysts.

According to public policy specialist Steven Manchester, members of his profession can bring skills to almost any cause or field.

"A public policy specialist thinks about the collective effort of society to make good decisions," he said. "There are public policy specialists in all sorts of areas."

In many ways the public policy specialist is an advocate for a particular cause or policy, according to Manchester.

"In my work I am constantly involved in convincing other policy makers, legislators in Michigan, and Congress to increase society's investment in children," he said.

As a public policy specialist, Manchester argues that the investments made by government setting good policies will have significant effect on all involved.

For those who wish to pursue a career as a public policy specialist, Manchester, a former Peace Corp Volunteer and legislative staff worker, recommends getting involved in the legislative process.

"Help someone get elected and get involved with the legislative process," Manchester suggests. "Young people who get into staff work in Washington, D.C., develop some insights on how to promote and drive public policy ideas, develop views on how to get society to collectively make decisions, and then make the messages so they are understandable to the general public.

"If you get a reputation for being reliable in the effort to influence public decisions, you will be like gold," he added. "Also, it doesn't hurt to realize that what's at stake is saving the world. It may sound hokey, but we really are involved in that."

Thinking of becoming a Public Policy Specialist?

Public policy specialists are experts in various academic disciplines that have broad real-world applications, such as adolescent science. Public officials turn to public policy specialists for background information and analysis of the issue at hand, as well as for their recommendations.

The career path for a public policy specialist sometimes begins with training in a scientific discipline such as psychology or sociology. Some specialists earn a master's or Ph.D. degree in their field, thus gaining thorough training and experience in research, before they move into public policy. Others complete a bachelor's degree in their field of interest and then obtain a master's degree in public policy administration. Other career paths are possible; some public policy specialists are scientists who made a midlife career change; others entered public policy careers after earning degrees in political science, law, or even business management. ■

across biological, cognitive, and social domains, and the boundaries between different subdisciplines will be blurred.

- The increasing racial, ethnic, linguistic, and cultural diversity of the U.S. population will lead the field to focus greater attention on issues of diversity.

- A growing number of professionals in a variety of fields will make use of adolescent science's research and findings. Educators, social workers, nurses, and other health-care providers, genetic counselors, social ethicists, and members of dozens of other professions will all draw on the field of adolescence.

- Work on adolescence will increasingly influence public policy issues. Discussion of many of the major social concerns of our time, including violence, prejudice and discrimination, poverty, changes in family life, and schooling will be informed by research on adolescence. Consequently, specialists in adolescent public policy are likely to make important contributions to 21st-century society (Benson et al., 2004; Lerner et al., 2005).

Review and Apply

Review

1. Major transitions in adolescence include reaching puberty, entering high school, getting one's first job, and becoming an adult.

2. The freedom that comes with a lack of rigid expectations can be either liberating or challenging.

3. The developmental tasks of adolescence include working out the meaning of physical maturity, achieving emotional and economic independence, and acquiring a set of ethics and values to guide life.

4. Researchers speak about influences through which people (including adolescents) pass either as a group or individually, including history-graded influences, age-graded influences, sociocultural-graded influences, and nonnormative life events.

5. Working out the influences of nature and nurture on adolescent development is the focus of a major strand of study among adolescent researchers.

Apply

1. Compared with less-affluent adolescents, are affluent adolescents more likely, less likely, or equally likely to feel like emerging adults instead of full adults? Why?

2. In what ways has adolescent development become a political issue?

EPILOGUE

In this chapter, we introduced many of the topics that we will look into more deeply in the chapters that follow. We examined the surprisingly broad range of subjects that adolescent researchers study, as well as the developmental changes that adolescents experience during the period.

Next, we considered the historical underpinnings of the study of adolescence as a scientific pursuit, and we discussed the major ways that researchers have designed to study the phenomenon of change in human development. We looked at the comparative advantages and shortcomings of longitudinal, cross-sectional, and sequential research in general and at the characteristics and limitations of major perspectives on adolescent development.

Finally, we examined the key transitions in adolescent development and the main tasks that adolescents face as they mature. We looked at the effects on adolescents' development of historical events, biological events, social and cultural events, and nonnormative life events.

Before moving on to the next chapter, let's go back to Elizabeth, Carly, Trevor, and Purva, the four adolescents who began our consideration of adolescence.

1. To what sort of events is Elizabeth's school success most likely attributable—history-graded influences, age-graded influences, sociocultural-graded influences, or nonnormative life events? Why?

2. If Carly's mother works as hard getting her daughter into a prestigious college as she worked to get her into a high school for gifted children, is this strategy guaranteed to earn Carly a successful life? Why or why not?

3. Which of the major tasks of adolescence is Trevor apparently addressing most directly by participating in the Boys and Girls Club?

4. Is Purva's relationship with her family typical or unusual for adolescents in the United States? Which aspects are typical and which are unusual? Why?

SUMMARY

REVIEW

● **What are the major topics and issues that researchers on adolescence study today?** *(p. 6)*

1. Adolescents face a constellation of changes relating to their "in-between" status as no longer children and not yet adults.

2. The number of years of adolescence has increased during recent decades, and yet those going through the period often remain dependent on their parents until well into their twenties.

3. The topics most often studied by adolescent researchers are physical development, cognitive development, and social/personality development.

4. Adolescents represent greater numbers than ever before and, despite negative stereotypes, are generally optimistic and happy.

● **How did the study of adolescence begin, and how has it developed historically?** *(p. 11)*

5. The founder of modern adolescent science is G. Stanley Hall, who characterized the period as one of storm and stress, giving rise to many modern stereotypes.

6. Although Hall is recognized for his views of the genetic origins of adolescence, subsequent studies have found his opinion that unusual turbulence marks the period to be exaggerated.

7. The study of adolescence has become increasingly scientific, focusing on the difficult topic of change through longitudinal, cross-sectional, and sequential studies.

● **What are some modern perspectives on adolescence?** *(p. 15)*

8. Modern perspectives on adolescence include the psychodynamic perspective attributed to Freud and the behavioral perspective of B. F. Skinner.

9. More recent perspectives include the contextual perspective and the evolutionary perspective.

10. No single perspective is right; rather, the different perspectives represent different ways of looking at important issues simultaneously.

● **What transitions and tasks are adolescents engaged in during the period?** *(p. 27)*

11. Adolescents face multiple tasks during the period, including identity exploration, feelings of instability, and the persistent sense that their lives are "in between" major periods.

12. The most important tasks during adolescence are due to adolescents' status as "emerging adults" rather than either full-fledged children or full-fledged adults.

13. The transitions of adolescence relate to physical maturity (e.g., reaching puberty), social maturity (e.g., entering high school), financial maturity (e.g., getting one's first job), and personal maturity (e.g., becoming an adult).

● **How do nature and nurture interact during adolescence?** *(p. 30)*

14. Adolescents are subject to history-graded influences (e.g., effects due to the cohort to which one belongs by birth year and birthplace) and age-graded influences (e.g., effects due to one's age, regardless of where one lives).

15. They are also subject to sociocultural-graded influences (e.g., effects due to one's social background and ethnicity) and nonnormative life events (e.g., the effects of occurrences happening to the individual rather than to the group as a whole).

16. Adolescents are also subject in important, but unresolved, ways to the competing effects of nature (genetic influences) and nurture (environmental influences).

17. Many of the issues affecting adolescents have social policy implications, which should be empirically based (i.e., based on observation, research, and the full arsenal of sound science) rather than political.

KEY TERMS AND CONCEPTS

adolescence (p. 5)

adolescent science: (p. 13)

scientific method (p. 13)

longitudinal research (p. 14)

cross-sectional research (p. 14)

sequential studies (p. 15)

psychodynamic perspective (p. 16)

psychoanalytic theory (p. 16)

psychosexual development (p. 16)

psychosocial development (p. 16)

behavioral perspective (p. 17)

cognitive perspective (p. 18)

information processing approaches (p. 19)

cognitive neuroscience approaches (p. 19)

contextual perspective (p. 20)

bioecological approach (p. 20)

sociocultural theory (p. 22)

evolutionary perspective (p. 22)

cohort (p. 29)

continuous change (p. 30)

discontinuous change (p. 30)

maturation (p. 30)

social policy (p. 31)

2

Physical Development

CHAPTER OUTLINE

PROLOGUE: The Cruelest Cut

H E ARRIVED 10 minutes before his fate, so Filip Olsson stood outside Severna Park High School and waited for coaches to post the cut list for the boys' soccer team.

Olsson, a sophomore, wanted desperately to make the junior varsity, but he also wanted justification for a long list of sacrifices. His family had rearranged a trip to Sweden so he could participate in a preparatory soccer camp; he'd crawled out of bed at 5:30 A.M. for two weeks of camp and tryouts and forced down Raisin Bran; he'd sweated off five pounds and pulled his hamstring.

Finally, a coach walked by holding a list, and Olsson followed him into the high school. He walked back out two minutes later, his hands shoved deep into his pockets and his eyes locked on the ground.

"It felt," he said later, "like a punch in the stomach." (Saslow, 2005, p. A1) ■

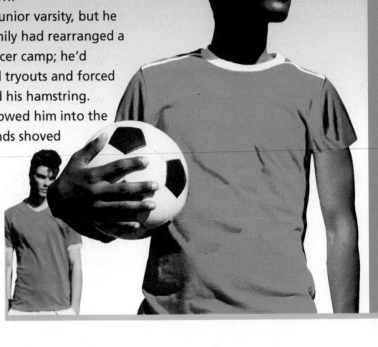

th!nk ABOUT THIS

FOR ADOLESCENTS LIKE Filip Olsson, their physical abilities are closely tied to who they are and how they view themselves. No wonder: The physical changes that occur during adolescence are so drastic that it is hard for adolescents to avoid viewing—and sometimes defining—themselves, in large part, in terms of their bodies.

In this chapter we consider the remarkable biological transitions of adolescence. We start by focusing on *puberty*, the period of rapid physical change characterized by the maturation of the sexual organs. We'll discuss the chemical changes that trigger puberty, concentrating on the hormones that initiate the period.

We then examine the outward physical changes that occur during puberty. We discuss the growth spurt in height and weight and the maturation of the reproductive organs that represent the awakening of sexuality. We also look at the ramifications of early and late maturation for adolescents' view of themselves.

Finally, we discuss health and wellness during adolescence. We will find that although adolescents are largely at the peak of health, relative to other periods of life, there are also a number of threats to their well-being. ■

- How and when does puberty begin, and what are its effects on maturing adolescents?
- How do the nervous system and brain develop during adolescence?
- What physical changes do adolescents experience as they grow?
- What are the psychological effects of sexual maturation in male and female adolescents?
- What is the typical state of adolescents' health, and what are some threats to health and wellness during adolescence?

Beginnings: The Start of Puberty

When I finally hit my growth spurt in high school ..., I just evened out. Even before I had finished growing, I found myself becoming more coordinated and more fluid in my motions. Looking back on that period of time I almost feel like as a kid, I was always a larger person trying to work in a smaller body, and when that body finally started to coincide with that inner sense of size, things smoothed out.

■ ■ ■

Puberty was not kind to me. I was the first to get pimples and the last to get a bra.

Puberty, the period of maturation during which the sexual organs mature, begins in a stealthy manner. The outward changes in the body that are the first sign of puberty—the tiny budding of breasts in females and the wispy beginnings of a beard in males—often go unnoticed. However, although the initial outward physical signs of puberty are small in scale, it's a different story inside adolescents' bodies, where significant changes are occurring.

Actually, those changes are determined at the moment of conception, when we receive our genetic makeup from our parents. The timing of puberty is encoded in a specific set of genes that determines when puberty starts and the order in which events unfold. However, as we'll see, the timing and sequence of puberty are not only a matter of genetics; environmental events, such as the adequacy of children's nutrition and the level of stress in their lives, also affect when and how puberty proceeds.

The biological events that mark the start of puberty are triggered by the endocrine system, the system in the body that exerts a powerful influence over the course of development.

The Endocrine System: Chemical Couriers

The **endocrine system** is a chemical communication network that sends messages throughout the body via the bloodstream. The endocrine system communicates via **hormones**, chemical messengers that circulate through the blood and affect the functioning or growth of other parts of the body (see Figure 2-1).

Hormones travel throughout the body in a manner similar to the way a radio station transmits a signal across the countryside. Just as the signal from a particular station produces a response only when a radio is tuned to that station, hormones flowing through the bloodstream activate only particular cells that are receptive and "tuned" to that particular hormone.

Pubertal development begins when the *pituitary gland* in the brain sends a signal via gonadotropins, specialized hormones that stimulate the sex glands, to increase the production of the sex hormones to adult levels. The pituitary gland is sometimes called the "master gland"

puberty   the period of maturation during which the sexual organs mature

endocrine system   a chemical communication network that sends messages throughout the body via the bloodstream

hormones   chemicals that circulate through the blood and affect the functioning or growth of other parts of the body

Structure

Function

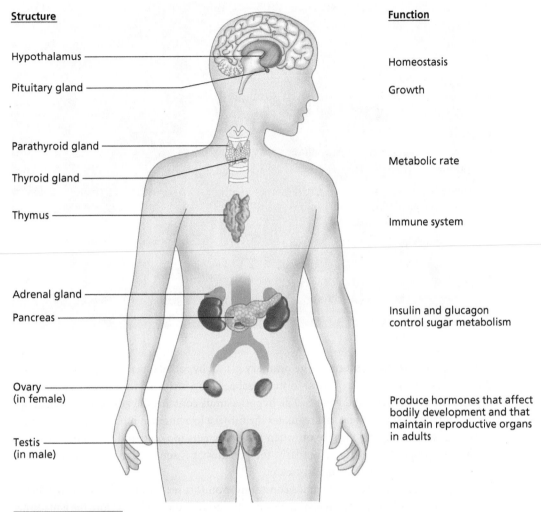

Hypothalamus

Pituitary gland

Parathyroid gland

Thyroid gland

Thymus

Adrenal gland

Pancreas

Ovary
(in female)

Testis
(in male)

Homeostasis

Growth

Metabolic rate

Immune system

Insulin and glucagon
control sugar metabolism

Produce hormones that affect
bodily development and that
maintain reproductive organs
in adults

▲ **FIGURE 2-1**

The Endocrine Glands   Location and function of the major endocrine glands. The pituitary
gland controls the functioning of the other endocrine glands and in turn is regulated by the
hypothalamus.

(*Source:* Mader, 2000)

because it controls the operation of the rest of the endocrine system. But it has important functions of its own. For example, hormones secreted by the pituitary gland control growth.

There are two major classes of sex hormones: *androgens* (the main category of male hormones) and *estrogens* (the main category of female hormones). Among the major androgens is
testosterone, which in males plays a particularly significant role during puberty. Greater concentrations of testosterone are related to the increase in height, weight, size of the male genitals, and deepening of the voice. Similarly, a major estrogen is *estradiol,* which has an important
role in determining female development during puberty. Estradiol is related to enlargement of
the breasts, development of the uterus, and increases in height and weight (Garnett et al., 2004;
Wang et al., 2004; Eriksson et al., 2005).

The pituitary gland works in tandem with the *hypothalamus,* the structure of the brain that
monitors and regulates basic drives such as eating, drinking, self-protection, and sexual behavior. Although the tiny hypothalamus, which is about the size of a fingertip, plays a powerful role in regulating the steady functioning of the body throughout life, it has an especially
important function during puberty as part of a complex feedback system involving the pituitary
gland and the sexual organs, as we will see next.

▶The significant differences in height that occur in adolescents of the same age highlight the role of unseen biological factors that determine the timing of maturation.

The HPG Feedback System. The pituitary gland, hypothalamus, and gonads (in males the testes, and in females the ovaries) form a feedback loop involving the *HPG axis*—short for *h*ypothalamus, *p*ituitary, and *g*onads. The hypothalamus contains the **gonadostat**, which operates a bit like the thermostat that regulates the furnace in a home. A home thermostat is sensitive to heat, turning the furnace on when the home gets too cold and off when the home reaches the proper temperature. Similarly, the gonadostat is sensitive to the amount of hormones circulating through the bloodstream.

The gonadostat in the hypothalamus constantly monitors sex hormone levels in an effort to maintain a consistent quantity circulating through the body. If the level is too low, the gonadostat signals the pituitary to work overtime to produce more hormones. If the sex hormones shoot above the desired level, the gonadostat inhibits the pituitary, thereby reducing the level of sex hormones (see Figure 2-2). During puberty, the hypothalamus calls for the release of greater quantitites of hormones than it did earlier in childhood.

The pituitary gland produces two hormones, known as FSH and LH, that determine the levels of sex hormones. *FSH (follicle-stimulating hormone)* stimulates sperm production in the testes of males and follicle production in the ovaries of females. *LH (lutenizing hormone)* regulates the production of testosterone in males and estrogen and eggs in females.

The start of puberty is not the first time that androgens and estrogens influence development in significant ways. In fact, the two classes of hormones are present in the body from the moment of conception, but at very low levels. Furthermore, although we associate androgens with males and estrogens with females, in fact both sexes produce the two types of sex hormones. It's just that males have a higher concentration of androgens and females a higher concentration of estrogens.

In fact, those androgens and estrogens play a significant role in the developing fetus prior to birth, organizing the brain and preparing the body to carry out functions that may not begin until adolescence. For example, in weeks 8 to 24 following conception, hormones are released that lead to the increasing differentiation of males and females. Specifically, high levels of androgen are produced in males that affect the size of brain cells and the growth of neural connections, which, some scientists speculate, ultimately may lead to differences in male and female brain structure and even to later variations in gender-related behavior during adolescence (Hines et al., 2002a; Berenbaum & Bailey, 2003; Reiner & Gearhart, 2004).

gonadostat a feedback loop mechanism that regulates the sex hormone concentration in blood through a complicated circuit involving the hypothalamus, pituitary, and gonads in males and ovaries in females

As the pituitary gland signals the body to increase its production of androgens and estrogens, it is also signals the endocrine system to produce growth hormones. These growth hormones interact with the sex hormones to cause the growth spurt and puberty.

Hormones and Emotions. Although scientists have a good understanding of how hormone production is related to the start of puberty, it is less clear how hormones are related to the emotions experienced by adolescents as puberty begins. But it is clear that there is an important link.

In certain respects, hormones directly affect adolescents' emotions. For example, high levels of certain hormones that are actively produced during puberty lead to the experience of depression or hostility. Exceptionally high levels of the male hormone testosterone are associated with antisocial behavior. There's also a gender difference: Males may have feelings of anger and annoyance that are associated with higher hormone levels. In females, the emotions caused by hormone production are somewhat different: Higher levels of hormones are associated with anger and depression (Buchanan, Eccles, & Becker, 1992; Rowe et al., 2004).

It's not just the presence of certain hormones that may influence emotions during puberty. It also seems that the rapid *increase* in hormone levels, independent of the specific hormone, affects mood. For instance, at the start of puberty, the concentration of sex hormones rises rapidly; mood swings at this time may reflect adolescents' efforts to adapt to the significant changes that are occurring in their bodies. Later in adolescence, even though hormone concentrations are still high, adolescents have adapted to the change, and their mood is not affected. Furthermore, it may be that the ability to adjust to the changes in hormone levels is related to genetic predispositions to psychological disorders (Brooks-Gunn & Warren, 1989; Walker, Sabuwalla, & Huot, 2004).

It's also possible that the very efficiency of the feedback loop that controls the HPG (hypothalamus–pituitary–gonad) axis is the source of the emotional mood swings found at puberty. Because the feedback system produces significant fluctuations, both up and down, in the concentration of hormones, adolescents may be reacting to the constant changes that are occurring in their bodies (Cameron, 2004; Tung et al., 2004).

In short, hormones appear to play a significant role in determining the emotional reactions experienced by adolescents passing through puberty. But clearly there are several routes through which hormones (and hormonal fluctuations) affect mood. In addition, hormones do not work in isolation from environmental stressors that have an impact on adolescents' lives. Adolescents who face significant stress in their family or school lives may be more susceptible to the effects of hormonal changes than those whose lives are more stable. In effect, changes in hormone levels become one more of several stressors that make life complicated, leading to greater emotionality and more pronounced mood swings (Paikoff & Brooks-Gunn, 1991; Young & Altemus, 2004).

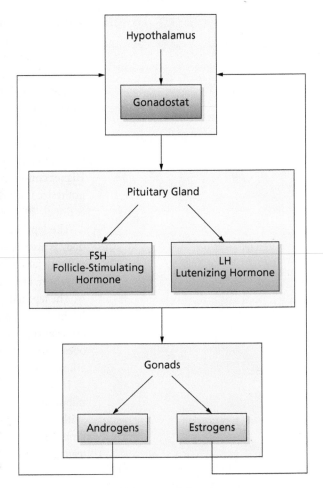

▲ FIGURE 2-2

Gonadostat Feedback Loop Hormone levels are constantly monitored by the gonadostat. If the hormone level is too low, the gonadostat signals the pituitary to work harder to produce more hormones. If the levels go too high, the gonadostat restricts the pituitary's output.

Adrenarche and Gonadarche: Prelude and Start of Puberty

Hormones play another role in the lead-up to puberty. Even though puberty doesn't formally start until later, *adrenarche,* hormonal changes in the adrenal glands, begins at around age 9 and sometimes as early as age 6. At that time, the adrenal glands start to produce adrenal androgens. These adrenal androgens continue to be manufactured throughout adolescence (Azziz et al., 2004; Dorn & Rotenstein, 2004; Remer et al., 2005).

Adrenarche may be the source of a surprising phenomenon: Sexual attraction to others begins even before the start of puberty. The average point at which children report experiencing sexual attraction is around the age of 10, and sometimes even earlier (Herdt & McClintock, 2000).

Gonadarche marks the actual beginning of puberty. Usually occurring about two years after adrenarche, gonadarche involves the start of maturation of the reproductive organs. As we'll discuss in greater detail later, gonadarche typically begins around the age of 9 to 10 years in Caucasian females and around 10 to 11 years in males. For African-American females, it begins even earlier.

What actually initiates the cascade of events that triggers puberty? We don't know for sure, but one possibility is an increase in levels of leptin. *Leptin* is a protein produced by fat cells. Higher concentrations of fat cells produce greater quantities of leptin, and some researchers hypothesize that when the amount of leptin reaches a critical quantity, puberty begins (Susman & Rogol, 2004; Veldhuis et al., 2005).

The leptin hypothesis is supported by clear evidence that the amount of fat stored in the body is associated with the onset of puberty. What isn't clear is whether it is the specific *amount* of body fat or the *proportion* of body fat to total weight that influences the start of puberty (Davison, Susman, & Birch, 2003).

The leptin hypothesis is also consistent with research showing delays in the onset of puberty in children who have suffered from illness and inadequate nutrition. Sustained, strenuous exercise also is related to delays in puberty, as are high levels of stress. In addition, girls who are obese are more likely to begin puberty earlier than girls who are not (Susman & Rogol, 2004; Dunger, Ahmed, & Ong, 2005; Torstveit & Sundgot-Borgen, 2005).

In addition to leptin, recent research suggests that a protein called *kisspeptin* also may be important in triggering puberty by sending a signal to the pituitary gland to release hormones. Without the production of kisspeptin, people never enter puberty and remain in a kind of limbo. The discovery of the role of kisspeptin may help in the development of treatments for teenagers in whom puberty has been significantly delayed (Gottsch et al., 2004; Vogel, 2005).

The Nervous System and Brain Development

The transformations that teenagers undergo during adolescence are accompanied—and often brought about—by dramatic changes in the nervous system and the brain. Scientists, armed with an increasingly sophisticated arsenal of tools that allow them to peer into the inner workings of the body, are identifying significant developmental advances in the nervous system and brain that occur during adolescence.

Neurons: The Building Blocks of the Nervous System and Brain.   To understand the changes that occur during adolescence, we first need to consider the building blocks of the nervous system: *neurons,* the basic cells of the nervous system. Figure 2-3 shows the structure of a neuron. Like all cells in the body, neurons have a cell body containing a nucleus. But unlike other cells, neurons have a distinctive ability: They can communicate with other cells, using a cluster of fibers called *dendrites* at one end. Dendrites receive messages from other cells. At their opposite end, neurons have a long extension called an *axon,* the part of the neuron that carries messages destined for other neurons. Neurons do not actually touch one another. Rather, they communicate with other neurons by means of chemical messengers, *neurotransmitters,* that travel across the small gaps, known as *synapses,* between neurons.

Although estimates vary, most scientists believe that we are born with between 100 and 200 billion neurons. At birth, most neurons in the brain have relatively few connections to other neurons. During the first years of life, however, our brains establish billions of new connections between neurons. Furthermore, the network of neurons becomes increasingly complex as we age. The intricacy of neural connections continues to increase throughout life. In fact, in adulthood a single neuron is likely to have a minimum of 5,000 connections to other neurons or other body parts.

We are actually born with many more neurons than we need. In addition, synapses are formed throughout life based on our changing experiences, but billions more are created than necessary. What happens to the extra neurons and synaptic connections?

Like a farmer who, in order to strengthen the vitality of a fruit tree, prunes away unnecessary branches, brain development enhances certain capabilities in part by "pruning down" unnecessary neurons. Neurons that do not become interconnected with other neurons become unnecessary. They eventually die out, increasing the efficiency of the nervous system.

As unnecessary neurons are being reduced, connections between remaining neurons are expanded or eliminated as a result of their use or disuse. If an individual's experiences do not stimulate certain nerve connections, these, like unused neurons, are eliminated—a process called *synaptic pruning*. The result of synaptic pruning is to allow established neurons to build more elaborate communication networks with other neurons. Unlike most other aspects of growth, then, the development of the nervous system proceeds most effectively through the loss of cells (Johnson, 1998; Mimura, Kimoto, & Okada, 2003; Iglesias et al., 2005).

From infancy on, neurons continue to increase in size. In addition to growth in dendrites, the axons of neurons become coated with **myelin**, a fatty substance that, like the insulation on an electric wire, provides protection and speeds the transmission of nerve impulses. So, even though many neurons are lost, the increasing size and complexity of the remaining ones contribute to impressive brain growth.

As they grow, the neurons also reposition themselves, becoming arranged by function. Some move into the *cerebral cortex*, the upper layer of the brain, while others move to *subcortical levels*, which are below the cerebral cortex. The subcortical levels, which regulate such fundamental activities as breathing and heart rate, are the most fully developed at birth. As time passes, however, the cells in the cerebral cortex, which are responsible for higher-order processes such as thinking and reasoning, become more developed and interconnected (Thompson & Nelson, 2001; Toga & Thompson, 2003).

The brain produces an oversupply of gray matter during early adolescence, which is later pruned back at the rate of 1 to 2% per year. Myelination—the process in which nerve cells are insulated by a covering of fat cells—increases and continues to make the transmission of neural messages more efficient. Both the pruning process and increased myelination contribute to the growing physical and cognitive abilities of adolescents, allowing increased physical coordination and more sophisticated kinds of thinking (Sowell et al., 2001, 2003).

One specific area of the brain that undergoes considerable development throughout adolescence is the prefrontal cortex, which is not fully developed until the early 20s. The *prefrontal cortex* is the part of the brain that allows people to think, evaluate, and make complex judgments in a uniquely human way (Giedd et al., 2004).

The prefrontal cortex also is the area of the brain that provides for impulse control. Rather than simply reacting to emotions such as anger or rage, an individual with a fully developed prefrontal cortex is able to inhibit the desire for action that stems from such emotions. However, because during adolescence the prefrontal cortex is biologically immature, the ability to inhibit impulses is not fully developed (see Figure 2-4).

As we discuss in the *Transitions* box, this brain immaturity may lead to some of the risky and impulsive behaviors that are characteristic of adolescence—and some behaviors that are even more extreme (Weinberger, 2001; Steinberg & Scott, 2003).

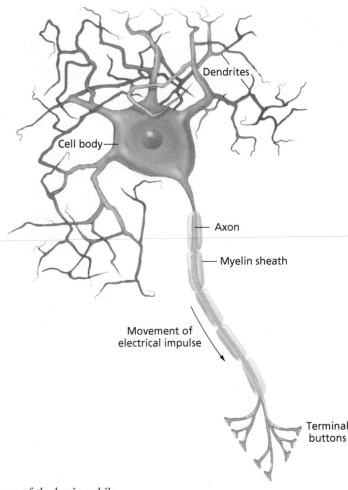

Dendrites

Cell body

Axon

Myelin sheath

Movement of electrical impulse

Terminal buttons

▲ **FIGURE 2-3**

The Neuron
The basic element of the nervous system, the neuron is comprised of a number of components.

(*Source:* Van de Graaff, 2000, p. 339)

myelin a protective coat of fat and protein that wraps around the axon

▶ **FIGURE 2-4**

Adolescent Brain Maturation Even in late teenage years, gray matter is replaced throughout the cortex.

(*Source: Science*, Vol. 305, 30 July 2004, p. 597)

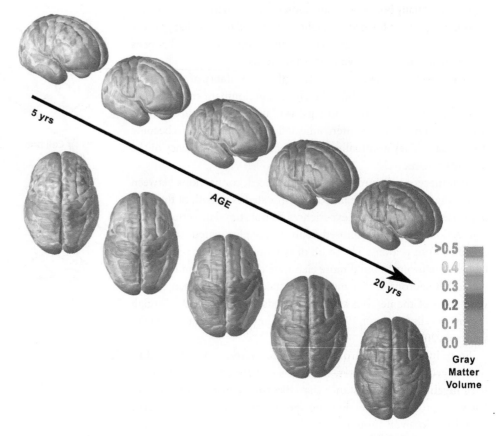

Adolescent brain development also produces changes in regions involving dopamine sensitivity and production. As a result of alterations in these areas, adolescents may become less susceptible to the effects of alcohol, needing a greater number of drinks before they experience the reinforcing qualities of intoxication. This can lead them to take in more alcohol than their older peers. In addition, alterations in dopamine sensitivity may make adolescents more sensitive to stress, leading to further alcohol use (Spear, 2002).

Finally, adolescence marks a period in which the brain shows unusual growth spurts that are linked to advances in cognitive abilities. One study that measured electrical activity in the brain found an unusual surge during late adolescence in the brain's occipital and parietal lobes (see Figure 2-5). The only other comparable level of activity was during the preschool years, which also are associated with significant cognitive growth.

▶ **FIGURE 2-5**

Brain Growth Spurt Electrical activity in the brain has been linked to advances in cognitive abilities at various stages across the life span. In this graph, activity increases dramatically between a year-and-half and 2 years, a period during which language rapidly develops.

(*Source:* Fischer & Rose, 1995)

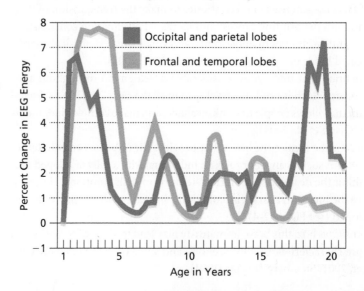

Transiti⬤ns

The Immature Brain Argument: Too Young for the Death Penalty?

Just after 2 A.M. on September 9, 1993, Christopher Simmons, 17, and Charles Benjamin, 15, broke into a trailer south of Fenton, Missouri, just outside of St. Louis. They woke Shirley Ann Crook, a 46-year-old truck driver who was inside, and proceeded to tie her up and cover her eyes and mouth with silver duct tape. They then put her in the back of her minivan, drove her to a railroad bridge and pushed her into the river below, where her body was found the next day. Simmons and Benjamin later confessed to the abduction and murder, which had netted them $6. (Raeburn, 2004, p. 26)

This horrific case sent Benjamin to life in prison, and Simmons was given the death penalty. But Simmons' lawyers appealed, and ultimately the U.S. Supreme Court ruled that he—and anyone else under the age of 18—could not be executed because of their youth.

Among the factors that the Supreme Court weighed in its decision was evidence from neuroscientists and child developmentalists that the brains of adolescents are still developing in important ways and that adolescents lack judgment because of their brain immaturity. According to this reasoning, adolescents are not fully capable of making reasonable decisions because their brains are not yet wired like those of adults.

The argument that adolescents may not be as responsible for their crimes stems from research showing that the brain continues to grow and mature during the teenage years, and sometimes beyond. For example, neurons that make up unnecessary gray matter of the brain begin to disappear during adolescence. In place of lost gray matter, the volume of white matter of the brain begins to increase. The decline in gray matter and increase in white matter permit more sophisticated, thoughtful cognitive processing (Beckman, 2004).

For instance, when the frontal lobes of the brain contain more white matter, they are better at restraining impulsivity. As neuroscientist Ruben Gur put it, "If you've been insulted, your emotional brain says, 'Kill,' but your frontal lobe says you're in the middle of a cocktail party, 'so let's respond with a cutting remark.'" (Beckman, 2004, p. 597)

In adolescents, that censoring process may not occur as efficiently. As a result, teenagers may act impulsively, responding with emotion rather than reason. Furthermore, adolescents' ability to foresee the consequences of their actions may also be hindered as a result of their less-mature brains.

Are the brains of adolescents so immature that teenage offenders should receive more lenient punishment for their crimes than those with older, and therefore more mature, brains? This is not a simple question, and those who study ethics will probably provide a more satisfying answer than scientists.

- Do you think that the penalty for criminal behavior should be tied to the brain maturity of the person who engaged in that behavior? Why or why not?

- Should other aspects of physical development be taken into consideration in determining a person's responsibility for criminal activity?

Of course, we do not yet know the direction of causality (does brain development produce cognitive advances, or do cognitive accomplishments fuel brain development?). However, it is clear that increases in our understanding of the physiological aspects of the brain have important implications for our comprehension of adolescents' behavior.

Brain Lateralization. The two halves of the brain illustrate significant differentiation and specialization. **Lateralization**, the process in which certain functions are located more in one hemisphere than the other, is pronounced during adolescence.

For most adolescents, the left hemisphere concentrates on tasks that necessitate verbal competence, such as speaking, reading, thinking, and reasoning. The right hemisphere develops its own strengths, especially in nonverbal areas such as comprehension of spatial relationships, recognition of patterns and drawings, music, and emotional expression (Koivisto & Revonsuo, 2003; McAuliffe & Knowlton, 2001; Pollak, Holt, & Wismer Fries, 2004; see Figure 2-6).

Each of the two hemispheres also processes information in a slightly different manner. Whereas the left hemisphere considers information sequentially, one piece of data at a time, the right hemisphere processes information in a more global manner, reflecting on it as a whole (Gazzaniga, 1983; Springer & Deutsch, 1989; Leonard et al., 1996).

lateralization the dominance of one hemisphere of the brain in specific functions

"Young man, go to your room and stay there until your cerebral cortex matures."

Credit: © The New Yorker Collection 1997 Barbara Smaller from cartoonbank.com. All Rights Reserved.

Still, although there is some specialization of the hemispheres, in most respects the two hemispheres act in tandem. They are interdependent, and the differences between the two are minor. Even the hemispheric specialization in certain tasks is not absolute. In fact, each hemisphere can perform most of the tasks of the other. For example, the right hemisphere does some language processing and plays an important role in language comprehension (Knecht et al., 2000; Corballis, 2003; Hutchinson, Whitman, & Abeare, 2003).

There are also individual differences in lateralization. For example, many of the 10% of people who are left-handed or ambidextrous (able to use both hands interchangeably) have language centered in their right hemispheres or have no specific language center (Banich & Nicholas, 1998; Compton & Weissman, 2002). Even more intriguing are differences in lateralization related to gender and culture, which we consider next.

Adolescent DIVERSITY

Are Gender and Culture Related to the Brain's Structure?

AMONG THE MOST controversial findings relating to the specialization of the hemispheres of the brain is evidence that lateralization is related to gender and culture. For instance, starting early in life, boys and girls show some hemispheric differences associated with lower body reflexes and the processing of auditory information. Males also clearly tend to show greater specialization of language in the left hemisphere; among females, language is more evenly divided between the two hemispheres (Gur et al., 1982; Grattan et al., 1992; Bourne & Todd, 2004).

According to psychologist Simon Baron-Cohen, the differences between male and female brains may help explain the puzzling riddle of *autism,* the profound developmental disability that produces language deficits and great difficulty in interacting with others. Baron-Cohen argued that adolescents with autism (who are predominately male) have what he calls an "extreme male brain." The extreme male brain, although relatively good at systematically sorting out the world, is poor at understanding the emotions of others and experiencing empathy for others' feelings. To Baron-Cohen, individuals with an extreme male brain have traits associated with the normal male brain, but display the traits to such an extent that their behavior is viewed as autistic (Baron-Cohen, 2003, 2005).

Although Baron-Cohen's theory is quite controversial, it is clear that gender differences exist in lateralization. But we still don't know the extent of the differences and why they occur. One explanation is genetic: that female brains and male brains are predisposed to function in slightly different ways. Such a view is supported by data suggesting that there are minor structural differences between males' and females' brains. For instance, a section of the corpus callosum is proportionally larger in women than in men. Furthermore, studies conducted among other species, such as primates, rats, and hamsters, have found size and structural differences in the brains of males and females (Witelson, 1989; Highley et al., 1999; Matsumoto, 1999).

However, before we accept a genetic explanation for the differences between female and male brains, we need to consider an equally plausible alternative: It may be that verbal abilities emerge earlier in girls because girls receive greater encouragement for verbal skills than do boys. For instance, even as infants, girls are spoken to more than boys (Beal, 1994). Such higher levels of verbal stimulation may produce growth in particular areas of the brain that does not occur in boys. Consequently, environmental factors rather than genetic ones may lead to the gender differences we find in brain lateralization.

Culture and Brain Lateralization.   Is the culture in which one is raised related to brain lateralization? Some research suggests it is. For instance, native speakers of Japanese process information related to vowel sounds primarily in the left hemisphere of the brain. In comparison, North and South Americans and Europeans—as well as people of Japanese ancestry who learn Japanese as a second language—process vowel sounds primarily in the brain's right hemisphere.

The explanation for this cultural difference in processing of vowels seems to rest on the nature of the Japanese language. Specifically, the Japanese language allows for the expression of complex concepts using only vowel sounds. Consequently, a specific type of brain lateralization may develop while learning and using Japanese at a relatively early age (Hiser & Kobayashi, 2003; Tsunoda, 1985).

This explanation, which is speculative, does not rule out the possibility that some type of subtle genetic difference may also be at work in determining the difference in lateralization. As always, teasing out the relative impact of heredity and environment is a challenging task.

Implications of Adolescent Brain Development.   The nature of brain development that occurs during adolescence has several significant implications. One is that the kinds of activities in which adolescents engage have a significant and lasting effect on the brain for the rest of their lives. The choices that adolescents make—participating in sports, the debating club, or playing video games—may hardwire the brain to specialize in certain functions. At the same time, adolescents who spend more of their time in passive activities such as watching a lot of television may miss an opportunity to stimulate brain growth, which can have a lasting effect throughout the remainder of the life span.

Yet we also know that the brain has considerable plasticity. *Plasticity* is the degree to which a developing behavior or physical structure is modifiable. For instance, rather than suffering permanent damage from a lack of certain kinds of stimulation, there is increasing evidence that later experiences can help to overcome earlier deficits. In addition, specific kinds of physical exercise can produce new brain cells (Cotman & Berchtold, 2002).

If the hemisphere that specializes in a particular type of information is damaged, the other hemisphere can take up the slack. For instance, when brain damage occurs to the left side of the brain (which specializes in verbal processing), producing a loss of language capabilities, the linguistic deficits are often not permanent. In such cases, the right side of the brain pitches in and may be able to compensate substantially for the damage to the left hemisphere (Hoptman & Davidson, 1994; Kempler et al., 1999; Slomine et al., 2002).

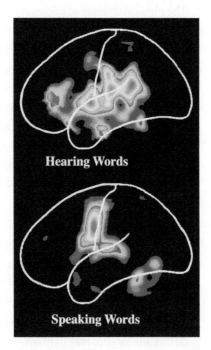

Hearing Words

Speaking Words

◄ **FIGURE2-6**

Looking into the Brain   These scans show how different parts of the brain are activated during particular tasks, illustrating the specialization of different areas of the brain. If one part of the brain is injured, will the functions associated with it be permanently lost?

◀ The culture to which an adolescent is exposed affects the nature of brain lateralization. In addition, there are gender differences in brain lateralization.

Review and Apply

Review

1. Puberty begins around ages 9 to 11, when biological changes are triggered by the endocrine system, which sends hormones called gonadotropins through the body to activate particular cells involved in sexual development and physical growth.

2. Hormones play a role in determining the emotional reactions of adolescents experiencing puberty, but stressors in the environment also affect adolescents' emotions.

3. The physical changes of adolescence are accompanied by changes in the nervous system and the brain, where needed neurons develop complexity and increased numbers of connections, and simultaneously, unnecessary neurons are pruned down and die out.

4. As they grow in size and complexity, neurons develop a protective coating called myelin, which speeds the transmission of nerve impulses. Neurons also arrange themselves in specific areas of the brain according to function.

5. Neuron pruning and ongoing myelination contribute to the growing cognitive abilities of adolescents, especially their ability to think, evaluate, make complex judgments, and control impulses. Brain lateralization, the specialization of the two hemispheres of the brain on different abilities and tasks, increases during adolescence, although both hemispheres continue to work mostly in tandem.

Apply

1. Describe a situation that arose during your adolescence in which your response today would be different from the response you made then. How might the difference relate to the developmental changes discussed in this chapter?

2. How is the phenomenon of synaptic pruning related to the fact that lifestyle choices made during adolescence may have lasting effects on the brain? How do you explain the brain's plasticity—its ability to overcome the effects of previous choices?

The Body Changes: The Physical Transformations of Puberty

For the male members of the Awa tribe, the beginning of adolescence is signaled by an elaborate and—to Western eyes—gruesome ceremony marking the transition from childhood to adulthood. The boys are whipped for two or three days with sticks and prickly branches. Through the whipping, the boys atone for their previous infractions and honor tribesmen who were killed in warfare. But that's just for starters; the ritual continues for days more.

Most of us probably feel gratitude that we did not have to endure such physical trials when we entered adolescence. But members of Western cultures do have their own rites of passage into adolescence, admittedly less fearsome, such as bar mitzvahs and bat mitzvahs at age 13 for Jewish boys and girls and confirmation ceremonies in many Christian denominations (Dunham, Kidwell, & Wilson, 1986; Delaney, 1995; Herdt, 1998; Eccles, Templeton, & Barber, 2003; Hoffman, 2003).

Regardless of the nature of the ceremonies celebrated by various cultures, their underlying purpose tends to be similar from one culture to the next—symbolically celebrating the onset of the physical changes that turn a child's body into an adult body capable of reproduction. With these changes the child exits childhood and arrives at the doorstep of adulthood.

Growth during Adolescence: The Rapid Pace of Physical and Sexual Maturation

I woke up after a seemingly 24 hour growth spurt a very, very big boy . . . already six feet and topping 200 pounds, and not quite fifteen. It was now almost impossible not to stand out. . . .

In only a few months, adolescents can grow several inches and require a virtually new wardrobe as they are transformed, at least in physical appearance, from children to young adults. One aspect of this transformation is the **adolescent growth spurt**, a period of very rapid growth in height and weight. On average, males grow 4.1 inches a year and females 3.5 inches a year. Some adolescents grow as much as 5 inches in a single year. This sudden spurt represents the most rapid period of physical growth since infancy and toddlerhood (Tanner, 1972; Caino et al., 2004).

Boys' and girls' adolescent growth spurts begin at different times. As you can see in Figure 2-7, girls begin their spurts around age 10, while boys start at about age 12. During the 2-year period starting at age 11, girls tend to be taller than boys. But by the age of 13, boys, on average, are taller than girls—a state of affairs that persists for the remainder of the life span.

Weight gain follows a similar path. Weight begins to increase rapidly at the start of puberty. At the time of their greatest weight gain at around the age of 12, girls gain an average of $1\frac{1}{2}$ pounds a month (or 18 pounds per year). Boys gain slightly more (around 20 pounds per year) during their peak growing year, which typically occurs between the ages of 13 and 14. For both boys and girls, the weight they attain represents half of their adult weight (Rogol, Roemmich, & Clark, 2002; Susman & Rogol, 2004).

As height and weight increase, the bones of the body become denser and stronger, but at the same time more brittle. Greater bone strength is related to the increased levels of physical activity in adolescents (Greene et al., 2005).

The shape and configuration of the body also change during the growth spurt. Girls' hips become wider (making it easier for them to give birth), and boys' shoulder width increases. Boys' legs also become proportionally longer. Even facial appearance changes, with the faces of boys becoming more angular and the faces of girls becoming softer and rounder.

adolescent growth spurt   a period of very rapid growth in height and weight

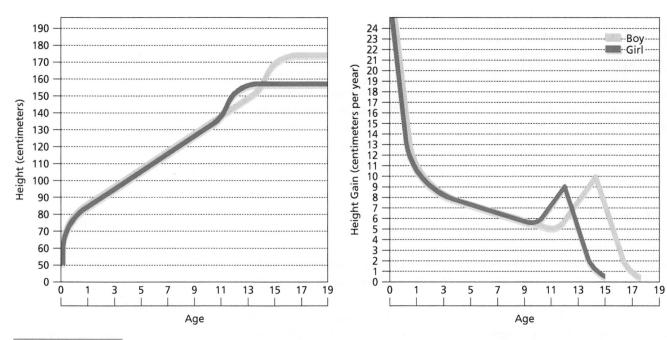

▲ FIGURE 2-7

Growth Patterns Patterns of growth are depicted in two ways. The figure on the left shows height at a given age, while the figure on the right shows the height *increase* that occurs from birth through the end of adolescence. Notice that girls begin their growth spurt around age 10 while boys begin the growth spurt at about age 12. However, by the age of 13, boys tend to be taller than girls. Why is it important that educators be aware of the social consequences of being taller or shorter than average for boys and girls?

(*Source:* Adapted from Cratty, 1986)

As they look at themselves in a mirror, young adolescents may be dismayed to notice that their bodies seem to be out of proportion—and they are, at least compared to the way they were prior to puberty. Although it may be a source of deep concern to some of them, they needn't be worried, because this disproportionality is only temporary. The source of the problem is that the various parts of the body grow at different rates and times. For example, hands, head, and feet are the first to grow, and they increase in size most rapidly. The arms and legs grow later, ultimately followed by the shoulders and torso. Eventually, all the components of the body catch up, and the parts of the body fit together in an adultlike fashion (Tanner, 1972; Goldberg et al., 1997; Nissinen et al., 2000).

The weight and height gains that occur during the growth spurt are driven, in part, by increases in body fat that occur in both males and females at that time. However, the rate of increase in body fat is greater for girls than boys and actually starts in the years just prior to puberty. Ultimately, boys end up with a muscle-to-fat ratio of 3:1, while girls end puberty with a 5:4 muscle-to-fat ratio.

The greater proportion of fat in girls produces two outcomes. First, it makes it more difficult for girls to compete athletically with boys because of natural strength differences. (Prior to adolescence there is little difference in strength between boys and girls.) Second, it may contribute to girls' susceptibility to societal messages regarding slimness. Even girls of normal weight may consider themselves fat and begin to diet unnecessarily (Sanborn & Jankowski, 1994; Cafri et al., 2005; Muris et al., 2005).

Boys, whose proportion of muscle is naturally increasing, also listen to societal messages about the "ideal" body shape and may turn their attention to becoming more "buff." Both girls' efforts to stay slim and boys' attempts to bulk up can lead to serious health problems involving eating disorders, as we'll discuss later in the chapter.

Coming of Age: Sexual Maturation

I had my first orgasm when I was about thirteen. . . . When the orgasm happened, I shouted "Oh, God," and immediately cursed myself for bringing God into it. . . . Surely something had gone terribly wrong.

■ ■ ■

In fifth grade we were doing book presentations. Before my turn I suddenly got my first period. My teacher wouldn't let me go to the bathroom, though; because it "would be rude to the people who were presenting." So by the time I went up, I had a blood stain on my pants. I sat on the yellow stool and gave my presentation. When I got up, there was blood on the stool, but I pretended not to notice. Minutes later my teacher said, "There's some blood on this stool. Can everyone check themselves to see if you have a cut that you didn't notice?" And eventually, of course, everyone found out where the blood came from. And it was all about the, "Ew. it was THAT kind of blood?" and the halls were filled with, "You guys! Did you know that Katie gets her period?!"

Puberty is not just a series of physical events brought about by an increase in levels of sex hormones. As these recollections make clear, sexual maturation often has deep psychological implications as well. In fact, the course of sexual maturation and its timing may have a lifelong impact on adolescents.

Like the growth spurt, sexual maturation begins earlier for girls than for boys. Girls start puberty at around age 11 or 12, and boys begin at around age 13 or 14. However, there are wide variations among individuals. For example, some girls begin puberty as early as 7 or 8 or as late as 16 years of age—differences that have considerable psychological impact, as we'll discuss later.

Furthermore, there is substantial variability in the timing of the development of primary and secondary sex characteristics. **Primary sex characteristics** are associated with the development of the organs and structures of the body that directly relate to reproduction. In contrast, **secondary sex characteristics** are the visible signs of sexual maturity that do not involve the sex organs directly. The development of secondary sex characteristics proceeds in fairly regular patterns, sometimes called *Tanner stages*, named after a British pediatrician who first identified them.

Because the nature and timing of puberty differs so much between males and females, we'll consider each gender separately.

Sexual Maturation in Females.   In most girls, the first sign of sexual maturation is the start of breast development in the form of *breast buds,* small swellings around the nipple area due to an increase in fatty and connective tissue. This occurs around 7 to 13 years of age. However, for about one third of girls, the first indication of puberty is the development of pubic hair around the age of 11. Underarm hair appears about 2 years later.

For some girls, changes in secondary sex characteristics start quite early. One out of 7 Caucasian girls develops breasts or pubic hair by age 8. Even more surprisingly, the figure is 1 out of 2 for African-American girls. The reasons for this earlier onset of puberty are unclear, and the demarcation between normal and abnormal onset of puberty is a point of controversy among specialists (Lemonick, 2000; The Endocrine Society, 2001; Ritzen, 2003).

At around the age of 12 to 13 years, girls typically experience **menarche**, the onset of menstruation. Although adolescents and parents often consider menstruation as the start of puberty, puberty actually has begun earlier with breast development and the growth of pubic hair. Still, menarche is a significant moment in most girls' lives because they must react to its occurrence.

The age at which menarche occurs varies greatly in different parts of the world. In poorer, developing countries, menstruation begins later than in more economically advantaged countries. Even within wealthier countries, girls in more affluent groups begin to menstruate earlier than less-affluent girls (see Figure 2-8).

Consequently, it appears that girls who are better nourished and healthier are more apt to start menstruation at an earlier age than those who suffer from malnutrition or chronic disease. In fact, some studies have suggested that weight or the proportion of fat to muscle in the body plays a role in the timing of menarche. For example, athletes with a low percentage of body fat

▲ The timing of menstruation is affecting by environmental factors such as nutrition, stress, and exercise. Athletes with a low percentage of body fat may experience a delay in menstruation compared to less active girls.

primary sex characteristics   characteristics that are associated with the development of the organs and structures of the body that directly relate to reproduction

secondary sex characteristics   the visible signs of sexual maturity that do not involve the sex organs directly

menarche   the onset of menstruation

▶ **FIGURE 2-8**

Onset of Menstruation The onset of menstruation occurs earlier in more economically advantaged countries than those that are poorer. But even in wealthier countries, girls living in more affluent circumstances begin to menstruate earlier than those living in less-affluent situations.

(*Source:* Adapted from Eveleth & Tanner, 1976)

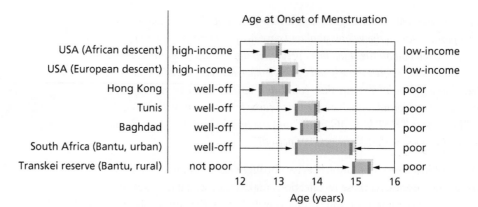

Age at Onset of Menstruation

USA (African descent)	high-income	low-income
USA (European descent)	high-income	low-income
Hong Kong	well-off	poor
Tunis	well-off	poor
Baghdad	well-off	poor
South Africa (Bantu, urban)	well-off	poor
Transkei reserve (Bantu, rural)	not poor	poor

Age (years)

may start menstruating later than less-active girls (Richards, 1996; Vizmanos & Marti-Henneberg, 2000).

Other factors can affect the timing of menarche. For instance, environmental stress due to such issues as parental divorce or high levels of family conflict can bring about an early onset (Kim & Smith, 1999; Kaltiala-Heino, Kosunen, & Rimpela, 2003; Ellis, 2004).

Over the past 100 years or so, girls in the United States and other cultures have been experiencing puberty at earlier ages. Near the end of the 19th century, menstruation began, on average, around age 14 or 15, compared with today's 11 or 12. Other indicators of puberty, such as the age at which adult height and sexual maturity are reached, have also appeared at earlier ages, probably due to reduced disease and improved nutrition.

The earlier start of puberty is an example of a significant **secular trend**, a pattern of change occurring over several generations. The earlier onset of menstruation and the increased height resulting from better nutrition are physical changes that have developed over centuries.

Sexual Maturation in Males. Boys' sexual maturation follows a somewhat different course. The penis and scrotum begin to grow at an accelerated rate around the age of 12, and they reach adult size about 3 or 4 years later. As boys' penises enlarge, other primary sex characteristics are also developing, such as the enlargement of the prostate gland and seminal vesicles, which produce semen (the fluid that carries sperm).

A boy's first ejaculation, known as *spermarche,* usually occurs around the age of 13, more than a year after the body has begun producing sperm. At first, the semen contains relatively few sperm, but the amount of sperm increases significantly with age. Secondary sex characteristics are also developing. Pubic hair begins to grow around the age of 12, followed by the growth of underarm and facial hair. Finally, boys' voices deepen as the vocal cords become longer and the larynx larger. (Figure 2-9 summarizes the changes that occur in sexual maturation during puberty.)

▶ **FIGURE 2-9**

The Changes of Sexual Maturation during Adolescence The changes in sexual maturation that occur for males and females during early adolescence.

(*Source:* Adapted from Tanner, 1978)

Average Male

Age in Years

Average Female

Age in Years

Height spurt   Penis growth
First ejaculation   Pubic hair

Height spurt   Pubic hair
Breast development
Onset of menstruation

Body Image: Reactions to the Physical Changes of Puberty

Unlike infants, who also undergo extraordinarily rapid growth, adolescents are well aware of what is happening to their bodies, and they may react with horror or joy, spending long periods in front of the mirror. Few, though, are neutral about the changes they are witnessing.

Some of the changes of adolescence do not show up as physical changes, but carry psychological weight. In the past, girls tended to react to menarche with anxiety because Western society tended to emphasize the more negative aspects of menstruation, such as the potential of cramps and messiness. Today, however, society's view of menstruation tends to be more positive, in part because menstruation has been demystified and is now discussed more openly. For instance, upbeat television commercials for tampons are commonplace. As a consequence, menarche is typically accompanied by an increase in self-esteem, a rise in status, and greater self-awareness, as adolescent girls see themselves becoming adults (Brooks-Gunn & Reiter, 1990; Johnson, Roberts, & Worell, 1999; Matlin, 2003).

A boy's first ejaculation is roughly equivalent to menarche in a girl. However, although girls generally tell their mothers about the onset of menstruation, boys rarely mention their first ejaculation to their parents or even their friends (Stein & Reiser, 1994). Why? One reason is that girls require tampons or sanitary napkins, and mothers provide them. It also may be that boys see the first ejaculation as an indication of their budding sexuality, an area about which they are quite uncertain and therefore reluctant to discuss.

Menstruation and ejaculations occur privately, but changes in body shape and size are quite public. Consequently, teenagers entering puberty frequently are embarrassed by the changes they are experiencing. Girls, in particular, are often unhappy with their new bodies. As we noted earlier, ideals of beauty in many Western countries call for an unrealistic thinness that is quite different from the actual shape of most women. Puberty brings a considerable increase in the amount of fatty tissue, as well as enlargement of the hips and buttocks—a far cry from the slenderness that society seems to demand (Attie & Brooks-Gunn, 1989; Crawford, & Unger 2004).

How children react to the onset of puberty depends in part on when it happens. Girls and boys who mature much earlier or later than most of their peers are especially affected by the timing of puberty.

The Timing of Puberty: The Consequences of Early and Late Maturation

Why does it matter when boys and girls reach puberty? The answer is that there are significant social and psychological consequences of early or late maturation. But these consequences vary considerably depending on the adolescent's gender.

Early Maturation.   For boys, early maturation is largely a plus. Beginning with the classic Berkeley Longitudinal Study conducted in the mid-1900s, researchers have found that early maturing boys tend to be more popular and to have a more positive self-concept, and they report more positive emotions. They also tend to be more successful at athletics, presumably because of their larger size. Generally, then, early maturation has a favorable impact on boys, who view themselves more positively (Jones, 1965; Ge et al., 2003).

On the other hand, early maturation in boys does have a downside. Boys who mature early are more apt to have difficulties in school, and they are more likely to become involved in delinquency and substance abuse. The reason: Their larger size makes it more likely that they will seek out the company of older boys who may involve them in activities that are inappropriate for their age. Overall, though, the pluses seem to outweigh the minuses for early maturing boys (Shulman & Ben-Artzi, 2003; Huddleston & Ge, 2003; Weichold, Silbereisen, & Schmitt-Rodermund, 2003).

The story is a bit different for early maturing girls. For them, the obvious changes in their bodies—such as the development of breasts—may lead them to feel uncomfortable and different from their peers. Moreover, because girls, in general, mature earlier than boys, early maturation tends to come at a very young age in the girl's life. Early maturing girls may have to endure ridicule from their less-mature classmates (Williams & Currie, 2000; Franko & Striegel-Moore, 2002; Olivardia & Pope, 2002).

On the other hand, early maturation is not a completely negative experience for girls. Girls who mature earlier tend to be sought after more as potential dates, and their popularity may enhance their self-concept. Still, this attention has a price. Early maturing girls may not be socially ready to participate in the kind of one-on-one dating situations that most girls deal with at a later age, and such situations may be psychologically challenging for them. Moreover, the conspicuousness of their deviance from their later-maturing classmates may have a negative effect, producing anxiety, unhappiness, and depression (Kaltiala-Heino, Kosunen, & Rimpela, 2003).

Cultural norms and standards regarding how women should look play a large role in how girls experience early maturation. For instance, in the United States, the notion of female sexuality is looked on with a degree of ambivalence, being promoted in the media yet frowned upon socially. Girls who appear "sexy" attract both positive and negative attention. Consequently, unless a girl who has developed secondary sex characteristics early can handle the disapproval she may encounter when she conspicuously displays her growing sexuality, the outcome of early maturation may be negative. In countries in which attitudes about sexuality are more liberal, the results of early maturation may be more positive. For example, in Germany, which has a more open view of sex, early maturing girls have higher self-esteem than such girls in the United States. Furthermore, the consequences of early maturation vary even within the United States, depending on the views of girls' peer groups and on prevailing community standards regarding sex (Silbereisen et al., 1989; Richards et al., 1990; Petersen, 2000).

Late Maturation. As with early maturation, the situation with late maturation is mixed, although in this case boys fare worse than girls. For instance, boys who are smaller and lighter than their more physically mature peers tend to be viewed as less attractive. Because of their smaller size, they are at a disadvantage when it comes to sports activities. Furthermore, boys are expected to be bigger than their dates, so the social lives of late-maturing boys may suffer. Ultimately, if these difficulties lead to a decline in self-concept, the disadvantages of late maturation for boys could extend well into adulthood (Ge et al., 2003).

On the other hand, coping with the challenges of late maturation may actually help males in some ways. Late-maturing boys grow up to have several positive qualities, such as assertiveness and insightfulness, and they are more creatively playful than early maturers. Furthermore, a prolonged preadolescence may offer late-maturing boys more time to ready themselves for the challenges of adolescence. Still, the overall consequences of late maturation for boys are more negative than positive (Livson & Peskin, 1980; Kaltiala-Heino, Kosunen, & Rimpela, 2003).

In contrast, the picture for late-maturing girls is actually quite positive. In the short term, girls who mature later may be overlooked in dating and other mixed-gender activities during junior high school and middle school, and they may have relatively low social status (Apter et al., 1981; Clarke-Stewart & Friedman, 1987). However, by the time they are in the tenth grade and have begun to mature visibly, late-maturing-girls' satisfaction with themselves and their bodies may be greater than that of early maturers. In fact, late-maturing girls may end up with fewer emotional problems. The reason? Late-maturing girls are more apt to fit the societal ideal of a slender, "leggy" body type than early maturers, who tend to look heavier in comparison (Simmons & Blyth, 1987; Petersen, 1988).

In sum, the reactions to early and late maturation present a complex picture. We need to take into consideration the complete constellation of factors affecting individuals to understand their development. Some developmentalists suggest that other factors, such as changes in peer groups, family dynamics, and particularly schools and other societal institutions, may be more pertinent in determining an adolescent's behavior than early and later maturation and the effects of puberty in general (Paikoff & Brooks-Gunn, 1991; Dorn, Susman, & Ponirakis, 2003; Stice, 2003).

Review and Apply

Review

1. Adolescents go through an adolescent growth spurt during which their height and weight increase rapidly. Girls' spurts begin earlier than boys', typically around age 10, but by age 13 most boys surpass same-age girls in height and weight.

2. Sexual maturation begins during adolescence, with girls generally maturing earlier than boys. Most girls experience the development of secondary sex characteristics before the teenage years and the onset of menstruation around age 12, while boys' primary and secondary sex characteristics typically develop around age 12, with the first ejaculation occurring around age 13.

3. The timing of sexual maturation varies across countries, with adolescents from more affluent countries experiencing maturation earlier than their peers in less-affluent countries. Differences in nutrition and health probably account for this.

4. Sexual maturation causes changes in adolescents' body images. Girls tend to be somewhat unhappy because their new bodies contrast with commercial ideals, while boys tend to be pleased with their increased size and weight.

5. Both early and late maturation may have social and psychological effects. In general, early maturation is a more positive experience for boys than girls, who may be ridiculed for being different and may have to deal with social and sexual attractiveness before they are ready. On the other hand, late maturation is more positive for girls than boys, whose social lives may suffer on account of their comparatively small size.

Apply

1. In addition to formal ceremonies marking the transition to adulthood, are there informal rites of passage for adolescents? What are some examples? Why are such ceremonies important to the culture and to the individual?

2. What sorts of messages do adolescents receive from the media regarding sexuality? Are the messages clear or mixed? Do the messages aimed at boys and girls differ or are they similar?

Health and Wellness

S pend some time with the Dettmann family in Emmetsburg, Iowa, and you'll know why so many school-age kids wish they could throw their alarm clocks out the window. Tyler, a 17-year-old high school senior, is usually up at dawn so he can make it to band or choir practice at 7:20 A.M. A couple of nights a week, he also works as a waiter at the local country club and doesn't get home until 9 P.M. Fifteen-year-old Travis, a sophomore, also gets to school early for choir and doesn't leave until after 6:30 because of football practice. Trevor, a 12-year-old seventh grader, plays football and participates in community theater. And every night, they all have at least an hour of homework. The biggest challenge for their mom, Sonya, is getting the boys to turn out the lights. "They don't think that they're tired," she says. "They look at the clock and say, 'I'm older this year. I shouldn't have to go to bed.'" (Kantrowitz & Springen, 2003, p. 75)

Going to bed is probably exactly what they should be doing. But don't tell that to the Dettmann brothers, who regard controlling their own bedtime and staying up late as an adolescent entitlement.

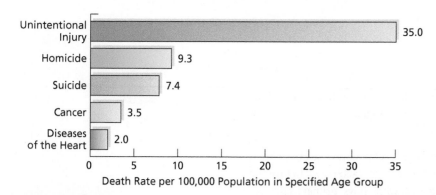

Death Rate per 100,000 Population in Specified Age Group

▲ **FIGURE 2-10**

Leading Causes of Death among Adolescents Although adolescents enjoy good health, the three leading causes of death can be prevented.

(*Source:* National Center for Health Statistics (NCHS), National Vital Statistics System, 2004).

In terms of health, adolescence is both the best of times and the worst of times. Adolescents are bigger, stronger, more energetic, and more coordinated than at any time in their lives. At the same time, though, their increasing independence and feelings of invulnerability can lead them to act in ways that not only are unhealthy—such as not getting enough sleep—but also may put themselves at great risk.

For most adolescents, though, the period is one of good health. In fact, the leading causes of death have nothing to do with physical illness (unlike in earlier generations, where illnesses were a more important factor). Instead, the three leading causes of death are accidents, homicide, and suicide (see Figure 2-10; National Center for Health Statistics, 2005).

Two thirds of adolescents' accidents involve motor vehicles. Not only is the incidence of DWI (driving while intoxicated) relatively high, but other risky behaviors, such as speeding, contribute to a high rate of vehicular deaths. The inexperience of new drivers only adds to the death rate from automobiles. In addition, teenage drivers are more likely to drive at night and to have cars packed with their friends, increasing even further the toll from accidents (Cvijanovich et al., 2001; Nell, 2002).

Homicide is the second most frequent cause of death in adolescence. Although the death rate from homicides is much lower than the death rate from accidents, some racial groups are particularly at risk. For example, African-American male adolescents are more likely to be killed than to die from any other cause.

Finally, a significant number of adolescents kill themselves. In fact, a teenager commits suicide in the United States every 90 minutes, and an even larger number attempt suicide. In the United States, 5% of females and 2% of males attempt suicide at some point during adolescence. More teenagers and young adults die from suicide than from cancer, heart disease, AIDS, birth defects, stroke, pneumonia and influenza, and chronic lung disease combined. Still, despite its prevalence, suicide is more common among adults than among adolescents (CDC, 2004).

We'll discuss the causes of suicide further in Chapter 14, as well as a number of other behaviors that contribute to physical problems in adolescents' lives. The central point to keep in mind is that health experts believe that the major threats to physical well-being among adolescents come from psychological, rather than physical, causes. Furthermore, many of these threats would be preventable if adolescents made better decisions (Ozer, Macdonald, & Irwin, 2002).

In short, health specialists now focus more on the prevention of illnesses and other physical dangers faced by adolescents, rather than on treating health-related problems after they occur. This viewpoint emphasizes a shift away from a *biomedical perspective,* in which the focus is on disease and disordered biological processes. Instead, adolescent health experts now take a *biopsychosocial perspective* that focuses on the interplay of biological, psychological, and social factors (Taylor, 2006).

Unlike the biomedical perspective, which focuses on illness, the biopsychosocial perspective concentrates on wellness. In the remainder of the chapter, we'll focus on several of the main factors that contribute to adolescents' physical well-being, including nutrition, exercise, and sleep.

Nutrition and Food: Fueling the Growth of Adolescence

I became anorexic when I was 12. I would starve myself but then give in and binge. . . . I've spent the last eight years of my life trying to get thin. I've never managed to get there. But it's all I want. Right now I am so far from thin, that it is killing me. Do you know what it's like to feel fat? It's the worst feeling in the world. Your skin feels tight. You look like a balloon.

And you are so ashamed you don't want anyone to see you. When I was in high school, I used to skip school when I felt too fat. I would pretend I was sick. But after missing 30 days or so of school because of supposed sickness, no one believes you anymore. . . . Two weeks ago I dropped out of college and came back home. The reason? I couldn't stand to let people see how fat I was. So now I'm back home and I need to concentrate on losing weight.

These comments, written by an adolescent girl who in fact was at a normal weight, illustrate the mind-set of a person with an eating disorder. No matter how thin they actually are, those with an eating disorder may still feel overweight.

As we have seen, the cultural ideal of slim and fit favors late-developing girls. But when those developments do occur, how do girls (and increasingly, boys) cope when the image in the mirror deviates from the ideal presented in the popular media?

The rapid physical growth of adolescence is fueled by an increase in food consumption. Particularly during the growth spurt, adolescents eat substantial quantities of food, increasing their intake of calories rather dramatically. During the teenage years, the average girl requires some 2,200 calories a day, and the average boy 2,800.

Of course, not just any calories help nourish adolescents' growth. Several key nutrients are essential, including in particular calcium and iron. The calcium provided by milk helps bone growth, which may prevent the development of osteoporosis—the thinning of bones—that affects 25% of women later in their lives. Similarly, iron is necessary to prevent iron-deficiency anemia, an ailment that is not uncommon among teenagers.

For most adolescents, the major nutritional issue is not regulating how much they eat but ensuring the consumption of a sufficient balance of appropriate foods. In fact, most adolescents are quite healthy, despite the fact that many do not eat a particularly nutritious diet. However, the quality of adolescents' diet is crucial in terms of their health in later parts of the life span.

Two extremes of nutrition are a major concern for a substantial minority of adolescents and can create immediate threats to health. Among the most prevalent problems: obesity and eating disorders like the one afflicting the adolescent whose blog comments started the section.

Obesity. The most common nutritional concern during adolescence is obesity. One in five adolescents is overweight, and 1 in 20 can be formally classified as *obese*, which means their body weight is more than 20% above the average for a person of their age and height. Moreover, the proportion of females who are classified as obese increases over the course of adolescence (Brook & Tepper, 1997; Critser, 2003; Kimm et al., 2002).

Although adolescents are obese for the same reasons as younger children, the psychological consequences may be particularly severe during a time of life when body image is of special concern. Furthermore, the potential health consequences of obesity during adolescence are also problematic. For instance, obesity taxes the circulatory system, increasing the likelihood of high blood pressure and diabetes. Finally, obese adolescents stand an 80% chance of becoming obese adults.

Obesity is caused by a combination of genetic and environmental factors. Particular inherited genes are related to obesity and predispose certain adolescents to be overweight. For example, adopted children tend to have weights that are more similar to those of their birth parents than to those of their adoptive parents (Zhang et al., 1994; Whitaker et al., 1997).

But it is not just a matter of a genetic predisposition that leads to weight problems. Poor diets also contribute to obesity. Despite recommendations regarding what foods are necessary

► **FIGURE 2-11**

Decline in Physical Activity Physical activity among both white and black adolescent females declines substantially over the course of adolescence. What might be the reasons for this decline?

(*Source: New England Journal of Medicine,* Kimm, et al., 2002)

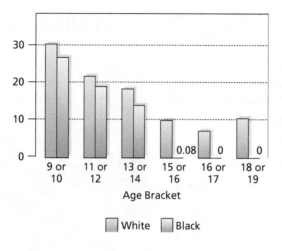

Age Bracket

☐ White ☐ Black

for a balanced, nutritious diet, most adolescents eat too few fruits and vegetables and more fats and sweets than experts recommend. But the biggest cause may be insufficient exercise.

Exercise and Sports. Lack of exercise is one of the main culprits behind the high rates of obesity found in adolescence. Despite recommendations that adolescents should engage in at least moderately intense physical activity for 30 minutes most days of the week, only around half of adolescents take part in vigorous exercise on a regular basis. A quarter report that they participate in no exercise at all (U.S. Department of Health and Human Services, 2001).

Ironically, the lack of exercise occurs at the same time that many adolescents have a strong interest in sports. In fact, the majority of boys and girls participate in some sports team, and the ability to participate and "make the team" is highly coveted (as the chapter opening prologue about Filip Olsson suggests). However, even if they do participate in an organized sport, participation is often seasonal. And for adolescents such as Olsson who are cut from a team, there may be no clear, desirable alternative (Pate et al., 2000; Trost, Saunders, & Ward, 2002).

The lack of exercise is more pronounced for girls than boys, with girls less likely to participate in regular physical activities than boys throughout adolescence. By the end of the teenage years, most females get virtually no exercise outside of physical education classes in school. In fact, the older they are, the less exercise female adolescents engage in. The problem is particularly pronounced for older black female adolescents, more than half of whom report *no* physical exercise outside of school, compared with about a third of white adolescents, who report no exercise (see Figure 2-11; Kimm et al., 2002).

Why do adolescent females get so little exercise? The failure to exercise may reflect a lack of organized sports or good athletic facilities for women. It may even be the result of lingering cultural norms suggesting that athletic participation is more the realm of boys than girls.

Another reason for the lack of exercise in both males and females is that many adolescents spend a significant proportion of their leisure time inside their homes watching television, playing video games, and surfing the Web. Such sedentary activities not only keep adolescents from exercising, but they often are also accompanied by snacks of junk foods (Gable & Lutz, 2000; Giammattei et al., 2003; Rideout, Vandewater, & Wartella, 2003; Tartamella, Herscher, & Woolston, 2005).

The importance of exercise has led to an increased emphasis on physical education in schools. As we discuss in the *Career Choices* box, physical education instruction is undergoing a revolution as teachers attempt to make exercise a lifelong activity.

The lack of exercise in adolescents makes treatment of obesity difficult. But as we discuss next, several strategies have proven effective.

BECOMING AN INFORMED CONSUMER OF ADOLESCENT SCIENCE

Reducing Obesity

A S OBESITY BECOMES an increasingly serious problem, not only in adolescence but also in later stages of life, you may be concerned about your own weight and wondering what you can do to prevent or reverse excessive weight gain during adolescence. These suggestions for starting a program of physical fitness will get you—and your waistline—moving in the right direction (President's Council on Physical Fitness and Sports, 2003; American Heart Association, 2005):

- Having the right attitude is critical for success. Be prepared to make fitness a part of your daily routine—it should become something that you just do every day without thinking twice, like brushing your teeth. A fitness program is not something you do for a while and then abandon once you reach your goal. It's a life commitment.

- Set reasonable goals and be patient. You can't undo in a week's time the effects of many months or even years of poor fitness decisions. The idea is to shift your lifestyle from a sedentary one that promotes weight gain to a reasonably active one that gradually creates and sustains physical fitness.

- Reduce the time you spend in sedentary activities. Limit your television watching, Web surfing, and other leisure activities that don't involve physical activity. Not only do such diversions reduce the time you spend being physically active each day, but they are also often associated with snacking—that's a two-fisted attack on your goal to become more physically fit.

- Get involved in physical activities that you enjoy doing. You can increase your activity level and your physical fitness simply by walking your dog, bicycling, swimming, roller skating, or playing lawn games. The key is choosing one or more activities that you'll enjoy and look forward to doing.

- Don't set yourself up for failure by overdoing it. Remember, to be successful at improving your physical fitness for the long term, you must make lifestyle changes that will stay with you for the rest of your life. An exercise regimen that is excessive and burdensome will be difficult to sustain over time.

Anorexia Nervosa and Bulimia.   The fear of fat and the desire to avoid obesity sometimes are displayed through eating disorders. One of the most profound problems is **anorexia nervosa,** a severe eating disorder in which individuals refuse to eat. Their troubled body image leads them to deny that their behavior and appearance, which may become skeletal, are out of the ordinary.

Anorexia is a dangerous psychological disorder; some 15 to 20% of people with the disorder literally starve themselves to death. It primarily afflicts women between the ages of 12 and 40; those most susceptible are intelligent, successful, and attractive white adolescent girls from affluent homes. Anorexia is also increasingly becoming a problem for boys. About 10% of persons with the disorder are male, a percentage that is increasing and is often associated with the use of steroids (Crosscope-Happel et al., 2000; Robb & Dadson, 2002; Jacobi et al., 2004; Ricciardelli & McCabe, 2004).

Even though they eat little, anorexics are often focused on food. They may go shopping often, collect cookbooks, talk about food, or cook huge meals for others. Although they may be incredibly thin, their body image is so distorted that they see their reflection in the mirror as disgustingly fat and try to lose more and more weight. Even when they look like skeletons, they are unable to see what they have become.

Bulimia, another eating disorder, is characterized by *bingeing,* eating large quantities of food, followed by *purging* of the food through vomiting or the use of laxatives. Bulimics may eat an entire gallon of ice cream or a whole package of tortilla chips. But afterwards they experience powerful feelings of guilt and depression and intentionally rid themselves of the food.

Although the weight of adolescents with bulimia remains fairly normal, the disorder is quite hazardous. The constant vomiting and diarrhea of the binge-and-purge cycles may produce a chemical imbalance that can lead to heart failure.

anorexia nervosa   a severe and potentially life-threatening eating disorder in which individuals refuse to eat while denying that their behavior or skeletal appearance is out of the ordinary

bulimia   an eating disorder that primarily afflicts adolescent girls and young women, characterized by binges on large quantities of food followed by purges of the food through vomiting or the use of laxatives

CAREER CHOICES

Physical Education Teacher

Name: Phil Lawler

Occupation: Physical Education Instructor

Education: BA, double major, physical education and history, Buena Vista College, Storm Lake, Iowa; MA, educational administration, Northern Illinois University, Dekalb, IL

PHIL LAWLER'S MIDDLE SCHOOL physical education classes used to be fairly traditional. He concentrated on teaching his students baseball and basketball, and his students participated in endless drills to improve their skills in those team sports.

No longer. Now, Lawler's classes are more like those you'd find in an upscale gym. Students at Madison Junior High in Naperville, Illinois, work out on an array of fitness equipment including treadmills, elliptical machines, and a rock-climbing wall (Bosman, 2005).

"One of the first things we did was focus on cardiovascular fitness and incorporated heart rate monitors," Lawler said. "We currently use high tech on other subjects, so why not in physical education. We have a tool to get an accurate assessment of how a student is doing."

According to Lawler's approach, students are graded on how well they stay within their heart rate zone, not on their success in specific sports.

"Instead of being compared to the athletes each student will get the same grade based on the number of minutes they put in their zone," explained Lawler. "If the best they can do is walk and they're in their zone, that's great."

The transformation in Lawler's classes reflects a change in philosophy that is sweeping the world of physical education instruction. Instead of concentrating on teaching skills aimed at helping potential big leaguers—skills that are unnecessary for the vast majority of adolescents—physical education instructors are moving toward instruction in skills that will lead to physical fitness throughout the entire life span.

"Statistics show that after age 24 less than 3% of the population uses a team sport as part of their normal physical activity," says Lawler. "So we mastered all these skills, for what?"

According to the new approach to physical education classes, the goal is to teach skills that will permit adolescents to build the habit of exercise and fitness. Consequently, adolescents are taught to use exercise equipment properly and to learn exercises that they can pursue when they are older. They are also taught to integrate exercise into their daily lives.

By teaching lifelong skills and making exercise a normal part of everyday life, the goal of this new breed of physical education instructor is to improve fitness and encourage adolescents to adopt healthy lifestyles. It's an approach that is bringing results: Researchers have found that overweight adolescents enrolled in middle school gym classes designed to improve fitness show improvements in body composition and fitness levels (Carrel et al., 2005).

Thinking of becoming a physical education teacher?

Teaching physical education in high school is a rewarding career for people who love sports and exercise and who would enjoy helping adolescents develop a lifelong appreciation for health and fitness. Physical education teachers conduct regular classes in movement and fitness, and they usually also serve as coaches for student athletic teams. They therefore must be widely knowledgeable about movement and motor skills, teaching and assessment of physical skills, gymnastics and sports fundamentals, athletics management, and general physical fitness. The best physical education teachers also have excellent communication skills, are sensitive to different students' abilities and needs, inspire trust and confidence in their students, and can motivate students to achieve their full potential.

High school physical education teachers typically hold at least a bachelor's degree in physical education. They also need to complete a teacher education program and must be certified to teach in their state. ■

As many as 10% of women suffer from bulimia at some point in their lives, and the onset of the disorder typically occurs between the ages of 15 and 29. Like anorexia, the incidence of bulimia in males is lower than in women, but the number of males diagnosed with bulimia is growing. Some groups of males are particular susceptible, such as male bodybuilders (Goldfield, Blouin, & Woodside, 2006; Hoek, 2006).

The exact reasons for the occurrence of eating disorders are not clear, although several factors appear to be implicated. Dieting often precedes the development of eating disorders, as even normal-weight individuals are spurred on by societal standards of slenderness to seek to lower their weight. The feelings of control and success may encourage them to lose more and more weight. Furthermore, girls who mature earlier than their peers and who have a higher level of body fat are more susceptible to eating disorders during later adolescence as they try to bring their maturing bodies back into line with the cultural standard of a thin, boyish physique. Adolescents who are clinically depressed are also more likely to develop eating disorders later, perhaps seeking to withhold the pleasure of eating food from themselves (Pratt, Phillips, & Greydanus, 2003; Walcott, Pratt, & Patel, 2003; Giordana, 2005).

Some experts suggest that a biological cause lies at the root of both anorexia nervosa and bulimia. In fact, studies of twins suggest that there are genetic components to the disorders. In addition, hormonal imbalances sometimes occur in sufferers (Condit, 1990; Irwin, 1993; Treasure & Tiller, 1993; Kaye et al., 2004).

Other attempts to explain the eating disorders emphasize psychological and social factors. For instance, some experts suggest that the disorders are a result of perfectionist, overdemanding parents or are by-products of other family difficulties. Culture also plays a role. Anorexia nervosa, for instance, is found only in cultures that idealize slender female bodies. Because in most places such a standard does not hold, anorexia is not prevalent outside the United States.

For example, anorexia is nonexistent in all of Asia, with two interesting exceptions: the upper classes of Japan and Hong Kong, where Western influence is greatest. Furthermore, anorexia nervosa is a fairly recent disorder. It was not seen in the 17th and 18th centuries, when the ideal of the female body was a plump corpulence. The increasing number of boys with anorexia in the United States may be related to a growing emphasis on a muscular male physique that features little body fat (Keel, Leon, & Fulkerson, 2001; Mangweth, Hausmann, & Walch, 2004).

Anorexia nervosa and bulimia are both difficult conditions to treat. Because they are products of both biological and environmental factors, treatment typically involves a mix of approaches. For instance, both counseling and behavior therapy and dietary modifications are likely to be needed for successful treatment. In addition to teaching strategies to change eating habits, therapists often focus on self-esteem issues and helping patients develop a more accurate body image. Often individual therapy is combined with group and family therapy. In more extreme cases, hospitalization may be necessary. (Miller & Mizes, 2000; Porzelius, Dinsmore, & Staffelbach, 2001; Stice & Shaw, 2004; Frisch, Herzog, & Franko, 2006).

Tired Teens: The Struggle to Get Enough Sleep

I'm really frustrated and tired all the time. I barely get any sleep. I look awful! But I hope it's just the start [of school]. Maybe I'll get used to these kind of things. I'm still familiarizing myself with my new surroundings and still making new friends. I expect high school to be more fun in the future . . . I really hope so . . .

For many adolescents—like this one, who is just starting high school—sleep is in short supply. With increasing academic and social demands placed on them, they go to bed later and get up earlier. As a result, they often lead their lives in something of a sleep-deprived daze.

Of course, adolescents are not the only ones who are sleep deprived: More than two thirds of adults sleep less than the 8 hours a day that sleep experts suggest is necessary to feel fully rested (see Figure 2-12). However, the sleep deprivation of adolescents comes at a time when their internal clocks are shifting. Older adolescents in particular experience the need to go to bed later and to sleep later in the morning, and they require 9 hours of sleep each night to feel rested. Because they typically have early morning classes but don't feel sleepy until late at night, they end up getting far less sleep than their bodies crave (Carpenter, 2001; National Sleep Foundation, 2002).

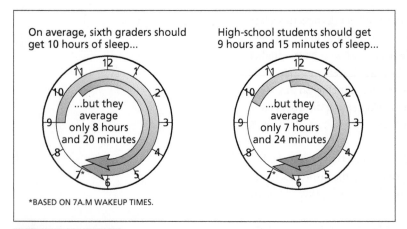

On average, sixth graders should get 10 hours of sleep...

...but they average only 8 hours and 20 minutes

High-school students should get 9 hours and 15 minutes of sleep...

...but they average only 7 hours and 24 minutes

*BASED ON 7A.M WAKEUP TIMES.

▲ **FIGURE 2-12**

Adolescent Sleep Requirements Sleep deprivation in adolescents comes at a time when their internal clocks are shifting, and many go to bed later and sleep later in the morning.

(Source: Mary Carskadon, National Sleep Foundation, 2002)

Adolescents' desire to go to bed later at night and sleep later in the morning, called the *delayed phase preference,* is the result of the other biological changes that are occurring during puberty. If permitted to follow their nature sleep preferences, adolescents will typically stay up until around 1:00 a.m. and sleep until 10 the next morning. Ultimately, the amount of sleep adolescents actually get is at its lowest point since birth (see Figure 2-13). Furthermore, it's only getting worse: surveys show that adolescents are getting less sleep now than they did 30 years ago (Carsakdon, 2002; Iglowstein et al., 2003).

Because their school schedules are at odds with the pattern of sleep their bodies desire, sleep deprivation takes its toll. Sleepy teens get lower grades, are more depressed and emotionally volatile, and have greater difficulty controlling their moods. In addition, they are at great risk for auto accidents (Fredriksen et al., 2004; Kurcinka, 2006).

Because of the toll that sleep deprivation takes, some school districts are revamping high school schedules and opening later in the day. For example, one Minnesota school district changed its opening time from 7:15 A.M. to 8:40 A.M. Students got more sleep on school nights, missed fewer classes, and got better grades. As a result of such successes, a number of politicians have introduced legislation to encourage school districts to start classes later in the morning (National Sleep Foundation, 2002; Wahlstrom et al., 2001).

Improving Adolescent Health

The period of adolescence represents an opportunity to teach good health habits that can last a lifetime. As we'll see when we discuss adolescent thinking processes in the next chapter, there are significant advances during the course of adolescence in the ability to think and reason in a more sophisticated manner. That means, of course, that the consequences of poor health habits should become increasingly apparent as adolescents age.

However, other factors work against the adoption of good habits. Adolescents become less compliant to parents' admonitions to practice healthful behaviors, and they may be less willing to follow the advice of health-care experts. They are also less willing to seek out medical services. Furthermore, they may see little immediate benefit from following health-care regimens, and future benefits may seem remote. The result is that adolescents often regress, showing poorer health habits than they did during their preadolescent childhood.

However, there's a long-term price to be paid for poor health habits adopted during adolescence. Adolescents may be starting on a path that will compromise their well-being for the rest of their lives. It's becoming increasingly clear that good health habits adopted during adolescence are a strong predictor of wellness after age 45 (Taylor, 2006).

School-Based Health Centers. To promote better health habits in adolescence, one promising approach has been the establishment of school-based health centers. *School-based health centers* are located in schools and provide a range of services to adolescents, including medical and mental health care. (*School-linked health centers* provide the same services, except they are located adjacent to schools, rather than in them.) About 1,500 such health centers are now open across the United States (Geierstanger & Amaral, 2005).

▼ **FIGURE 2-13**

Total Sleep Duration As one approaches adolescence the total number of hours slept decreases and is at its lowest point since birth. Trends show that adolescents are sleeping less than they did 30 years ago.

(Source: Iglowstein et al., 2003, p. 303)

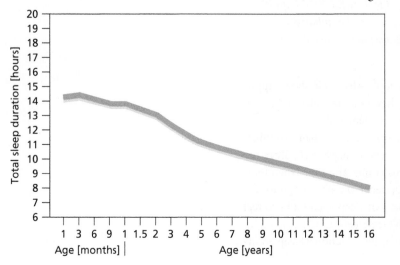

Such health centers provide a range of services and typically are multidisciplinary, involving nurse practitioners, physicians and physician assistants, social workers, and alcohol and drug counselors. The caregivers provide services confidentially—an important feature in eliciting adolescents' involvement. Not only do they seek to provide health services to adolescents, but they also aim at preventing problems such as drug abuse and sexually transmitted infections. In addition, because healthier adolescents make better students, school-based health centers seek to improve the academic performance of students.

Are school-based health centers effective? The research evaluation evidence is promising, but not definitive. It's clear that the accessibility of school-based centers increases the use of medical and health services. Their presence also improves the mental health of those who use them and reduces the hospitalization rate for children with some kinds of chronic diseases, such as asthma (Webber et al., 2003; Geierstanger et al., 2004).

It's less clear that school-based centers achieve the more difficult goal of improving students' academic performance. It is also true that school-based centers are better at increasing adolescents' knowledge of health-related issues and promoting more positive attitudes than they are at bringing about improvements in health-related preventive behaviors. This is not surprising: In the domain of health care, it's always considerably easier to bring about changes in knowledge and attitudes than in actual behavior (Geierstanger & Amaral, 2005; Taylor, 2006).

Socioeconomic Factors and Adolescent Health Care.   Vast socioeconomic disparities exist in health care in the United States. Adolescents who live in poverty experience far greater stress in their lives than those living in relative affluence, and the stress puts them at greater risk for health problems (Isaacs & Schroeder, 2004; Steinbrook, 2004).

For example, lower socioeconomic status is related to greater use of alcohol and tobacco, higher levels of obesity, and higher cholesterol levels at all age levels. Adolescents living in poverty have less social support to deal with problems that may arise. Ultimately, the result is to increase both the risk and the actual incidence of poorer health (House, 2002; Cubbin et al., 2005; Lantz et al., 2005).

Racial and ethnic minorities also experience generally poorer health. For example, African Americans are more likely to suffer from general health problems and are at greater risk for chronic diseases. Some of the racial differences are due to lower socioeconomic status of racial

◀ Racial and ethnic minority adolescents may suffer poorer health in part because of the stress of prejudice and racism that they encounter.

minorities, but some of the difference is likely due to the stresses of racism (Karlsen et al., 2005; Taylor, 2006).

The disparities between adolescents from different socioeconomic levels, as well as racial and ethnic groups, is not only limited to the social environment; it has practical consequences. Poorer adolescents have less access to good medical care. Many poorer families do not have medical insurance, and there is pressure on adolescents to avoid incurring medical bills unless absolutely necessary. Resource limitations also lead adolescents to make more use of emergency rooms rather than turning to a family physician for medical treatment. Asians, Hispanics, and African Americans are less likely than whites to visit a physician, dentist, or other health professional (Feinberg et al., 2001; Shi & Stevens, 2005).

The impact of socioeconomic status on adolescents' health is not limited to the United States. Adolescents growing up in poorer countries throughout the world face greater health challenges than those in more affluent countries. The extreme poverty found in poorer countries reduces access to medical care and leads to a greater possibility of exposure to environmental risks. In some cases, malnutrition is prevalent (Licari, Nemer, & Tamburlini, 2005; UNESCO, 2005).

Poverty, then, places adolescents at risk for a variety of health-related problems. On the other hand, risk is not destiny. Living in a lower socioeconomic status household does not doom adolescents to physical (as well as social) problems. Some individuals have a quality termed *resilience*, the ability to overcome circumstances that place an adolescent at high risk for psychological or physical damage, such as extreme poverty, violent homes, or other social ills. Several factors seem to reduce, and in certain cases eliminate, the reactions of some adolescents to difficult circumstances that produce negative consequences in others (Luthar, Cicchetti, & Becker, 2000; Trickett, Kurtz, & Pizzigati, 2004).

According to developmental psychologist Emmy Werner and other researchers who have investigated resilience, the adolescents who are the most resilient often have personalities that elicit positive responses from others. They are more socially pleasant and outgoing, and they have good communication skills. They also have relatively high self-esteem and are more intelligent than average. Finally, resiliency is more likely for adolescents who have a close relationship with at least one of their parents (Werner, 1995; Resnick et al., 1997; Werner & Smith, 2002).

In short, resilient adolescents have skills that permit them to cope more effectively with the stress of living in poverty. Clearly, though, the long-term goal is not to expect adolescents to develop coping skills to deal with the pressures of poverty. Instead, we need to change social conditions to maximize the opportunities available for all adolescents, regardless of the socioeconomic circumstances in which they are raised.

Review and Apply

Review

1. In many ways, adolescents are at the peak of their personal health, but they also face challenges to their wellness. The most common risk is obesity, which is caused by both genetic and environmental factors.

2. Because of the focus on body image, adolescent obesity has psychological consequences and can lead to eating disorders such as anorexia nervosa and bulimia.

3. Adolescents have difficulty getting enough sleep, a situation aggravated by the natural desire to stay up and get up later than is commonly allowed.

4. Health and wellness are susceptible to socioeconomic factors. In general, poor health is associated with lower socioeconomic status both in the United States and around the world.

Apply

1. Should schools compel students to engage in healthy habits by banning junk food and increasing the hours devoted to physical education or after-school athletics? Why or why not?

2. What is the proper role of federal and local governments in improving the health of their citizens? Should they legislate against unhealthy activities? Provide universal health care regardless of lifestyle?

EPILOGUE

In this chapter, we considered physical development during adolescence, focusing on the emergence of, and adjustment to, puberty. We discussed physical changes such as the development of primary and secondary sexual characteristics and analyzed the role of hormones secreted by the endocrine system in adolescent development. We noted that the physical changes of sexual maturation are accompanied by developments in the nervous system and the brain, and that they have considerable psychological effects as well. We traced the increasing complexity of the connections between neurons in the nervous system, leading to improved cognitive abilities. We looked at the effects of early and later maturation on boys and girls, noting that the effects are different across the genders. Finally, we examined the general state of adolescents' health and discussed some of the major threats that adolescents face, including obesity, sleep deprivation, and susceptibility to behaviors that can lead to accidents.

Before turning to the next chapter, which focuses on cognitive development, reread the Prologue to this chapter about Filip Olsson being cut from his soccer team. Consider the following questions based on what you have learned while reading this chapter:

1. Why do think Filip was so upset at being cut from the team?

2. Do you think he would have been upset to the same degree if he had the same experience either prior or subsequent to adolescence? Why?

3. Do you think Filip's advances in brain development made the experience of being cut more or less difficult emotionally? Why?

4. If you could have talked to Filip after he learned that he hadn't made the team, what would your advice have been?

SUMMARY

REVIEW

- **How and when does puberty begin, and what are its effects on the maturing adolescent?** *(p. 38)*
    1. Puberty begins with subtle bodily changes, typically commencing between ages 11 and 14. The biological changes of puberty are triggered by the endocrine system, which sends messages through the body by means of hormones specialized to activate particular cells.

2. The two major classes of sex hormones are androgens and estrogens. Testosterone, one of the androgens, stimulates the development of the male sex characteristics, while estradiol, one of the estrogens, is responsible for determining female development during puberty.

3. In addition to physical effects, the hormone activity of puberty affects adolescents' emotions, often causing hostility, depression, and antisocial behavior. Hormones are themselves affected by environmental stresses in adolescents' lives.

● **How do the nervous system and brain develop during adolescence?** *(p. 42)*

4. Major developmental advances occur in the nervous system and brain during adolescence. Connections between neurons, the basic cells of the nervous system, grow more complex through pruning, and the production of myelin increases, making the transmission of neural messages more efficient.

5. These developments contribute to the growing cognitive abilities of adolescents. The prefrontal cortex of the brain, in particular, undergoes considerable development, which improves the ability to reason, evaluate, and make complex judgments and to control dangerous impulses.

6. Other brain developments during adolescence include alterations in dopamine sensitivity, which can make adolescents less susceptible to the effects of alcohol and more sensitive to stress, and an increase in brain lateralization, by which the two hemispheres of the brain specialize in different mental tasks.

● **What physical changes do adolescents experience as they grow?** *(p. 49)*

7. The most noticeable physical change during adolescence is the adolescent growth spurt. As body size, weight, and strength increase, so does body shape, a development that can play into adolescents' natural sensitivity to body image.

8. Sexual maturation occurs during adolescence, with girls typically developing earlier than boys. Girls experience menarche, the onset of menstruation, around age 12, while boys experience spermarche, the first ejaculation, at around age 13.

● **What are the psychological effects of sexual maturation in male and female adolescents?** *(p. 53)*

9. The timing of puberty can have consequences for adolescents of both sexes. Among boys, early maturation leads to enhanced popularity and self-concept. On the other hand, early maturing boys tend to have academic difficulties and are more likely to engage in harmful activities.

10. Late-maturing boys are often less athletic and less popular than their peers but may have more time to prepare for the challenges of adolescence.

11. Among girls, early maturation may lead to discomfort with their changing bodies, but may also enhance popularity and self-concept. In addition, early maturing girls may be drawn to activities for which they are physically, but not emotionally, ready.

12. Late-maturing girls are at a disadvantage at first because they tend to be overlooked socially, but when they mature, they may be readier for the emotional challenges of adolescence.

● **What is the typical state of adolescents' health, and what are some threats to health and wellness during adolescence?** *(p. 55)*

13. Adolescence is the time of greatest physical strength and health, and yet adolescents are susceptible to threats linked to their own development and their growing ability to make choices. The leading causes of death in adolescence are accidents, homicide, and suicide.

14. One problem faced by adolescents is obesity, which is caused by both genetic factors and environmental factors, such as poor nutrition and a lack of exercise. Eating and exercise habits formed during adolescence are likely to have lifelong effects.

15. The fear of obesity among adolescents and their concerns about body image can lead to eating disorders, of which the two most common are anorexia nervosa and bulimia.

16. Inadequate sleep is another problem that confronts adolescents, whose natural rhythms lead to a preference for staying up late and sleeping late. The need to rise early for school and/or work conflicts with these preferences and often leads to sleep deprivation.

17. Adolescents' health can be improved through preventive actions, such as the encouragement of good habits and the availability of health centers at schools. Socioeconomic factors have a significant impact on adolescents' health, with less-affluent adolescents experiencing greater health challenges than their more affluent peers.

KEY TERMS AND CONCEPTS

puberty (p. 38)

endocrine system (p. 38)

hormones (p. 38)

gonadostat (p. 40)

myelin (p. 43)

lateralization (p. 44)

adolescent growth spurt (p. 49)

primary sex characteristics (p. 51)

secondary sex characteristics (p. 51)

menarche (p. 51)

secular trend (p. 52)

anorexia nervosa (p. 59)

bulimia (p. 59)

3

Cognitive Development

CHAPTER OUTLINE

PROLOGUE Satellite Vision

COULD SATELLITES in space help the visually impaired navigate through daily life?

That's what Ameen Abdulrasool, an 18-year-old high school student, figured when he invented a system that promises independence for the visually impaired. Ameen, who attends high school in Chicago, was inspired by automobile navigation systems that use Global Positioning System satellites to help car drivers avoid getting lost.

Ameen, whose father and several other relatives are blind, wanted to devise a system that would let the visually impaired know where they were and how to reach particular destinations. To do this, he put together an iPod-size instrument that would receive the satellite signals, bracelets to be worn on each arm, and earphones. After users program in a destination, they receive voice commands telling them what direction to turn. At the same time, the bracelets vibrate to indicate the right direction. In addition, an infrared sensor helps users avoid obstacles.

It took 3 years of trial and error, but the system has proven highly effective. It promises to expand the world of the visually impaired, who now may be able to plot a course through the world as never before (Adams, 2005). ■

th!nk ABOUT THIS

CONSIDER THE INTELLECTUAL processes that were involved in Ameen's invention: Understanding the global positioning satellite system. Reasoning about ways that one could adopt those satellites for the use of the visually impaired. Thinking creatively to identify how the navigational system could provide directions to a person. Formulating a way to test out his reasoning.

All these sophisticated cognitive processes were unlikely to occur just a few years earlier. Not only would Ameen have lacked basic knowledge about technology, but it's unlikely that he would have the logical ability to deduce novel ways of approaching the problem and creating the solution.

In this chapter, we'll examine the extraordinary advances in cognitive development that are the hallmarks of adolescence. We first discuss several theoretical perspectives that seek to explain intellectual development, focusing on Piaget's theory, information processing, and Vygotsky's approaches to cognition.

We'll then consider intelligence and how it is measured. We discuss the development and use of IQ tests, and consider several alternatives to traditional measures of intelligence. We also look at the controversy surrounding differences in IQ test results for members of different racial groups.

Finally, we consider cognitive changes that affect the way in which adolescents view themselves and others. We discuss the cognitive changes that underlie risk-taking behavior, and we examine how decision making and critical thinking can improve during the adolescent years. ■

YOU WILL BE ABLE TO
ANSWER THESE QUESTIONS:

- How does thinking develop during adolescence, and how have the major developmental researchers explained these changes?

- What are some of the traditional and alternative views of intelligence?

- How is intelligence measured, and what are some of the pitfalls in traditional IQ testing?

- Why are egocentrism and risk taking such central elements of adolescent development?

- How do creativity, decision making, and critical thinking develop during adolescence?

Intellectual Development

*M*s. Cortina smiled *as she read a particularly creative paper. As part of her eighth-grade American government class every year, she asked students to write about what their lives would be like if America had not won its war for independence from Britain. She had tried something similar with her sixth-graders, but many of them seemed unable to imagine anything different from what they already knew. By eighth grade, however, they were able to come up with some very interesting scenarios. One boy imagined that he would be known as Lord Lucas; a girl imagined that she would be a servant to a rich landowner; another that she would be helping to plot an overthrow of the government.*

What is it that sets adolescents' thinking apart from that of young children? One of the major changes is the ability to think beyond the concrete, current situation to what *might* or *could* be. Adolescents are able to keep in their heads a variety of abstract possibilities, and they can see issues in relative, as opposed to absolute, terms. Instead of viewing problems as having black-and-white solutions, they are capable of perceiving shades of gray.

▲ Significant advances in cognitive development occur during adolescence.

Adolescent scientists employ several approaches to explain adolescents' cognitive development. We'll begin by considering a broad theory of cognitive development devised by the developmentalist Jean Piaget. Piaget's approach has had a significant influence on how developmentalists think about thinking during adolescence.

Piagetian Approaches to Cognitive Development

Fourteen-year-old Leigh is asked to solve a problem that anyone who has seen a grandfather's clock may have pondered: What determines the speed at which a pendulum moves back and forth? In the version of the problem that she is asked to solve, Leigh is given a weight hanging from a string. She is told that she can vary several things: the length of the string, the weight of the object at the end of the string, the amount of force used to push the string, and the height to which the weight is raised in an arc before it is released.

Leigh doesn't remember, but she was asked to solve the same problem when she was 8 years old, as part of a longitudinal research study. At that time, she was in the concrete operational period, and her efforts to solve the problem were not very successful. She approached the problem haphazardly, with no systematic plan of action. For instance, she simultaneously tried to push the pendulum harder and shorten the length of the string and increase the weight on the string. Because she was varying so many factors at once, when the speed of the pendulum changed, she had no way of knowing which factor or factors made a difference.

Now, however, Leigh is much more systematic. Rather than immediately beginning to push and pull at the pendulum, she stops a moment and thinks about what factors to take into account. She considers how she might test which of those factors is important, forming a hypothesis about which is most important. Then, just like a scientist conducting an experiment, she varies only one factor at a time. By examining each variable separately and systematically, she is able to come to the correct solution: The length of the string determines the speed of the pendulum.

Leigh's latest approach to the pendulum question, a problem devised by psychologist Jean Piaget, illustrates the newfound sophistication of her thinking—and that she has moved into a newer, higher-level form of thinking.

A Swiss psychologist who lived from 1896 to 1980, Piaget proposed that all people pass in a fixed sequence through a series of universal stages of cognitive development (summarized in Table 3-1). The four stages are the *sensorimotor stage* (from birth until around age 2); the *preoperational stage* (from around ages 2 to 5); the *concrete operational stage* (from around ages 6 to 12); and the *formal operational stage* (from around age 12 onward).

Piaget argued that movement from one stage to the next occurs when an individual reaches an appropriate level of physical maturation *and* is exposed to relevant experiences. Without such experience, people are assumed to be incapable of reaching their cognitive potential. Some approaches to cognition focus on changes in the *content* of children's knowledge about the world, but Piaget argued that it was critical to also consider the changes in the *quality* of children's and adolescents' knowledge and understanding as they move from one stage to another (Piaget, 1952, 1962, 1983).

Piaget further suggested that human thinking is arranged into *schemes*, organized mental patterns that represent behaviors and actions. In infants, such schemes represent concrete behavior—a scheme for sucking, for reaching, and for each separate behavior. In older children and adolescents, the schemes become more sophisticated and abstract. Schemes are like intellectual computer software that directs and determines how data from the world are looked at and dealt with (Parker & Taylor, 2005).

Piaget suggested that two principles underlie the growth in schemes: assimilation and accommodation. **Assimilation** is the process by which people understand an experience in terms of their current stage of cognitive development and way of thinking. Assimilation occurs, then, when a stimulus or event is acted on, perceived, and understood in accordance with existing

assimilation the process in which people understand an experience in terms of their current stage of cognitive development and way of thinking

TABLE 3-1 Piaget's Stages of Cognitive Development

Cognitive Stage	Approximate Age Range	Major Characteristics
Sensorimotor	Birth–2 years	Development of object permanence (idea that people/objects exist even when they can't be seen); development of motor skills; little or no capacity for symbolic representation
Preoperational	2–7 years	Development of language and symbolic thinking; egocentric thinking
Concrete operational	7–12 years	Development of conservation (idea that quantity is unrelated to physical appearance); mastery of concept of reversibility
Formal operational	12 years–adulthood	Development of logical and abstract thinking

patterns of thought. In contrast, when we change our existing ways of thinking, understanding, or behaving in response to encounters with new stimuli or events, **accommodation** takes place.

For example, consider a 15-year-old adolescent girl who purchases a new mobile phone. She may have little trouble turning it on and making calls because the phone is similar enough to her prior phone. In Piaget's words, she assimilates her use of her new phone to her previous scheme for operating mobile phones.

But because her new phone has certain new features, such as new ways to store phone numbers in memory and download ringtones, she may have difficulty in making use of the phone. It is necessary for her to accommodate her existing scheme, modifying it by reading the phone's instruction book or asking a friend for help.

Because Piaget argued that movement from one stage to the next was brought about by a combination of biological maturation and experience, he viewed adolescence—with its significant biological changes and simultaneous transformations in the demands of the environment—as a particularly important period of cognitive growth.

Using Formal Operations to Solve Problems.   Returning to our example of Leigh and the pendulum, Piaget would argue that what allows Leigh to better understand the problem during adolescence is that she has moved into the formal operational period of cognitive development (Piaget & Inhelder, 1958). At the **formal operational stage**, people develop the ability to think abstractly. Piaget suggested that people reach it at the start of adolescence, around the age of 12. Leigh, now 14, was able to think about the various aspects of the pendulum problem in an abstract manner and understand how to test the hypotheses that she had formed.

By bringing formal principles of logic to bear on problems they encounter, adolescents are able to consider problems in the abstract rather than only in concrete terms. They are able to test their understanding by systematically carrying out basic experiments on problems and situations and observing what their experimental "interventions" bring about.

Adolescents in the formal operational stage use *hypotheticodeductive* reasoning, in which they start with a general theory about what produces a particular outcome and then deduce explanations for specific situations in which they see that particular outcome. Like scientists who form hypotheses, they can then test their theories. What distinguishes this kind of thinking

accommodation   changes in existing ways of thinking that occur in response to encounters with new stimuli or events

formal operational stage   the stage at which people develop the ability to think abstractly

from earlier cognitive stages is the ability to start with abstract possibilities and move to the concrete; in previous stages, children are tied to the concrete here and now. For example, at age 8, Leigh just started moving things around to see what would happen to the pendulum—a concrete approach. As she reached adolescence, however, she started with the abstract idea that each variable—the string, the size of the weight, and so forth—should be tested separately.

Adolescents also are able to employ propositional thought during the formal operational stage. *Propositional thought* is reasoning that uses abstract logic in the absence of concrete examples. For example, propositional thinking allows adolescents to understand that if certain premises are true, then a conclusion must also be true. For example, consider the following:

All men are mortal.   [*premise*]
Jake Gyllenhaal is a man.   [*premise*]
Therefore, Jake Gyllenhaal is   [*conclusion*]
mortal.

Not only can adolescents understand that if both premises are true, then so is the conclusion, but they are also capable of using similar reasoning when premises and conclusions are stated more abstractly, as follows:

All As are B.   [*premise*]
C is an A.   [*premise*]
Therefore, C is a B.   [*conclusion*]

Although Piaget proposed that we enter the formal operational stage at the beginning of adolescence, he also hypothesized that—as with all the stages of cognitive development—full capabilities do not emerge suddenly, at one stroke. Instead, they gradually unfold through a combination of physical maturation and environmental experiences. According to Piaget, it is not until adolescents are around 15 years old that they are fully settled in the formal operational stage.

In fact, some evidence suggests that a sizable proportion of people hone their formal operational skills at a later age and in some cases never fully employ formal operational thinking at all. For instance, most studies show that only 40 to 60% of college students and adults achieve

◀ Cognitive tasks ranging from figuring out the features on a cell phone to using propositional thought is possible because adolescents have reached the formal operations stage, according to Piaget's theory of cognitive development.

formal operational thinking completely, and some estimates run as low as 25%. But many of those adults who do not show formal operational thought in every domain are fully competent in *some* aspects of formal operations (Sugarman, 1988; Keating, 1990).

Why are there Inconsistencies in the Use of Formal Operations?

Why don't older adolescents consistently use formal operational thinking?

One reason is that all of us often are cognitively lazy, relying on intuition and mental short-cuts rather than formal reasoning. In addition, we are more apt to think abstractly and use formal operational thought on tasks in which we have considerable experience; in unfamiliar situations we find it more difficult to apply formal operations. An English major may find it easy to identify the themes of a Faulkner play, while a biology major may struggle. On the other hand, the biology major may find the concept of cell division simple, whereas the English major may find it baffling (Keating, 1990; Klaczynski, 2004).

Furthermore, adolescents differ in their use of formal operations because of the culture in which they were raised. People who live in isolated societies that lack a scientific orientation and who have little formal education are less likely to perform at the formal operational level than formally educated persons living in more technologically oriented societies (Jahoda, 1980; Segall et al., 1990; Erlbaum, 2000).

Does this mean that adolescents (and adults) from cultures in which formal operations tend not to emerge are incapable of attaining them? Not at all. A more probable conclusion is that the scientific reasoning that characterizes formal operations is not equally valued in all societies. If everyday life does not require or promote a certain type of reasoning, it is unreasonable to expect people to employ that type of reasoning when confronted with a problem (Shea, 1985; Gauvain, 1998).

The Consequences of Adolescents' Use of Formal Operations.

Adolescents' ability to reason abstractly, embodied in their use of formal operations, leads to a change in their every-day behavior. Whereas earlier they may have unquestioningly accepted rules and explanations set out for them, their increased abstract reasoning abilities may lead them to question their parents and other authority figures far more strenuously. Advances in abstract thinking also lead to greater idealism, which may make adolescents impatient with imperfections in institutions such as schools and the government.

In general, adolescents become more argumentative. They enjoy using abstract reasoning to poke holes in others' explanations, and their increased abilities to think critically make them acutely sensitive to parents' and teachers' perceived shortcomings. For instance, they may note the inconsistency in their parents' arguments against using drugs, even though they know that their parents used them when they were adolescents, and nothing much came of it. At the same time, adolescents can be indecisive, as they are able to see the merits of multiple sides to issues (Elkind, 1996).

Coping with the increased critical abilities of adolescents can be challenging for parents, teachers, and other adults who deal with them. But it also makes adolescents more interesting, as they actively seek to understand the values and justifications that they encounter in their lives.

Evaluating Piaget's Approach.

Piaget was a masterly reporter of children's and adolescents' behavior, and his descriptions of cognitive growth across the life span remain a monument to his powers of observation. Furthermore, the broad outlines sketched out by Piaget of the se-quence of cognitive development and the increasing cognitive accomplishments that occur dur-ing childhood and adolescence are generally accurate (Gratch & Schatz, 1987; Kail, 2004).

However, it is important to consider Piaget's approach to cognitive development within the appropriate historical context and in light of more recent research findings. His theory is based on extensive observations of relatively few children and adolescents, and despite his insightful and groundbreaking observations, recent experimental investigations have suggested a number of limitations to Piaget's theory. Let's summarize the issues here:

- Piaget suggests that cognitive development proceeds in universal, step-like advances that occur at particular stages. Yet we find significant differences in cognitive abilities from one person to the next, especially when we compare individuals from different cultures. Furthermore, we find inconsistencies even within the same individual. People may be able to accomplish some tasks that indicate they have reached a certain level of thinking, but not others. If Piaget were correct, a person ought to perform uniformly well once she or he reaches a given stage (Siegler, 1994).

- The notion of stages proposed by Piaget suggests that cognitive abilities do not grow gradually or smoothly. Instead, the stage point of view implies that cognitive growth is typified by relatively rapid shifts from one stage to the next. In contrast, many developmentalists argue that cognitive development proceeds in a more continuous fashion, increasing not so much in qualitative leaps forward as in quantitative accumulations. They also contend that Piaget's theory is better at *describing* behavior at a given stage than *explaining* why the shift from one stage to the next occurs (Case, 1991).

- Because of the nature of the tasks Piaget employed to measure cognitive abilities, critics suggest that he underestimated the age at which certain capabilities emerge. It is now widely accepted that cognitive developmental skills emerge at an earlier age than Piaget asserted (Bornstein & Lamb, 2005).

- Piaget had a relatively narrow view of what is meant by *thinking* and *knowing*. To Piaget knowledge consisted primarily of the kind of understanding displayed in the pendulum problem. However, as we will discuss later, developmentalists such as Howard Gardner have suggested that we have many kinds of intelligence, separate from and independent of one another (Gardner, 2000).

- Finally, some developmentalists have argued that formal operations do not represent the epitome of thinking and that more sophisticated forms of thinking do not actually emerge until early adulthood. Developmental psychologist Giesela Labouvie-Vief argued that the complexity of society requires thought that is not necessarily based on pure logic. Instead, a kind of thinking is required that is flexible, allows for interpretive processes, and reflects the fact that reasons behind events in the real world are subtle—something that Labouvie-Vief calls *postformal thinking* (Labouvie-Vief, 1986; Labouvie-Vief & Diehl, 2000).

These criticisms and concerns regarding Piaget's approach to cognitive development have considerable merit. On the other hand, Piaget's theory has been the impetus for an enormous number of studies on the development of thinking capacities and processes, and it also spurred a good deal of classroom reform. Finally, his bold statements about the nature of cognitive development provided a fertile soil from which several alternative positions on cognitive development bloomed, such as information-processing perspectives, to which we turn next (Zigler & Gilman, 1998; Parker, 2005).

Information-Processing Perspectives: Gradual Transformations in Abilities

To proponents of information-processing approaches to cognitive development, adolescents' mental abilities grow gradually and continuously. Unlike Piaget's view that the increasing cognitive sophistication of adolescents is a reflection of stage-like spurts, the **information-processing perspective** sees changes in adolescents' cognitive abilities as evidence of gradual transformations in the capacity to take in, use, and store information.

information-processing perspective the model that seeks to identify the way that individuals take in, use, and store information

Rather than seeking to identify the universal, broad milestones in cognitive development through which all adolescents pass, as Piaget tried to do, information-processing theorists consider the specific processes by which individuals acquire and use the information to which they are exposed. They focus less on the qualitative changes in adolescents' mental lives and consider more closely their quantitative capabilities.

From this perspective, cognitive growth is characterized by increasing sophistication, speed, and capacity in information processing. If we can compare Piaget's schemes to computer software, telling the computer how to deal with data from the world, we might compare information-processing improvements to the use of more efficient programs that enable users to process information with increased speed and sophistication. Information-processing approaches, then, focus on the types of "mental programs" that people use when they seek to solve problems (Reyna, 1997; Siegler, 1998; Cohen and Cashon, 2003).

Encoding, Storage, and Retrieval: The Foundations of Information Processing.
Information processing has three basic aspects: encoding, storage, and retrieval (see Figure 3-1). *Encoding* is the process by which information is initially recorded in a form usable to memory. Like all of us, adolescents are exposed to a massive amount of information; if they tried to process it all, they would be overwhelmed. Consequently, they encode selectively, picking and choosing the information to which they will pay attention.

Even if someone has been exposed to the information initially and has encoded it in an appropriate way, there is still no guarantee that he or she will be able to use it in the future. Information must also have been stored in memory adequately. *Storage* refers to the placement of material into memory. Finally, success in using the material in the future depends on being able to retrieve it when it is needed. *Retrieval* is the process by which material in memory storage is located, brought into awareness, and used.

We can use our comparison to computers again here. Information-processing approaches suggest that the processes of encoding, storage, and retrieval are analogous to different parts of a computer. Encoding can be thought of as a computer's keyboard, through which one inputs information; storage is the computer's hard drive, where information is stored; and retrieval is analogous to software that accesses the information for display on the screen. Only when all three processes are operating—encoding, storage, and retrieval—can information be processed.

Automatization.   In some cases, encoding, storage, and retrieval are relatively automatic, while in other cases they are deliberate. *Automatization* is the degree to which an activity requires attention. Processes that require relatively little attention are automatic; processes that require relatively large amounts of attention are controlled. For example, some activities such as walking, eating with a fork, or reading may be automatic for you, but at first they required your full attention.

Automatic mental processes help adolescents in their initial encounters with the world by enabling them to easily and "automatically" process information in particular ways. For instance, adolescents automatically encode information in terms of frequency. Without a lot of attention to counting or tallying, they are aware of how often they have encountered particular people, which helps them navigate socially and determine who might be romantically interested in them (Hasher & Zacks, 1984; Collin, 2006).

▶ FIGURE 3-1

Information processing, the method by which information is encoded, stored, and retrieved.

Furthermore, without intending to and without being aware of it, adolescents develop a sense of how often different stimuli are found together simultaneously. This permits them to develop an understanding of *concepts*, categorizations of objects, events, or people that share common properties. For example, by encoding the information that four legs, a wagging tail, and barking are often found together, we learn very early in life to understand the concept of "dog." Adolescents are rarely aware of how they learn such concepts, and they are often unable to articulate the features that distinguish one concept (such as dog) from another (such as cat). (Try it—it's not so easy.) Instead, learning tends to occur automatically.

Improvements in Information Processing during Adolescence.

A number of progressive changes occur in the ways adolescents organize their thinking about the world, develop strategies for dealing with new situations, sort facts, and achieve advances in memory capacity and perceptual abilities. Adolescents' general intelligence—at least as measured by traditional IQ tests that we'll discuss later in the chapter—remains stable, but there are dramatic improvements in the specific mental abilities that underlie intelligence (Pressley & Schneider, 1997; Luna et al., 2004; Wyer, 2004).

For example, verbal, mathematical, and spatial abilities increase, making many adolescents quicker with a comeback and turning some into impressive sources of information and accomplished athletes. Processing speed increases from early childhood through midadolescence. As illustrated in Figure 3-2, memory capacity grows, continuing a trend that began in the preschool years. In addition, adolescents become more adept at effectively dividing their attention across more than one stimulus at a time—such as simultaneously studying for a biology test and listening to a Green Day CD.

Furthermore, as Piaget also noted, adolescents grow increasingly sophisticated in their understanding of problems, their ability to grasp abstract concepts and to think hypothetically, and their comprehension of the possibilities inherent in situations. This permits them, for instance, to endlessly dissect the course that their relationships might hypothetically take.

▲ Improvements in the speed and capacity of information processing underlie adolescents' abilities to make increasingly proficient split-second decisions.

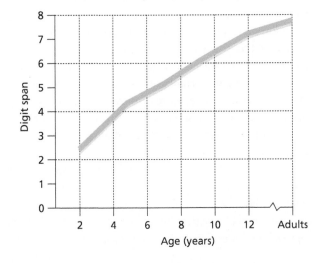

◀ **FIGURE 3-2**

The processing of information begins early with memory capacity growing quickly into adolescence.

(*Source:* Dempster, 1981)

Adolescents know more about the world, too. Their store of knowledge increases as the amount of material to which they are exposed grows and their memory capacity enlarges. Older adolescents also are better at monitoring and managing how they learn. They improve in their capabilities to make use of their intellectual resources. Taken as a whole, the mental abilities that underlie intelligence show a marked improvement during adolescence (Kail, 2003, 2004; Kuhn, 2006).

According to information-processing explanations of cognitive development during adolescence, one of the most important reasons for advances in mental abilities is the growth of metacognition. **Metacognition** is the knowledge that people have about their own thinking processes and their ability to monitor their cognition. Although school-age children can use some metacognitive strategies, adolescents are much more adept at understanding their own mental processes.

For example, as adolescents improve their understanding of their memory capacity, they get better at gauging how long they need to study a particular kind of material to memorize it for a test. Furthermore, they can judge when they have fully memorized the material considerably more accurately than when they were younger. These improvements in metacognitive abilities permit adolescents to comprehend and master school material more effectively (Nelson, 1994; Kuhn, 2000; Desoete, Roeyers, & De Clercq, 2003).

Information-Processing Theories in Perspective.   According to information-processing approaches, cognitive development consists of gradual improvements in the ways people perceive, understand, and remember information. With age and practice, children process information more efficiently and with greater sophistication as they age, and they are able to handle increasingly complex problems. In the eyes of proponents of information-processing approaches, it is these quantitative advances in information processing—and not the qualitative changes suggested by Piaget—that constitute cognitive development (Case & Okamoto, 1996; Goswami, 1998; Zhe & Siegler, 2000).

For supporters of information-processing approaches, the reliance on well-defined processes that can be tested, with relative precision, by research is one of the perspective's most important features. Rather than relying on concepts that are somewhat vague, such as Piaget's notions of assimilation and accommodation, information-processing approaches provide a comprehensive, logical set of concepts.

Proponents of information-processing theory have also been successful in focusing on important cognitive processes to which alternative approaches traditionally have paid little attention, such as the contribution of mental skills like memory and attention to adolescents' thinking. They suggest that information processing provides a clear, logical, and full account of cognitive development.

Yet information-processing approaches have their detractors, who raise significant points. For one thing, the focus on a series of single, individual cognitive processes leaves out of consideration some important factors that appear to influence cognition. For instance, information-processing theorists pay relatively little attention to social and cultural factors—a deficiency that the approach we'll consider next attempts to remedy.

An even more important criticism is that information-processing approaches "lose the forest for the trees." In other words, information-processing approaches pay so much attention to the detailed, individual sequence of processes that compose cognitive processing and development that they never adequately paint a whole, comprehensive picture of cognitive development—which Piaget clearly did quite well.

Developmentalists using information-processing approaches respond to such criticisms by saying that their model of cognitive development has the advantage of being precisely stated and capable of leading to testable hypotheses. They also argue that far more research supports their approach than alternative theories of cognitive development. In short, they suggest that their approach provides a more accurate account than any other.

metacognition   the knowledge that people have about their own thinking processes and their ability to monitor their cognition

Information-processing approaches have been highly influential over the past several decades. They have inspired a tremendous amount of research that has helped us gain some insights into how adolescents develop cognitively.

Vygotsky's View of Cognitive Development: Taking Culture into Account

As her daughter intently watches, a member of the Chilcotin Indian tribe prepares a salmon for dinner. When the daughter asks a question about a small detail of the process, the mother takes out another salmon and repeats the entire process. According to the tribal view of learning, understanding and comprehension can come only from grasping the total procedure, and not from learning about the individual subcomponents of the task (Tharp, 1989).

The Chilcotin view of how learning takes place stands in contrast to the prevalent view of Western societies, in which the general assumption is that only by mastering the separate parts of a problem can one fully comprehend it. Do differences in the ways different cultures and societies approach problems have an influence on cognitive development? According to Russian developmental psychologist Lev Vygotsky, who lived from 1896 to 1934, the answer is a clear "yes."

In an increasingly influential view, Vygotsky argued that the focus of cognitive development should be on an individual's social and cultural world. Instead of concentrating on individual performance, as do Piagetian and many alternative approaches, Vygotsky focused on the social aspects of development and learning. He held that cognitive development proceeds as a result of social interactions in which partners jointly work to solve problems. Because of the assistance that such adult and peer partners provide, adolescents grow intellectually and begin to function on their own (Vygotsky, 1978, 1926/1997; Wertsch & Tulviste, 1992).

Vygotsky contended that the nature of the partnership that adults and peers provide is determined largely by cultural and societal factors. For instance, culture and society establish the institutions, such as schools, clubs, and other social activities, that promote development by providing opportunities for cognitive growth. Furthermore, because the challenges that adolescents face as they move through the teenage years increase, adolescence is a particularly challenging period.

In addition, by emphasizing particular tasks that adolescents are expected to accomplish, culture and society shape the nature of specific cognitive advances. Consequently, unless we look at what is important and meaningful to adolescents in a given society, we may seriously underestimate the nature and level of cognitive abilities that ultimately will be attained. (Belmont, 1995; Tappan, 1997).

Vygotsky's approach is therefore quite different from that of Piaget. Whereas Piaget looked at developing adolescents and saw junior scientists, working on their own to develop an independent understanding of the world, Vygotsky saw something quite different. In his view, adolescents' cognitive development was dependent on interaction with others. Vygotsky argued that it was only through partnership with other people—peers, parents, teachers, and other adults—that adolescents could fully develop their knowledge, thinking processes, beliefs, and values (Kitchener, 1996).

The Zone of Proximal Development and Scaffolding: Foundations of Cognitive Development. Vygotsky proposed that cognitive abilities increase through exposure to information that resides within an adolescent's zone of proximal development. The **zone of proximal development**, or **ZPD**, is the level at which an individual can *almost*, but not fully, comprehend or perform a task, but can learn to do so with the assistance of someone more competent. When appropriate instruction is offered within the ZPD, adolescents are able to increase their understanding or master new tasks. For cognitive development to occur, then, new

zone of proximal development (ZPD) according to Vygotsky, the level at which a child can almost, but not fully, comprehend or perform a task without assistance

Lev Vygotsky's approach to cognitive development is having an increasing influence on our understanding of cognitive development, despite his death 75 years ago.

information must be presented—by parents, teachers, or more skilled peers—within the zone of proximal development (Blank & White, 1999; Chaiklin, 2003; Kozulin, 2004).

The concept of the zone of proximal development suggests that even though two adolescents can achieve the same amount without help, receiving aid may lead one to improve substantially more than another. The greater the improvement that comes with help, the larger is the zone of proximal development.

The assistance provided by others has been termed scaffolding. **Scaffolding** is the support for learning and problem solving that encourages independence and growth. To Vygotsky, not only does scaffolding promote the solution of specific problems, it also aids in the development of overall cognitive abilities (Puntambekar & Hübscher, 2005).

Scaffolding takes its name from the scaffolds that are put up to aid in the construction of a building and removed once the building is complete. In education, scaffolding involves, first, helping adolescents think about and frame a task in an appropriate manner. In addition, a parent or teacher is likely to provide clues to task completion that are appropriate to the adolescent's level of development and to model behavior that can lead to completion of the task. As in construction, the scaffolding that more competent people provide, which facilitates the completion of identified tasks, is removed once adolescents are able to solve a problem on their own (Rogoff, 1995; Warwick & Maloch, 2003).

Aid provided learners by more accomplished individuals comes in the form of cultural tools. *Cultural tools* are actual, physical items (e.g., pencils, paper, calculators, computers, and so forth), as well as an intellectual and conceptual framework for solving problems. The intellectual and conceptual framework available to learners includes the language that is used within a culture, its alphabetical and numbering schemes, its mathematical and scientific systems, and even its religious systems. These cultural tools provide a structure that can be used to help adolescents define and solve specific problems, as well as an intellectual point of view that encourages cognitive development.

For example, consider how people talk about distance. In cities, distance is usually measured in blocks ("the store is about 15 blocks away"). To an adolescent from a rural background, such a unit of measurement is meaningless, and more meaningful distance-related terms may be used, such as yards, miles, such practical rules of thumb as "a stone's throw," or references to known distances and landmarks ("about half the distance to town"). To make matters more complicated, "how far" questions are sometimes answered in terms not of distance, but of time ("it's about 15 minutes to the store"), which will be understood variously to refer to walking or riding time, depending on context—and, if riding time, to different forms of riding. For some adolescents the ride to the store will be conceived of as being by ox cart, for others, by bicycle, bus, canoe, or automobile, again depending on cultural context. The nature of the tools available to children to solve problems and perform tasks is highly dependent on the culture in which they live.

Vygotsky and Educational Practices. Vygotsky's approach has been particularly influential in the development of several classroom practices based on the proposition that adolescents should actively participate in their educational experiences. Consequently, classrooms are seen as places where adolescents should have the opportunity to experiment and try out new activities (Holzman, 1997; Vygotsky, 1926/1997).

According to Vygotsky, education should focus on activities that involve interaction with others. Both adolescent–adult and adolescent–adolescent interactions can provide the poten-

scaffolding the support for learning and problem solving that encourages independence and growth

tial for cognitive growth. The nature of the interactions must be carefully structured to fall within each individual adolescent's zone of proximal development.

Several current and noteworthy educational innovations have borrowed heavily from Vygotsky's work. For example, *cooperative learning*, in which students work together in groups to achieve a common goal, incorporates several aspects of Vygotsky's theory. Students working in cooperative groups benefit from the insights of others, and if they get off on the wrong track, they may be brought back to the correct course by others in their group. On the other hand, not every peer is equally helpful to members of a cooperative learning group: As Vygotsky's approach would imply, individual students benefit most when at least some of the other members of the group are more competent at the task and can act as experts (Karpov & Haywood, 1998; Jarvella & Hakkinen, 2005; Veenman et al., 2005).

Reciprocal teaching is another educational practice that reflects Vygotsky's approach to cognitive development. *Reciprocal teaching* is a technique to teach reading comprehension strategies. Students are taught to skim the content of a passage, raise questions about its central point, summarize the passage, and finally predict what will happen next. A key to this technique is its reciprocal nature, its emphasis on giving students a chance to take on the role of teacher. In the beginning, teachers lead students through the comprehension strategies. Gradually, students progress through their zones of proximal development, taking more and more control over use of the strategies, until the students are able to take on a teaching role (Palincsar, Brown, & Campione, 1993; Greenway, 2002; Byra, 2004).

Reciprocal teaching has shown impressive success in raising reading comprehension levels, particularly for students experiencing reading difficulties, and the process illustrates the influence of Vygotsky's work on contemporary education. Another area in which Vygotsky's theorizing has been influential is illustrating the importance of culture on learning, as we consider next.

Adolescent DIVERSITY How Culture Influences How We Learn

DOES THE CULTURE in which we live influence the way we learn?

The answer seems to be "yes," at least according to research on adolescents' *learning styles,* the characteristic ways of approaching material based on an individual's cultural background and unique pattern of abilities (Chi-Ching & Noi, 1994a; Sternberg & Grigorenko, 1997; Evans, 2004).

Learning styles vary along several dimensions. For example, adolescents vary in terms of whether their typical way of learning is analytical or relational. Those with an *analytical learning style* learn most readily if they are first exposed to the individual components and principles behind a phenomenon or situation. By understanding those components and principles, they are better able to grasp the broad picture.

In contrast, those with a *relational learning style* master material best through exposure to a presentation of a complete phenomenon or unit. Parts of the unit are understood only when their relationship to the whole is understood. Rather than focusing on the individual components of a problem, students with relational learning styles learn best when they are first presented with the full picture. Then they can take this broad view and break it down into its components.

For example, suppose an adolescent is trying to learn how food is converted to energy in a cell. A more analytic learner would learn best by considering each individual step in the process sequentially. On the other hand, someone with a relational style would be more apt to consider the big picture, focusing on the general, overall process and its purpose (see Table 3-2).

TABLE 3-2 Characteristics of Relational and Analytical Learning Styles	
Relational Style	**Analytical Style**
1. Perceive information as part of total picture	1. Able to dis-embed information from total picture (focus on detail)
2. Exhibit improvisational and intuitive thinking	2. Exhibit sequential and structured thinking
3. More easily learn materials that have a human, social content and are characterized by experimental/cultural relevance	3. More easily learn materials that are inanimate and impersonal
4. Have a good memory for verbally presented ideas and information, especially if relevant	4. Have a good memory for abstract ideas and irrelevant information
5. Are more task oriented concerning nonacademic areas	5. Are more task oriented concerning academics
6. Are influenced by authority figures' expression of confidence or doubt in students' ability	6. Are not greatly affected by the opinions of others
7. Prefer to withdraw from unstimulating task performance	7. Show ability to persist at unstimulating tasks
8. Style conflicts with the traditional school environment	8. Style is consistent with school environments

What is particularly interesting about learning styles is that there may be cross-cultural differences in learning styles. Although their work is controversial, some educational researchers suggest that particular gender, racial, and ethnic groups display characteristic learning styles. According to James Anderson and Maurianne Adams (1992), Caucasian women and African-American, Native American, and Hispanic-American males and females are more likely to use relational styles of learning. In contrast, Caucasian and Asian-American males are more apt to favor an analytical learning style.

The assumption that different cultural groups have different learning styles is contentious, with critics arguing that there is so much variability among members of different groups that it is hard to generalize. These critics suggest that a discussion of group learning styles is misguided and that the focus should be on determining specific individuals' learning styles, not group differences (an argument that we'll see again later in the chapter when we discuss group differences in IQ scores). Still, it is clear that learning styles do play a role in determining how students learn and their preferred way of obtaining information, and that culture plays a role in determining how those learning styles develop (Kennedy, 2002; Rodrigues, 2005).

Evaluating Vygotsky's Contributions. Vygotsky's view—that the specific nature of cognitive development can be understood only by taking into account the cultural and social context—has become increasingly influential in the last decade. In some ways, this is surprising, in light of the fact that Vygotsky died over seven decades ago at the young age of 37 (Van Der Veer & Valsiner, 1993, 1994; Winsler, 2003).

Several factors explain Vygotsky's growing influence. One is that until recently, he was largely unknown to developmentalists. His writings are only now becoming widely disseminated in the United States due to the growing availability of good English translations. In fact, for most of the 20th century Vygotsky was not widely known even within his native land. His work was banned for some time, and it was not until the breakup of the Soviet Union that it became freely available in the formerly Soviet countries. Thus, Vygotsky, long hidden from his fellow developmentalists, only emerged onto the scene long after his death.

Even more important, though, is the quality of Vygotsky's ideas. They represent a consistent theoretical system and help explain a growing body of research attesting to the importance of social interaction in promoting cognitive development. The idea that children and adolescents' comprehension of the world is an outcome of their interactions with their parents, peers, and other members of society is both appealing and well supported by research findings. It is also consistent with a growing body of multicultural and cross-cultural research, which finds evidence that cognitive development is shaped, in part, by cultural factors (Daniels, 1996; Scrimsher & Tudge, 2003).

Of course, not every aspect of Vygotsky's theorizing has been supported, and he can be criticized for a lack of precision in his conceptualization of cognitive growth. For instance, such broad concepts as the zone of proximal development are not terribly precise, and they do not always lend themselves to experimental tests (Wertsch, 1999).

Furthermore, Vygotsky was largely silent on how basic cognitive processes such as attention and memory develop and how adolescents' natural cognitive capabilities unfold. Because of his emphasis on broad cultural influences, he did not focus on how individual bits of information are processed and synthesized. These processes, which must be taken into account if we are to have a complete understanding of cognitive development, are more directly addressed by information-processing theories.

Still, Vygotsky's melding of the cognitive and social worlds of adolescents has been an important advance in our understanding of cognitive development. We can only imagine what his impact would have been if he had lived a longer life. (See Table 3-3 for a comparison of Piaget's theory, information-processing theories, and Vygotskian approaches.)

TABLE 3-3 Comparison of Piaget's Theory, Information-Processing Theories, and Vygotsky's Approach to Cognitive Development			
	Piaget	**Information Processing**	**Vygotsky**
Key concepts	Stages of cognitive development; qualitative growth from one stage to another	Gradual, quantitative improvements in attention, perception, understanding, and memory	Culture and social context drive cognitive development
Role of stages	Heavy emphasis	No specific stages	No specific stages
Importance of social factors	Low	Low	High
Educational perspective	Children must have reached a given stage of development for specific types of educational interventions to be effective	Education is reflected in gradual increments in skills	Education is very influential in promoting cognitive growth; teachers serve as facilitators

▶ Adolescents' improving cognitive abilities, particularly in terms of abstract thought, makes them more likely to become engaged in social issues.

Review and Apply

Review

1. Thinking during adolescence becomes more abstract and less tied to the concrete here and now.

2. Piaget suggested that people pass through four stages of cognitive development, entering the formal operational stage at adolescence.

3. The information-processing perspective regards development as gradual and largely quantitative, attributable to adolescents' increasing ability to encode, store, and retrieve information and to use metacognition.

4. Vygotsky's approach focuses on the social and cultural aspects of development, in which interactions with others help individuals to develop cognitively.

5. All three major approaches have bred numerous studies and further theories, as well as educational applications, but no single theory is complete and all-encompassing.

Apply

1. Do you agree with Labouvie-Vief that there is a developmental stage beyond formal operations in which flexible, interpretive thinking becomes important? Why? If this stage exists, does this support or contradict Piaget's general approach?

2. Do you think that Vygotsky's social and cultural approach would argue for or against home schooling as an effective way to learn and develop? Why?

Intelligence: Determining Individual Strengths

"Why should you tell the truth?" "How far is Los Angeles from New York?" "A table is made of wood; a window of _____."

As 13-year-old Hyacinth sat hunched over her desk, trying to answer a long series of questions like these, she tried to guess the point of the test she was taking in her seventh-grade classroom. Clearly, the test didn't cover material that her teacher, Ms. White-Johnston, had talked about in class.

"What number comes next in this series: 1, 3, 7, 15, 31, ___?"

As she continued to work her way through the questions, she gave up trying to guess the rationale for the test. She'd leave that to her teacher. She sighed to herself. Rather than attempting to figure out what it all meant, she simply tried to do her best on the individual test items.

Hyacinth was taking an intelligence test. She might be surprised to learn that she was not alone in questioning the meaning and import of the items on the test. Intelligence test items are painstakingly prepared, and intelligence tests show a strong relationship to success in school (for reasons we'll soon discuss). Many developmentalists, however, would admit to harboring their own doubts as to whether questions such as those on Hyacinth's test are entirely appropriate to the task of assessing intelligence.

Understanding just what is meant by the concept of intelligence has proven to be a major challenge for researchers interested in delineating what separates intelligent from unintelligent behavior. Although nonexperts have their own conceptions of intelligence (one survey found, for instance, that laypersons believe that intelligence consists of three components: problem-solving ability, verbal ability, and social competence), it has been more difficult for experts to concur (Sternberg et al., 1981; Howe, 1997). Still, a general definition of intelligence is possible: **Intelligence** is the capacity to understand the world, think with rationality, and use resources effectively when faced with challenges (Wechsler, 1975).

▲ Intelligence tests seek to assess adolescents' intellectual capabilities.

intelligence the capacity to understand the world, think rationally, and use resources effectively when faced with challenges

Part of the difficulty in defining intelligence stems from the many—and sometimes unsatisfactory—paths that have been followed over the years in the quest to distinguish more intelligent people from less-intelligent ones. To understand how researchers have approached the task of assessing intelligence by devising *intelligence tests,* we need to consider some of the historical milestones in the area of intelligence.

Intelligence Benchmarks: Differentiating the Intelligent from the Unintelligent

The Paris school system was faced with a problem at the turn of the 20th century: A significant number of students were not benefiting from regular instruction. Unfortunately, these students—many of whom we would now call mentally retarded—were generally not identified early enough to shift them to special classes. The French minister of instruction approached psychologist Alfred Binet with this problem and asked him to devise a technique for the early identification of students who might benefit from instruction outside the regular classroom.

Binet's Test.   Binet tackled his task in a thoroughly practical manner. His years of observing school-age children and adolescents suggested to him that previous efforts to distinguish intelligent from unintelligent students—some of which were based on reaction time or keenness of sight—were off the mark. Instead, he launched a trial-and-error process in which items and tasks were administered to students who had been previously identified by teachers as being either "bright" or "dull." Tasks that the bright students completed correctly and the dull students failed to complete correctly were retained for the test. Tasks that did not discriminate between the two groups were discarded. The end result of this process was a test that reliably distinguished students who had previously been identified as fast or slow learners.

Binet's pioneering efforts in intelligence testing left several important legacies. The first was his pragmatic approach to the construction of intelligence tests. Binet did not have theoretical preconceptions about what intelligence was. Instead, he used a trial-and-error approach to psychological measurement that continues to serve as the predominant approach to test construction today. His definition of intelligence as that which his test measured has been adopted by many modern researchers, and it is particularly popular among test developers, who respect the widespread utility of intelligence tests but wish to avoid arguments about the underlying nature of intelligence.

Binet's legacy extends to his linking intelligence and school success. Binet's procedure for constructing an intelligence test ensured that intelligence—defined as performance on the test—and school success would be virtually one and the same. Thus, Binet's intelligence test, and today's tests that follow in Binet's footsteps, have become reasonable indicators of the degree to which students possess attributes that contribute to successful school performance. On the other hand, they do not provide useful information regarding a vast number of other attributes that are largely unrelated to academic proficiency, such as social skills or personality characteristics.

Finally, Binet developed a procedure of linking each intelligence test score with a **mental age**, the age of the children taking the test who, on average, achieved that score. For example, if a 6-year-old girl received a score of 30 on the test, and this was the average score received by 10-year-olds, her mental age would be considered 10 years. Similarly, a 15-year-old boy who scored a 90 on the test—thereby matching the mean score for 15-year-olds—would be assigned a mental age of 15 years (Wasserman & Tulsky, 2005).

Although assigning a mental age to students provides an indication of whether or not they are performing at the same level as their peers, it does not permit adequate comparisons between students of different **chronological (physical) ages**. By using mental age alone, for instance, it would be assumed that a 15-year-old responding with a mental age of 17 years would be as bright as a 6-year-old responding with a mental age of 8 years, when actually the 6-year-old would be showing a much greater *relative* degree of brightness.

mental age   the typical intelligence level found for people of a given chronological age

chronological (physical) age   a person's age according to the calendar

A solution to this problem comes in the form of the **intelligence quotient**, or **IQ**, a score that takes into account a student's mental *and* chronological age. The traditional method of calculating an IQ score uses the following formula, in which MA stands for mental age and CA for chronological age:

$$\text{IQ score} = \frac{\text{MA}}{\text{CA}} \times 100$$

As a bit of trial and error with this formula demonstrates, people whose mental age (MA) is equal to their chronological age (CA) will always have an IQ of 100. Furthermore, if the chronological age exceeds the mental age—implying below-average intelligence—the score will be below 100; and if the chronological age is lower than the mental age—suggesting above-average intelligence—the score will be above 100.

Using this formula, we can return to our earlier example of a 15-year-old who scores at a 17-year-old mental age. This student's IQ is $\frac{17}{15} \times 100$, or 113. In comparison, the IQ of a 6-year-old scoring at a mental age of 8 is $\frac{8}{6} \times 100$, or 133—a higher IQ score than the 15-year-old's.

Although the basic principles behind the calculation of an IQ score still hold, scores today are calculated in a more mathematically sophisticated manner and are known as *deviation IQ scores*. The average deviation IQ score remains set at 100, but tests are now devised so that the degree of deviation from this score permits the calculation of the proportion of people who have similar scores. For instance, approximately two thirds of all people fall within 15 points of the average score of 100, achieving scores between 85 and 115. As scores rise or fall beyond this range, the percentage of people in the same score category drops significantly (see Figure 3-3).

Measuring IQ: Present-Day Approaches to Intelligence.   Since the time of Binet, tests of intelligence have become increasingly accurate measures of IQ. Most of them can still trace their roots to his original work in one way or another. For example, one of the most widely used tests, the *Stanford-Binet Intelligence Scale*, began as an American revision of Binet's original test. The test consists of a series of items that vary according to the age of the person being tested. For instance, younger children are asked to answer questions about everyday activities or to copy complex figures. Adolescents and adults are asked to explain proverbs, solve analogies, and describe similarities between groups of words. The test is administered orally, and test takers are given progressively more difficult problems until they are unable to proceed.

intelligence quotient (IQ)   a score that expresses the ratio between a person's mental and chronological ages

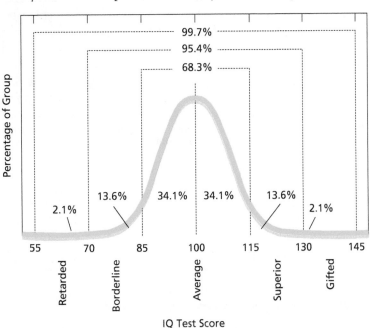

◄ **FIGURE 3-3**

This graph shows that 68.3% of all people fall within 15 points of the most common and average IQ score of 100. About 95% have scores that are within 30 points above or below 100. Fewer than 3% score below 55 or above 145.

The *Wechsler Intelligence Scale for Children Revised—Fourth Edition (WISC-IV)* is another widely used intelligence test for adolescents up to the age of 17. The test, and its adult counterpart, the *Wechsler Adult Intelligence Scale—Third Edition (WAIS-III)*, provides separate measures of verbal and performance (or nonverbal) skills, as well as a total score. As you can see from the sample items in Figure 3-4, the verbal tasks are traditional word problems testing skills

	WAIS-III	
NAME	**GOAL OF ITEM**	**EXAMPLE**
VERBAL SCALE		
Information	Assess general information	Who wrote Tom Sawyer?
Comprehension	Assess understanding and evaluation of social norms and past experience	Why is copper often used for electrical wires?
Arithmetic	Assess math reasoning through verbal problems	Three women divided eighteen golf balls equally among themselves. How many golf balls did each person receive?
Similarities	Test understanding of how objects or concepts are alike, tapping abstract reasoning	In what way are an circle and a triangle alike?
PERFORMANCE SCALE		
Digit symbol	Assess speed of learning	Test-taker must learn what symbols correspond to what digits, and then must replace a multidigit number with the appropriate symbols. 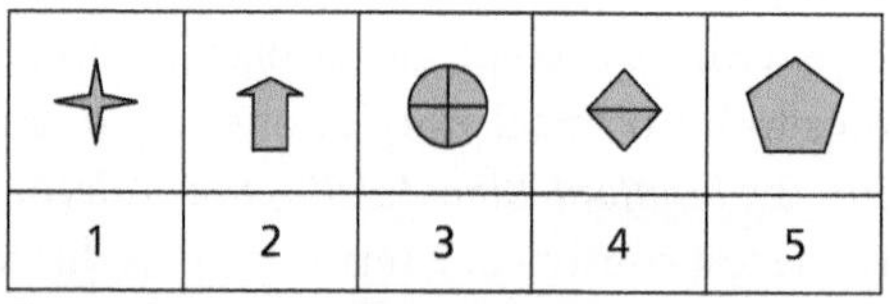
Matrix reasoning	Tests spatial reasoning	Test-taker must decide which of the five possibilities replaces the question mark and completes the sequence. 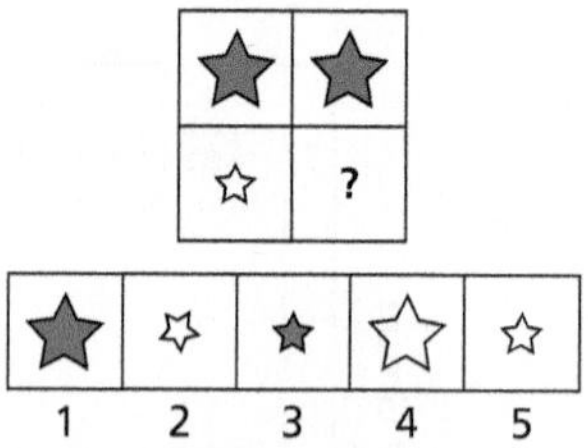
Block design item	Test understanding of relationship of parts to wholes	Problems require test-takers to reproduce a design in fixed amount of time. 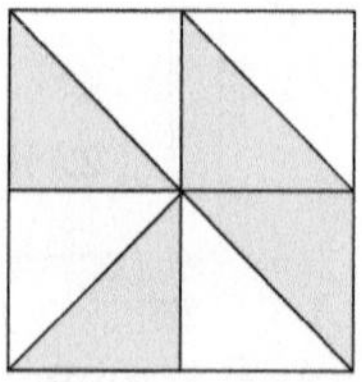

▲ **FIGURE 3-4**

The Wechsler Adult Intelligence Scales (WAIS-III) includes items such as these.

(*Source:* The Psychological Corporation, 1997).

	WISC-IV	
NAME	**GOAL OF ITEM**	**EXAMPLE**
VERBAL SCALE		
Information	Assess general information	How many nickels make a dime?
Comprehension	Assess understanding and evaluation of social norms and past experience	What is the advantage of keeping money in the bank?
Arithmetic	Assess math reasoning through verbal problems	If two buttons cost 15 cents, what will be the cost of a dozen buttons?
Similarities	Test understanding of how objects or concepts are alike, tapping abstract reasoning	In what way are an hour and a week alike?
PERFORMANCE SCALE		
Digit symbol	Assess speed of learning	Match symbols to numbers using key. 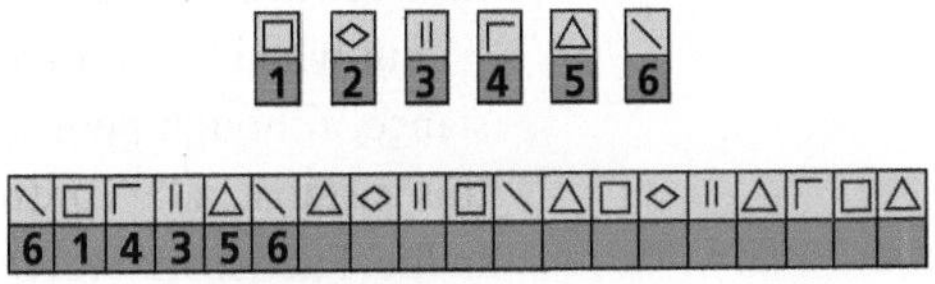
Picture completion	Visual memory and attention	Identify what is missing. 
Object assembly	Test understanding of relationship of parts to wholes	Put pieces together to form a whole. 

▲ **FIGURE 3-4 (continued)**

such as understanding a passage, while typical nonverbal tasks are copying a complex design, arranging pictures in a logical order, and assembling objects. The separate portions of the test allow for easier identification of any specific problems a test taker may have. For example, significantly higher scores on the performance part of the test than on the verbal part may indicate difficulties in linguistic development (Zhu & Weiss, 2005).

The **Kaufman Assessment Battery for Children, 2nd Edition (KABC—II)** takes a different approach than the Stanford-Binet and WISC-IV. In it, children and adolescents up to the age of 18 are tested on their ability to integrate different kinds of stimuli simultaneously and to use systematic thinking. The KABC—II minimizes verbal instructions and responses. It allows those administering the test the ability to use alternative wording or gestures, or even to pose questions in a different language, to maximize a test taker's performance. This capability of the KABC—II makes testing more valid and equitable for children to whom English is a second language (Kaufman et al., 2005).

What do the IQ scores derived from IQ tests mean? For most adolescents, IQ scores are reasonably good predictors of their school performance. That's not surprising, given that the initial impetus for the development of intelligence tests was to identify children who were having difficulties in school (Sternberg & Grigorenko, 2002).

But when it comes to performance outside academic spheres, the story is different. For instance, although people with higher IQ scores are apt to finish more years of schooling, once this is statistically controlled for, IQ scores are not closely related to income and later success in life. Furthermore, IQ scores are frequently inaccurate when it comes to predicting a particular individual's future success. For example, two people with different IQ scores may both finish their bachelor's degrees at the same college, and the person with a lower IQ might end up with a higher income and a more successful career. Because of these difficulties with traditional IQ scores, researchers have turned to alternative approaches to measuring intelligence (McClelland, 1993).

What IQ Tests Don't Tell: Alternative Conceptions of Intelligence

The intelligence tests used most frequently in school settings today are based on the idea that intelligence is a single factor, a unitary mental ability. This one main attribute has commonly been called *g* (Spearman, 1927; Lubinski, 2004). The *g* factor is assumed to underlie performance on every aspect of intelligence, and it is the *g* factor that intelligence tests presumably measure.

However, many theorists dispute the notion that intelligence is one-dimensional. Some developmentalists suggest that in fact two kinds of intelligence exist: fluid intelligence and crystallized intelligence (Catell, 1967, 1987). **Fluid intelligence** reflects information-processing capabilities, reasoning, and memory. For example, a student asked to group a series of letters according to some criterion or to remember a set of numbers would be using fluid intelligence. In contrast, **crystallized intelligence** is the accumulation of information, skills, and strategies that people have learned through experience and that they can apply in problem-solving situations. A student would likely be relying on crystallized intelligence to solve a puzzle or deduce the solution to a mystery, in which it was necessary to draw on past experience (Alfonso, Flanagan, & Radwan, 2005; McGrew, 2005).

Other theorists divide intelligence into an even greater number of parts. For example, psychologist Howard Gardner has suggested that we have eight distinct intelligences, each relatively independent (see Figure 3-5). Gardner suggested that these separate intelligences operate not in isolation, but together, depending on the type of activity in which we are engaged (Gardner, 2000, 2003; Chen & Gardner, 2005).

The Russian psychologist Lev Vygotsky, whose approach to cognitive development we discussed earlier in the chapter, took a very different approach to intelligence. He suggested that

Kaufman Assessment Battery for Children, 2nd Edition (KABC—II) an intelligence test permitting unusual flexibility in its administration

fluid intelligence the ability to deal with new problems and situations

crystallized intelligence the store of information, skills, and strategies that people have acquired through education and prior experiences

1. *Musical intelligence* (skills in tasks involving music). Case example:
When he was 3, Yehudi Menuhin was smuggled into the San Francisco Orchestra concerts by his parents. The sound of Louis Persinger's violin so entranced the youngster that he insisted on a violin for his birthday and Louis Persinger as his teacher. He got both. By the time he was 10 years old, Menuhin was an international performer.

2. *Bodily kinesthetic intelligence* (skills in using the whole body or various portions of it in the solution of problems or in the construction of products or displays, exemplified by dancers, athletes, actors, and surgeons). Case example:
Fifteen-year-old Babe Ruth played third base. During one game, his team's pitcher was doing poorly and Babe loudly criticized him from third base. Brother Mathias, the coach, called out, "Ruth, if you know so much about it, *you* pitch!" Babe was surprised and embarrassed because he had never pitched before, but Brother Mathias insisted. Ruth said later that at the very moment he took the pitcher's mound, he *knew* he was supposed to be a pitcher.

3. *Logical mathematical intelligence* (skills in problem solving and scientific thinking). Case example:
Barbara McClintock won the Nobel Prize in medicine for her work in microbiology. She describes one of her breakthroughs, which came after thinking about a problem for half an hour...: "Suddenly I jumped and ran back to the [corn]field. At the top of the field [the others were still at the bottom] I shouted, 'Eureka, I have it!'"

4. *Linguistic intelligence* (skills involved in the production and use of language). Case example:
At the age of 10, T.S. Elliot created a magazine called *Fireside*, to which he was the sole contributor. In a 3-day period during his winter vacation, he created eight complete issues.

5. *Spatial intelligence* (skills involving spatial configurations, such as those used by artists and architects). Case example:
Navigation around the Caroline Islands...is accomplished without instruments....During the actual trip, the navigator must envision mentally a reference island as it passes under a particular star and from that he computes the number of segments completed, the proportion of the trip remaining, and any corrections in heading.

6. *Interpersonal intelligence* (skills in interacting with others, such as sensitivity to the moods, temperaments, motivations, and intentions of others). Case example:
When Anne Sullivan began instructing the deaf and blind Helen Keller, her task was one that had eluded others for years. Yet, just 2 weeks after beginning her work with Keller, Sullivan achieved a great success. In her words, "My heart is singing with joy this morning. A miracle has happened! The wild little creature of 2 weeks ago has been transformed into a gentle child."

7. *Intrapersonal intelligence* (knowledge of the internal aspects of oneself; access to one's own feelings and emotions). Case example:
In her essay "A Sketch of the Past," Virginia Woolf displays deep insight into her own inner life through these lines, describing her reaction to several specific memories from her childhood that still, in adulthood, shock her: "Though I still have the peculiarity that I receive these sudden shocks, they are now always welcome; after the first surprise, I always feel instantly that they are particularly valuable. And so I go on to suppose that the shock-receiving capacity is what makes me a writer."

8. *Naturalist intelligence* (ability to identify and classify patterns in nature). Case example:
In prehistoric periods, hunter-gatherers required naturalist intelligence in order to identify what types of plants were edible.

▲ **FIGURE 3-5**

Psychologist Howard Gardner suggested there are eight distinct intelligences, each relatively independent.

(*Source:* Adapted from Walters & Gardner, 1986)

to assess intelligence, we should look not only at those cognitive processes that are fully developed, but at those that are currently being developed as well. To do this, Vygotsky contended that assessment tasks should involve cooperative interaction between the individual who is being assessed and the person who is doing the assessment—a process called *dynamic assessment*. In short, intelligence is seen as being reflected not only in how adolescents can perform on their own, but also in terms of how well they perform when helped by adults (Vygotsky, 1927/1976; Daniels, 1996; Brown & Ferrara, 1999).

Sternberg's Triarchic Theory of Intelligence. Taking yet another approach, psychologist Robert Sternberg (1987, 1990, 2003) suggested that intelligence is best thought of in terms of information processing. In this view, the way in which people store material in memory and later use it to solve intellectual tasks provides the most precise conception of intelligence. Rather than focusing on the various subcomponents that make up the *structure* of intelligence, then, information-processing approaches examine the *processes* that underlie intelligent behavior (Floyd, 2005).

Studies of the nature and speed of problem-solving processes show that people with higher intelligence levels differ from others not only in the number of problems they ultimately are able to solve, but in their method of solving the problems as well. People with high IQ scores spend more time on the initial stages of problem-solving, retrieving relevant information from memory. In contrast, those who score lower on traditional IQ tests tend to spend less time on the initial stages, instead skipping ahead and making less-informed guesses. The processes used in solving problems, then, may reflect important differences in intelligence (Sternberg, 1990, 2005).

In his **triarchic theory of intelligence**, Sternberg suggested that intelligence is made up of three major components: componential, experiential, and contextual (see Figure 3-6). The *componential* aspect consists of the mental components involved in analyzing data used in solving problems, especially problems involving rational behavior. It relates to people's ability to

triarchic theory of intelligence the belief that intelligence consists of three aspects of information processing: the componential element, the experiential element, and the contextual element

Componential Aspect of Intelligence
(Analysis of data to solve problems, using previously-learned information)

Contextual Aspect of Intelligence
(How intelligence is used to face real-world demands; practical intelligence)

Experiential Aspect of Intelligence
(How prior experiences are used in problem solving; abililty to cope with new situations)

▲ **FIGURE 3-6**

Sternberg's Triarchic Theory of Intelligence.
(*Source:* Based on Sternberg, 1985, 1991).

select and use formulas, to choose appropriate problem-solving strategies, and in general to make use of what they have been taught. The *experiential* component refers to the relationship between intelligence, people's prior experience, and their ability to cope with new situations. This is the insightful aspect of intelligence, which allows people to relate what they already know to a new situation and an array of facts never before encountered. Finally, the *contextual* component of intelligence involves the degree of success people demonstrate in facing the demands of their everyday, real-world environments. For instance, the contextual component is involved in adapting to on-the-job professional demands (Sternberg, 1985a; 1991).

Traditional intelligence tests, which yield an IQ score, tend to focus on the componential aspect of intelligence. Yet increasing research suggests that a more useful measure, particularly when one is looking for ways to compare and predict adult success, is the contextual component—the aspect of intelligence that has come to be called practical intelligence.

Practical and Emotional Intelligence.   According to Robert Sternberg, the IQ score that most traditional tests produce relates quite well to academic success. However, IQ seems to be unrelated to other types of achievement, such as career success. For example, although it is clear that success in business settings requires some minimal level of the sort of intelligence measured by IQ tests, the rate of career advancement and the ultimate success of business executives is only marginally related to IQ scores (McClelland, 1993; Sternberg & Wagner, 1986; 1993; Wagner & Sternberg, 1991).

Sternberg contends that success in a career necessitates a type of intelligence—called **practical intelligence**—that is substantially different from that involved in traditional academic pursuits (Sternberg et al., 1997). While academic success is based on knowledge of particular types of information, obtained largely from reading and listening, practical intelligence is learned primarily by observing others and modeling their behavior. People who are high in practical intelligence can extract and deduce broad principles and norms about appropriate behavior and apply them in particular situations. (See Figure 3-7 for a sample item from a

practical intelligence   intelligence that is learned primarily by observing others and modeling their behavior

◀ **FIGURE 3-7**
Practical intelligence tests such as this one measure the ability to utilize a wide range of principles in solving everyday problems. (*Source*: Sternberg, 2000, pg. 389).

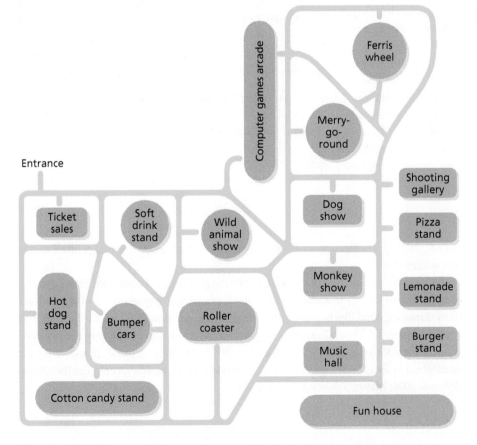

Following a map of an amusement park you walk from the lemonade stand to the computer games arcade. Your friend walks from the shooting gallery to the roller coaster. Which landmark will BOTH of you most likely pass? (1) the merry-go-round, (2) the music hall, (3) the pizza stand, or (4) the dog show.

Transiti⊃ns

Too Smart to Get the Job You Want?

Sam Brock had wanted to be in law enforcement as long as he could remember. Just before graduating with a community college degree, he began to apply for police officer's jobs. But after taking several initial screening tests offered by local police departments looking for new police recruits, he came up empty-handed. The reason, he later found out, was not that he'd scored too low on the test—he had scored too high, and was considered too smart for the job.

Sam was not the only one to feel the sting of rejection because of scoring too high on the test. For instance, anyone who applied to the New London, Connecticut, police department was faced with an official hiring policy that prevented people who scored too low or too high on an employment test to be considered for a police officer position (Allen, 1999).

These hiring standards came to light during a prolonged court battle waged by an unsuccessful applicant. He was denied employment because he scored 33 out of 50, and anyone with a score over 27 was considered too skilled to do a good job as a police officer.

The test used by the police department was the Wonderlic Personnel Test (WPT), which is used by thousands of employers across the United States. The WPT provides a range of scores for applicants who are most likely to succeed in a given profession (see Figure 3-8). The test assesses both fluid intelligence and crystallized intelligence by measuring a variety of cognitive skills, including learning ability, skill in understanding instructions, and problem-solving potential (Bell et al., 2002; Wonderlic, 2003).

Although typically the WPT is used to provide a minimum score, in some cases it provides a cutoff at the high end. The rationale is that for professions involving a great deal of routine, and sometimes tedious, activities, people who are easily bored are more likely to leave the job soon after they receive expensive training.

Critics of the approach of setting maximum scores point out that the test needlessly rejects those who are highly motivated and who

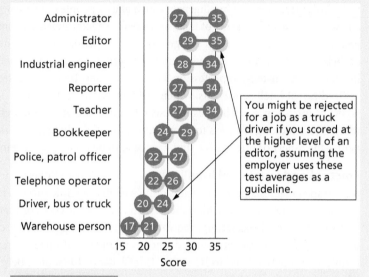

> You might be rejected for a job as a truck driver if you scored at the higher level of an editor, assuming the employer uses these test averages as a guideline.

▲ FIGURE 3-8

Developed by a private human resources firm, and based on a scale of 1 to 50, these are minimum and maximum scores for selected professions.
(*Source:* Wonderlic, 1999).

might enjoy the work. Furthermore, a significant number of police activities require quick, complicated decision making, skills that would benefit from higher intelligence (Bulmahn & Krakel, 2002).

Despite these criticisms, the courts have ruled in favor of the use minimum and maximum cutoffs. When seeking a job, then, job applicants have an additional worry—appearing too smart.

● Do you agree that setting a maximum test score is appropriate for certain jobs? Is it possible to be "overqualified," or should only your personal preferences determine which jobs you seek?

---

test of practical intelligence, and also see the *Transitions* box for more on intelligence and career success.)

Another type of intelligence involves emotional domains. **Emotional intelligence** is the set of skills that underlie the accurate assessment, evaluation, expression, and regulation of emotions. Emotional intelligence underlies the ability to get along well with others, to understand what others are feeling and experiencing, and to respond appropriately to the needs of others. It permits people to tune into others' feelings, allowing them to respond appropriately. Emotional intelligence is also of obvious value to personal success as an adolescent (Zeidner, Matthews, & Roberts, 2004; Mayer, Salovey, Caruso, 2004).

emotional intelligence the set of skills that underlie the accurate assessment, evaluation, expression, and regulation of emotions

Group Differences in IQ

A jontry is an example of a

(a) rulpow

(b) flink

(c) spudge

(d) bakwoe

If you were to find an item composed of nonsense words such as this on an intelligence test, your immediate—and quite legitimate—reaction would likely be to complain. How could a test that purports to measure intelligence include test items that incorporate meaningless terminology?

Yet for some people, the items actually used on traditional intelligence tests might appear equally nonsensical. To take a hypothetical example, suppose children living in rural areas were asked details about subways, while those living in urban areas were asked about the mating practices of sheep. In both cases, we would expect that the previous experiences of test takers would have a substantial effect on their ability to answer the questions. And if questions about such matters were included on an IQ test, the test could rightly be viewed as a measure of prior experience rather than of intelligence.

Although the questions on traditional IQ tests are not so obviously dependent on test takers' prior experiences as are our examples, cultural background and experience do have the potential to affect intelligence test scores. In fact, many educators suggest that traditional measures of intelligence are subtly biased in favor of white, upper- and middle-class students and against groups with different cultural experiences (Ortiz & Dynda, 2005).

Explaining Racial Differences in IQ. The issue of how cultural background and experience influence IQ test performance has led to considerable debate among researchers. The debate has been fueled by the finding that IQ scores of certain racial groups are consistently lower, on average, than the IQ scores of other groups. For example, the mean score of African Americans tends to be about 15 IQ points lower than the mean score of whites—although the measured difference varies a great deal depending on the particular IQ test employed (Fish, 2001; Maller, 2003).

The question that emerges from such differences, of course, is whether they reflect actual differences in intelligence or, instead, are caused by bias in the intelligence tests themselves in favor of majority groups and against minorities. For example, if whites perform better on an IQ test than African Americans because of their greater familiarity with the language used in the test items, the test hardly can be said to provide a fair measure of the intelligence of African Americans. Similarly, an intelligence test that solely used African-American Vernacular English could not be considered an impartial measure of intelligence for whites.

The question of how to interpret differences between intelligence scores of different cultural groups lies at the heart of one of the major controversies in adolescent development: To what degree is an individual's intelligence determined by heredity and to what degree by environment? The issue is important because of its social implications. For instance, if intelligence is primarily determined by heredity and is therefore largely fixed at birth, attempts to alter cognitive abilities later in life, such as by schooling, will meet with limited success. On the other hand, if intelligence is largely environmentally determined, modifying social and educational conditions is a more promising strategy for bringing about increases in cognitive functioning (Weiss, 2003).

***The Bell Curve* Controversy.**   Although investigations into the relative contributions of heredity and environment to intelligence have been conducted for decades, the smoldering debate became a raging fire with the publication of a book by Richard J. Herrnstein and Charles Murray (1994), titled *The Bell Curve*. In the book, Herrnstein and Murray argued that the average 15-point IQ difference between whites and African Americans is due primarily to heredity rather than environment. Furthermore, they argued that this IQ difference accounts for the higher rates of poverty, lower employment, and higher use of welfare among minority groups as compared with majority groups.

The conclusions reached by Herrnstein and Murray raised a storm of protest, and many researchers who examined the data reported in the book came to conclusions that were quite different. Most developmentalists and psychologists responded by arguing that the racial differences in measured IQ can be explained by environmental differences between the races. In fact, when a variety of indicators of economic and social factors are statistically taken into account simultaneously, mean IQ scores of black and white children turn out to be actually quite similar. For instance, children from similar middle-class backgrounds, whether African American or white, tend to have similar IQ scores (Brooks-Gunn, Klebanov, & Duncan, 1996; Alderfer, 2003).

Furthermore, critics maintained that there is little evidence to suggest that IQ is a cause of poverty and other social ills. In fact, some critics suggested, as mentioned earlier in this discussion, that IQ scores were unrelated in meaningful ways to later success in life (e.g., McClelland, 1993; Nisbett, 1994; Sternberg, 1995, 1997a; Reifman, 2000).

Finally, members of cultural and social minority groups may score lower than members of the majority group due to the nature of the intelligence tests themselves. It is clear that traditional intelligence tests may discriminate against minority groups who have not had exposure to the same environment as majority group members have experienced.

Most traditional intelligence tests are constructed primarily using white, English-speaking, middle-class populations as their test participants. As a result, children from different cultural backgrounds may perform poorly on the tests—not because they are less intelligent, but because the tests use questions that are culturally biased in favor of majority group members. In fact, a

▲ The causes of group racial differences in IQ are difficult to ascertain.

classic study found that in one California school district, Mexican-American students were 10 times more likely than whites to be placed in special education classes (Mercer, 1973). More recent findings show that nationally twice as many African-American students as white students are classified as mildly retarded, a difference that experts attribute primarily to cultural bias and poverty (Reschly, 1996; Terman et al., 1996). Although certain IQ tests (such as the *System of Multicultural Pluralistic Assessment,* or *SOMPA*) have been designed to be equally valid regardless of the cultural background of test takers, no test can be completely without bias (Sandoval et al., 1998).

In short, most experts in the area of IQ were not convinced by *The Bell Curve* contention that differences in group IQ scores are largely determined by genetic factors. Still, we cannot put the issue to rest, largely because it is impossible to design a definitive experiment that can determine the cause of differences in IQ scores between members of different groups. Thinking about how such an experiment might be designed shows the futility of the enterprise: One cannot ethically assign children to different living conditions to find the effects of environment, nor would one wish to genetically control or alter intelligence levels in unborn children.

Today, IQ is seen as the product of *both* nature and nurture interacting with one another in a complex manner. Rather than seeing intelligence as produced by either genes or experience, genes are seen to affect experiences, and experiences are viewed as influencing the expression of genes. For instance, psychologist Eric Turkheimer has found evidence that although environmental factors play a larger role in influencing the IQ of poor children, genes are more influential in the IQ of affluent children (Turkheimer et al., 2003).

Ultimately, it may be less important to know the absolute degree to which intelligence is determined by genetic and environmental factors than it is to learn how to improve children's living conditions and educational experiences. By enriching the quality of children's environments, we will be in a better position to permit all children to reach their full potential and to maximize their contributions to society, whatever their individual levels of intelligence (Wachs, 1996; Wickelgren, 1999).

Achievement and Aptitude Tests

During the course of your schooling, you may or may not have taken an IQ test. But what is almost certainly true is that you took one of the other forms of tests that are administered routinely to students before they enter college—an achievement or aptitude test.

An **achievement test** is a test that measures a person's level of knowledge in a specific subject area. Instead of measuring overall general ability, as intelligence tests are designed to do, an achievement test concentrates on specific material a person is supposed to have learned. For instance, high school students may have to pass an achievement test in a specific area such as American literature or calculus to obtain advanced college credit (the CLEP, or College-Level Examination Program). Similarly, lawyers need to pass the bar exam to practice law. (Also see the *Career Choices* box.)

An **aptitude test** is designed to predict a person's ability in a particular area or line of work. Most adolescents are asked to take the SAT or ACT exam as part of the process of applying to college. The SAT and ACT are designed to predict how well a high school student will do in college, and they do so reasonably well (Hoffman, 2001).

Although the distinction between achievement tests (which measure specific knowledge), aptitude tests (which predict performance), and traditional IQ tests (which assess general intelligence) are theoretically clear, the reality is different. For instance, it is hard to devise an aptitude test like the SAT that does not involve at least some aspects of underlying intelligence and past academic achievement. In practice, then, the differences between the various kinds of tests are not clear-cut.

In addition, the use of achievement and aptitude tests like the SAT, ACT, and standardized high school graduation tests has been the source of considerable controversy. Some critics argue

achievement test a test designed to determine a person's level of knowledge in a given subject area

aptitude test a test designed to predict a person's ability in a particular area or line of work

CAREER CHOICES

Test Designer

Name: Heather S. Klesch

Occupation: Test developer, National Evaluation Systems

Education: BA, English Literature, Florida State University, Tallahassee

ACHIEVEMENT AND APTITUDE tests are two of many different approaches used to determine people's abilities and skills, and every test is designed to a specific set of required measurements, according to test developer Heather Klesch. Klesch works at National Evaluation Systems, a test development firm that creates assessments in more than 100 content areas, teaching competency exams, and the basic skills of reading, writing, and mathematics.

"For example, a state's history curriculum changes over time and has to be updated periodically," Klesch explained. "Or at some point the state decides it wants its teachers to demonstrate they have the knowledge and skills in a particular area. The state would then want to offer a test that is customized and aligns with the state curriculum."

But before a test is considered an accurate and practical measurement tool, it must pass through a series of developmental steps.

"The first thing that needs to be done is to develop a framework which explains the test and its content," Klesch said. "There has to be an outline and resource for examinees to be able to understand what is expected of them."

Once test developers have designed a test framework, some type of job analysis is conducted in which those who are already working in the field for which the test is being designed are surveyed. This job analysis, according to Klesch, helps to ensure that the content and the framework of the exam truly is applicable to the job.

"The next step would be the development of specific items, or questions, which are then field tested," Klesch said.

The final phase of test development is to determine what a passing grade will be. The specific passing score that is chosen depends on the reason the test is being given.

"What you have to make sure of is that the purpose of the test is defined up front rather than letting the test itself define the purpose," Klesch noted.

Thinking of working in the test construction field?

Test development is a growing field, as increasing numbers of states require that students pass competency tests before graduation. People who create tests such as these, as well as those we're all familiar with such as the SAT, come from a variety of backgrounds. A college bachelor's degree is always required, but the specific major is less important, because tests cover a broad variety of topical areas. The exception would be if you were interested in working on the statistical basis of test construction, in which case a Ph.D. in psychometrics—the field of study concerned with educational and psychological measurement—or a related doctoral degree in social science is required. ■

---

that too much emphasis is placed on the results of a single test and that the real-world significance of test performance is minimal. Furthermore, because economically disadvantaged adolescents sometimes perform worse than adolescents from more affluent homes, some complain that the tests may be biased. Consequently, some colleges and universities no longer use the SAT and ACT in their admissions process (Banerji, 2006).

Review and Apply

Review

1. Intelligence is a difficult concept to define precisely, and modern theories suggest that humans have multiple kinds of intelligence.

2. Intelligence tests were originally created to differentiate persons who would be successful in school from those who would not. Current IQ tests maintain a focus on academic knowledge and abilities.

3. Newer theories of intelligence, such as Catell's, Sternberg's, and Gardner's, identify several different components or types of intelligence.

4. Group differences in IQ test results are most likely attributable to the tests' inability to assess the person without assessing the environment as well.

5. In addition to intelligence tests, two other types of tests are achievement tests and aptitude tests.

Apply

1. Sternberg's triarchic theory of intelligence is related to the information-processing approach to cognitive development. Do you think Piaget had a theory of intelligence? What would a Piagetian theory of intelligence be like?

2. An achievement test measures what individuals have learned, whereas an aptitude test predicts the extent to which they are capable of learning. Which type of test is more appropriate for making college admissions decisions? Why?

Social Cognition: Thinking in a Social Context

It was my last night in Russia, and we had a party on board a ship, floating down the Volga River. As the evening proceeded, and we furtively passed around bottles of vodka, I thought over the incredible experiences I'd had and the friends I'd made during my month-long visit as an exchange student. My Russian had improved a lot, but the best part was the memories that I knew would last a lifetime. As the evening wore on, and vodka flowed freely, we sang Russian folk songs. From what I remember—and I don't remember much, 'cause I got myself drunker than I'd ever been in my life—the high point of the evening came when I went to the back of the boat, where for some reason a Russian friend and I flung some ugly wooden chairs into the river to celebrate the evening. It seemed to make sense at the time, although I can't remember now, a day later, exactly why we did it.

It's not hard to enumerate the various acts of folly involved in this 15-year-old's account of his boat ride down the Volga River in Russia: The drinking of enough vodka to get drunk. The destruction of property. The polluting of the river. Being in a foreign country where the judicial system may not presume innocence. The possibility of ending up in a foreign jail, which may lack the niceties of American prisons (which are not so nice themselves).

Why would anyone take such chances? One major reason is the risk-taking behavior characteristic of adolescence. Adolescents' newly developed ability to think in a more sophisticated manner also produces outcomes that can lead to self-absorption and risk taking. As we will see in the remainder of the chapter, advances in adolescents' *social cognition*—how they understand and make sense of others and themselves—are not always matched by advances in judgment and critical thinking.

Egocentrism in Thinking: Adolescents' Self-Absorption

Carlos thinks of his parents as "control freaks." He cannot figure out why his parents insist that, when he borrows their car, he call home and let them know where he is. Jeri is thrilled that Molly bought earrings just like hers, thinking it is the ultimate compliment, even though it's not clear that Molly even knew that Jeri had a similar pair when she bought them. Lu is upset with his biology teacher, Ms. Sebastian, for giving a long, difficult midterm exam on which he didn't do well.

Adolescents' newly sophisticated metacognitive abilities enable them to readily imagine that others are thinking about them, and they may construct elaborate scenarios about others' thoughts. These abilities are also the source of the egocentrism that sometimes dominates adolescents' thinking. **Adolescent egocentrism** is a state of self-absorption in which the world is viewed from one's own point of view. This egocentrism—which largely occurs because of adolescents' newly developed capabilities to introspect and examine their own thinking—makes them highly critical of authority figures such as parents and teachers. In addition, they are less willing to accept criticism and quick to find fault with the behavior of others (Elkind, 1985; Rycek et al., 1998; Greene, Krcmar, & Rubin, 2002).

The kind of egocentrism we see in adolescence helps explain why adolescents sometimes perceive that they are the focus of everyone else's attention. In fact, particularly in early adolescence, some teenagers develop what has been called an **imaginary audience**, fictitious observers who pay as much attention to the adolescents' behavior as adolescents do themselves. The imaginary audience is a reflection of the same kind of egocentrism that dominates the rest of adolescents' thinking. For instance, a student sitting in a class may be sure a teacher is focusing on her, and a teenager at a basketball game is likely to be convinced that everyone around him is focusing on the pimple on his chin.

Egocentrism leads to a second distortion in thinking—the notion that one's experiences are unique. Adolescents often develop **personal fables**, the view that what happens to them is unique, exceptional, and shared by no one else. For instance, teenagers whose romantic relationships have ended may feel that no one has ever experienced the hurt they feel, that no one has ever been treated so badly, that no one can understand what they are going through.

Although personal fables are hardly unique to adolescence—ask any adult who has just lost a long-held job, but who felt he or she was immune to job cuts—personal fables play a particularly prominent role during early adolescence. Furthermore, as we consider next, one result of the belief in one's own personal fable is the development of one of the most prominent characteristics of adolescents: risk taking (Frankenberger, 2000; Vartanian, 2000).

Risk Taking

As we first noted in Chapter 2, adolescents are more likely to behave in ways that put themselves at risk, both physically and psychologically, than at other periods of life. For example, not only are they less likely to take preventive measures to avoid potential problems (such as using condoms during sex or fastening a seatbelt), they are more apt to abuse drugs or drive recklessly.

Such recklessness starts early in adolescence. For example, 20% of seventh graders engage in sex, and half the time it is unprotected sex. Two thirds of sixth graders have tried alcohol. Later in adolescence, they drive while intoxicated or ride in cars with those who are drunk (Ozer et al., 2002).

Why are adolescents such risk takers? It's not because they are bad at making decisions generally. Although there are significant advances in decision-making capabilities from childhood to adolescence, by the time they reach the age of 15, they use pretty much the same decision-making rules as adults. Poor decision-making processes, by themselves, do not seem to account for the riskiness of adolescents' behavior (Steinberg & Cauffman, 1995).

But even if they follow sound decision-making rules, adolescents may make poor decisions if they initially weigh or define the pros and cons differently. It's as if someone learns the rules of addition, but instead of adding 2 + 2 and getting 4, they answer the wrong problem. The addition adds up, but it's not the correct problem.

For example, an adolescent may have more inaccurate information about the risks involved in unprotected sex than a better-informed older adult. Then, when weighing the likelihood of

adolescent egocentrism   a state of self-absorption in which the world is viewed from one's own point of view

imaginary audience   fictitious observers who pay as much attention to adolescents' behavior as they do themselves

personal fables   the view held by some adolescents that what happens to them is unique, exceptional, and shared by no one else

contracting a sexually transmitted disease, the misinformation is used in the calculation, making the ultimate decision a poor one.

Adolescents are also highly attuned to their peers, as we'll discuss in Chapter 7. If they perceive that their peers tend to behave in a risky manner, they may be more likely to take risks themselves. In fact, adolescents take more risks in groups than they do alone (Gardner & Steinberg, 2005).

Furthermore, much of adolescents' risk taking may well be traced to the personal fables they construct for themselves. Their personal fables may make them feel invulnerable to the risks that threaten others. They may think that there is no need to use condoms during sex because, in the personal fables they construct, pregnancy and sexually transmitted diseases such as AIDS only happen to other kinds of people, not to them. They may drive after drinking, because their personal fables paint them as careful drivers, always in control (Ponton, 1999; Greene et al., 2000; Vartanian, 2000).

Adolescent risk taking is also related to personality factors such as sensation seeking. Adolescents who have a higher motivation to engage in activities that offer physiological arousal—such as skydiving, gambling, and even criminal activity—may be responding to an internal motivation to increase sensation seeking. Consistent with this hypothesis, adolescents who engage in risky health-related behaviors, such as smoking, are more likely to score high on measures of sensation seeking (Frankenberger, 2004). (To get a sense of your own level of sensation seeking, complete and score the questionnaire in Table 3-4.)

Creativity: Novel Thought

For many adolescents, the teenage years mark the blossoming of a personal style and way of thinking that individuals embrace as their own. It is, in short, a period marked by significant creativity.

Creativity is the ability to combine responses or ideas in novel ways. It's a tricky topic for psychologists and educators to understand because it's much easier to come up with *examples* of creativity than to determine its *causes* (Csikszentmihalyi, 1997; Simonton, 2003; Niu & Sternberg, 2003; Kaufman & Baer, 2005).

For instance, consider how you might respond to the question "How many uses can you think of for a newspaper?"

creativity the ability to combine responses or ideas in novel ways

◀ Not only do adolescents have less experience driving, but their tendency to take risks leads them to take chances that older drivers would avoid. Such risk-taking can have deadly consequences.

TABLE 3-4   Do You Seek Out Sensation?

How much stimulation do you crave in your everyday life? You will have an idea after you complete the following questionnaire, which lists some items from a scale designed to assess your sensation-seeking tendencies. Circle either *A* or *B* in each pair of statements.

1. *A* I would like a job that requires a lot of travelling.

   B I would prefer a job in one location.

2. *A* I am invigorated by a brisk, cold day.

   B I can't wait to get indoors on a cold day.

3. *A* I get bored seeing the same old faces.

   B I like the comfortable familiarity of everyday friends.

4. *A* I would prefer living in an ideal society in which everyone was safe, secure, and happy.

   B I would have preferred living in the unsettled days of our history.

5. *A* I sometimes like to do things that are a little frightening.

   B A sensible person avoids activities that are dangerous.

6. *A* I would not like to be hypnotized.

   B I would like to have the experience of being hypnotized.

7. *A* The most important goal of life is to live it to the fullest and to experience as much as possible.

   B The most important goal of life is to find peace and happiness.

8. *A* I would like to try parachute jumping.

   B I would never want to try jumping out of a plane, with or without a parachute.

9. *A* I enter cold water gradually, giving myself time to get used to it.

   B I like to dive or jump right into the ocean or a cold pool.

10. *A* When I go on a vacation, I prefer the comfort of a good room and bed.

    B When I go on a vacation, I prefer the change of camping out.

11. *A* I prefer people who are emotionally expressive, even if they are a bit unstable.

    B I prefer people who are calm and even-tempered.

12. *A* A good painting should shock or jolt the senses.

    B A good painting should give one a feeling of peace and security.

13. *A* People who ride motorcycles must have some kind of unconscious need to hurt themselves.

    B I would like to drive or ride a motorcycle.

Scoring Give yourself one point for each of the following responses: 1*A*, 2*A*, 3*A*, 4*B*, 5*A*, 6*B*, 7*A*, 8*A*, 9*B*, 10*B*, 11*A*, 12*A*, 13*B*. Find your total score by adding up the number of points and then use the following scoring key:

  0–3 very low sensation seeking
  4–5 low
  6–9 average
10–11 high
12–13 very high

Keep in mind, of course, that this short questionnaire, for which the scoring is based on the results of college students who have taken it, provides only a rough estimate of your sensation-seeking tendencies. Moreover, as people get older, their sensation-seeking scores tend to decrease. Still, the questionnaire will at least give you an indication of how your sensation-seeking tendencies compare with those of others.

Now compare your solution with this one proposed by a boy just about to begin adolescence:

You can read it, write on it, lay it down and paint a picture on it . . . You could put it in your door for decoration, put it in the garbage can, put it on a chair if the chair is messy. If you have a puppy, you put newspaper in its box or put it in your backyard for the dog to play with. When you build something and you don't want anyone to see, it, put newspaper around it. Put newspaper on the floor if you have no mattress, use it to pick up something hot, use it to stop bleeding, or to catch the drips from drying clothes. You can use a newspaper for curtains, put it in your shoe to cover what is hurting your foot, make a kite out of it, shade a light that is too bright. You can wrap fish in it, wipe windows, or wrap money in it . . . You put washed shoes in newspaper, wipe eyeglasses with it, put it under a dripping sink, put a plant on it, make a paper bowl out of it, use it for a hat if it is raining, tie it on your feet for slippers. You can put it on the sand if you had no towel, use it for bases in baseball, make paper airplanes with it, use it as a dustpan when you sweep, ball it up for the cat to play with, wrap your hands in it if it is cold. (Ward, Kogan, & Pankove, 1972)

Creativity is associated with **divergent thinking,** the ability to generate unusual, yet nonetheless appropriate, responses to problems or questions. Divergent thinking contrasts with *convergent thinking,* thinking that produces responses that are based primarily on knowledge and logic. If, for example, you responded to the newspaper question with "you learn about the news from it" and stopped there, you were using convergent thinking (Baer, 1993; Runco & Sakamoto, 1993; Finke, 1995; Sternberg, 2001; Ho, 2004).

Cognitive complexity, the preference for elaborate, intricate, and complex stimuli and thinking patterns, is another aspect of creativity. Creative adolescents often have a wider range of interests, and they are more independent and less conforming. In addition, they are more interested in philosophical or abstract problems (Barron, 1990).

Something that is *not* closely tied to creativity is intelligence, at least as measured by traditional intelligence tests. Intelligence tests tend to penalize the divergent thinking of highly creative adolescents. Furthermore, although it is clear that many creative adolescents are also highly intelligent, it's also true that one can be a highly intelligent adolescent without showing any significant degree of creativity. In short, research finds only a modest relationship between school grades and intelligence, when intelligence is measured using traditional intelligence tests (Hong, Milgram, & Gorsky, 1995; Sternberg & O'Hara, 2000).

One reason for the blossoming creativity of adolescence may be that later in life creativity can be stifled by a situation that psychologist Sarnoff Mednick (1963) described as "Familiarity breeds rigidity." By this he meant that the more people know about a subject, the less likely they are to be creative in that area. According to such reasoning, adolescents may show increased creativity because many of the problems they encounter are new to them. As they get older, however, and become more familiar with the problems, their creativity may be stymied.

Adolescents may also show increased creativity because of a willingness to take risks that may result in potentially high payoffs (Sternberg & Lubart, 1992). Creative individuals are analogous to successful stock market investors, who try to follow the "buy low, sell high" rule. They are more likely to endorse ideas that are unfashionable or regarded as wrong ("buying low"). They assume that eventually others will see the value of the ideas and embrace them ("selling high"). In short, the increased riskiness of adolescents, which in other domains may be a drawback, actually helps them to be more creative.

Decision Making during Adolescence

Whether an adolescent is trying to decide whether to attend an expensive private college or a less-expensive state college, take a calculus or an art class, or simply choose a vegetarian or pepperoni pizza, every choice requires a decision to be made. Some of these decisions are simple,

divergent thinking the ability to generate unusual, yet nonetheless appropriate, responses to problems or questions

while others are more agonizing. Regardless of the complexity of the decision, it is clear that adolescents must make an increasing number of decisions.

As adolescents' thinking and other intellectual capabilities grow, it seems reasonable that the quality of their decision making also would improve. And that does seem to be the case, but perhaps not as much as we'd expect.

First, it is clear that adolescents are better decision makers than preadolescents. They are able to generate more options, take a variety of perspectives, think more abstractly about problems, and take a number of possibilities into account simultaneously. Furthermore, the processes that adolescents follow to make decisions increasingly mimic those of adults (Keating, 1990; Bosma & Koops, 2004).

In an absolute sense, however, it's less clear that adolescents are optimal or even good decision makers. In fact, both adolescents and adults suffer from a variety of impediments that reduce their ability to make good decisions. Like adults, adolescents use *heuristics,* personal principles or rules of thumb that permit people to make decisions on the basis of limited information and with relatively little cognitive effort. Heuristics are mental shortcuts that we employ to make decisions and solve problems (Borders, Earleywine, & Huey, 2004).

Although heuristics permit adolescents (and adults) to deal with the enormous amount of information they encounter every day, their use also may lead to relatively unreflective decision making. For example, the *availability heuristic* is a cognitive rule that is applied in judging the likelihood of an event by considering the ease with which it can be recalled from memory. For instance, adolescents generally are more fearful that they will be involved in a fatal crash when they take an airplane flight than when they go for a car ride—despite statistics showing that airplanes are much safer than cars. The reason for their fear is that airplane crashes are much more widely publicized than auto crashes and therefore much more easily retrievable from memory. The availability heuristic, then, leads to assume that they are more likely to crash in a plane than in a car (Vaughn & Weary, 2002; Oppenheimer, 2004).

The availability heuristic can skew adolescents' beliefs about others. For instance, students attending a high school with many liberal classmates may assume that because most of their acquaintances share their liberal views on abortion, the general population also shares those views. However, once they leave campus and interact with a broader cross-section of the population, these students may be surprised to learn the degree of variability in viewpoints.

In short, adolescents' use of heuristics hinders their ability to make logical decisions. At the same time, there are small improvements in metacognitive skills that help adolescents to better resist the faulty application of heuristics. Because these metacognitive skills improve with age, adolescents' decision-making capabilities improve modestly as they move through adolescence (Jacobs & Klaczynski, 2002; Klaczynski, 2004).

Thinking Critically

Critical thinking is the process involving reanalysis, questioning, and challenging of underlying assumptions. Critical thinking skills involve the ability to think divergently, to consider the source of information when evaluating its reliability, and to identify the assumptions that underlie a statement. It also calls for understanding the facts that are necessary to support a claim and the ability to discount irrelevant information (Feldman, Coats, & Schwartzberg, 1994; Halpern, 1998; Gong, 2005).

During adolescence, the ability to think critically increases considerably. Adolescents process information more rapidly and automatically, offering the opportunity to free up cognitive resources for more analytic thinking. In addition, adolescents increasingly become more critical of authority figures (as we'll discuss more in Chapter 6), meaning that they question assertions and assumptions (Keating, 1990).

The increased capacity of adolescents to think critically is also made possible by their greater, and ever-increasing, knowledge about the world. Such knowledge, in a variety of areas, permits adolescents to think more broadly and apply a greater array of facts to new situations.

Techniques for Effective Problem Solving

PROBLEM SOLVING is an important skill for success in a career and in life, but it's not a skill that people just "grow into"; instead, it has to be learned. Furthermore, the problems we face—and the decisions we need to make—become increasingly complex as we grow older. Here are some specific problem-solving strategies that research has shown to be effective (Tillery, 1974; Halpern, 1998; Feldman, 2006):

- Be sure that you understand the problem thoroughly. You can't begin to solve a problem until you have all the information you need—including a firm grasp of what the problem is.

- Be active in working the problem out. Drawing a sketch or a diagram may help you to visualize a problem more clearly. Organizing your thoughts on paper or even just talking through the problem can also be very helpful.

- Break the problem down. Some problems are just too big to be tackled whole. You might try to break the problem into manageable pieces, or to take it one step at a time.

- Check your progress. Be sure that you haven't gotten off track at an earlier step, lest you find yourself at the end of a blind alley. Take the time to verify that your current progress is headed in the right direction before proceeding to each successive step.

- Keep a positive attitude. Staying focused is easier when you have confidence that the problem will eventually be solved. It may take some diligence, but you'll eventually work it through if you complete all the steps.

- Practice! Problem solving is like any other skill—the more you do it, the better you get.

Finally, adolescents have a broader range of thinking strategies that they can call on to obtain information they need to reason, make judgments, and solve problems more effectively. They are able to apply this capacity to novel situations and use it to reach better solutions.

In short, there are several reasons why adolescents are increasingly capable of effective critical thinking. On the other hand, having the ability to think critically does not mean that adolescents will automatically engage in critical thinking. In fact, there is considerable evidence that even older adolescents do not use critical thinking much of the time. Because it takes cognitive effort to think critically, adolescents may lack both the motivation and skills to use critical thinking. Furthermore, traditional educational practice focuses on *what* to think, rather than *how* to think (Gong, 2005).

The good news is that it is possible to teach critical thinking; critical thinkers are made, not born. For example, educators and researchers have developed several programs that directly teach critical thinking skills. Students are taught to redefine problems, use analogies, reanalyze and review their conclusions, question outcomes, and identify their assumptions and challenge them. They are also taught strategies for thinking divergently (Klaczynski, Fauth, & Swanger, 1998; Zwiers, 2004; Lauer, 2005).

Other approaches to teaching critical thinking are more indirect. Rather than teaching specific techniques, students are taught abstract rules of logic and reasoning. Research shows that learning these rules can improve reasoning and problem-solving capabilities (Lehman & Nisbett, 1990).

As we discuss above in the Becoming an Informed Consumer of Adolescent Science box the techniques developed by educators and researchers for enhancing critical thinking can be incorporated into our everyday lives to help us to solve the problems that we encounter. (For practice in critical thinking, try completing the problems in Figure 3-9.)

Exercise Your Problem-Solving Skills

To help you devise solutions, a hint regarding the best strategy to use is included after each problem.

1. One cold, dark, and rainy night, a college student has a flat tire on a deserted stretch of country road. He pulls onto the shoulder to change it. After removing the four lug nuts and placing them into the hub cap, he removes the flat tire and takes his spare out of the trunk. As he is moving the spare tire into position, his hand slips and he upsets the hub cap with the lug nuts, which tumble off into the night where he cant fin d them. What should he do? (*Hint*: Instead of asking how he might find the lug nuts, reframe the problem and ask where else he might find lug nuts).

2. Cheryl, who is a construction worker, is paving a walk, and she needs to add water quickly to the concrete she has just poured. She reaches for her pail to get water from a spigot in the front of the house, but suddenly realizes the pail has a large rust hole in it and cannot be used. As the concrete dries prematurely, She fumbles through her toolbox for tools and materials with which to repair the pail. She finds many tools, but nothing that would serve to patch the pail. The house is locked and no one is home. What should she do?
(Hint: When is a pail not a pail?)

3. What day follows the day before yesterday if 2 days from now will be Sunday?
(*Hint*: Break it up or draw a diagram.)

4. A caterpillar has to climb up the muddy wall of a well that is 12 feet deep. Each day the caterpillar advances 4 feet, but each night as he sleeps, he slips back 2 feet How many days will it take him to get out? (*Hint*: Draw it.)

5. Carrie has four chains, each three links long. She wants to join the four chains into a single, closed chain. Having a link opened costs 2 cents and having a link closed costs 3 cents. How can Carrie have the chains joined for 15 cents?
(Hints: Can only end links be opened?)

6. What is two-thirds of one-half? (*Hint*: Reverse course.)

7. Juan has three separate large boxes. Inside each large box are two separate medium-sized boxes, and inside each of the medium boxes are four small boxes. How many boxes does Juan have altogether? (*Hint*: Draw it.)

   After working to solve these problems, consider these questions: Which problems were the easiest to solve, and which were more difficult? Why? Were the hints helpful? Do you think there was more than one solution to any of the problems? Did your initial assumptions about the problem help or hinder your efforts to solve it? (*Note*: Answers to the problems are found on page xx.)

Answers

7. 33 boxes (3 large, 6 medium, 24 small).

6. It is the same as one-half of two-thirds, or one-third.

5. Open all three links on one chain (cost = 6 cents) and use them to fasten the other three chains together (cost = 9 cents; total cost = 15 cents).

4. Five days' on the fifth day the caterpillar will reach the top and will not have to slide down again.

3. Thursday.

2. Take the tools out of the toolbox and use it as a pail.

1. Remove one lug nut from each of the other three tires on the car and use these three to attach the spare tire. This will hold until four more lug nuts can be obtained.

▲ **FIGURE 3-9**
Exercise your problem-solving skills

Review and Apply

Review

1. Adolescents' increased cognitive and metacognitive skills can lead to egocentrism, belief in an imaginary audience, and reliance on personal fables.

2. Adolescents are prone to risk-taking behavior, which is supported by personal fables of invulnerability and personality factors such as sensation seeking.

3. Creativity blossoms in adolescence as divergent thinking improves and cognitive complexity develops. Creativity is not closely associated with intelligence.

4. Decision making improves with better metacognitive skills, but the quality of decisions is limited by faulty heuristics (such as the availability heuristic) and a tendency to ignore base-rate information about the probability of events.

5. During adolescence, the ability to think critically increases, enhanced by improvements in information processing, factual knowledge, and strategies for problem solving.

Apply

1. In what ways do middle and high schools help or hinder the development of creativity, decision making, and critical thinking? How effective are they in dealing with egocentrism and risk taking? Can schools be made to fit adolescents' developmental needs more effectively?

2. Can you think of any heuristics (rule-of-thumb principles) you habitually use when confronted with novel decisions? How do you test the validity of your heuristics? Have they changed over time?

EPILOGUE

In this chapter, we discussed cognitive development during adolescence, considering several different approaches. We noted that Piaget's stage theory and the information-processing approach focus on the individual, whereas Vygotsky's theories consider the individual in social and cultural contexts. We also addressed intelligence, considering its origins and nature. We also looked at IQ testing and discussed some of the major controversies and issues that surround it. Finally, we considered adolescent egocentrism, which can lead to a lack of concern about risks and an unrealistic belief that they are the center of everyone's attention. We saw how creativity relates to adolescents' growing individualism, and we discussed the growth of decision-making abilities and critical thinking during the period.

Before turning to the next chapter, think back to the Prologue. There we met Ameen Abdulrasool, who at age 18 has developed a promising new way to help the visually impaired navigate through the world. Consider the following questions.

1. What aspects of Abdulrasool's personal development might have caused him at his age to focus on satellite technology as a possible way to help the visually impaired?

2. How might divergent thinking have helped Abdulrasool to look for a solution to the problem he was addressing? Do you think divergent thinking gave him an advantage over scientists focusing on more traditional approaches?

3. As he devised his approach, what other aspects of his adolescent cognitive development probably came into play?

4. Do you think that Vygotsky's social theories of cognitive development apply to Abdulrasool's creativity? How?

SUMMARY

REVIEW

- **How does thinking develop during adolescence, and how have the major developmental researchers explained these changes?** *(p. 70)*

  1. The ability to think improves dramatically as adolescents become capable of abstract thinking and viewing issues in shades of gray instead of black and white.

  2. One of the earliest and most influential developmental researchers was Jean Piaget, who concluded that adolescence marks the stage when most people reach the formal operational stage of development.

  3. Piaget suggested that adolescents use sophisticated schemes to organize their thinking about the world and for the first time apply abstract thinking to the problems they face.

  4. Information-processing approaches attribute adolescents' increased mental abilities to the growth of metacognition and to quantitative improvements in the encoding, storage, and retrieval of information.

  5. Lev Vygotsky regarded cognitive development as largely a social, not an individual, phenomenon, which is facilitated by interactions with others.

- **What are some of the traditional and alternative views of intelligence?** *(p. 85)*

  6. Intelligence—generally understood as the capacity to understand the world, think rationally, and solve problems resourcefully—is difficult to define with precision.

  7. Alfred Binet regarded intelligence as the quality that differentiates successful students from unsuccessful ones. Other theorists found Binet's approach one dimensional.

  8. Catell distinguished two kinds of intelligence, fluid and crystallized, while Howard Gardner suggested that there are eight distinct intelligences, and Robert Sternberg's triarchic theory of intelligence describes three main components of intelligence.

  9. The concepts of practical and emotional intelligence have expanded our understanding and have suggested additional areas of research.

- **How is intelligence measured, and what are some of the pitfalls in traditional IQ testing?** *(p. 95)*

  10. Binet developed the first IQ test, which focused on differences between mental age and chronological age. IQ testing is slanted toward academic abilities.

  11. IQ testing is controversial because of its limited focus, the lack of a relationship between IQ and career success, and the tendency of IQ tests to produce different results for different groups of test takers.

  12. In addition to intelligence tests, achievement tests and aptitude tests are also used widely.

- **Why are egocentrism and risk taking such central elements of adolescent development?** *(p. 99)*

  13. As adolescents advance in social cognition, they are likely to become egocentric, believing that others think about them as much as they think about themselves.

  14. Adolescent egocentrism often leads to belief in an imaginary audience and personal fables.

  15. Personal fables may also encourage risk-taking behavior by supporting the belief that the odds can be beaten and universal dangers do not apply to the individual.

● **How do creativity, decision making, and critical thinking develop during adolescence?**
(p. 103)

16. Adolescents' development of individuality often enhances creativity, especially the use of divergent thinking to address and solve problems.

17. Adolescents experience slight improvements in decision making, but are neither more nor less able than adults to avoid fallacies in their decision strategies.

18. Critical-thinking abilities improve in adolescence as information processing becomes faster and more automatic and adolescents' stores of knowledge and information increase.

KEY TERMS AND CONCEPTS

assimilation (p. 71)

accommodation (p. 72)

formal operational stage (p. 72)

information-processing perspective (p. 75)

metacognition (p. 78)

zone of proximal development (ZPD) (p. 79)

scaffolding (p. 80)

intelligence (p. 85)

mental age (p. 86)

chronological (physical) age (p. 86)

intelligence quotient (IQ) (p. 87)

Kaufman Assessment Battery for Children, 2nd Edition (KABC-II) (p. 90)

fluid intelligence (p. 90)

crystallized intelligence (p. 90)

triarchic theory of intelligence (p. 92)

practical intelligence (p. 93)

emotional intelligence (p. 94)

achievement test (p. 97)

aptitude test (p. 97)

adolescent egocentrism (p. 100)

imaginary audience (p. 100)

personal fables (p. 100)

creativity (p. 101)

divergent thinking (p. 103)

Social Development:
Adolescent Roles,
Personality, and Morality

CHAPTER OUTLINE

THE SOCIAL TRANSITIONS OF ADOLESCENCE

The social construction of adolescence: Inventing a phase of life
The social roles of adolescence

PERSONALITY DEVELOPMENT

Psychodynamic approaches to personality
Trait approaches to personality
Adolescent personality in perspective

**MORAL DEVELOPMENT IN ADOLESCENCE:
TREATING OTHERS FAIRLY**

Piaget's approach to moral development
Moral reasoning: Kohlberg's approach
Gilligan's account of moral development in girls
Social learning perspectives on morality: Focusing on behavior
Moral behavior and moral reasoning: Why the disconnect?
Prosocial reasoning and prosocial behavior: The other side of the coin
Volunteerism: Sustained helping
Honesty and lies in everyday life: Is the truth dead?

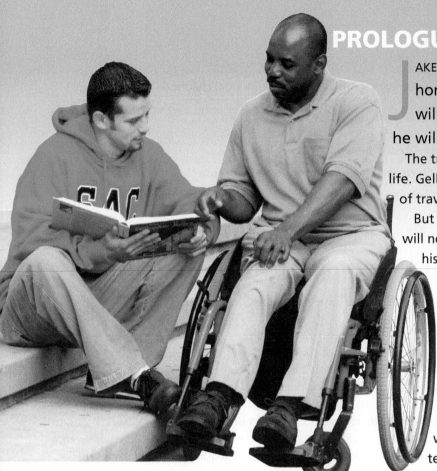

PROLOGUE: Help is on the Way

Jake Geller will leave his Medway [Massachusetts] home this morning in a lift-equipped van that will take him and his parents to Phoenix, where he will be a freshman at Arizona State University.

The trip will be one of the longest and most difficult of his life. Geller, 19, has muscular dystrophy, which makes any type of travel an elaborate effort.

But after Geller's parents drop him off on August 17, he will not be alone. His lifelong friend, Jack Buchholz, will be his roommate and serve as his personal care attendant.

While many people have been amazed by Buchholz's dedication to his friend, Buchholz himself is unfazed.

"It's not that big a deal," he insisted. "Waking up a half hour earlier in the morning is not that difficult."

Buchholz will get Geller, who uses a wheelchair, out of bed every morning, dress him, and help him shave and shower. At night, he will undress him, help him with such routine bathroom chores as brushing his teeth, and put him into bed. . . .

Geller says he is grateful to Buchholz for the sacrifices he has made, and Geller hopes to hire a personal care attendant in the next few months to help him at school and take the burden off his friend.

But do not expect them to be spending any less time together.

"As a pair, they're inseparable," said George Murphy, the director of the computer camp where the two have spent the last few summers. "Their personalities mesh together so well that they're a great team. I think of them as a pair of super-heroes, each with his own strength." (Kiehl, 1998, p. C1.) ■

th!nk ABOUT THIS

In an era in which the news is often bad, Jack Buchholz's willingness to sacrifice his energies and time for Jake Geller stands out. Jack, and others like him who make exceptional sacrifices, may seem unusual. Yet such behavior is an essential—and not, it turns out, altogether rare—part of adolescent behavior.

In this chapter, we consider the social context of adolescent development, examining the substantial changes that occur in the way that adolescents increasingly become a part of the groups and cultures to which they belong. Although these social transitions occur on many levels—and will be discussed in greater detail in future chapters—here we lay the groundwork for understanding the nature of social development by examining key areas of personality and moral development during adolescence.

We begin by considering how society defines adolescence. We examine how adolescence came to be seen as a distinct period, and we look at some of the rituals that are used to mark the beginning of the period. We also look at the key roles that adolescents play and how these roles affect their behavior.

We then turn to personality development. We look at a variety of perspectives that explain personality development during adolescence and how genetics and the environment shape personality.

Finally, we examine moral development. We see how reasoning about moral dilemmas changes in adolescence, and how the expression of moral and helping behavior develops. We also look at volunteerism, trying to tease out the reasons why people volunteer and the consequences of helping others through volunteerism. ■

- How—and why—do cultures mark the transition from childhood to adolescence?
- What sorts of roles do people play during adolescence, and why are these roles important?
- How are personality and temperament related?
- In what ways do we develop morally during adolescence?
- As adolescents become more sophisticated morally, how does their behavior change?

The Social Transitions of Adolescence

Being an adolescent is not easy, even if they tell you that it is. People that say that clearly were never in my shoes.

The physical and cognitive transitions of adolescence that we've considered in the two previous chapters are accompanied by changes in the social sphere that are equally significant. Adolescents find themselves in novel social situations, forced to relate to others in new ways, and expected by society to act as adults more than children.

Part of the challenge faced by adolescents is the lack of clarity in society's expectations. In large part, this ambiguity is brought about by a lack of agreement not only on when adolescence starts and ends, but also—as we'll discuss next—on the meaning and significance of the period.

The Social Construction of Adolescence: Inventing a Phase of Life

There have always been 13- to 19-year-olds, but there haven't always been adolescents. The period of time known as "adolescence" is a social construction. A *social construction* is a shared notion of reality, one that is widely accepted but is a function of society and culture at a given time.

In this view, adolescence, like the period of childhood before it and adulthood after it, is in many ways arbitrary and culturally derived. For example, although the start of adolescence is biologically determined as the onset of puberty, the *label* of that moment as the start of adolescence is arbitrary. It is meaningful only because society says it is meaningful.

Similarly, the end of adolescence, typically pegged at the age of 19, is equally arbitrary. The age of 19 is notable only because it marks the end of the teens. In fact, for many people, such as those enrolled in higher education, the age change from 19 to 20 has little special significance, coming as it does in the middle of the college years. For them, more substantial changes often occur when they leave college and enter the workforce, which is more likely to happen around age 22. Furthermore, in some non-Western cultures, the end of adolescence and the start of adulthood occurs much earlier, when children whose educational opportunities are limited begin full-time work.

Adolescence is not the only period that is socially constructed. For example, there was a historical period when childhood didn't even exist, at least in the minds of adults. According to Philippe Ariès, who studied paintings and other forms of art, children in medieval Europe were not given any special status before 1600. Instead, they were viewed as miniature, somewhat imperfect adults. They were dressed in adult clothing and not treated specially in any significant way. Childhood was not seen as a stage qualitatively different from adulthood (Ariès, 1962; Acocella, 2003; Hutton, 2004).

Although the view that children during the Middle Ages were seen simply as miniature adults may be somewhat exaggerated—Ariès's arguments were based primarily on art depicting the European aristocracy, a very limited sample of Western culture—it is clear that childhood had a considerably different meaning than it does now. Moreover, the idea that childhood could be studied systematically did not take hold until later.

Views of Adolescence.   The social construction of adolescence has attracted attention from a variety of observers, starting with the ancient Greek philosophers. For instance, in the fourth century B.C.E., Aristotle called teenagers "passionate, irascible, and apt to be carried away by their impulses." Several centuries later, in the 1700s, philosopher Jean-Jacques Rousseau wrote that adolescence was a period of "tumultuous change," so much so that it represented a reenactment of earlier stages of life.

In the modern era, one of the first psychologists to focus on adolescence was G. Stanley Hall, the first president of the American Psychological Association and a man who shaped the field of developmental psychology. Hall (1916), followed in the footsteps of his philosopher predecessors, arguing that adolescence was a time of stormy upheaval unlike any other developmental period.

As we first saw in Chapter 1, Hall also believed that adolescence was a period that recapitulated the evolutionary development of the human species. As such, he saw adolescence as a time of biologically determined "storm and stress." It was society's job to tame the "raging hormones" that would unfailingly produce problems if left unchecked.

At the same time, though, Hall suggested that adolescence offered an opportunity. Because it was a kind of rebirth from earlier evolutionary periods in which morality and reasoning were unsophisticated, adolescence was also a time when adolescents could be unusually flexible and creative and were open to new ideas.

Hall's view on the volatile nature of adolescence continues to influence the popular, stereotypical perception of the period. In fact, even as adolescent scientists are increasingly providing objective evidence that adolescence is not such an extreme and stormy period, the popular media continue to present a persistent view of adolescence as a time of profound upheaval. When, and whether, the stereotypic view of adolescence as a period of "storm and stress" will shift to match the realties of the scientific evidence are open questions.

What is clear is that current social constructions of adolescence still view it as a uniquely important period. In fact, as we see next, societies around the world offer ritualized ceremonies at the start of adolescence to mark a child's entry into the period in a formal manner.

Adolescent DIVERSITY   The Rituals of Adolescence: Celebrating the Social Redefinition of Children

As children move into adolescence, society helps define the period by providing rituals that celebrate the transition in very obvious ways. **Rites of passage** are ceremonies or rituals that mark a person's transition from one stage of life to another. They are a public indication that an individual has reached a new stage of development. Central to the rite of passage is the notion that a person is expected to have achieved a new level of understanding, enlightenment, or spirituality. But the rite of passage is also expected to produce a new level of responsibility at its conclusion (Delaney, 1995; Scott, 1998).

Rites of passage typically involve some temporary period of separation and removal from society, formal preparation for the new phase of life, a public ceremony, and finally, a welcoming back to society. At the end, participants in the rite are considered more fully integrated into society.

rites of passage   ceremonies or rituals that mark a person's transition from stage of life to another

▲ Modern rites of passage include the Jewish *bar* and *bat mitvah* and the *quinceanera* for Latino girls.

Many traditional, non-Western societies have rites of passage to mark the beginning of adolescence. Typically these occur at the start of puberty, and they are a reaction to the obvious physical maturation that is occurring. In addition, many societies separate girls from boys at the beginning of puberty, often when girls have their first menstrual period.

For example, according to an account by the famous anthropologist Margaret Mead (1935), girls in the Arapesh culture of New Guinea are removed from their family at the time of their first menstrual period. They are assigned an older woman who attends to them in a ritual that lasts several days. The girls discard their arm and leg bands and earrings, and they are rubbed with stinging thorns with the purpose of stimulating breast growth. The girls also fast for up to six days. The purpose is to provide a clear demarcation between childhood and the childbearing years.

The separation of Arapesh girls during this rite of passage is an example of a broader phenomenon in which children starting adolescence are either symbolically or actually separated from their parents. Sometimes they spend days with their parents and nights with another family; sometimes they live in a dwelling designed to house preadolescents. There was once a time when children in the United States were separated from their parents to gain professional skills when they worked as apprentices with a master craftsman, learning a trade.

Contemporary Rites of Passage.   If you think such separations are no longer a part of modern life, consider this: Many contemporary child-rearing practices reflect parents' (and society's) push to make children more independent. Think, for example, about the practice of sending children to camp. The idea is that children will have the opportunity to learn new skills and gain social competencies by interacting with a group of friends. Attendance at college away from home serves a similar purpose.

Furthermore, adolescents in Western societies also participate in formal rites of passage. For example, Jewish boys (at the age of 13) and girls (at the age of 12) traditionally have a *Bar Mitzvah* or *Bat Mitzvah,* which is celebrated at a synagogue and followed by a sometimes an elaborate party. The religious ceremonies occur after a period of formal training in which children learn prayers that allow them to help lead services. Following Bar and Bat Mitzvahs, Jewish children are considered adults, at least from a religious standpoint, and can participate fully in religious services. Among Christians, the confirmation ceremony serves a similar purpose.

The *quinceañera* celebration is another contemporary rite of passage. The quinceañera is a ritual that honors Latino girls when they reach the age of 15. It can be quite elaborate, combining a church celebration with dinner and dancing. Girls wear white or pale pink gowns, sometimes with a matching headdress.

Finally, school graduations are also rites of passage. Whether they come at the start of adolescence (graduation from elementary school), during adolescence (middle- and high school), or at the end of adolescence (college), graduation ceremonies are formal celebrations of an educational achievement and the graduate's progression into a new phase of life. Although not associated with physical maturation, graduation ceremonies do mark the completion of a formal period of instruction and often include ritualistic advice—in the form of a graduation speech—on the new responsibilities that lie ahead.

Other important milestones mark the end of adolescence. In fact, surveys of adults in the United States suggest that the completion of formal schooling is viewed as only one event signaling the entry into adulthood. Other important events are gaining full-time employment and attaining financial independence from one's parents (see Table 4-1).

The Social Roles of Adolescence

Given that the period of adolescence is a social construction, it is not surprising that adolescents have some difficulty defining who they are and deciding what behavior will be appropriate. This difficulty is largely due to the shifting roles of adolescence.

How adolescents act is in part a result of prescribed **roles**, the behaviors that are associated with and come to be expected of people in a given position. We are all familiar with the attributes of certain important roles. For instance, the role of student encompasses the behaviors of studying, listening to teachers, and attending class. The role of employee involves coming to work, completing assigned tasks, and collecting a paycheck. Like a theatrical role, then, the roles of everyday social interaction prescribe the routine, appropriate conduct associated with a given position.

roles   behaviors that are associated with and come to be expected of people in a given position

TABLE 4-1	Milestones in the Transition to Adulthood	
Life Event	Expected Age	Percentage of People Who View Event as Extremely/ Quite Important
Financial independence from parents/guardians	20.9 years	80.9%
Separate residence from parents	21.1	57.2
Full-time employment	21.2	83.8
Completion of formal schooling	22.3	90.2
Capability of supporting a family	24.5	82.3
Marriage	25.7	33.2
Parenthood	26.2	29.0

Note: Based on the 2002 General Social Survey of 1,398 people.

But the roles of adolescence do more than just provide direction on how to behave. They also influence the attitudes that adolescents hold. In fact, carrying out the behaviors associated with a role may ultimately lead adolescents to adopt attitudes consistent with the role.

Consider, for instance, the results of psychologist Philip Zimbardo's stunning demonstration of the power of roles. In his study, Zimbardo and colleagues set up a mock prison in the basement of the Stanford University psychology department, complete with cells, solitary confinement cubicles, and a small recreation area. The researchers then advertised for college students who would be willing to spend two weeks participating in a study of prison life. Once they identified the study participants, a flip of a coin designated who would be a prisoner and who would be a prison guard. Neither prisoners nor guards were told how to fulfill their roles (Haney, Banks, & Zimbardo, 1973; Zimbardo, 1973; Haney & Zimbardo, 1998).

On the first day of the study, prisoners were picked up unexpectedly at their homes and brought, by police car, to the basement "prison." They were given loose-fitting, baggy prison smocks, and each had a chain clamped to his ankle. The guards received uniforms, nightsticks, handcuffs, and whistles. Apart from a few rules, the guards and prisoners were given little direction on what to do; they had only their conception of what the roles of guard and prisoner required of them.

After just a few days, it became apparent that no direction was necessary: Both parties had a clear, and ultimately frightening, conception of the behavior and expectations associated with their roles. The guards became abusive to the prisoners, waking them at odd hours and subjecting them to arbitrary punishment. They withheld food and forced their prisoners to perform hard labor. Their attitudes toward the prisoners matched their actions: The guards saw the prisoners as unruly, uncooperative, and deserving of the treatment they were receiving.

The prisoners were initially rebellious, but they soon became docile and subservient to the guards. They became extremely demoralized, and one slipped into a depression so severe that he was released after just a few days. In fact, after only six days of captivity, the remaining prisoners' reactions became so extreme that the study was terminated—to the disappointment of the guards, who were enjoying their taste of power over what they had come to believe were good-for-nothing prisoners.

The experiment (which, incidentally, drew harsh criticism on both methodological and ethical grounds) delivered a clear lesson: Roles have a powerful effect on how people behave and the attitudes that they hold.

Key Roles. Obviously, most important roles played by adolescents are not temporary like those encountered in research studies, but are enacted over the long term. Among the primary roles of adolescence are the following:

- *Family member.* Whether their relationship with other members of their family is tranquil or stormy (and most of the time, as we will see in Chapter 6, it is generally positive), families play a central role in the lives of adolescents. The family member role is of considerable importance during adolescence, although its importance declines throughout the period. Parents' expectations regarding their children do not always match up with how their children view their roles as family members, and this mismatch may lead to tension. For example, adolescents see themselves as worthy of increasing independence, while parents need to relinquish their previous views of their children as dependent and see them more as worthy of the autonomy they are seeking.

  For some adolescents who live in blended families in which there is at least one step-parent due to death or divorce, family roles are particularly challenging. There often is a fair amount of *role ambiguity,* in which roles and expectations are unclear. Children may be uncertain about their responsibilities, how to behave toward stepparents and stepsiblings, and how to make a host of decisions that have wide-ranging implications for their role in the family. For instance, an adolescent in a blended family may have to choose which parent to spend each vacation and holiday with or to decide between the conflicting advice coming from biological parent and stepparent (Dainton, 1993; Cath & Shopper, 2001; Belcher, 2003).

- *Friend.* Friendships become increasingly important during adolescence, as we will discuss in detail in Chapter 7. Adolescents spend increasing time with their peers, and the importance of peer relationships grows as well. In fact, there is probably no time during life when peer relationships are as central to one's life as adolescence (Youniss & Haynie, 1992).

  Enacting the role of friend, then, increasingly takes precedence over other roles. For example, consider an adolescent whose parents want him to accompany them on a visit to his aging grandparents (the role of family member) but who wants to go to a movie with some buddies (the role of friend). The conflict between roles is likely to be resolved ultimately in favor of the movie, if the adolescent prevails (de Bruyn, 2005).

- *Student.* Adolescents spend a substantial amount of time involved in academic endeavors. Consequently, the role of student is a central one in their lives, certainly in terms of the amount of time spent on academic tasks during the school year. On the other hand, for adolescents who are less invested in academics, the role is less central, despite the fact that they spend significant periods of the day in classes and at school.

  Like other roles, the student role can come into conflict with other roles that adolescents play. Take, for example, student–athletes. Students who participate in team sports have enormous pressure to spend time at practices and games, stay in shape, and follow certain training requirements. Such requirements may at times conflict with the role of student, making adolescents feel torn between competing demands (Killeya-Jones & Ley, 2005).

Although the roles of family member, friend, and student are among the most important, adolescents also inhabit a variety of lesser roles. Some are fleeting (such as being an actor in a school play), while others are more consistent during adolescence (like being a member of the school orchestra throughout the years of middle and high school).

▼ Adolescents may seek to distance themselves from other family members, sometimes quite literally.

Furthermore, adolescents typically "try on" various roles, experimenting with them for a period of time and later accepting some and rejecting others. Society aids this process by providing a number of options, both educationally and in terms of activities in which adolescents can engage. The choices that adolescents make have significant implications for their ultimate view of who they are and how they view themselves—the topic of the next chapter.

Review and Apply

Review

1. The period of adolescence is a social construction that is marked by cultures in different ways that underline its importance to the individual and society.

2. The rites of passage that societies use to mark the transition to adolescence typically emphasize separation from the parents and integration with society.

3. Adolescents play different roles during the period, which involve the performance of prescribed, socially defined actions and the assumption of associated attitudes.

4. The major roles played by adolescents include family member, friend, and student.

5. Performance of these roles involves a redefinition of the self and the need to deal with a certain amount of role conflict.

Apply

1. In what ways do you think popular culture helps to define adolescence? How do you think that TV and movies, in particular, encourage adolescents to understand roles and role conflict? Are they good influences?

2. People sometimes say that, with all the pressures put on them, children are no longer allowed to be children. Do you think adolescents are allowed to be adolescents? Should they be?

Personality Development

I just look for a great personality. That's it! I mean gosh how hard is it to have a great personality?

Most adolescents would probably agree with this teenage blogger that one of the things they look for in others is a good personality. But they also might believe that having a "great personality" is, in fact, not so easy to achieve. In fact, presenting oneself to the world effectively can be one of the most overwhelming developmental tasks facing adolescents.

In studying personality, adolescent developmentalists don't focus on whether an adolescent's personality is "good" or "bad." Instead, they look at personality in terms of how it paints a psychological portrait of an individual. Adolescents (like the rest of us) are assumed to have a unique combination of characteristics that, taken collectively, provide a summary description of who they are.

In a formal sense, **personality** is the pattern of enduring characteristics that differentiate people—the behaviors that make each adolescent a unique individual. An adolescent's person-

personality the pattern of enduring characteristics that differentiate people—the behaviors that make each adolescent a unique individual

ality also leads him or her to behave consistently in different situations and over extended periods.

Adolescent scientists take a variety of approaches to personality. We'll consider several of the most influential.

Psychodynamic Approaches to Personality

According to the **psychodynamic approach to personality,** personality is shaped by inner forces and conflicts about which adolescents have little awareness or control. *Psychoanalytic theory,* which was devised by Sigmund Freud in the early 1900s, is the most influential of the psychodynamic approaches. Freud argued that much of behavior is motivated by the *unconscious,* a part of personality of which a person is not aware.

To Freud, the memories, knowledge, beliefs, and feelings of the unconscious are far more extensive and influential than the material that resides in the conscious. To understand an adolescent's personality, we have to expose what is in the unconscious.

Freud also suggested that personality was composed of three components: the id, ego, and superego. The *id* is the raw, unorganized, inherited portion of personality that seeks to fulfill our primitive urges relating to hunger, sex, and aggression. In contrast, the *ego* is the part of personality that seeks to balance the desires of the id with the realities of the objective, rational world. The ego acts as a check on the id. Finally, the *superego* represents the rights and wrongs of society as taught by an individual's parents and society. It is the part of personality that impels adolescents to behave in a moral way.

Freud argued that adolescence marked the end point of personality development. He suggested that people pass through a series of stages, beginning at birth, in which they must resolve conflicts involving sexual gratification and that are centered on particular parts of the body. He suggested that adolescence marks the end of a latency period that extends from around the age of six until puberty. During latency, he assumed that little personality development is occurring.

However, things change when people reach puberty. At that point, adolescents enter the *genital stage* of personality development, which lasts throughout the remainder of life. According to Freud, adolescents' psychic energy becomes focused on the genitals and on mature, adult sexuality, which he defined as sexual intercourse. At the same time, personality continues to be influenced by the earlier stages of personality development and, in fact, by unconscious forces about which an adolescent may have little awareness.

Evaluating Psychoanalytic Explanations of Personality. Was Freud's description of personality accurate? Freud was clearly on the right track in thinking that personality, and behavior in general, is influenced by the unconscious. Current neuroscientific evidence on memory and dreams supports the view that adolescent and adult behavior are influenced by the unconscious. For example, there is evidence that the brain's limbic system may be the source of unconscious motivations (Westen, 2000; Guterl, 2002; Messer & McWilliams, 2003; Heller, 2005).

On the other hand, although Freud's view was highly influential in the realms of psychology, literature, and even philosophy, his theory is controversial. Furthermore, significant changes in personality can occur during the latency period, and it's hardly the case that personality is fixed during adolescence at the entry to the genital stage. The kinds of experiences adolescents encounter clearly can produce profound changes in personality.

For example, an adolescent who undergoes a traumatic experience such as rape may become withdrawn and fearful. Other personality changes can be more gradual, yet no less real. For instance, some individuals become increasingly serious as they move through adolescence and must, because of family circumstances, take on more adultlike responsibilities. In addition,

psychodynamic approach to personality the approach to the study of development that states behavior is shaped by inner forces and conflicts about which adolescents have little awareness or control

conflicts with parents can lead to greater depression in adolescents (Brockman, 2003; Brendgen et al., 2005; Resnick et al., 2005).

Because of the drawbacks to psychoanalytic approaches to personality, more contemporary approaches employ a different perspective. In particular, they focus on the kinds of traits that make up the central core of personality.

Trait Approaches to Personality

Roberto is moody, and it makes him hard to get along with.

Jake is a happy-go-lucky, cheerful kind of guy who has a lot of friends.

Rebecca is hard-working and conscientious, a very serious person, and that's why she's at the top of her high school class.

Moody . . . happy-go-lucky . . . cheerful . . . hard-working . . . conscientious. When we describe adolescents and seek to understand the reasons behind their behavior, we typically use specific traits to describe them. Furthermore, we usually assume that if someone is happy-go-lucky and cheerful in one situation, he or she is happy-go-lucky and cheerful in other situations (Gilbert et al., 1992; Gilbert, Miller, & Ross, 1998; Mischel, 2004).

But adolescents have many traits. How do we decide which of the traits are the most important ones, the traits that are central to describing their personality? To answer the question, personality theorists have developed a perspective known as trait theory. **Traits** are enduring dimensions of personality characteristics along which adolescents differ.

traits enduring dimensions of personality characteristics along which adolescents differ

▲ Trait approaches explain personality in terms of traits, enduring characteristics that distinguish adolescents. What traits might characterize these adolescents?

Trait approaches do not assume that some adolescents have a trait and others do not. Instead, they suggest that all adolescents have certain traits, but to a greater or lesser degree. For example, all adolescents might be assumed to have a "trustworthiness" trait, except that some are relatively trustworthy, while others are relatively untrustworthy. In this case, the trustworthy adolescents would be said to have the trait to a large degree, while others have it to a lesser extent.

The Big Five Personality Traits: Mapping Personality.   Using a variety of sophisticated statistical techniques, personality research specialists have identified a set of five broad trait factors that describe basic personality. Known as the *Big Five personality traits,* these traits are *openness to experience, conscientiousness, extraversion, agreeableness,* and *neuroticism (emotional stability).* (Table 4-2 presents a summary of the Big Five, which you can remember most easily by using the acronym OCEAN for the first letters of each trait.)

The Big Five have been found to reflect the basic core traits not only in adolescents but also in a variety of populations, including children, older adults, and non-English speakers. Furthermore, cross-cultural studies have found them in a variety of cultures ranging from across the Americas and Europe to the Middle East to Africa (Paunonen, 2003; Rossier, Dahourou, & McCrae, 2005; McCrae et al., 2005).

Although most work examining the Big Five has involved adults, research involving adolescents has been highly supportive of the trait approach. For example, the Big Five trait of conscientiousness was associated with more decisiveness about career choices in adolescents in middle and high school. In addition, Big Five traits are related to deviant behavior in adolescents. For instance, one study found that low agreeableness is associated with impulsivity, instability, and social deviance in 13- and 16-year-old boys (Lounsbury, Hutchens, & Loveland, 2005; Lynam et al., 2005).

TABLE 4-2   The Big Five Personality Factors and Dimensions of Sample Traits

Openness to experience

Independent—Conforming
Imaginative—Practical
Preference for variety—Preference for routine

Conscientiousness

Careful—Careless
Disciplined—Impulsive
Organized—Disorganized

Extraversion

Talkative—Quiet
Fun-loving—Sober
Sociable—Retiring

Agreeableness

Sympathetic—Fault-finding
Kind—Cold
Appreciative—Unfriendly

Neuroticism (Emotional Stability)

Stable—Tense
Calm—Anxious
Secure—Insecure

The Stability of Personality in Adolescence and Beyond.   It's clear that the Big Five approach to personality, and trait approaches more broadly, provide a good description of personality in adolescence. But an important question remains: How stable are personality traits during adolescence? Specifically, is there significant growth and change in personality during adolescence, or is personality relatively consistent during the period?

The answer is that although personality traits are somewhat less stable in adolescence than in the later stages of life, they are relatively consistent. The personality traits that adolescents hold may manifest themselves in different ways over the life span, but the particular constellation of traits that describe an individual are fairly consistent (Costa, McCrae, & Siegler, 1999; Whitbourne, 2001).

For example, an adolescent who is high on the Big Five trait of Conscientiousness as an adolescent may be a highly organized student who takes pains to meet deadlines and carefully completes assignments. When he was in kindergarten, he may have carefully arranged his toys, neatly placing each of his action figures on shelves over his bed. As an older adult, he may demonstrate his high Conscientiousness by precisely arranging the tools in his garage.

In the same way, we find that adolescents who are well adjusted tend to have been well adjusted during middle childhood—and are more likely to be well adjusted in later adulthood. Similarly, infants and toddlers who are easily frustrated and angered and who show more negative emotions as infants are more likely to evolve into adolescents who are easily frustrated and angered and behave more aggressively (Hart, et al., 1997; Leve, Kim, & Pears, 2005).

Temperament: Stability in Arousal and Emotionality.   Although the specific types of behavior change over the course of life, the underlying traits that guide behavior remain relatively constant. One reason for this stability is that we all inherit broad personality temperaments. **Temperaments** are patterns of arousal and emotionality that are consistent and enduring.

For example, one central dimension of temperament is *activity level,* which reflects the degree of overall movement. From the time of birth, some infants are relatively placid, and their movements are slow and almost leisurely. In contrast, the activity level of other infants is quite high, with strong, restless movements of the arms and legs. As adolescents, individuals still show equivalent sorts of activity levels (think of an adolescent who is relaxed and laid-back compared with a jittery, nervous one).

Another important dimension of temperament is the nature and degree of an adolescent's *irritability.* Adolescents who are easily upset and get bothered with little provocation were likely easily disturbed, cried easily, and fussed a great deal as infants. Other important dimensions of temperament include adaptability, moodiness, intensity of reaction, and attention span (Thomas, Chess, & Birch, 1968; Brendgen et al., 2005).

Temperaments are inherited from our parents at the moment of conception. For example, consider the consistency from infancy to adolescence that we find in such traits as physiological reactivity, a characteristic of temperament that relates to the degree of physical reaction a person displays when faced with a novel stimulus. This high reactivity, which has been termed *inhibition to the unfamiliar,* is exhibited as shyness.

There is a clear biological basis underlying inhibition to the unfamiliar, in which any novel stimulus produces a rapid increase in heartbeat, blood pressure, and pupil dilation, as well as high excitability of the brain's limbic system. For example, people who were categorized as inhibited at two years of age show high reactivity in their brain's amygdala in adulthood when viewing unfamiliar faces. The shyness associated with this physiological pattern seems to continue through childhood and into adolescence and adulthood (McCrae et al., 2000; Arcus, 2001; Schwartz et al., 2003).

Personality and the Interaction of Genetics and the Environment.   Traits related to temperament are not the only personality characteristics that are affected by heredity. The importance of genetics in shaping personality in general is highlighted by the work of behavioral

temperaments   patterns of arousal and emotionality that are consistent and enduring

geneticists and evolutionary psychologists. These scientists believe that personality is determined largely by combinations of inherited genes, similar to the way in which our height and eye color are largely an outcome of genetic contributions from our ancestors. The evolutionary approach argues that personality traits that were beneficial to the survival and reproductive success of our ancestors are more likely to be maintained and passed on to subsequent generations.

Studies of personality traits in genetically identical twins illustrate the importance of heredity in personality development (Tellegen et al., 1988). Identical twins who were raised apart from one another have similar personalities on a number of major dimensions, even when they were separated at an early age and experienced dissimilar upbringings. For example, the traits of social potency (the degree to which a person assumes mastery and leadership roles in social situations) and traditionalism (the tendency to follow authority) have particularly strong genetic components. In contrast, other traits, such as achievement and social closeness, have relatively weak genetic components (see Figure 4-1).

Although it is clear that genetics plays an important role in determining the personality of adolescents, environmental influences also play a significant role in making these traits consistent throughout the life span. In fact, the environment tends to reinforce inherited traits. For example, an adolescent who is active and aggressive might gravitate toward sports, while a more

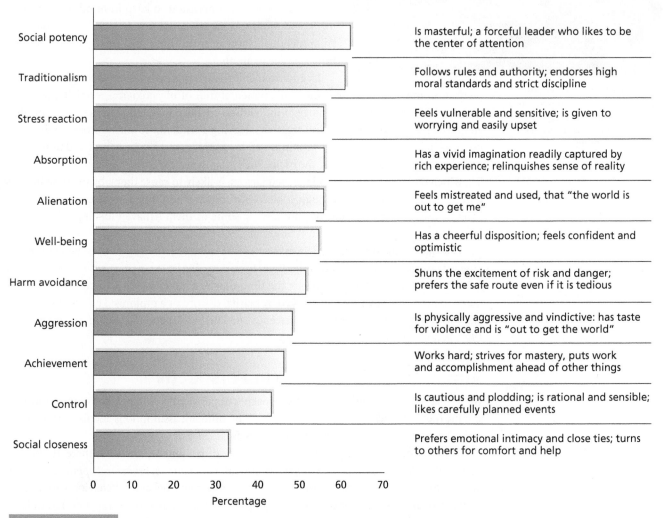

▲ **FIGURE 4-1**

The influence of the degree of heredity of these 11 personality characteristics is indicated by the percentages noted.

(*Source:* Tellegen et al., 1988).

▲ Adolescents are drawn to activities available in their social environments that are consistent with their genetic endowment, illustrating the interplay of heredity and the environment.

reserved adolescent may be more engaged by academics or solitary pursuits, such as computer games or drawing. At the same time, both adolescents may pay less attention to those aspects of the environment that are less compatible with their genetic endowments.

Thus, two adolescents may be checking out school announcements on their high school's Web page. One may notice an announcement advertising tryouts for an intramural baseball team, wheareas her less-coordinated but more musically endowed friend might be more apt to pay attention to the notice recruiting students for an after-school chorus. In each case, the adolescent is attending to those aspects of the environment in which her genetically determined temperament can flourish.

In other cases, the genetically driven temperament of an adolescent may *evoke* certain environmental influences. For instance, an adolescent's demanding behavior may cause parents to be more attentive to the adolescent's needs than would be the case if the adolescent were less demanding. In this case, the inherited traits are influencing the environment.

Furthermore, it is important to keep in mind that temperament, and more specific traits, are not destiny. For instance, certain individuals show relatively little consistency in temperament from one age to another.

In addition, child-rearing practices can alter temperamental predispositions. An example is the temperamental trait of physiological reactivity, which we discussed earlier. A small percentage of individuals are born with temperaments that produce an unusual degree of physiological reactivity. Having a tendency to shrink from anything unusual, as infants they react to novel stimuli with a rapid increase in heartbeat and unusual excitability of the limbic system of the brain. Such heightened reactivity to stimuli at the start of life, which seems to be linked to inherited factors, is likely to cause them, by the time they are four or five and continuing through adolescence and later adulthood, to be considered shy by parents, teachers, and friends. But not always: some of them behave indistinguishably from their peers at the same age (Kagan & Snidman, 1991; McCrae et al., 2000).

What makes the difference? The answer seems to be the environment in which they are raised. Those whose parents encourage them to be outgoing by arranging new opportunities for them may overcome their shyness by the time they reach adolescence. In contrast, children raised in a stressful environment marked by marital discord or a prolonged illness may be more likely to retain their shyness into adolescence and later adulthood (Kagan, Arcus, & Snidman, 1993; Pedlow et al., 1993; Joseph, 1999).

Adolescent Personality in Perspective

We've focused on two quite different approaches to personality: the psychodynamic approach and the trait approach. Each perspective is built on different assumptions and focuses on somewhat different aspects of personality (Larsen & Buss, 2005).

Furthermore, we've only scratched the surface of personality theories; there are literally dozens of explanations of personality development. For example, *behavioral approaches* to personality focus on the external world that shapes adolescents' behavior. Behavioral approaches view personality as the sum of learned responses, and they pay little or no attention to inner thoughts and feelings. *Humanistic approaches* to personality see adolescents as inherently good and having a tendency to function at more sophisticated levels as they age. They view adolescence as a period of change, growth, and improvement, and it is this ability to grow that makes up the core of personality.

Although the various approaches are quite different from one another, they all agree on the significance of personality in shaping an adolescent's behavior. Moreover, the various approaches see adolescent personality as developing along a fairly level path that starts at birth.

In short, despite the stereotype that the period of adolescence is markedly different from an individual's earlier life, in fact, personality is generally stable throughout the life span. An adolescent's personality is predicted to a large degree by his or her temperament and personality traits at the beginning of life. The adolescent who emerges from adolescence into adulthood is not terribly different, at least in terms of underlying personality, from the one who began it.

Review and Apply

Review

1. The psychodynamic approach to personality, pioneered by Sigmund Freud, focuses on the unconscious nature of the personality, while the trait approach seeks to identify the traits that are central to personality.

2. In general, personality traits are fairly stable throughout life, with only slightly more volatility during adolescence than in other periods.

3. Temperament refers to the broad patterns of arousal and emotionality that underlie personality traits and are surprisingly consistent throughout the life span.

4. Personality and temperament have both genetic and environmental components, with many basic tendencies being inherited and later being influenced by and influencing the environment.

Apply

1. In what ways are trait theories of personality more "scientific" than the psychodynamic approach of Freud? Can you devise an experiment to examine the relative influences of the id, ego, and superego on personality? Why or why not?

2. What are the educational implications of the finding that some personality traits are inherited and remain consistent over time? Is it wiser for schools to try to change personalities or accommodate to them? Why?

Moral Development in Adolescence: Treating Others Fairly

The first thing I ever remember stealing was a pack of gum from Food Town in Waterville, OH when I was probably 9 or 10. Yes, I got an early start . . . but when you have an older teenage brother with a lot of pull on his younger brother, things are sort of out of my control.

Junior High, now it was time for me to realize that I was never going to be as smart as the girl sitting next to me. And it was also time to learn how to be really good at cheating on tests. Yes, I admit it . . . I pretty much cheated my way through the following classes: (High School) anatomy & physiology, algebra, biology, Mr. Murphy's senior math class;

(College) college Algebra, trigonometry, statistics, economics, Gale Vere's accounting class . . . , and at least a couple marketing classes. What can I say . . . I was good, and I never got caught.

■ ■ ■

Cheating on exams was a foreign thing . . . . Then came the difficult years of college. It was a great test of honesty and conviction, not to cheat in spite of the great temptation. A classmate who was as desperate as I was somehow got hold of a copy of an old exam that was surely to be given that day, that seemingly hopeless day that I needed to make up for lost points in previous exams. It was a do or die thing. I took the papers she handed me, the world stopping for a moment as I wrestled with the idea. It's in my hands. This may be the break that I needed. Everyone is doing it anyway, so why not me? That would make things even, I reasoned. Time is ticking . . . Principles finally won and I handed the papers back without even taking a peek. I took the exam . . . armed with nothing but a clear conscience. . . .

Two adolescents, two different approaches to morality. What makes them so different?

To answer the question, we need to consider **moral development,** changes in one's sense of justice and of what is right and wrong, and our behavior related to moral issues. Moral development has been considered in terms of adolescents' reasoning about morality, their attitudes toward moral lapses, and their behavior when faced with moral issues. In the process of studying moral development, several approaches have evolved (Langford, 1995; Grusec & Kuczynski, 1997).

Piaget's Approach to Moral Development

Developmental psychologist Jean Piaget, whose work on cognitive development we discussed in Chapter 3, was one of the first to study questions of moral development. He suggested that moral development, like cognitive development, proceeds in stages (Piaget, 1932). The earliest stage is a broad form of moral thinking that he called *heteronomous morality,* in which rules are seen as invariant and unchangeable. During this stage, which lasts from about age 4 through age 7, children play games rigidly, assuming that there is one, and only one, way to play and that every other way is wrong. At the same time, though, preschool-age children may not even fully grasp game rules. Consequently, a group of children may be playing together, with each child playing according to a slightly different set of rules. Nevertheless, they enjoy playing with others. Piaget suggests that every child may "win" such a game, because winning is equated with having a good time, as opposed to truly competing with others.

This rigid heteronomous morality is ultimately replaced by two later stages of morality: incipient cooperation and autonomous cooperation. As its name implies, in the *incipient cooperation stage,* which lasts from around age 7 to age 10, children's games become more clearly social. Children learn the actual formal rules of games, and they play according to this shared knowledge. Consequently, rules are still seen as largely unchangeable. There is a "right" way to play the game, and preschool children play according to these formal rules.

It is not until the *autonomous cooperation stage,* which begins at about age 10, that children become fully aware that formal game rules can be modified if the people who play them agree. The later transition into more sophisticated forms of moral development—which we will consider in Chapter 12—also is reflected in school-age children's understanding that rules of law are created by people and are subject to change according to the will of people.

Until these later stages are reached, however, children's reasoning about rules and issues of justice is bounded in the concrete. For instance, consider the following two stories:

A little boy who is called John is in his room. He is called to dinner. He goes into the dining room. But behind the door there was a chair, and on the chair there was a tray with fifteen cups on

moral development   changes in one's sense of justice and of what is right and wrong, and our behavior related to moral issues

it. John couldn't have known there was all this behind the door. He goes in, the door knocks against the tray, bang go the fifteen cups, and they all get broken!

■ ■ ■

Once there was a little boy whose name was Marcello. One day when his mother was out he tried to get some jam out of the cupboard. He climbed up on to a chair and stretched out his arm. But the jam was too high up and he couldn't reach it and have any. But while he was trying to get it he knocked over a cup. The cup fell down and broke. (Piaget, 1932, p. 122)

Piaget found that a preschool child in the heteronomous morality stage judges the child who broke the 15 cups worse than the one who broke just one. In contrast, children who have moved beyond the heteronomous morality stage consider the child who broke the one cup naughtier. The reason: Children in the heteronomous morality stage do not take *intention* into account. Children who have moved beyond the heteronomous morality stage have come to understand that one must make judgments about the severity of a transgression based on whether the person intended to do something wrong.

Children in the heteronomous stage of moral development also believe in immanent justice. *Immanent justice* is the notion that rules that are broken earn immediate punishment. Preschool children believe that if they do something wrong, they will be punished instantly—even if no one sees them carrying out their misdeeds. In contrast, older children understand that punishments for misdeeds are determined and meted out by people.

Evaluating Piaget's Approach to Moral Development.   Recent research suggests that although Piaget was on the right track in his description of how moral development proceeds, his approach suffers from the same problem we encountered in his theory of cognitive development. Specifically, Piaget underestimated the age at which children's moral skills are honed.

It is now clear that preschool-age children understand the notion of intentionality by about age 3, and this allows them to make judgments based on intent at an earlier age than Piaget supposed. Specifically, when provided with moral questions that emphasize intent, preschool children judge someone who is intentionally bad as more "naughty" than someone who is unintentionally bad, but who creates more objective damage. Moreover, by the age of 4, they judge intentional lying wrong (Yuill & Perner, 1988; Bussey, 1992).

Moral Reasoning: Kohlberg's Approach

Your wife is near death from an unusual kind of cancer. One drug exists that the physicians think might save her—a form of radium that a scientist in a nearby city has recently developed. The drug, though, is expensive to manufacture, and the scientist is charging ten times what the drug costs him to make. He pays $1,000 for the radium and charges $10,000 for a small dose. You have gone to everyone you know to borrow money, but you can get together only $2,500—one-quarter of what you need. You've told the scientist that your wife is dying and asked him to sell it more cheaply or let you pay later. But the scientist has said, "No, I discovered the drug and I'm going to make money from it." In desperation, you consider breaking into the scientist's laboratory to steal the drug for your wife. Should you do it?

According to developmental psychologist Lawrence Kohlberg and his colleagues, the answer that adolescents give to this question reveals central aspects of their sense of morality and justice. He suggests that adolescents' reasoning about moral dilemmas such as this one reveal the stage of moral development they have attained—as well as yielding information about their general level of cognitive development (Kohlberg, 1984; Colby & Kohlberg, 1987).

Kohlberg contends that people pass through a series of stages as their sense of justice evolves and in the kind of reasoning they use to make moral judgments. Primarily due to cognitive characteristics that we discussed earlier, younger school-age children tend to think either in terms of concrete, unvarying rules ("It is always wrong to steal" or "I'll be punished if I steal") or in terms of the rules of society ("Good people don't steal" or "What if everyone stole?").

By the time they reach adolescence, however, individuals are able to reason on a higher plane, typically having reached Piaget's stage of formal operations. They are capable of comprehending abstract, formal principles of morality, and they consider cases such as the one presented in terms of broader issues of morality and of right and wrong ("Stealing may be acceptable if you are following your own conscience and doing the right thing").

Kohlberg suggested that moral development emerges in a three-level sequence, which is further subdivided into six stages (see Table 4-3). At the lowest level, *preconventional morality* (Stages 1 and 2), people follow rigid rules based on punishments or rewards. For example, a student at the preconventional level might evaluate the moral dilemma posed in the story by saying that it was not worth stealing the drug because if you were caught, you would go to jail.

In the next level, that of *conventional morality* (Stages 3 and 4), people approach moral problems in terms of their own position as good, responsible members of society. Some at this level would decide *against* stealing the drug because they think they would feel guilty or dishonest for violating social norms. Others would decide *in favor* of stealing the drug because if they did nothing in this situation, they would be unable to face others. All of these people would be reasoning at the conventional level of morality.

Finally, individuals using *postconventional morality* (Level 3, Stages 5 and 6) invoke universal moral principles that are considered broader than the rules of the particular society in which they live. People who feel that they would condemn themselves if they did not steal the drug because they would not be living up to their own moral principles would be reasoning at the postconventional level.

Kohlberg's theory proposes that people move through the periods of moral development in a fixed order and that they are unable to reach the highest stage until adolescence, due to deficits in cognitive development that are not overcome until then (Kurtines & Gewirtz, 1987). However, not everyone is presumed to reach the highest stages: Kohlberg found that postconventional reasoning is relatively rare.

Although Kohlberg's theory provides a good account of the development of moral *judgments,* the links with actual moral *behavior* are less strong. Furthermore, some critics have questioned Kohlberg's methodology of inferring moral level from their responses to his particular scenarios (Durm & Pitts, 1993).

Still, students at higher levels of moral reasoning are less likely to engage in antisocial behavior at school (such as breaking school rules) and in the community (such as engaging in juvenile delinquency) (Richards et al., 1992; Langford, 1995; Carpendale, 2000).

Furthermore, one experiment found that 15% of students who reasoned at the postconventional level of morality—the highest category—cheated when given the opportunity, although they were not as likely to cheat as those at lower levels, where more than half of the students cheated. Clearly, though, knowing what is morally right does not always mean acting that way (Snarey, 1995; Killen & Hart, 1995; Hart, Burock, & London, 2003).

Kohlberg's theory has also been criticized because it is based solely on observations of members of Western cultures. In fact, cross-cultural research finds that members of more industrialized, technologically advanced cultures move through the stages more rapidly than members of nonindustrialized countries. Why? One explanation is that Kohlberg's higher stages are based on moral reasoning involving governmental and societal institutions like the police and the court system. In less-industrialized areas, morality may be based more on relationships between people in a particular village. In short, the nature of morality may differ in diverse cultures, and Kohlberg's theory is more suited for Western cultures (Snarey, 1995).

An aspect of Kohlberg's theory that has proved even more problematic is the difficulty it has explaining girls' moral judgments. Because the theory initially was based largely on data from males, some researchers have argued that it does a better job describing boys' moral development than girls' moral development. This would explain the surprising finding that women

TABLE 4-3 Kohlberg's Sequence of Moral Reasoning

Level	Stage	Sample Moral Reasoning	
		In Favor of Stealing	**Against Stealing**
LEVEL 1 **Preconventional morality:** At this level, the concrete interests of the individual are considered in terms of rewards and punishments.	**STAGE 1** Obedience and punishment orientation: At this stage, people stick to rules to avoid punishment, and obedience occurs for its own sake.	"If you let your wife die, you will get in trouble. You'll be blamed for not spending the money to save her, and there'll be an investigation of you and the druggist for your wife's death."	"You shouldn't steal the drug because you'll get caught and sent to jail if you do. If you do get away, your conscience will bother you thinking how the police will catch up with you at any minute."
	STAGE 2 Reward orientation: At this stage, rules are followed only for a person's own benefit. Obedience occurs because of rewards that are received.	"If you do happen to get caught, you could give the drug back and you wouldn't get much of a sentence. It wouldn't bother you much to serve a little jail term, if you have your wife when you get out."	"You may not get much of a jail term if you steal the drug, but your wife will probably die before you get out, so it won't do much good. If your wife dies, you shouldn't blame yourself; it isn't your fault; she has cancer."
LEVEL 2 **Conventional morality:** At this level, people approach moral problems as members of society. They are interested in pleasing others by acting as good members of society.	**STAGE 3** "Good boy" morality: Individuals at this stage show an interest in maintaining the respect of others and doing what is expected of them.	"No one will think you're bad if you steal the drug, but your family will think you're an inhuman husband if you don't. If you let your wife die, you'll never be able to look anybody in the face again."	"It isn't just the druggist who will think you're a criminal; everyone else will, too. After you steal the drug, you'll feel bad thinking how you've brought dishonor on your family and yourself; you won't be able to face anyone again."
	STAGE 4 Authority and social-order-maintaining morality: People at this stage conform to society's rules and consider that "right" is what society defines as right.	"If you have any sense of honor, you won't let your wife die just because you're afraid to do the only thing that will save her. You'll always feel guilty that you caused her death if you don't do your duty to her."	"You're desperate and you may not know you're doing wrong when you steal the drug. But you'll know you did wrong after you're sent to jail. You'll always feel guilty for your dishonesty and law-breaking."
LEVEL 3 **Postconventional morality:** At this level, people use moral principles, which are seen as broader than those of any particular society.	**STAGE 5** Morality of contract, individual rights, and democratically accepted law: People at this stage do what is right because of a sense of obligation to laws which are agreed upon within society. They perceive that laws can be modified as part of changes in an implicit social contract.	"You'll lose other people's respect, not gain it, if you don't steal. If you let your wife die, it will be out of fear, not out of reasoning. So you'll just lose self-respect and probably the respect of others, too."	"You'll lose your standing and respect in the community and violate the law. You'll lose respect for yourself if you're carried away by emotion and forget the long-range point of view."
	STAGE 6 Morality of individual principles and conscience: At this final stage, a person follows laws because they are based on universal ethical principles. Laws that violate the principles are disobeyed.	"If you don't steal the drug, and if you let your wife die, you'll always condemn yourself for it afterward. You won't be blamed and you'll have lived up to the outside rule of the law, but you won't have lived up to your own standards of conscience."	"If you steal the drug, you won't be blamed by other people, but you'll condemn yourself because you won't have lived up to your own conscience and standards of honesty."

(*Source:* Adapted from Kohlberg, 1969.)

▶ Kohlberg's theory of moral development has been criticized for focusing on Western cultures' conceptions of morality.

typically score at a lower level than men on tests of moral judgments using Kohlberg's stage sequence. This result has led to an alternative account of moral development for girls.

Gilligan's Account of Moral Development in Girls

Psychologist Carol Gilligan (1982, 1987) has suggested that differences in the ways boys and girls are raised in our society lead to basic distinctions in how men and women view moral behavior. According to her, boys view morality primarily in terms of broad principles such as justice or fairness, while girls see it in terms of responsibility toward individuals and willingness to sacrifice themselves to help specific individuals within the context of particular relationships. Compassion for individuals, then, is a more prominent factor in moral behavior for women than it is for men (Gilligan, Ward, & Taylor, 1988; Gilligan, Lyons, & Hammer, 1990; Gump, Baker, & Roll, 2000).

Gilligan views morality as developing among females in a three-stage process (summarized in Table 4-4). In the first stage, called "orientation toward individual survival," females first concentrate on what is practical and best for them, gradually making a transition from selfishness to responsibility, in which they think about what would be best for others. In the second stage, termed "goodness as self-sacrifice," females begin to think that they must sacrifice their own wishes to what other people want.

Ideally, women make a transition from "goodness" to "truth," in which they take into account their own needs plus those of others. This transition leads to the third stage, "morality of nonviolence," in which women come to see that hurting anyone is immoral—including hurting themselves. This realization establishes a moral equivalence between themselves and others and represents, according to Gilligan, the most sophisticated level of moral reasoning.

Clearly, Gilligan's sequence of stages charts a very different path of moral development from that described by Kohlberg. Some developmentalists have suggested that her rejection of Kohlberg's work is too sweeping and that gender differences are not as pronounced as first thought (Colby & Damon, 1987). For instance, some researchers argue that both males and females use similar "justice" and "care" orientations in making moral judgments. Clearly, the question of how boys and girls differ in their moral orientations, as well as the nature of moral development in general, is far from settled (Haviv & Leman, 2002; Tangney & Dearing, 2002; Weisz & Black, 2002).

TABLE 4-4 Gilligan's Three States of Moral Development for Women		
Stage	**Characteristics**	**Example**
Stage 1 Orientation toward individual survival	Initial concentration is on what is practical and best for self. Gradual transition from selfishness to responsibility, which includes thinking about what would be best for others.	A first-grader may insist on playing only games of her own choosing when playing with a friend.
Stage 2 Goodness as self-sacrifice	Initial view is that a woman must sacrifice her own wishes to what other people want. Gradual transition from "goodness" to "truth," which takes into account needs of both self and others.	Now older, the same girl may believe that to be a good friend, she must play the games her friend chooses, even if she herself doesn't like them.
Stage 3 Morality of nonviolence	A moral equivalence is established between self and others. Hurting anyone—including one's self—is seen as immoral. Most sophisticated form of reasoning, according to Gilligan.	The same girl may realize that both friends must enjoy their time together and look for activities that both she and her friend can enjoy.

The lingering questions about the nature of moral reasoning have not deterred people from applying what has been learned about morality to everyday life. For example, as we discuss in the *Career Choices* box, professional mediators offer good solutions for resolving disputes.

Social Learning Perspectives on Morality: Focusing on Behavior

Social learning approaches to moral development stand in stark contrast to those of Piaget, Kohlberg, and Gilligan. Instead of focusing on how adolescents' level of cognitive development leads to particular forms of moral *reasoning,* social learning approaches focus more on how the environment in which adolescents operate produces moral *behavior* (Eisenberg et al., 1999).

Social learning approaches build on the behavioral approaches that we first discussed in Chapter 1. They acknowledge that some instances of adolescents' prosocial behavior stem from situations in which they have directly received positive reinforcement for acting in a morally appropriate way. For instance, when Mia's mother tells her she has been "terrific" for helping her younger brother complete a difficult homework assignment, her mother has reinforced that helping behavior. As a consequence, Mia is more likely to engage in such prosocial behavior in the future.

However, social learning approaches take behavioral approaches a step further, arguing that not all prosocial behavior has to be performed and subsequently directly reinforced for learning to occur. According to social learning approaches, we also learn moral behavior more indirectly by observing the behavior of others, called *models* (Bandura, 1977). Children and adolescents imitate models who receive reinforcement for their behavior, and ultimately they learn to perform the behavior themselves. For example, when Mia's boyfriend Jake watches Mia help her brother with the assignment and be praised for it, Jake is more likely to engage in prosocial behavior himself at some later point.

CAREER CHOICES

Mediator

Name: Jelani Quinn

Education: BA, Psychology, University of Washington, Seattle: BA, Business Administration, University of Washington, Seattle

Position: Program Director and Lead Trainer, CRU Institute, Bellevue, WA

CONFLICTS AND DISAGREEMENTS are common among high school students, ranging from conflicts about stereotypes and cultural misunderstandings to teacher–student grading arguments. However, trained mediators can help defuse many situations in a fair and equitable way.

Although different approaches are used depending on the conflict situation, mediators generally ask the parties involved to follow several basic ground rules, according to Jelani Quinn. Quinn was a student mediator for three years before joining the CRU Institute, a nonprofit organization whose goal is to teach young people effective, peaceful ways to resolve conflict and to develop understanding, respect, and the ability to cooperate with others.

"When students come to mediation, they are asked to sign a mediation contract and agree to abide by some basic rules," Quinn explained. "The rules are to make a commitment to solve the problem; don't interrupt; no name calling or putting down; tell the truth; no physical fighting; and everything is kept confidential except if someone is threatening to hurt themselves or another."

Once the mediation agreement is signed, the mediator opens up a dialogue, giving each student the opportunity to offer his or her side of the story.

"One of the most important things in mediation is to get their feelings out," Quinn said. "It may be the first time they are able to express that feeling. If someone says something important, we try to get the other person to state what was said in the hope that some empathy is created between the two parties."

"If I can't keep them from arguing, I ask them what would happen if they can't settle their problem," he added. "I try to get them to look at the options they have."

Sometimes a mediation just doesn't seem to work, but according to Quinn, that doesn't always produce a negative outcome.

"Sometimes there is no solution, but that can be a good thing," he explained. "The solution is not always the most important aspect of mediation. The most important part is that these two people were able to sit down and talk about the situation. A lot of the communications skills that I'm using as a mediator is reflected to these students and they can transfer that to their own actions."

Thinking of becoming a mediator?

Mediation, an informal process that is an alternative to legal actions, is a rapidly growing profession. Mediators help in disputes ranging from custody battles and job issues to arguments about real estate and finances. Mediators don't make decisions but, as neutral parties, clarify positions and lead people to think creatively about solutions. Good mediators are good listeners and unemotional communicators, thinking about the underlying issues rationally and dispassionately.

Mediators typically hold at least a bachelor's degree. They also need to complete specific mediation training, which is offered at many colleges and universities.

Ultimately, modeling paves the way for the development of more general rules and principles in a process called *abstract modeling*. Rather than always modeling the specific behavior of others, adolescents rely on generalized principles that underlie the behavior that they observe. After observing repeated instances in which a model is rewarded for acting in a morally desirable way, children begin the process of inferring and learning the general principles of moral conduct (Bandura, 1991).

Moral Behavior and Moral Reasoning: Why the Disconnect?

Except for social learning perspectives, most of the approaches to moral development in adolescence (such as those of Kohlberg and Gilligan) focus on moral reasoning. Why has the research spotlight shone more brightly on reasoning about moral behavior, as opposed to examining actual behavior?

One reason is that the researchers have assumed that moral reasoning lies at the heart of moral behavior. If adolescents don't have a clear internal moral compass, it seems unreasonable to expect that they will behave in a moral way. Unfortunately, though, there has been a persistent disconnect between prosocial *reasoning* and prosocial *behavior*. Obviously, we'd expect moral reasoning and judgments to be closely associated, but that doesn't seem to be the case. Why?

One reason is that in the real world circumstances often override our internal moral compass. Although we may know and truly believe that it is wrong to break to the law by not fully stopping at a stop sign, we may feel that because no one is around, we don't have to come to a complete stop. Or perhaps we're driving someone to a hospital emergency department, and our internal principles about aiding someone in distress are more salient at that moment than our principles about obeying traffic laws. Unlike when they are measured in experiments, moral principles in the real world occur in a particular context that brings its own situational pressures.

In addition, moral judgements are made in a variety of contexts, and it may be an oversimplification to expect that morality will be displayed in similar ways across different domains and situations. According to the *social domain approach,* adolescents' moral reasoning needs to be considered in the context in which judgments are being made at a given time. Major contexts include the *moral domain* (contexts that focus on concerns about justice), the *social-conventional domain* (contexts involving the need for social groups to function well), and the *personal domain* (contexts involving matters of personal choice). The particular moral judgments made by adolescents are likely to vary according to the domain (Smetana & Turiel, 2003; Turiel, 2006).

Finally, adolescents sometimes look at situations through the lens of personal choices and freedom, rather than in terms of ethical dilemmas. For example, consider the decision to engage in premarital sex. For some people, premarital sex is always ethically wrong, and to engage in it is, by definition, an immoral act. But to others, premarital sex is a choice to be decided on by the individuals who are involved. Similarly, alcohol use—although illegal for adolescents younger than a certain age—may be viewed in terms of a fairly rational, cost-benefit analysis (drinking provides certain benefits, but also accrues certain costs), rather than in terms of morality. The view that such activities as taking drugs, engaging in sex, and drinking are personal, not moral, choices, helps explain the lack of relationship between risk taking and moral reasoning (Kuther, 2000; Kuther & Higgins-D'Alessandro, 2000, 2003; Eisenberg & Morris, 2004).

Prosocial Reasoning and Prosocial Behavior: The Other Side of the Coin

We've been focusing on situations in which adolescents are faced with situations involving some form of wrongdoing—breaking a rule, violating a moral principle, disobeying a law. But what

◀ Rather than looking at drinking as a moral issue, adolescents may view it in terms of rewards and costs the behavior produces.

about the other side of the coin—doing positive, unselfish, or altruistic deeds that benefit others, sometimes at the expense of oneself?

Although there is considerably less research in this area, emerging work suggests that adolescents generally become more sophisticated in their thinking about **prosocial behavior,** helping behavior that benefits others. For example, their growing cognitive abilities allow them to distinguish between prosocial behavior that is self-serving (done to gain something, such as looking better in others' eyes) or truly *altruistic* (done to help others and requiring clear self-sacrifice).

In addition, adolescents who are unusually helpful to others also tend to show more sophisticated moral reasoning than adolescents who are less prosocially active. For instance, we might assume that Jack Buchholz, whose helpfulness to his friend Jake Geller was described in the chapter prologue, would show more advanced levels of moral reasoning (Eisenberg, Zhou, & Koller, 2001).

Furthermore, adolescents who show more sophisticated levels of prosocial reasoning are generally more sympathetic. Moreover, there's a persistent sex difference: Females tend to demonstrate higher levels of prosocial reasoning than males (Eisenberg & Morris, 2004).

On the other hand, it's harder to make generalizations about adolescent prosocial *behavior*. Although some adolescents become increasingly helpful as they move through adolescence, others do not. In a way, the difficulty in finding a relationship between prosocial behavior and personal characteristics is not surprising, given the difficulty that researchers have had in finding any particular personality characteristics related to helpfulness. Most research suggests that people are not invariably helpful or, for that matter, unhelpful. Instead, whether particular individuals act in a prosocial manner depends on their personality *and* the specifics of the situation. Furthermore, no single pattern of specific, individual personality traits determines prosocial behavior. Rather, the way that specific personality factors fit together, as well as the demands of the particular situation, determines whether a person will help (Carlo et al., 1991; Knight et al., 1994; Eisenberg & Morris, 2004).

Empathy and Moral Behavior.   According to some developmentalists, **empathy,** the understanding of what another individual feels, lies at the heart of many kinds of moral behavior. Although the roots of empathy grow early (one-year-old infants cry when they hear other infants crying, for example), it is not until around the start of adolescence that the most sophisticated kinds of empathy begin to emerge. Adolescents experience empathy not only in specific situations, but also empathy for collective groups, such as people living in poverty or victims of racism (Hoffman, 1991, 2001).

For example, in early adolescence, a teenager may experience empathy when she learns a friend is ill. Understanding the emotions that the friend is experiencing—concerns about missing classes, fear about falling behind, and so forth—may lead the teenager to offer help to her classmate. On the other hand, when hearing about victims of an outbreak of bird flu in China, the same girl may be emotionally unmoved.

However, later in adolescence, as her cognitive abilities increase and she can reason on more abstract levels, the same girl may feel empathy for collective groups. Not only may she feel emotionally involved over victims of specific situations (such as people who lost their homes as a consequence of Hurricane Katrina), but she may also experience deep emotional responses toward abstract groups such as the homeless, whose experiences may be completely unfamiliar to her.

Gender and Cultural Differences in Prosocial Behavior.   Both gender and culture are related to prosocial behavior during adolescence. For example, quite consistently, girls are more helpful than boys in adolescence. They are more caring about others, and they act in a more prosocial manner. (By the way, not only are males less likely to provide help, they are also less willing to ask for help than females—something we might call the males-hating-to-ask-for-directions-even-when-they-are-lost phenomenon; Wills & DePaulo, 1991; Eisenberg & Morris, 2004).

prosocial behavior   helping behavior that benefits others

empathy   the understanding of what another individual feels

On the other hand, males don't always act less helpfully than females (Eagly & Crowley, 1986). If the situation is one in which their behavior is public and visible to others, and the person needing help is female, males are more likely to be helpful. Having the opportunity to act like a "knight in shining armor" and come to the rescue of a damsel in distress elevates the level of male helpfulness beyond its typically more modest level.

The typically higher levels of prosocial behavior displayed by females reflect their tendency to hold a *communal* orientation, centering on an interest in relationships and community. In contrast, males are more likely to have an *agentic* orientation, which focuses on individuality and getting things done. Communal orientations lead to greater prosocial behavior (Mosher & Danoff-Burg, 2005; Salmivalli et al., 2005).

Culture, too, affects the extent to which adolescents behave prosocially. For instance, people living on Israeli kibbutzim, or collective farms, tend to show greater helpfulness and even different reasoning about morality than members of the dominant culture in the United States. Similarly, adolescents raised in the United States use more rights-based reasoning about morality than adolescents in other societies. In *rights-based reasoning,* certain rights (such as freedom of speech) are assumed; they don't have to be earned, but are the birthright of every citizen. In contrast, adolescents in India are more likely to use reasoning based on *duty-based reasoning,* in which people are expected to behave in a certain way because it is their responsibility (Mann, 1980; Fuchs et al., 1986; Shweder, Much, & Mahapatra, 1997).

Parents' child-rearing practices produce different forms of helping behavior, which emerge even prior to adolescence. For example, the level of helping behavior that children display while playing varies substantially in different cultures. Children raised in cultures in which children are taught to cooperate with other family members to do chores or to help in the upbringing of younger children (such as in Kenya, Mexico, and the Philippines) show relatively high levels of prosocial behavior. In contrast, cultures that promote competition—such as the United States—produce lower levels of prosocial behavior (Whiting & Whiting, 1975; Whiting & Edwards, 1988; Carlo et al., 1999).

Furthermore, the degree to which adolescents view helping in the context of reciprocity— the view that we should help because we expect to receive help from others in the future—is related to cultural factors. For example, Hindu Indians see reciprocity as a moral obligation, whereas college students in the United States consider reciprocity as more of a personal choice (Moghaddam, Taylor, & Wright, 1993; Miller & Bersoff, 1994; Miller, 1997; Chadha & Misra, 2004).

Volunteerism: Sustained Helping

Every Tuesday, Emily goes to a local hospital to assist nurses in the children's unit care for "crack babies," who are suffering painful withdrawal symptoms from drugs used by their mothers during pregnancy. Anthony spent last summer working with a church group to renovate rundown homes in his community. As a trained volunteer at the zoo, Alicia spends one day each week showing school-children the wonders of animal life. (Taylor, Peplau, & Sears, 2006, p. 395)

What each of these adolescents has in common is that they devote a substantial amount of time volunteering to aid their community. In contrast to one-time, unplanned helping behavior, volunteerism requires a sustained commitment over a lengthy period (Snyder & Omoto, 2001; Omoto & Malsch, 2005).

Why do adolescents volunteer? They have a variety of motives, some of which are entirely altruistic and others of which are actually somewhat self-serving. Volunteering can be an expression of personal values and compassion, reflecting the wish to truly provide help to others, even, sometimes, at significant personal expense. It can provide greater self-understanding and can be personally challenging, supporting personal growth. Volunteers can also learn new skills.

But volunteerism also provides some less-noble benefits to those providing help. For instance, acting as a volunteer can win the social approval of others. In addition, it can be a résumé builder, helping adolescents to get into the college of their choice or to enhance the possibilities of getting a good job in the future (Snyder, Clary, & Stukas, 2000; Snyder & Clary, 2004).

Regardless of the motivation behind volunteerism, several generalizations can be made about adolescent volunteerism. First, volunteers are more likely to be female than male, consistent with the findings about prosocial behavior that we discussed earlier. Second, adolescents who volunteer are more altruistic than their nonvolunteering peers. Third, they are more likely to have parents who engage in volunteer work of their own in their community (Flanagan, 2004).

It's harder to figure out what effects acting as a volunteer has on adolescents, because volunteers are already different from their nonvolunteering peers even before they start to volunteer. Still, researchers have found some differences. Participation in volunteerism produces improvements in social responsibility. It makes participants feel that helping others is of greater importance, and they end up feeling more obligated to act with tolerance towards others (Flanagan, 2004; Bertelsen & Flanagan, 2005).

But what of adolescents whose volunteerism is not so voluntarily? In many schools, completing a certain number of hours of community service is a requirement. Do adolescents benefit from participation in community service if they are forced to do so? We discuss the answer in the accompanying *Transitions* box.

Honesty and Lies in Everyday Life: Is the Truth Dead?

Although volunteerism and service learning certainly represent important instances of prosocial behavior, they occur on a scheduled, occasional basis. But what of those more frequent episodes of everyday life, when adolescents can choose to be honest or can behave dishonestly to obtain some ordinary gain?

The findings from a variety of areas are, in many ways, disheartening. For example, let's consider what adolescent developmentalists have found about academic honesty and cheating. Some surveys show that a majority of adolescents report cheating on a test in the previous year. Others show that almost half of adolescents report plagiarizing a passage, either from written materials or the Web (Whitley, 1998; Jensen et al., 2002).

In one comprehensive study of academic cheating, Lene Jensen and colleagues found that the acceptability of cheating was linked to the motives of the cheater. For example, cheating to get a good grade to obtain a job that would let someone help her family and cheating to avoid disappointing parents were seen as relatively acceptable (Jensen et al., 2002).

Furthermore, cheating seems to decline as adolescents age: High school students are more likely to cheat than college students. There are also gender differences: As shown in Figure 4-2 on page 138, boys are more likely to cheat than girls.

The frequency of cheating in academic settings mirrors findings of adolescent honesty during everyday conversations. For example, researchers who were examining lying in everyday life asked previously unacquainted undergraduate students to try to get to know one another during a 10-minute encounter that was secretly videotaped. Later, participants viewed the videotape of themselves and indicated each time they had said something that was not entirely accurate.

The results were disquieting. Around 60% of the participants lied at least once during the 10 minutes, and the average number of lies—in just a 10-minute period—was three. There was also a gender difference. Although men and women produced approximately the same number of lies, what they lied about was different. Women lied more to make their partner feel better ("That sweater looks great on you"). In contrast, men lied more to make themselves look better ("I aced the test") (Feldman, Forrest, & Happ, 2002; Tyler & Feldman, 2005).

Transiti⦿ns

Mandatory Volunteerism: A Contradiction in Terms?

By the end of their senior year, all students must have engaged in some form of community service of at least five hours a week over the course of a term. Examples of community service include working at a shelter for the homeless or a soup kitchen, tutoring, holding an internship in a human service agency, or working with children in an after-school program.

Sound like a good idea for a school requirement? It does to many high schools and colleges, which have instituted required community service programs to encourage students to become involved in their community. One reason for such requirements is to increase the probability that people will volunteer in the future, resulting in an increase in community volunteers.

There's a hitch, though: According to a study by psychologist Arthur Stukas and colleagues, such programs may have unintended consequences. In fact, these researchers found that people who felt forced into volunteering due to a requirement ended up saying they were *less* likely to volunteer in the future (Stukas, Snyder, & Clary, 1999; Clary & Snyder, 2002).

In the first of two studies, the researchers surveyed a group of students required to enroll in a college service-learning course. They

▲ Mandatory volunteerism may lead to a decline in adolescents' willingness to engage in volunteer work in the future.

found that students who had prior volunteer experience, but who saw themselves as required to participate in the service-learning course, had *lowered* intentions to volunteer in the future. Participation in the course, then, had the ironic effect of reducing their interest in future volunteer work.

In the subsequent study, the results of the survey were supported. In the experiment, a group of participants were required to carry out a "volunteer" activity—reading to the blind. For participants who before the experiment said they were unlikely to volunteer in the future, being forced to volunteer led to lower intentions to volunteer. On the other hand, for those who felt before the experiment that they would have volunteered even if they were weren't required to, being forced to volunteer had little effect on their willingness to participate in the future.

Why would requiring volunteer work make participants less likely to volunteer in the future? One explanation is that community service requirements may alter people's perceptions of why they help. Instead of seeing themselves as willing volunteers, their forced participation may lead to the view that the sole reason they are helping is to fulfill a requirement. Consequently, they are unable to view themselves as volunteers doing good deeds, and they may be less eager to volunteer in the future. Furthermore, forced participation in any activity may lead to *reactance,* hostility and anger that results from the restriction of one's freedom (Brehm & Brehm, 1981). If people experience reactance as a result of being required to volunteer, they may seek to reestablish their sense of freedom by downgrading volunteerism.

The results of the studies suggest that mandatory volunteerism may have a downside. Rather than producing a corps of willing volunteers, community service requirements may lead to volunteers who are actually less likely to volunteer in the future. To be successful, then, community service programs must encourage people to volunteer in as noncoercive a manner as possible.

- Knowing what you know about prosocial behavior and adolescents' motivations, how would you introduce a community service policy at the high school level?

- Some people have argued that compulsory national service—either military or nonmilitary—would be a reasonable way to introduce a military draft while also encouraging a culture of helpfulness. How do the results of the studies described earlier relate to this idea? Would giving citizens a choice between military and nonmilitary service lessen reactance? Why or why not?

MOTIVE	MALE	FEMALE
Needed to pass the class in order to get a job that would let her help her family	2.88	2.65
Didn't want to disappoint her parents	2.22	1.97
Would be put on academic probation if she didn't pass	2.29	1.88
Didn't have enough time to study because of her job	2.07	1.85
"Froze" and couldn't recall the answers	2.03	1.89
Thought the instructor had treated her unfairly	2.08	1.86
Needed a good grade to maintain athletic eligibility	2.04	1.71
Knew the class was very competitive and it would be tough to get a good grade	2.02	1.69
Was depressed and didn't have the energy to prepare for the exam	1.86	1.73
Knew everyone else was cheating	2.10	1.76
Felt the instructor deliberately made the exam too hard	1.95	1.59
Knew no one else would suffer since the exam was not on a curve	1.91	1.59
Knew she wouldn't get caught	1.89	1.45
Wanted to maintain her class ranking	1.68	1.50
Knew the instructor wouldn't do much if she were caught	1.78	1.42
Was very competitive by nature	1.74	1.46
Didn't think it was a big deal	1.68	1.39
Had cheated in other classes and gotten away with it	1.49	1.31
Wanted to see if she could get away with it	1.40	1.28

Rating scale: 1 = totally unacceptable; 2 = somewhat unacceptable; 3 = somewhat acceptable; 4 = totally acceptable

▲ FIGURE 4-2

In addition to showing that almost half of all adolescents have participated in some sort of academic dishonesty, studies have also noted that boys are more likely to cheat than girls.

(*Source:* Jensen, Arnett, Feldman, & Cauffman, 2002.)

In addition, adolescents become more effective liars as they get older. They are less likely to be detected when they lie and are therefore better able to get away with their lies. Moreover, there is a relationship between social skills and lying, with the most effective liars having the greatest level of popularity. It's probably not so much that lying enhances an adolescent's popularity as that adolescents derive a social advantage from knowing when to avoid the sort of bluntness that can hurt someone's feelings ("You look like you're putting on weight") (Feldman, Tomasian, & Coats, 1999; Tyler, Feldman, & Reichart, 2006).

In short, cheating, deception, and lying are part of everyday adolescent life. Academic cheating, in particular, is on the rise, with increasing numbers of adolescents believing that it is permissible to cheat (Murdock et al., 2001).

Yet these disheartening generalizations are far from the full story of adolescence. We need only recall the story that began this chapter of Jake Geller, who for years has been helped by his friend Jack Buchholz. Such examples of the bright side of adolescent behavior are far from unique.

Furthermore, the number of adolescents engaged in civic activities, community service, and local community organizations is growing. With increasing participation comes involvement in the exercise of governance and the determination of the activities in which these organizations engage. In turn, this permits adolescents to try out ideas, make contributions, work out disagreements, and otherwise make their voices heard—all of which leads to greater civic engagement (Flanagan, 2004; Bertelson & Flanagan, 2005).

In addition, as adolescents become increasingly involved with others on the level of civic engagement and volunteerism, they become more connected with their peers, families, and other representatives of the social world in which live. These social interactions help in achieving one of the central developmental tasks facing adolescents—acting as interdependent, contributing members of society.

BECOMING AN INFORMED CONSUMER OF ADOLESCENT SCIENCE

Increasing Prosocial Behavior

HOW CAN WE increase adolescents' helpfulness, moral reasoning levels, and civic engagement? Adolescent developmentalists have devised a number of strategies:

- *Increase opportunities to participate in community service.* Although we've seen that *forcing* adolescents to become involved in community service may not produce optimal outcomes, generally the research data suggest that participation in community service and other volunteer activities is associated with higher levels of helping. Making it easier for adolescents to participate and encouraging them to take advantage of opportunities is a reasonable strategy.

- *Create youth charters.* According to developmental psychologist William Damon, one of the best ways to increase prosocial behavior is through the creation of youth charters (Damon, 1997). *Youth charters* consist of a set of principles, guidelines, and action plans that are meant to foster prosocial behavior, academic success, and civic engagement. Youth charters are jointly created by adolescents and important people in their lives, such as parents, teachers, friends, and others in the community. Charters specify expectations about significant behaviors that affect honesty, civility, respect, and excellence.

- *Teaching moral behavior.* Although programs that seek to teach adolescents to behave more morally aren't very effective if they rely on preaching ("You'll be a better person if you are more honest"), more targeted approaches do work. For example, programs that teach social decision-making strategies have helped adolescents to behave more prosocially (Gibbs, 2003).

- *Influence public policy.* The development of prosocial, civically engaged adolescents must be supported by public policies. Public institutions such as schools must assist and encourage parents in their efforts to raise morally committed children. Parents must have the resources to fulfill adolescents' basic needs and to encourage the establishment of positive values (Flanagan, Gill, & Gallay, 2005). ■

Review and Apply

Review

1. Researchers focusing on moral development include Piaget, who identified three stages of moral development; Kohlberg, who established six stages of moral reasoning; and Gilligan, who focused on girls' moral behavior and found significant gender differences.

2. In contrast to the focus on moral reasoning of other approaches, social learning approaches study ways—such as modeling—in which adolescents learn moral behavior.

3. Adolescents' growing sophistication enables them both to consider and to evaluate prosocial behavior. The likelihood that a person will act prosocially depends on both the individual and the situation rather than on personality traits alone.

4. There are clear gender and cultural differences in both empathy and prosocial behavior during adolescence.

5. Cheating and lying are prevalent during adolescence, although reasoning about both becomes more sophisticated, taking into account social issues such as motivation and the need to avoid hurting people's feelings.

Apply

1. Do you think that gender differences in empathy and prosocial behavior (e.g., communal vs. agentic orientations) are primarily genetic in nature or caused by environmental factors, such as child-rearing practices and attitudes? Why?

2. How might a rights-based orientation, such as is found in the United States, tend to decrease prosocial behavior, while a duty-based orientation encourages prosocial behavior? Can government policies that encourage volunteerism bring about a change in U.S. attitudes?

EPILOGUE

In this chapter, we discussed the development of personality, focusing first on two major theoretical approaches. We discussed the psychodynamic approach pioneered by Sigmund Freud, with its emphasis on the unconscious, and the trait approach, which emphasizes specific personality characteristics. We also considered temperament, which underlies personality and accounts for the general consistency of personality throughout the life span, including adolescence. Finally, we turned to moral development, observing approaches that emphasize moral reasoning and approaches that focus on moral behavior. We discovered that moral reasoning and moral behavior are not the same thing.

Before we move on to the next chapter, let's return briefly to the Prologue. Consider the friendship between Jake Geller and Jack Buchholz and the help that Jack willingly provides to his friend. Answer the following questions.

1. What do you think is the primary motivation behind Jack Buchholz's willingness to help Jake Geller?

2. Do you think Jack's help would have been as extensive if he did it to receive credit as part of a mandatory service-learning experience?

3. Using Kohlberg's approach and based on what you know of Jack's behavior, at what level of moral reasoning might he fall?

4. Do you think that Jack sees his actions primarily as a duty or as something else? Why?

SUMMARY

REVIEW

● **How—and why—do cultures mark the transition from childhood to adolescence?** *(p. 112)*

1. The period of adolescence, stretching from ages 13 to 19, is a social construction that many cultures mark with rituals and ceremonies known as rites of passage.

2. Adolescence is regarded as socially important because it signals the transition from a life of dependence on parents to an independent life in which the individual becomes an adult, starts a new family, and becomes a full member of society.

3. The most widespread modern rite of passage is the transition from schooling to full-time work, which is celebrated with graduation rituals.

- **What sorts of roles do people play during adolescence, and why are these roles important?** *(p. 115)*

4. The main roles that adolescents play are family member, friend, and student.

5. Roles—expected behaviors associated with people who occupy a given position—are important because they help adolescents define themselves in new ways by adopting shifting patterns of behavior.

6. Roles influence not only behaviors, but also the attitudes that adolescents hold.

- **How are personality and temperament related?** *(p. 122)*

7. Personality, the pattern of enduring characteristics that makes each person an individual, causes a person to behave consistently over time and in different situations.

8. Two main approaches to the study of personality are the psychodynamic approach and the trait approach.

9. Temperament is the underlying pattern of traits that determine personality.

10. Personality and temperament are a combination of genetic and environmental elements. Both are influenced by and influence the environment in which the adolescent lives.

- **In what ways do people develop morally during adolescence?** *(p. 125)*

11. Researchers have used several approaches to study adolescents' reasoning about moral issues, moral behavior, and attitudes toward moral and immoral behavior.

12. Piaget, Kohlberg, and Gilligan focused mainly on moral reasoning, while social learning theorists have focused more on ways in which the environment influences moral behavior.

13. Moral reasoning approaches identify a series of stages through which people pass, concluding that they achieve a sophisticated level of moral reasoning by the end of adolescence.

- **As adolescents become more sophisticated morally, how does their behavior change?** *(p. 133)*

14. Moral reasoning is not the same as moral behavior, as researchers with a social learning orientation have noted. Adolescents who understand moral issues do not invariably behave in a moral manner.

15. Adolescents understand prosocial behavior and can evaluate the motivations behind it, which may be altruistic or self-serving.

16. There are gender and cultural differences in empathy and prosocial behavior.

17. Adolescents have a sophisticated understanding of the motivations behind lying and cheating, but their sophistication does not produce notable gains in honesty.

KEY TERMS AND CONCEPTS

rites of passage (p. 114)
roles (p. 115)
personality (p. 118)
psychodynamic approach
  to personality (p. 119)

traits (p. 120)
temperaments (p. 122)
moral development (p. 126)

prosocial behavior (p. 134)
empathy (p. 134)

5

Self and Identity

PROLOGUE

DEAR BETH:
I'm a senior, a cheerleader, considered pretty and popular. Everyone thinks I have a perfect life, but I feel like I don't know who I am anymore. What is my personality really like? What is important to me? What should I be doing?

It's all in there someplace inside of me, but it's hidden and confused. I always felt so secure before. I told my most trusted friend, and she says everyone goes through this, but I don't know. I feel worried and confused all the time.

If it's a phase, when will I get over it? I'm sick of being lifeless and withdrawn. I don't mean I think about suicide, I just want to get rid of this worry.

—Confused (Ask Beth, 1988) ■

th!nk ABOUT THIS

ADVICE COLUMNISTS, THERAPISTS, friends, and—occasionally—parents face similar questions from adolescents. Answering the question "Who am I?" is one of the primary developmental tasks faced during adolescence.

In this chapter, we'll address the topic of self and identity, discussing the ways that adolescents think about and determine who they are and their place in the world. We start by addressing self-concept, looking at how adolescents view their own characteristics and how their identity is shaped.

We then turn to the critical of issue of self-esteem. We consider how adolescents make judgments about themselves and the importance of self-esteem to the well-being of adolescents.

Finally, we look at emotional development during adolescence. We discuss the kinds of emotions experienced by adolescents and the functions that they play. We also consider cross-cultural differences in emotion and how emotional competence is developed. ■

- **How do individuals develop a sense of identity during adolescence?**
- **What challenges are there to successful identity formation?**
- **How important is self-esteem, and what are the consequences of both low and high self-esteem?**
- **Why is emotional development important in adolescence?**
- **Are there cultural differences in emotional development and expression?**

Identity: Asking "Who Am I?"

Thirteen is a hard age, very hard. A lot of people say you have it easy, you're a kid, but there's a lot of pressure being 13—to be respected by people in your school, to be liked, always feeling like you have to be good. There's pressure to do drugs, too, so you try not to succumb to that. But you don't want to be made fun of, so you have to look cool. You gotta wear the right shoes, the right clothes.

The thoughts expressed here by a 13-year-old demonstrate a clear awareness—and self-consciousness—regarding his newly forming place in society and life. During adolescence, questions like "Who am I?" and "Where do I belong in the world?" begin to take a front seat.

Why should issues of identity become so important during adolescence? One reason is that adolescents' intellectual capacities become more adultlike. They are able to see how they stack up to others and become aware that they are individuals, apart not just from their parents, but from all others. The dramatic physical changes during puberty make adolescents acutely aware of their own bodies and aware that others are reacting to them in ways to which they are unaccustomed. Whatever the cause, adolescence often brings substantial changes in teenagers' self-concepts and self-esteem—in sum, their notions of their own identity.

Self-Concept: What Am I Like?

Ask Valerie to describe herself, and she says, "Others look at me as laid-back, relaxed, and not worrying too much. But really, I'm often nervous and emotional."

The fact that Valerie distinguishes others' views of her from her own perceptions represents a developmental advance of adolescence. In childhood, Valerie would have characterized herself according to a list of traits that would not differentiate her view of herself and others' perspectives. However, adolescents are able to make the distinction, and when they try to describe who they are, they take both their own and others' views into account (Harter, 1990a; Cole et al., 2001; Updegraff et al., 2004).

This broader view of themselves is one aspect of adolescents' increasing understanding of who they are. They can see various aspects of the self simultaneously, and this view of the self becomes more organized and coherent. They look at the self from a psychological perspective, viewing traits not as concrete entities but as abstractions (Adams, Montemayor, & Gullotta, 1996). For example, teenagers are more likely than younger children to describe themselves in terms of their ideology (saying something like "I'm an environmentalist") than in terms of physical characteristics (such as "I'm the fastest runner in my class").

Furthermore, as illustrated in Figure 5-1, adolescents' views of themselves become divided into increasingly differentiated spheres. For example, one important dimension is the nonaca-

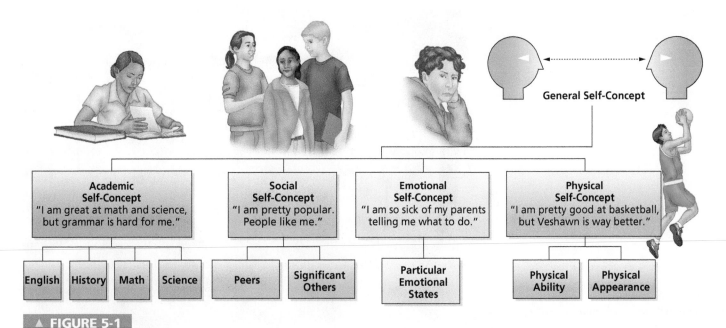

Looking Inward: The Development of Self Adolescents' views of themselves becomes divided into increasingly differentiated spheres. What cognitive changes make this possible?

(*Source:* Adapted from Shavelson, Hubner, & Stanton, 1976.)

demic self-concept, which includes the components of physical appearance, peer relations, and physical ability. Academic self-concept is similarly divided. Research on students' self-concepts in English, mathematics, and nonacademic realms has found that the separate self-concepts are not necessarily viewed in similar ways, although there is some overlap. For example, an adolescent who sees herself as an ace math student is not necessarily going to see herself as great in English. During adolescence, these views become increasingly refined (Burnett, Pillay, & Dart, 2003; Marsh & Ayotte, 2003; Marsh & Perry, 2005).

The broader, more multifaceted view of self-concept that expands during adolescence is a mixed blessing, especially during the earlier years of adolescence. At that time, adolescents may be troubled by the multiple aspects of their personalities. During the beginning of adolescence, for instance, teenagers may want to view themselves in a certain way ("I'm a sociable person and love to be with people"), and they may become concerned when their behavior is inconsistent with that view ("Even though I want to be sociable, sometimes I can't stand being around my friends and just want to be alone"). By the end of adolescence, however, teenagers find it easier to accept that different situations elicit different behaviors and feelings (Harter, 1990b; Pyryt & Mendaglio, 1994; Trzesniewski, Donnellan, & Robins, 2003).

Possible Selves and Identity. Identity not only shapes the way adolescents view themselves in the here and now, but it also shapes the way they view themselves in their future lives. **Possible selves** are those aspects of the self that relate to the future. Possible selves reflect adolescents' aspirations, concerns, and views of what is likely to happen to them. For instance, a high school student who is vaguely thinking of becoming a lawyer may hold several possible views about her future, seeing herself as a defense lawyer, a prosecuting attorney, or a Supreme Court justice. However, not every possible self is necessarily positive. For instance, possible selves may include a view of being extremely overweight, developing a brain tumor, or becoming a homeless drug addict (Shepard & Marshall, 1999; Shepard, 2004; Abrams & Aguilar, 2005).

possible selves those aspects of the self that relate to the future

▶ Adolescents develop more complex, differentiated views of themselves as they age.

Obviously, such alternative possible selves represent only possibilities, but they influence adolescents' current behavior and the choices they make. They may act as incentives (for example, inspiring an adolescent to study hard to be successful in the future) or as barriers (for example, motivating an adolescent to avoid overeating to prevent future weight gains). In fact, people make use of possible selves to consider their future throughout life, not only in adolescence.

In addition to considering the self in terms of possible selves, adolescents "package" their identities, in terms of both the categories that are important to them and the meanings that they attach to the categories. For example, when several Hispanic first-year college students were asked to list their identities and the characteristics associated with each identity, they came up with very different representations of the same identity (Ethier & Deaux, 1990). As you can see in Table 5-1, a comparison of two of the participants' reports reveals very different patterns of responses.

Social Comparison: Making Judgments of Oneself

If someone asks you how good you are at math, how would you respond? Most of us would compare our performance to others who are roughly of the same age and educational level. It is unlikely that we'd answer the question by comparing ourselves either to Albert Einstein or to a kindergartner just learning about numbers.

Adolescents begin to follow the same sort of reasoning when they seek to understand how able they are. When they were younger, they tended to consider their abilities in terms of some hypothetical standard, making judgments that they were good or bad in an absolute sense. Now they begin to use social comparison processes, comparing themselves to others, to determine their levels of accomplishment (Weiss, Ebbeck, & Horn, 1997).

Social comparison is the desire to evaluate one's own behavior, abilities, expertise, and opinions by comparing them to those of others. The concept of social comparison suggests that when concrete, objective measures of ability are lacking, people turn to social reality to evaluate themselves. *Social reality* refers to understanding that is derived from how others act, think, feel, and view the world.

For instance, suppose an adolescent wants to know how good a tennis player she is. Because objective means are usually lacking, she needs to compare herself to others to see how she stacks

social comparison the desire to evaluate one's own behavior, abilities, expertise, and opinions by comparing them to those of others

TABLE 5-1	Self-Identities of Two Hispanic Students	
Identity	**Participant 1**	**Participant 2**
Hispanic	Confused	Proud
	Proud	Loyal
	On guard	Happy
	Representative	Part of a big family
	Questioning	Lucky
	Aware	Cared for
	Token	Stand out in good and bad ways
	Excluded	Social
		Religious
Student	Conscientious	Hard
	Flexible	Big change
	Self-sacrificing	Pressure
	Curious	Freedom
	Assertive	Responsibilities
	Demanding	New environment

Source: Ethier & Deaux, 1990.

up. But who is the most useful comparison person? Unless she is a top-ranked pro, she already knows she doesn't play as well as Lindsay Davenport or Serena Williams. At the same time, she is probably certain that she plays better than someone who has just taken up the game. Consequently, the most likely candidates for comparison are tennis players who consistently play at a level fairly similar to her own.

This example illustrates a general rule: People generally determine their abilities by comparing themselves to others who are similar to themselves along relevant dimensions. Consequently, when adolescents cannot objectively evaluate their abilities, they look to others who are comparable to themselves (Suls & Wills, 1991 Summers, Schallert, & Ritter, 2003).

Upward and Downward Social Comparison. Although adolescents typically compare themselves to those who are similar to themselves, they sometimes choose others who are different from themselves. In some cases, they use upward *social comparison,* in which they compare themselves to those who are slightly more proficient or skilled than they are. Upward social comparison with others who are slightly more capable provides the possibility of ultimately attaining the comparison person's higher level of competence (Burleson, Leach, & Harrington, 2005).

In other cases—particularly when adolescents' self-esteem is at stake—they choose to make downward social comparisons. In *downward social comparisons,* adolescents compare themselves with others who are obviously less competent or successful. Downward social comparison is used because it protects adolescents' view of themselves. By comparing themselves to those who are less able, adolescents ensure that they will come out on top and thereby preserve an image of themselves as successful (Aspinwall & Taylor, 1993; Vohs & Heatherton, 2004).

Downward social comparison helps explain why some students who don't perform all that well academically sometimes have more positive academic self-concepts than very capable students in schools that have high academic standards and many successful students.

The reason is that students in the schools with generally low-achieving students observe others who are not doing terribly well academically, and they feel relatively good by comparison. In contrast, students in the schools with a high proportion of high-achieving students find themselves competing with a more academically proficient group of students, and their perception of their performance may suffer in comparison. In short, it is often better to be a big fish in a small pond than a small fish in a big one—at least in terms of how adolescents view themselves academically (Marsh & Hau, 2003; Borland & Howsen, 2003; Chanal, Marsh, & Sarrazin, 2005).

Identity Formation: Change or Crisis?

Psychoanalyst Erik Erikson, who lived from 1902 to 1994, provided a psychodynamic view in his theory of psychosocial development, which emphasizes our social interaction with other people. In Erikson's view, society and culture both challenge and shape us. *Psychosocial development* encompasses changes in our interactions with and understandings of one another, as well as in our knowledge and understanding of ourselves as members of society (Erikson, 1963; Côté, 2005).

Erikson's theory suggests that developmental change occurs throughout our lives in eight distinct stages corresponding to periods of the life span (see Table 5-2). The stages emerge in a fixed pattern and are similar for all people. Erikson argued that each stage presents a crisis or conflict that the individual must resolve.

In Erikson's view, passing through the stages is an inevitable part of getting older. He represented each stage as a pairing of the most positive and most negative aspects of the crisis of the period. For example, during the first 18 months of life, we pass through the *trust-versus-mistrust stage*. During this period, infants develop a sense of trust or mistrust, largely depending on how well their needs are met by their caregivers. Erikson suggested that if infants are able to develop

TABLE 5-2 A Summary of Erikson's Stages

Stage	Approximate Age	Positive Outcomes	Negative Outcomes
1. Trust-versus-mistrust	Birth–1½ years	Feelings of trust from environmental support	Fear and concern regarding others
2. Autonomy-versus-shame-and-doubt	1½–3 years	Self-sufficiency if exploration is encouraged	Doubts about self, lack of independence
3. Initiative-versus-guilt	3–6 years	Discovery of ways to initiate actions	Guilt from actions and thoughts
4. Industry-versus-inferiority	6–12 years	Development of sense of competence	Feelings of inferiority, no sense of mastery
5. Identity-versus-identity-confusion	Adolescence	Awareness of uniqueness of self, knowledge of role to be followed	Inability to identify appropriate roles in life
6. Intimacy-versus-isolation	Early adulthood	Development of loving, sexual relationships and close friendships	Fear of relationships with others
7. Generativity-versus-stagnation	Middle adulthood	Sense of contribution to continuity of life	Trivialization of one's activities
8. Ego-integrity-versus-despair	Late adulthood	Sense of unity in life's accomplishments	Regret over lost opportunities of life

(*Source:* Erikson, 1963).

trust, they experience a sense of hope, which permits them to feel as if they can fulfill their needs successfully. On the other hand, feelings of mistrust lead infants to see the world as harsh and unfriendly, and they may have later difficulties in forming close bonds with others.

Although each crisis is never fully resolved—life becomes increasingly complicated as people grow older—every crisis has to be resolved sufficiently to deal successfully with the increasingly complicated demands made during the following stage of development. The success with which adolescents meet the demands of adolescence depends on how well they resolved the crises they encountered during earlier psychosocial stages.

Identity-Versus-Role-Confusion Stage. Erikson argued that during adolescence teenagers try to figure out what is unique and distinctive about themselves. They strive to discover their particular strengths and weaknesses and the roles they can best play in their future lives. This discovery process often involves "trying on" different roles or choices to see if they fit an adolescent's capabilities and views about himself or herself. Through this process, adolescents seek to understand who they are by narrowing and making choices about their personal, occupational, sexual, and political commitments. Erikson called this the **identity-versus-role-confusion stage.**

In Erikson's view, adolescents who stumble in their efforts to find a suitable identity may go off course in several ways. They may adopt socially unacceptable roles as a way of expressing what they do *not* want to be, or they may have difficulty forming and maintaining long-lasting close personal relationships. In general, their sense of self becomes "diffuse," failing to organize around a central, unified core identity.

▲ Erik Erikson.

On the other hand, those who are successful in forging an appropriate identity set a course that provides a foundation for future psychosocial development. They learn their unique capabilities and believe in them, and they develop an accurate sense of who they are. They are prepared to set out on a path that takes full advantage of what their unique strengths permit them to do (Blustein, & Palladino, 1991; Archer & Waterman, 1994; Allison & Schultz, 2001).

But finding the appropriate identity is not simple, in part because—in addition to self-generated identity concerns—societal pressures are high during the identity-versus-role-confusion stage. For example, many adolescents face repeated questioning by parents and friends regarding whether their post–high school plans include work or college and, if they choose work, which occupational track they plan to follow. Prior to adolescence, students' educational lives have been pretty much programmed by U.S. society, which lays out a universal educational track.

However, during adolescence, the universal track ends. Students must face decisions about whether they should follow a college or vocational track, sometimes choosing early in adolescence a series of courses that will make it either easier or more difficult to attend college. Consequently, adolescents face difficult choices about which of several possible future paths they will follow (Kidwell et al., 1995).

During this period, adolescents increasingly rely on their friends and peers as sources of information, as we'll discuss in greater detail in Chapter 7. At the same time, their dependence on adults declines. This increasing dependence on the peer group enables adolescents to forge close relationships. Comparing themselves to others helps them clarify their own identities.

This reliance on peers to help adolescents define their identities and learn to form relationships is the link between the identity-versus-role-confusion stage of psychosocial development and the next stage Erikson proposed, known as the *intimacy-versus-isolation stage.* It also relates to the question of the nature of gender differences in identity formation.

When Erikson developed his theory, he suggested that males and females move through the identity-versus-role-confusion period differently. He argued that males are more likely to

identity-versus-role-confusion stage according to Erikson the stage where adolescents seek to understand who they are by narrowing and making choices about their personal, occupational, sexual, and political commitments

▲ Erikson suggested that males tend to develop a stable identity prior to committing to an intimate relationship, whereas females followed an opposite sequence—ideas that reflected the social conditions of the time he was writing. Today, males and females follow similar patterns during the identity-versus-role-confusion stage.

proceed through the social development stages in the order they are shown in Table 5-2, developing a stable identity before committing to an intimate relationship with another person. In contrast, he suggested that females reverse the order, seeking intimate relationships and then defining their identities through these relationships. These ideas largely reflect the social conditions at the time he was writing, when women were less likely to go to college or establish their own careers and instead often married early. Today, however, the experiences of boys and girls seem relatively similar during the identity-versus-role-confusion period.

Psychological Moratorium.   Because of the pressures of the identity-versus-role-confusion period, Erikson suggested that many adolescents pursue a "psychological moratorium." The *psychological moratorium* is a period during which adolescents take time off from the upcoming responsibilities of adulthood and explore various roles and possibilities. For example, many college students take a semester or year off to travel, work, or find some other way to examine their priorities.

On the other hand, many adolescents cannot, for practical reasons, pursue a psychological moratorium involving a relatively leisurely exploration of various identities. Some adolescents, for economic reasons, must work part time after school and then take jobs immediately after graduation from high school. As a result, they have little time to experiment with identities and engage in a psychological moratorium. Does this mean such adolescents will be psychologically damaged in some way? Probably not. In fact, the satisfaction that can come from successfully holding a part-time job while attending school may be a sufficient psychological reward to outweigh the inability to try out various roles.

Limitations of Erikson's Theory.   One criticism that has been raised regarding Erikson's theory is that he used male identity development as the standard against which to compare female identity. In particular, he saw males as developing intimacy only after achieving a stable identity, which is viewed as the normative pattern. To critics, Erikson's view is based on male-oriented concepts of individuality and competitiveness. In an alternative conception, psychologist Carol Gilligan has suggested that women develop identity through the establishment of relationships. In this view, a key component of a woman's identity is the building of caring networks between herself and others (Gilligan, Brown, & Rogers, 1990; Gilligan, 2004).

Marcia's Approach to Identity Development: Updating Erikson

Using Erikson's theory as a springboard, psychologist James Marcia suggests that identity can be seen in terms of which of two characteristics—crisis or commitment—is present or absent. *Crisis* is a period of identity development in which an adolescent consciously chooses between various alternatives and makes decisions. *Commitment* is psychological investment in a course of action or an ideology. We can see the difference by comparing an adolescent who careens from one activity to another, with no interest lasting more than a few weeks, with an adolescent who becomes totally absorbed in volunteer work at a homeless shelter (Marcia, 1980; Peterson, Marcia, & Carpendale, 2004).

After conducting lengthy interviews with adolescents, Marcia proposed four categories of adolescent identity (see Table 5-3).

1. *Identity achievement.*   Teenagers in this identity status have successfully explored and thought through who they are and what they want to do. Following a period of crisis during which they considered various alternatives, these adolescents have committed to a

---

TABLE 5-3 Marcia's Four Categories of Adolescent Identity Development

The four categories in Marcia's theory of adolescent development are illustrated in this table, along with sample responses to the question, "Have you ever had any doubts about your religious beliefs?"

		Commitment	
		Present	Absent
Exploration	**Present**	Identity achievement ("I've had plenty of doubts in the past, but for the most part I've resolved them.")	Moratorium ("I'm in a phase right now where I'm trying to figure it out. I just don't know where I stand.")
	Absent	Identify foreclosure ("I've known where I stand for as long as I can re-member.")	Identity diffusion ("Sometimes I have doubts, and sometimes I'm pretty sure of where I stand. I guess I can't make up my mind.")

(*Source:* Marcia, 1980.)

---

particular identity. Teens who have reached this identity status tend to be the most psychologically healthy, higher in achievement motivation and moral reasoning than adolescents of any other status.

2. *Identity foreclosure.* These are adolescents who have committed to an identity, but who did not do it by passing through a period of crisis in which they explored alternatives. Instead, they accepted others' decisions about what was best for them. Typical adolescents in this category are a son who enters the family business because it is expected of him and a daughter who decides to become a physician simply because her mother is one. Although foreclosers are not necessarily unhappy, they tend to have what can be called "rigid strength": Happy and self-satisfied, they also have a high need for social approval and tend to be authoritarian.

3. *Moratorium.* Although adolescents in the moratorium category have explored various alternatives to some degree, they have not yet committed themselves. As a consequence, Marcia suggested, they show relatively high anxiety and experience psychological conflict. On the other hand, they are often lively and appealing, seeking intimacy with others. Adolescents of this status typically settle on an identity, but only after something of a struggle.

4. *Identity diffusion.* Adolescents in this category neither explore nor commit to a consideration of various alternatives. They tend to be flighty, shifting from one thing to the next. Although they may seem carefree, according to Marcia, their lack of commitment impairs their ability to form close relationships. In fact, they are often socially withdrawn.

It is important to note that adolescents are not necessarily stuck in one of the four categories. In fact, some move back and forth between moratorium and identity achievement in what has been called a "MAMA" cycle (**m**oratorium—identity **a**chievement—**m**oratorium—identity **a**chievement). For instance, even though a forecloser may have settled on a career path during early adolescence with little active decision making, he or she may reassess the choice later and move into another category. For some individuals, then, identity formation may take place beyond the period of adolescence. However, identity gels in the late teens and early twenties for most people (Kroger, 2000; Meeus, 1996, 2003).

Identity, Race, and Ethnicity

[I] was one of "a few" in the honor/advanced placement track in high school and white kids frequently couldn't remember my name . . . or called me Mario, the name of the other black kid in my classes . . .

Although the path to forming an identity is often difficult for adolescents, it presents a particular challenge for members of racial and ethnic groups that have traditionally been discriminated against. Society's contradictory values are one part of the problem. On the one hand, adolescents are told that society should be color-blind, that race and ethnic background should not matter in terms of opportunities and achievement, and that if they do achieve, society will accept them. Based on a traditional *cultural assimilation model,* this view holds that individual cultural identities should be assimilated into a unified U.S. culture—this is the proverbial "melting pot" model.

On the other hand, the *pluralistic society model* suggests that U.S. society is made up of diverse, coequal cultural groups that should preserve their individual cultural features. The pluralistic society model grew in part from the belief that the cultural assimilation model denigrates the cultural heritage of minorities and lowers their self-esteem. According to this view, then, racial and ethnic factors become a central part of adolescents' identity and are not submerged in an attempt to assimilate into the majority culture.

There is a middle ground. Minority group members can form a *bicultural identity* in which they draw from their own cultural identity while integrating themselves into the dominant culture. This view suggests that an individual can live as a member of two cultures, with two cultural identities, without having to choose one over the other (Garcia, 1988; LaFromboise, Coleman, & Gerton, 1993). The choice of a bicultural identity is increasingly common. In fact, the number of individuals who think of themselves as belonging to more than one race is considerable, according to data from the 2000 U.S. census (see Figure 5-2; Schmitt, 2001).

► Forming an identity can be particularly challenging for members of minority groups.

The process of identity formation is not simple for anyone and may be doubly difficult for minority group members, as we'll consider in detail when we consider ethnic identity in detail in Chapter 12. Racial and ethnic identity takes time to form, and for some individuals it may occur over a prolonged period. Still, the ultimate result can be the formation of a rich, multifaceted identity (Roberts et al., 1999; Grantham & Ford, 2003; Nadal, 2004; Umaña-Taylor & Fine, 2004).

The Self in a Cultural Context: Squeaky Wheel or Pounded Nail?

In Western cultures, the "squeaky wheel gets the grease." In Asian cultures, "the nail that stands out gets pounded down."

These two maxims represent quite different views of the world held by adolescents and their parents. The Western saying suggests that to get the attention one deserves, it is best to be special and different and to make one's concerns known to others. The Asian perspective is quite the opposite, suggesting that one ought to try to blend in with others in society and refrain from making waves or being noticed.

The two maxims, and the reasoning that lies behind them, illustrate profound cultural differences in the view of the self. By the time they reach adolescence, people in most Asian societies have an interdependent view of themselves. They see themselves as part of a larger social network in which they work with others to maintain social harmony. Individuals in such societies strive to behave in accordance with the ways that others think, feel, and behave.

These beliefs are typical of collectivistic cultures. *Collectivism* is the notion that the well-being of the group is more important than that of the individual. People in collectivistic cultures emphasize the welfare of the groups to which they belong, sometimes at the expense of their own personal well-being.

Adolescents living in many Western countries, in contrast, have an independent perspective on the self. They tend to see themselves as self-contained and autonomous, competing with others to better their own lot in life. Individuals in independent societies strive to behave in ways that express their uniqueness. They consider that their behavior is brought about by their own special configuration of personal characteristics (see Figure 5-3).

These Western beliefs are characteristic of individualistic cultures. Societies reflecting *individualism* hold that the personal identity, uniqueness, freedom, and worth of the individual person are central. People in individualistic societies emphasize that their own goals should hold greater weight than the goals of the groups to which they belong.

This difference between collectivistic Asian views and individualistic Western views of the self has several consequences. For instance, college students in India see themselves as more similar

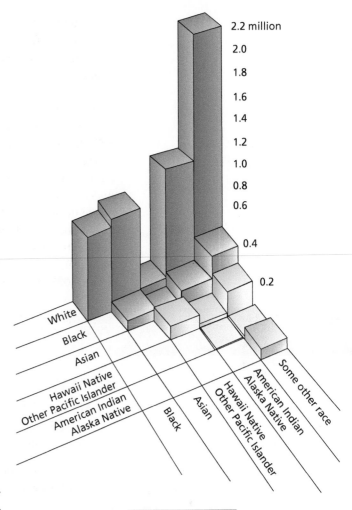

▲ **FIGURE 5-2**

Multiracial Rising Almost 7 million people indicated they were multiracial on the 2000 Census.

(*Source:* U.S. Census Bureau, 2000.)

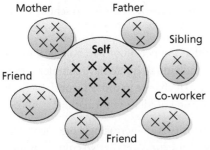

Independent View of Self

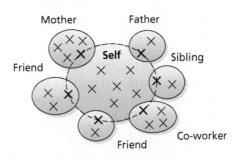

Interdependent View of Self

◄ **FIGURE 5-3**

Cultural Representation of the Self Western adolescents view themselves as being independent, self-contained, and autonomous. In contrast, Asian adolescents see themselves as interdependent, related to a large social network with others.

(*Source:* Markus & Kitayama, 1991, p. 227.)

to one another than do American college students. While American students emphasize qualities that they feel differentiate themselves from others, Indian students emphasize qualities that they share with others.

Similarly, people living in individualistic cultures see achievement in terms of personal gains, viewing themselves as better or worse achievers than others. They compare their salaries and their grades with those of their peers, and they seek and receive individual rewards for good performance. The self-concepts of people in independent cultures, then, are based on personal, individual successes and failures.

The perspective of those in collectivistic cultures is different. In these cultures, people are rewarded on the basis of their contributions to group achievement. For example, a high school student who works part time pumping gas might be evaluated more in terms of her contribution to the gas station's overall profits, rather than her own individual contribution. If the gas station does well, all employees receive benefits; if it does not do well, everyone suffers. It is as if students in a class received grades based not just on their own performance but also on the performance of their classmates, as a whole, on the final exam (Fiske et al., 1998; Hoppe-Graffe & Kim, 2005; Yamaguchi et al., 2005).

Review and Apply

Review

1. Adolescence brings changes in self-concept, including the ability to differentiate others' views of oneself from one's own views, to see different aspects of the self simultaneously, and to explore possible selves that may be adopted in the future.

2. In developing an understanding of their identity, adolescents make social comparisons with others, typically measuring themselves against others who are similar to them.

3. Erik Erikson's psychodynamic view of development assigns adolescents primarily to the identity-versus-role-confusion stage. Those who manage this conflict are free to move on to the intimacy-versus-isolation stage.

4. Erikson's theory has been criticized for focusing excessively on male developmental patterns and for being limited by the times in which it was developed. Carol Gilligan and James Marcia have both provided updated views.

5. Cultural factors complicate the development of identity by adding cultural identity to the dimensions that must be addressed. Adolescents from collectivistic cultures regard identity issues differently than those from individualistic cultures.

Apply

1. Is the trying on of different selves unique to adolescence? How is it different from "reinventing oneself" in later life by adopting a different career, returning to school, or exploring some other new path?

2. Do you believe that there is an optimal time that the period of psychological moratorium should last, and at what point do you think an individual should have completed the process of identity formation? Why? Has the rapid pace of change in today's world, fueled by technological advances, had implications for the timing of identity formation?

3. Why do you think that adopting a bicultural identity is an increasingly prevalent strategy for persons of nonmajority backgrounds? Which of the individual's two cultures is more likely to accept the bicultural identity?

Self-Esteem: Evaluating the Self

*W*hat's failure? *The answer would be me. I AM a failure. A pathetic looking one. Lost in her own world, dark and cold, not knowing what kind of life she will lead next time. Always plan what to do, but seldom act on it. This is what you call a failure. Me! Me! Me! . . . Being a teenager is really hard. People always say that the best moment in your life is when you're a teenager. How can a teenage life be fun and interesting if it's so miserable for me?—17-year-old girl*

Like the adolescent who wrote the sad blog entry above, most of us don't view ourselves in dispassionate, neutral terms. Instead, we evaluate ourselves in terms of positive or—like this blogger—negative dimensions. If we're students, we don't only see ourselves as a student, but as a good, bad, or indifferent one.

When it comes to the self, adolescents are not neutral, unbiased observers. Instead, they evaluate the self, considering it in terms of positive and negative dimensions. Moreover, they try to protect their view of self, reacting to threats by attempting to change either the situation or the way in which they view it. As we will see, these self-protective efforts sometimes color both their behavior and the way that they view the world.

Self-Esteem: Rating the Self

Self-esteem is the affective component of self, an individual's general and specific positive and negative self-evaluations. In contrast to self-concept, which reflects an adolescent's beliefs and cognitions regarding his or her self, self-esteem is more emotionally oriented (Baumeister, 1993, 1998; see Table 5-4).

Just as the self is composed of multiple self-schemas, self-esteem is not one dimensional. Instead, adolescents view particular parts of the self in more positive or less positive ways. For instance, a teenager may hold his academic self-schemas in high regard but consider his weight and body-type self-schema negatively (Marsh, 1986; Pelham & Swann, 1989; Moretti & Higgins, 1990; Baumeister, 1998).

Adolescents construct a mental hierarchy of which domains of self-esteem are most important to them. Overall, physical appearance may be the most important domain, particularly for girls. Academic abilities, athletic skill, and moral behavior tend to be less important. Some gender differences also determine which domains are most important to overall self-esteem. As

---

TABLE 5-4 Self-Esteem Scale
Indicate whether each item is true (T) or false (F) for you.
_____1. I feel that I have a number of good qualities.
_____2. I feel I do not have much to be proud of.
_____3. At times I think I am no good at all.
_____4. I feel I am a person of worth, at least on an equal basis with others.
_____5. All in all, I feel that I am a failure.
_____6. On the whole, I am satisfied with myself.
If you answered "true" on items 1, 4, and 6, you scored high on self-esteem. If you answered: "true" to items 2, 3, and 5, you scored low on self-esteem.
Source: Adapted from M. Rosenberg, Society and the adolescent self-image. Copyright © 1965 by Prin University Press. © renewed.

self-esteem the affective component of self, an individual's general and specific positive and negative self-evaluations

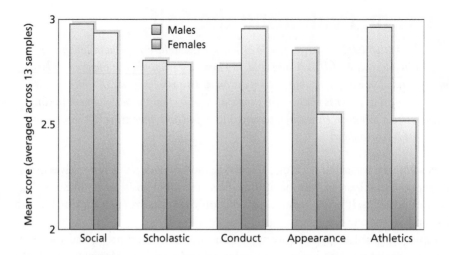

▶ **FIGURE 5-4**

Importance of Domains of Self-Esteem
Adolescent males tend to be more concerned than adolescent females about athletics, while females tend to view conduct as more important. When it comes to social activities, males and females express similar levels of concern.

(*Source:* Harter, 1999.)

you can see in Figure 5-4, males are considerably more concerned about success in the athletic domain than females, whereas females place greater emphasis on conduct (Harter, 1999).

The constituents of self-esteem vary according to cultural factors. For example, having high *relationship harmony*—a sense of success in forming strong bonds with others—is more important to self-esteem in collectivistic Asian cultures than in more individualistic Western societies (Kwan, Bond, & Singelis, 1997).

The complexities of self-esteem have made it challenging to measure. According to psychologist Susan Harter, who devised a widely used self-esteem questionnaire called the Self-Perception Profile for Adolescents, it is insufficient to solely obtain a global measure of self-worth. Arguing that self-esteem is a consequence of competence in the particular domains that are personally important to adolescents and which earns them approval of others who are significant to them, she believes that self-esteem should be measured in terms of separate domains (Harter, 2001; Harter & Whitesell, 2003).

Consequently, her questionnaire measuring adolescent self-esteem assesses self-esteem in eight key areas: scholastic competence, athletic competence, social acceptance, physical appearance, behavioral conduct, close friendship, romantic appeal, and job competence. Furthermore, because different aspects of self-esteem unfold across different parts of the life span, Harter has devised separate questionnaires for preadolescents, working adults, and the elderly, as well as adolescence (Harter, Whitesell, & Junkin, 1998; Harter, 2006).

The Consequences of Self-Esteem

Although everyone occasionally goes through periods of low self-esteem, such as after an undeniable failure, some adolescents are chronically low in self-esteem. For them, life can be painful. For instance, those adolescents with low self-esteem respond more negatively to failure than those with high self-esteem, in part because those with low self-esteem focus on their shortcomings after experiencing failure.

In contrast, adolescents with high self-esteem focus on their strengths following failure. In short, the consequences of chronic low self-esteem can be profound, including physical illness, psychological disturbance, and a general inability to cope with stress. In addition, low self-esteem is related to higher levels of aggression, antisocial behavior, and delinquency in adolescence (Baumeister, 1993; Dodgson & Wood, 1998; Donnellan et al., 2005).

One reason that low self-esteem is damaging is that it can become part of a cycle of failure that is difficult to break—a kind of self-fulfilling prophecy in which adolescents act in a way that is consistent with their expectations and beliefs and thereby increase the likelihood that the event or behavior will occur. For example, consider middle school students with low self-esteem who are facing an upcoming test. As a result of their low self-esteem, they expect to do poorly. In turn, this expectation produces high anxiety and may lead them to reduce the amount of effort they apply to studying. After all, why should people who expect to do badly bother to work very hard? Ultimately, of course, the high anxiety and lack of effort produce just what was expected—failure on the test. Unfortunately, as seen in Figure 5-5, the failure simply reinforces the low self-esteem, and the cycle continues.

On the other hand, high self-esteem produces the reverse effect. Adolescents with high self-esteem hold more positive expectations about their future performance. This reduces their anxiety and leads them to study more effectively. Subsequently, their lower anxiety and more effective studying lead to higher performance. Ultimately, their success reinforces their higher self-esteem—causing the cycle to persist.

Clearly, positive self-esteem is associated with desirable consequences, and lower self-esteem is related to negative results. However, this doesn't mean that we should seek to boost the self-esteem of adolescents at any cost. For example, although higher self-esteem is associated with positive outcomes such as academic achievement, the relationship between the two

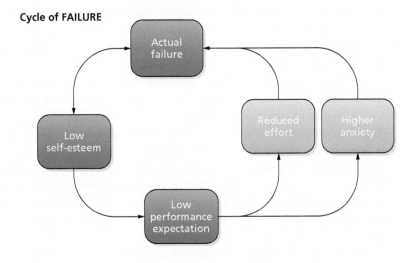

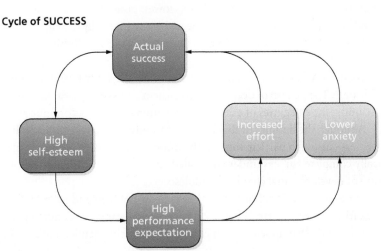

◄ **FIGURE5-5**

Cycles of Self-Esteem Middle school students who are low in self-esteem may expect to do poorly on a test. This expectation produces high anxiety and may lead them to reduce the amount of effort they apply to studying because they expect to do poorly anyway. Ultimately, of course, the high anxiety and lack of effort produce just what was expected—failure on the test. In contrast, those with high self-esteem hold more positive expectations about their future performance, thereby reducing their anxiety and leading them to study more effectively. Subsequently, their lower anxiety and more effective studying lead to higher performance. In the end, their success reinforces their higher self-esteem.

factors is merely correlational. The association simply means that people with higher self-esteem are more likely to have better academic performance, and those with lower self-esteem are more likely to have poorer academic performance.

However, there are several possible explanations for the relationship between self-esteem and academic performance. First, it may in fact mean that higher self-esteem causes better academic performance. On the other hand, it may be the reverse, that doing well academically causes higher self-esteem. Or, finally, there may be some third factor (intelligence seems like a reasonable possibility) that produces both higher self-esteem and better academic performance (Crocker & Knight, 2005).

In short, high self-esteem does not necessarily lead to positive outcomes. In fact, as we will discuss in the accompanying *Transitions* box, it may well be that high self-esteem can have a significant downside.

Changes in Self-Esteem During Adolescence

Adolescent self-esteem shows clear variations over time. Some of this change is due to specific experiences and can occur fairly rapidly. Depending on the situation, adolescents sometimes feel quite good about themselves, and other times quite bad, with the result that self-esteem can rise and fall over relatively short periods. Students may feel better about themselves after learning they did particularly well on a test and worse after learning they failed.

Generally, adolescents' evaluation of themselves is particularly unstable during the early part of adolescence. During later parts of adolescence, self-esteem becomes less volatile. Adolescents seem to have an increasingly clear picture of themselves as they become older, leading to stability in their self-evaluations. They also become less susceptible to specific experiences and situations. It's as if their evaluation of themselves becomes firmer and their view of themselves grows more influential in determining their reactions (Heatherton & Polivy, 1991; Alasker & Olweus, 1992; Trzesniewski, Donnellan, & Robins, 2003).

Although it is clear that the stability of adolescent self-esteem increases throughout the period of adolescence, this only means that day-to-day changes become less pronounced. What it doesn't tell us is whether the specific nature of self-esteem changes over the course of time.

The question of how self-concept changes during adolescence has proven difficult to answer. Some studies have shown increases in self-esteem across adolescence, whereas some have shown the opposite. The inconsistency of results has made it a challenge to form generalizations.

However, a recent research study provides a clearer picture. The study was conducted using the Web and included over 300,000 participants. Keeping in mind that researchers have little control over who volunteers to complete a survey over the Web—and thus the sample may not be representative of the population at large—we can observe a number of broad trends in the results. Specifically, self-esteem is relatively high during the years preceding adolescence, but drops sharply during adolescence. It reaches its lowest point during late adolescence and young adulthood (18–22). However, self-esteem begins to rise gradually throughout adulthood until old age, when it declines significantly (see Figure 5-6 on page 160; Robins et al., 2002; Robins & Trzesniewski, 2005).

Focusing specifically on the adolescent years, the study found that self-esteem declined significantly. The pattern of decline was consistent across every demographic category in the study, including the categories of ethnic group, nationality, socioeconomic status, and gender.

Although the findings of this Web-based study seem clear, more traditional, non-Web-based studies—in which participants may be more representative of the population at large and typically complete surveys under controlled conditions—continue to paint a more complex picture of developmental changes in adolescence.

For example, according to researchers Scott Baldwin and John Hoffman (2002), who used data from the Family Health Study, a large, seven-year study conducted in a metropolitan area, found that changes in self-esteem reflected adolescents' gender and specific events in their lives.

Transiti⬤ns

The Downside of High Self-Esteem

According to many, low self-esteem lies at the heart of a variety of social ills, ranging from teenage pregnancy to gang violence to drug abuse. For example, government officials in California set up a task force to encourage self-esteem, arguing that increased self-esteem might raise the general psychological health of the population and even help the state balance its budget.

But not everyone agrees with this view. According to psychologist Roy Baumeister and colleagues, if high self-esteem is unjustified by actual accomplishment, it can actually be psychologically damaging. In fact, unwarranted high self-esteem can lead to a variety of social problems, including violence (Baumeister et al., 2003; Baumeister et al., 2005).

Consider, for example, adolescents who have high, but unjustified, self-esteem—a personality type called *narcissism*. When their unwarranted positive view of themselves is disputed, they may view the challenge as so threatening that they lash out at others, behaving in a violent manner. Consequently, efforts to reduce the violence of bullies (who are typically viewed as low in self-esteem) by raising their self-esteem may backfire, unless there are actual accomplishments to accompany their raised self-esteem (Baumeister, Bushman, & Campbell, 2000).

Similarly, efforts to boost the self-esteem of students who are facing academic difficulties to improve their performance may provoke the opposite result. For example, in one study, students who were receiving Ds and Fs in one class were divided into two groups. One group received the message that good grades were caused by a lack of confidence and low self-esteem. The other group received a different message; they were told that it was hard work that produced good grades. At the end of the semester, the group that received the self-esteem message ended up with significantly lower grades than the group that received the hard work message (Forsyth & Kerr, 1999).

Of course, such findings don't mean that high self-esteem is a bad thing. In fact, people with high self-esteem are significantly happier than those with low self-esteem, and they are less likely to be depressed. Still, the research has relevance to programs that seek to raise self-esteem in everyone. Feel-good messages ("We're all special"

▲ Having unwarranted high self-esteem can leave adolescents vulnerable when they experience failure.

and "We applaud ourselves") may be off base, leading adolescents to develop unwarranted self-esteem. Instead, schools and parents should help adolescents *earn* high self-esteem through actual accomplishments (Begley, 1998; Crocker & Park, 2004).

- Under what circumstances should a school or a society seek to raise the academic self-esteem of adolescents? Is the situation different if the adolescents have high self-esteem in other areas, such as athletics or artistic accomplishments?

- How would you go about designing a program to address the self-esteem issues of adolescents?

Specifically, female self-esteem decreased substantially from age 12 to age 17. In comparison, male self-esteem increased until age 13, decreased until age 16, and then increased as the males moved into early adulthood. Furthermore, females were more sensitive to stressful life events, reacting to them with greater reductions in self-esteem.

Why this gender difference? It may have to do with the specific experiences of the two genders. For instance, the decline in male self-esteem at age 14 may be related to their transition from middle school to high school, where they face a sudden fall in their social status. The decline in females' self-esteem, which occurs earlier, may be due to the start of puberty, when females may be dissatisfied with the changes in their body image.

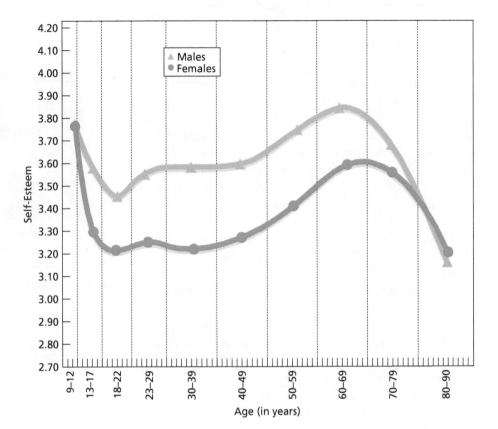

Drop of Self-Esteem During Adolescence
A recent study involving more than 300,000 participants using the Web has found that although self-esteem was relatively high during the years before adolescence showed a sharp decline during adolescence. However, self-esteem begins to climb throughout adulthood until declines occur again in old age.

(*Source:* Adapted from Robins et al., 2002, Figure 1, pg. 428.)

Gender and Self-Esteem. The Family Health Study findings present a consistent conclusion: During adolescence, the self-esteem of males is generally higher than that of females. In fact, this difference is fairly consistent across the life span, although it narrows after adolescence (see Figure 5-6) (Watkins, Dong, & Xia, 1997; Byrne, 2000; Miyamoto et al., 2000; Birndorf et al., 2005).

One reason is that, compared to adolescent boys, adolescent girls tend to be more concerned about physical appearance and social success—in addition to academic achievement. Although boys are also concerned about these things, their attitudes are often more casual. In addition, societal messages suggesting that female academic achievement is a roadblock to social success can put girls in a difficult bind: If they do well academically, they jeopardize their social success. No wonder the self-esteem of adolescent girls is more fragile than that of boys (Unger, 2001; Ricciardelli & McCabe, 2003).

Although generally self-esteem is higher in adolescent boys than girls, boys do have vulnerabilities of their own. For example, society's stereotypical gender expectations may lead boys to

feel that they should be confident, tough, and fearless all the time. Boys facing difficulties, such as not making a sports team or being rejected by a girl they wanted to date, are likely to feel not only miserable about the defeat they face, but also incompetent because they don't measure up to the stereotype (Pollack, 1999; Pollack, Shuster, & Trelease, 2001).

Socioeconomic Status and Race Differences in Self-Esteem.   Socioeconomic status (SES) and race also influence self-esteem. Adolescents of higher SES generally have higher self-esteem than those of lower SES, particularly during middle and later adolescence. It may be that the social status factors that especially enhance one's standing and self-esteem—such as having more expensive clothes or a car—become more conspicuous in the later periods of adolescence (Savin-Williams & Demo, 1983; Van Tassel-Baska et al., 1994).

Race and ethnicity also play a role in self-esteem, but their impact has lessened as prejudicial treatment of minorities has eased. Early studies argued that minority status would lead to lower self-esteem, and this idea was initially supported by research. African Americans and Hispanics, researchers explained, had lower self-esteem than Caucasians because prejudicial attitudes in society made them feel disliked and rejected, and this feeling was incorporated into their self-concepts.

More recent research paints a different picture. Most findings suggest either that African American adolescents differ little from whites in their levels of self-esteem or actually have higher levels than white adolescents (Harter, 1990b; Twenge & Crocker, 2002). Why should this be?

One explanation is that social movements within the African American community that bolster racial pride help support African American adolescents. In fact, research finds that a stronger sense of racial identity is related to a higher level of self-esteem in African Americans and Hispanics (Phinney, Lochner, & Murphy, 1990; Gray-Little & Hafdahl, 2000; Verkuyten, 2003).

Another reason for the higher levels of self-esteem in African Americans is that teenagers in general focus their preferences and priorities on those aspects of their lives at which they excel. Consequently, African American adolescents may concentrate on the domains that they find most satisfying and gain self-esteem from being successful at them (Gray-Little & Hafdahl, 2000; Yang & Blodgett, 2000; Phinney, 2005).

Finally, African American adolescents may experience a sense of solidarity by being members of an outgroup in U.S. society that is often the target of prejudice. Living in a world in which discrimination is commonplace may make African American adolescents feel particularly united with others who experience the same negative incidents (Birndof et al., 2005).

Although African Americans outscore whites on self-esteem, the same is not true for members of other ethnic and racial groups. In fact, both African Americans and whites have higher self-esteem than Hispanic American, Asian American, or Native American adolescents (Twenge & Crocker, 2002).

Ultimately, self-esteem may be influenced not by race alone, but by a complex combination of factors. For instance, some developmentalists have considered race and gender simultaneously, coining the term *ethgender* to refer to the joint influence of race and gender. One study that took both race and gender into account simultaneously found that African-American and Hispanic males had the highest levels of self-esteem, whereas Asian and Native American females had the lowest levels (Dukes & Martinez, 1994; King, 2003; Romero & Roberts, 2003; Saunders, Davis, & Williams, 2004).

Contingent Self-Worth: The Costs of the Pursuit of Self-Esteem

We've seen that understanding self-esteem in adolescence is not simple. Some studies show that self-esteem falls during the period, whereas others find that it's fairly stable. Other research shows significant differences between adolescent boys and girls, but other work shows only small discrepancies.

contingent self-worth   a concept that is composed of beliefs that one has value and worth that are related to accomplishments in specific, important domains

According to psychologists Jennifer Crocker and Katherine Knight, one explanation for the inconsistent findings is that self-esteem is actually of less importance than what they call contingent self-worth. **Contingent self-worth** is composed of beliefs that one has value and worth that are related to accomplishments in specific, important domains.

Unlike global self-esteem, which is a general measure of self-evaluation, contingent self-worth is built on what an adolescent believes he or she must do to be successful. Contingent self-worth may be related to performance in academic, athletic, artistic, or other specific domains (Harter, 1999; Crocker & Knight, 2005).

To understand how contingent self-worth operates, let's consider adolescents whose contingent self-worth revolves around their academic accomplishments. For such students, doing well on school tasks is viewed as a demonstration of their intelligence. Because doing poorly on an academic task may threaten their underlying self-esteem, they will be particularly motivated to do well—a positive result of contingent self-worth. On the other hand, if the task is unusually difficult and they sense they are likely to fail at it, they may give up prematurely and make up excuses in an effort to make the task less threatening to their self-esteem ("This set of math problems is impossible; no one could do well on it, so I'm not even going to try").

In short, pursuing self-esteem that is tied to contingent self-worth has a number of potential costs. In particular, it can produce these consequences (Crocker & Knight, 2005):

- *Costs to learning.* When students are motivated to perform well not because of the intrinsic pleasure of learning but because doing well increases their self-esteem, they may seek success at all costs or may choose to disengage from particular academic tasks, depending on how difficult they seem to be.

- *Costs to relationships.* People who use relationship success as a source of self-esteem may focus more on their own needs than those of their relationship partner, making them less than supportive.

- *Costs to mental and physical health.* People who view their self-worth in terms of performance in a particular area are likely to experience ups and downs in self-esteem. The stress of constantly having to prove themselves is bound to affect their physical and mental well-being.

Clearly, the effort to increase one's self-esteem has a number of potential costs. At the same time, we know that low self-esteem is associated with a variety of consequences. Is it possible to help adolescents increase their self-esteem in a way that improves their overall well-being and avoids the costs associated with the pursuit of self-esteem? A number of adolescent specialists have tried. As we consider next, they have devised several promising strategies to raise self-esteem.

Strategies for Raising Self-Esteem: Where Feeling Good Is *Not* the Goal

Although we've seen that having high self-esteem does not always result in positive outcomes for adolescents, it is clear that in most cases holding a realistic positive view of oneself is associated with desirable consequences. Certainly, adolescents who see themselves as valuable, worthy members of society are in a better position to withstand the challenges of the period than those who view themselves in a negative light. And those with low self-esteem—like the adolescent who wrote the passage at the beginning of this part of the chapter and who views herself as a failure—would benefit from a more positive view of themselves.

The question becomes, then, how to raise self-esteem most effectively. Clearly, it's a poor strategy to shower adolescents with unconditional praise that is unrelated to their conduct. Telling adolescents to feel good about themselves brings little benefit except to produce an inflated view of oneself (Harter, 1990a, 1998).

Instead, more effective strategies involve providing opportunities for gaining expertise and mastery in a variety of domains. By offering adolescents a range of experiences in which they

CAREER CHOICES

Recreational Program Worker

Name: Theresa Ryan

Position: Youth Service Center Coordinator, Doss High School, Louisville, Kentucky

Education: BS, Business Administration, University of Louisville; MS, Education, Guidance Counseling, University of Louisville

SELF-ESTEEM IS an important issue in the lives of adolescents, especially at a time when they are learning new skills and ways of interacting with their peers and others.

At Doss High School, the Youth Service Center works primarily with students in the 9th and 10th grades and provides them with services ranging from educational to recreational, according to director Theresa Ryan.

"We have what is basically a mentoring program for young women called *Teen Youth Program of Encouragement,* or *TYPE,*" said Ryan. "Several social workers from a local social services organization coordinate the meetings."

"In addition, we schedule professional women or specialists in various areas who will come in to lead a group with the students," she added. "At the end of the program, they serve with a local service agency. For example, the last group worked with the Salvation Army."

Among the topics chosen by the young women are careers, grooming, dating and domestic violence, and sexuality, according to Ryan. In addition, the program places emphasis on self-improvement.

Results so far have been good, according to Ryan.

"There are a number of young women who went through the program who now serve on my advisory council," she noted, "and in some cases serve as peer mediators. I've found that most students really like being part of peer mediation. It's a skill they can use on a daily basis and provides opportunities for leadership and building self-esteem."

Ryan is enthusiastic about a new program that just started for young men in grades 9 and 10 called Empowering Young Men with Skills for Success.

"With this program we work with young men on improving interpersonal social skills, getting along with people, and conflict resolution," she said. "We look for those young men who have difficulty connecting with others or who are isolated. Some may have problems with disrupting classes.

"We start with an experiential activity, something that is hands-on in which everyone has to engage," Ryan said, "and we encourage teamwork. Because the teams are small everyone has a chance to be heard."

Thinking of working in the recreational program field?

Recreational program workers assist in the operation of a variety of leisure and recreational facilities, such as parks, camps, community centers, and tourist attractions. They facilitate recreational activities at all stages, from initial planning and organization to directing activity participants. Depending on the setting, recreation workers may provide instruction and coaching in sports, aquatics, arts and crafts, music and dance, camping, and other leisure pursuits. Recreation directors supervise recreation workers and develop entire recreation programs.

Some recreation workers—such as summer camp counselors—have little formal preparation beyond a passion for outdoor leisure and experience in one or more activities, such as dance or team sports. Most career recreation workers have a bachelor's degree, often with a major in parks and recreation or leisure studies. ◼

---

can develop competence, they can come to view themselves as "experts" in particular areas. This expertise can be attained in a variety of settings, such as participating in recreational programs designed to teach new skills (see, also, the Career Choices box).

Ultimately, the goal is to develop *self-efficacy,* which is the learned expectation that one is capable of carrying out a behavior or producing a desired outcome in a particular situation. Adolescents who are high in self-efficacy tend to exert greater effort and show greater persistence when faced with challenging tasks—thereby increasing their likelihood of success and positive emotions (DuBois et al., 2003).

Positive self-esteem is also enhanced when adolescents are given the freedom to make choices between various alternatives. Although they may not succeed in every domain in which they choose to participate, the very act of making a choice can be of benefit. The important point is that they become engaged in activities in which feel they have the opportunity to make contributions to their communities and society, as well as to enhance the quality of their own lives (Brooks, 1994).

Another approach to raising self-esteem is to provide therapy and counseling to adolescents who suffer from unusually negative views of themselves. Like most therapeutic interventions, little definitive evidence exists to show that therapy is generally effective. Still, there are many reports of success using a variety of therapies (Rosselló & Bernal, 1999; Hall & Torres, 2002; Shirk, Burwell, & Harter, 2003).

Finally, educators have developed a variety of school-based programs that seek to raise self-esteem. They fall into two broad categories: socioemotional programs and skill-based programs. In socioemotional programs, the focus is on directly raising self-esteem by making adolescents feel good about themselves. Participants are praised for their accomplishments, and efforts are made to teach them to evaluate their accomplishments, whatever they may be, in a way that is more positive (Hamilton & Oswalt, 1998; Field, 2003).

In contrast, skill-based programs seek to provide specific skills to be successful in areas that adolescents identify as important to themselves. The idea is to increase the likelihood that adolescents will be successful in meaningful domains. In turn, it is hoped that this success will lead to a subsequent rise in self-esteem (Harter, 1999).

Of the two sorts of programs meant to raise self-esteem, socioemotional programs have been less successful. That's not surprising. As we've noted, simply telling individuals that they are good people may have little impact, especially on those whose self-esteem is so low that they see everything through a negative lens. Furthermore, as we discussed earlier, self-esteem that is unjustified by objective accomplishments may actually be detrimental in the long run.

On the other hand, skill-based programs, which seek to teach specific competencies, are more likely to succeed. Yet even these programs are not entirely successful. For instance, if the domains in which skills are being taught are not those that are important to a particular adolescent, then the program may have little impact on self-esteem. It is only when there is a match between the skills being taught and what is important to the individual that success in raising self-esteem is likely.

In short, raising self-esteem through formal, school-based programs is a challenging task. In the long run, a more successful strategy may be to focus on the parents of adolescents. Parents who provide a warm, supportive environment for their children are more likely to raise adolescents who have a strong sense of self and high self-esteem.

The Benefits of Illusions: Is It Better to Be Wrong than Right?

Most of us would probably endorse the notion that one of the hallmarks of good mental health during adolescence is holding a clear, accurate view of oneself, and that distorted and inaccurate self-perceptions are a sign of disorder.

However, this may not be true. For instance, adolescents who suffer from depression and those with low self-esteem often see themselves clearly and accurately—warts and all. Their negative view of themselves—"I'm not very smart" or "I'm really unattractive" or "People don't really like me"—may, in fact, be quite accurate, so unfortunately accurate that the adolescent can't help feeling miserable (Taylor & Brown, 1994; Brown & Dutton, 1995).

In fact, the peril of having an accurate view of the world and of oneself seems so pronounced that certain types of inaccuracies about oneself and others may actually promote good mental health (Taylor & Brown, 1988; Aspinwall & Taylor, 1992). Specifically, three basic illusions are associated with better psychological functioning: holding unrealistically positive evaluations of oneself, having an exaggerated sense of control over occurrences in one's life, and being unrealistically optimistic. These positive illusions are related to happiness and contentment, productivity and creativity, and the ability to care about others.

Obviously there are limits to how far someone can twist reality, and sometimes it is clearly maladaptive to ignore objective threats and to assume that one can always exert control over any situation. In fact, holding overly positive illusions may well produce poor, biased decisions and inappropriate behavior based on erroneous assumptions. Consequently, the view that positive illusions are beneficial is quite controversial. Still, it's possible that holding some degree of illusion promotes good mental health (Colvin & Block, 1994; Colvin, Block, & Funder, 1995; Salovey et al., 1998).

Review and Apply

Review

1. Self-esteem, the emotional aspect of self-concept, varies over time during adolescence and according to gender, socioeconomic status, and cultural background.

2. Adolescents with low self-esteem can experience negative physical and psychological consequences and can be caught in a self-fulfilling cycle of low expectations and low performance, thereby reinforcing their low self-esteem.

3. High self-esteem usually, but not always, leads to positive outcomes. The downside appears when the self-esteem is unjustified by high achievement.

4. Contingent self-worth is essentially self-esteem that is tied to specific goals and values held by the individual. If self-esteem depends too closely on contingent self-worth, there can be negative consequences.

5. Efforts to raise self-esteem have met with uneven success. In general, efforts that focus on making adolescents feel good about themselves are less effective than programs that focus on developing self-efficacy.

Apply

1. What effects are traditional, academically focused school curricula likely to have on students' self-esteem? What sorts of school programs might improve feelings of self-esteem among the full range of students?

2. Why are "feel-good" programs designed to enhance self-esteem likely to be less effective among adolescents than among younger children?

Emotional Development

Sometimes I have to stop and ask myself what kind of mood I'm in. Am i happy? sad? contemplative? usually contemplative, if i'm bothering to contemplate what kind of mood I'm in. I'm kind of sad because Kyle can't come tonight. . . , but kind of worried because he's sick. I'm kind of depressed feeling, too. It finally started sinking in a while ago that he's not coming back, that he has finally dropped out of my life as I feared he would.

Happy . . . sad . . . contemplative . . . worried . . . depressed . . . feared. The feelings experienced by adolescents range from the positive to the negative, as this blog comment illustrates. In fact, a traditional view of the adolescent period is that it is among the most emotionally volatile of the entire life span.

How accurate is this view? To answer the question, we first need to consider the role that emotions play during adolescence. **Emotions** are feelings that have both physiological and cognitive elements and that influence behavior.

For example, consider an adolescent girl who is experiencing sadness. As the definition suggests, sadness produces a feeling that can be differentiated from other emotions. She likely experiences physiological reactions, too, such as an increase in heart rate or sweating, that are

emotions feelings that have both physiological and cognitive elements and that influence behavior

part of her emotional reaction. In addition, the sadness has a cognitive element, in which her understanding and evaluation of the meaning of what is happening to her prompt her feelings of sadness.

It's also possible, however, to experience an emotion without the presence of cognitive elements. For example, adolescents may feel the sadness of depression without knowing why they are feeling that way. In the same way, they may react with fear to an unusual or novel situation without having an awareness or understanding of what is so frightening.

The Nature and Functions of Emotions

Emotions serve several functions in the daily lives of adolescents (Averill, 1994; Scherer, 1994; Oatley & Jenkins, 1996). For one thing, they prepare them for action. They link events that occur in their lives and the responses to them. If, for example, an adolescent is suddenly confronted by a mugger, her emotional reaction of fear would be associated with physiological arousal that activates a "fight-or-flight" response. The arousal of the nervous system would help the girl evade the mugger.

Emotions also help adolescents prepare for the future, shaping upcoming behavior. For example, the emotional response that occurs when an adolescent has an unpleasant encounter—such as a fight with a girlfriend—may help him in the future to avoid similar circumstances or to improve the way he deals with the situation.

Finally, emotions help adolescents interact more effectively with other people in their lives. By displaying their emotions through their verbal and nonverbal behavior, adolescents are able to communicate what they are experiencing. These behaviors can act as a signal to others, permitting them to understand what the adolescent is experiencing and helping them to predict the behavior of the adolescent more accurately. Similarly, displays of emotions in others allows an adolescent to better understand what *they* are experiencing. In short, emotional displays allow better and more accurate communication.

The Instability of Emotions in Adolescence

Are adolescent emotions more volatile than at other stages of life? That's certainly the stereotype. Adolescence has traditionally been viewed as a period in which emotions run high and are easily triggered.

The stereotype does have some truth to it. Although not as extreme as the outmoded "storm and stress" view of adolescence would have us believe, emotions do tend to be more volatile during early adolescence. Younger adolescents experience emotional highs and lows, often in rapid succession. In addition, as they enter adolescence, teenagers report that they are less happy than in prior years. They are also more likely to experience mildly negative emotions as they move into adolescence (Larson & Lampman-Petraitis, 1989; Rosenbaum & Lewis, 2003; Ackerman & Izard, 2004).

Not only are the emotions more negative than they were in middle childhood, but in adolescents' emotional responses are also often more extreme than one would expect from the nature of the situation. For example, an adolescent may react with fury to a parent's suggestion that he might consider wearing a jacket to school because it is chilly. Even seemingly innocuous suggestions may be viewed as critical and reacted to with extremes of emotion.

If there is a positive side to the more explosive nature of adolescents' emotions, it is that even though they may be extreme, they don't necessary last very long. Partly because adolescents' moods change so frequently, any given emotional response is apt to be replaced by another before much time passes (Rosenbaum & Lewis, 2003).

Why are emotions so unstable during adolescence? One answer comes from work on the neurological underpinnings of emotion that we discuss next.

The Neurological Basis of Emotion.   Emotions produce activation of specific parts of the brain. For instance, the *amygdala,* in the brain's temporal lobe, is central to the experience of emotions. It provides a link between the perception of an emotion-producing stimulus and later memory of that stimulus. For example, someone who was once frightened by a vicious dog is likely to respond with fear when he later sees the dog. Because of neural pathways connecting the amygdala, visual cortex, and the *hippocampus* (a part of the brain that is involved in the storage of memories), the emotion of fear is experienced nearly instantly. The response occurs so quickly that rational thought may not be involved at first—the fear response is literally a kind of "gut reaction" produced by the brain. It is only later that the response will be evaluated more thoroughly using rational thought processes (Adolphs, 2002; Dolan, 2002; Monk et al., 2003).

Studies of brain activity help explain the greater volatility of emotions in adolescence than later in life. For example, in one study, adolescents and adults repeatedly viewed faces showing different emotions. Although both age groups showed engagement of the *left ventrolateral prefrontal cortex,* adolescents showed more activity in certain other areas of the brain when viewing familiar faces, depending on the kind of emotion being displayed (see Figure 5-7). These differences suggest emotional responses may be particularly pronounced during adolescence and affect the rationality of adolescents' evaluation of challenges they encounter and their responses to them (Nelson et al., 2003).

On the other hand, the physiological reactivity of emotions is not the full story of emotional responses during adolescence. As we'll see next, adolescents have considerable (and increasing) control over their emotions.

Emotional Self-Regulation

Throughout adolescence, both boys and girls become more adept at controlling their emotions. **Emotional self-regulation** is the ability to adjust emotions to a desired state and level of intensity. When adolescents seek to "keep cool," they are relying on emotional self-regulation.

It's not easy for any of us to regulate our emotions. For example, people asked to hide their responses to the observation of gruesome photos of accident victims show high levels of physiological reactivity as a result of their efforts to suppress their actual emotion. They also have difficulty later in recalling what they viewed. In short, emotional regulation takes both cognitive and physical effort (Richards & Gross, 2000; Richards, Butler, & Gross, 2003; Ochsner & Gross, 2005).

During childhood, emotional regulation skills improve considerably, and that trend continues throughout adolescence. The demands and challenges that adolescents face lead to improvements in emotion management (Zahn-Waxler et al., 2000; Eisenberg, Sprinrad, & Smith, 2004; Graber, 2004).

Adolescents use several strategies to regulate their emotional responses. One is to try to cognitively reappraise events that produce emotional responses. Specifically, they may try to change

emotional self-regulation   the ability to adjust emotions to a desired state and level of intensity

◀ **FIGURE 5-7**

Brain Activity and Emotions
Although both adolescents and adults viewing pictures of faces displaying different emotions showed activation of the left ventrolateral prefrontal cortex, compared with adults, adolescents showed more activity in other areas of the brain. This suggests emotional responses may be particularly pronounced during adolescence.

(*Source:* Nelson et al., 2003. Journal of Child Psychology and Psychiatry, 44, 1020, Bottom of Figure 2.)

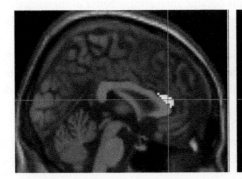
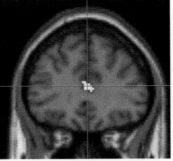

the way they think about something they have encountered, making it seem less bothersome. For example, an adolescent might try to convince himself that his girlfriend's decision to break up is really a good thing, because he didn't like being tied down. If he is able to convince himself of this, his initial sadness or anger might be replaced with more positive (or at least neutral) emotions.

Another emotion-regulating strategy that adolescents can use is to suppress troubling emotions. Using such a strategy involves inhibiting the outward signs of inner emotional states, despite experiencing particular emotions internally. Although such a strategy may not make the individual who is suppressing the emotion feel better about negative emotions they might be experiencing, it can be effective in making others feel better. In fact, learning to "put on" a face appropriate to a particular social situation is an important advance in emotional self-regulation that occurs during adolescence, as we see next.

Display Rules: Presenting Oneself Well to Others.   By the time they reach their early teens, most adolescents have learned to avoid frowning, pouting, or otherwise showing displeasure even when they have received even the most unwelcome and disappointing gift. Instead, they know it is appropriate to smile and express great pleasure over the gift.

The guidelines that govern what society sees as appropriate nonverbal behavior are known as display rules. *Display rules* are the implicit rules that define what type of nonverbal behavior is appropriate for a given situation or interpersonal relationship, and what type is not. Display rules are learned during childhood and adolescence as cognitive abilities and control of facial muscles increase (Halberstadt et al., 1992; Matsumoto et al., 2005; Gosserand & Diefendorff, 2005).

There are at least four strategies through which display rules can modify the expression of emotion: amplification, deamplification, neutralizing, and masking. In *amplification,* an adolescent exaggerates an expression, such as a smile, to convey the appearance of a stronger emotion than he or she is actually feeling. In *deamplification,* the opposite occurs: The communication of a felt emotion is minimized. For example, an adolescent who bests someone in a video game may try not to show how happy he is but instead may try to minimize his true delight (Matsumoto et al., 2005).

When adolescents *neutralize* an expression, they attempt to withhold any indication of how they actually feel. The term *poker face* characterizes someone's attempt to show no emotion of any sort. This is accomplished by neutralizing the nonverbal expressions representative of emotions that are actually being experienced.

The most extreme form of modification of nonverbal behavior occurs when someone masks one expression with another. For instance, a high school student might mask her pleasure when a rival for an academic award fails. Similarly, an adolescent might smile and congratulate the classmate who just beat him in a race. In both examples, the expression being displayed is precisely the opposite of the feeling being experienced.

How successful are adolescents at self-presentation through the modification of facial expressions? It turns out that they are pretty good at it, and their skill increases throughout adolescence. For example, in one experiment, a group of 11- to 16-year-old adolescents were asked to fool someone by saying that a foul-tasting drink actually tasted good—and vice versa. The results showed that the participants became increasingly better at masking their true feelings about the drink the older they were (Feldman, Tomasian, & Coats, 1999; Hrubes, Feldman, & Tyler, 2004).

Even more important, the emotional self-regulation displayed by participants was related to their general social competence. Specifically, the better participants were able to hide their actual emotions, the more socially skilled they were in their interactions with friends, teachers, and family members.

In short, adolescents become increasingly skilled at the self-regulation of emotions. Furthermore, the better able they are to regulate their emotions, the more effective they are at successfully interacting with others (Eisenberg, Sprinrad, & Smith, 2004; Philippot & Feldman, 2004).

▲ FIGURE 5-8

Which Is the True Smile? The smile shown in (a) is a true smile of happiness, while those in (b) and (c) are false.

(*Source:* Ekman, Friesen, & O'Sullivan, 1988.)

True Versus False Displays of Emotion: What's the Difference? Although adolescents become increasingly successful at displaying the nonverbal message that they seek to portray, they are never entirely successful. For example, no matter how much an adolescent seeks to communicate happiness in the face of disappointment, it's likely that her true emotion will "leak" out. No matter how much effort one employs, there are nearly always visible differences between true and feigned emotional displays.

For instance, consider the photos in Figure 5-8 of a smiling girl. Can you tell which is the true smile of happiness? If you look closely, you should be able to, because one of them portrays a smile in reaction to positive emotion, whereas two of them are false smiles.

The difference between the true and fake smiles rests on a subtle difference in the use of facial muscles. True smiles, known as *Duchenne smiles,* involve a unique pattern of facial muscles that does not appear in false ones (Frank, Ekman, & Friesen, 1997; Harris & Alvarado, 2005).

Adolescent
DIVERSITY   Cultural Differences in Displays of Emotion

GIVEN THAT DISPLAY rules are learned through socialization during childhood and adolescence, it is not surprising that the rules vary greatly across cultures and ethnicities. For instance, in Asian cultures it is generally considered inappropriate to display emotions, whereas in Mediterranean and Latin cultures volatile nonverbal displays are expected in social interactions (Matsumoto & Yoo, 2005).

In addition to general differences in nonverbal expressiveness, cultures sometimes differ in the display of a particular emotion. For example, one study found that the Japanese, whose collectivistic culture places a strong emphasis on group harmony and cohesion, felt that nonverbal displays of anger and disgust were more appropriately shown to members of other ethnic and cultural groups than to members of their own cultural groups. In contrast, citizens of the United States, which is a more individualistic culture, felt that displays of anger, disgust, and sadness were more permissible toward members of their own group than to members of other groups (Matsumoto, 1990; Lee et al., 1992).

Cultural differences even may extend to the experience of particular emotions by adolescents belonging to different cultures. For example, Westerners are more apt to experience emotions that are related to their view of themselves as independent, unconnected individuals—emotions such as jealousy and anger. In contrast, people living in Japan are more likely to experience "other-focused" emotions, which are related to cooperation with others. Specifically, the Japanese language describes emotions that are not even present in the English vocabulary, such as feeling "oime," which refers to being indebted to another (Markus & Kitayama, 1994; Chua, Leu, & Nisbett, 2005; Soto, Levenson, & Ebling, 2005).

Although it is clear that culture seems to shape our *expression* of emotion (recall, for example, the well-known reserve and lack of emotional expression in Asians compared with Westerners), do such differences extend to the actual *experience* of emotion? Specifically, although people from Asian cultures *express* emotions less obviously than people from Western cultures, do Asians actually *feel* emotions less intensely than Westerners?

Researchers most often have investigated this question using two types of measures of emotional experience: physiological response (such as heart rate, respiration, and skin temperature) and self-reported emotional intensity. Participants are induced to feel specific positive or negative emotions by undergoing experiences such as watching an emotional film clip or recalling an emotional event from their past.

When Asian and Western participants' physiological responses to emotion are compared, little or no difference can be found, suggesting that there are minimal differences in how intensely emotions are felt. On the other hand, when directly asked about the intensity of their emotions, the results are less clear. Sometimes Asian participants indicate feeling less emotion than do Western participants, while other times they do not. In short, whether a cultural difference exists in the subjective experience of emotional intensity is still an open question (Levenson et al., 1992; Tsai & Levenson, 1997; Drummond & Quah, 2001; Tsai et al., 2002).

Developing Emotional Competence

Most of us have met adolescents (and perhaps some adults, as well) who don't make eye contact when they speak to us. Looking down at the floor, they mumble or giggle when talking, and they seem embarrassed at the very notion of speaking to someone who isn't their peer.

Such individuals are lacking in emotional competence. Their emotions are inappropriate, and—because they are so focused on their own discomfort—they miss social signals from the person with whom they are conversing. The result is a conversation that is awkward for everyone involved.

Adolescents vary greatly in their levels of *emotional competence,* the ability to effectively understand and manage emotional situations. According to psychologist Carolyn Saarni (2002), emotional competence involves a variety of skills, including these:

- Awareness of one's own emotions at a given moment and knowledge of why the emotions are being elicited.

- The understanding that one can experience several emotions at the same time.

- The ability to read others' emotions from their verbal and nonverbal behavior, as well as understanding individual differences in the way that people express emotions.

- The ability to experience empathy and sympathy for others.

- The ability to cope with negative emotions in a positive way.

- The awareness that emotions play a central role in relationships, and that different relationships involve different emotions.

- Experiencing emotional self-efficacy, the perception that one has effective mastery over one's emotions.

Although no adolescent is likely to have mastered all these skills, it is clear that the more effectively adolescents are able to master their emotions, the better they are able to successfully navigate the challenges of adolescence. But what of those adolescents who are deficient in emotional competence? Can they be taught the skills they need to improve their performance in the emotional domain?

The answer is a qualified "yes." Some research findings suggest that in fact it is possible to improve the emotional competence of adolescents. For example, educators have devised techniques to teach individuals to decode the emotions of others more effectively. In addition, programs have been designed to help students to better understand the intentions behind their classmates' behavior so that they may react more effectively (Beck & Feldman, 1990; Buckley, Storino, & Saarni, 2003; Maurer, Brackett, & Plain, 2004).

On the other hand, many of the programs for increasing emotional competence are not well validated scientifically. Consequently, it is not clear how effective they really are in improving adolescents' emotional competence. Still, the efforts to improve emotional competence are promising. Furthermore, they have been helpful in identifying some specific ways that adolescents can be encouraged to improve their level of emotional competence, as we consider next.

BECOMING AN INFORMED CONSUMER OF ADOLESCENT SCIENCE

Promoting Emotional Competence

DRAWING ON CAROLYN SAARNI'S list of skills associated with emotional competence, educators have developed specific strategies for adolescents who want to sharpen their emotional competence skills. One approach focuses on becoming more mindful of oneself, and it offers the following suggestions:

- Be observant. Take note of what is happening to you at the moment—both externally and internally. Notice what is going on around you, and how you are reacting to those events. Allow your thoughts to flow naturally without trying to stop them or control them; instead, just take note of what they are.

- Describe your experiences. Distinguish thoughts, feelings, and events and label them appropriately. Then think through how you might explain to someone else what is happening to you. What words would you use?

- Describe your emotions. Don't be vague about what you are feeling. Put a label on your emotions. Are you feeling sad? Angry? Fearful?

- Resist being judgmental. Observe and describe the events around you and your own thoughts and feelings without evaluating them. Don't make judgments about whether they are good or bad, or what you should or should not think and feel. (Weiner, 2004)

Review and Apply

Review

1. Emotions serve several functions, including preparing people for action, shaping future behavior, and helping people interact with others more effectively.

2. Emotions in adolescence tend to be more changeable and more extreme than in other periods of life.

3. During adolescence, people become more effective at emotional self-regulation and at using display rules to produce socially appropriate nonverbal behaviors in different situations.

4. Cultural differences in the expression of emotions do not correspond perfectly with actual differences in the experience of emotions by people from different cultures.

5. One task of adolescence is the development of emotional competence, the ability to understand and manage emotional situations.

Apply

1. In what ways does the emotion of sadness differ from feelings of depression in adolescence? How can one tell the difference?

2. What are some advantages and disadvantages of emotional self-regulation? Are there dangers in too much self-regulation?

EPILOGUE

This chapter focused on the development of the self and the definition of an identity with which one can be comfortable. We discussed the formation of self-concept and explored the theories of researchers regarding the challenges and stages of identity development. We turned next to a look at self-esteem, which takes on particular importance during adolescence. We saw that self-esteem is a complex matter, in that high self-esteem can be both beneficial and harmful. We also looked at strategies for improving self-esteem by relating it firmly to actual achievements and basing it on an accurate appreciation of self-worth. Finally, we discussed emotions in adolescents. We examined the notion that adolescents are emotional whirlwinds and addressed ways in which people learn to regulate their emotions and develop emotional competence.

Before we proceed to the next chapter, recall "Confused," the popular cheerleader with identity confusion. Remember what you have learned about identity development and answer the following questions.

1. Into which of Marcia's categories of adolescent identity does "Confused" seem to fall, and why?

2. What could "Confused" do to raise her self-esteem?

3. What neurological explanation can you offer for "Confused's" apparently volatile emotions?

4. "Confused" asks when she will "get over" her worry and confusion. How would you answer her question?

5. If Erik Erikson were writing this advice column, how might he reply to "Confused"?

SUMMARY

REVIEW

● **How do individuals develop a sense of identity during adolescence?** *(p. 144)*

1. Identity issues become especially important during adolescence as physical and other changes focus attention on defining the self.

2. Adolescents grow increasingly able to differentiate their own views of themselves from those of others, to understand abstract and psychological aspects of themselves, and to distinguish separate aspects of the self.

3. The primary way in which adolescents develop their sense of identity is through social comparison with others who are generally similar in abilities, expertise, behavior, and attitudes.

- **What challenges are there to successful identity formation?** *(p. 148)*

  4. Erik Erikson associates adolescence with a conflict between identity and role confusion. During adolescence, people try on different identities and roles and, largely through interactions with peers, begin to clarify their identities.

  5. Carol Gilligan has extended Erikson's male-centered theory to females, observing that women tend to develop their identities through caring relationships.

  6. James Marcia has updated Erikson's work by interpreting identity formation in terms of crisis and commitment.

  7. Race, ethnicity, and culture play complex and significant roles in the formation of identity.

- **How important is self-esteem, and what are the consequences of both low and high self-esteem?** *(p. 155)*

  8. Self-esteem is the emotional side of self-concept, involving the self-evaluative feelings that people have about various aspects of themselves.

  9. In general, adolescents with higher self-esteem hold more positive expectations about their abilities and performance, and adolescents with lower self-esteem hold more negative expectations.

  10. Adolescent self-esteem changes over time, with boys and girls experiencing increases and decreases at different times. Males and females also differ in the aspects of themselves that they consider to be particularly important for self-esteem.

  11. Socioeconomic status, race, and ethnicity also affect self-esteem, with African American and white adolescents generally having higher self-esteem than other groups.

  12. Contingent self-worth involves self-evaluation focused on areas that an adolescent believes to be most important. If self-esteem is linked too closely with contingent self-worth, there can be negative consequences.

  13. Broad, unfocused efforts at increasing self-esteem are less successful than focused efforts aimed at improving self-efficacy.

- **Why is emotional development important in adolescence?** *(p. 165)*

  14. Emotions play an important role in adolescents' lives, preparing them for action, shaping future behavior, and enabling effective interactions with others.

  15. Emotions are more intense and changeable in adolescence than at other periods of the life span, and adolescents face the task of regulating their emotions and developing emotional competence.

- **Are there cultural differences in emotional development and expression?** *(p. 169)*

  16. There are cultural differences in the range and types of emotions that are normally learned and expressed in a given culture.

  17. Culture clearly shapes the expression of emotion, but it is less clear if it also affects the experience of emotions.

KEY TERMS AND CONCEPTS

possible selves (p. 145)
social comparison (p. 146)
identity-versus-role-
  confusion stage (p. 149)

self-esteem (p. 155)
contingent self-worth
  (p. 161)

emotions (p. 165)
emotional self-regulation
  (p. 167)

6 Adolescents and Their Families

CHAPTER OUTLINE

CONFLICT, AUTONOMY, AND ATTACHMENT

The generation gap: Myth or reality?
The nature of conflict
The quest for autonomy: The reasons behind conflict
Attachment: Maintaining connectedness

PARENTING: RAISING ADOLESCENTS IN THE 21st CENTURY

Parenting styles
Reciprocal socialization: The two-way street of parent–adolescent influence

Cultural differences in child-rearing practices
Parental development: Middle adulthood meets adolescence

ADOLESCENTS AND THE DIVERSITY OF THEIR FAMILIES

Single-parent families, divorce, blended families
Siblings: Adolescents and their brothers and sisters
The bottom line: Families matter

PROLOGUE

S LIM AND DARK, with a passing resemblance to actress Demi Moore, Leah is dressed up and ready to go to the first real formal dance of her life. True, the smashing effect of her short beaded black dress is marred slightly by the man's shirt she insists on wearing to cover her bare shoulders. And she is in a sulk. Her boyfriend, Sean Moffitt, is four minutes late, and her mother, Linda, refuses to let her stay out all night at a coed sleepover party after the dance. . . .

Leah's father, George, suggests a 2 a.m. curfew: Leah hoots incredulously. Sean pitches the all-nighter, stressing that the party will be chaperoned. Leah's mother has already talked to the host's mother, mortifying Leah with her off-hand comment that a coed sleepover seemed "weird." Rolling her eyes, Leah persists: "It's not like anybody's really going to sleep!" (E. Graham, 1995, p. B1) ■

th!nk ABOUT THIS

IN MANY WAYS, THIS snippet of Leah's life sums up adolescent–parent relations. There's the obvious conflict over staying out all night and the postprom coed sleepover arrangements, as well as Leah's embarrassment over her mother's articulating that the sleepover is "weird." At the same time, though, it's also clear, probably even to Leah, that her parents' behavior is motivated by their support and concern for her welfare. And, if you asked them directly, both she and her parents would admit that most of the time they actually get along pretty well, despite periods of conflict.

In this chapter, we look at adolescents and their families. Families provide the grounding for adolescents' lives and in many ways are the most important factor in determining their well-being.

We first consider the degree and nature of conflict between adolescents and their families. We look at the so-called generation gap and examine its reality. We will also look at adolescents' efforts to

gain autonomy and how that relates to the attachment bonds that link them and their parents.

Next, we turn to a consideration of how adolescents are raised by their parents. We look at different parenting styles and also consider how adolescents influence their parents. We then examine cultural differences in child rearing and the differing roles played by mothers and fathers.

Finally, we consider the diversity that characterizes family life. We discuss single-parent families, multigenerational and blended families, the effects of divorce, and the role of race and ethnicity in family life. We also look at relationships between adolescents and their siblings. We then consider the effects of poverty on family life, ending the chapter with the bottom-line conclusion that family life plays a central role in adolescents' lives. ■

- How characteristic of adolescence is conflict within the family?
- How do adolescents balance their need for attachment with their desire for autonomy?
- What roles and styles of parenting are typical in families with adolescents?
- How are adolescents affected by diverse and changing family arrangements?

Conflict, Autonomy, and Attachment: Negotiating Family Life

My idiot father just came in and drove me insane, . . . and asking me why Mozilla is different from IE. I told him to look it up on the internet because he wouldn't understand it and I couldn't be bothered to waste my time answering stupid, pointless questions. He said he didn't have time to look it up. Yeah, whatever. No time to look it up, and yet he throws away hours of his life watching lame-ass television shows that rots his mind.

Then he came in and started driving me nuts about typing some stupid letter for him. . . . He got mad and told me it was only 3 lines, so I told him to type it himself. What really annoys me is that I especially woke up this morning so I could get ready and relax for once, and he drove me nuts all morning. . . . He's such a moron.

If we relied on teenage blogs like this one, we might believe that most teenagers are members of unhappy, dysfunctional families. In this blogger's world, parents (who have low IQs and short memories) appear to live in some alternative universe, making occasional unwelcome journeys into their children's lives. Their intrusion is marked by unreasonable demands that have the effect of making their children miserable.

Similarly, if we took our cues from television entertainment, we'd find families typically portrayed in disarray (think of most of the families on *The O.C.* or *Nip/Tuck*). In such shows, serious, ongoing conflicts between adolescents and their parents are often featured story-lines.

The portrayals of adolescents and their families in other media mirror the sense of upheaval featured on television shows. Walk into any bookstore and you'll find rows of books meant to help parents deal with their supposedly unruly, difficult, or disturbed adolescent. Titles such as *Get Out of my Life, but First Could You Drive Me and Cheryl to the Mall* or *Stop Negotiating With Your Teen: Strategies for Parenting Your Angry, Manipulative, Moody, or Depressed Adolescent* are the norm.

While books about infants and toddlers focus on normal development, books about adolescents focus on problem behaviors and how parents can "survive" the period. Even books targeted toward adolescents mirror the theme of difficulty in parent–child relations (consider the title *Yes, Your Parents are Crazy: A Teen Survival Handbook*) (Steinberg, 2001; Bradley, 2004).

The Generation Gap: Myth or Reality?

generation gap a divide between adolescence and other periods of life that supposedly reflects profound differences in behavior, values, attitudes, lifestyle choices, and experiences

Blogs, television, books, and other media reflect the common view that there is a significant generation gap. The **generation gap** is a divide between adolescence and other periods of life. The divide supposedly reflects profound differences in behavior, values, attitudes, lifestyle choices, and experiences.

◀ Most adolescents have deep love, affection, and respect for their parents.

Yet if we relied on popular opinion to inform our understanding of adolescence, we'd come to the wrong conclusions. Yes, adolescence is a period in which parent–child difficulties can escalate. And certainly some adolescents have serious problems in their relationships with their parents and other adults. And it is true that many adolescents are unhappy with their parents, seeing them at best as clueless and overly restrictive and at worst as mean, malicious, and abusive.

Overall, though, the past two decades of careful scientific research have come to a clear conclusion that differs significantly from popular opinion: By far the majority of adolescents have deep love, affection, and respect for their parents—and parents feel the same way about their children. Although some parent–adolescent relationships are seriously troubled, the majority of relationships are more positive than negative and help adolescents avoid the kind of peer pressure we'll discuss in Chapter 7 (Gavin & Furman, 1996; Resnick et al., 1997; Black, 2002; Granic, Dishion, & Hollenstein, 2005).

Furthermore, even though adolescents spend decreasing amounts of time with their families in general, the amount of time they spend alone with each parent remains remarkably stable across adolescence (see Figure 6-1). In short, there is no evidence suggesting that family problems are worse during adolescence than at any other stage of development (Steinberg, 1993; Larson et al., 1996; Granic, Hollenstein, & Dishion, 2003).

In fact, in many respects, the differences in terms of fundamental social and psychological characteristics *between* generations are smaller than the differences *within* a particular generation. Put another way, if we look closely at adolescents, we are likely to encounter more differences between adolescents than between adolescents and members of other age groups. (The same is true for periods other than adolescence. For instance, there is greater diversity *within* the group of people who are in middle adulthood than there is between people in middle adulthood and adolescents.)

For example, adolescents whose parents went to college are likely to mirror their parents' behavior and aspire to attend college, and adolescents and their parents tend to see eye-to-eye in a variety of domains. Republican parents generally have Republican children; members of the Christian right have children who espouse similar views; parents who advocate for abortion rights have children who are pro-choice.

In short, on social, political, and religious issues, parents and adolescents tend to be in synch, and children's worries match those of their parents. Adolescents' concerns about society's

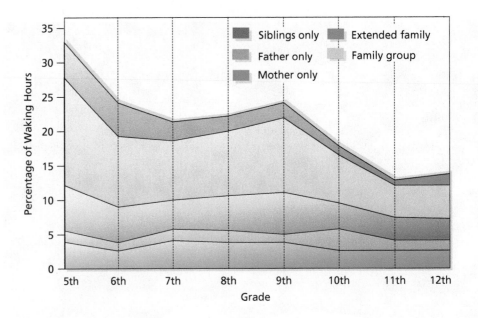

▶ **FIGURE 6-1**

Time Spent with Parents At the same time adolescents seek independence and autonomy, most have great love, affection, and respect for their parents, and the amount of time spent alone with each parent remains quite stable.

(*Source:* Larson et al., 1996.)

problems (see Figure 6-2) are ones with which most adults would probably agree. In fact, the behavior of their parents is often a larger determinant of adolescent behavior than the behavior of members of their own generation (Flor & Knap, 2001; Knafo & Schwartz, 2003; Smetana, 2005).

The Nature of Conflict

My stupid parents have stupid curfewed me for this weekend and told me im not allowed out late at all during the week, just cos i didnt come home til 3 in the morning on saturday nite. they are being completely unreasonable, but apart from just walking out the house and getting into even more trouble there isnt much i can do about it, tho hopefully they will have forgotten about it by wednesday and I can go out Wednesday nite!!

Although it's clear that there is no significant generation gap between adolescents and their parents, it is also true that adolescents often are in conflict with their parents, as this blog excerpt indicates. For instance, careful analysis of the level of conflict shows that during certain periods conflict does escalate. In one study, researchers asked boys and their mothers to discuss family problems every other year for a decade. The videotapes of the discussions showed that conflict increased during early adolescence (in 13- to 14-year olds) and peaked around age 15 to 16. But then conflict declined to earlier levels, as illustrated in Figure 6-3 (Granic, Dishion, & Hollenstein, 2005).

Although the degree of conflict between parents and adolescents is, by and large, not great, between 5 and 20% do experience major, sustained clashes. However, when substantial parent–adolescent conflict exists, it usually is not new to adolescence. In many cases, parents and children had rocky relationships before the period, and the conflict they experience during the period is an extension of earlier battles. In short, there is continuity in patterns of conflict, which has the effect of extending preadolescent levels of conflict into adolescence (Collins, 1990; Offer & Schonert-Reichl, 1992; Laursen & Collins, 2004).

In most cases, the conflicts that do occur between parents and adolescents involve rather ordinary situations. Unlike G. Stanley Hall's view of adolescence as a period characterized by turbulence, most conflict does not involve serious problems such as drug use or criminal activity. Instead, parents and adolescents are more likely to squabble about mundane sorts of things: keeping one's room clean, talking on the phone too much, taking out the garbage, choosing

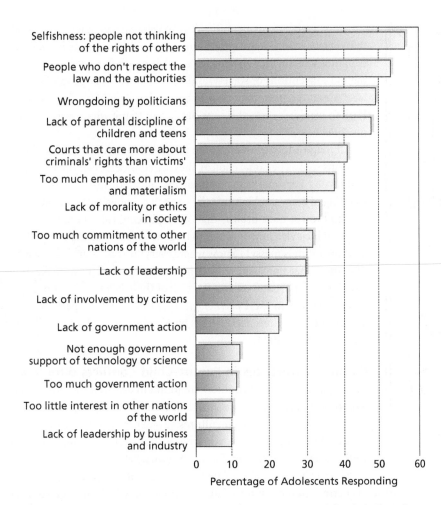

Adolescent Concerns about Society
Both adolescents and their parents view the problems of society similarly.
(*Source:* PRIMEDIA/Roper, 1999.)

clothes to wear, deciding to get a tattoo or a piercing. Furthermore, most of the time these low-level conflicts are resolved with the adolescent giving in to the parents (Montemayor, 1983; Holmbeck & Hill, 1988; Steinberg & Silk, 2002).

Part of the reason that even these low-level conflicts persist is that adolescents and their parents define issues in different ways. According to psychologist Judith Smetana, adolescents see many issues in terms of personal lifestyle choices. The choice of clothing is a personal choice determined by the social environment in which they live. They want to conform to the norms of their peers, not those of their parents. An adolescent girl who says that "everybody wears dresses this short" is saying that she is simply making a personal choice that permits her to fit into her own peer group (Smetana & Gaines, 1999; Daddis & Smetana, 2005).

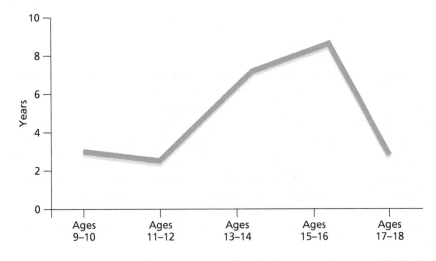

◄ **FIGURE 6-3**
Conflicts with Parents   Although there is no significant generation gap between adolescents and their parents, this study of boys and their mothers discussing family problems shows an increase in conflict during early adolescence, peaking around ages 15–16. Why do conflicts peak at this point and not earlier?
(*Source:* Granic, Dishion & Hollenstein, 2005, pg. 73.)

"Dear Mom and Dad: Thanks for the happy childhood. You've destroyed any chance I had of becoming a writer."

In contrast, parents are more likely to view choices in terms of social conventions that dictate what is appropriate and what is inappropriate in *their* view. When his daughter wears a very short skirt, a father may believe it is a sign that she is defying the conventions of society, and he may worry that people "may get the wrong idea" about the meaning of her behavior. His daughter might reply that "Maybe a Puritan wouldn't dress this way, but it's up to me what I wear" (Smetana & Daddis, 2002).

Although adolescents are apt to resist their parents' cautions when they relate to domains seen as personal choices, they are considerably more willing to accept rules that involve personal safety or basic morality. For instance, they are more understanding of a no-smoking rule (because they know it stems from their parents' desires to protect their health) than a no-piercing rule (because that is viewed as a personal lifestyle choice). Rules that make no sense to them—"What does it matter if my room is messy? I know where everything is"—are less likely to be followed than those that they believe their parents have the right to make. In general, adolescents find parental efforts to control their *behavior* as more legitimate than parental efforts to exert *psychological control* (in which parents seek to influence adolescents' emotions and feelings by, for example, inducing guilt or withdrawing love) (Silk et al., 2003).

Cultural Differences in Parent–Child Conflicts during Adolescence. Although parent–child conflicts are found in every culture, there does seem to be less conflict between parents and their teenage children in "traditional," preindustrial cultures. Teens in such cultures also experience fewer mood swings and instances of risky behavior than do teens in industrialized countries (Schlegel & Barry, 1991; Arnett, 2000; Nelson, Badger, & Wu, 2004).

Why? The answer may relate to the degree of independence that adolescents expect and adults permit. In more industrialized societies, in which the value of individualism is typically high, independence is an expected component of adolescence. Consequently, adolescents and their parents must negotiate the amount and timing of the adolescent's increasing independence—a process that often leads to strife.

In contrast, in more traditional societies, individualism is not valued as highly, and therefore adolescents are less inclined to seek out independence. Compared to adolescents from more individualistic societies, those in more collectivistic cultures tend to feel a greater obligation to their families, accepting that they have a duty to fulfill family expectations and to provide assistance, show respect, and support their families in the future (see Figure 6-4). The result of such views is less parent–child conflict (Dasen, 2000; Dasen & Mishra 2002; Chao, 2001; Fuligni & Zhang, 2004).

The Quest for Autonomy: The Reasons Behind Conflict

One reason that parent–child conflict rises during adolescence relates to the growing cognitive abilities of adolescents. An eight-year-old child's more limited cognitive abilities make it more likely that he or she will accept a parent's admonitions at face value. An explanation of "clean your room because I tell you to clean your room" is acceptable during middle childhood.

On the other hand, as their cognitive abilities grow, adolescents are more likely to demand a valid reason for the rules they are asked to follow. In fact, parents who are accustomed to having their rules accepted without an explanation may grow weary at having to provide a rationale each time they ask their adolescent son or daughter to do something.

But it's not only the growing cognitive abilities of adolescents that lead to conflict with parents. Even more important is the quest for autonomy that adolescents increasingly engage in.

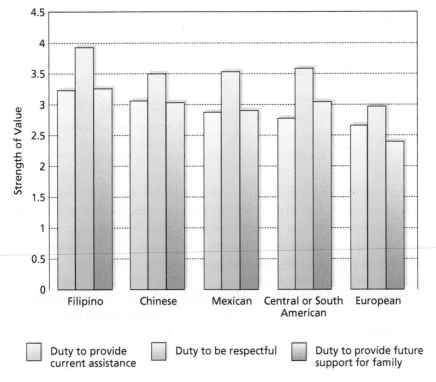

Duty to provide current assistance

Duty to be respectful

Duty to provide future support for family

◀ **FIGURE 6-4**
Obligations to Family Asian and Latin-American adolescents feel a greater sense of respect and responsibility toward their families than their European counterparts. How might this attitude carry over in the classroom?

(*Source:* Fuligni, Tseng, & Lam, 1999.)

Autonomy is the development and expression of independence. Gaining a sense of autonomy is one of the primary developmental tasks of adolescence. The emotional experience of feeling autonomous, as well as having the knowledge and ability to achieve one's own goals, provides adolescents with a sense of themselves as individuals.

In order to attain autonomy, adolescents must develop a view of themselves as unique and different from others, at least in some ways. This is a gradual process. In early adolescence, individuals become increasingly dependent on feedback from others to understand who they are. In midadolescence, there is a near preoccupation with the opinions and judgments of others, as well as with their expectations.

It is only in late adolescence that individuals begin to set their own standards and form a coherent view of themselves, which leads to a sense of autonomy. In addition, adolescents learn to do things because they are important to them ("I do my homework because I want to learn") instead of because they are important to someone else ("I do my homework because my teacher or parents make me") (Harter, 2003; Collins & Laursen, 2004; Ryan & Deci, 2004).

Furthermore, adolescents begin to perceive parents less in idealized terms and more as persons in their own right. For example, rather than seeing their parents as authoritarian disciplinarians mindlessly reminding them to do their homework, they may come to see their parents' emphasis on excelling in school as evidence of parental regrets about their own lack of education and a wish to see their children have more options in life. At the same time, adolescents come to depend more on themselves and to feel more like separate individuals (see Figure 6-5).

The increase in adolescent autonomy changes the relationship between parents and teenagers. At the start of adolescence, the relationship tends to be asymmetrical: Parents hold most of the power and influence. By the end of adolescence, however, power and influence have become more balanced, and parents and children end up in a more symmetrical, or egalitarian, relationship. Power and influence are shared, although parents typically retain the upper hand (Gehring et al., 1990; Wentzel & Feldman, 1996; Noack & Buhl, 2005).

The Development of Autonomy. Although it was once thought that developing autonomy was another demonstration of the presumed defiance of those passing through

autonomy the development and expression of independence

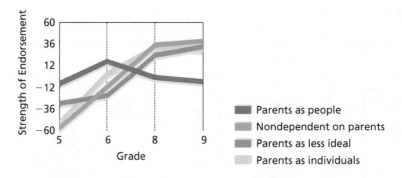

► **FIGURE 6-5**

Changing Views of Parents As they become older, adolescents see their parents more as individuals and less in idealized terms. What effect is this likely to have on family relations?

(*Source:* Adapted from Steinberg & Steinberg, 1986.)

Legend:
- Parents as people
- Nondependent on parents
- Parents as less ideal
- Parents as individuals

adolescence, today we know otherwise. Most researchers believe that establishing a sense of autonomy is a significant and necessary milestone in adolescent development. Rather than being a sign of rebellion, the quest for autonomy is a central passage of adolescence. Furthermore, for most adolescents the growth of autonomy is an often gradual change, lacking in drama.

In fact, in psychologically strong and supportive families, adolescents are encouraged in their quest for autonomy. They are increasingly treated in more adultlike ways, and they are increasingly included in decision making. Such gains in autonomy are beneficial. As autonomy intensifies during middle and late adolescence, adolescents are more likely to adopt attitudes and opinions that are their own and are less influenced by peers—despite the rise in peer pressure that occurs at that time (Zimmer-Gembeck & Collins, 2005).

Furthermore, as they pass through adolescence, individuals see an increasing number of domains as legitimately under their control and less under that of their parents. As a result, there is a significant amount of negotiation—and renegotiation—between adolescents and their parents. In fact, part of the adolescent experience that parents often find exhausting is the continual process of negotiation and compromise that occurs, even when adolescents are compliant with parental rules—which are themselves continually shifting (Smetana & Daddis, 2002; Daddis & Smetana, 2005).

Consequently, there is often a tension between parents' views of how much autonomy their children should have and how much autonomy adolescents seek. Parents themselves may be un-

▲ Adolescents who come from psychologically strong and supportive families are encouraged to seek autonomy.

sure of the degree of independence that is reasonable. Furthermore, because of the significant physical, cognitive, and social advances that occur during adolescence, the amount of independence that it is reasonable to grant to one's son or daughter at age 15 may be insufficient just a year later.

Although society helps by providing a few arbitrary milestones—such as a set age at which it is legal to get a driver's license—in most cases parents have few concrete guidelines to follow. For example, is it reasonable for a 15-year-old to go to a sleepover in a house where the parents will be away for the weekend? What if the 15-year-old is a girl, and it's a mixed-gender sleepover? How convinced should parents be by their daughter's argument that "all my friends are doing it"?

One reason for parent–adolescent conflict, then, is that adolescents and their parents may differ in their view of the proper timetable for the development of autonomy. In addition, autonomy develops across several levels simultaneously. Specifically, we can view autonomy in terms of three separate, although interdependent, domains (Steinberg, 1990; Noom, Dekovie, & Meeus, 2001; Steinberg & Silk, 2002; Beyers et al., 2003):

- *Emotional autonomy.* Emotional autonomy focuses on adolescents' close relationships with others, and particularly with their parents. The ability of adolescents to separate and understand their emotional reactions to their parents is a crucial aspect of adolescent development. Starting in early adolescence, individuals become less emotionally dependent on their parents—although not, at least initially, emotionally autonomous from their friends. In later adolescence, they become more emotionally autonomous generally.

- *Behavioral autonomy.* Behavioral autonomy relates to the growing ability of adolescents not only to make their own decisions but also to carry them out. Although behavioral autonomy increases during adolescence, adolescents, like the rest of us, are never free from the influence of others on decisions and judgments. Individuals learn early to rely on others as important sources of information, particularly when a situation or issue is ambiguous. Hence, behaviorally autonomous individuals are able to take advantage of the knowledge and advice of others, but to weigh it and accept or reject it appropriately.

- *Attitudinal and value autonomy.* Attitudinal and value autonomy encompasses the development of independence in the realm of attitudes and values. During adolescence, individuals begin to adopt attitudes and values that represent more who they are and less what their parents and other authority figures want them to be. Furthermore, as they get older and their attitudinal and value autonomy increases, adolescents begin to rely more on broad, general principles to guide their behavior, and their thinking about issues becomes more abstract. For example, a 14-year-old girl may be in favor of a particular political position (such as drilling for oil in the National Wildlife Refuge in Alaska) largely because her parents are strong supporters of that position. When she is older, she may reject that view as she develops her own personal political philosophy with regard to environmentalism.

Cultural and Gender Differences in the Development of Autonomy. Autonomy is highly valued in the United States and other individualistic cultures of the sort we first discussed in Chapter 5. In individualistic cultures, where the focus is on personal identity, uniqueness, freedom, and the worth of the individual person, the development of autonomy is viewed in a highly positive manner. Although parents in individualistic cultures may sometimes resist the specific ways in which their children seek to demonstrate autonomy, by and large they encourage their children to make their own decisions and take on growing responsibility (Cooper, 1994; Cooper et al., 2005; Zimmer-Gembeck & Collins, 2005).

In contrast, the expectations for children differ in collectivistic cultures, in which the well-being of the group is emphasized more than that of the individual. The societal push for autonomy is less strong, and the timetable during which autonomy is expected to develop is slower (Fuligni, 1998; Fuligni & Zhang, 2004).

For example, when asked at what age an adolescent would be expected to carry out certain behaviors (such as going to a concert with friends), adolescents and parents provide different answers depending on their cultural background. In comparison to Asian adolescents and parents, Caucasian adolescents and parents indicate an earlier timetable, anticipating greater autonomy at an earlier age (Feldman & Rosenthal, 1991; Feldman & Wood, 1994).

Does the more extended timetable for the development of autonomy in more collectivistic cultures have negative consequences for adolescents in those cultures? Apparently not. The more important factor is the degree of match between cultural expectations and developmental patterns. What probably matters most is how well the development of autonomy matches societal expectations, not the specific timetable of autonomy (Rothbaum et al., 2000; Zimmer-Gembeck & Collins, 2005).

In addition to cultural factors affecting autonomy, gender also plays a role. In general, male adolescents are permitted more autonomy at an earlier age than female adolescents. The encouragement of male autonomy is consistent with more general traditional male stereotypes, in which males are perceived as more independent and females, conversely, more dependent on others. In fact, the more parents hold traditional stereotypical views of gender, the less likely they are to encourage their daughters' autonomy (Bumpus, Crouter, & McHale, 2001).

Attachment: Maintaining Connectedness

Although establishing autonomy is a central task for adolescents, this doesn't mean that the ideal situation is one in which adolescents grow so independent that their ties with their family become unimportant. In fact, just the opposite is true: The best-adjusted adolescents are those who, while attaining autonomy, maintain close, warm relationships with their parents.

Attachment is the positive emotional bond that develops between a child and particular, special individuals. Attachment bonds form during infancy between children and their primary caregivers. The nature of that attachment has wide-ranging implications for the nature of a person's relationships and functioning, reaching into adolescence and beyond.

Attachment serves two primary functions during the earliest stages of life. First, attachment provides children with a sense of security based on the presence of the person with whom they are attached. When faced with an anxiety-producing situation, securely attached children can turn to this individual for support and comfort. Second, the attached person can provide information about the situation. In an unfamiliar situation, the child can look to this person for hints about how to respond. In contrast, children who are not securely attached may actively avoid or show ambivalence toward their caregivers (Grossman, Grossman, & Waters, 2005).

Much of our understanding of attachment comes from observations of infants and toddlers and their parents, where the roots of attachment are thought to form. According to British psychiatrist John Bowlby (1951) and American psychologist Mary Ainsworth (Ainsworth et al., 1978), attachment is based primarily on infants' needs for safety and security—their genetically determined motivation to avoid predators. As they develop, infants come to learn that their safety is best provided by a particular individual. This realization ultimately leads to the development of a special relationship with that individual, who is typically the mother. The relationship with the primary caregiver is qualitatively different from the bonds formed with others.

Attachment is important during adolescence because the attachment style that develops during infancy continues into adolescence. Specifically, adolescents typically show one of three major patterns: securely attached, avoidant, and ambivalent (summarized in Table 6-1).

Adolescents who have a **secure attachment pattern** (which characterizes the majority of them) are well adjusted, having positive self-esteem and social competence. Because they received consistently warm and nurturing care during infancy, they tend to be trusting and open.

In contrast, adolescents with an **avoidant attachment pattern** steer clear of relationships. Often the product of distant, aloof caretakers who have ignored or rejected them during their

attachment the positive emotional bond that develops between a child and particular, special individuals

secure attachment pattern a pattern of attachment in which the adolescent is well adjusted, having positive self-esteem and social competence as the result of receiving consistently warm and nurturing care during infancy

avoidant attachment pattern a pattern of attachment in which the adolescent steers clear of relationships; often the product of distant, aloof caretakers who have ignored or rejected them during their early childhood

TABLE 6-1 Attachment Patterns		
Pattern	Caretaker Behavior during Infancy	Adolescent Behavior Associated with Pattern
Securely Attached	Caretaker provides consistently warm and nurturing care	Adolescents are well adjusted, having positive self-esteem and social competence.
Avoidant	Caretaker was distant, aloof, and ignored or rejected infant	Adolescents are so fearful of being hurt that they shut down emotionally. In such cases, adolescents and parents may pay little attention to one another.
Ambivalent	Caretaker provides inconsistent treatment, sometimes being highly attentive, while other times they ignored the child.	Adolescents will need frequent reassurance that they are loved, and they are afraid that they will be abandoned. Their insecurity results in shifts from appearing overly attached to their parents and showing unusual hostility to them.

early childhood, adolescents showing the avoidant attachment pattern are so fearful of being hurt that they shut down emotionally. In such cases, adolescents and parents may pay little attention to one another.

Adolescents with an **ambivalent attachment pattern** most likely received inconsistent treatment as young children. Sometimes their caregivers were highly attentive, but at other times they ignored their child. This background is related to adolescents who display a combination of positive and negative reactions to their parents. They need frequent reassurance that they are loved, and they are afraid that they will be abandoned. Their insecurity produces a pattern of shifts in which they sometimes appear overly attached to their parents and sometimes show unusual hostility to them.

The quality of attachment between infants and their mothers has significant consequences, affecting relationships with family, peers, and others. For example, boys who are securely attached at the age of 1 year show fewer psychological difficulties at older ages than do avoidant or ambivalent children. Similarly, children who are securely attached as infants tend to be more socially and emotionally competent later, and others view them more positively.

Furthermore, securely attached adolescents show better coping skills than those who are insecurely attached. Even the success of romantic relationships during adolescence is associated with the kind of attachment style that was developed during infancy (Waters et al., 2000; Schneider, Atkinson, & Tardif, 2001; Aviezer, Sagi, & Resnick, 2002; Mikulincer & Shaver, 2005; Seiffge-Krenke & Beyers, 2005).

Autonomy and Attachment: Finding the Balance

Both autonomy and attachment are necessary components of good adjustment during adolescence. Parents who encourage their daughters and sons to develop autonomy and a clear sense of themselves, within a context of warmth and support, provide the healthiest environment (Noom, Dekovic, & Meeus, 1999; Grolnick, 2003).

Furthermore, the research on attachment shows that parental support is important not only in adolescence but early in life as well. The way in which caregivers treat their children as infants has important consequences for the later success of their children.

ambivalent attachment pattern a pattern of attachment in which the adolescent displays a combination of positive and negative reactions to their parents; these adolescents received inconsistent treatment as young children

▶ Appropriate parental support, encouraging autonomy, helps adolescents to reach their potential.

In fact, the optimal situation may be one in which parents encourage adolescents to think for themselves and express differing opinions, and adolescents understand that the conflict that may come from espousing divergent views does not put them at risk of losing their parents' affection and emotional support. The combination of parental support for finding their adolescent's own voice, and accepting that voice, seems to maximize adolescent adjustment (Cooper & Cooper, 1992; Grotevant & Cooper, 1998).

Does this mean that adolescents who have suffered a less-than-ideal upbringing are unlikely to pass through the period successfully? Not at all. Adolescents have a considerable degree of **resilience,** the ability to overcome circumstances that place them at high risk for psychological or physical damage, such as extremes of poor parenting, poverty, or homes that are racked with violence or other forms of social disorder (Olsson et al., 2003; Barrera, Hageman, & Gonzales, 2004).

Resilient adolescents are particularly independent, feeling that they can shape their own fates. They tend to rely less on others, and they believe less in luck and more in their own abilities to determine what occurs in their lives. For them, family plays a less central role in their psychological world, and other people and social institutions may serve as substitutes, as we'll discuss in later chapters (Werner & Smith, 2002; Curtis & Cichetti, 2003; Kim & Cicchetti, 2003).

As we'll see in the remainder of the chapter, there are many ways that parents and adolescents interact with one another, just as there are many different family configurations. The resilience of adolescents reminds us that a variety of paths through adolescence can produce healthy development.

resilience   the ability to overcome circumstances that place adolescents at high risk for psychological or physical damage

Review and Apply

Review

1. Conflict between adolescents and caregivers is typically minor and manageable, and the depth of the supposed "generation gap" has been greatly exaggerated.

2. The main reason for conflict is the necessary development of autonomy during adolescence, when adolescents seek to make more of their own decisions and parents gradually relax their control.

3. The development of autonomy is best managed when adolescents negotiate and renegotiate an acceptable amount of independence with their parents.

4. There are cultural differences in the timetable of autonomy, with earlier development in individualistic societies and later development in more collectivistic societies.

5. Attachment patterns developed in infancy—whether secure, avoidant, or ambivalent—can have effects well into adolescence and later life.

Apply

1. Is the need to negotiate the line between autonomy and dependence confined only to adolescence? Does negotiation of this type occur later in life too? How, and when, might it occur?

2. Should societies be more involved in defining the timetable of autonomy by setting more age-related milestones for permissible actions (in the way that obtaining a driver's license is now set at a certain age)? Would this help or hinder adolescent development?

Parenting: Raising Adolescents in the 21st Century

I do love my parents, but never have I found the courage to say so. I really wonder which is worst, having parents who don't scold you at all and give you a lot of freedom but hardly ever talk to you, or having parents who do talk a lot with you and there are lots of laughter but even more fighting?

As this adolescent blogger observes, finding the right style of parenting is not a simple task. Consider the following situation, and think how you'd respond:

Fourteen-year-old Maria is a few dollars short of what she needs to buy some earrings she's been wanting. She's asked her parents for an advance on her allowance, but they've refused. Knowing that she will be going to the mall with her friends later that day, Maria goes into her younger brother Alejandro's bedroom. She furtively takes the cash she needs from the metal box in which Alejandro stores his allowance, which he's been saving for the last two months. Maria plans to pay back the "loan," but she doesn't want to tell Alejandro that she's taking the cash, because she knows he'd refuse to let her borrow the money. Just as she reaches into the box to take the money, her mother walks into the room and immediately takes in the situation.

If you were Maria's mother, which of the following reactions seems most reasonable?

1. Tell Maria that she is grounded for the next month and can't leave the house except to go to school.

2. Mildly tell Maria that what she did was not such a good idea and that she shouldn't do it in the future.

3. Talk about the morality of the situation, explaining why her brother Alejandro is going to be upset, and ground her for the day as punishment. In addition, tell Maria that she will have to apologize to Alejandro.

4. Forget about it and let the two children sort it out themselves; it's not worth getting involved.

Parenting Styles

Each of these four alternative responses represents one of the major parenting styles identified by Diana Baumrind (1971, 1980) and later updated by Eleanor Maccoby and colleagues (Baumrind, 1971, 1980; Maccoby & Martin, 1983).

Authoritarian parents respond as in the first alternative. They are controlling, punitive, rigid, cold. Their word is law, and they value strict, unquestioning obedience from their children. They also do not tolerate expressions of disagreement.

Permissive parents, in contrast, provide lax and inconsistent feedback, as in the second alternative. They require little of their children, and they don't see themselves as holding much responsibility for how their children turn out. They place few or no limits on their children's behavior.

Authoritative parents are firm, setting clear and consistent limits. Although they tend to be relatively strict, like authoritarian parents, they are loving and emotionally supportive. They also try to reason with their children, giving explanations for why they should behave in a particular way ("Alejandro is going to be upset"), and communicating the rationale for any punishment they may impose. Authoritative parents encourage independence in their offspring.

Finally, **uninvolved parents** show little interest in their children, displaying indifferent, rejecting behavior. They are detached emotionally and see their role as no more than feeding, clothing, and providing shelter for their child. In its most extreme form, uninvolved parenting results in *neglect*, a form of child abuse. (The four patterns are summarized in Table 6-2.)

Does the particular style of discipline that parents use result in differences in adolescents' behavior? The answer is a very strong yes—although, as you might expect, there are many exceptions (Steinberg et al., 1994; Parke & Buriel, 1998; Collett, Gimpel, & Greenson, 2001; Snyder et al., 2005):

- The offspring of authoritarian parents tend to be withdrawn, showing relatively little sociability. They are not very friendly, often behaving uneasily around their peers. Girls who are raised by authoritarian parents are especially dependent on their parents, whereas boys are unusually hostile.

- Adolescents with permissive parents in many ways share the undesirable characteristics of those with authoritarian parents. Adolescents with permissive parents tend to be dependent and moody, and they are low in social skills and self-control.

- Adolescents with authoritative parents fare best. They generally are independent, friendly with their peers, self-assertive, and cooperative. They have strong motivation to achieve, and they are typically successful and likable. They regulate their own behavior effectively, exercising control over their relationships with others and their own emotions.

  Some authoritative parents also display characteristics that produce a style that has come to be called *supportive parenting*. The characteristics include parental warmth, proactive teaching, calm discussion during disciplinary episodes, and interest and involvement in children's peer activities. Compared to other adolescents, those whose parents engage in supportive parenting show better adjustment and are better protected from the consequences of later adversity they may encounter (Pettit, Bates, & Dodge, 1997; Belluck, 2000; Kaufmann et al., 2000).

- Finally, adolescents whose parents show uninvolved parenting styles are the worst off. Their parents' lack of involvement disrupts their emotional development considerably, leading them to feel unloved and emotionally detached. It also impedes their physical and cognitive development.

Although such classification systems are useful ways of categorizing and describing parents' behavior, they are not a recipe for success. Parenting and growing up are more complicated than that! For instance, in a significant number of cases, adolescents with authoritarian and permissive parents develop quite successfully.

authoritarian parents parents who are controlling, punitive, rigid, and cold. Their word is law, and they value strict, unquestioning obedience from their children

permissive parents parents who provide lax and inconsistent feedback and require little of their children

authoritative parents parents who are firm, setting clear and consistent limits; although they tend to be relatively strict, like authoritarian parents, they are loving and emotionally supportive

uninvolved parents parents who show little interest in their children, displaying indifferent, rejecting behavior; in its most extreme form, uninvolved parenting results in *neglect*, a form of child abuse

TABLE 6-2	Parental Discipline Styles		
Parenting Style	**Nature of Demands and Responsiveness to Children**	**Characteristics**	**Relationship With Child**
Authoritarian	High demands; low responsiveness	Controlling, punitive, rigid, cold	Parent's word is law; they value strict, unquestioning obedience from their child. They do not tolerate expressions of disagreement.
Authoritative	High demands; high responsiveness	Firm, setting clear and consistent limits	They are relatively strict but emotionally supportive; they encourage independence. They try to reason with their child and give the rationale for an imposed punishment.
Permissive	Low demands; high responsiveness	Lax and inconsistent feedback	They require little of their child, and they don't see themselves as holding much responsibility for how their child turns out. They place little or no limits or control on their child's behavior.
Uninvolved	Low demands; low responsiveness	Displaying indifferent, rejecting behavior	They are detached emotionally and see their role as only providing food, clothing, and shelter. In its extreme form, this parenting style results in *neglect,* a form of child abuse.

(*Sources:* Baumrind, 1971; Maccoby & Martin, 1983.)

Furthermore, most parents are not entirely consistent: Although the authoritarian, permissive, authoritative, and uninvolved patterns describe general styles, sometimes parents switch from their dominant mode to one of the others. For instance, when an adolescent is arrested for drunk driving, even the most laid-back and permissive parent is likely to react in a harsh, authoritarian manner, laying down strict demands about safety. In fact, in such cases authoritarian styles may be most effective (Janssens & Dekovic,1997; Holden & Miller, 1999; Eisenberg & Valiente, 2002; Gershoff, 2002).

Updating Baumrind: Beyond Discipline Styles. Why does authoritative parenting seem to have the best result? Building on the research on parenting styles, more recent work has focused on the specific dimensions of parenting that lead to adolescent success. Adolescent developmentalist Brian Barber and colleagues (Barber, Stoltz, & Olsen, 2005) have identified three sets of behaviors that are associated with successful adolescent functioning. They are

▲ Authoritative parenting, in which parents are relatively strict but emotionally supportive, generally provides the most effective discipline style.

- *Parental support. Parental support* involves creating an emotionally positive environment. Supportive parents are nurturant and provide companionship. Parental support is associated with higher levels of interpersonal competence and confidence in adolescents.

- *Lack of psychological control. Psychological control* refers to excessive parental control that impedes the psychological and emotional development of adolescents. It includes efforts to change children's feelings or thoughts to those that the parent feels are more acceptable, threats of withdrawal of love, and parental behavior designed to induce guilt. High levels of psychological control are associated with higher levels of depression in adolescents.

- *Behavioral control. Behavioral control* refers to the degree to which parents monitor their offspring's activities and provide consistent, clear guidelines for acceptable behavior. Higher levels of behavioral control are associated with lower levels of antisocial behavior on the part of adolescents.

Furthermore, it's becoming increasingly clear that parenting is not a one-way street; certain kinds of behavior on the part of children and adolescents may evoke specific behaviors from their parents. Adolescents who are dependable, conscientious, and confident tend to draw out more effective, authoritative parenting (Cook, 2001, 2005).

On the other hand, adolescents who are hostile or needy are more likely to bring about less-than-optimum parental practices. Parents of difficult children are more likely to use strict or even harsh discipline, or they may simply ignore their adolescents' behavior.

Reciprocal Socialization: The Two-Way Street of Parent–Adolescent Influence

reciprocal socialization   the process by which at one and the same time parents socialize their children and adolescents, and children and adolescents socialize their parents

The interplay between parents and their children reflects the phenomenon of reciprocal socialization. **Reciprocal socialization** is the process by which at one and the same time parents socialize their children and adolescents, and children and adolescents socialize their parents. That is, adolescent behavior is not only the *result* of parental child-rearing practices, but also in part the *cause* of parental behavior (Patterson & Fisher, 2002; Granic et al., 2003).

For example, when a 17-year-old boy breaks his curfew and comes in an hour late, his mother's initial response may be to yell at him and threaten to take away permission to use the family car. As a result, the son may respond with hostility that extends beyond the source of the mother's anger. In turn, the son's hostility may be interpreted by the mother as a sign that her son is difficult and stubborn, and she is more likely to respond with anger in the future when he creates even a minor provocation. This cycle may play out over days, weeks, months, and even years, creating a negative spiral that has an impact on both mother and son.

In short, the mother's behavior affects her adolescent son and produces various reactions on his part. But at the same time, the adolescent's behavior affects his mother and determines how she treats him.

It's clear that adolescents affect their parents' behavior and emotional reactions, sometimes even in ways that extend beyond the parent–child relationship. In fact, the presence of an adolescent in the home can affect the quality of the parents' married life. For instance, in surveys of parents, they report being least satisfied with their marriages when their children are teenagers. Marital satisfaction is higher in the periods that surround adolescence, when their offspring are younger or are adults (Benin & Robinson, 1997).

There are several reasons for the decline in marital satisfaction during adolescence. Not only are adolescents psychologically taxing, but they are economically costly. The expenses involved in feeding, clothing, and providing support for teenage activities are higher than in other, earlier periods of life (Collins & Laursen, 2004).

Continuity and Discontinuity in Parent-Child Relationships. The phenomenon of reciprocal socialization raises a chicken-versus-egg kind of question: Which comes first—parental or adolescent behavior? Because the two sets of reciprocal influences are so closely interwoven, it's a difficult, and perhaps ultimately impossible, question to answer.

Some adolescent developmentalists suggest that the roots of parent–child ways of relating to one another are found early in life. The *continuity approach* suggests that the way that parents and adolescents relate to one another is determined when the child is very young. As Ainsworth and other attachment theorists argued, the early interactions we have with our primary caregivers set the stage for our future relationships. These early relationships provide a kind of template for our subsequent interactions with others. The basic nature of parent–adolescent relations, then, has been determined far earlier in life than during adolescence (Roisman et al., 2005; Sroufe et al., 2005).

In fact, in some cases, continuity in the nature of relationships extends not only to parents and their children, but also across additional generations. For example, a father's relationship with his adolescent son may reflect the type of relationship the father had with *his* own father. And it may be that the adolescent will one day in the future have a similar type of relationship with his own son (Pratt & Fiese, 2004; Cowan, Bradburn, & Cowan, 2005).

In contrast to the continuity approach, the *discontinuity approach* argues that significant growth and change can occur in how one approaches relationships over the course of development. As adolescents and their parents develop, they encounter new types of relationships with others that can modify the way that they typically interact. In this view, relationship styles are constantly evolving as people form new relationships. This is particularly true of the adolescent period, when adolescents' relationships with peers become increasingly influential.

Cultural Differences in Child-Rearing Practices

It's important to keep in mind that the findings regarding child-rearing styles we have been discussing are chiefly applicable to Western societies. The style of parenting that is most successful may depend quite heavily on the norms of a particular culture—and what parents in a particular culture are taught regarding appropriate child-rearing practices (Papps et al., 1995; Rubin, 1998; Claes, Lacourse, & Bouchard, 2003; Giles-Sims & Lockhart, 2005).

For example, the Chinese concept of *chiao shun* suggests that parents should be strict, firm, and in tight control of their adolescents' behavior. Parents are seen to have a duty to train their offspring to adhere to socially and culturally desirable standards of behavior, particularly those manifested in good school performance. An adolescent's acceptance of such an approach to discipline is seen as a sign of parental respect (Chao, 1994; Wu, Robinson, & Yang, 2002).

Korean adolescents view strict parental control as signifying warmth and interest in their lives, in contrast to adolescents in the United States, who see the same behavior as oppressive. Similarly, parents in China are typically highly directive with their children, pushing them to excel and controlling their behavior to a considerably higher degree than parents typically do in Western countries. And it works: Generally speaking, adolescents with Asian parents tend to be quite successful, particularly academically (Steinberg, Dornbusch, & Brown, 1992; Collins & Laursen, 2004; Kim, 2005).

In contrast, U.S. parents typically are advised to use authoritative methods and explicitly to avoid authoritarian measures. Interestingly, it wasn't always this way. Until World War II, the point of view that dominated the advice literature was authoritarian, apparently founded on Puritan religious influences that suggested that children had "original sin" or that they needed to have their wills broken (Smuts & Hagen, 1985).

Ethnicity and Child-Rearing Practices.   Members of different ethnic groups within the United States also engage in parenting practices that reflect the norms of their own subcultural group. For example, authoritative parenting is less frequent in African-American, Asian-American, and Hispanic families than in Caucasian-American families. At the same time, authoritarian styles of parenting are more common among ethnic minority groups in the United States.

Although research on Caucasian-American adolescents finds that authoritarian parenting methods have generally harmful consequences, the consequences of authoritarian parenting for minority children may be less negative. For one thing, ethnic minorities may be more economically disadvantaged and live in more dangerous neighborhoods. In such a situation, strict parenting may reflect the need to protect adolescents from the dangers around them (Caughy & Franzini, 2005).

In addition, the parental styles of minority parents actually may consist of a combination of several styles. For example, minority parents may be quite strict (as in an authoritarian style) but also show great warmth (as in an authoritative style). Such a combination may be quite successful if it is congruent with the norms of child rearing that exist in a particular ethnic minority group (Formoso, Gonzales, & Aiken, 2000; Deardoff, Gonzales, & Sandler, 2003; Daddis & Smetana, 2005).

In short, the child-rearing practices that parents follow reflect cultural perspectives about the nature of children as well as parental perceptions regarding the appropriate role of parents and their support system. No single parenting pattern or style, then, is likely to be universally appropriate or invariably to produce successful adolescents (Harwood et al., 1996; Hart et al., 1998; Wang & Tamis-LeMonda, 2003).

Adolescent DIVERSITY   **Transcultural Adoptions**

Although most adolescents are raised by parents that share their own racial and ethnic identities, some aren't. Instead, they have been placed in a *transcultural adoption*, adopted by parents who belong to a different racial or ethnic group from their own.

By one estimate, transcultural adoptions account for nearly 15% of all nonrelative adoptions in the United States. Parents may adopt children from a different culture for several reasons. In some cases, transcultural adoptions occur because few children from the parents' own ethnic group are available for adoption, because parents feel connected to their adopted child's culture, or for humanitarian reasons. Opinions on transcultural adoptions among adoption experts are mixed; although some feel that matching race and ethnicity is less important than finding good homes for children in need, others point out that having a same-race family is important for the development of a strong racial identity (National Adoption Information Clearinghouse, 1994; Steinberg & Hall, 2000).

How well do children adjust to being transculturally adopted? The research evidence suggests that they fare pretty well in general. Their attachment to their adoptive families, self-esteem, academic achievement, and other indicators of adjustment don't seem to differ from those of children adopted into same-race families (Weinberg et al., 2004).

One way that transculturally adopted children do seem to differ from children in same-race families is in their racial identities. When the adopted children are very young, they actually seem to have a better sense of racial identity—perhaps because frequent reactions of other people to the racial composition of their families emphasizes their race at an early age. But by adolescence, a greater degree of racial confusion seems to emerge. Researchers have found that transculturally adopted adolescents may tend to feel discomfort with their appearance, to identify more with their parents' racial group than with their own, and to handle racial bias incidents poorly. This seems to be particularly the case when their adoptive parents minimize the importance of their racial identities (Friedlander, 1999; Nickman et al., 2005).

▲ Transcultural adoptions generally work well, although some degree of racial confusion may emerge during adolescence.

Parental Development: Middle Adulthood Meets Adolescence

It's not only their adolescent children who are changing in significant ways during adolescence. Parents, too, are facing their own challenges and encountering significant physical and psychological changes as their offspring pass through adolescence.

During their children's adolescence, most parents are passing through the period of middle adulthood. It's a time of significant physical and psychological change, as significant in some ways as what occurs during adolescence.

During middle adulthood, most parents are putting on weight, their vision and hearing are declining, and their reaction times are slowing down. Middle-aged parents are having sex less often, just as their children are having a sexual awakening and exploring their sexuality. Many mothers experience the *female climacteric,* the change from being able to bear children to no longer being able to do so. The most notable sign is *menopause,* the cessation of menstruation, which is often accompanied by physical and emotional discomfort. Fathers face the *male climacteric,* in which they slow down sexually, with periods between ejaculations becoming longer and sexual problems becoming more prevalent (Boul, 2003; Stewart, 2005).

In part because of these physical changes, middle adulthood is also a challenging period on a psychological level. Although research has shown that the "midlife crisis" is something of a myth, middle adulthood often brings the sometimes painful realization that one's life is more or less half over (Wethington, Kessler, & Pixley, 2004).

In substantial ways, the die is cast regarding one's career during middle adulthood. Mothers and fathers may realize that they are not going to be promoted beyond a certain level in their jobs, and they become more concerned about the here-and-now qualities of work and less on building careers. Parents must deal with the fact that they may not have achieved their early aspirations—aspirations that may have been nurtured during their own adolescence (Simonton, 1997; Jepsen & Sheu, 2003).

In addition, parents of adolescents may face another challenge: growing responsibility for the care of their own aging parents. The term *sandwich generation* has come to be applied to those middle-age adults who feel squeezed between the needs of both their children and their aging parents (Riley & Bowen, 2005).

The pressures of middle adulthood make for challenges that are in many ways the reverse of those faced by their adolescents. Adolescents are looking ahead, seeing the future as limitless and boundless in possibilities; their parents are looking back, contemplating opportunities missed and focusing on the limitations of life.

Furthermore, adolescents are coming into their own physically, facing increasing strength, the flowering of an adult body, and a sexual awakening. Their parents are looking at declines in their physical abilities and their sexual functioning. Particularly in Western societies, with their emphasis on youth and physical attractiveness, the physical aging of middle adulthood can be difficult.

How do these changes in parents' development affect their relationship with their adolescent children? In the worst case, parents feel jealous or act competitively with their adolescent. For instance, a mother may dress in a seductive manner, or a father may flirt with his son's girlfriends. Such behavior, although far from typical, obviously can be a source of substantial parent–child conflict.

In more usual cases, the physical and psychological changes being experienced by parents result in an increase in stress. Because adolescence already is a difficult period—most parents rate it as the toughest and most demanding period of child rearing—the transformations of middle adulthood add a further layer of stress to parent–adolescent relations (Steinberg & Steinberg, 1994; Bonds et al., 2002).

Who Parents?: The Differing Roles of Mothers and Fathers

After his mother—usually the more permissive of his parents—denied Bob permission to go to the beach for a weekend with his friend George, Bob decided to appeal to a different, if not higher, authority. Before his mother could talk to his father about her decision, Bob e-mailed his father, who was at work. He asked the same question about the proposed weekend trip, neglecting to mention that his mother had already said no. He figured he had nothing to lose—if his father said no, too, then it was pretty clear his chances were pretty slim. But if his father said it was OK, then Bob felt that he could at least negotiate some sort of compromise, even though he knew his parents would be annoyed with him for not accepting his mother's initial response. But, he reasoned, they'd end up being more annoyed at each other, rather than him.

The divide-and-conquer strategy of playing one parent off against another is a longstanding method used by adolescents seeking to get a desired response. Its use highlights the fact that up to now we've been considering "parents" in fairly imprecise terms.

We need to realize that the term "parents" encompasses both mothers and fathers, and that they do not necessarily act in tandem and think in precisely the same ways. In fact, the relationship between adolescents and their mothers is quite different from the one between adolescents and their fathers.

Mothers and Parenting. Mothers generally are more involved in the upbringing of their adolescents. Adolescents spend more time with their mothers than with their fathers, and adolescents report that they are more at ease talking about things with their mothers than their fathers. In particular, they are more comfortable talking about difficulties and emotional matters with their mothers (Updegraff et al., 2001).

In addition, mothers are more knowledgeable about their adolescents' interactions with their friends than are their fathers. There is also a gender difference relating to the sex of the adolescent: Mothers spend more time with their daughters than they do with their sons (see Figure 6-6).

Finally, there is greater emotional intensity in mother–adolescent relationships than in father–adolescent relationships. But this cuts both ways: Although the emotional connection between adolescents and their mothers can be positive and can provide support to the adolescent, the great emotionality can also have negative consequences, adding an emotional volatility to the relationship that father–adolescent relationships lack (Larson & Richards, 1994).

The picture painted of adolescent–mother relations is very much congruent with the gender stereotype of mothers and, more generally, females and reflects the reality that the major responsibility for parenting remains the burden of the mother. Mothers are more likely to be at home, rather than working outside the home, than fathers, and this affords mothers more opportunity to interact with their children. Furthermore, the psychological qualities associated with the traditional gender role of women, who are viewed as being more emotionally expressive and placing greater importance on interpersonal connections, may help to make mothers more accessible (Hyde & Delamter, 2006).

Fathers and Parenting.

My parents don't know me at all. Well, that's not exactly fair. My dad knows me pretty well, because he's actually sat down and we've talked about almost everything at some point.

Until the last three decades, the role of the father in parenting was considered secondary. In the traditional view of fatherhood, fathers' primary responsibilities were to be the breadwinner for the family and, to a lesser extent, to act as a role model (primarily for sons) and provide the moral underpinnings of the family. The day-to-day nitty-gritty of child care was left to the mother.

In the 1970s and 1980s, that view began to change. Fathers began to be seen as playing a significant role in the upbringing of their children, and engagement in child rearing was seen as an important component of fatherhood. Today fathers are recognized as playing a critical role in child and adolescent development (Day & Lamb, 2004; Parke, 2004; Parke et al., 2005).

For example, adolescents who report strong, accessible, and supportive fathers are better adjusted, reporting lower conflict and more positive emotions. They also report fighting less with their fathers than their mothers (Flouri & Buchanan, 2003; Flouri, 2005; Renk et al., 2005).

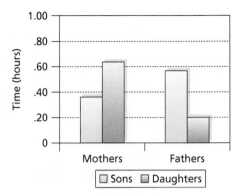

▲ **FIGURE 6-6**

Time Spent with Adolescent Sons and Daughters Time spent with adolescents breaks down along gender lines, as mothers spend more time with their daughters, and fathers spend more time with their sons. The figure represents the time (in hours) spent with the adolescent.

(*Source:* Updegraff et al., 2001, Table 1.)

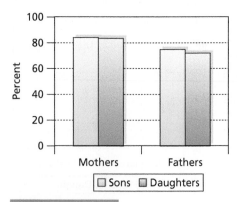

Knowledge of Adolescents' Friends
Adolescents report they are more comfortable talking with their mothers about difficult issues. In addition, mothers are more knowledgeable about their adolescents' interactions with their friends than are their fathers.

(*Source:* Updegraff et al., 2001, Table 1.)

Despite the acknowledged importance of fathers, they still don't play as important a role in adolescents' lives as do mothers. For many adolescents, fathers are seen as relatively distant, and they are most often viewed as the parent who provides material support or offers information—not unlike the traditional view of fatherhood (Steinberg & Silk, 2002; Collins & Laursen, 2004).

As seen in Figure 6-6, fathers spend less time with their adolescents than do mothers. However, there is also a difference in terms of the sex of their child: Like mothers, they spend more time with their same-sex adolescent, typically spending nearly twice as much time with their sons as with their daughters.

In addition, fathers are less well informed about what their adolescents are doing and whom they're doing it with. As shown in Figure 6-7, knowledge of their adolescents' lives and friends is lower among fathers than among mothers (Updegraff et al., 2001).

Coparenting: The Joint Effects of Mothers and Fathers.   In households that contain both a mother and father (and many don't, as we'll see in the last part of the chapter), coparenting takes on an important role. **Coparenting** is the process by which mothers and fathers coordinate their child-rearing practices (McHale, Kuersten-Hogan, & Rao, 2004).

The term *coparenting* was first used of divorced parents seeking to cooperate in caring for their offspring. But the term has been expanded to encompass parents living together in intact families. Specifically, adolescent specialists have sought to understand the effects of parental coordination and agreement regarding child-rearing practices on adolescent development (McHale & Kuersten-Hogan, 2004).

It turns out that effective coparenting is an important component of adolescent success. Parents who cooperate, agree on disciplinary tactics, present a united front, and have a warm relationship themselves are more likely to have well-adjusted adolescents. In contrast, adolescents whose parents don't coordinate child-rearing practices, are uncooperative with one another, or have different philosophies are placed at risk. Parents who contradict one another and undermine each other's authority can be particularly detrimental to adolescent development (Tamis-LeMonda & Cabrera, 2002; McHale, Kuersten-Hogan, & Rao, 2004).

The notion of coparenting is based on the premise that there are multiple individuals who are involved in the upbringing of an adolescent. However, in many situations this is not true. In the remainder of the chapter, we'll examine the variety of arrangements that make up families in the 21st century, and we'll consider their impact on adolescents.

coparenting   the process by which mothers and fathers coordinate their child-rearing practices

"Is everything all right, Jeffrey? You never call me 'dude' anymore."

Review and Apply

Review

1. Four major parenting styles have been identified by researchers, each of which affects adolescents' behavior differently.

2. Parental support, lack of psychological control, and behavioral control are three sets of parental behaviors that are associated with successful adolescent functioning.

3. As adolescents and parents interact, they engage in a process of reciprocal socialization in which the actions of each affect the future actions and attitudes of the other.

4. There are notable cultural and ethnic differences in child-rearing beliefs and practices, with no single style being universally appropriate or effective.

5. Fathers and mothers play different roles in their interactions with adolescent children, with mothers generally being more involved and more emotional.

Apply

1. What is the difference between psychological control and behavioral control? What are some examples of each, and what are the effects of each on adolescent behaviors?

2. If socialization is reciprocal, how might parents and their adolescents be helped to affect one another's behavior in positive rather than negative ways? Can the spiral of behaviors and attitudes go upward as well as downward?

Adolescents and the Diversity of their Families

If you asked most people in the United States, they would say the traditional **nuclear family**—a married couple and their unmarried children living together—is the preferred arrangement for families. And they might think that such an arrangement represents the reality of family life.

Yet only a third of families in the United States fit this description, and the number is shrinking. Over the last four decades, the number of households composed of a married heterosexual couple with children has been steadily declining, and this downward trend is predicted to continue.

In addition, the number of single-parent households has grown (see Figure 6-8). A quarter of all families with children and adolescents are headed by single parents (and 4% of children and adolescents grow up in households with no parent). Of those children living with single parents, the vast majority live with their mother. Furthermore, 65% of African American children and 37% of Hispanic children live in single-parent households (U.S. Bureau of the Census, 1998; ChildStats.gov, 2005).

Furthermore, the average size of families is shrinking. Today, on average, there are 2.6 persons per household, compared to 2.8 in 1980. The number of people living in nonfamily households (without any relatives) is close to 30 million.

The traditional nuclear family has also changed in terms of the roles that parents play. Families consisting of a wage-earning husband and a wife who stays at home have largely been replaced with *dual-income households* in which both parents work. For married couples, 96% of men and 70% of women work outside the home.

nuclear family a married couple and their unmarried children living together, considered by most to be the preferred arrangement for families

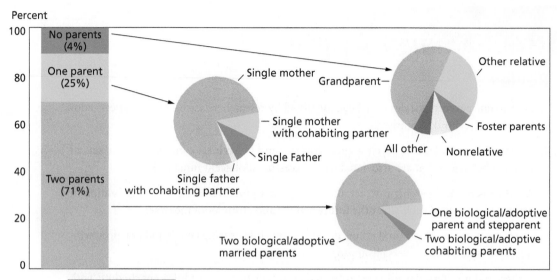

▲ FIGURE 6-8

Single-Parent Households Increasing The proportion of single-parent households is substantial and has increased dramatically over the past 50 years. What are some of the reasons for this trend?

(*Source:* U.S. Census Bureau, Survey of Income and Program Participation, 2001.)

These changes in the structure of the family have occurred for a number of reasons. One is economic need: The income of families in which both partners are employed is 85% higher than in families in which there is only one wage earner. But that's not the whole story. The number of dual-income households also has increased because women have become better educated, the economy of the United States has shifted its emphasis from manufacturing to more service-oriented industries, and the feminist movement has brought about a philosophical change in which women feel it is appropriate to hold a job outside the home (Bureau of the Census, 2002).

Perhaps even more important are changes in the view of single parenthood held by society. The stigma of being a single parent has declined significantly in the last few decades as divorce has become more common. Let's consider some of the different family configurations and their effects on adolescents.

Single-Parent Families

If present demographic trends continue, almost three quarters of American adolescents and children will spend some portion of their lives in a single-parent family before they are 18 years old. For members of minority groups, the numbers are even higher: Two thirds of African American adolescents and children and more than a third of Hispanic adolescents and children under the age of 18 live in single-parent homes (U.S. Bureau of the Census, 2000; see Figure 6-9).

In a small minority of cases, death is the reason for single parenthood. More frequently, either no spouse was ever present (that is, the mother never married), the spouses have divorced, or the spouse is absent. In the vast majority of cases, the single parent who is present is the mother.

What consequences are there for adolescents living in homes with just one parent? This is a difficult question to answer. Much depends on whether a second parent was present earlier and the nature of the parents' relationship at that time. Furthermore, the economic status of the single-parent family plays a role in determining the consequences for children. Single-parent families are often less well-off financially than two-parent families, and living in relative poverty has a negative impact on children (Davis, 2003; Harvey & Fine, 2004).

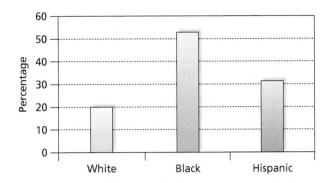

◀ **FIGURE 6-9**

Single-Parent Minority Households
Almost one quarter of all children in the
United States under the age of 18 live with
one parent. The figures are highest for
Blacks and Hispanics.

(*Source:* Childstats, 2006.)

In sum, the impact of living in a single-parent family is not, by itself, invariably negative or positive. Given the large number of single-parent households, the stigma that once existed toward such families has largely declined. The ultimate consequences for children depend on a variety of factors that accompany single parenthood, such as the economic status of the family, the amount of time that the parent is able to spend with the adolescent, and the degree of stress in the household.

Divorce

Having divorced parents is no longer very distinctive. Only around half the adolescents in the United States spend their entire preadult lives in the same household with both their parents. The rest will live in single-parent homes or with stepparents, grandparents, or other nonparental relatives, and some will end up in foster care (Harvey & Fine, 2004).

How do adolescents react to divorce? The answer depends on how soon you ask the question following a divorce as well as how old the children are at the time of the divorce.

Although researchers agree that the short-term consequences of divorce can be quite devastating, the longer-term consequences are less clear. Some studies have found that 18 months to 2 years later, most children begin to return to their predivorce state of psychological adjustment. For many children, there are minimal long-term consequences (Hetherington & Kelly, 2002; Guttmann & Rosenberg, 2003; Harvey & Fine, 2004).

On the other hand, there is evidence that the fallout from divorce lingers. For example, twice as many children of divorced parents enter psychological counseling as children from intact families (although sometimes counseling is mandated by a judge as part of the divorce). In addition, people who have experienced parental divorce are more at risk for experiencing divorce themselves later in life (Wallerstein et al., 2000; Amato & Booth, 2001; Wallerstein & Resnikoff, 2005).

How adolescents react to divorce depends on several factors. One is the economic standing of the family with which the adolescent is living. In many cases, divorce brings a decline in both parents' standard of living. When this occurs, adolescents may be thrown into poverty (Ozawa & Yoon, 2003).

In other cases, the negative consequences of divorce are less severe because the divorce reduces the hostility and anger in the home. If the household before the divorce was overwhelmed by parental strife—as is the case in around 30% of divorces—the greater calm of a postdivorce household may be beneficial to their offspring. This is particularly true for adolescents who maintain a close, positive relationship with the parent with whom they do not live (Davies et al., 2002).

For some adolescents, then, divorce is an improvement over living with parents who have an intact but unhappy marriage, high in conflict. But in about 70% of divorces, the predivorce level of conflict is not high, and adolescents in these households may have a more difficult time adjusting to divorce (Amato & Booth, 1997).

▲ Divorce can be quite devastating for adolescent children in the short term, but less so as time passes.

BECOMING AN INFORMED CONSUMER OF ADOLESCENT SCIENCE

Coping with Divorce

MUCH OF THE available advice on helping adolescents cope with the divorce of their parents is directed at parents themselves. Here are some coping tips specifically for adolescents (Nemours Foundation, 2004):

● Adolescents need to understand that the divorce is not their fault. Married couples divorce for many reasons, including personal or financial problems or simply falling out of love. Adolescents should try to understand that their parents have their own reasons for divorcing, which almost certainly had nothing to do with them. It's not something they could have prevented.

● Adolescents should expect a range of emotions. Adolescents whose parents are divorcing may feel a flood of emotions, and these may change from one day to the next. They may feel angry at one or both parents, worried about their future, or sad that their parents are unhappy. They might at times feel guilty for causing problems, or even relieved to have less tension and strife at home. These feelings are all a normal part of adjusting to divorce.

● Adolescents should prepare for changes in their lives. Some things will be different after their parents divorce. They may have to move to a different home and school, see their parents separately (perhaps spending a lot of time traveling between them), or adjust to a smaller household income.

● Adolescents should try to stay neutral to both parents. Their parents may say unkind things about each other or try to get their child to "takes sides." An adolescent should respectfully remind the critical parent that the former spouse is still the adolescent's mother or father. The adolescent should keep in mind that the bickering is between the parents and try not to get drawn into it.

● Adolescents should try to maintain contact with both parents. Although they may see one parent much less frequently than the other, or even live far apart, staying in touch by telephone or e-mail can help them both maintain a sense of closeness and stay informed about each other's lives.

● Adolescents should talk to their parents about their concerns. They may be worried about changes in family finances or their college or career plans. It can help them to know that their parents have them in mind, too. Talking about these issues is the first step to finding appropriate solutions. It can also be reassuring.

● Finally, adolescents should seek support from others. They should talk to trusted friends and family members about their concerns and feelings. They might even find it comforting to talk with a school counselor or a therapist, or to join a support group for adolescent children of divorced parents.

Multigenerational Families

Some households consist of several generations, with adolescents and their siblings, parents, and grandparents all living together. The presence of multiple generations in the same house can make for a rich living experience for adolescents, who may benefit from the influence of both their parents and their grandparents. On the other hand, multigenerational families also have the potential for conflict, with several adults acting as disciplinarians without coordinating their actions.

◀ The presence of multiple generations living together in a household can provide a rich experience for adolescents.

The prevalence of three-generation families who live together is greater among African Americans than among Caucasians. In addition, African American families, which are more likely than white families to be headed by single parents, often rely substantially on the help of grandparents in everyday child care, and cultural norms tend to be highly supportive of grandparents taking an active role (Budris, 1998; Baydar & Brooks-Gunn, 1998; Baird, John, & Hayslip, 2000; Crowther & Rodriguez, 2003).

Blended Families: Living with Stepparents and Stepsiblings

Today I had a lazy, slow wakeup and then spent the afternoon with my stepbrother, Jeff, who was up from Calgary for the day. My dad and his mom starting dating when I was 15 or 16 and Jeff was the cool, older brother that I always wished that my real brother had been.[5]

For many children, the aftermath of divorce includes the subsequent remarriage of one or both parents. For some adolescents, the addition of a stepparent and stepbrothers and stepsisters proceeds relatively smoothly and even may offer real benefits—as in the situation just described. But for other adolescents, the blending of families is difficult.

More than 10 million households in the United States contain at least one spouse who has remarried. More than 5 million remarried couples have at least one stepchild living with them in situations that have come to be called **blended families.** Overall, 17% of all children and adolescents in the United States live in blended families (U.S. Bureau of the Census, 2001; Bengtson et al., 2004).

Living in a blended family is challenging for adolescents. Often, a fair amount of *role ambiguity* occurs, in which roles and expectations are unclear. Adolescent children may be uncertain about what their responsibilities are, how to behave toward stepparents and stepsiblings, and how to make a host of decisions that have wide-ranging implications for their role in the family. For instance, an adolescent in a blended family may have to choose which parent to spend each vacation and holiday with or to decide between the conflicting advice coming from biological parent and stepparent (Dainton, 1993; Cath & Shopper, 2001; Belcher, 2003).

In comparison to younger children, who often adjust quite well, adolescents often find it difficult to become a part of a blended family. Despite the fact that the financial situation in a

blended famili
couples with a

Children
lar rel
n of heter

blended family may improve after a parent remarries and there are more people to share the burden of household chores, adolescents may be resentful of the new living arrangement. They may be particularly resistant to efforts by a stepparent to regulate their behavior (Hetherington & Clingempeel, 1992; Greene, Anderson, & Hetherington, 2003; Hetherington & Elmore, 2003).

Furthermore, adolescents may find the disruption of routine and of established networks of family relationships difficult to deal with. This is particularly true for girls, who generally have a harder time adjusting to blended families than do boys (Hetherington et al., 1989; Gunnoe & Hetherington, 2004).

Ultimately, both male and female adolescents usually manage to adjust to blended families. The most successful blending occurs when the parents create an environment that supports adolescents' self-esteem and a climate in which all family members feel a sense of togetherness (Buchanan, Maccoby, & Dornbusch, 1996; Sage, 2003).

Families with Gay and Lesbian Parents

An increasing number of adolescents have two mothers or two fathers. Estimates suggest that there are between one and five million families in the United States headed by parents who are both lesbians or gay men, and some 6 million adolescents and children have lesbian or gay parents (Patterson & Friel, 2000).

Relatively little research has been done on the effects of same-sex parenting on adolescents, and the results are not definitive. However, most studies find that the adolescents who grow up in lesbian and gay households develop similarly to those in heterosexual families. Their sexual orientation is unrelated to that of their parents, their behavior is no more or less gender-typed, and they seem equally well adjusted (Patterson, 2002, 2003; Parke, 2004).

Furthermore, children of lesbian and gay parents have similar relationships with their peers as children of heterosexual parents. They also relate to adults—both those who are gay and those who are straight—no differently from children whose parents are heterosexual. Furthermore, adolescents' romantic relationships and sexual behavior are no different from those of adolescents living with opposite-sex parents (Patterson, 1995; Golombok et al., 2003; Wainright, Russell, & Patterson, 2004).

In short, a growing body of research suggests that there is little developmental difference between children whose parents are gay or lesbian and those whose parents are heterosexual. What is clearly different for children with same-sex parents is the possibility of discrimination and prejudice based on their parents' homosexuality. As U.S. citizens engage in an ongoing and highly politicized debate regarding the legality of gay and lesbian marriage, children of such unions may feel singled out and victimized because of societal stereotypes and discrimination. (We'll consider gay and lesbian relationships between adolescents in Chapter 9).

Race, Ethnicity, and Family Life

Although there are as many types of families as there are individuals, there are consistencies related to race and ethnicity. For example, African-American families often have a particularly strong sense of family. Members of African-American families are frequently willing to offer welcome and support to extended family members in their homes. Because the level of female-headed households among African Amer-

of lesbian and gay parents
ationships with their peers
osexual parents.

icans is relatively high, the social and economic support of the extended family often is critical. In addition, there is a relatively high proportion of families headed by older adults, such as grandparents, and some studies find that children in grandmother-headed households are particularly well adjusted (McLoyd et al., 2000; Smith & Drew, 2002; Taylor, 2002; Parke, 2004).

Hispanic families also often stress the importance of family life, as well as community and religious organizations. Adolescents are taught to value their ties to their families, and they come to see themselves as a central part of an extended family. Ultimately, their sense of who they are becomes tied to the family. Hispanic families also tend to be relatively larger, with an average size of 3.71, compared to 2.97 for Caucasian families and 3.31 for African-American families (Cauce & Domenech-Rodriguez, 2000; U.S. Census Bureau, 2003).

Adolescents whose parents are immigrants face particular challenges. Not only must they make their way in schools in which they are most likely members of minority groups, but they must also help their parents and other family members navigate life in a foreign culture, as we discuss in the accompanying *Transitions* box.

Siblings: Adolescents and Their Brothers and Sisters

Siblings also have an important influence on adolescents, for good and for bad. Although brothers and sisters can provide support, companionship, and a sense of security, they can also be a source of strife.

Sibling relationships are generally fairly stable over the course of adolescence. Adolescents who were close to their siblings during middle childhood tend to remain close, whereas those with more distant relationships tend to remain distant. Adolescents who have good relationships with friends are also likely to have positive relationships with their siblings (Kramer & Kowal, 2005).

Some changes do occur in the nature of sibling relations over the course of adolescence. Generally, sibling relationships become more positive and egalitarian, with older siblings treating younger ones more respectfully and more as equals. As you can see in Figure 6-10 on page 205, adolescents asked to rate various relationships in their lives feel significant affection for their siblings, particularly compared to the degree of affection they feel for those outside their family. In some other respects, however, siblings are viewed as more similar to their friends than to other family members, such as in terms of the companionship they provide. At the same time, relationships with siblings may involve more conflict than any other relationship in their lives—even the relationship with parents (Furman & Buhrmester, 1992; Richmond, Stocker, & Rienks, 2005).

One cause of sibling conflict is *sibling rivalry,* the situation in which siblings compete with one another. Such rivalry may be most intense when siblings are similar in age and of the same gender. Parents may intensify sibling rivalry when they are perceived as favoring one child over another. Such perceptions may or may not be accurate. For example, older adolescents are likely to be permitted more freedom, which a younger sibling may interpret as favoritism. In some cases, perceived favoritism not only leads to sibling rivalry, but may also damage the self-esteem of the younger sibling (Howe & Ross, 1990; Ciricelli, 1995; Tseung & Schott, 2004).

What about "only children"—adolescents who have no siblings? Although only children have no opportunity to develop sibling rivalry, they also miss out on the benefits that siblings can bring. Generally, despite the stereotype that only children are spoiled and self-centered, the reality is that they are as well-adjusted as children with brothers and sisters. In fact, in some ways, only children are better-adjusted, often having higher self-esteem and stronger motivation to achieve. This is particularly good news for parents in the People's Republic of China, where a strict one-child policy is in effect. Studies there show that Chinese only children often perform better than children with siblings (Jiao, Ji, & Jing, 1996; Miao & Wang, 2003).

Transitions

Adolescents as Culture Brokers for their Families

*The whole thing, being an interpreter for my parents, my family—
I feel it is too much sometimes. . . . I need to deal with everything
from the simple matters to complicated matters. I feel I am like a
translating machine. It is not fun at all. I have my school work to do
too, and helping my parents after school. (Hall & Sham, 1998, p. 7)*

■ ■ ■

*Sometimes I am in control because I can make a decision on be-
half of my parents or a person I help as an interpreter. They all
depend on me. I feel great. My parents are so proud of me. They
think I am their good boy and they can depend on me when they
grow older. (Hall & Sham, 1998, p. 4)*

These children of immigrant parents are describing different reactions to their roles as culture brokers—go-betweens for their
families and the culture of their new country. Adolescents who
perform this function may be called on to translate documents and
mail, to answer the telephone, to help with shopping and business
transactions, to make medical appointments, and more. They help
their parents and other family members to communicate with the
outside world as well as to negotiate the norms, customs, and laws
of their new country. This responsibility tends to fall on the shoulders of immigrant children in part because they, more than their
parents, become immersed in their new culture through school and
peer interactions (Jones & Trickett, 2005).

As the earlier quotations suggest, acting as a culture broker can
be both a rewarding and a stressful experience for adolescent children of immigrants. On the one hand, this role can place a substantial burden on adolescents by giving them increased
responsibility or, in making the parents dependent on the adolescent,
disrupting the usual family structure. On the other hand, it may
give an adolescent feelings of pride and accomplishment in fulfill-

ing an important role within the family (Puig, 2002; Jones & Trickett, 2005).

One study of 226 adolescents and their mothers who immigrated
to the United States from the Soviet Union explored the culture-
broker role and its effects on these adolescents' lives. Nearly 90% of
these adolescents engaged in at least some culture brokering. The
demands placed on them varied, but they mainly involved translation and simple tasks such as answering the door and the telephone.
Not surprisingly, culture-broker duties were more common for adolescents whose parents were older, less educated, or less proficient in
English and for adolescents whose families arrived in the United
States more recently (Jones & Trickett, 2005).

Studies of the effects of culture brokering on adolescents suggest
that performing this function can be burdensome. Culture brokering was associated with emotional stress, decreased feelings of school
membership, and problems with friends. It was also related to the
frequency and intensity of family disagreements. However, culture
brokering was not associated with adolescents' scholastic performance or absenteeism at school, suggesting that the role of culture
broker isn't so burdensome that it interferes with immigrant adolescents' academic achievement.

In short, culture brokering represents a challenge for adolescents
who must play that role. At the same time, it makes an essential contribution to the family, helping older generations become more integrated into their new society.

- Do you think that adolescent boys and girls who assume the
culture-broker role experience the same feelings and have the
same experiences? How do you think they might differ?

- In what situations involving interactions between parents and
society do you think culture brokering by an adolescent child
would not be advisable? Why?

Family Systems

The complexity of families has led some researchers and theoreticians to view them as a system
in which the family members try to maintain some sort of equilibrium, or *homeostasis*. In this
view, families have their own rules and hierarchies, in which some members have higher status
than others. These rules and hierarchies implicitly direct the behavior of family members, determining in part their behavior within the family and even sometimes outside the family
(Menuchin, 2002).

In this *family systems perspective*, family members participate in a variety of subunits, such
as relationships between adolescents and their fathers, adolescents and their mothers, and adolescents and their individual siblings. In addition, there may be psychological alliances built between particular family members; conversely, certain pairs (or larger subunits) of family
members habitually may not get along well with one another.

Family systems may themselves be generally psychologically healthy, or they may be dysfunctional. Family systems that are healthy support the growth of the individual members and
accept change as adolescents develop.

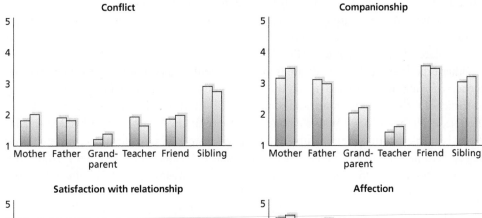

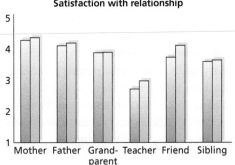

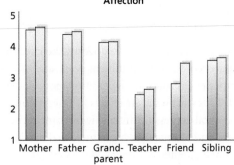

◄ **FIGURE 6-10**

Adolescent Relationships   Ratings of adolescents' relationships with significant people in their lives for whom they have affection.

(*Source:* Furman & Buhrmester, 1985.)

On the other hand, dysfunctional family systems may discourage growth on the part of family members, making the passage through adolescence difficult. Some dysfunctional families are inflexible, showing resistance to change and having difficulties when children move into adolescence. Other dysfunctional families are enmeshed, being so highly involved in each others' lives that the members may feel overly controlled. In either case, the nature of the family dysfunction can affect children as they pass through adolescence (Kaslow & Celano, 1995; Pinsof & Lebow, 2005).

Group and Foster Care: When Families Fail

If the thought of adolescents living in group care evokes images of pitiful, poorly clothed youngsters in huge, prison-like orphanage—like the portrayal in John Irving's book *Cider House Rules*—you need to revise your view, because it's quite out of date. The reality today is different. Even the term *orphanage* is rarely used, having been replaced by *group home, residential treatment center,* or *foster care.* Typically housing a relatively small number of adolescents, group homes are used for adolescents whose parents are no longer able to care for them adequately. They are typically funded by a combination of federal, state, and local aid.

The number of children and adolescents in group care grew significantly in the 1990s and then leveled off. In fact, in some cities, the number of children in out-of-home care declined somewhat in the early 2000s. Still, more than one-half million children in the United States live in foster care (Berrick, 1998; Roche, 2000; Jones-Harden, 2004).

About three quarters of children in group care are victims of neglect and abuse. Most of them can be returned to their homes following intervention with their families by social service agencies. But some are so psychologically damaged due to abuse or other causes that once they are placed in group care, they are likely to remain there throughout adolescence. Adolescents who have developed severe problems, such as high levels of aggression or anger, have difficulty finding adoptive families, and in fact it is often difficult to find even temporary foster families who are able to cope with their emotional and behavioral problems (Bass, Shields, & Behrman, 2004).

Although some politicians have suggested that an increase in group care is a solution to complex social problems associated with unwed mothers who become dependent on welfare, experts in providing social services and psychological treatment are not so sure. For one thing, group homes cannot always consistently provide the support and love potentially available in a family setting. Moreover, group care is hardly cheap: It can cost some $40,000 per year to support an adolescent in group care—about ten times the cost of maintaining a child in foster care or on welfare (Roche, 2000; Allen & Bissell, 2004).

Other experts argue that group care is inherently neither good nor bad. Instead, the consequences of living away from one's family may be quite positive, depending on the particular characteristics of the staff of the group home and the ability of the youth care workers to develop an effective, stable, and strong emotional bond with a specific child. On the other hand, if an adolescent is unable to form a meaningful relationship with a worker in a group home, the results may well be harmful (Shealy, 1995; McKenzie, 1997; Reddy & Pfeiffer, 1997). (For a discussion with someone who works with group care residents, see the accompanying *Career Choices* interview.)

Poverty: The Toll of Being Raised Poor

For adolescents living in poverty, the challenges of the period are intensified. Lacking the resources of their more affluent peers, and often living in families in which the parents themselves experience economic deprivation, poor adolescents face more than their share of difficulties.

Let's start with the effects of poverty on parents of adolescents. Economic strain increases parental depression, intensifies arguments between parents, produces worry about money matters, and ultimately leads to increased marital conflict and shaky marriages (Conger et al., 1999; Conger, Reuter, & Conger, 2000; Conger, & Lorenz, 2005).

Clearly, poverty has negative consequences on parents, and it affects their ability to parent their offspring successfully. Parents with marriages possibly dissolving under the strain of economic hardship may be focused on their own difficulties, and consequently they may spend less time providing direct care to their adolescents. In addition, they may work long hours at multiple jobs to make ends meet (Luster & Okagaki, 2005).

The stress on parents may be reflected in their child-rearing practices. They may provide harsh or inconsistent parenting, or they may be relatively uninvolved with their children. As we've seen earlier in the chapter, such disciplinary styles typically result in negative consequences. Furthermore, adolescents and their parents may squabble over money, with adolescent children feeling deprived in relation to their more affluent peers (Johnson et al., 2003; Felner, 2005; Gutman, McLoyd, & Tokoyawa, 2005).

It is clear that poverty places adolescents at risk for negative outcomes. But this doesn't mean that adolescents raised in poverty are destined to have difficulties. As we discussed earlier in the chapter, adolescents have enormous resiliency, which permits them to weather less-than-ideal circumstances. In addition, the extent of poverty can be reduced. With appropriate governmental intervention, such as the institution of programs to fight poverty, increases in the minimum wage, and good child care that allows the parents of adolescents with younger siblings to work, the negative consequences of economic deprivation can be diminished (Felner, 2005).

The Bottom Line: Families Matter

In meeting the challenges of adolescence, families have an enormous impact. The research findings from literally thousands of studies are indisputable: Adolescents who feel connected to their families and perceive that they are supported and loved pass through the period more successfully than those who feel unconnected to their families.

Whether it is a single-parent or a dual-parent family, whether the parents are heterosexual or homosexual, whether the family is affluent or poor, whether the structure is a traditional nuclear family or a blended family, the results are similar. The particular family structure is less important than the degree of connection and support offered to the adolescent.

The centrality of family was made clear by a massive questionnaire and interview study involving almost 100,000 U.S. adolescents. The major finding: The single most important deter-

CAREER CHOICES

Social Worker

Name: Paul J. Detaege, LCSW

Education: B.A., Sociology, Cardinal Stritch University, Milwaukee, WI; MS, Social Work, Loyola University, Chicago, IL

Position: Licensed clinical social worker in the Department of Psychiatry section of Child and Adolescent clinic

Home: Chicago, IL

ADOLESCENTS WHO need help in dealing with the many significant issues that arise during their teenage years require a specialized approach to addressing their problems, according to adolescent social worker Paul Detaege.

Detaege, who sees as many as 600 youth a year in his capacity as social worker, says that developing a bond with adolescents is crucial in understanding what their problems are and helping to resolve them.

"For many adolescents it is very difficult to come in and talk to someone, so I try to focus on developing a therapeutic relationship as the real key," Detaege explained. "When you build that relationship, it is then that you get at what is really going on. You have to develop a trust."

Detaege says he starts with the basics by creating an environment of consistency in his meetings with adolescents.

"The first thing I would do is establish a consistent meeting time and let them know I will be there," he said. "If I say I'm going to do something, I will do it. They can rely on and can create a structure they can depend on. Modeling consistency, predictability, and structure are important."

Detaege noted that adolescents have a difficult time acknowledging sadness and anger, as well as feelings of loneliness and not having friends.

"I try to talk to them on how long they have been feeling this way, and then we set up a task plan," he said. "I ask if there are some things we can brainstorm about and whether there is something they can plug into, perhaps at school. I try to help them put together a plan."

One area in which Detaege has found success is a group adolescent program he started a number of years ago.

"I could be working with an adolescent for a number of weeks, with just the two of us. But once I put him in a group, it would be amazing the new things one would hear him talk about. Being among one's peers can be very therapeutic and also provides a support system," he said.

Thinking of becoming a social worker?

Social workers help people to overcome adversity or to improve their lives. They provide services to people who need help dealing with personal, family, or social problems, such as drug addiction, spousal abuse, or unemployment. Some social workers specialize in families and children; they may help single parents to cope with the competing demands of work and family, or they may help place abused or neglected children in appropriate foster homes. These social workers typically work for family service agencies or for state or local government agencies.

Good social workers are mature, responsible, and sensitive people who are able to work independently and have a passion for helping others. The minimum preparation for a social work career is a bachelor's degree in social work (BSW), although many positions require a master's degree (MSW), which includes a lengthy internship. Social workers must be licensed or certified by the state in which they intend to practice. ■

minant of adolescent well-being was the family environment (Blum & Rinehart, 2000). Regardless of an adolescent's gender, race, socioeconomic status, personality, or any other factor, what fundamentally matters is having a family member who provides love and support—a simple, and reassuring, conclusion.

Review and Apply

Review

1. The traditional nuclear family is the pattern in only a minority of families in the United States today. For adolescents living in single-parent families, the effects mostly depend on factors other than the lack of a second parent, such as economic conditions.

2. The effects of divorce depend on family economic conditions, the level of parental conflict before the divorce, the quality of the postdivorce relationship between the adolescent and both parents, and the time that has elapsed since the divorce.

3. Blended and multigenerational families have become common and may present both challenges and opportunities for adolescents.

4. Adolescents with gay or lesbian parents generally turn out the same as adolescents with heterosexual parents in terms of later relationships, sexual orientation, and other factors.

5. Siblings have an important influence on adolescents, providing support and companionship as well as conflict.

Apply

1. Why does the myth of the nuclear family persist so strongly in U.S. popular culture? Do the media help to sustain this myth or combat it?

2. Given the importance of families, should the federal government adopt policies to encourage and support families? What sorts of policies would work? What sorts of policies are unlikely to work?

EPILOGUE

In this chapter we looked at the role of the family in the lives of adolescents. We examined the myth of conflict and tumult that is supposed to infect family relations during the period, and we found it to be largely inaccurate. We considered adolescents' increasing need for autonomy as a natural part of the period, and we balanced it with a discussion of the adolescent's continuing need for attachment with parents and caregivers. Next we looked at the roles and styles that parents employ in exercising their responsibilities, and the effects of their different approaches on their adolescent children. We found that adolescents influence their parents nearly as much as parents influence their children. Finally, we explored the many different patterns and structures that constitute "families" in the United States, including nuclear families, single-parent families, coparenting arrangements, families headed by gay or lesbian parents, blended and multigenerational families, and other arrangements. We found that the quality of relationships within families is the most important factor, not the structure of the family itself.

Before we move on to the next chapter, let's return for a second look at Leah as she prepares to attend her first formal dance. Consider the following questions:

1. What do you think might be the consequences of Leah's mother and father apparently having different ideas regarding Leah's curfew?

2. What seems to be at the heart of the conflict between Leah and her parents?

3. Which of Baumrind's parenting styles do you think Leah's parents best typify? Why?

4. How do you think Leah's parents should resolve this disagreement? Why?

SUMMARY

REVIEW

- **How characteristic of adolescence is conflict within the family?** *(p. 176)*

    1. Some conflict is unavoidable during adolescence as adolescents seek to increase their autonomy and caregivers struggle with releasing control.

2. The extent of conflict in adolescence is mostly minor and focuses on ordinary everyday matters rather than serious issues.

3. The "generation gap" has been exaggerated; in fact there is typically more agreement between adolescents and their parents than between adolescents and their peers.

● **How do adolescents balance their need for attachment with their desire for autonomy?** *(p. 185)*

4. The development of autonomy is one of the major tasks of adolescence.

5. To develop autonomy, adolescents have to develop their own unique view of themselves and learn to do things because they are important to them instead of to others.

6. Although autonomy is important, attachment between adolescents and others, especially parents, is also important because patterns of attachment affect social competence and relationships throughout life.

● **What roles and styles of parenting are typical in families with adolescents?** *(p. 188)*

7. Four major parenting styles—authoritarian, permissive, authoritative, and uninvolved—have been identified by adolescent researchers. These parenting styles can have long-term effects on children, but there is no universally successful style that works in all cases.

8. Parental support, a lack of psychological control, and sound behavioral control are sets of behaviors that are associated with successful parenting.

9. Just as parents influence their adolescent children's behavior, so too do adolescent children influence their parents' behavior. This is called reciprocal socialization.

10. Culture, ethnicity, and gender influence parenting practices. In general, mothers are involved and emotional in their interactions with their children.

● **How are adolescents affected by diverse and changing family arrangements?** *(p. 197)*

11. The traditional nuclear family has given way in the United States to single-parent families, coparenting by divorced parents, blended families, families headed by gay and lesbian couples, multigenerational families, and other family structures.

12. In general, diverse and changing family structures have less of a direct impact on adolescents than other factors that are associated with the functioning of families, such as economic conditions.

13. Different ethnic and culture groups in the United States display different family arrangements. No single arrangement is universally correct or successful, and all are subject to threats and challenges.

14. Group and foster care arrangements are neither good nor bad on their own, but may have positive or negative effects depending on the quality of staff and services.

KEY TERMS AND CONCEPTS

generation gap (p. 177)
autonomy (p. 181)
attachment (p. 184)
secure attachment pattern (p. 184)
avoidant attachment pattern (p. 184)
ambivalent attachment pattern (p. 185)

resilience (p. 186)
authoritarian parents (p. 188)
permissive parents (p. 188)
authoritative parents (p. 188)
uninvolved parents (p. 188)

reciprocal socialization (p. 190)
coparenting (p. 196)
nuclear family (p. 197)
blended families (p. 201)

7 Peers

CHAPTER OUTLINE

PROLOGUE Web of Friends

WAY BEFORE GEORGIA State University freshman Rebecca Hickom ever set her sneakers on campus for the first time, the Cartersville teenager had already chatted with her roommates, checked out her dorm-hall neighbors and met another freshman who shares her love of indie-rock music—a guy, "just a friend," she's been hanging out with "like every single night. . . ."

Trevor Stittleburg, a Georgia Tech freshman from Kennesaw, registered on Facebook this summer before he got to campus. As Stittleburg waited in front of the Theta Chi fraternity house recently, he spotted one of his new Facebook friends across the street and waved.

Erika Gemzer, 18, clad in green capri pants for her first day of sorority rush, flitted across Techwood Drive to say hello. The two met at a freshmen orientation party a few evenings before and had already exchanged e-mails through the Web site.

"It's great because you can see what interests people have and what you have in common," Stittleburg said, as Gemzer nodded. "It's a really excellent tool."

"Everybody's Facebooking each other," Gemzer said. "It's a verb." (Jones, 2005, p. 1E) ∎

th!nk ABOUT THIS

ONLY A FEW YEARS AGO—eons in cybertime—the physical reality of adolescents' lives defined who their peers were. No longer. For many, like Trevor Stittleburg and Erika Gemzer, online peers are as important, and influential, as those they encounter in their schools and neighborhoods. But whether peers are found in cyberspace or in the house next door, they play a central role in the lives of adolescents.

In this chapter we examine the role of peers in adolescents' lives. We begin by considering how adolescents increasingly characterize who they are in relation to others of the same age. We'll see that other adolescents—even those who aren't close friends—have considerable influence over adolescents' attitudes and behavior, and that there are significant developmental changes in peer relationships during the course of adolescence.

Next, we examine peer groups—all the groups to which adolescents belong. Everywhere they turn, adolescents encounter groups ranging from formal groups to informal cliques and crowds, and we'll observe the various ways that such groups exert significant conformity pressures.

Finally, we consider what makes some adolescents popular with their peers—and the factors that lead others to experience the status of social outsiders. We'll consider the nature of popularity and its advantages (there are many) and shortcomings (there are a few). We'll also look at ways adolescents can improve their social standing. ∎

YOU WILL BE ABLE TO ANSWER THESE QUESTIONS:

- Why are peer relationships important during adolescence?
- How do adolescents choose the people who will become their peers?
- What are the characteristics of the groups to which adolescents belong?
- What determines an adolescent's popularity or unpopularity?
- Can an adolescent take steps to become more popular?

Connections with Peers

First day of HIGH SCHOOL!
Well, I can't say I'm particularly fond of high school. At all. It was a little weird, didn't expect to have such a new group of friends, but that's awesome, friends rock! Woo!

1st: Geography. A lot of people from [middle school]. It's like going back . . .

2nd: Biology 1. With Janet and Jamie! Friends!

3rd: Theatre Arts 1. Why did Janet, Stephanie and Alex get the same class but I'm left all alone?

Lunch. Had FIVE MINUTES TO EAT. Alex and I were standing in LINE THE WHOLE TIME. Talking about how we already hated almost all of these people.

4th: Study Hall. Easy pass, no one to talk to.

5th: English. Jamie's in my class. Zach too. Sit near both of them.

6th: German 1. . . .

7th: Algebra 2. Alecko and Taylor Osbourne in my class. You know how much I just love those guys . . .

As this 14-year-old's description of her first day of school indicates, friends play a central role in adolescents' lives. They clearly constituted what was important to this adolescent—far more important than the new academic challenges that she presumably faced.

One of the most visible transitions from childhood to adolescence is the stronger reliance on friendships. In contrast to children, adolescents increasingly define themselves by the kind of friends they have—or don't have. Friends offer support and acceptance that become increasingly important as reliance on parents and families decreases. Furthermore, adolescents' relationships with peers become increasingly complex and intense (Brown, 2004).

But it's not only friends who are important. Even peers who are not counted as friends become extraordinarily influential in the lives of adolescents. **Peers** are individuals who are about the same age or level of maturity, and they play a potent role in the development of adolescents—in part because of the educational and social practices that characterize the adolescent period.

Adolescents spend an enormous amount of time with their peers. In fact, they spend more time interacting with their peers than on *anything* else. Even without counting the time they spend in their classes, high school students spend twice as much time with peers as they do with their families, teachers, or other adults. They see their friends at school, in the evenings, and on weekends. If adolescents are asked to identify their *significant others*—the people who are most important to them—close to half of the people named are of the same age as they are (Csikszentmihalyi & Larson, 1984; Brown, 2004).

As peers grow in importance, time spent with parents declines. In fact, one of the most significant changes in the transition from childhood to adolescence is the reduction in time spent with parents. But the nature of the change is not the same for boys and girls. For girls, time

peers individuals who are about the same age or level of maturity

spent with parents is replaced during early adolescence by time spent with friends. For boys, the reduction in time with parents is replaced by an increase in time spent alone (see Figure 7-1). In addition, there are some racial differences: The increase in time spent with peers is more pronounced for Caucasian girls than for Caucasian boys and African-American boys and girls (Larson & Richards, 1991; Larson et al., 2001).

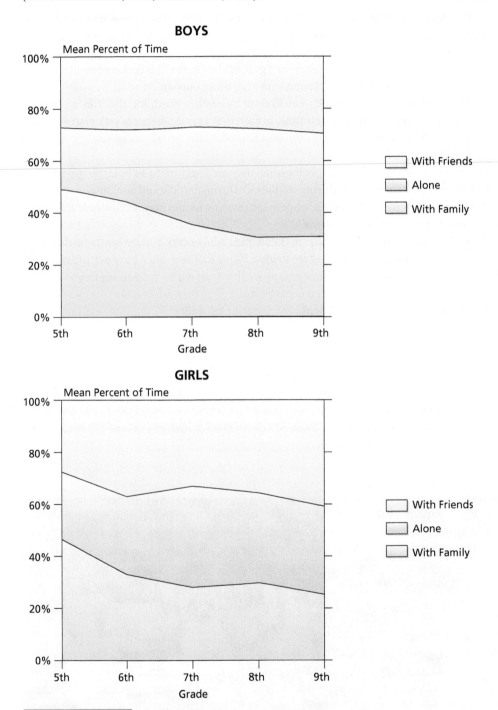

▲ **FIGURE 7-1**

Time Spent with Parents While time spent with parents declines as peers play a more important role in adolescents' lives, the change is different for boys and girls. For girls, time spent with parents is replaced with time spent with friends, while with boys, time spent with parents is replaced with time spent alone.

(*Source:* Larson & Richards, 1991.)

Furthermore, although time with parents declines as time spent with peers begins to increase, this does not mean that peers replace parents in terms of their psychological influence, but instead they supplement parental influence. Depending on the domain, either parents or peers may be more influential (Blyth, Hill, & Thiel, 1982; Munsch & Blyth, 1993; Schwartz, Bukowski, & Aoki, 2006).

As the amount of time spent with peers grows during adolescence, the degree of adult supervision declines. Adolescents increasingly function on their own, outside the scrutiny of parents and other adult figures. Prior to adolescence, children's activities usually occur under the watchful eye of an adult, typically in organized groups such as the Cub Scouts or in after-school programs. Even when children are playing with each other outside, an adult is nearby.

During adolescence, teenagers are more likely to be unsupervised, and they take on increasing responsibility for structuring their time. In fact, they may deliberately seek places to hang out where parents are not present, as the nearness of adults becomes disliked and resented (Brown, 1990, 2004).

Furthermore, when adolescents get together, they are likely to do so in larger groups than those in which they congregated during childhood. During middle and late childhood, typical groups consisted of pairs of children, or perhaps three or four others. In contrast, adolescent groups often consist of larger collectives.

As we'll discuss in greater detail later in the chapter, adolescents come to see themselves (and others) as parts of specific groups that are so identifiable that they often have particular names, such as the "jocks" or the "Goths." These groups are characterized by the clothing they wear, their activities, the places they frequent, and even the vocabulary they use. It is not until adolescence that such distinctions can be made with any degree of reliability.

Developmental Changes in Peer Relationships

Not only do adolescents spend more time with their peers than they did earlier, but *what* they do also changes in adolescence. In middle childhood, peer interaction is largely about sharing activities. There is enjoyment simply from doing things with another child. Furthermore, the choice of peers is oriented toward those who have similar interests (Berndt & Perry, 1986; Brown, 2004; Brown & Klute, 2006).

▶When adolescents spend time together, they are usually in larger groups than when they were younger.

However, as individuals enter adolescence, their choices of peers are based more on psychological factors. Adolescents seek to share concerns, secrets, and hopes for the future. Trust becomes as central to friendship as companionship. Furthermore, adolescents expect their trust to be reciprocated.

In addition, the heterogeneity of peers becomes greater. Adolescents typically move into larger schools that include a wider array of individuals, differing with respect to racial, ethnic, and socioeconomic characteristics. Whereas elementary schools typically draw from small, relatively homogeneous neighborhoods, and children's neighborhood playmates are often similar to themselves, the situation typically changes in larger middle schools. The pool of peers becomes larger, offering the opportunity to meet more—and different—peers.

Yet in terms of one characteristic—age—relationships remain extremely homogeneous. Most peer relationships involve adolescents of similar ages. In fact, age segregation remains a very strong characteristic of peer interaction throughout adolescence, largely due to historical reasons, as we see next.

Peers, Age Segregation, and Age Grading

When U.S. educators developed the notion of universal, free education in the mid-1800s, the organizing principle was to group students according to age—a practice called *age grading*. In making this decision, educators played a large role in determining whom adolescents would spend most of their time with. Ultimately, their decision guaranteed that there would be a significant degree of age segregation within adolescent peer groups.

In fact, the degree of age segregation among adolescents in the United States is quite remarkable. For example, surveys of adolescents find that the large majority name people in their own grade when asked to identity those who are important to them. Age segregation is extensive even in extracurricular activities, where there's at least the potential for cross-age interaction (Blyth, Hill, & Thiel, 1982; Brown & Klute, 2006).

Middle and high schools actually foster age grading. Not only do they create segregation by separating students into particular grades, but they also encourage students to frame their identity around a particular class level by the use of labels such as "the sophomore class" or "the senior class." Furthermore, there is often open—and encouraged—competition between members of different grades. (We'll discuss the consequences of school structure further in Chapter 10, when we focus on schooling.)

The widespread and extreme age segregation of adolescence is a relatively recent phenomenon, at least in a historical sense. Postelementary school education was relatively restricted prior to the 1930s, with high school being available almost exclusively to members of higher socioeconomic classes. Furthermore, particularly in rural areas, preadolescents were often educated in one-room schools that included classmates of a wide range of ages. Such schools fostered interaction between individuals of different ages. Thus, although we don't know for sure, it seems reasonable to assume that in earlier periods there was less age segregation than we find now (Devin-Sheehan, Allen, & Feldman, 1976; Allen, 1989; Merrow, 2004).

Finally, during the first third of the 20th century, before the onset of child labor laws, most adolescents joined the workforce instead of continuing their education. At the workplace they encountered people of different ages and were likely to interact with them from early adolescence on. After the adoption of stricter legal regulations on when children and adolescents could work—and controls on the kind of work they could do—the probability of adolescents interacting with a significant number of adults declined (Modell & Goodman, 1990; Hindman, 2002; Whittaker, 2003).

Parental Pressure Supporting Age Segregation. The age grading found in schools and the decline in adolescent work experiences with older individuals are two historical causes of the prevalence of age segregation in adolescence. An additional cause is parental pressure on adolescents to stick to their own age group. Parents may fear that friendships that deviate too much from the peer group may jeopardize their sons' and daughters' relationships with people their own age. For example, they may feel that adolescents who become close friends with a younger child may be hindered in their social development and miss out on significant social milestones.

Parents tend to be even more concerned about adolescent sons and daughters who become close to older adolescents or young adults. The fear is that older friends will lure younger adolescents into questionable activities, such as the use of illegal drugs, sexual experiences, and delinquency (Galambos, Barker, & Tilton-Weaver, 2003).

Their fears are not unfounded: There is some evidence that adolescents with older friends are somewhat more likely to become involved in undesirable behavior than those who stick with friends their own age. However, it's not clear whether having older friends leads younger adolescents toward unwelcome consequences, or whether adolescents who are already prone to undesirable behaviors are more likely to seek out older individuals who are engaged in such behaviors (Dishion, Nelson, & Bullock, 2004; Laird et al., 2005).

The Sex Cleavage: Gender and Peers

As young people begin the transition from middle childhood to adolescence, their groups of friends are composed almost universally of same-sex individuals. Boys hang out with boys and girls hang out with girls. Both organized activities—such as the Brownies and Cub Scouts—and more informal play reflect this sex segregation, which technically is called the **sex cleavage.**

However, the situation changes as members of both sexes enter puberty. Boys and girls experience the hormonal surge that marks puberty and causes the maturation of the sex organs. At the same time, societal pressures suggest that the time is appropriate for romantic involvement. These developments lead to a change in the ways adolescents view the opposite sex.

Whereas a 10-year-old is likely to see every member of the other sex as "annoying" and "a pain," heterosexual teenage boys and girls begin to regard each other with greater interest in terms of both personality and sexuality. (For gays and lesbians, pairing off holds its own complexities, as we will discuss in Chapter 8, when we consider adolescent dating.)

As they move into puberty, boys' and girls' peer groups, which previously had moved along parallel but separate tracks, begin to converge. Adolescents begin to attend boy–girl dances or parties, although most of the time the boys still spend their time with boys, and the girls with girls (Richards et al., 1998).

A little later, however, adolescents increasingly spend time with members of the other sex. New peer groups emerge, composed of both males and females. Not everyone participates initially: Early on, the teenagers who are leaders of the same-sex groups and who have the highest status lead the way. Eventually, however, most adolescents find themselves in groups that include both boys and girls.

sex cleavage sex segregation in which boys interact primarily with boys and girls primarily with girls

Adolescent
DIVERSITY
Race Segregation: The Great Divide of Adolescence

*W*hen Philip McAdoo . . . stopped one day to see a friend who worked on his college campus, a receptionist asked if he would autograph a basketball for her son. Because he was African American and tall, "she just assumed that I was on the basketball team," recounted McAdoo.

Jasme Kelly, an African American sophomore at the same college, had a similar story to tell. When she went to see a friend at a fraternity house, the student who answered the door asked if she was there to apply for the job of cook.

White students, too, find racial relations difficult and in some ways forbidding. For instance, Jenny Johnson, a white 20-year-old junior, finds even the most basic conversation with African American classmates difficult. She describes a conversation in which African American friends "jump at my throat because I used the word 'black' instead of African American. There is just such a huge barrier that it's really hard . . . to have a normal discussion." (Sanoff & Minerbrook, 1993, p. 58)

The pattern of race segregation found at this college is repeated over and over in schools and colleges throughout the United States: Even when they attend desegregated schools with significant ethnic and racial diversity, people of different ethnicities and races interact very little. Moreover, even if they have a friend of a different ethnicity within the confines of a school, most adolescents don't interact with that friend outside school (DuBois & Hirsch, 1990).

Evidence for this ethnic and race segregation comes from a study of Hispanic adolescents in which researchers Grace Kao and Elizabeth Vaquera (2006) explored friendship choices. Using questionnaire data from the National Longitudinal Study of Adolescent Health, a study that used a large representative sample of adolescents in grades 7 through 12, they compared Hispanic participants' own self-reported racial and ethnic identities to those of their closest same-sex friends. They found that ethnic background tended to be matched between Hispanic friends. For example, about 90% of Mexican adolescents listed another Mexican adolescent as their closest same-sex friend, 66% of Cubans listed another Cuban, and 54% of Puerto Ricans listed another Puerto Rican.

The racial and ethnic segregation typical of adolescence doesn't start out this way. During elementary school and even during early adolescence, there is a fair amount of integration among students of differing ethnicities. However, by middle and late adolescence, the

▲ Even when cross-racial friendships arise in school, most adolescents do not interact with that friend outside of school.

amount of segregation is striking (Shrum, Cheek, & Hunter, 1988; Spencer & Dornbusch, 1990; Spencer, 1991; Ennett & Bauman, 1996).

Why should racial and ethnic segregation be the rule, even in schools that have been desegregated for some time? One reason is that minority students may actively seek support from others who share their minority status (where "minority" is used in its sociological sense to indicate a subordinate group whose members lack power, compared to members of a dominant group). By associating primarily with other members of their own group, members of minority groups are able to affirm their own identity.

Members of different racial and ethnic groups may be segregated in the classroom as well. As we will discuss in Chapter 12, because members of certain minority groups have been historically discriminated against, they tend to experience less school success than members of the majority group. It may be that ethnic and racial segregation in high school is based not on ethnicity itself, but on academic achievement.

If minority group members experience less academic success, they may find themselves in classes with proportionally fewer majority group members. Similarly, majority students may be in classes with few minority students. Such class assignment practices, then, may inadvertently maintain and promote racial and ethnic segregation. This pattern would be particularly prevalent in schools where rigid academic tracking is practiced, with students assigned to "low," "medium," and "high" tracks, depending on their prior achievement (Lucas & Behrends, 2002).

The lack of contact among students of different racial and ethnic backgrounds in school may also reflect prejudice, both perceived and real, toward members of other groups. Students of color may feel that the white majority is prejudiced, discriminatory, and hostile, and they may prefer to stick to same-race groups. Conversely, white students may assume that minority group members are antagonistic and unfriendly. Such mutually destructive attitudes reduce the likelihood that meaningful interaction can take place (Phinney, Ferguson, & Tate, 1997; Tropp, 2003).

Is this sort of voluntary segregation along racial and ethnic lines found during adolescence inevitable? No. Adolescents who have interacted regularly and extensively with those of different races earlier in their lives are more likely to have friends of different races. Schools

"Gee, Tommy, I'd be lost without your constant peer pressure."

Transiti◑ns

How Adolescents Influence Their Friends to Be Helpful

Attention is often focused on the ways in which adolescents are influenced by their friends to engage in various risky or antisocial behaviors, such as drug use or crime. But how much do friends influence each other to engage in beneficial, helpful behavior—known as *prosocial behavior?*

There is good reason to suppose that friends can influence one another to behave more prosocially to others. For one thing, friendships provide a context for adolescents to develop a sense of concern and caring for others. In addition, adolescents can model prosocial behaviors for their friends, which may in turn increase their friends' motivation to be more socially positive themselves. Furthermore, adolescents can provide reinforcement to their friends for engaging in prosocial behaviors (Barry & Wentzel, 2006).

In fact, research confirms that adolescent friends tend to be similar in their level of prosocial motivation and behaviors. However, we cannot be sure that this similarity results from friends influencing each other. Instead, it may be the case that adolescents who already have similar prosocial values are simply more likely to become friends (Wentzel, Barry, & Caldwell, 2004).

To determine if friends influence each other to behave in a more prosocial manner, researchers Carolyn Barry and Kathryn Wentzel (2006) conducted a longitudinal study to investigate the ways in which adolescents influence their friends. They were specifically interested in whether friends' prosocial behaviors predict whether adolescents will put their own prosocial motivations into action, and whether the quality of the friendship makes a difference.

Barry and Wentzel asked almost 300 9th- and 10th grade students to indicate who their best friends were, the quality of these friendships, and their own level of prosocial motivation and to estimate their friends' levels of prosocial behaviors. Participants also rated nonfriend peers on a measure of prosocial behavior. The researchers then returned 1 year later and obtained the same measures a second time.

The researchers found that adolescents who perceived a best friend as behaving in a more prosocial way tended to behave more prosocially themselves a year later. In other words, the adolescents' prosocial motivations were influenced by their friends' prosocial behaviors.

Furthermore, the quality of the friendship was an important variable, too. Adolescents were most influenced by friends with whom they held a strong bond and had frequent interaction.

These results are consistent with the more general conclusion showing the powerful effect of peers on one another. Depending on the behavior of one's friends, that influence can be positive or negative.

- What kinds of prosocial behaviors might adolescents learn from their friends?

- Why might adolescents have prosocial motivations but not put them into action?

that actively promote contact among members of different ethnicities in classes help create an environment in which cross-race friendships can flourish (Hewstone, 2003).

Still, the task is daunting. Many societal pressures act to keep members of different races from interacting with one another. For example, prior experience with members of different groups may be minimal for adolescents who grew up in neighborhoods with little diversity. Peer pressure, too, may discourage adolescents from crossing racial and ethnic lines to form new friendships.

Do Peers Matter? The Influence of Peers on Development

Peers play an important role in an adolescent's development. For example, during early adolescence, school adjustment is related to the kind of peer support that the adolescent experiences, as well as to parental support. Students whose peers support academic achievement are more likely to be successful in school than those whose peers are less supportive of academic endeavors. In addition, adolescents can influence their friends to behave in a more positive, helpful manner to others, as we discuss in the *Transitions* box (Kurdek, Fine, & Sinclair, 1995; Kurdek & Sinclair, 2000; Barry & Wentzel, 2006).

Peers can be so influential, in fact, that they can compensate for negative circumstances in other realms of an adolescent's life. For instance, one large study of close to a thousand fifth and eighth graders found that difficulties in the family or school could be counteracted by the support of peers (Barber & Olsen, 1997, 2004; Bradford et al., 2004).

Things also worked the other way: Problems with peers can be offset by family and school support. Adolescents who lack a network of close peers can still be well adjusted if they are the recipients of sufficient and appropriate parental support (Gauze et al., 1996; Bierman, 2003).

Review and Apply

Review

1. Because adolescents spend more time with peers than with anyone else, peer relationships are of great importance.

2. Age segregation is the prevalent pattern governing adolescent interactions in the United States, mainly because of schooling policies and parental preferences.

3. During adolescence, the sex cleavage typical of the middle school years diminishes, and teenage boys and girls begin to show more interest in each other and spend more time together.

4. Even when adolescents attend desegregated schools, a pattern of racial and ethnic segregation persists, sometimes self-determined and sometimes subtly imposed by school practices and policies.

5. Peers play an important role in adolescents' development, with strong influence in such areas as academic achievement and prosocial behaviors.

Apply

1. Do you think that reducing age segregation in schools (for example, by encouraging multigrade classes and discouraging "class pride") would have mostly positive or mostly negative effects? Why?

2. What are two policies that schools could institute to decrease racial segregation among students? Why are these steps not being taken?

Peer Groups

*A*aron called and *wanted to know if I wanted to go and see a movie. Marie and myself had planned to go out to have something to eat, and since Aaron doesn't really know that Marie and me are going together, nor that she was there at my house, I didn't know what to say. Finally, I told him Marie was there, and then asked her if she'd like to go along with us, and she said yes. So we went to McDonald's (not exactly the Ritz) to eat, since I had a ton of gift certificates to use, and then we met Aaron, Benji, Bill and Paul at the theater. Benji and Aaron wanted to see "Breakin' 2," as did Marie, but they wanted to see it to make fun of it, unlike Marie. So originally Bill, Paul, Aaron, Benji, Marie and myself all went to see that.*

Aaron, Marie, Benji, Bill, Paul . . . For most adolescents, life is a complicated mix of friends and acquaintances linked by phone calls, instant messaging, text messages, and e-mail, allowing them to produce complex plans that change from one moment to the next.

The seemingly compulsive need to interact with friends is a reflection of the central role that peers play in adolescence. And it's not only the amount of time spent with peers that increases; peer groups assume greater importance in many other ways as well. **Peer groups** are informal or formal groups composed of individuals of approximately the same age and status. There may be no period of life in which peer groups are as influential as they are in adolescence (Youniss & Haynie, 1992; Richard & Schneider, 2005).

Several factors account for the importance of peer groups in the lives of adolescents. For one thing, peers can help adolescents satisfy personal interests and can provide them with information that they feel they need for their own purposes. For instance, an interest in conservation may cause adolescents to become part of a group dedicated to stamping out pollution. Or they may join a high school gay, lesbian, and bisexual alliance not only because of their interest in supporting people with different sexual orientations, but also because they themselves are questioning their sexual identity.

In addition, some groups provide prestige. Membership on a cheerleading squad or service on the school council may be an honor in some middle schools. (In others, membership on a cheerleading squad or school council may be a source of derision, with prestige reserved for other groups and activities.)

The Characteristics of Adolescent Peer Groups

Like all groups, adolescent peer groups, whether formal or informal, have certain characteristic features and functions. Among the most important:

- *Peer groups have their own roles.* As we first discussed in Chapter 4, *roles* are the behaviors that are associated with and come to be expected of people in a given position. Sometimes roles evolve during the course of group interaction, as in the case of a person who comes to play a leadership role or another who acts like the class clown. In other cases, roles are more formal, and they are assigned to people on group membership. For example, a person who is elected treasurer of the school council enters the group with an established role. In either case, roles have a considerable impact on people's behavior in the group (McMahon & Goatley, 1995; Stevenson & Wright, 1999).

  Roles not only provide information on expected behavior, but they also influence attitudes and how adolescents view themselves. This is because various roles confer different degrees of status. *Status* is the social rank a person holds within a group. Individuals of higher status have greater access to the group's resources, and they have the authority either to tell others what to do directly or to wield influence over them indirectly. In contrast, group members of lower status tend to follow the lead of higher-status members.

  Although holding a particular role or position in a group can determine an adolescent's status within the group, personal characteristics also play a part. Adolescents who are more intelligent, friendlier, and physically more attractive, or who have other positively valued characteristics, will typically be of higher status than those with fewer valued attributes (Ridgeway, Diekema, & Johnson, 1995; Stormshak et al., 1999).

- *Peer groups provide social comparison opportunities.* Peer groups also become more important in adolescence because they provide individuals with the opportunity to compare and evaluate opinions, abilities, and even physical changes—a process called *social comparison,* as we first noted in Chapter 5. Because the physical and cognitive changes of adolescence are so unique to this age group and are so pronounced, especially during the early stages of

peer groups informal or formal groups composed of individuals of approximately the same age and status

puberty, adolescents turn increasingly to others who share, and consequently can shed light on, their own experiences (Paxton et al., 1999; Schutz, Paxton, & Wertheim, 2002; Rankin, Lane, & Gibbons, 2004).

Parents are unable to provide social comparison opportunities. Not only are parents well beyond experiencing the changes that adolescents undergo, but also adolescents' tendency to question adult authority and motivation to become more autonomous make parents, other family members, and adults in general inadequate and invalid sources of knowledge. Who is left to provide such information? Peers.

- *Peer groups act as reference groups.* As we have repeatedly seen, adolescence is a time of experimentation, of trying out new identities, roles, and conduct. Peers provide information about what roles and behavior are most acceptable by serving as a reference group. **Reference groups** are groups of people with whom one compares oneself. Just as professional ballplayers are likely to compare their performance against that of other professional players, so do teenagers compare themselves to those who are similar to them.

Reference groups present a set of *norms,* or standards, against which adolescents can judge their abilities and social success. An adolescent need not even belong to a group for it to serve as a reference group. For instance, unpopular adolescents may find themselves belittled and rejected by members of a popular group, yet use that more popular group as a reference group (Berndt, 1999).

Adolescent Cliques: Belonging to a Group

I transferred schools starting my first year of HS. This gave me the opportunity (or disadvantage) of being a new student in school. I could start fresh, start with a clean slate. I remember my first-year self thinking that I wouldn't be a nerd anymore . . .

I found myself being welcomed by the 'cool' clique, or so I christened them. This lasted all of 1 semester. It's not that I disliked my new-found clique, it's just that we sort of had different views of things . . . .

I shifted to another clique, and it was a triumvirate this time. We weren't the 'coolest' but we weren't pariahs, either. Perhaps the best word to describe us would be 'under the radar.' I kept a low profile in my social life, although, with my high grades, it was only a matter of time 'til I got stuck with the 'nerd' label again.

As this boy's blog suggests, cliques play a central role in the social lives of adolescents. A **clique** (pronounced "kleek" or "klik") is a group of from 2 to 12 people whose members have frequent social interactions with one another. On average, high school cliques average about 5 people, and pairs of adolescents who consider themselves best friends are usually in the same clique (Urberg et al., 1995; Brown & Klute, 2006).

Even if they are not in a clique, adolescents may be friends of clique members and participate in some of their activities. They are known as *liaisons,* and they may interact with members of several different cliques. In other cases, some adolescents, called *isolates,* either have friendships with a single member of a clique (but don't interact with other clique members) or, in rarer cases, have no friends. Figure 7-2 illustrates the relationships among a subset of adolescents in one high school.

Similarity of Clique Members.   One central feature of adolescent cliques is the high degree of similarity among members, particularly in terms of age and gender. As we noted earlier, the age segregation we see in friendships is largely due to the structure of schools. Gender segregation, too, is typical of cliques, although less strongly so than age segregation. For example, gender similarity within cliques is less significant in late adolescence than earlier.

In addition, race is a significant determinant of clique membership, with cliques generally showing a high degree of similarity in racial composition. In fact, the closer the members of a

reference groups   groups of people with whom one compares oneself.

cliques (pronounced "kleeks")   groups of from 2 to 12 people whose members have frequent social interactions with one another

clique are to one another, the less likely it is that the clique will include members of different races. Segregation according to race is substantial even in schools that are quite heterogeneous in terms of racial composition, as we discussed in the "Adolescent Diversity" section earlier in the chapter (Zisman & Wilson, 1992; Urberg et al., 2000; Tatum, 2003).

Social class is also involved in the organization of cliques. Members of cliques tend to be similar in terms of their family income. In part this is due to the extracurricular interests and activities of adolescents, which vary significantly according to economic status. For instance, adolescents from more affluent families might be able to take dance and horse-riding lessons, and they develop cliques that include others who are able to afford the same activities. Adolescents from less-affluent backgrounds are less able to afford such lessons, and their interests are bound to differ. Ultimately this self-separation may lead to socioeconomic similarities within cliques.

The similarity found in cliques is not limited to demographic characteristics such as race and socioeconomic status; behavioral characteristics, as well, help shape the composition of cliques. For example, one important behavior relates to substance use. Specifically, adolescents tend to choose friends who use alcohol and other drugs to the same extent that they do (Bukowski, Sippola, & Newcomb, 2000; Bukowski, 2003).

In addition, members of cliques are also often similar in terms of their academic success, although this is not always true. One factor that lessens academic similarity is the fact that, during early adolescence, there is a reduction in attraction to peers who are particularly well behaved. At the same time, those who act more aggressively become more attractive—a kind of "bad-boys look good" phenomenon. This phenomenon leads to cliques that include students of differing academic abilities (Farmer, Estell, & Bishop, 2003; Kupersmidt & Dodge, 2004).

Changes in Cliques during Adolescence: Developmental Patterns. Cliques become more coordinated and stable during the course of adolescence. Initially, there are few cliques, but they increase in number and kind as children enter adolescence. As individuals proceed

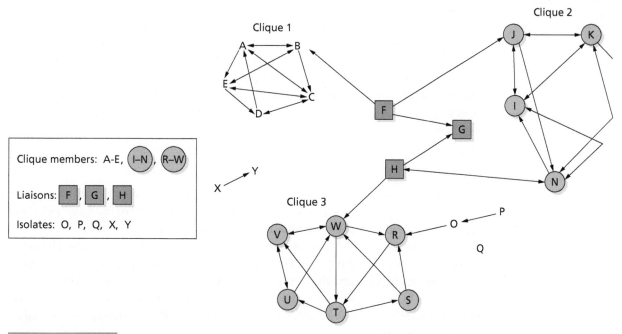

▲ **FIGURE 7-2**

Adolescent Social Networks and Friendship Patters An illustration of the intricacies of peer networks. The patterns are based on the responses of adolescents who were asked to list their closest friends.

(*Source:* Ennett & Bauman, 1996.)

▲ Members of crowds share particular characteristicas, but they do not necessarily interact much with each other.

through adolescence there are increasing status differences among cliques, with some cliques clearly enjoying higher status than others (Brown & Klute, 2006).

Australian sociologist Dexter Dunphy (1963) carried out a classic observational study of the development of cliques nearly five decades ago, which mirrors the work on friendship patterns that we discussed earlier in the chapter. He found that early in adolescence, same-sex groups were most common. But as adolescence progressed, high-status members of the same-sex groups began to form mixed-sex groups, which eventually led to the decline of the same-sex groups. By later adolescence, group membership became less influential as males and females developed more serious relationships, and individual pairings became more prominent.

One of the most obvious places that cliques manifest themselves is the school cafeteria, where student seating patterns offer an insight into clique formation. In one study, for instance, researchers found that sixth graders' seating patterns were not very stable, with a fair amount of intermingling among students from one day to the next. In seventh grade, seating patterns became more stable, and students might sit together for weeks and eventually months (Eder, 1985; Eder & Nenga, 2003).

By eighth grade, seating patterns reflected cliques comprising students with similar activities and status, and seating was stable across the entire school year. For example, the cheerleaders sat together at one set of tables, and members of the student government sat at other tables. In addition, seating patterns were associated with the socioeconomic status of the students.

Membership in cliques is most obvious during the early years of adolescence. In later stages, the number of liaisons and isolates—those who are not members of a clique—actually increases. In addition, cliques eventually become less distinctive and rigid, and membership in cliques shows a fair amount of turnover. In the later stages of adolescence, cliques become less stable, and social interactions revolve around more flexible groups that are tied together by liaisons who move between members of different groups (Ennett & Bauman, 1996; Brown & Klute, 2006).

Crowds

In contrast to cliques, **crowds** are larger and looser groups, comprising individuals who share particular characteristics but who may not interact with one another. For instance, "jocks" and "nerds" are representative of crowds found in many high schools.

There is a surprisingly high level of agreement among adolescents regarding the characteristics of members of particular groups. For instance, one study found that "jocks" and "normals" were seen as dressing casually, where as "populars" were viewed as more stylish dressers. "Normals" and "jocks" were perceived as friendly, while "populars" were cliquish. "Populars" and "jocks" tried hard in school, where as "druggies" and "toughs" hated it (Brown, Lohr, & Trujillo, 1990; see Figure 7-3).

Membership in crowds can cut across different cliques. For example, the "jock" crowd is typically made up of members of different cliques who participate in athletics, with not every member of a particular clique belonging to the jocks.

Crowds, like cliques, can reflect the socioeconomic status of members. In some schools, for example, the nature (and expense) of dress signifies membership in a particular crowd, with

crowds in contrast to cliques, crowds are larger and looser groups, comprising individuals who share particular characteristics but who may not interact with one another

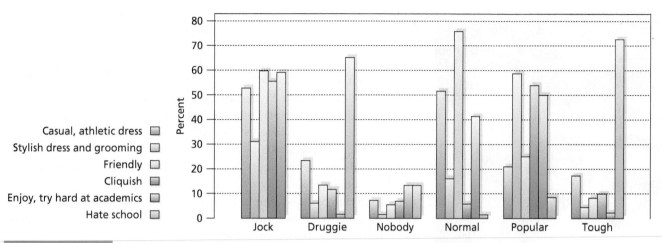

The Characteristics of Cliques There is a high level of agreement among adolescents regarding the characteristics of members of specific groups.

(*Source:* Adapted from Brown, Lohr, & Trujillo, 1990.)

students of a more affluent background dressing in a similar—and upscale—manner to distinguish themselves from those who can't afford to dress the same way.

Furthermore, crowds reflect the racial and ethnic nature of a community. In racially homogeneous schools, crowd identity reflects individual interests ("jocks") or competencies ("brains") or social status ("populars"). However, in more racially or ethnically heterogeneous communities, crowds may form along racial and ethnic lines.

Furthermore, parallel crowds may evolve within different racial groups. For example, there may be a crowd of white "jocks" that coexists in the same high school with a separate crowd of African-American "jocks" (Matute-Bianchi, 1986; Thurlow, 2001).

Crowds, Status, and Self-Esteem. Crowds differ significantly in social status. For instance, in some schools the "jocks" are most esteemed, whereas the "Goths" may be at the bottom of the social ladder. Such differences in social status have an effect on how adolescents view themselves. In particular, those who are associated with high-social status groups may have higher self-esteem than those who belong to crowds of lower status.

For those who find themselves associated with certain types of low-status crowds during adolescence, ultimately they may derive a certain kind of liberation from their low-status position, at least over the long term. For example, one study that examined the long-term personal adjustment of "brains"—members of a crowd that was not viewed as high status—found that they were better off psychologically as adults than those who belonged to higher-status crowds during adolescence (Barber, Eccles, & Stone, 2001).

However, even adolescents associated with low-status crowds may derive psychological comfort from their identification with *any* crowd. In general, membership in any group is used as a source of pride and self-worth. However, to feel such pride, adolescents make the assumption that their group is, in fact, superior to others. As a result, positive aspects of groups to which an adolescent belongs—called *ingroups*—are exaggerated and inflated. At the same time, *outgroups* (those groups or crowds to which an adolescent does not belong) are scorned and disparaged (Stroebe, Lodewijkx, & Spears, 2005).

The differentiation of crowds into one's own ingroup and other people's outgroups leads to a bias in how members of outgroup crowds are perceived; this is called the outgroup homogeneity bias. The *outgroup homogeneity bias* is the perception that there is less variability among the members of outgroups than there is in one's own ingroup. Adolescents assume that members

▲ Crowd membership is related to social status.

of other crowds are similar to one another, whereas they are keenly aware of the differences among members of their own crowd.

The outgroup homogeneity bias occurs in part because of a lack of contact with outgroup members. If adolescents interact with members of outgroup crowds only infrequently, they are less likely to view them as individuals with differing beliefs, opinions, values, and traits. Even when they do interact with members of different crowds, the circumstances may be so limited that they are prevented from developing more complex, multifaceted views of outgroup members (Linville, Fischer, & Yoon, 1996; Judd et al., 2005).

Particularly during the earlier years of adolescence, rivalries among different crowds can be significant. Higher-status crowd members mock and tease lower-status crowd members, and lower-status members may be accepting of such ridicule. More often, higher-status crowd members simply ignore those who are in different crowds (Kinney, 1993; Brown, 2004).

The degree to which members of different crowds interact depends largely on the nature of the norms of a given situation. For example, in some high schools—particularly those that track students into different academic groups—there is relatively little interaction between members of different crowds. In other schools, there is considerably more cross-crowd interaction.

Furthermore, because the significance of crowd membership changes depending on the norms in a given environment, membership in a particular crowd has different effects on self-esteem depending on the context. For example, in some schools with a strong academic emphasis, high-achieving "brains" may be positively regarded, and membership in the "brain" crowd is therefore a source of self-esteem. In other schools, membership in the "brain" crowd may result in ridicule.

This phenomenon is also reliably related to race. Specifically, high academic achievers in predominately African-American schools may be labeled as "Brainiacs." Buying into academics is seen as "acting white," and adolescents who excel academically may be shunned as a result (Fordham & Ogbu, 1986).

The Developmental Course of Crowds. As with cliques, there is a developmental progression in the identification and formation of crowds. Crowds begin to emerge in midadolescence, and by the time adolescents reach ninth grade, 95% of them can articulate and distinguish different crowds.

However, crowds become less distinct in later adolescence. The rigid lines that earlier precluded membership in multiple crowds become more flexible. Furthermore, different crowds may merge, and adolescents may be members of multiple crowds. Ultimately, the perceived importance of membership in a crowd declines with age (see Figure 7-4; Brown, Eicher, & Petrie, 1986; Brown & Klute, 2006).

During adolescence, membership in some types of crowds is more stable than it is in others. For example, the crowd orientations of "all-around" and "studious" are more stable than others, meaning that it is less likely that their membership will change during the course of adolescence. Furthermore, when adolescents do shift from one crowd to another, the change that occurs is typically between crowds that have similar reputations and status, as in the case of a high school student who moves from the "nerds" to the "brains" (Strouse, 1999; Brown, 2004).

The emergence of distinct crowds during middle adolescence reflects in part the increased cognitive capabilities of adolescents. Crowd labels are abstractions, requiring teens to make judgments of people with whom they may interact only rarely and of whom they have little direct knowledge. It is not until mid-adolescence that teenagers are sufficiently sophisticated cognitively to make the subtle judgments that underlie distinctions between crowds.

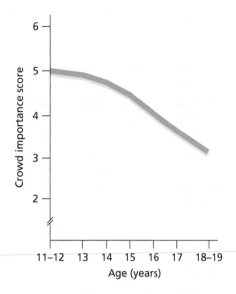

◄ **FIGURE 7-4**
The Importance of Belonging Being part of a group becomes less important as adolescents grow older. Why do you think this change occurs?
(*Source:* Adapted from Brown, Eicher, & Petrie, 1986).

It's important to keep in mind that the descriptions used to identify particular crowds are stereotypes, and they do not necessarily represent the actual characteristics of individual crowd members. Still, the stereotypes are powerful and widespread, and the expectation that people in a particular crowd behave in a certain way may constrain the behavior of both non–crowd members and members.

In fact, the stereotype may actually bring about the expected behavior—an example of a self-fulfilling prophecy, in which people act in a way that is consistent with their expectations, beliefs, or cognitions about an event or behavior, thereby increasing the likelihood that the expected event or behavior will occur (Olson, Roese, & Zanna, 1996; Rosenthal, 2006).

Conformity, Peer Pressure, and Crowd Membership. Crowds affect their members in several ways. For one thing, they influence what people do by exerting peer pressure to conform. **Conformity** is a change in behavior or attitudes brought about by a desire to follow the beliefs or standards of others.

Conformity is induced through two types of social pressure. *Informational social influence* is pressure to conform that emanates from adolescents' assumption that others have knowledge that they lack. Adolescents rely on the perceptions, experience, and knowledge of others because they are unable to experience firsthand certain aspects of the world, and their crowd can provide that information.

However, another type of pressure explains why adolescents conform to others in their crowd. *Normative social influence* is pressure that reflects group norms, the expectations regarding appropriate behavior held by those belonging to groups. Normative social influence operates because of adolescents' desire to meet the expectations of a group. They know that transgressors against group norms are punished in some way by the other members of the group. Consequently, adolescents may agree with others in their crowd to avoid the anticipated unpleasant consequences of violating group standards.

Normative social pressures from adolescent crowds are particularly high because the crowds typically are strong in cohesiveness. *Cohesiveness* is the extent to which the members of a peer group find the group attractive. Cohesiveness in crowds generally is high because the members are strongly identified with a group and intensely attracted to it.

Although the social pressure that causes conformity can be strong, it is rare that it is imposed directly. For example, adolescents don't usually overtly tell their peers they ought to conform because they'll experience some sort of retaliation if they don't go along. Instead, adolescent conformity pressure typically occurs through *normative regulation,* in which there is an implicit

conformity a change in behavior or attitudes brought about by a desire to follow the beliefs or standards of others

appreciation that youth in the same crowd should stick together, behave in similar ways, and generally conform to the implicit norms of the crowd.

Furthermore, adolescents do not unquestioningly follow the dictates of their peer group. Whether they listen to their peers or to others depends largely on the situation. For example, they are more likely to conform to the will of their crowd on everyday social matters such as what to wear and preferences for television shows or music groups, especially during the early years of adolescence. But when it comes to major lifestyle choices, they are less willing to conform to their peers and more likely to follow their parents' beliefs and values. They are also more willing to listen to adults rather than their peers on more objective matters, such as how to avoid sexually transmitted diseases or which methods of birth control are most effective (Chen-Yu & Seock, 2002; Moutappa et al., 2003).

In short, particularly in middle and late adolescence, teenagers turn to those they see as experts on a given dimension. If they have social concerns, they turn to the people most likely to be experts—their peers. If the problem is in an area about which parents or other adults are most likely to have expertise, teenagers tend to turn to them for advice and are most influenced by their opinions (Young & Ferguson, 1979; Perrine & Aloise-Young, 2004).

Overall, then, it does not appear that susceptibility to peer pressure suddenly soars during adolescence. Instead, adolescence brings about a change in the people to whom an individual conforms. Whereas children conform fairly consistently to their parents during childhood, in adolescence conformity shifts to the peer group, in part because pressures to conform to peers increase as adolescents seek to establish their identity apart from their parents.

Ultimately, however, adolescents conform less to both peers *and* adults than they did earlier as they develop increasing autonomy over their lives. As they grow in confidence and in the ability to make their own decisions, adolescents are more apt to remain independent and to reject pressures from others, no matter who those others are (Steinberg, 1993; Crockett & Crouter, 1995).

On the other hand, adolescents are never totally immune to the social pressures of others. Even when they move into adulthood, they are at least somewhat susceptible to group pressure. In addition, there are significant individual differences in resistance to social pressures, with some adolescents better able to maintain independence from peer social pressures than others.

Formal Groups and Organizations

Up to now, we've been talking about membership and associations with informal cliques and crowds. Because they don't exist officially, there are no stated membership requirements, no forms to complete, and no leadership structure, such as a president or vice president. Membership in cliques and crowds is in many ways unspoken.

Formal groups and organizations, on the other hand, do require that adolescents make a formal decision to join. They also play a significant role in the lives of adolescents.

There are hundreds of formal national organizations, and thousands of more local organizations, that adolescents are able to become part of. Some are career oriented, such as the Future Business Leaders of America and National FFA (Future Farmers) Organization; others have religious affiliations, such as the Catholic Youth Organization or B'nai B'rith Youth Organization; and some are service oriented, such as Big Brothers Big Sisters.

The most common type of formal group membership for adolescents involves an *extracurricular activity,* voluntary, school-sponsored activities for students that lie outside the normal school curriculum. Almost two-thirds of high school students take part in one or more extracurricular activity. The most common is athletics, in which almost half of all adolescents are involved. In addition, membership in music and academically oriented clubs (such as a science club or language club) are particularly prevalent (Simpkins et al., 2006).

Participation in extracurricular activities and in formal organizations during adolescence is associated with several positive outcomes. Adolescents who participate are more likely to have higher self-esteem than those who are not members of voluntary groups. In addition, they are more likely to participate in formal groups and organizations when they are adults (Youniss, Bales, & Christmas-Best, 2002; Flanagan & Van Horn, 2003; Fredricks & Eccles, 2006).

On the other hand, because participation in organizations is self-selected, those adolescents who might benefit the most from membership may be the least likely to join. For instance, adolescents who are social isolates or those who are heavily involved in antisocial or delinquent activities may not be attracted to such groups.

Why does participation in extracurricular activities and other formal groups benefit adolescents? One reason may be that adolescents' self-confidence and self-images improve as a consequence of participation. Furthermore, participants may learn new skills and develop a stronger self-efficacy. Finally, another possibility is that participants are exposed to positive adult role models who advise extracurricular activities and groups and who reinforce positive values or may act as supportive confidantes (Simpkins et al., 2006).

Participation in voluntary organizations shows a developmental pattern across the life span. Participation is likely to peak in high school and college, during late adolescence. In part, this reflects the wide range of extracurricular activities that are available during the high school years, as well as the pressure on youth who are applying to college to make themselves more attractive to selective colleges (Jennings & Stoker, 2001).

After high school and college, participation in formal groups and organizations declines during the time of early adulthood, probably because people are raising families and have less time for voluntary activities. However, participation in formal groups and organizations increases during middle adulthood, as adults' children begin to leave home and parents have more time available.

Participation in Formal Groups and Socioeconomic Status.

Not all socioeconomic groups participate equally in formal groups and organizations. There is a persistent linkage between socioeconomic status (SES) and participation in voluntary group activities, with members of lower SES groups showing significantly lower rates of participation (Flanagan, 2004).

There are several reasons for the lack of participation of members of lower SES groups. One is that poorer adolescents are more likely to be holding after-school jobs and are therefore less able to participate in extracurricular activities (a point we'll discuss more fully in Chapter 11 when we cover work issues). In addition, schools in poorer neighborhoods often do not have the resources to develop and sustain a wide array of extracurricular activities, thereby limiting the choices of adolescents residing in those less-affluent areas (Hart & Atkins, 2002).

The lack of opportunities for lower SES adolescent participation in voluntary organizations has real implications for future civic engagement. For example, participation in extracurricular activities in eighth grade has been linked to a higher likelihood of voting during adulthood. In general, the lessons that adolescents learn about civic engagement affect their level of participation in volunteer activities as adults (Flanagan, 2004).

To increase the participation of adolescents who are members of lower SES and other groups that traditionally have had less participation in volunteer activities, some national groups are seeking to make themselves more attractive to a more diverse membership. For example, Boys and Girls Clubs are working with the U.S. Department of Justice to target and recruit adolescents who are at risk for delinquency, inviting them to participate in clubs established in inner-city locations (Chaiken, 2000).

Civic Engagement and Community Service Programs.

Programs that involve individuals in community service are among the most important recent innovations in helping to involve adolescents in formal organizations. **Community service programs** involve groups that engage in activities meant to improve the social welfare of a town, city, or even the nation.

Almost two-thirds of adolescents have engaged in some form of community service activity by the time they graduate from high school. The range of community service activities in which

community service programs programs that involve groups that engage in activities meant to improve the social welfare of a town, city, or even the nation

▶ Participation in formal group activities typically is most frequent during high school and college, in late adolescence.

they participate is vast (see Table 7-1). For instance, some adolescents tutor elementary school children in after-school programs. Others volunteer at a halfway house for patients with severe psychological disorders (Youniss, McClellan, & Yates, 1997; McIntosh, Metz, & Youniss, 2005).

Participation in community service activities increases adolescents' awareness of the needs of others and makes them more likely to be helpful to others. In addition, they are more likely to volunteer, vote, work on political campaigns, and demonstrate in support of various causes (Reinders & Youniss, 2006).

Ultimately, membership in community service organizations can provide opportunities for critical thinking about social questions and can bring about a more sophisticated understanding of political issues. Adolescents' awareness of issues involving social justice may be enhanced, and their sense of responsibility for improving their communities can be increased (Smetana & Turiel, 2006).

TABLE 7-1 Community Service Possibilities
Here are just a few possibilities for community service activities:
• Develop a Web site for a social service agency.
• Participate in a "Big Brother" or "Big Sister" program.
• Raise funds for a local food bank.
• Register voters for the next election.
• Volunteer at a local government office.
• Help organize a Special Olympics for people with disabilities.
• Participate in an educational program to protect the environment.
• Help staff a shelter for battered women.
• Volunteer to feed the homeless.
• Organize a blood drive.

CAREER CHOICES

Community Group Director

Name: Deborah Tuttle-Nelson

Education: Bachelor of Science, Organizational Communications, Ohio University, Athens, Ohio

Position: Volunteer Coordinator, Dayton, Ohio, Habitat for Humanity

HABITAT FOR HUMANITY has built more than 200,000 homes worldwide with the help of millions of volunteers, but that could not have been done without careful plans for coordinating volunteers, who arrive with all levels and kinds of skills.

According to Deborah Tuttle-Nelson, volunteer coordinator for the Dayton, Ohio, branch of Habitat for Humanity, every volunteer goes through an extensive application process before coming on board. Dayton utilizes about 6,000 volunteers every year.

"We try to look for a good skill blend among the 6 to 10 volunteers we have per building site," said Tuttle-Nelson. "Our application process asks each person to provide a self-skills analysis based on a rating of 1 to 4, novice through expert."

Volunteers come from all walks of life, including many high school students.

"One of my personal missions is to communicate to young people that they do not have to wait until they are older to contribute to their community," said Tuttle-Nelson. "Adolescents tend to feel a great sense of accomplishment when they use a new skill they have learned as a result of their service. In addition, their self-worth is positively impacted when they contribute to the organization using a skill they already have."

It is one thing for a volunteer to be enthusiastic, but it is also important that the individual leaves with a positive experience. Making sure this happens, according to Tuttle-Nelson, requires an approach known as "relationship management."

"We have to give people a positive experience on the job site," she said. "If we have jobs they can't do because they didn't know how, they don't have a positive experience. This is one reason we try to match people with their abilities on the job.

"Because we rely on volunteers and their donations of time and material, we want to be gentle and loving with people as much as we can to help them have a positive experience and tell others. Word-of-mouth is the best advertising."

Habitat for Humanity also has many student chapters at colleges and universities across the United States.

"Many times a student chapter will work in conjunction with the alumni association to volunteer for a build," Tuttle-Nelson said. "This gives both groups an opportunity to work side-by-side."

Thinking of becoming a community group director?

Community groups include civic and social organizations such as scouting troops, sports leagues, and interest groups, as well as social advocacy groups that promote a cause, such as human rights or a clean environment. These types of nonprofit organizations rely heavily on volunteer service to function, but they often also employ a director or manager and a small paid staff. People are drawn to careers within local nonprofit organizations for a variety of reasons, but they usually share a desire to use their skills and talents to help others in their communities.

Community group directors plan and organize the group's activities as well as overseeing the budget; they may also be involved in writing grant proposals and other fund-raising activities. They usually have experience as volunteers themselves, as well as education and experience in business management. Many colleges and universities offer courses and even entire degree programs in the management of nonprofit organizations. ■

The growing importance of community service organizations has led to an increasing need for community group directors and administrators. See the *Career Choices* box for more on this field.

Online Social Networks: Cyberspace Peers

As we saw in the chapter Prologue, adolescents are increasingly involved in groups comprising people that they've never met in person, but with whom they are well acquainted—online. Cyberspace social networks are a growing aspect of adolescent social life, acting as virtual community centers where adolescents socialize, sometimes for hours at a time (Hempel, 2005).

▶ Even the youngest adolescents are involved in online social networks.

One of the major sites, MySpace.com, has some 40 million members and is ranked fifteenth in popularity among all Web sites. Adolescents may flirt online with total strangers or ask a person to be their friend. They are able to keep up with the latest music and films, discussing what's hot and what's out of favor.

Using virtual social networks, adolescents can also make contact with people they know in real life, as well as finding new individuals with whom to network. Several social-networking sites, such as Facebook.com, offer the opportunity to construct an elaborate Web page, post photos and favorite songs, and list the friends each member of the network has.

It's too early to tell if Web-based social networks will simply augment or actually replace more traditional forms of peer relationships. What is clear is that they offer adolescents a major new way both to interact with existing acquaintances and to make new friends.

Review and Apply

Review

1. Peer groups are of great importance during adolescence, providing a way to meet personal interests, acquire information, and gain prestige.

2. Peer groups offer adolescents distinctive roles, provide opportunities for social comparison, and serve as reference groups for experimenting with identities, roles, and conduct.

3. Groups may be cliques, which feature a high degree of similarity among members, or crowds, which are larger and looser than cliques and can contribute to self-esteem. Online social networks are an emerging form of group interaction.

4. Crowds exert pressure to conform to group behaviors and attitudes through informal social influence and normative social influence.

5. In addition to informal groups, adolescents have the opportunity to join a large number of formal organizations, which can enhance self-esteem and lead to community service in later life.

Apply

1. Should schools attempt to diminish the influence of crowds and cliques and address the overt stereotyping that they represent, or should they just let adolescents be adolescents? Why?

2. Does the popularity of online networking indicate a greater or lesser tendency to engage in social activities than face-to-face networking? Why?

Popularity

It was a humiliation that Hector Vasquez has never forgotten. When he was 12 years old, his classmate Nicole planned what was to be the first boy–girl party among his classmates. Everyone in the class knew about it, because Nicole had mentioned it to several friends, and it had been talked about for almost a week.

Hector already was well aware that he was not among the more popular kids in his sixth-grade class. But because he had known Nicole since first grade, he thought he would be invited. Every evening for a week he waited near the telephone, hoping for an invitation.

But the call never came, and Hector's worst fears were realized. Hector spent the night of the party at home with his parents, who never knew why he was so down-cast. The rejection hurt for weeks, and Hector never did make it into the social circle of what he thought of as "the popular kids."

Adolescents like Hector can have a difficult time. Some are rejected outright and are the constant butt of jokes and teasing, while others are simply ignored and are left out of the social mainstream of adolescence.

Actually, the social world of adolescents is more complex than a simple division into popular and unpopular individuals (see Figure 7-5). For instance, some adolescents are controversial; in contrast to *popular* adolescents, who are mostly liked, **controversial adolescents** are liked by some and disliked by others. A controversial adolescent may be highly popular within a particular group, such as the string orchestra, but not popular among other classmates. Furthermore, there are **rejected adolescents,** who are uniformly disliked, and **neglected adolescents,** who are neither liked nor disliked. Neglected adolescents are the forgotten students—the ones whose status is so low that they are overlooked by almost everyone.

In most cases, popular and controversial adolescents tend to be similar in that their overall status is higher, while rejected and neglected adolescents share a generally lower status. Popular and controversial adolescents have more close friends, engage more frequently in activities with their peers, and disclose more about themselves to others than less-popular students. They are also more involved in extracurricular school activities. In addition, they are well aware of their popularity, and they are less lonely than their less-popular classmates (Franzoi, Davis, & Vasquez-Suson, 1994; Englund et al., 2000; Farmer et al., 2003; Zettergren, 2004).

In contrast, the social world of rejected and neglected adolescents is considerably more bleak. They have fewer friends, engage in social activities less often, and have less contact with the opposite sex. They see themselves—accurately, it turns out—as less popular, and they are more likely to feel lonely.

controversial adolescents adolescents who are liked by some and disliked by others

rejected adolescents adolescents who are uniformly disliked

neglected adolescents adolescents who are neither liked nor disliked

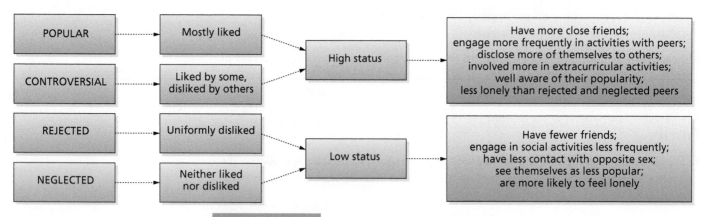

▲ **FIGURE 7-5**

An Adolescent's Social World
Adolescents' social lives are complex. Based on the opinions of their peers, adolescents fall into four categories of popularity.

Rather than dividing them into rejected and neglected youth, some researchers have used a different categorization to look at unpopular youth. For instance, one three-part categorization divides unpopular adolescents into those who are (a) excessively *aggressive* (showing overt violence or bullying or sometimes *relational aggression,* which is nonphysical aggression meant to hurt another person's psychological well-being), those who are (b) *withdrawn* (being shy, timid, and often the victims of bullying), and those who are (c) *aggressive-withdrawn* (showing overt aggression, but also having difficulty initiating relationships). Each of three kinds of behavior evokes negative reactions from other adolescents (Bendixen, Endresen, & Olweus, 2003; Coie, 2004; Kiesner & Pastore, 2005; Zimmer-Gembeck, Geiger, & Crick, 2005).

What is it that determines status in high school? As illustrated in Table 7-2, men and women have different perceptions. For example, although college men suggest that physical attractiveness is the most important factor in determining high school girls' status, college women believe that a girl's grades and intelligence determine high school status (Suitor et al., 2001).

The Roots of Popularity

When you were in high school, did you ever wonder how membership into higher-status, more popular cliques and crowds might be attained? When they are asked this question, adolescents give several answers, although the answers differ for males and females. For example, in one study, college students were asked to identify the ways in which boys and girls could have increased their level of prestige in the high school from which they graduated (Suitor & Reavis, 1995).

The answers they gave were quite consistent and, in fact, had changed little from those provided during a similar study conducted a decade earlier. For boys, the perception was that the way to achieve status was through sports, grades, and intelligence. In contrast, the primary routes to status for girls were seen as physical attractiveness, sociability, and school achievement.

How accurate were these adolescents in their perceptions of the factors that underlie prestige in high school? Adolescent experts have sought to discover the roots of popularity among adolescents, and as we see next, in many ways their answers are similar to the factors identified by adolescents themselves.

Personal Qualities and Popularity.　It's hardly surprising that adolescents' personal qualities—their personality, intelligence, and social skills—are significant factors in determining their level of popularity. Those with positive qualities are more popular than those with more disagreeable qualities.

TABLE 7-2 High School Status

What Makes High School Girls High in Status		What Makes High School Boys High in Status	
According to College Men	According to College Women	According to College Men	According to College Women
1. Physical attractiveness	1. Grades/intelligence	1. Participation in sports	1. Participation in sports
2. Grades/intelligence	2. Participation in sports	2. Grades/intelligence	2. Grades/intelligence
3. Participation in sports	3. General sociability	3. Popularity with girls	3. General sociability
4. General sociability	4. Physical attractiveness	4. General sociability	4. Physical attractiveness
5. Popularity with boys	5. Clothes	5. Car	5. School clubs/government

Note: Students at the following universities were asked in which ways adolescents in their high schools had gained prestige with their peers: Louisiana State University, Southeastern Louisiana University, State University of New York at Albany, State University of New York at Stony Brook, University of Georgia, and the University of New Hampshire.

(*Source:* Suitor et al., 2001)

What are the positive qualities that matter during adolescence? Popular boys and girls have high emotional intelligence, knowing how to act appropriately in a particular situation. They are enjoyable to be around—friendly, cheerful, smart, and with a good sense of humor.

But the sheer number of qualities is not the whole story. Sometimes adolescents prefer those who have at least a few negative qualities over those who are seemingly flawless. The negative aspects of their personality make them more human and approachable (Hawley, 2003).

Furthermore, some less-than-admirable qualities are associated with popularity. For example, adolescents who lie most effectively are more popular than those who lie less well. The explanation is not that lying produces popularity. Instead, effective lying may act as a kind of social skill, allowing an adolescent to say the right thing at the right moment. In contrast, adolescents who are always truthful may hurt others' feelings with their bluntness (Feldman, Tomasian, & Coats, 1999; Feldman, Forrest, & Happ, 2002).

Culture also plays a role in determining what qualities are associated with popularity. In Western cultures, for example, extroversion is related to popularity, while introverted adolescents are generally less popular. In contrast, in Asian cultures, shyness is viewed as a desirable trait, and introversion is more closely related to popularity (Chen, Rubin, & Li, 1995; Chen et al., 2002).

Physical Attractiveness and Popularity. As much as we might like to think otherwise, physical attractiveness is a significant determinant of adolescent popularity. This powerful phenomenon—which holds not only for adolescence but across the entire life span—flies in the face of the idea that judgments of others should be based on accomplishments, not looks (Aboud & Mendelson, 1998; Nikitaras & Ntoumanis, 2003).

With startling consistency, adolescents who are physically attractive are liked more than unattractive ones. In addition, a physically attractive adolescent's behavior is interpreted more positively than the behavior of those who are less attractive.

The reason why physical attractiveness is so important in determining popularity is a pervasive *beautiful-is-good stereotype,* in which physically attractive people are assumed to possess a wide range of positive characteristics. Adolescents (again, like adults) assume that more

▲ Participation in athletics is typically a high-status activity and a route to popularity in most high schools.

physically attractive peers also hold such traits as higher sociability, greater dominance, and better social skills. In addition, those who are physically attractive are thought to be more intelligent, sexually warmer, and in better mental health than less physically attractive people (Feingold, 1992; Locher et al., 1993; Kalick et al., 1998).

How accurate is the beautiful-is-good stereotype? Although the physically attractive do have better social lives, better social skills, and more sexual experiences, they do not differ from the less-attractive in basic personality dimensions, such as emotional stability, self-esteem, and dominance (Kalick et al., 1998). Further, intelligence and academic ability show no relationship to attractiveness (thereby putting the lie to the myth of the "dumb blonde"; attractive people are neither more nor less intelligent that unattractive people).

Despite the inaccuracy of the beautiful-is-good stereotype, it remains a pervasive force that determines popularity during adolescence. One reason is that the entertainment media, particularly television and film, portray a world in which the key players are exceptionally attractive. Both male and female leading actors are unusually handsome or beautiful, and they are also charming and sensual. In addition, other actors surrounding the stars are often relatively unattractive, and they frequently play bumbling, socially inept roles. (The television show *My Name Is Earl* is a classic example of this phenomenon.) Based on what the media present, it is little wonder that adolescents, along with the rest of society, expect physically attractive people to have exceptionally good personalities as well.

Membership in Organizations and Popularity. Greater popularity comes to adolescents who are highly involved in particular activities. Those who are members of multiple groups, clubs, and other activities are more popular than those who are less involved (Eder & Kinney, 1995).

The relationship between amount of participation and popularity certainly makes intuitive sense, because greater organizational membership provides the opportunity to come into contact with a greater number of people. As the number of acquaintances increases, there is more opportunity for an adolescent's popularity to grow.

Furthermore, membership in groups provides frequent occasions for interaction, and frequent interaction is associated with liking. Adolescents can obtain social rewards—such as social approval, companionship, and help—at relatively little cost from those with whom they interact frequently. Conversely, it is hard to maintain close contact with those with whom one does not interact frequently. Ultimately, adolescents are more apt to value those whose friendship is relatively more rewarding and less costly (DuBois & Hirsch, 1993; McPherson, Smith-Lovin, & Cook, 2001).

Activity-Based Popularity: It's Not Who You Are, It's What You Do. Consider this strategy for becoming popular:

> *I was a nerd in primary school, for whom my few friends and many foes made the pet names, 'Coon Cheese' or 'Mega Brain.' Upon reaching my high school years I vowed to turn my back on my bookish ways in favor of the pursuit of popularity.*

The idea of becoming less "bookish" suggests some sensitivity to the activities that are associated with popularity. For instance, in the typical high school, star athletes have little trouble being part of a high-status, popular crowd. Their achievements are sufficient to bring about acceptance and popularity, even if in other regards they do not have the personal qualities that are usually associated with popularity.

On the other hand, not every activity is held in equal regard. For example, academic success may not hold the same social prestige as athletic success. Generally, there are no cheerleaders for the students with the highest grade point averages, and the number of spectators at high school math tournaments is a lot lower than the number at the average Friday night football game.

In fact, some research finds a negative association between success in math and science and high school popularity. On the other hand, all is not lost, popularity-wise, for academically talented adolescents: If their success in academics is paired with success in athletics, they are often the most popular high schoolers of all (Landsheer et al., 1998; Maassen & Landsheer, 2000; Kessels, 2005).

The negative relationship between academic success and popularity is particularly pronounced for members of certain racial and ethnic minority groups. For example, one large-scale analysis of 9,000 students in grades 7 through 12 found that African-American and Hispanic students who excelled academically were less popular than Caucasian youth who performed well academically. These findings suggest that the importance of academic achievement, and the esteem accorded to it, may vary in different cultures (see Figure 7-6; Fryer, 2005).

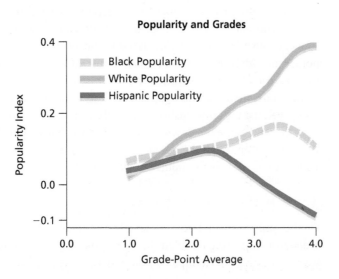

Popularity and Grades

◄ **FIGURE 7-6**

Academic Success and Popularity One large study found that black and Hispanic students who do well academically were less popular that white students who do well academically. If you were an educator, what kinds of approaches would you use to reverse this phenomenon among black and Hispanic students?

(*Source:* Fryer, 2005).

Conformity and Popularity: Going Along to Get Along. Earlier in the chapter, we discussed how peer pressure leads adolescents to conform to the cliques and crowds to which they belong. One of the reasons that such peer pressure is successful in producing conformity is that conforming is associated with popularity.

The ability of conformity to bestow popularity rests on social psychological findings about the fate of those in groups who remain independent and do *not* conform. Typically, nonconformers are disliked and ridiculed by the typical group member, and group members redouble their efforts to produce conformity. When such efforts fail, nonconformers face an ugly fate: The other group members typically ignore them, eventually even seeking to exclude nonconformers from the group (Levine & Moreland, 2002; Poole et al., 2004).

Consequently, acting in conformity with the norms of a clique or crowd enables group members to avoid the fate of nonconformers. At the same time, slavish adherence to group norms may be counterproductive, especially in crowds that embrace norms that promote independence of behavior. The irony is that such crowds may produce as strong a degree of conformity pressure as more traditional crowds.

The Downside of Popularity

Popular adolescents seem to have it all. They're socially skilled, they have a lot of friends and social interactions, they are involved in a lot of activities, and generally they're smart enough that they do at least reasonably well in school.

The reality is, however, that even highly popular adolescents face challenges in their day-to-day lives. They may be different from the challenges faced by their less-popular peers, but they are challenges nonetheless, particularly during early adolescence.

For example, one study that delved deeply into the lives of highly popular girls found that there were times when, paradoxically, these highly admired girls had difficulty making new friends. Because of their high prestige, girls of lower prestige often avoided them because they feared being socially rejected (Eder, 1985; Eder & Nenga, 2003).

Furthermore, even when less-popular girls did approach them, sometimes the highly popular girls felt they had so many friends that they couldn't deal with additional ones, and thus they were unreceptive to friendship overtures. The result was that the popular girls were labeled as "cold" or "mean."

In fact, highly popular adolescents may turn on members of their own high-status cliques and crowds. For instance, one study of highly popular adolescent junior high school girls found that if a member of a clique became *too* popular, the other clique members acted in a nasty and even cruel manner. They gossiped about their too-popular peer, started rumors, and even took action to upset their friendship (Merten, 1997).

The difficulties faced by popular adolescents underscore another important point: Being popular is not the same as having close friends. Popularity occurs when one is liked by a large number of other individuals, whereas friendship involves a degree of intimacy and closeness with another individual. Although it is uncommon, adolescents can be popular but simultaneously lack close friends (Asher, Parker, & Walker, 1998).

Still, more often than not, popular adolescents also have close friendships. That's not surprising, because the same qualities that make an individual popular are associated with friendships. In fact, despite the downside of popularity that we've been considering, the benefits of popularity far outweigh the potential problems, especially when viewed from the perspective of adolescents who are unpopular, as we see next.

Unpopularity and Rejection

Whether you are an adolescent or an adult, it's hard to face rejection. And it's not just the immediate sting of being rebuffed that hurts; the long-term consequences of unpopularity can be quite negative. For example, rejection is associated with academic problems, loneliness, depression, and behavior problems (Asher, Rose, & Gabriel, 2001; Asher & Paquette, 2003; Prinstein et al., 2005).

For some adolescents, the source of rejection rests on their inability to accurately interpret the meaning of their peers' behavior. According to developmental psychologist Kenneth Dodge and his colleagues, some unpopular adolescents have the tendency to assume that the behavior of their peers is motivated by negative, aggressive intent. They are unable to pay attention to the appropriate cues in a situation and incapable of interpreting the behaviors in a given situation accurately. Instead, such adolescents assume—often erroneously—that what is happening is related to others' hostility. Subsequently, in deciding how to respond, they base their behavior on their inaccurate interpretation of behavior. In sum, they may behave aggressively in response to a situation that never, in fact, existed (Dodge & Coie, 1987; Dodge & Crick, 1990; Petit & Dodge, 2003).

In this view, unpopular, rejected adolescents are unskilled at social problem solving. **Social problem solving** refers to the use of strategies for solving social conflicts in ways that are satisfactory both to oneself and to others. Successful strategies for dealing with conflicts are an important element of social success (Laursen, Hartup, & Koplas, 1996; Rose & Asher, 1999; Murphy & Eisenberg, 2002).

Successful social problem solving proceeds through a series of steps that correspond to information-processing strategies (see Figure 7-7). Dodge argued that the manner in which social problems are solved is a consequence of the decisions that children and adolescents make at each point in the sequence (Dodge & Crick, 1990; Dodge & Price, 1994; Dodge et al., 2003).

social problem solving the use of strategies for solving social conflicts in ways that are satisfactory both to oneself and to others

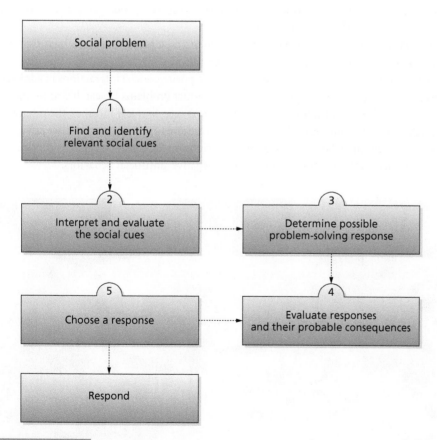

Successful Problem Solving The way in which social problems are solved is a consequence of the decisions that adolescents make at each point in the sequence illustrated in the figure. How might an educator use adolescents' problem-solving skills as a learning tool?

(*Source:* Adapted from Dodge, 1985).

By carefully delineating each of the stages, Dodge provides a means by which interventions can be targeted toward a specific child's deficits. For instance, some adolescents routinely misinterpret the meaning of others' behavior (Step 2), and then respond according to their misinterpretation.

Generally, adolescents who are popular are better at interpreting the meaning of others' behavior accurately. Furthermore, they possess a wider inventory of techniques for dealing with social problems. In contrast, less-popular adolescents tend to be less effective at understanding the causes of others' behavior, and because of this their reactions to others may be inappropriate. In addition, their strategies for dealing with social problems are more limited; they sometimes simply don't know how to apologize or help someone who is unhappy feel better (Vitaro & Pelletier, 1991; Rose & Asher, 1999; Rinaldi, 2002).

Teaching Social Competence.   Can anything be done to help unpopular adolescents learn social competence? Happily, the answer appears to be yes. Several programs have been developed to teach adolescents a set of social skills that seems to underlie general social competence.

For example, in one experimental program, a group of unpopular fifth- and sixth-graders were taught how to hold a conversation with friends. They were taught ways to disclose material about themselves, to learn about others by asking questions, and to offer help and suggestions to others in a nonthreatening way.

Compared with a group of children who did not receive such training, the children who were in the experiment interacted more with their peers, held more conversations, developed higher self-esteem, and—most critically—were more accepted by their peers than before training (Asher & Rose, 1997; Bierman, 2004).

Fast Track is an even more extensive program to teach children who are at high risk the social and emotional skills that will help them when they reach adolescence. The program aims to prevent serious antisocial behavior and encourage positive social interactions in adolescents by working with them beginning in first grade (Conduct Problems Research Group, 2004a).

Targeting children in communities with high crime rates and low incomes, the program focuses on those who are unprepared for school, who are already impulsive and disruptive as they enter kindergarten, and who are primed for aggression and failure. Such children are also at risk for being rejected by their peers because of their negative, antisocial behaviors.

▶ Several programs have been developed to teach the social skills that underlie social competence.

The program includes a classroom curriculum designed to teach self-control, social understanding, and understanding of one's own and others' emotions. Children participate in social skills training groups, called Friendship Groups, and efforts are made to help the children develop friendships. Parents of children in the program also receive training to help them effectively manage their children's behavior (Lavallee et al., 2005).

The *Fast Track* program continues into adolescence. Adolescents in grades 6 through 10 receive individualized support personalized to their own needs, including tutoring, encouragement to be involved positively with peers, and support for their families.

According to extensive evaluations, the program has had a significant positive effect on participants, compared with those who did not receive the interventions. For example, participants showed improvements in their social and cognitive skills. By the beginning of adolescence, a third of those in the intervention group were on a path toward decreasing behavior problems, compared with around a quarter of nonparticipants. Special education placements were also lower for those who received program support (Conduct Problems Research Group, 2004b; Kupersmidt & Dodge, 2004).

BECOMING AN INFORMED CONSUMER OF ADOLESCENT SCIENCE

Developing Your Social Skills

Just like any other valuable skill, social skills take time and practice to master. Ironically, adolescents with unpolished social skills may tend to shy away from opportunities to practice them. Here, then, are some suggestions to enable an adolescent to become more sociable.

- Like yourself. If adolescents want other people to like them, they first have to like themselves. Many adolescents who are socially awkward fear criticism and rejection, so they focus on their shortcomings and become their own worst critics. Adolescents should instead focus on their positive qualities that make them attractive to others and pursue their interests, which will help them to be more interesting persons.

- Practice, practice, practice. Adolescents should try not to shy away from groups or gatherings or avoid invitations to join in with others. Even though they may not shine at social interactions, they need practice to polish their skills. Getting involved in group activities is a good way to meet people with similar interests.

- Rehearse. Before adolescents enter a situation where they might feel socially awkward, they should give some thought to what they will say and do. It is wise to plan out some appropriate things to say. They should imagine themselves interacting with others calmly and confidently, perhaps even practicing in front of a mirror!

- Monitor body language. Although adolescents may be preoccupied with the words they say to others, they should not forget that that they actually say a lot before they even speak! They should try to move about confidently rather than lingering in a corner, and they should be sure to smile and make eye contact. If they show interest in other people, they will make themselves more approachable.

- Put on an act. Some sociologists believe that social interaction is much like a stage play in which we all play out roles. Adolescents don't necessarily have to feel socially confident to act as if they are. They might try acting as if they were someone whose social skills they admire.

- Acknowledge progress. No one suddenly emerges as a social butterfly. Mastering new social skills takes time, and adolescents are likely to make some mistakes along the way. They shouldn't punish themselves for getting tongue-tied at a party—instead, they should congratulate themselves for getting out and taking chances (Lyness, 2004).

Review and Apply

Review

1. The degrees of popularity common in adolescence include popular, unpopular, controversial, rejected, and neglected.

2. Popularity is most directly associated with personality, intelligence, social skills, and physical attractiveness. Popularity in a group also typically entails conformity.

3. Although it is better to be popular than unpopular, popularity can cause adolescents to be considered mean and can lead to rivalries. It can even impede the formation of new friendships.

4. Adolescents who are unpopular can learn social skills that may increase their popularity.

Apply

1. Do you think TV and movie portrayals of popular and unpopular characters in high school settings are helpful or harmful to adolescents wrestling with popularity issues? Why?

2. Do you think social skills training should be a standard part of the curriculum for every student at the middle school level? Do you think such a requirement could be successful? Why or why not?

EPILOGUE

In this chapter we examined the nature and importance of peers during adolescence. We saw how peers play an increasing role in adolescents' lives, helping them to define themselves and influencing their attitudes toward academics and affecting their social behavior. We discussed formal and informal peer groups and observed how they form and develop during adolescence. Finally, we took a close look at popularity, even discussing practical steps that adolescents can take to increase their popularity.

Before we move to the next chapter, take a look back to the Prologue of this chapter, about Rebecca Hickom's Internet-enabled social life. Consider the following questions.

1. In what ways might social networking Web sites change the ways in which adolescents meet friends?

2. Do you think that crowd membership still matters in adolescents' Internet friendships?

3. How important is face-to-face contact in the development and maintenance of adolescent friendships?

4. In what ways might social networking Web sites enhance or diminish adolescents' social skills?

SUMMARY

REVIEW

- **Why are peer relationships important during adolescence?** *(p. 212)*

    1. One of the most noticeable changes from childhood to adolescence is the greater reliance on friendships, which help adolescents define who they are.

2. In addition to friends, other peers play an influential role during adolescence as parents' supervisory role begins to diminish.

3. Peers influence one another in many ways during adolescence, providing support for academic achievement and prosocial behavior and compensation for negative school or family situations.

● **How do adolescents choose the people who will become their peers?** *(p. xxx)*

4. Adolescents' choice of peers is determined largely by psychological factors based on mutual trust and understanding.

5. In the United States, adolescents' peers tend to be of the same or a similar age, mostly because of schooling policies and parental preferences that favor age segregation.

6. Adolescents gradually diminish the sex cleavage that is the rule in middle childhood, but peer segregation by race and ethnicity remains a prevalent pattern.

● **What are the characteristics of the groups to which adolescents belong?** *(p. 221)*

7. Peer groups provide loosely defined roles for their members, offer opportunities for social comparison, and serve as reference groups for their members.

8. One type of peer group is the clique, a comparatively small group of people who interact socially, exhibit similar characteristics and attitudes, and gain status through their membership.

9. Another type of group is the crowd, which is larger and looser than the clique and comprises individuals who share particular characteristics and interests and have ingroup status that distinguishes them from members of outgroups.

10. Crowds are based on stereotypical characterizations of people and impose a degree of conformity on their members.

11. In addition to cliques and crowds, adolescents also join formal groups and organizations that appeal to their prosocial inclinations and interests.

● **What determines an adolescent's popularity or unpopularity?** *(p. 234)*

12. Several characteristics are associated with popularity among adolescents including physical attractiveness, personality, social skills, intelligence, and athletic ability.

13. Especially in the area of academic ability, cultural differences influence perceptions of popularity among adolescents.

14. Although it is better to be popular than unpopular, even popularity has its downside. Popular adolescents risk being perceived as mean and standoffish and can threaten other popular adolescents and incite rivalries.

● **Can an adolescent take steps to become more popular?** *(p. 241)*

15. Adolescents who are members of organizations and participate in activities increase their chances of making friends and becoming popular.

16. Adolescents can learn skills associated with popularity, including social problem-solving skills and social interaction skills.

KEY TERMS AND CONCEPTS

peers (p. 212)
sex cleavage (p. 216)
peer groups (p. 221)
reference groups (p. 222)
cliques (pronounced "kleeks") (p. 222)

crowds (p. 224)
conformity (p. 227)
community service programs (p. 229)
controversial adolescents (p. 233)

rejected adolescents (p. 233)
neglected adolescents (p. 233)
social problem-solving (p. 239)

8 Intimacy

CHAPTER OUTLINE

PROLOGUE

IRST THERE WAS sweet, long-legged Tammy. Then came OnRae: really goofy, plays a mean saxophone. Then a cello player named Asia, followed by a cheerleader named Brookie. Then the punk-rock India. Then the art-loving Lenita. And now Holly.

"She plays soccer. She's a dancer. She's hot," says Richard "Ricky" Reiter, a popular and well-liked senior—he wasn't elected band president for nothing—at Suitland High School in Forestville. He started dating at the end of eighth grade. Everyone went bowling on the last day of school. Ricky and Tammy were on the same team. They won. He asked her out. She said yes. . . .

He can't seem to walk around a hallway without greeting a good-looking girl. "Hey, Tootie! Hey, Epiphany! What's up?"

"I prefer girls who can accept my sense of humor, 'cuz I make a lot of silly jokes," he says. "I prefer girls that are my height, but that's not, like, final. I prefer long hair, but that's not final, either." (Vargas, 2005, p. W28) ■

th!nk ABOUT THIS

RICKY REITER IS NOT looking for a long-term relationship; he may not be looking for a relationship at all. Instead, his adolescence—at least so far—has featured a series of relationships with a variety of girls, each very different from the others.

Ricky's romantic involvements represent only a few of his connections with other people. In fact, one of the major tasks of adolescence is learning how to interact with others, to form increasingly close relationships with friends and romantic partners.

In this chapter, we focus on the development of intimacy during adolescence. We start with a look at the theoretical foundations of intimacy, considering adolescents' interpersonal needs and how intimacy relates to the formation of identity.

Next, we consider the development of friendship in adolescents. We look at the role of friendship in adolescents' lives and how they view the concept of friendship. We also consider the qualities that adolescents look for in their friends.

Finally, we turn to romance and dating. We examine the functions of dating and look at the many different dating patterns that characterize romance in the 21st century. We also take a close (but dispassionate) view of love, consider how it develops, and consider how intimacy provides some of the underpinnings for development across the life span. ■

- Why is the development of intimacy important during adolescence?
- In what ways does friendship grow and change during adolescence?
- What is the nature of loneliness, and what are its effects?
- How do adolescents understand and manage dating?
- What sorts of romantic relationships do adolescents have?

Intimacy and Adolescents

I think it's important to realize that in any relationship, you care about the other person, and the other person cares about you. . . . It's based on friendship, principles of kindness, reciprocation. It just has more intimacy to it, and there are different degrees of intimacy in any friendship. I'm closer with some friends than others, and I realize they feel the same about me, on a continuum with their other friends. . . . It's normal to have different feelings for different people, and in most cases, friends don't need to confirm to each other their friendship.

Developing intimacy with one or more close friends is a central aspect of adolescence. The friendships of childhood, built on shared activities, give way to relationships in which there is a psychological closeness that can emerge only during adolescence.

The ability to experience **intimacy,** the feeling of emotional closeness and interconnectedness with another person, develops during adolescence because of the cognitive, social, and physical advances that occur during that period. Adolescents' growing cognitive abilities allow them to develop a more sophisticated understanding not only of others but also of themselves. Socially, as adolescents begin to better understand the motivations and needs of others, they can establish friendships that are deeper and more meaningful. Finally, on a physical level, the growing sexual interests of adolescents also propel them to seek greater intimacy.

Keep in mind that although intimacy can be reflected through sexuality—which we'll discuss in the next chapter—most intimate relationships during adolescence are nonsexual in nature. Instead, intimacy may arise between close friends, as well as potentially with parents, siblings, and other family members.

We'll begin our look at intimacy during adolescence by examining the ideas of two major theorists who studied intimacy extensively: psychoanalysts Harry Stack Sullivan and Erik Erikson. As we'll see, they have quite different conceptions of the topic.

Sullivan's Theory of Interpersonal Development

Maybe my problem is with intimacy. Not sex, but intellectual intimacy. Letting people know what I'm really like on the inside.

As this comment suggests, distinguishing between intimacy and sex is not always easy. But to at least one theorist on adolescent development, the development of intimacy is based, in part, on expressing one's sexuality. In fact, to psychoanalytic theorist Harry Stack Sullivan, the needs for sexual contact and intimacy are a driving force during middle adolescence.

One of the most influential adolescent personality theorists, Sullivan (1892–1949) wrote extensively on adolescent development from a psychoanalytic perspective. More than other theorists from the psychoanalytic tradition, Sullivan emphasized the importance of social factors. In particular, he argued that to understand adolescent personality development, we need to

intimacy the feeling of emotional closeness and interconnectedness with another person, develops during adolescence because of the cognitive, social, and physical advances that occur during that period

focus on adolescents' relationships with others and how their interpersonal needs influence their behavior.

Sullivan's **theory of interpersonal development** focuses on the specific needs that must be resolved to attain growth. Sullivan suggested that we have particular interpersonal needs that dominate our social lives at different stages of life. If the needs are satisfied, the satisfaction leads to feelings of security; if the needs are frustrated, the frustration leads to feelings of anxiety.

To Sullivan, interpersonal needs are in many ways as important as biological needs, such as the need for sleep and food, and the degree to which children's and adolescents' needs are fulfilled affects their later development in significant ways. The more that early interpersonal needs are satisfied, the greater the security that an individual experiences later in life. Conversely, if early needs go unfulfilled, the anxiety that the individual feels spills over into later interpersonal relationships. In cases of unfulfilled needs, later relationships must overcome the deficits in security that the person has built up from earlier relationship failures.

As you can see in Table 8-1, the interpersonal needs that are dominant as children and adolescents develop differ significantly over time (Sullivan, 1953; Perry, 1982). In the first stages of life, needs include the *needs for contact and tenderness* (infancy), the *need for adult participation* (early childhood), and *needs for peer interaction and acceptance* (middle childhood).

However, as children approach adolescence, their major interpersonal needs reflect the growing desire for closeness with others. In preadolescence, the *need for intimacy* predominates. Preadolescents begin to focus on a few close friends, typically of the same sex. Their relationships with close friends fulfill their need for intimacy with others, and they learn the value of supportive, caring relationships with those outside their families. On the other hand, if they are unable to engage in close friendships, preadolescents will feel insecurity that may hamper their ability to form close relationships for the remainder of their lives.

As preadolescents enter puberty, they begin to experience the *need for sexual contact*. As powerful urges for sexual involvement begin to take hold and at least partially to direct their behavior, adolescents experience strong needs for sexual involvement. These needs lead to a shift from a focus on same-sex friendships to a focus on more intimate, romantic sexual relationships with persons of the other sex.

The need for sexual contact leads some adolescents to engage in a significant amount of sexual experimentation with multiple partners. Others fulfill their intimacy needs by becoming involved with a single individual in a long-term relationship that may last for years.

▲ To Harry Stack Sullivan the needs for sexual contact and intimacy are a driving force during middle adolescence.

TABLE 8-1 Sullivan's Interpersonal Needs at Different Developmental Stages	
Developmental Stages	**Interpersonal Needs**
Infancy (0 to 2–3 years)	Need for contact and tenderness
Early childhood (2–3 to 6–7 years)	Need for adult participation in play
Middle childhood (6–7 to 8–10 years)	Need for peer interaction and acceptance
Preadolescence (8–10 to 12–14 years)	Need for intimacy
Early adolescence (12–14 to 17–18 years)	Need for sexual contact
Late adolescence (17–18 years to adult)	Need for integration into adult society
(Source: Sullivan, 1963.)	

theory of interpersonal development Sullivan's theory that focuses on the specific needs that must be resolved in order to attain growth

▶ Sullivan believed that strong same-sex bonds were necessary to later experience intimate relationships with the other sex.

Sullivan believed that success in opposite-sex relationships was built on a foundation of success in same-sex relationships. Specifically, he argued that for an adolescent to be successful in intimate other-sex bonds that have a sexual component, it was first necessary for the adolescent to have experienced strong same-sex bonds (male–male and female–female). (Sullivan focused almost exclusively on heterosexual relationships and said little about homosexual intimacy, which—reflecting the views of the era in which he was writing—he viewed as disordered. As we'll discuss later, this is one of the major drawbacks to Sullivan's theory.)

Finally, in late adolescence, the primary interpersonal needs shift once more. If adolescents have been largely successful in achieving intimate, romantic relationships, they are ready to confront the next challenge by seeking to fulfill their *need for integration into adult society*. During this stage, needs for same-sex friendships and for sexual expression become merged into the desire to become a functioning, productive member of society.

To Sullivan, then, one of the major challenges of adolescence is to move beyond the close, same-sex, nonsexual relationships that are formed in preadolescence to intimate, other-sex sexual relationships during middle adolescence. The intimate and romantic sexual relationships of middle adolescence are seen as paving the way for integration into adult society. Ultimately, success in interpersonal, and more specifically intimate, relationships leads to the development of a full, coherent, and integrated adult identity.

Assessing Sullivan's Theory of Interpersonal Development. In some ways, Sullivan anticipated the work of later adolescent specialists. Many of his speculations have been supported by later research findings, and he influenced an entire generation of researchers examining adolescent development.

For example, consider Sullivan's view that the success of early relationships with parents and other adults affects the success of later relationships. This hypothesis has been confirmed by more recent research showing that the nature of attachment between infants and parents is related to the course of adult relationships, as we first discussed in Chapter 6 (Aviezer, Sagi, & Resnick, 2002; Mikulincer & Shaver, 2005; Seiffge-Krenke & Beyers, 2005).

Similarly, Sullivan's view that intimacy initially develops between same-sex boys and girls in the context of friendship has been borne out by more recent research. Without a foundation of successful, same-sex intimate relationships, adolescents have a more difficult time navigating romantic relationships later.

One area in which Sullivan's theory clearly falters is his concentration on male–female romantic relationships and his disregard for same-sex relationships. He largely ignored the possibility of mature, loving gay and lesbian relationships. However, there is certainly every reason to believe that the need for intimate relationships is just as strong in homosexuals as it is in heterosexuals. Consequently, Sullivan's focus on heterosexual intimacy represents a significant shortcoming of his theory.

In addition, some research findings question Sullivan's view of the timing of developmental change. For instance, although Sullivan suggested that intimacy with same-sex friends is important primarily during preadolescence, more recent research shows that it actually may be more critical later, during early adolescence (Buhrmester, 1998; Berndt, 2004).

Ultimately, Sullivan's major contribution was to highlight the developmental task of integrating adolescents' existing needs for intimacy with their emerging sexuality. Sullivan helped us to understand that desires for intimacy emerge even before puberty, and that the success of close friendships provides the foundation for intimacy in romantic relationships. Furthermore, he introduced the idea that the development of intimacy during middle adolescence paves the way for integration into society as an adult.

Erikson's Approach to Intimacy

Think back, for a moment, to Erik Erikson's theory of psychosocial development that we first discussed in Chapter 5, when we examined the development of the self during adolescence. You may recall that, like Sullivan, Erikson proposed that people move through a series of stages throughout their lives, each of which presents a crisis or conflict that the individual must resolve. However, unlike Sullivan, Erikson focused less on intimacy and more on identity.

In fact, Erikson believed that the development of a firm identity must precede the development of deep intimacy. He argued that when true intimacy arose between two people, their identities became, in a way, merged. This merger not only affected and modified both their individual identities, but also produced a new, joint identity for the couple. This didn't mean that the individuals lost their individual identities, but that, at least ideally, their individual identities were enhanced (Erikson, 1963; Côté, 2005).

Erikson thought that teenagers were passing through the *identity-versus-role-confusion stage* during most of adolescence, a stage in which their focus was on forming an acceptable identity. To him, then, the major task of adolescence was identity formation. It was only after adolescence, in early adulthood, as they entered the intimacy-versus-isolation stage, that the major focus of psychosocial development was on intimacy. In the *intimacy-versus-isolation stage,* the focus is on developing close, intimate relationships with others.

Erikson's idea of intimacy encompasses several components. One is a degree of selflessness, involving the sacrifice of one's own needs to those of another. A further component involves sexuality, the experience of joint pleasure from focusing not just on one's own gratification but also on that of one's partner. Finally, there is deep devotion, marked by efforts to fuse one's identity with the identity of a partner.

Erikson suggested that those who experience difficulties in forming intimacy are often lonely, isolated, and fearful of relationships with others. Their difficulties may stem from an earlier failure to develop a strong identity. In contrast, those who successfully resolve the crisis of the stage are able to form intimate relationships with others on a physical, intellectual, and emotional level.

In short, Erikson suggested that true intimacy does not emerge until after the end of adolescence and the beginning of early adulthood. He saw the strong sexual desires of adolescence as producing a kind of pseudo-intimacy, in which adolescents form relationships that lack deep intimacy. Instead of depth, their intimacy is shallow, and their professed love for each other masks a deeper fear or distrust.

Reconciling Erikson's and Sullivan's Views

There are clear differences in the accounts of Erikson and Sullivan regarding the development of intimacy. Erikson said that true intimacy does not emerge until early adulthood, after adolescents develop a firm, coherent identity in adolescence. In contrast, Sullivan suggested that intimacy develops in several stages beginning in preadolescence and continuing throughout adolescence. It is only after adolescents have the capacity for true intimacy that they are able to form their identity.

Given that two prominent theorists suggest quite different sequences (Erikson's identity-development-leads-to-intimacy-development view and Sullivan's intimacy-development-leads-to-identity-development view), how do we reconcile the theories? The most reasonable way to shed light on the issue is by moving beyond theory and looking at research findings. In fact, several questionnaire studies have addressed the issue in an effort to determine which of the two accounts is the more accurate.

Unfortunately, no definitive answer to the question has emerged. Although studies often find an association between identity and intimacy in which people with a strong sense of identity also are successful in forming intimate relationships (and people with less-established identities are less successful in forming close, intimate relations), no clear temporal sequence has emerged (Dyk & Adams, 1990; Crawford et al., 2002; Montgomery, 2005; Kroger, 2006).

What research does suggest is that the issue of sequence may be less important than the fact that the development of identity and intimacy are closely linked throughout adolescence. A firm, coherent sense of identity facilitates the formation of deep, intimate relationships with both friends and romantic partners. Conversely, engaging in intimate relationships assists in the development of identity. The two domains of psychosocial development build on one another and help adolescents face the later challenges of adulthood.

Review and Apply

Review

1. The ability to experience intimacy develops during adolescence because of the cognitive, social, and physical advances of the period.

2. Sullivan's theory of interpersonal development holds that the need for intimacy and the need for sexual contact become dominant during adolescence.

3. According to Sullivan, individuals have to fulfill their intimacy needs successfully if they are to develop an integrated adult identity.

4. Erikson's theory of psychosocial development suggests that the development of intimacy flows from the development of a firm identity during adolescence.

5. According to Erikson, adolescents have to resolve the identity-versus-role-confusion stage if they are to achieve intimacy during early adulthood.

Apply

1. Do you think that the increasing incidence of Internet relationships aids or hinders the development of intimacy? Why?

2. Why do you think that the questionnaire studies aimed at resolving whether intimacy precedes identity formation or vice versa were inconclusive? Can you tell whether intimacy or identity came first in your adolescent years?

Friends

S *hannon and I met in 7th grade, towards the end of it. She was the quiet girl, Miss Gymnastics, and I was Miss Bubbly—the total opposite of each other. I think we got introduced to each other because we started hanging around the same group of friends.*

She helped pull me out of deep depression after some devastation in March of 8th grade. I seriously believe that I would not be here if it wasn't for her. She helped keep me going through high school. I was her cheerleader for all the sports she participated in and she was my life's cheerleader.

Endless letters, phone calls, hugs, smiles, words of love and encouragement. . . .

I was always told that I was lucky to have that special friend. I am blessed beyond blessed for her. She is truly my angel.

A friend is much more than a peer. Peers are simply those who are of the same status. In contrast, **friendships** are relationships in which there is a positive, reciprocal relationship between two people.

Friendships are a central component of adolescents' lives. There's nothing that adolescents like to do more than spend time with their friends. Friends provide a sounding board to try out ideas, a respite from adult idiosyncrasies, a relief from the pressures of school and parents, and a group of confidants with whom to share secrets.

Adolescents' Understanding of Friendship: What's a Friend?

What's a friend? To young children, a friend is someone to share activities with. A friend is a peer with whom one plays ball, goes to Girl Scout meetings, shares a toy, or helps out with a chore.

However, by the time they reach adolescence, boys' and girls' conceptions of friendship change. For adolescents, friendship involves more than it used to; now its components include intimacy and loyalty. Although helpfulness and availability to do things are qualities that are consistently cited as central to friendship throughout childhood and adolescence, it is only during adolescence that intimacy and loyalty are seen as primary components of friendship (Berndt, 1981, 2004).

friendships relationships in which there is a positive, reciprocal relationship between two people

◀ The nature of friendships changes during adolescence.

In part, this shift in the conception of friendship reflects the growing cognitive sophistication of adolescents. Rather than seeing friends in concrete terms ("we spend two hours a day together after school"), friendship can be seen more abstractly ("she is so loyal to me; I can count on her to stand up for me").

In sum, close friendships are characterized by three main qualities: emotional attachment, need fulfillment, and interdependence. Emotional attachment relates to typically positive (although sometimes negative) feelings for another person. Need fulfillment suggests that friends help fulfill significant psychological or physical needs. Finally, the interdependence component presumes that adolescents involved in a close relationship have an impact on one another, affecting each other's lives (Brehm, 1992; Coontz, 2006).

The Role of Friendship in Adolescents' Lives

Friendships play a variety of roles in the lives of adolescents. Among the most important (Gottman & Parker, 1986; Richard & Schneider, 2005):

- *Companionship.* At their most basic level, friendships offer the opportunity to carry out activities together.

- *Stimulation.* Have you ever had a friend call and say, "I'm bored . . . want to do something?" Friends offer something to do and a way to pass the time.

- *Physical support.* Friends help out. An adolescent who wants to rearrange her room may call a friend to help move the furniture around.

- *Psychological support.* Friends can bolster each other's ego, affirming that the other person is worthwhile and offering support when the friend is psychologically in need of bolstering.

- *Social comparison.* As we noted when we discussed peers in Chapter 7, one of the ways adolescents assess their own capabilities and success is by comparing themselves to others. Similar others—a description that typically applies to friends—are a pool of useful individuals with whom to compare oneself.

- *A safe environment.* Adolescents are able to discuss intimate thoughts with friends, who are typically perceived as being less judgmental and more tolerant of unusual ideas and feelings with their parents or other adults.

- *Intimacy and affection.* Friends offer close relationships with strong components of intimacy and affection. The understanding that another person is close and feels affection is a central role of friendship.

In short, friendship plays a range of roles in the lives of adolescents. However, not all friendships play all of these roles. In some cases, adolescents may have some friends that offer a certain set of functions but not others. Thus, one friend may offer companionship and stimulation, while another friend may provide primarily physical support. However, the more roles a particular friendship encompasses, the closer and more intimate is that friendship.

The Benefits (and Risks) of Friendship

There are clear psychological benefits from having close friends. Adolescents are happier, more cooperative, more helpful, and more socially skilled when they are part of a social network of friends. They are also better adjusted, in part because they share their inner feelings and receive emotional support from their friends, and their self-esteem is higher (Berndt, 2004; Brown & Klute, 2006).

And it is not the quantity of friendships that is critical. Having just one close friend is often sufficient to shield an adolescent from the feelings of loneliness and isolation that might afflict unpopular adolescents (Bishop & Inderbitzen, 1995; Brown, 2004).

Still, having close, intimate friendships is not a universally positive experience—despite the benefits that are associated with them. Friendships vary in quality. Having friends who are not supportive or who have low social skills may in some ways be worse than having no friends at all, because such friends undermine the self-esteem of an adolescent. Consequently, adolescents with high-quality friendships tend to be better adjusted emotionally (Brown & Klute, 2006).

On the other hand, adolescents with high-quality friendships may be more at risk for deviant behavior if their friends engage in antisocial activities. High-quality friendships may actually encourage drug use or delinquency if the close friends engage in those behaviors (Dishion, Haas, & Poulin, 1999; Dishion & Dodge, 2005).

Furthermore, a downside of close relationships is the risk of rejection and betrayal, an experience that can be extraordinarily painful to an adolescent. An adolescent who is, for whatever reason, rejected or betrayed by a close friend experiences a loss of trust that can be devastating. The experience can lead the rejected individual to feel reluctant to seek out new friends or to open up to others in the future. Rejection or betrayal is painful at any stage of life, but it is particularly distressing during adolescence (Way, 2004).

Still, despite their risks, the bottom line on close friendships is that their consequences are largely positive. Given the clear benefits of close, intimate friendships, does this mean that adolescents who experience little of the intimacy of close friendships are at risk for future problems? Not necessarily. No relationship has been found that shows that adolescents who lack intimate friendships are more prone to major psychological disorders, criminal activities, or other serious antisocial behaviors. Intimacy levels in adolescence do relate to the level of intimacy experienced in adult friendships, but otherwise the consequences are not severely negative (Giordano et al., 1998; Berndt, 2004; Noack & Buhl, 2004).

Self-Disclosure and Adolescent Friendships

As children move into adolescence, the nature of their conversations with parents and peers shifts. In particular, **self-disclosure,** in which information about the self is exchanged with others, changes. During childhood, self-disclosure is directed more toward parents than friends. But during adolescence, the target of self-disclosing conversations shifts dramatically, with friends being the recipients of more personal information than parents. See Figure 8-1 (Buhrmester & Prager, 1995).

self-disclosure conversation in which information about the self is exchanged with others

◀ Adolescents with high-quality friendships may be more at risk for deviant behavior if their friends engage in antisocial activities.

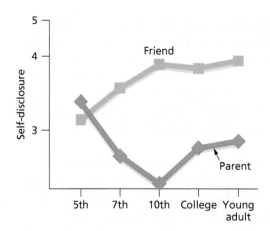

▶ **FIGURE 8-1**

Self-Disclosing Conversations   As adolescents get older, self-disclosing conversations with their peers increase dramatically. However, the trend shifts in the college years, with more self-disclosing conversations with parents. Why do you think this shift occurs?

(*Source:* Baumester, 1996.)

Self-disclosure leads to an increase in the level of intimacy in social interactions, which in turn provides several advantages to adolescents. For instance, higher levels of intimacy may provide social support that can help reduce stress. Self-disclosure also may promote more honest responses from friends, who may then become more useful sounding boards because their feedback is more honest. As a result of self-disclosure, adolescents come to feel better understood, cared for, and validated by their friends (Ben-Ari, 1995; Waring, Schaefer, & Fry, 1994; Dolgin & Minowa, 1997).

There are several varieties of self-disclosure, of course; revealing your AOL password is quite different from discussing your sexual fantasies. One of the key distinctions in self-disclosure is the difference between descriptive self-disclosure and evaluative self-disclosure. In **descriptive self-disclosure,** people share *facts* about their lives. Revealing your place of birth and your parents' professions are examples of descriptive self-disclosure. In contrast, **evaluative self-disclosure** communicates information about personal *feelings.* Expressing shame—an emotion—over a past misdeed is an illustration of evaluative self-disclosure (Laurenceau et al., 1998).

The two types of self-disclosure occur in different contexts and result in different degrees of intimacy. Descriptive self-disclosure is apt to result in less intimacy among friends than evaluative self-disclosure (Berg & Archer, 1982).

Furthermore, the timing of self-disclosure may vary according to the degree of intimacy that adolescents believe their relationship holds. An adolescent may tentatively offer limited amounts of information about himself to test the reaction of a friend, particularly if the friendship is in its formative stages. For example, a high school student may make a joking comment about the difficulty of an upcoming exam to judge the listener's reaction. If the comment is met with sympathy, the student may then make a fuller disclosure regarding the strong anxiety that actually underlies his anticipation of the exam. Conversely, if no sympathy or reciprocal self-disclosure is forthcoming, the student may drop the topic (Duck, 1986; Duck, 1988).

Self-disclosure increases as friends become better acquainted and their relationship and its level of intimacy become deeper. Initially, adolescents reveal relatively little about themselves, providing friends with only superficial information through descriptive self-disclosure. However, as the relationship becomes more intimate, both the level and the degree of disclosure increase. The information becomes broader, encompassing more areas of the adolescent's life; and it becomes deeper, embodying more delicate, hidden material that is revealed through evaluative self-disclosure. Although self-disclosure continues to be an important factor throughout the life of a friendship, it may reach its highest level as soon as 6 weeks into the development of a new relationship. After that point the rate of disclosure tends to level off (Hays, 1985; Cooper & Sportolari, 1997; Matsushima & Shiomi, 2002).

Although self-disclosure to friends generally yields positive results by increasing the level of intimacy in the relationship, in some cases it has negative consequences. For example, if

descriptive self-disclosure   self-disclosure in which people share *facts* about their lives

evaluative self-disclosure   self-disclosure that communicates information about personal *feelings*

adolescents disclose that there are aspects of their friend that they don't like or, even worse, imply that they actually don't like their friend that much, then self-disclosure may be harmful. Furthermore, too much disclosure in the early stages of a relationship can be unsettling and sometimes off-putting. An adolescent who reveals details of, for instance, her difficult family life without building the proper foundation of intimacy may be viewed as inappropriately self-disclosing (Tolstedt & Stokes, 1984; Kogan, 2004).

Generally, though, self-disclosure is an important component of adolescent friendships, and higher levels of self-disclosure lead to great intimacy. Adolescents who don't self-disclose to friends, either because they are afraid of a friend's reactions or because they do not feel they are in a close enough relationship, may feel lonely and sometimes confused about how much to reveal. For example, adolescents' fears of disclosing their sexual orientation are particularly strong, in part because of society's often negative attitudes toward homosexuality. But keeping their sexual orientation hidden from friends may have significant negative consequences, both on the friendships themselves and on the general psychological health of the adolescent hiding the secret. As we'll discuss further in Chapter 9, making a decision about disclosing sexual orientation to friends—"coming out"—is often one of the greatest challenges faced by gay, lesbian, and bisexual adolescents (Matsushima & Shiomi, 2001; Ford, 2003).

Becoming Friends: The Qualities that Lead to Friendship

How do adolescents choose their friends? Several qualities are involved in determining which adolescents develop, and maintain, friendships with one another.

Similarity between Friends.   Do birds of a feather flock together? Or—as an equally popular maxim would have it—do opposites attract?

There's a clear answer when it comes to adolescent friends: Similarity is a key component of friendship. Adolescent friends tend to be similar to one another in a variety of dimensions. Similarity—in terms of age, sex, ethnicity, attitudes, values, and personality traits—is a central basis for most adolescent friendships, just as we saw was the case when we looked at cliques and crowds in Chapter 7. Adolescents are especially likely to choose same-gender and same-race peers (Brown, 2004; Noack & Buhl, 2004).

There are some exceptions. For example, compared with white adolescents, black adolescents may choose close friends who are relatively less similar in attitudes and values because there are simply fewer same-race peers available to choose from, particularly in predominately white schools and neighborhoods. In addition, some research shows African-American adolescents are more accepting of dissimilarities in friends than are white adolescents (Clark, 1989; Brown & Klute, 2006).

Furthermore, it may be that friends are similar to one another, but that different friends represent similarity along different dimensions. For example, one friend may be similar to a teenager in terms of a common taste in music, another in terms of the kinds of books they both enjoy, and yet another in terms of a shared interest in athletics. Each of these three friends may be relatively dissimilar to one another, yet each may share a bond of similarity with the same teenager and be that teen's close friend (Kiesner, Kerr, & Stattin, 2004).

Why is similarity so important a factor in adolescent friendships? One reason is geographic: Adolescents and their families often live in homogeneous neighborhoods with others of similar socioeconomic status, race, and other demographic categories. Consequently, teenagers are more likely to have contact with those who are similar to themselves, both in their neighborhoods and in schools that draw from the same neighborhoods.

Other explanations for the similarity we see in adolescent friendships rest on two alternative, and quite different, processes: selection and socialization. *Selection* suggests that adolescents

Similarity is a key aspect of friendship during adolescence.

choose their friends, and the choices with which they are most comfortable are those based on similarity. In this view, teens choose friends who are most like them.

In contrast, the *socialization* view suggests that the similarity within adolescent friendships is the result of having friends with certain characteristics, which adolescents adopt and learn. In this view, it is conformity pressure that leads adolescents to adopt attitudes, values, and likes and dislikes that are similar to their friends'.

Both selection and socialization are at work in determining friendships. Adolescents are drawn to those who have similar attitudes, values, and behavior. At the same time, their friends exert explicit and implicit pressure to maintain those attitudes, values, and behavior (see Figure 8-2).

Reciprocity of Friendship. Adolescents like those who like them. Although this is true for adults as well, reciprocity is one of the central, defining characteristics of friendship among adolescents (Taniguchi & Ura, 2005).

Reciprocity is important not only in terms of liking, but also in the degree of intimacy of the relationship. An adolescent who perceives a friend demonstrating a deepening degree of intimacy is likely to reciprocate such feelings. In addition, adolescents expect that their friends will show as much loyalty and trust as they themselves demonstrate in the relationship.

However, there are several exceptions to the reciprocity-of-liking principle. One exception occurs for those with unusually low self-esteem (Shrauger, 1975). For adolescents in this category, who don't much like themselves, finding that someone likes them is at odds with their own self-concept. In such a case, they may consider that a person who likes them is insensitive or undiscerning, and their liking for that person actually may decline as a consequence. Such a perception on the part of an adolescent is obviously self-defeating and only acts to reinforce the person's low self-esteem.

Another exception to the reciprocity-of-liking rule occurs when an adolescent suspects that a potential friend is saying positive things out of a desire to ingratiate. *Ingratiation* is a deliberate effort to make a favorable impression, often through flattery. Unless it is used with subtlety, ingratiation may fail to bring about the desired result and sometimes may totally backfire, leading the individual using the tactic to be disdained rather than to be regarded as more likeable (Jones & Jones, 1964; Cantor, Jones & Pittman, 1982; Brodsky, 2004).

Proximity: The Architecture of Friendship. Circumstances of geography determine friendships. Consider, for example, who your closest friends were when you were growing up. In most cases, they were probably children and teenagers who lived close to you. The reason is that *proximity,* the degree to which people are geographically close to one another, plays a central role in determining who we like.

The importance of proximity is often seen in college dorms: Students are often friendliest with people whose rooms are nearby and least friendly with those who are assigned to rooms farthest away. Perhaps more surprisingly, a similar situation occurs with more intimate rela-

▶ **FIGURE 8-2**

Selection and Socialization of Friendships Friendships among adolescents are determined by both selection and socialization. Adolescents are drawn to others who have similar attitudes, values and behavior, while at the same time their friends exert pressure to maintain those attitudes, values, and behavior.

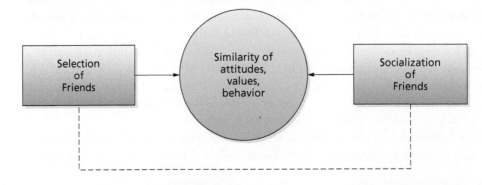

tionships, such as dating relationships and even marriage (Newcomb, 1961; Whitbeck & Hoyt, 1994; Smith & Weber, 2005).

Gender and Friendship.   Male and female adolescents have different types of friendships. Males are more likely to build a friendship with other males based on shared activities such as sports, music, or working on cars. In contrast, the friendships of female adolescents center around social–emotional aspects of the relationship, such as support for one another and shared intimacies (Eshel & Kurman, 1994).

There's also a difference in self-disclosure. Although self-disclosure increases for both females and males over the course of adolescence, females place a higher value on self-disclosure and intimacy than males and are more likely to disclose information that they see as reflecting their innermost thoughts. In contrast, males are less likely than females to share personal information and are less apt to regard intimacy as an important goal of close relationships. Furthermore, females tend to create intimacy through discussion and self-disclosure. In contrast, males create intimacy through shared activities (McNelles & Connolly, 1999).

But what of friendships with the other sex? It is not until late adolescence that many close friendships arise between boys and girls. Prior to that time, the sex segregation that is characteristic of children's friendships remains a defining feature of friendships, and it is relatively rare for a young teenager to be close to a member of the opposite sex. The exception seems to be among male homosexual teenagers, who are more likely to have close friendships with females than males. Homosexual males also report being closer to their best friends than are heterosexual males (Diamond & Dubé, 2002).

Part of the reason for the strong sex segregation is that activities in which boys and girls engage are quite segregated along gender lines. Furthermore, during early adolescence, there is some reluctance among boys and girls to maintain a close friendship for fear that contact between them will be misinterpreted as romantic involvement.

These perceptions change during middle and late adolescence. At that point, adolescents are more willing to engage in romantic involvements and even seek them out. Furthermore, it becomes more acceptable socially to hold a nonromantic friendship with a member of the other sex, even while engaging in a romantic relationship with someone else. Still, even in later adolescence, most close friendships are between adolescents of the same sex.

Conflict and Friendships

Even the closest of friends encounter rough spots in their relationships. Sometimes the issue may be momentary anger over an act of thoughtlessness. Other times it may involve a deeper dispute, one that threatens the very foundation of the friendship.

What leads adolescent friends to fight one another? Generally, the origin is the violation of the implicit rules that govern the relationship. The violation may involve being untrustworthy, a perceived lack of interest or attention, or acting in an unkind manner. Younger adolescents are more likely to experience conflict over a lack of dependability or an exhibition of public disrespect. Older adolescents are more likely to have conflicts over private disrespect (Collins & Repinski, 1994; Shulman & Laursen, 2002; Noack & Buhl, 2005).

Early adolescence is a period in which conflict between friends may be particularly intense. In fact, interpersonal theorist Harry Stack Sullivan argued that conflict of such a high level was likely to occur that it would ultimately destroy many friendships.

It is true that conflicts between friends during early adolescence can be stormy. Younger adolescents often have unrealistic and sometimes rigid expectations of their friends, insisting that they be consistently and totally supportive. If they perceive that their friends are disappointing them, which inevitably happens, they may feel sufficiently hurt and angry to break off the friendship.

Furthermore, conflicts experienced by female adolescents typically take different paths from those experienced by male adolescents. Male conflicts tend to come in briefer, more intense

▲ Conflict between friends may be particularly intense during adolescence.

stretches that may escalate into physical violence. But they tend to be resolved fairly rapidly, without explicit acknowledgement, as the situation calms down and the conflict is put aside. Very often, the end of the dispute is not explicitly acknowledged.

In contrast, female conflicts last longer, and they often revolve around some perceived betrayal, personal insult, or affront. They are not settled until explicit apologies are made, and accepted, between the individuals involved (Raffaelli, 1997; Peets & Kikas, 2006).

The Value of Conflict. It's important to keep in mind that conflict between friends is not necessarily all bad. Learning to manage conflict and control anger is an important developmental task that adolescents face, and conflict among friends may represent a "safe harbor" in which to develop and practice conflict-management skills (von Salisch & Vogelgesang, 2005; Schneider et al., 2005).

Conflicts among friends differ from conflicts with parents. Parental conflicts are more likely to involve direct assertions of power ("Do this because I'm your father and I'm telling you to do it"). Adolescents realize that they are not likely to be booted out of their family if they boldly try to assert a position. This leads them to be less willing to try to negotiate with their parents and more willing to push hard for what they wish to achieve.

In contrast, conflict with friends is more apt to involve negotiation and persuasion, as well as more give-and-take. Because negotiation and persuasion are strategies that will be useful in later life, conflict between friends can provide important lessons in social competence (Laursen, 1993; Laursen, Finkelstein, & Townsend Betts, 2001; von Salisch & Vogelgesang, 2005).

Some changes in how friends handle conflict occur as they move into later adolescence. In the preadolescent period and during early adolescence, friends are more likely to yield to the demands of their peers. In contrast, during later adolescence, as they become more certain of their own identity, individuals are less likely to feel that they need to comply unquestioningly with their friends' demands. They no longer believe that the friendship will inevitably dissolve if they don't yield to the demands of a friend. Instead, they see that friendships involve compromise. When conflicts arise, this understanding more often leads to negotiated settlements rather than to the breakup of the friendship (Hartup, 1993; Cillessen et al., 2005).

Loneliness: Alone in a Social World

Cammy told me all about her family in Jamaica and her puppy Sparkle-something and how popular she was in elementary school in Jamaica and she had a "crew" who would "bust some heads" if she asked them to. I guess she is lacking that here and she kept crying and talking about how she had no friends and it hurts so bad that she cries every night.

If you have ever felt lonely, you are not alone: One survey found that more than one quarter of people polled in a national survey stated that they had felt "very lonely or remote" from others during the prior few weeks. In fact, if you are an adolescent or an adult in your early twenties, you are within the age segment of society that reports being the loneliest of all. Despite the conventional wisdom that elderly people are most apt to be lonely, loneliness actually declines with increasing age—at least until someone's activities must be restricted due to health or other problems (Schultz & Moore, 1984; Wagner, Schuetze, & Lang, 1999; de Minzi & Sacchi, 2004).

Loneliness is the inability to maintain the level of affiliation one desires. It is a subjective state relating to how an individual defines a situation. Loneliness and being alone are not the same thing: Adolescents can be alone and not feel lonely or be in a crowd and feel lonely. The partners in a long-term dating relationship can experience loneliness, whereas an adolescent with few friends may not feel lonely. Loneliness occurs only when an adolescents' actual level of relationships with others does not correspond to the desired level (Tornstam, 1992; Andersson, 1998).

Loneliness occurs in two forms. In **emotional isolation,** adolescents feel a lack of deep emotional attachment to one specific person. By contrast, adolescents who experience **social isolation** suffer from a lack of friends, associates, or relatives (Dugan & Kivett, 1994; Clinton & Anderson, 1999; Flanagan, Gill, & Gallay, 2005).

The two types of loneliness often do not go hand in hand. For example, an adolescent may have many friends and acquaintances and a large, extended family, yet lack any single person with whom to share a deep relationship. Similarly, adolescents who frequently attend parties or eat in crowded cafeterias with many others may still experience a sense of loneliness if they feel emotionally detached from the people who surround them. Although they might not feel socially isolated in such cases as these, they may experience emotional isolation.

Of course, being alone is not invariably bad. Many adolescents crave time by themselves. What is critical in producing loneliness, then, are the attributions that a person makes regarding the experience of being alone (Archibald, Bartholomew, & Marx, 1995; Tur-Kaspa et al., 1998; Toner & Heaven, 2005).

Those who view isolation as largely attributable to factors outside themselves ("I've got a lot of tough classes this year and because of those classes I don't have much time to socialize") are unlikely to experience loneliness. On the other hand, adolescents who attribute isolation to their own stable, uncontrollable personal shortcomings ("I'm by myself because I'm not very likable or interesting") are much more likely to experience loneliness.

The social expectations of adolescence add to the possibility that a teenager will feel lonely. If adolescents believe that they *should* be out every weekend night attending parties and hanging out with their friends, the failure to meet such expectations may lead to loneliness. Such loneliness may be the result of false expectations, because the reality may be that a sizeable number of their peers are sometimes (and perhaps even often) not socializing consistently.

Review and Apply

Review

1. Friendships are important during adolescence, offering emotional attachment, need fulfillment, and interdependence and serving a range of functions from companionship to the sharing of intimacy and affection.

loneliness   the inability to maintain the level of affiliation one desires

emotional isolation   loneliness in which adolescents feel a lack of deep emotional attachment to one specific person

social isolation   loneliness in which adolescents suffer from a lack of friends, associates, or relatives

2. In adolescence, friendships are mainly built on similarity, reciprocity, and proximity and depend on self-disclosure, including descriptive self-disclosure and evaluative self-disclosure.

3. Conflict in friendships is inevitable and not all bad because it can strengthen conflict-management and anger-control skills.

4. Loneliness is the subjective feeling of not having the desired level of attachment with others.

5. Loneliness may be of two types: emotional isolation and social isolation.

Apply

1. Do you think self-disclosure in male–female friendships during adolescence is symmetrical (i.e., practiced equally by both parties)? Why? Should it be?

2. Why would adolescents have an expectation that to be happy they should be alone less often than the actually are? How does popular culture contribute to this expectation?

Romance and Dating

My high school dating life was pretty awful . . . I mean, I had girlfriends and did okay I guess, but there was a lot of rejection as well. I would have done much better had I just lowered my standards a bit. . . . But the problem I had is, every now and then I would land a girl who was way out of my league, and that would skew my self image and make me think I could get hot girls on a regular basis . . . which it turned out I couldn't do.

■ ■ ■

"How about her?" "No, she's going steady." "And her?" "OK, we'll fix it up." I had once again engaged in my high school dating ritual.

For over four years my choice of dates was determined by the yearbook of St. Joseph girls' high school. My best friend and his girl friend . . . used this means to make our weekends a foursome. It was convenient, it was easy, it was wonderful. . . . It was also debilitating.

Intimacy moves to new levels when an adolescent begins to be romantically involved with a peer in a dating relationship. Clearly, dating encompasses more than friendship, typically involving a different level of intimacy. But not always: Some nonromantic friendships may involve a level of closeness that eludes adolescent romantic dating relationships (Giordano, Manning, & Longmore, 2006).

Although we will focus on the traditional view of **dating**—individual-choice courtship in which boys and girls pair off together as couples in committed relationships—the traditional practices of dating are evolving. Specifically, dating, in which two adolescents are identified as a couple and the boy asks the girl out in advance for a date on an upcoming weekend night, has been replaced to some extent, particularly among older adolescents. Dating is often less formal and exclusive, and when a boy and girl are involved romantically, dating may occur in the context of larger groups of friends.

In fact, the term *dating* is sometimes viewed as archaic, being used less than such labels as "being boyfriend and girlfriend" or being involved in relationships involving "hooking up." "Hooking up" is a more ambiguous term, which may imply a more short-term relationship or only a physical encounter that involves anything from kissing to sexual intercourse (as we'll consider in greater detail in the next chapter). Hooking up may last only one night and may or may not involve commitment or even affection (Furman & Hand, 2006).

In fact, one survey showed that by the time they reach their senior year of college, only half of women report being asked out on a formal date by a male more than six times, and one third of women were asked out on two dates or fewer. In college, men and women were more likely

dating individual-choice courtship in which boys and girls pair off together as couples in committed relationships—the traditional practices of dating are evolving

◀ Today, dating between adolescents is less formal and exclusive than in earlier generations.

to hang out in groups together. Sometimes women repeatedly "hook up" with the same male and yet still don't identify themselves as being in a long-term relationship, or even know if they are (Glenn & Marquardt, 2001).

Despite the prevalence of nontraditional conceptions of dating in late adolescence, dating remains an important adolescent practice, certainly for younger adolescents (like Ricky Reiter in the chapter Prologue) as well as for many older ones. In fact, forming close, intimate romantic relationships (however they are labeled) is an important developmental milestone in adolescence. Although the practice of dating is evolving in important ways, boys still agonize about deciding whom to invite to the high school prom, and girls still wonder if certain boys are really interested in them. And the hormonal surges that accompany puberty certainly prime adolescents for becoming interested in romance and sexual encounters.

For the remainder of the chapter, we'll focus on the increasing intimacy that leads adolescents to pair off as couples. And in the next chapter we'll discuss the sexual behavior that accompanies the higher levels of intimacy.

The Functions of Dating

Dating fulfills several functions during adolescence. Not only can it have a recreational quality—it is a kind of entertainment—but it also can be a source of status and prestige, assuming one dates someone who fits that role. Adolescents who start dating early may be viewed by their peers as socially advanced.

Dating also helps adolescents build their own identities. As they form greater intimacy with a partner, they are at the same time separating themselves from their families and peers and developing a more independent identity. Furthermore, if there is a sexual component to the relationship, it can help define heterosexual, homosexual, or bisexual identities.

Finally, dating also fulfills needs for both companionship and intimacy, permitting adolescents to draw close to one another. In one sense, dating provides practice for future intimate relationships. Adolescents learn effective ways of interacting with others as they become socialized into effective courtship strategies (e.g., understanding the importance of offering social support or learning that an apology or a gift of flowers can help resolve a misunderstanding).

Just how well dating serves the function of developing psychological intimacy is an open question. What specialists in adolescence do know, however, is surprising: Dating in early and middle adolescence is not terribly successful at facilitating intimacy. On the contrary, dating is often a superficial activity in which the participants so rarely let down their guards that they never become truly close and never expose themselves emotionally to each other. Psychological intimacy may be lacking even when sexual activity is part of the relationship (Douvan & Adelson, 1966; Savin-Williams & Berndt, 1990).

True intimacy becomes more common during later adolescence. At that point, the dating relationship may be taken more seriously by both participants, and it may be seen as a way to select a mate and as a potential prelude to marriage. In fact, in later adolescence, dating still plays one of its original roles: as a way-station along the path to long-term mate selection. When dating first arose—and it is a relatively recent practice, originating in the early 1900s in the United States—it was carefully controlled by parents and was quite formal. Males had to get the permission of a female's parents to initiate a relationship, and parents often accompanied their children during their encounters. Males and females were not permitted to be alone together until they were actually married, which was the explicit goal of dating.

Although most adolescents (and their parents) no longer see dating as explicitly tied to marriage, it still serves that function. Couples in the United States rarely marry without some period of dating in which they get to know one another well.

Dating in Minority Groups. Cultural influences affect dating patterns among minority adolescents, particularly those whose parents have come to the United States from other countries. Minority parents may try to control their children's dating behavior in an effort to preserve the minority group's traditional values (Spencer & Dornbusch, 1990).

For example, Asian parents may be especially conservative in their attitudes and values, in part because they themselves may have had no experience of dating. (In many cases, the parents' marriage was arranged by others, and the entire concept of dating is unfamiliar.) They may insist that dating be conducted with chaperones, or not at all. As a consequence, they may find themselves involved in substantial conflict with their children (Sung, 1985).

Similarly, traditional Latino parents may find it difficult to adjust to typical U.S. dating patterns, seeing dating as a practice that has the potential to bring dishonor to their families. The result is that parents enforce restrictive boundaries regarding dating, especially on girls, who begin to date at a later age than non-Latinos. However, these restrictions often lead to an increase in tension and conflict revolving around dating. Ultimately, the result may be that Latino adolescents secretly date, hiding the activity from their parents. In fact, in one study, more than half of Latino girls reported dating during adolescence without their parents' knowledge or permission (Raffaelli & Ontai, 2001; Raffaelli, 2005).

Cross-Cultural Variations in Dating.   In many parts of the world, dating simply does not exist. Particularly in nonindustrialized, agriculturally-based cultures, there is no dating prior to marriage, and the first time a couple who are to marry meet one another is just before the marriage ceremony. The arrangements are made through the parents.

Through the lens of Western culture, a lack of dating and choice of partner prior to marriage may seem antiquated. But many adolescents in non-Western cultures prefer parent-arranged marriages and find nothing unusual about not engaging in a process of premarital dating.

Furthermore, concrete advantages exist for adolescents who are not expected to date. There are no concerns over rejection, and couples do not have to wonder if they have actually found their true love. Commitment on the part of a partner is not a source of concern; it is simply assumed that commitment and faithfulness are present in arranged marriages.

Finally, because their parents and other family members are so invested in making the relationship work, couples whose marriages are based on parental choice typically get along quite well. In fact, parent-arranged marriages almost never end in divorce (Olson & DeFrain, 2006).

Adolescent DIVERSITY Relationship Intimacy in African-American Adolescents

Are there subcultural differences in how romantic relationships play out during adolescence? There is some reason to think that there might be. African-American family life tends to be relatively close and involved, with ties extending across generations. It might be the case that such family unity comes with added family obligations, reducing African-American adolescents' capacity to become closely involved with dating partners (Burton & Jarrett, 2000; Giordano, Manning, & Longmore, 2005).

To investigate this issue, data were examined from the National Longitudinal Study of Adolescent Health, a long-term study of a large sample of adolescents in grades 7 through 12. Consistent with the hypothesis, African-American adolescents reported having less interaction with their dating partners than did white adolescents. For example, the African-American adolescents were less likely to have spent time with their dating partners during the previous weekend, to have spent time together after school, or to have gone to their dating partners' homes. They were also less likely to discuss a problem with their dating partner or to engage in romantic behaviors (such as kissing, holding hands, or exchanging gifts). African-American adolescents were also more likely than white adolescents to report having more than one current relationship (although a wide majority of adolescents in both groups reported that their current relationship was exclusive). Perhaps most tellingly, African-American adolescents rated having a future romantic relationship within the coming year as less important to them than did white adolescents.

African-American adolescents seem to have a less intimate relationship style than do white adolescents. This difference appears to arise from different parenting styles and family dynamics as well as a cultural difference rooted in different historical, social, and economic experiences.

Developmental Patterns in Dating

Saying that they "like" someone—in a romantic sense—is often the earliest forerunner of dating, and it is a phrase used even before children reach adolescence. In fact, one survey found that almost 20% of fourth graders said that they "liked" someone in a romantic sense. By the time they reach 12th grade, that percentage increases to around 95% (Burhmester, 2001; see Figure 8-3).

Actual dating among heterosexual adolescents starts later. By the time they are in 8th grade, 40% of adolescents have gone out with the same person three or more times, and almost 20% have had an exclusive relationship with another person that lasted for more than 2 months. Furthermore, more than half of 12- to 18-year-olds say they have been involved in a romantic relationship within the prior 18 months, and most fall in love for the first time during early adolescence (Montgomery & Sorell, 1998; Furman & Shaffer, 2003, 2006).

For many younger adolescents, though, dating doesn't consist of one-on-one activities. Instead, dating involves hanging out with a group of friends. In such cases, younger adolescents say they are "going out" with someone but the two of them never actually do anything by themselves. Instead, a couple who see themselves as going out may go to the mall, hang out at friends' houses, or go a movie within the context of a larger group of friends.

The reason for this lack of one-to-one activity is that for younger adolescents, dating involves more companionship and less genuine intimacy. In fact, in many cases, such early relationships are not seen as a way to fulfill needs for sexual activity or affiliation. Instead, they serve a more social and informational purpose, permitting adolescents to learn about norms of dating and helping them to understand how to navigate through the complex social waters of dating. Typically, it is not until younger adolescents have had some experience with dating and romance that needs for intimacy and sex become a more central part of the relationship (Furman & Wehner, 1998; Furman & Hand, 2006).

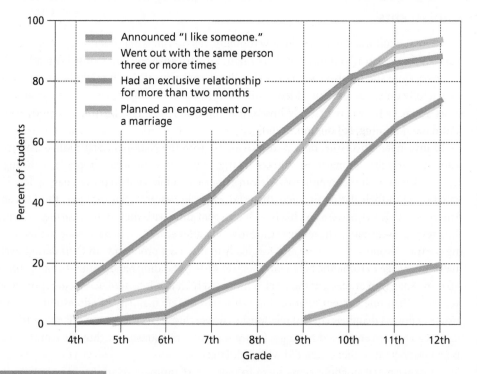

▲ FIGURE 8-3

The Development of Dating   "Liking" someone in a romantic sense is often considered the forerunner of dating. By the time they are in 12th grade, most adolescents indicate they have "liked" someone in a romantic sense. (*Source:* Burhmerster, 2001.)

Although common stereotypes suggest that girls are more interested in romance than boys, the reality of romantic interests in adolescence is different. Boys report becoming romantically interested in girls at an earlier age than girls report a romantic interest in boys. In addition, adolescent boys are more likely than girls to say that they are currently in love, and they report more frequently than girls that they have been in love in the past (Montgomery & Sorell, 1998).

Furthermore, boys and girls concentrate on somewhat different aspects of their partner, at least until late adolescence. In early and middle adolescence, boys are more focused on physical attractiveness. In contrast, girls are more interested in interpersonal characteristics such as supportiveness and understanding. However, by late adolescence, boys and girls become more similar in what they say is important in a partner. Both males and females believe that characteristics such as communication, emotional support, and passion are critical in making a relationship work—characteristics that are not all that different from the characteristics that adults cite as important in their relationships (Connolly et al., 1999; Collins, 2003; Collins & van Dulman, 2006).

The fact that boys and girls have different conceptions of dating points to a potential source of difficulty for girls who begin dating early, particularly if they are dating older boys. If younger girls are most interested in companionship and older boys are more focused on sex and passion, such mismatched expectations can lead the less-experienced girls to be pressured into behavior that they may be detrimental to their well-being (McNelles & Connolly, 1999; Crouter & Booth, 2006; Giordano, Manning, & Longmore, 2006).

"Sure I'm Alfred the Great now, but in high school I couldn't get a date."

Credit: © The New Yorker Collection 2000 Charles Barsotti from cartoonbank.com. All Rights Reserved.

Dating Scripts.   What happens on dates—what has been called the "dating script"—also differs according to gender. **Dating scripts** are cognitive models of what behavior and expectations are appropriate and inappropriate within the context of a dating relationship. Dating scripts are learned from peers, family, and the mass media, and they can have a powerful impact on the way in which adolescents evaluate what is supposed to happen within a dating relationship (Gershon et al., 2004).

For example, girls and boys typically differ in their conception of what should happen on a first date, often following traditional gender stereotypes. Boys traditionally believe that they should be proactive, asking for the date and suggesting an activity. In contrast, the female dating script has traditionally been more passive, with girls waiting to be asked out. In addition, gender stereotypes lead males to be more concerned with public domains (initiating activities and driving the car) and females to be more interested in private domains (such as appearance). Such scripts are changing, however, as both males and females adopt more egalitarian views (Rose & Frieze, 1993; Rose, 2000; Wiederman, 2005).

Demographic Factors in Dating.   Traditionally, most dating has occurred with a partner who is a member of an adolescent's racial, ethnic, and religious group. In part, this is a reflection of the pool of potential romantic partners who are available because schools tend to draw from neighborhoods that are relatively homogeneous (Giordano, Manning, & Longmore, 2006).

On the other hand, when the pool of potential romantic partners is broader, adolescents are beginning to cross racial, ethnic, and religious boundaries in greater numbers. For example, around a quarter of college students reported in one survey that they had dated interracially, and almost one half were open to the idea of crossing racial lines in forming a relationship (Knox, Zusman, Buffington, et al., 2000).

dating scripts   cognitive models of what behavior and expectations are appropriate and inappropriate within the context of a dating relationship

The Phases of Intimacy.   One way of looking at the development of romance and dating during adolescence is to consider it in terms of a series of phases of increasing intimacy. In this view, adolescents' romantic relationships proceed in four phases (Brown, 1999; Brown & Klute, 2006):

Phase 1. Infatuation. In the first stage of romance, adolescents are infatuated with one another. Although they may be smitten by their partner, relationships actually are not very serious, because adolescents focus more on learning about themselves and are only beginning to think of themselves as romantic partners. Relationships are generally short during this time, and partners are viewed more in terms of superficial criteria.

Phase 2. Status. In the second phase, adolescents date to maintain or improve their status among their peers. Dating is seen as a social activity, and dating the "right" person can be helpful in improving one's popularity. Conversely, dating an "inappropriate" person—where inappropriate is measured in the eyes of peers, and not parents—can damage one's social standing.

Phase 3. Intimacy. The intimate phase of romance represents a more authentic type of romance. Partners become more concerned with their relationship and less concerned with how their peers are viewing them. They experience true, deep feelings for the partner, and they are preoccupied with him or her and with the relationship itself.

Phase 4. Bonding. In this last stage, romantic partners begin to consider the issue of long-term commitment. They ask themselves whether the relationship will last and whether their partner is someone with whom they would like to share, at least on a theoretical level, a potentially lifelong, caring relationship. Although most adolescents are not contemplating marriage at this point—this typically occurs after adolescence for most youth today—they are thinking about the relationship in terms of how long it can last. To some extent, then, passion becomes less important than the sense of caring commitment within the relationship.

Dating in Sexual Minority Youth

Gay, lesbian, and bisexual adolescents—known collectively as *sexual minority youth*—face dating issues that are significantly different from those faced by their heterosexual peers. Because nonheterosexual relationships typically face significant social condemnation and because their own sexuality is sometimes unclear to them, members of sexual minorities may find it difficult to act on their romantic interests. Furthermore, because there is a smaller pool of individuals who are also members of the sexual minority youth population, they have fewer opportunities to form romantic relationships than heterosexual youth (Savin-Williams & Cohen, 2004).

These challenges mean that sexual minority youth do not follow consistent patterns in their dating behavior, and it is hard to make generalizations. Many gays and lesbians initially participate in dating with the other sex, and they may feel romantically involved and experience some genuine degree of sexual attraction in such relationships.

On the other hand, other gays and lesbians are never attracted to members of the other sex, and they experience similar romantic interests, except for the sex of the individual, as do heterosexual adolescents. And sometimes their interest in becoming involved with others of the same sex is purely sexual and has little to do with emotional, romantic involvement—as is also the case with some heterosexual adolescents (Diamond, Savin-Williams, & Dubé, 1999; Savin-Williams, 2003).

In short, adolescents who are members of sexual minorities engage in heterogeneous patterns of dating behavior. In considering dating behavior among gays, lesbians, and bisexuals, however, it is important not to assume that their behavior is similar to heterosexual youth except for the sex of the target of their affection. Instead, adolescent researchers need to determine the different patterns of dating and romance and ultimately (as we'll discuss in Chapter 9) sexual behavior exhibited by adolescents who belong to sexual minorities.

Love: It's Different from Liking

Is "love" between adolescents just a lot of "liking"? Most adolescent specialists would answer negatively; love not only differs quantitatively from liking, but it also represents a qualitatively different state. For example, love, at least in its early stages, involves relatively intense physiological arousal, an all-encompassing interest in another individual, recurrent fantasies about the other individual, and rapid swings of emotion. As distinct from liking, love includes elements of closeness, passion, and exclusivity (Connolly et al., 1999; Schwartz, 2006).

Not all love is the same, however. Adolescents who are in love don't love their girlfriends and boyfriends in the same way they love their siblings or parents. What distinguishes these different types of love? Some psychologists suggest that adolescent love relationships fall into two different categories: passionate or companionate.

Passionate (or romantic) love is a state of powerful absorption in someone. It includes intense physiological interest and arousal, and caring for another's needs. In comparison, **companionate love** is the strong affection that we have for those with whom our lives are deeply involved (Hatfield, 1988; Lamm & Wiesman, 1997; Hatfield & Rapson, 2002).

What is it that fuels the fires of passionate love? According to one theory, anything that produces strong emotions—even negative ones such as jealousy, anger, or fear of rejection—may be the source of deepening passionate love.

In psychologists Elaine Hatfield and Ellen Berscheid's *labeling theory of passionate love,* individuals experience romantic love when two events occur together: intense physiological arousal and situational cues that indicate that "love" is the appropriate label for the feelings that are being experienced (Berscheid & Walster, 1974). The physiological arousal can be produced by sexual arousal, excitement, or even negative emotions such as jealousy. Whatever the cause, if that arousal is subsequently labeled as "I must be falling in love" or "she makes my heart flutter" or "he really turns me on," then the experience is attributed to passionate love.

The theory is particularly useful in explaining why adolescents may feel deepened love even when they experience continual rejection or hurt from someone to whom they are attracted. It suggests that such negative emotions can produce strong physiological arousal. If this arousal is interpreted as being caused by "love," then people may decide that they are even more in love than they were before they experienced the negative emotions.

But why should adolescents label an emotional experience as "love" when there are so many possible alternatives? One answer is that in Western cultures, passionate love is seen as possible, acceptable, desirable—an experience to be sought. The virtues of passion are extolled in love songs, advertisements, television shows, and films. Consequently, adolescents are primed and ready to experience love in their lives (Dion & Dion, 1988; Hatfield & Rapson, 1993).

It is interesting to note that this is not the way it is in every culture. For instance, in many cultures, passionate, romantic love is a foreign concept. As we noted earlier, marriages may be arranged on the basis of economic and status considerations. Even in Western cultures, the concept of love is of relatively recent origin. In fact, the notion that couples need to be in love was not "invented" until the Middle Ages, when social philosophers first suggested that love ought to be a requirement for marriage. Their goal in making such a proposal: to provide an alternative to the raw sexual desire that had served as the primary basis for marriage before (Lewis, 1958; Xiaohe & Whyte, 1990).

Sternberg's Triangular Theory: The Three Faces of Love. To psychologist Robert Sternberg, love is more complex than a simple division into passionate and companionate types. He suggested instead that love is made up of three components: intimacy, passion, and decision/commitment. The **intimacy component** encompasses feelings of closeness, affection, and

▲ Passionate (or romantic) love is a state of powerful absorption in another person.

passionate (or romantic) love   a state of powerful absorption in someone that includes intense physiological interest and arousal, and caring for another's needs

companionate love   the strong affection that we have for those with whom our lives are deeply involved

intimacy component   the component of love that encompasses feelings of closeness, affection, and connectedness

connectedness. The **passion component** comprises the motivational drives relating to sex, physical closeness, and romance. This component is exemplified by intense, physiologically arousing feelings of attraction. Finally, the third aspect of love, the **decision/commitment component,** embodies both the initial cognition that one loves another person and the longer-term determination to maintain that love (Sternberg, 1998, 2004).

By jointly considering whether each of the three components is either present or missing from a relationship, eight unique combinations of love can be formed (see Table 8-2). For instance, *nonlove* refers to people who have only the most casual of relationships; it consists of the absence of the three components of intimacy, passion, and decision/commitment. *Liking* develops when only intimacy is present; *infatuated love* exists when only passion is felt; and *empty love* exists when only decision/commitment is present.

Other types of love are more complex. For instance, *romantic love* occurs when intimacy and passion are present, and *companionate love* when intimacy and decision/commitment occur

TABLE 8-2   The Combinations of Love

| Type of Love | Component | | | Example |
	Intimacy	Passion	Decision/ Commitment	
Nonlove	Absent	Absent	Absent	The way you might feel about the person who takes your ticket at the movies.
Liking	Present	Absent	Absent	Good friends who have lunch together at least once or twice a week.
Infatuated love	Absent	Present	Absent	A "fling" or short-term relationship based only on sexual attraction.
Empty love	Absent	Absent	Present	An arranged marriage or a couple who have decided to stay married "for the sake of the children."
Romantic love	Present	Present	Absent	A couple who have been happily dating a few months, but have not made any plans for a future together.
Companionate love	Present	Absent	Present	A couple who enjoy each other's company and their relationship, although they no longer feel much sexual interest in each other.
Fatuous love	Absent	Present	Present	A couple who decides to move in together after knowing each other for only two weeks.
Consummate love	Present	Present	Present	A loving, sexually vibrant, long-term relationship.

passion component   the component of love that comprises the motivational drives relating to sex, physical closeness, and romance and is exemplified by intense, physiologically arousing feelings of attraction

decision/commitment component   the component of love that embodies both the initial cognition that one loves another person and the longer-term determination to maintain that love

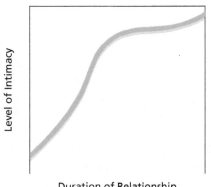

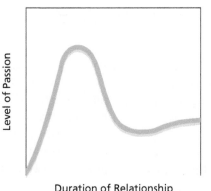

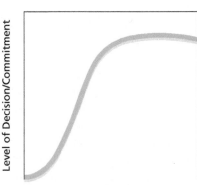

Duration of Relationship · Duration of Relationship · Duration of Relationship

▲ **FIGURE 8-4**

The Three Aspects of Love The strength of the three aspects of love—intimacy, passion, and decision/commitment—varies over the course of a relationship.

(*Source:* Sternberg, 1986.)

jointly. When two people experience romantic love, they are drawn together physically and emotionally, but they do not necessarily view the relationship as lasting. Companionate love, on the other hand, may occur in long-lasting relationships in which physical passion has taken a backseat.

Fatuous love exists when passion and decision/commitment, without intimacy, are present. Fatuous love is a kind of mindless loving in which there is no emotional bond between the partners.

Finally, the eighth kind of love is *consummate love*. In consummate love, all three components of love are present. Although we might assume that consummate love represents the "ideal" love, such a view may well be mistaken. Many long-lasting and entirely satisfactory relationships are based on types of love other than consummate love. Furthermore, the type of love that predominates in a relationship varies over time. As shown in Figure 8-4, in strong, loving relationships the level of decision/commitment peaks and remains fairly stable. By contrast, passion tends to peak early in a relationship, but then declines and levels off. Intimacy also increases fairly rapidly, but can continue to grow over time. (For more on different sorts of romantic relationships, see the *Transitions* box.)

The Biochemistry of Romance. The newest approach to understanding romantic love comes from research on the physiological changes that occur in the brain. Noting that some degree of passion is involved in attraction to mates in virtually every culture, researchers have sought to find if there are specific neurological mechanisms relating to the experience of passionate love.

The initial answer suggests that there are certain areas of the brain, associated with reward and motivational brain systems, that are activated when a person thinks about a loved one. For example, in one study, 18- to 25-year-olds who reported being intensely in love were shown photos of their beloved and photos of a nonloved acquaintance while experiencing an fMRI (functional magnetic resonance image) brain scan (Aron et al., 2005; Aron, Fisher, & Mashek, 2005).

The results found clear differences in brain activation depending on which photo participants were viewing. In particular, the right ventral tegmental area and right caudate nucleus—both areas of the brain associated with reward and high motivation—were activated when looking at loved ones (see Figure 8-5 on page 271).

The End of Romance: Breaking Up Is Hard to Do

I really liked Trini. I guess my friends put the pressure on, because he did ask me out, but after exactly one week . . . he broke up with me. My 13-year-old heart was broken.

The end of a romantic relationship between adolescents can represent a major crisis, even in relationships that have not lasted very long. This is often puzzling to parents and other adults, who have greater experience and realize that relationships come and go, especially during adolescence.

Transiti⊃ns

Falling in Love: How Do Adolescent Relationships Blossom?

When we talk about "romantic relationships," we often assume that the meaning of that term is clear. Yet for many adolescents—and for many adults—the point at which a relationship transitions from one sort to another isn't very clear at all. One reason the early days of a new dating relationship are so exciting (some might call them nerve-racking) is the uncertainty over where the relationship is heading. Is it just a one-time affair, or is it a nonexclusive dating arrangement? If so, at what point does it cross over into a serious committed relationship?

Researcher Louisa Allen (2004) recognized that the notion of a romantic relationship can have diverse meanings to adolescents. In contrast to the view that adolescents' relationships tend to develop predictably in stages of increasing intimacy and commitment, another possibility is that adolescents may switch among different relationship options to meet different needs. Allen investigated adolescents' varied understandings of romantic relationships through a series of structured discussions involving groups of 17- to 19-year-old adolescents who were friends.

Each session began by asking the adolescents to comment on the first thing that came to mind when they heard the word *relationships,* followed by specific questions about the participants' understanding of the meaning and function of relationships. The results showed that there were four distinct relationship types: one-night stands, short-term relationships, casual dating, and going out.

Adolescent participants used the term *one-night stand* to refer to one-time sexual encounters. These might occur between strangers who just met or between adolescents who had known each other previously but not in any intimate way. The sexual activity that adolescents ascribed to one-night stands wasn't necessarily sexual intercourse; it might, for example, simply entail kissing.

Short-term relationships were described by adolescents as something beyond a one-night stand, lasting anywhere from less than a day to a few weeks. Short-term relationships may or may not involve sexual activity, as that was not the defining characteristic. Instead, this type of relationship was primarily distinguished by its recognition by others; that is, by having others refer to the couple as boyfriend and girlfriend. This type of relationship could sometimes be quite superficial, involving little actual interaction beyond the use of the "boyfriend" and "girlfriend" labels.

Casual dating was described by adolescents as essentially a repetitive one-night stand. Adolescents engaging in this type of relationship saw themselves as uncommitted but available to each other for sexual activity (which may or may not include sexual intercourse). Casual dating may or may not be exclusive; that is, adolescents might have one casual dating partner or more than one at the same time. This type of relationship was the one most likely to produce confusion and anxiety over the possibility of increasing the level of commitment.

Finally, adolescents used the term *going out* to refer to a relationship that was exclusive, committed, and recognized by others. It included an expectation of monogamy as well as a sense of emotional attachment.

Clearly, the various levels of relationships had a fair amount of overlap. But each had a distinct meaning to adolescents, who were able to distinguish different levels of romance and had a common vocabulary that helped to categorize the different kinds of relationships. Moreover, the differences among these relationship types were not just a matter of increasing intimacy and commitment levels; other important factors were the amount of time spent together, exclusivity, emotional attachment, and sexual activity. Adolescents' recognition of these different options underscores the point that relationships serve a variety of functions for them.

- Which components of Sternberg's triangular theory of love seem to be present or absent from each of the types of romantic relationships described in Allen's research?

- Why might adolescents call someone their "boyfriend" or "girlfriend" even though they have no special relationship with that person?

But adolescents are particularly vulnerable when breakups occur. Their sense of themselves and their self-worth are still evolving and sometimes fragile, and they may not have the cognitive sophistication to understand or accept the reasons behind the dissolution of the romance. In addition, they simply don't have experience dealing with a breakup, making it more difficult to cope with the situation. As a consequence, relationship difficulties are among the most frequently cited causes of adolescent depression and suicide (Knox, Zusman, Kaluzny et al., 2000; Smith, Buzi, & Weinman, 2001; Welsh, Grello, & Harper, 2003).

Adolescents react to romantic conflict in a number of ways. In some cases, they get angry and lash out at their partner. In other cases, they seek the comfort and consolation of their friends and peers, who can provide social support. Adolescents also may try to disregard problems in their relationships, holding onto an idealized view of their partner and trying to ignore issues that are detrimental to the relationship (Laursen, 1995; Coontz, 2006).

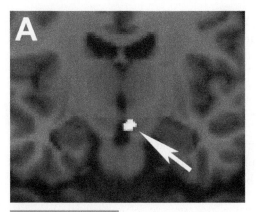 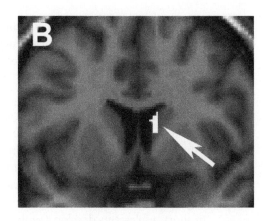

▲ **FIGURE8-5**

Passion in the Brain   In these fMRI brain scans, two areas of the brain were activated when exposed to a photo of an individua with whom the viewer was passionately in love. In (a), the right ventral tegmental area (arrow) is activated, and in (b), the right caudate nucleus (arrow) is activated.

BECOMING   AN INFORMED CONSUMER OF ADOLESCENT SCIENCE

Coping with a Breakup

For most adolescents, the end of a romantic relationship is an emotionally painful event. Feelings of sadness, loss, regret, and even anger are all common and normal reactions.

If you were to give advice to an adolescent who was suffering through a breakup, here are some tips for coping that you might pass on, based on the work of researchers who have studied relationships (Sprecher et al., 1998; Hardcastle, 2003; Mikulincer, Dolev, & Shaver, 2004; Sbarra & Emery, 2005; Sbarra, 2006):

- Don't take it personally. It's easy to think that when someone falls out of love with you, it must be because there is something wrong with you. But relationships lose their spark for many reasons; often the couple simply grows apart. A breakup doesn't mean that you're a bad or unlovable person—it just means that you weren't right for this one particular person at this time.

- Keep your perspective. Even if your former intimate identifies something specific about you or your behavior that led to the breakup, remember that different people have different likes and dislikes. Of course it's a good idea to learn from your mistakes, but keep in mind that no one is perfect—and the quirks that your former intimate found distasteful about you might be the same ones that someone else will find attractive!

- Accept your former intimate's decision. Breaking up with someone is not easy—it's often just as painful for the person making the breakup decision as it is for the person hearing it. Your former partner knew that this news would probably shock and upset you, yet he or she felt strongly enough to deliver it anyway. You can't persuade or shame another person into loving you, and if you try these tactics, you'll only prolong the anguish for both of you.

- Let your feelings out. After a breakup you might feel a confusing jumble of emotions, including sadness, anger, grief, embarrassment, and so on. This is perfectly normal—breakups hurt! Seek out support from family and friends; a sympathetic ear can help you work through your emotions and get past them.

- Give yourself time to adjust. It takes some time to recover from a painful experience such as a breakup. You may need to adjust to becoming a single person again after a period of identifying yourself as one half of a couple. You may need to reevaluate plans that you had made for your immediate or long-term future together. And of course, you need to get past your feelings of sadness and loss. All of this takes time. ■

Family Conflict and Relationship Scripts. The way in which adolescents experience and attempt to resolve conflict reflects, in part, their own family history. Adolescents typically display the same level of conflict in their romantic relationships that they have witnessed in their own families. Furthermore, they tend to employ with their romantic partner the conflict-resolution strategies that were most prevalent between their parents and themselves and their siblings (Reese-Weber & Kahn, 2005).

In short, adolescents develop cognitive scripts for handling conflict (similar to the more general dating scripts we discussed earlier) that are based on their experience in their own families, as well as the media and society in general. Adolescents who have witnessed high levels of conflict and verbal aggression in their families form scripts that involve similar levels of argumentativeness. In a sense, they are primed to expect conflict and are not surprised when it actually occurs. Furthermore, they may not deal with clashes in the most effective manner, because their cognitive models of conflict resolution reflect the dysfunction they have seen in their own families (Gray & Steinberg, 1999; Doyle et al., 2003; Shulman, 2003).

However, in some cases, rather than adopting a relationship script based on their parents' level of conflict, adolescents may take a very different path. For example, an adolescent who witnesses her parents fighting a great deal may throw herself into dating, seeking to find a "perfect" relationship in which there is no conflict. To attain this (largely unattainable) goal, she may gloss over sources of conflict and try to maintain a relationship in which conflict does not occur. Obviously, such an effort is unhealthy and ultimately unsustainable, because some conflict is part of every relationship.

Furthermore, it's not only parents who provide models of conflict and conflict resolution. Siblings, too, affect the manner in which adolescents deal with disagreements. Adolescents who have difficult, conflict-ridden relationships with their siblings can experience difficulties in their romantic relationships as a consequence. Counseling and therapy can help such individuals deal with the relationship problems they face (Bigelow, Tesson, & Lewko, 1999). (To get insight into how family counseling operates, see the *Career Choices* box.)

Long-Term Development and Intimacy

We began this chapter by discussing Sullivan's and Erikson's views on the role of intimacy in adolescent development. Both argued that the building of intimate relationships was an essential task of adolescence, and that success in finding intimacy was an important determinant of how relationships played out for the remainder of a person's life.

Clearly, both were correct. In developing increasingly close relationships with friends and dating partners, adolescents not only learn how to navigate the complex social waters of the period, but they also learn about themselves. Intimates provide a sounding board for one's thoughts and ideas, they can offer social support, and they present an opportunity to engage in enjoyable activities. Furthermore, having even just one close friend is tied to higher self-esteem and better mental health.

Although not all close relationships foster constructive development—we've seen that close relationships with peers who hold antisocial values and engage in delinquent acts can have negative consequences—generally speaking, having close friends is an important and positive aspect of adolescents' lives. As they develop increasing and more meaningful levels of intimacy with others, adolescents prepare themselves for the developmental tasks that are central to adulthood.

Finally, you've probably noticed that we've largely disregarded the sexual aspects of intimacy. That's about to change, though. In the next chapter, we'll consider the role of gender and sexuality in adolescent relationships, considering sex as both a reflection and a source of intimacy.

CAREER CHOICES

Family Counselor

Name: Ernie Reilly

Education: Bachelor of Science Degree with dual majors in psychology and philosophy, Florida State University, Tallahassee, Florida; master's degree in clinical social work, Florida State University, Tallahassee.

Position: Child and Family Therapist; Director of The Counseling Center, Orlando, Florida.

Home: Orlando, Florida

ALMOST ALL ADOLESCENTS experience conflict with their parents or other family members at some point. Although most parents and adolescents work things out on their own, there are situations in which a family counselor can provide much-needed guidance.

According to child and family therapist Ernie Reilly, adolescents typically have some degree of internal, as well as external, conflict about who they are and how they function within their families.

"One of the things I do is take a coaching role with adolescents," he explains. "We try to figure out what their strengths and weaknesses are and what they want to accomplish.

"When we analyze what adolescents want, we find that most kids want to do well in life, have good relationships, and be successful in school, whether it's in athletics or academics."

However, the process of getting adolescents to see what they really want can be slow, according to Reilly.

"Oftentimes parents are upset with their adolescent resisting what they want him or her to do, and the adolescent reacts to their parents' concern. This creates a cycle of resistance and reaction," he said. "We can be successful if the adolescent can see me as someone who can help them accomplish what they want in life—which is usually not a whole lot different from what the parents want."

Reilly noted that counseling adolescents with parental conflicts can be difficult. One must walk a thin line and not appear to be taking sides.

"I meet with the parents on a fairly regular basis, and I have to take a careful role to avoid appearing as if I'm an extension of the parent," he explained. "You need to control the perception as well as the reality of the situation.

"If the adolescent does perceive me to be an extension of the parent, then I won't be any more effective than the parent," Reilly added.

Thinking of working in the family counseling field?

Family counselors help families and couples who are experiencing relationship difficulties or conflicts. They use individual, family, and group therapy to help family members work through their emotional problems and develop important relationship skills, such as open communication. They may work in private practice, at mental health clinics, or at family service agencies. Many family counselors specialize in a particular area, such as sex counseling or couples counseling.

Preparation for a career as a family counselor usually requires at least a master's degree, and often a Ph.D., including coursework as well as a supervised counseling internship. Almost all states require family counselors to pass an exam to be licensed and to complete annual continuing education as well. ■

Review and Apply

Review

1. Dating, which is undergoing significant changes in U.S. society, is an important component of adolescent development because it helps adolescents build their identities and learn intimacy.

2. Dating behavior and norms in the United States differ substantially across cultural and ethnic groups, and "dating scripts" differ across the genders and in sexual minority adolescents.

3. Love is recognized by adolescents as being qualitatively different from liking, involving physiological arousal, intense interest, and feelings of closeness and exclusivity.

4. Relationships serve a number of different needs for adolescents, and relationship types range from the highly casual to the more exclusive and romantic.

5. Conflict in romantic relationships is unavoidable and can be difficult for adolescents to handle. Adolescents' scripts for dealing with conflict are based on their experiences in their own families and in the media.

Apply

1. Can you think of examples from literature, movies, or TV shows of the eight combinations of love suggested by Sternberg's triangular theory of love? Which type is easiest to find in popular culture? Which is hardest? Why?

2. Do you believe that changing relationship patterns among adolescents have had mostly positive or mostly negative effects on U.S. society? Why?

EPILOGUE

In this chapter we covered the topic of intimacy. We began with a consideration of the theoretical underpinnings of intimacy and the relationship between intimacy and identity. We then discussed adolescents' understanding of friendships, exploring why they are important, what roles they play, and the qualities that lead to friendship. We also took a look at the issue of loneliness. We finished the chapter with a consideration of the changing world of dating and romance during adolescence. We examined how dating is changing, why love is different from liking, what the components of a romance are, and how adolescents deal with romantic breakups.

Before we move to the next chapter, recall the experiences of Ricky Reiter, an adolescent seemingly inundated with relationships. Consider the following questions.

1. Considering the attributes he focuses on in a romantic partner, in what ways is Ricky like a boy in middle adolescence and in what ways is he like a boy in late adolescence?

2. If you were studying a group of high school seniors like Ricky, who have had relationships with a substantial number of girls, what questions would you ask to try to determine whether identity precedes intimacy (as Erikson says) or intimacy precedes identity (as Sullivan believes)?

3. Based on the information in the Prologue, what sorts of friendships do you think Ricky would have had in high school, in terms of the roles friendships play, self-disclosure, reciprocity, and other characteristics?

4. Given Ricky's experience and personality, how hard do you think it will be for him to achieve intimacy? Why?

SUMMARY

REVIEW

● **Why is the development of intimacy important during adolescence?** *(p. 246)*

1. Because of their developmental advances, adolescents are able to experience intimacy, an emotional closeness with other people that will have long-lasting effects on their later relationships.

2. In the view of Harry Stack Sullivan, it is during adolescence that the preadolescent need for intimacy gives way to the adolescent need for sexual contact.

3. According to Sullivan, individuals must successfully resolve their need for intimacy if they are to develop a fully coherent identity during adulthood.

4. Erik Erikson regards the development of intimacy as an outcome of adolescents' resolution of the identity-versus-role-confusion stage of psychosocial development.

5. Whether intimacy precedes identity development (Sullivan) or vice versa (Erikson) is an unresolved question.

● **In what ways does friendship grow and change during adolescence?** *(p. 251)*

6. The childhood idea of friendship as a way to share activities shifts during adolescence to include intimacy and loyalty.

7. Friendships serve many functions during adolescence, including companionship, stimulation, support, social comparison, a safe environment, and intimacy and affection.

8. Friendships bring many advantages, including happiness and improved social skills, and comparatively few risks, including a risk of rejection and betrayal.

9. A characteristic of friendships during adolescence is self-disclosure, including descriptive self-disclosure and, especially, evaluative self-disclosure.

10. Friendships most often are built on similarity, reciprocity, and proximity. Other-sex friendships develop in late adolescence about the same time as, and in parallel with, romantic relationships.

● **What is the nature of loneliness and what are its effects?** *(p. 259)*

11. Loneliness is a subjective state in which a person's actual level of relationships does not correspond to the desired level.

12. Psychologists recognize two types of loneliness: emotional isolation and social isolation.

● **How do adolescents understand and manage dating?** *(p. 260)*

13. The traditional view of dating has been evolving to include more options for male–female relationships and to include gay, lesbian, and bisexual relationships as well.

14. Dating serves several functions during adolescence, including providing recreation, helping adolescents construct their identities, increasing their independence from families and peers, and enabling them to achieve intimacy.

15. Dating behavior develops as adolescents age, shifting from hanging out with a group, to going out casually with one other person, to developing intimacy with one person exclusively.

● **What sorts of romantic relationships do adolescents have?** *(p. 267)*

16. Love differs qualitatively from liking and involves closeness, passion, and exclusivity.

17. According to Sternberg, love consists of three components: intimacy, passion, and decision/commitment.

18. When asked to explain relationships, adolescents identified one-night stands, short-term relationships, casual dating, and going out as specific types of relationships.

19. Relationships typically involve conflict, and breaking up can be particularly difficult for adolescents to deal with, given the issues of identity and self-worth with which they are wrestling.

KEY TERMS AND CONCEPTS

intimacy (p. 246)

theory of interpersonal development (p. 247)

friendships (p. 251)

self-disclosure (p. 253)

descriptive self-disclosure (p. 254)

evaluative self-disclosure (p. 254)

loneliness (p. 259)

emotional isolation (p. 259)

social isolation (p. 259)

dating (p. 260)

dating scripts (p. 265)

passionate (or romantic) love (p. 267)

companionate love (p. 267)

intimacy component (p. 267)

passion component (p. 268)

decision/commitment component (p. 268)

9 Adolescent Sexuality

CHAPTER OUTLINE

PROLOGUE Virginity, Renewed

LUCIAN SCHULTE HAD always planned to wait until he was married to have sex, but that was before a warm night a couple of years ago when the green-eyed, lanky six-footer found himself with an unexpected opportunity. "She was all for it," says Lucian, now 18. "It was like, 'Hey, let's give this a try.'" The big event was over in a hurry and lacked any sense of intimacy. "In movies, if people have sex, it's always romantic," he says. "Physically, it did feel good, but emotionally, it felt really awkward. It was not what I expected it to be."

Lucian, raised Roman Catholic, was plagued by guilt. "I was worried that I'd given myself to someone and our relationship was now a lot more serious than it was before," he says. "It was like, 'Now, what is she going to expect from me?'" Lucian worried, too, about disease and pregnancy. He promised himself never again.

Lucian, now an engineering major at the University of Alberta in Canada, is a "renewed virgin." His parents are strong proponents of chastity, and he attended school-sponsored abstinence classes. But the messages didn't hit home until he'd actually had sex. . . . He has dated since his high-school affair, and is now hoping a particular cute coed from Edmonton will go out with him. "But I'll try to restrict myself to kissing," he says. (Ali & Scelfo, 2002, p. 61) ■

th!nk ABOUT THIS

WE'LL PROBABLY NEVER know whether Lucian Schulte will be successful in his quest to abstain from sex prior to marriage. But the issues of sexuality he is grappling with are those that virtually every adolescent thinks about at one point or another.

In this chapter we consider adolescent sexuality. We begin by examining sexual behavior during adolescence, starting with the basic biology of sex. We look at a range of behavior, including masturbation and sex with a partner. We also consider sexual orientation.

Next we turn to adolescent pregnancy. We examine recent trends in teenage pregnancy rates and try to explain why the rate of pregnancy has changed in the last decade. We also look at abortion and adoption.

Finally, we discuss sexual disorders and difficulties. We consider how disorders affect and adolescents look at sexually transmitted infections. We also examine sexual harassment and rape. ■

- What sexual activities are common among adolescents?
- Why are there different sexual orientations, and what determines one's orientation?
- What are the issues associated with adolescent pregnancy, and how can it be prevented?
- What sorts of difficulties may adolescents encounter as they negotiate their sexuality?
- Why are sexual harassment and rape particular threats during adolescence?

Becoming Sexual

*W*hen I started *"tuning out," teachers thought I was sick—physically sick that is. They kept sending me to the school nurse to have my temperature taken. If I'd told them I was carrying on with Beyoncé in their classes, while supposedly learning my Caesar and my Latin vocabulary, they'd have thought I was—well, delirious. I was! I'd even think of Beyoncé while jogging; I'd have to stop because it'd hurt down there! You can't run and have sex—or can you?*

Not every adolescent's sexual fantasies are as consuming as those of this teenage boy. But the hormonal changes of puberty bring with them maturation of the sexual organs and a new range of feelings and possibilities in their relations with others. Sexual behavior and thoughts are among the central concerns of adolescents. Almost all adolescents think about sex, and many think about it a good deal of the time (Kelly, 2001; Ponton, 2001).

Adolescence is not the first time individuals think about sex. You probably know this from your own experiences. Perhaps you "played doctor" as a preschooler. Or maybe you had an erection as a child. Or perhaps you were curious about the pubic hair a sibling was growing.

In fact, even infants and preschoolers experience some sort of sexuality, because it is clear that they do take pleasure from touching their genitals and apparently enjoy the stimulation it produces. Later, preadolescents report experiencing sexual pleasure from kissing and touching themselves and others, and some even report going through the motions of sexual intercourse during middle childhood.

But it is not until adolescence, and the onset of puberty, that sexuality becomes a central aspect of everyday life. However, although the increased emphasis on sexuality during adolescence is related to puberty, physical maturation does not fully account for the phenomenon. In fact, another aspect of maturation also plays a key role. The growing cognitive maturity of adolescents allows them to think about sex in a more abstract and hypothetical way. Adolescents are capable of playing out different scenarios in their minds ("If we don't have sex will he drop me?" or "If we do have sex will he think I'm too eager?"). They may try to figure out how sex enters into their relationships—and how engaging (or not engaging) in sex might change the nature of a relationship.

Prior to adolescence, sexuality has little of the cognitive significance that it takes on during adolescence. The erotic feelings preadolescents experience don't carry the meaning they do in adolescence, and the sexual drives brought about by the hormonal surges of puberty are clearly not as strong until adolescence (Thanasiu, 2004; Firestone, Firestone, & Catlett, 2006).

In short, the combination of physical and cognitive changes that occur during adolescence makes sexual behavior a significant focus of adolescents' lives. This budding sexuality raises several distinct developmental challenges. First, adolescents must come to terms with their changing bodies. They need to recognize that the changes are inevitable and that they are unfolding automatically. In addition, they need to accept that the sexual feelings they are experiencing are a typical, and an acceptable, part of their increasing maturity.

Furthermore, adolescents must begin to make choices about what is and isn't acceptable for themselves in terms of their own sexual behavior, drawing on their knowledge of sexuality and society's norms for appropriate conduct. Finally, if they do decide to engage in sexual activity, they have to learn to do so responsibly, engaging in safe-sex practices that provide protection from sexually transmitted infections and pregnancy (Brooks-Gunn & Paikoff, 1997; O'Sullivan & Brooks-Gunn, 2005).

Not all adolescents meet these developmental challenges successfully, and even in adulthood, sexuality may be an emotionally charged and difficult topic. But whether sexual development proceeds smoothly or follows a rocky path, it is an important part of adolescents' lives.

Let's begin our exploration of adolescent sexuality by reviewing a bit about the biology that underlies sex. As you'll see, that biology encompasses both the sexual organs and, in some ways even more importantly, the brain.

The Biology of Sex

As we discussed in Chapter 2, at the start of puberty, the testes accelerate their production of *androgens,* the male sex hormone. These androgens not only produce secondary sex characteristics such as the growth of body hair and the deepening of the voice, but they also increase the sex drive. Because the production of androgen is fairly constant, adolescent boys are capable of and interested in sex independent of any biological cycles.

In females, puberty produces the secretion of *estrogens* and *progesterone,* female sex hormones, and *androgens,* male sex hormones. In women, the sex hormones are produced inconsistently. Their production follows a cyclical pattern in which greatest output occurs during *ovulation,* when an egg is released from the ovaries, making the chances of fertilization by a sperm cell highest. Although there is some research suggesting that in some cases women are more receptive to sex in the period around ovulation (which is true among nonhumans), most findings suggest that women are receptive to sex throughout their monthly cycle (Pillsworth, Haselton, & Buss, 2004).

Is there a difference in the strength of the sex drive between males and females? Some evidence suggests there is, although this difference may have more to do with society's reluctance to acknowledge female sexuality than with biological differences between the sexes. What is clear is that males *think* about sex more than females, with some studies showing that about half of males, but only around 20% of females, report thinking about sex every day (Baumeister, Twenge, & Nuss, 2002; Peplau, 2003; Mendelsohn, 2003; Gangestad et al., 2004).

Adolescents have a rich sexual fantasy life. Thinking about being sexually irresistible and about engaging in oral–genital sex are the most common fantasies for college students (see Figure 9-1). Generally, there is little difference in the fantasies of male and female adolescents. Keep in mind that fantasies are just fantasies; thinking about something doesn't mean that an adolescent actually wants it to happen in real life (Jones & Barlow, 1990; Hsu et al., 1994).

Although we usually think of the genitals as the center of sexuality, in reality what constitutes a sexual turn-on for adolescents depends more on their brains than on their genitals. There is no part of the body that automatically produces sexual arousal when touched. Although a number of areas of the body, called *erogenous*

B. Smaller

"I think I'll be more relaxed once my secondary sex characteristics kick in."

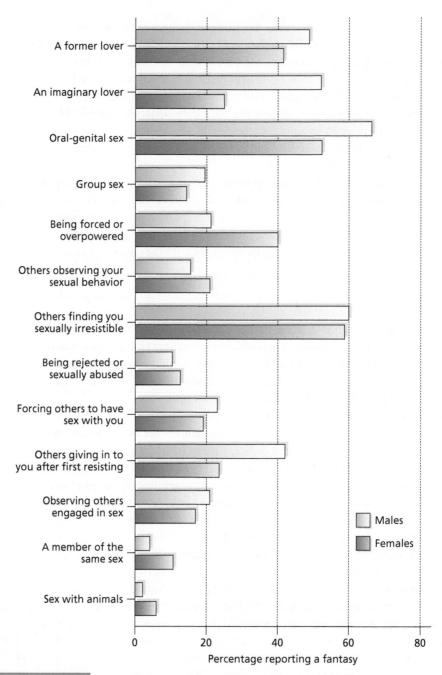

▲ **FIGURE 9-1**

Although adolescents have a wide range of sexual fantasies, there is little difference in the types of fantasies that men and women have (Sue, 1979). Do you think this is the case in non-Western cultures?

zones, have an unusually high number of nerve receptors and are sensitive to a sexual touch, they are also receptive to nonsexual stimulation as well. What determines whether a touch is perceived as sexually stimulating is the brain. For example, when someone touches an adolescent male's penis, the reaction to the touch is dependent on whether the situation is seen as sexual (a lover touching it) or nonsexual (a physician touching it) (Gagnon, 1977; Goldstein, 2000).

In addition, there is significant agreement within a culture as to which specific parts of the body are viewed as sexually of interest. For example, in Western cultures, a woman's breast size is considered to contribute particularly to her allure. In other cultures, however, breast size is uninteresting. Similarly, there are subcultural differences in the degree to which a plump figure is seen by adolescent males as erotic. Specifically, black males are more likely to value plumpness in their partners than whites. In some traditional Arab cultures, obese females are valued so much that parents force-feed their daughters to make them more desirable (Rothblum, 1990; Mills et al., 2002; Naik, 2004; Pettijohn, 2004).

Let's turn now from fantasies to actual sexual behavior. We'll start with solitary sexual experiences and move on to sex with a partner.

Masturbation

The first type of sex in which adolescents engage is often solitary sexual self-stimulation, or **masturbation**. By the age of 15, some 80% of teenage boys and 20% of teenage girls report that they have masturbated. The frequency of masturbation in males is greatest in the early teens and then begins to decline, while in females, the frequency is lower initially and increases throughout adolescence. In addition, patterns of masturbation frequency show differences according to race. For example, African-American men and women masturbate less than whites (Oliver & Hyde, 1993; Schwartz, 1999; Hyde & DeLamater, 2003).

Although masturbation is widespread, it still may produce feelings of shame and guilt. There are several reasons for this. One is that adolescents may believe that masturbation signifies the inability to find a sexual partner—an erroneous assumption because statistics show that three quarters of married men and 68% of married women report masturbating between 10 and 24 times a year (Hunt, 1974; Davidson, Darling, & Norton, 1995).

For some there is also a sense of shame about masturbation, the result of a lingering legacy of misguided views of masturbation. For instance, 19th-century physicians and laypersons warned of horrible effects of masturbation, including "dyspepsia, spinal disease, headache, epilepsy, various kinds of fits. . . , impaired eyesight, palpitation of the heart, pain in the side and bleeding at the lungs, spasm of the heart, and sometimes sudden death" (Gregory, 1856). Suggested remedies included bandaging the genitals, covering them with a cage, tying the hands, male circumcision without anesthesia (so that it might better be remembered), and for girls, the administration of carbolic acid to the clitoris. One physician, J. W. Kellogg, believed that certain grains would be less likely to provoke sexual excitation—leading to his invention of cornflakes (Hunt, 1974; Michael et al., 1994).

The reality of masturbation is different. Today, experts on sexual behavior view it as a normal, healthy, and harmless activity. In fact, some suggest that it provides a useful way to learn about one's own sexuality (Else-Quest, Hyde & DeLamater, 2005).

Sex with a Partner

As adolescence proceeds, sexual behavior involving a partner increases, both in terms of the proportion of adolescents who engage in sex and in the frequency of sexual activity. In most cases, sexual behaviors tend to follow a fairly regular progression, or *sexual script*. Most adolescents begin with kissing, proceed to French kissing, petting, and breast and genital fondling, and move on to oral–genital sex.

Still, although it may be preceded by many different types of sexual intimacy, engaging in sexual intercourse remains a major milestone in the perceptions of most adolescents. Consequently, the main focus of researchers investigating sexual behavior has been on the act of heterosexual intercourse.

Most people learn about sexual intercourse before the start of adolescence. For instance, one survey found that almost two thirds of women had learned about intercourse by the age of 12. The news often produces shock, disgust, and incredulity, largely because it is unimaginable that one's parents would have engaged in such behavior. Because preadolescents often have only a

▲ As adolescence unfolds, sexual activity involving a partner increases.

masturbation solitary sexual self-stimulation

vague understanding of human anatomy (even of their own bodies), it is hard for them to comprehend the process. Consider, for example, this college woman's description of learning about sexual intercourse:

> *One of my girlfriends told me about sexual intercourse. It was one of the biggest shocks of my life. She took me aside one day, and I could tell she was in great distress. I thought she was going to tell me about menstruation, so I said that I already knew, and she said, "No, this is worse!" Her description went like this: "A guy puts his thing up a girl's hole, and she has a baby." The hole was, to us, the anus, because we did not even know about the vagina and we knew that the urethra was too small I pictured the act as a single, violent and painful stabbing at the anus by the penis. Somehow, the idea of a baby was forgotten by me. I was horrified and repulsed . . . We held each other and cried. We insisted that "my parents would never do that," and "I'll never let anyone do it to me." We were frightened, sickened, and threatened by the idea of some lusty male jabbing at us with his horrid penis. (Hyde & DeLameter, 2006, p. 266)*

Obviously, both girls and boys get over their initial misgivings about sexual intercourse, because it is not too long after hearing about intercourse that many adolescents are engaging in it. The average age at which adolescents first have sexual intercourse has been steadily declining over the last 50 years, and about one in five adolescents has had sex before the age of 15. Overall, around half of adolescents begin having intercourse between the ages of 15 and 18, and at least 80% have had sex before the age of 20 (see Figure 9-2).

Although adolescents who are having sex are doing so at earlier ages, the number who are postponing sex is growing. For example, the number of adolescents who say they have never had sexual intercourse increased by nearly 10% from 1991 to 2001, largely as a response to the threat of infection by the virus that causes AIDS (Seidman & Reider, 1994; Centers for Disease Control & Prevention, 1998; NCPYP, 2003).

Race and ethnicity also are related to the timing of first intercourse. On average, African Americans have intercourse for the first time at age 15.7 years, whites at 16.6 years, Hispanics at 17 years, and Asian Americans at 18.1 years. Such racial differences probably are a consequence of differences in cultural norms, family structure, and economic status (Upchurch et al., 1998; Hyde & DeLameter, 2007).

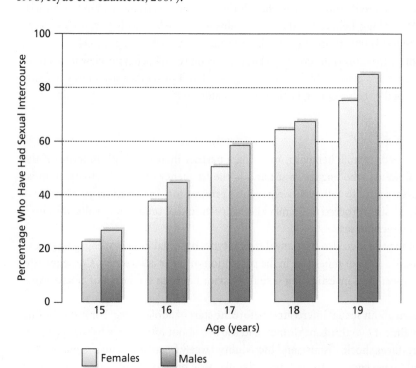

▶ **FIGURE 9-2**

Currently 80% of adolescents have sex before the age of 20, indicating that the age at which adolescents have sexual intercourse for the first time is declining.

(*Source:* Kantrowitz & Wingert, 1999, p. 38.)

Societal Norms About Sex: Double Standard, Permissiveness with Affection, and Friends with Benefits.   It is impossible to consider sexual activities without also looking at the societal and cultural norms related to sexual conduct. (Norms are informal, widely held views and attitudes about a particular topic.) Several decades ago, the prevailing norm in U.S. society about sexual conduct was the *double standard,* in which premarital sex was considered permissible for males but not for females. Women were told by society that "nice girls don't," while men heard that premarital sex was permissible—although they should be sure to marry virgins.

As recently as the 1960s, most adult Americans supported the double standard, and most thought that premarital sex was always inappropriate. However, there has been a dramatic shift of opinion, and today 60% believe that premarital sex is permissible (see Figure 9-3).

These beliefs reflect the fact that the double standard has largely given way to a new norm, called *permissiveness with affection.* According to this standard, premarital intercourse is viewed as permissible for both men and women if it occurs in the context of a stable, committed, and loving relationship (Hyde & DeLameter, 2007).

To proponents, the permissiveness-with-affection norm is a more egalitarian viewpoint because it does not say that sexual intercourse is more permissible for one sex than the other. Sex is viewed as okay for both women and men, as long as the couple are in a relationship and have deep fondness for one another.

One of the most recent societal norms to evolve around adolescent sexuality has been called *friends with benefits,* referring to sex between adolescents who are not interested in a long-term, committed relationship. "Friends-with-benefits" sexual encounters involve individuals who may be close friends (or even not-so-close friends). The key characteristic of a friends-with-benefits sexual encounter—which may involve kissing, oral sex, or (more rarely) intercourse—is that the two parties are looking for sexual involvement with no strings attached. The extent to which the friends-with-benefits norm is accepted is not clear, and some experts believe that it is more talked about than acted on by adolescents (Denizet-Lewis, 2004; Rosenblum, 2006).

Probably the most prevalent norm among adolescents today is permissiveness with affection. However, a significant number of adolescents (and even more parents of adolescents) believe

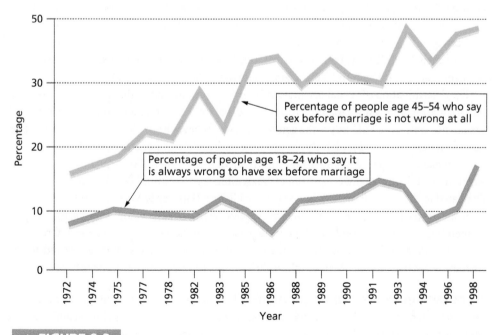

▲ **FIGURE 9-3**

The percentage of adults who feel that premarital sex is not wrong has risen sharply over the past 25 years, while the percentage of adults who think it is always wrong has increased slightly.

(*Source:* Gallup Poll News Service, 1998.)

in a norm of *abstinence,* in which sex outside marriage is viewed as morally wrong. Furthermore, the demise of the double standard is far from complete. Attitudes toward sexual conduct are still typically more lenient for males than for females, even in relatively socially liberal cultures (Laumann et al., 1994; Castañeda & Burns-Glover, 2004; Savin-Williams and Diamond, 2004; Tangmunkongvorakul, Kane, & Wellings, 2005).

In addition, in some non-Western cultures, the standards for men and women are quite distinct. For example, in North Africa, the Middle East, and the majority of Asian countries, most women conform to societal norms suggesting that they abstain from sexual intercourse until they are married. In Mexico, where there are strict standards against premarital sex, males are also considerably more likely than females to have premarital sex. In contrast, in sub-Saharan Africa, women are more likely to have sexual intercourse prior to marriage than in other cultures, and intercourse is common among unmarried teenage women (Spira et al., 1992; Johnson et al., 1992; Singh, 2000).

Sexual Orientation: Heterosexuality, Homosexuality, and Bisexuality

When we consider adolescents' sexual development, the most frequent pattern is *heterosexuality,* sexual attraction and behavior directed to the other sex. Yet some teenagers are *homosexual,* in which their sexual attraction and behavior are oriented to members of their own sex. (Many male homosexuals prefer the term *gay* and female homosexuals the term *lesbian* because these words refer to a broader array of attitudes and lifestyle than the term *homosexual,* which focuses on the sexual act.) Other adolescents find that they are *bisexual,* sexually attracted to people of both sexes.

Many teens experiment with homosexuality. At one time or another, around 20 to 25% of adolescent boys and 10% of adolescent girls have at least one same-sex sexual encounter. In fact, homosexuality and heterosexuality are not completely distinct sexual orientations. Alfred Kinsey, a pioneer sex researcher, argued that sexual orientation should be viewed as a continuum in which "exclusively homosexual" is at one end and "exclusively heterosexual" at the other (Kinsey, Pomeroy, & Martin, 1948). In between are people who show both homosexual and heterosexual behavior. Although accurate figures are difficult to obtain, most experts believe that between 4 and 10% of both men and women are exclusively homosexual during extended periods of their lives (Kinsey, Pomeroy, & Martin, 1948; McWhirter, Sanders, & Reinisch, 1990; Michael et al., 1994; Diamond, 2003a, 2003b; Russell & Consolacion, 2003).

The determination of sexual orientation is further complicated by distinctions between sexual orientation and gender identity. Although sexual orientation relates to the object of one's sexual interests, *gender identity* is the gender a person believes he or she is psychologically. Sexual orientation and gender identity are not necessarily related to one another: A man who has a strong masculine gender identity may be attracted to other men. Consequently, the extent to which men and women enact traditional "masculine" or "feminine" behavior is not necessarily related to their sexual orientation or gender identity (Hunter & Mallon, 2000).

Some people feel they were born the wrong physical sex, believing, for example, that they are women trapped in men's bodies. These *transgendered* individuals may pursue sexual reassignment surgery, a prolonged course of treatment in which they receive hormones and reconstructive surgery to enable them to take on the physical characteristics of the other sex.

What Determines Sexual Orientation?　The factors that induce people to develop as heterosexual, homosexual, or bisexual are not fully understood, although increasing evidence suggests that genetic and biological factors play an important role. Studies of twins show that identical twins are more likely to both be homosexual than are pairs of siblings who don't share their genetic makeup. Other research finds that various structures of the brain are different in homosexuals and heterosexuals, and hormone production also seems to be linked to sexual orientation (Berenbaum & Snyder, 1995; Meyer-Bahlburg et al., 1995; Lippa, 2003; Rahman & Wilson, 2003).

Other researchers have suggested that family or peer environmental factors play a role. For example, Freud argued that homosexuality was the result of inappropriate identification with the opposite-sex parent (Freud, 1922/1959). The difficulty with Freud's theoretical perspective and other, similar perspectives that followed is that there simply is no evidence to suggest that any particular parental identification pattern, family dynamic, or child-rearing practice is consistently related to sexual orientation. Similarly, explanations based on learning theory, which suggest that homosexuality arises because of rewarding, pleasant homosexual experiences and unsatisfying heterosexual ones, have received little support (Bell & Weinberg, 1978; Isay, 1990; Golombok & Tasker, 1996).

In short, there is no fully accepted explanation of why some adolescents develop a heterosexual orientation and others a homosexual orientation. Most experts believe that sexual orientation develops from a complex interplay of genetic, physiological, and environmental factors (LeVay & Valente, 2003).

What is clear is that adolescents who find themselves attracted to members of the same sex may face a more difficult time than other teens. U.S. society still harbors great ignorance and prejudice regarding homosexuality, persisting in the belief that people have a choice in the matter—which they do not. Gay and lesbian teens may be rejected by their family or peers or even harassed and assaulted if they are open about their orientation. The result is that adolescents who find themselves to be homosexual are at greater risk for depression, and suicide rates are higher for homosexual adolescents than heterosexual adolescents (Ryan & Rivers, 2003; Harris, 2004; Murdock & Bolch, 2005; Joyner, Udry, & Suchindran, 2005).

Ultimately, though, most people are able to come to grips with their sexual orientation and become comfortable with it. Although lesbians, gays, and bisexuals may experience mental health difficulties as a result of the stress, prejudice, and discrimination they face, homosexuality is not considered a psychological disorder by any of the major psychological or medical associations. All of them endorse efforts to reduce discrimination against homosexuals (Stone, 2003; van Wormer & McKinney, 2003; Davison, 2005).

◀ Although gays, lesbians, and bisexuals may be the target of prejudice and discrimination, most accept and embrace their sexual orientation.

Adolescent
DIVERSITY   Disclosing Same-Sex Attraction to Parents

A S YOU MIGHT IMAGINE, the decision to disclose to one's parents that one is attracted to persons of the same sex is not an easy one. For sexual minority adolescents, such disclosure is an important event in their sexual development. It's also an event that is fraught with anxiety; adolescents typically fear that their parents will react negatively to their coming out, possibly even by throwing them out of the house. Yet many sexual minority adolescents do tell at least one of their parents of their same-sex attraction, although the how, when, why, and to whom of disclosure vary from person to person (Savin-Williams, 1998; Rotheram-Borus & Langabeer, 2001).

According to the results of research on the issue, gender turns out to be an important factor in the disclosure of sexual orientation. Adolescents are more likely to disclose a same-sex attraction to their mothers than to their fathers, and if they disclose to both parents, they usually disclose to their mothers first. Most often this disclosure comes in a face-to-face meeting. Fathers, on the other hand, are most likely to learn of their adolescent's same-sex attraction by accident or through someone else. Adolescents of both sexes disclose to their mothers because they share a closer relationship with them—in fact, in most cases, the mothers simply asked them whether they were gay. Their reasons for disclosing to their fathers differed, however; male adolescents most frequently did so to seek support, while female adolescents most often simply wanted to get it over with (Savin-Williams & Ream, 2003).

Adolescents' reasons for choosing *not* to come out to their parents differ for mothers versus fathers. Mothers are most often kept in the dark because adolescents perceive that the time is not yet right or because they fear damaging their relationship with their mother. Fathers, on the other hand, are most frequently not told of their children's same-sex attractions because they are less important in their sons' or daughters' lives.

Are adolescents' fears of parental rejection well founded? Usually, no. Parental reactions typically are similar for male and female adolescents and for mothers and fathers, and both parents tend to be either supportive or slightly negative (a frequent reaction is to express disbelief). Moreover, in the overwhelming majority of cases, parent–child relations stay the same or even improve over time. In only about 5% of cases do adolescents report a decrease in relationship quality (Savin-Williams & Ream, 2003).

Sexually Active Adolescents: Who Is Having Sex, and Why?

There was a time when adolescents who engaged in sexual activity were thought to be psychologically disturbed. Having sex was viewed as an indication that an adolescent was poorly adjusted and likely to have problems in other areas of life.

That view, though, turns out to be a myth. Considerable research suggests that adolescents who engage in sexual activity are no more likely to be maladjusted than those who do not (Savin-Williams & Diamond, 2004).

In addition, the timing of sex is unrelated to adolescent adjustment. Youth who have sexual intercourse earlier than their peers do not suffer psychologically as a result. Specifically, well-adjusted adolescents who have sex earlier than their most of their peers are just as well adjusted later; and poorly adjusted adolescents who engage in sex earlier than their peers are no worse off as a result of having sex (Bingham & Crockett, 1996; Crockett, Raffaelli, & Moilanen, 2006).

On the other hand, adolescents who engage in early sexual encounters, such as having sexual intercourse before age 16, are more likely to experiment with drugs and engage in other risky behavior, be less interested in academics and less intelligent, and be more independence oriented. That doesn't mean that having sex early in adolescence produces these behaviors and attitudes, nor that these behaviors and attitudes lead adolescents to have sex early. There may be some additional factor that leads to the emergence of both early sex and such behavior and attitudes (Halpern et al., 2000; Cleveland, 2003; Florsheim, 2003).

Parents' behavior is also related to sexual activity. More parent–child conflict is associated with early sexual activity and riskier sexual behavior (such as not using safer sex practices). In contrast, the adolescent offspring of authoritative parents, who set boundaries but do so in the context of a warm, supportive environment, are more likely to postpone sexual intercourse (Capaldi et al., 2002; McBride, Paikoff, & Holmbeck, 2003; Bersamin et al., 2006).

Family socioeconomic status also is related to the onset of sexual activity in adolescents. Adolescents from less-affluent households are likely to have sexual intercourse at an earlier age than those from more affluent households. One reason for this is that adolescents in poorer households may have less parental supervision, thereby providing more opportunities to engage in sex. Consistent with this speculation, adolescents who are by themselves after school are more likely to have intercourse earlier. The bedroom at home (usually the boy's bedroom) is a more likely place for adolescents to lose their virginity than the back seat of a car. And sex is more likely to occur during the weekday, after school, than on the weekend (Woody, Russel, & D'Souza, 2000; Cohen et al., 2003).

The Motives behind Sex.   Why do adolescents have sex? The answer seems as if it should be straightforward: Adolescents have sex because there is a natural, built-in drive to have sex. Hormonal changes create strong sexual tensions that are relieved by sexual activity. In addition, as they reach puberty, adolescents receive implicit and explicit messages from their peers and the media that it is appropriate for them to seek sexual activity.

But it's important to keep in mind that sexual desire is not the only reason that adolescents engage in sex. Psychologists Ritch Savin-Williams & Lisa Diamond (2004) suggested that several other factors are central to adolescent sexuality:

- *Curiosity.* Hearing descriptions of others' sexual encounters (sometimes real, sometimes exaggerated) may lead adolescents to seek sex. In addition, the availability of sexually explicit material on the Web, in films, television programs, and commercials, and in other media may trigger great interest in sex (Brown, 2002).

◀ Media images of sexuality encourage sexual activity in adolescents.

- *Peer pressure.* Peer pressure, whether real or implied, plays a role in the decision of adolescents to have sex. Sexual activity may be seen as one route to social status and may be perceived as part of a typical (and desirable) developmental course during adolescence. In this view, then, sex is a means to obtain social benefits.

- *Asserting independence by rejecting parental and societal norms.* Some adolescents engage in sexual activity in part to demonstrate their independence from their parents. They may also wish to reject religious views that hold that sex outside of marriage is wrong.

- *Romantic relationships.* Because adolescents who are involved in romantic relationships are more likely to become sexually aroused on a more frequent basis, they are more likely to become sexually involved with their partner. Sex provides a means of demonstrating and maintaining emotional intimacy.

- *Emotion regulation.* Finally, sex may be a way of coping with anxiety and other negative emotions. Sexual activity may permit adolescents to put aside their problems, at least for a while, and may help bring about emotional closeness with a partner.

In short, there are a number of reasons why adolescents engage in sex. Sexual desire, per se, is only one of them.

Contraceptive Use

The only foolproof method to avoid both sexually transmitted infections and pregnancy is abstinence from sex. However, many adolescents are unwilling to make that choice and instead rely on *contraception,* the intentional prevention of conception.

Unfortunately, because the sex lives of adolescents often play out in unplanned, haphazard ways, the use of contraceptives can also be somewhat chaotic. Consider the steps that are necessary for an adolescent to effectively employ contraception:

1. Being aware of the different types of contraceptives

2. Deciding on what contraceptive to use

3. Obtaining the contraceptive of choice

4. Deciding to have sex with a particular individual

5. Communicating that decision to one's partner

6. Having the contraceptive available at the appropriate time prior to having sex

7. Using the contraceptive properly

Ignoring any step in the sequence can lead to the risk of sexually transmitted infection or pregnancy. Furthermore, each step not only requires cognitive effort, but also involves psychological and moral issues. For example, a boy may wonder whether having a conversation about sex prior to a date will "ruin" his chances of spontaneous sex or make it seem that all he is interested in sex. A girl may believe that, if she has a condom available "just in case" she and her boyfriend decide to have sex, she will be seen as sexually promiscuous (Creighton & Miller, 2003).

In some cases, adolescents, especially younger ones, lack basic knowledge about sex and contraceptive use. They may minimize the risks of pregnancy, or they may have an unrealistic, romanticized view of pregnancy as not an occurrence that needs to be actively avoided. In some cases, adolescents with low self-esteem or high social anxiety may be drawn into sexual activity without weighing the risks (Hart & Heimberg, 2005; Ethier et al., 2006).

In addition, the more limited cognitive abilities of younger adolescents may prevent them from thinking about the hypothetical consequences of becoming pregnant and raising a child and the impact it would have on their lives. Furthermore, the generally higher level of risk taking that is typical of adolescents may lead them to feel invulnerable to the possibility of pregnancy and sexually transmitted diseases.

Increased Contraceptive Use.   Despite the complications involved in using contraceptives, adolescents are increasingly using them and thereby reducing the risks of sexually transmitted infection and pregnancy. According to surveys, adolescents currently are more likely than ever to use contraception (usually a condom) the first time they have sex. Furthermore, a growing number of adolescent girls use the pill and a condom at first intercourse, thereby protecting themselves not only from pregnancy but also from sexually transmitted diseases. Finally, the percentage of adolescents using *no* contraception at first intercourse has declined (Mosher et al., 2004).

The increased use of contraceptives is good news, because it has reduced the rate of teenage pregnancy (as we'll discuss later in the chapter). However, contraceptive use by adolescents remains a controversial topic, because views among lawmakers (and their constituents) regarding teenage sex are quite ambivalent. Consequently, less than half of the 50 states permit adolescents who are legally still minors to obtain contraceptives without a parent's consent. Because many adolescents will not seek out contraception services if they have to tell their parents they are sexually active, the result is that many young adolescents forgo contraception. Either they are legally barred from obtaining contraceptives, or, in some cases, they don't know where to purchase them (Guttmacher Institute, 2006).

Consequently, younger adolescents are less likely to use contraception than older ones, and when they do employ contraceptives, they are inconsistent in their use. Whereas older adolescents are more likely to use birth control pills or diaphragms, which are generally effective, younger adolescents are more likely to rely on condoms or withdrawal (Greydanus, Patel, & Rimsza, 2001; Mosher et al., 2004).

Withdrawal, in particular, is an inadequate method. In withdrawal, the penis is withdrawn from the vagina before orgasm; this method has a high failure rate. Other adolescents attempt to use the rhythm method, timing sexual intercourse to coincide with periods of lowest fertility. However, the rhythm method is based on careful calibration of menstrual cycles, which requires a degree of care that most adolescents find difficult to apply. In addition, adolescent female menstrual cycles are often irregular.

Review and Apply

Review

1. Physical maturation combines with increased cognitive maturity to make concerns about sex centrally important during adolescence.

2. The first type of sexual activity in which adolescents engage is typically masturbation, which is now considered normal and healthy.

3. Sexual intercourse remains the final, major step in sexual relations with partners during adolescence. Many adolescents postpone intercourse until the late teens.

4. Adolescents must establish their sexual orientation. Although most are heterosexual, same-sex relations are common during adolescence, despite continuing taboos against homosexuality.

5. To avoid pregnancy and sexually transmitted diseases, adolescents must learn to use contraception properly. Younger adolescents have more difficulty with this than their older peers.

Apply

1. Do you think the double standard, which approved male sexual activity but condemned female sexual activity, has entirely disappeared? Does popular culture work to eliminate or perpetuate the double standard?

2. *From the perspective of an educator:* Many politicians are opposed to schools providing contraceptive information or distributing condoms to adolescents. Their argument is typically that these practices actually encourage teens to have sex and increase the incidence of teen pregnancy. Do you agree or disagree, and why?

Adolescent Pregnancy

Night has eased into day, but it is all the same for Tori Michel, 17. Her 5-day-old baby, Caitlin, has been fussing for hours, though she seems finally to have settled into the pink-and-purple car seat on the living-room sofa. "She wore herself out," explains Tori, who lives in a two-bedroom duplex in this St. Louis suburb with her mother, Susan, an aide to handicapped adults. "I think she just had gas."

Motherhood was not in Tori's plans for her senior year at Fort Zumwalt South High School—not until she had a "one-night thing" with James, a 21-year-old she met through friends. She had been taking birth-control pills but says she stopped after breaking up with a long-term boyfriend. "Wrong answer," she now says ruefully. (Gleick, Reed, & Schindehette, 1994, p. 38)

Feedings at 3:00 A.M., diaper changes, and visits to the pediatrician are not part of most people's vision of adolescence. Yet, every year, around 800,000 adolescents in the United States give birth. Most of these pregnancies are unintended. For these teenagers, life becomes increasingly challenging as they struggle with the demands of parenthood while still facing the complexities of adolescence.

The United States has the highest rate of teenage pregnancy in the developed world. Almost a quarter of U.S. teenagers become pregnant prior to the age of 18, with the number rising to 45% before the age of 21. An American adolescent is twice as likely to become pregnant as a Canadian adolescent, four times more likely than a French adolescent, and six times more likely than a Swedish adolescent. In Japan and Korea, only 1% of teenagers become pregnant (Darroch, Singh, & Frost, 2001).

Why is the teenage pregnancy rate so much higher in the United States than in other developed countries? One reason is a lack of adequate sex education, reflecting conflicted attitudes on the part of the adult population. Sex and sex education are viewed with considerable ambivalence in the United States. On the one hand, advertisements and the media promote sexuality. On the other hand, there is a strong Puritan view that sex among teenagers is problematic and should be strongly discouraged. Consequently, American teenagers are often poorly educated in sexual matters compared with their counterparts in other developed countries (Boonstra, 2002).

Another reason for the poor record of U.S. teenagers in preventing pregnancy is the lack of availability of good contraceptive services. Many teenagers do not have health insurance, or their insurance does not provide them with birth control. In other countries, which have universal health care, family planning is free and integrated into other types of primary health care.

The good news, though, is the overall number of teenage pregnancies is declining. In the last 10 years, the teenage birthrate has dropped 30%. Births to African-American teenagers have shown the steepest decline, down by more than 40% in a decade. Overall the pregnancy rate of

◄ Although the number of teenage pregnancies has declined it remains a serious problem in the United States.

teenagers is 43 births per 1,000, a historic low (see Figure 9-4; Centers for Disease Control and Prevention, 2003).

Although the overall birthrate has been declining among teenagers, the proportion of teens who give birth and who are unmarried has increased significantly. Whereas 13% of the teenage mothers who gave birth were unmarried in 1950, that figure rose to almost 80% in 2000 (see Figure 9-5; National Center for Health Statisics, 2001).

The increase in the proportion of adolescent mothers who are unmarried has occurred for two reasons. One is that teenage marriage, in general, is quite unusual. (The average age of marriage is now 25 for women and 27 for men.) Perhaps even more important, social norms have changed, softening the stigma of being an unwed mother. The days of "shotgun marriages," in

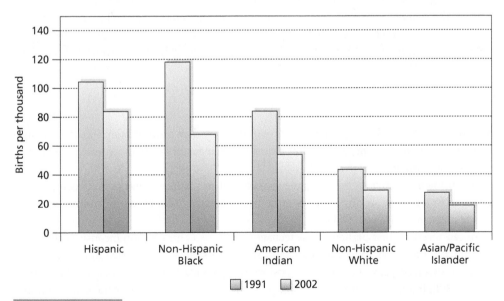

▲ **FIGURE 9-4**

The rate of teenage pregnancy in the United States has declined significantly over the last decade among all ethnic groups.

(*Source:* Centers for Disease Control, 2003.)

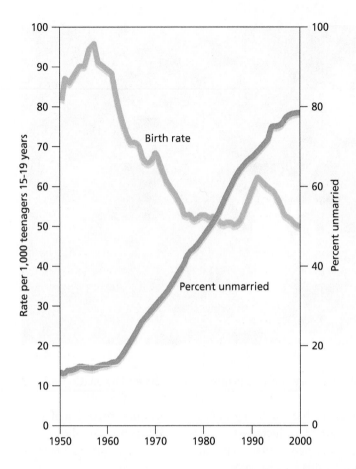

Although the birthrate among teenagers has declined over the past 50 years, the proportion of teens who give birth and who are unmarried has increased significantly.

(*Source:* National Center for Health Statistics, 2001.)

which a disgraced pregnant girl and the boy who got her pregnant are forced to marry by their embarrassed parents, are behind us (Boonstra, 2002).

The rise in the proportion of teenage mothers who are unmarried has significant social implications. Unmarried teenage mothers are considerably more likely to live in poverty, and having a baby decreases their chances of rising above their economic deprivation. Poverty thus increases the chances of having a baby—motherhood is sometimes said to be a career choice for poor teenagers with few employment options—and motherhood during adolescence makes remaining in poverty more likely, which produces a challenging cycle from which to break out (Darroch et al., 2001).

Who Gets Pregnant?

As we've noted, teenagers living in poverty are more likely than more affluent teens to become pregnant during their teenage years. But a host of other factors contribute to the likelihood that a teenager will become pregnant.

One of the most obvious factors is the inconsistent or ineffectual use of birth control. Although most teenagers say they don't want to become pregnant, their use of contraception is often inadequate, as we saw earlier.

We can speculate that perhaps those teenagers who use contraception inconsistently actually want, on some level, to become pregnant. Such a possibility is supported by data showing that the more a teenager views pregnancy positively, the less likely she is to use birth control consistently. Still, it appears that most teenage pregnancies are, in fact, unintended, and that inconsistent use of birth control is a consequence not of a deep-down longing to have a child but of other factors (Unger, Molina, & Teran, 2000; Jaccard, Dodge, & Dittus, 2003).

It is also clear that an adolescent's relationship with her parents is related to teenage pregnancy. Adolescents who have a close, warm relationship with their parents are less likely to become pregnant as teenagers than those who are less close to their parents. In part, this may be because teenagers in close, warm families tend to delay the first time they have intercourse, have fewer sexual partners, and use contraception more consistently (Miller, Benson, & Galbraith, 2001).

But it is not just having a close, warm relationship that reduces the risk of teenage pregnancy. Parents who set limits and discourage premarital sex (or at least unprotected sex) and unequivocally object to pregnancy are less likely to have pregnant teenage daughters than those with more ambiguous values (Jaccard, Dodege, & Dittus, 2003; Miller et al., 2006).

Finally, peer pressure is associated with teenage pregnancy. It's not so much that teenagers get pregnant because they want to conform to the behavior of their teenage peers who become pregnant. Instead, teenagers are influenced by their peers to engage in risky behavior, such as unprotected, and early, sex. Such risky behaviors increase the chances of pregnancy (Miller-Lewis et al., 2006).

Ultimately, teenage pregnancy and subsequent parenthood are the result of a series of complex choices that have to be made by adolescents, whose decision-making capabilities are not as sophisticated as they will be later in life. These choices are presented as the series of turning points illustrated in Figure 9-6 (Miller et al., 2006).

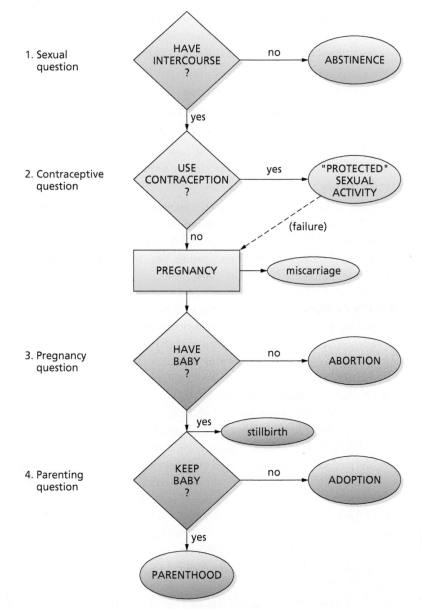

◄ **FIGURE 9-6**
This flowchart reflects the major turning points and outcomes of adolescent pregnancy.
(*Source:* Miller, et al., 2006.)

The first choice is whether to have sexual intercourse or to choose abstinence. The next turning point involves the decision to use contraception (and, if the decision is yes, to use it correctly). If a teenager chooses not to use contraception, or if contraception fails, pregnancy may occur. In this case, the next choice that the prospective mother faces, potentially along with the father, her parents, and perhaps others, is whether to have the baby or to seek an abortion. Assuming she chooses to have the baby, the next choice is whether to put the child up for adoption or to raise it herself.

At each point in the decision-making sequence, adolescents are influenced by their own attitudes, as well as a variety of individuals, including parents and family, the sexual partner, and friends. In addition, the availability of health, family planning, and adoption services influences the decisions.

Explaining the Decline in Adolescent Pregnancy

As we discussed earlier, the positive news about adolescent pregnancy is that the percentage of teenagers who get pregnant—although still high—has declined significantly in the last decade. Several factors account for this drop in pregnancies:

- New initiatives have raised awareness among teenagers of the risks of unprotected sex (as discussed in the *Transitions* box). For example, about two thirds of high schools in the United States have established comprehensive sex education programs (Villarosa, 2003).

- The rate of sexual intercourse among teenagers has declined. The percent of teenage girls who have ever had sexual intercourse dropped from 51% to 43% between 1991 and 2001.

- The use of condoms and other forms of contraception has increased. For example, 57% of sexually active high school students reported using condoms.

- The legality of abortions has made it easier for teenagers to terminate their pregnancies. Around a third of teenage pregnancies are terminated through abortion, and around 10% end in miscarriage.

- Substitutes for sexual intercourse may be more prevalent. For example, data from the National Survey of Adolescent Males found that about half of 15- to 19-year-old boys reported having received oral sex, an increase of 44% since the late 1980s. It is possible that oral sex, which many teenagers do not even consider "sex," may increasingly be viewed as an alternative to sexual intercourse (Bernstein, 2004).

Virginity Pledges.   One thing that apparently *hasn't* led to a reduction in teenage pregnancies is asking adolescents to take a virginity pledge. Public pledges to refrain from premarital sex—a centerpiece of some forms of sex education—have a mixed record. Initial studies of virginity pledges were promising, showing that adolescents who took a pledge to defer sexual intercourse until marriage delayed sex about 18 months longer than those who had never taken such a pledge (Bearman & Bruckner, 2001).

But even this early research called virginity pledges into question. For example, the effectiveness of pledging depended on a student's age. For older adolescents (18 years old and above), taking a pledge had no effect. Pledges were effective only for 16- and 17-year-olds. Furthermore, the pledges worked only when a minority of people in a school took such a pledge. When more than 30% took such a pledge, the effectiveness of the pledge diminished substantially.

The reason for this surprising finding relates to why virginity pledges might work: They offer adolescents a sense of identity, similar to the way joining a club does. When a minority of students take a virginity pledge, they feel part of a special group, and they are more likely to adhere to the norms of that group—in this case, remaining a virgin. In contrast, if a majority of students take a pledge of virginity, the pledge becomes less unique and adherence is less likely.

Most recent research finds that virginity pledges are ineffective. For example, in one study of 12,000 teenagers, 88% reported eventually having sexual intercourse, although taking a pledge did delay the start of sex (Bearman et al., 2004). (For more on pregnancy reduction strategies—some of which are far more successful than the use of virginity pledges—see the accompanying *Transitions* box.)

Consequences of Teenage Pregnancy

Even with the decline in the birthrate for U.S. teenagers, the rate of teenage pregnancy in the United States is 2 to 10 times higher than that of other industrialized countries. The results of an unintended pregnancy can be devastating to both mother and child. In comparison to earlier times, teenage mothers today are much less likely to be married. In a high percentage of cases, mothers care for their children without the help of the father. Without financial or emotional support, a mother may have to abandon her own education, and consequently she may be relegated to unskilled, poorly paying jobs for the rest of her life. In other cases, she may develop long-term dependency on welfare. An adolescent mother's physical and mental health may suffer as she faces unrelenting stress due to continual demands on her time (Manlove et al., 2004).

These difficulties affect the children of teenage mothers, who also do not fare well. Children of teenage mothers are more likely to suffer from poor health and to show poorer school performance when compared to children of older mothers. Later, they are more likely to become teenage parents themselves, creating a cycle of pregnancy and poverty from which it is very difficult to extricate themselves (Carnegie Task Force, 1994; Spencer, 2001.)

Abortion

For pregnant teenagers, one alternative to having the child is abortion. Almost one in five women having abortions in the United States are adolescents, although the number of abortions has declined over the last decade. Teenagers are more likely than older women to wait until later in their pregnancies to have an abortion, making the procedure riskier (Jones, Darroch, & Henshaw, 2002).

For some adolescents, abortion is impossible on moral and religious grounds. For others, it is impossible to have an abortion due to legal restrictions or practical constraints, such as the lack of availability of abortion medical services. But even when abortion is an available and practical possibility, it represents a difficult choice for most adolescents.

When teenagers do choose to have an abortion, they do so for a variety of reasons. Some may lack economic resources to support a child, or they may feel that they are unable to care for a child on their own. In other cases, an unplanned pregnancy would disrupt school or work plans. In some cases, a teenager faces relationship problems that may mean she would be a single parent, and she feels overwhelmed by the prospect (Donovan, 1995; Finken, 2005).

Involving a complex set of physical, psychological, legal, and ethical issues, abortion is a difficult choice for any woman, let alone a teenager. A task force of the American Psychological Association, which looked at the aftereffects of abortion, found that, following an abortion, most women experienced a combination of relief over terminating an unwanted pregnancy and regret and guilt. However, in most cases, the negative psychological aftereffects did not persist, except for a small proportion of women who already had serious emotional problems. In all cases, abortion is a difficult choice (APA Reproductive Choice Working Group, 2000; Andrews & Boyle, 2003).

Adoption

Another option available to teenagers who become pregnant is to deliver the baby, but then place it for adoption. Like abortion, adoption represents a difficult choice for an adolescent mother, who gives up the right to raise her child and have it as a part of her life. On the other hand, unlike abortion, it does not involve the moral and religious issues that come with choosing to terminate the life of the fetus and, in fact, evokes the support of religious organizations.

Safer Choices: Helping Adolescents to Avoid Unwanted Pregnancy

Given the well-known risks that unintended pregnancies pose to adolescents, educators and psychologists have sought to develop a number of intervention programs to help prevent teen pregnancy. Many of these programs focus primarily (or solely) on encouraging abstinence from sexual intercourse. They teach adolescents that abstinence is the only guaranteed way of preventing pregnancy and other complications from sexual activity, such as sexually transmitted diseases. They also teach that sexual activity before marriage can have various harmful effects and that abstinence has social and psychological benefits. To support adolescents in their efforts to abstain, these programs teach strategies for declining sexual advances and for avoiding risky situations (Santelli et al., 2006).

It's true that abstinence is a healthy choice for adolescents, and that it's theoretically the most effective way to prevent pregnancy. There is also a great deal of public support for efforts to encourage abstinence. But programs that focus on abstinence as the only way to reduce teen pregnancy are controversial. The concern is that abstinence may not be a realistic option for many adolescents, and in cases where abstinence-only education fails, adolescents may become sexually active with little awareness of other options.

As a result, some researchers have called for more comprehensive education programs to replace ones that focus on abstinence as the only option. Most parents and teachers agree that abstinence education should be emphasized, but that information on contraception and safer sex practices should be included as well. Research supports these beliefs: Although abstinence-only programs and programs that include contraception education do not clearly differ in their effects on adolescents' sexual activity, the addition of contraception education does improve adolescents' understanding and use of birth-control strategies (Dailard, 2001; Manlove et al., 2002; Bennett & Assefi, 2005; Santelli et al., 2006).

Safer Choices, a two-year program for adolescents in high school, is one such program that combines encouragement of abstinence with education on contraceptive use. Its goals are to reduce the number of students who are sexually active while in high school and to increase condom usage in students who do have sex by addressing adolescent sexual activity on multiple fronts. The program attempts to modify students' attitudes and norms about sexual behavior, abstinence, and condom use (including adolescents' perceived barriers to condom use). It also addresses students' confidence in their ability to refuse sex, to discuss safer sex with their partners, and to use a condom, and it teaches students about sexually transmitted diseases and their risks of infection. Finally, the program seeks to improve students' communication with their parents about sex (Advocates for Youth, 2003; Kirby et al., 2004).

Safer Choices accomplishes all of this with a multiple-component plan that attempts to modify the entire school environment in a way that supports abstinence and safer sex practices. It addresses the school organization by forming a school health promotion council consisting of students, teachers, parents, and others for the purpose of coordinating program activities. These activities include a 20-lesson curriculum for students in the 9th and 10th grades that teaches interactive lessons on pregnancy and sexually transmitted diseases, communication skills, and contraceptive use. Other activities focus on reinforcing these messages throughout the school environment with events and media such as dramatic productions, guest speakers, articles in the school newspaper, and posters. The idea here is not only to remind students of the lessons they learned, but also to foster a social norm of sexual responsibility.

In addition to conducting in-school activities aimed at adolescents, the *Safer Choices* program also targets parents and the wider community for involvement. Parent education efforts include regular newsletters as well as homework assignments requiring students to discuss issues of sexuality with their parents. Students are encouraged to learn about resources within their community through homework assignments.

Is the *Safer Choices* program worth all this effort? The answer is a cautious yes. Although *Safer Choices* does not appear to be effective at delaying adolescents from having sex, it also does not appear to hasten sexual activity. More importantly, students who participate in the program are more knowledgeable about sexually transmitted diseases and perceive themselves at greater risk for infection, have more positive attitudes toward and greater confidence in condom use, are more likely to use contraception, and are specifically more likely to use condoms compared to adolescents who do not participate in the program. There also is some evidence that *Safer Choices* may be more effective for adolescent males than it is for females, which may be because males have greater control over the decision to use a condom (Advocates for Youth, 2003; Kirby et al., 2004).

How does the *Safer Choices* program fare in comparison to other programs designed to reduce teen pregnancy? Similar sexuality education programs have been less successful at encouraging condom use, although a few are better at delaying sexual activity. Other types of intervention programs exist, and several of these are effective in various ways. For example, some programs that get adolescents involved in community service have been shown to delay sexual activity and to reduce the incidence of pregnancy (Manlove et al., 2002, 2004).

- Sophisticated abstinence-only programs offer a range of theoretical, practical, moral, and information-based approaches to enabling adolescents to avoid intercourse. Does such a multi-component approach coincide effectively with the various aspects of adolescent development? Why?

- Should schools be involved in sex-education and pregnancy-prevention instruction at all, or is sex education purely a moral or family matter? Why?

Formal adoption is chosen more frequently by adolescents who are relatively more financially well off and who have higher educational aspirations. However, informal adoptions occur relatively frequently in poor African-American communities, where a family member—often the newborn's grandmother—cares for the child. The advantage to informal adoption is that it permits the mother to continue playing a significant role in the child's life (Resnick et al., 1990; Miller & Coyl, 2000).

The long-term consequences for teenagers who place their infants for adoption are typically favorable. Not only are their attitudes generally positive about the adoption experience, but also their educational and vocational attainment ultimately is higher compared with teenagers who raise their children (Donnelly & Voydanoff, 1996; Wiley & Baden, 2005).

BECOMING AN INFORMED CONSUMER OF ADOLESCENT SCIENCE

How Adolescents Can Prevent Unwanted Pregnancy

F YOU'RE CONCERNED about the possibility of an unwanted pregnancy and its harmful consequences, your first line of defense is to educate yourself on prevention methods. A number of birth control options are available that are appropriate for adolescents, each with its own advantages and disadvantages. A physician can help choose the method that is best for each individual. Following are some recommendations that are effective (Food and Drug Administration, 2003; Knowles, 2005).

▲ Advertisements such as this have proven effective in encouraging adolescents to use condoms.

● *Abstinence.* Abstaining from sex is the only birth control method that is guaranteed to be 100% effective. Abstinence requires no special equipment or medical supervision, costs nothing, and prevents sexually transmitted disease as well as unwanted pregnancy. The downside of abstinence is that some people find it difficult to refrain from sex, and if they have not explored alternative methods of birth control, they may not be prepared to protect themselves from unwanted pregnancy when they do become sexually active.

● *Outercourse.* Outercourse is sexual activity that does not involve vaginal intercourse. It may include kissing, masturbation, massage, or oral sex. Outercourse is 100% effective against pregnancy as long as no semen comes in contact with the vaginal area.

● *Condoms.* A condom, a sheath that covers the penis during intercourse, provides a barrier against the transmission of semen. Condoms are 85 to 98% effective against pregnancy, depending in part on how they are used (the addition of a spermicidal lubricant enhances their effectiveness). Condoms also provide protection against sexually transmitted diseases, and they are widely available and generally inexpensive. Relying on condoms to prevent unwanted pregnancy means that a condom must be used every time sexual intercourse occurs.

● *Birth control pills.* Birth control pills contain hormones that prevent pregnancy by interfering with egg fertilization. They are 92 to 99% effective against pregnancy, but they must be prescribed by a physician. Birth control pills have the advantage of providing continuous protection against unwanted pregnancy—you don't have to remember to do anything special at the time of intercourse. Their main disadvantage is that they must be taken daily, whether or not one is having sex.

● *Prescription barriers.* A prescription barrier, such as a diaphragm, is treated with spermicide and then inserted into the vagina before intercourse, where it blocks the transmission of semen. Prescription barriers are an alternative to daily hormone use for women who have intercourse only occasionally. They are available through a physician, and they are 84 to 94% effective against pregnancy. However, barriers can be difficult to use correctly, and like condoms, must be used every time one has intercourse.

Review and Apply

Review

1. Although the number of teenage pregnancies has declined in recent years, the United States has the highest rate of teenage pregnancy among industrialized nations.

2. A number of factors determine who is likely to get pregnant, including family affluence, the quality of the family relationship, tendency toward risky behaviors, and awareness of contraceptive methods.

3. Abstinence-only approaches to pregnancy prevention are only partially effective and can leave adolescents without knowledge of contraceptive strategies when they most need them.

4. The consequences of teenage pregnancy can be highly negative for the parent and the child, leading to a cycle of poverty from which it is nearly impossible to escape.

5. When a teenager becomes pregnant, she is faced with a difficult decision. Keeping the child can lead to a very hard life, abortion is a difficult and controversial choice, and adoption can cause a painful sense of loss.

Apply

1. If you had to advise a relative who became pregnant at age 15, how would you tailor your advice to her age?

2. *From the perspective of a health care provider:* Why do you think the United States is a world leader in teenage pregnancies? Can this be changed? How?

Sexual Issues and Difficulties

*C*asey Letvin, like *hundreds of other recently arrived University of Colorado freshmen, was looking for a party. The students milling about the streets of Boulder seemed convivial, and Casey and her roommate thought nothing of stopping four upperclassmen to ask where the parties were. "We just wanted to meet new people and have fun," says Casey, now 20. The four young men offered to take them to a nearby off-campus house where about twenty students were gathered. But approximately four hours later, the evening ended in a brutal breach of trust. At 12:30 A.M., Casey Letvin was taken back to her dormitory and raped on her own narrow bed by a man she might never have spoken to had he not been a fellow student. (Freeman, 1990, p. 94)*

What happened to Casey Letvin unfortunately is not rare. When sex—an activity that has the potential to bring people to the deepest levels of intimacy—goes wrong, it can be the ultimate betrayal. Furthermore, because sexual activity is so loaded with meaning in Western societies, even mild sexual dysfunctions can be a source of great anxiety.

Let's consider some of the most common sexual difficulties, along with date rape and, more broadly, the problem of sexual harassment and sexual assault.

Sexual Disorders

Even though the newly matured sex organs function normally in the vast majority of adolescents, because sexual activity is new, adolescents are often quite uncertain about just what is normal. Consequently, sex can be a source of considerable anxiety and self-consciousness.

Some sexual disorders are relatively common among adolescents. Among the most frequent are these:

- *Premature ejaculation.* In *premature ejaculation,* a male is unable to delay orgasm as long as he wishes. Because "as long as he wishes" is clearly subjective, the problem of premature ejaculation may disappear if a male and his partner redefine how long ejaculation needs to be delayed. Furthermore, because adolescent boys typically have little sexual experience, their excitement at becoming sexually active may be so strong that even minimal amounts of stimulation may bring about an orgasm. In addition, early sexual encounters are often furtive because of a fear of being caught in the act. Consequently, adolescents may be in such a rush to culminate sexual acts that premature ejaculation becomes a learned habit. Simply having greater sexual experiences, under more relaxed conditions, may be sufficient to reduce the problem (Astbury-Ward, 2002).

- *Erectile dysfunction. Erectile dysfunction* is the inability of a male to achieve or maintain an erection. Erectile dysfunction is not uncommon, and almost 10% of 18- to 29-year-olds have experienced it at least once.

  In most cases, erectile dysfunction is a temporary condition. The ability to achieve and maintain an erection is sensitive to alcohol, drugs, performance fears, and anxiety—factors that are hardly rare in adolescent sexual encounters. However, when it does occur, erectile dysfunction is probably one of the most embarrassing of disorders for an adolescent male.

Those who suffer from it may have severe psychological distress, causing them to avoid sexual contact (Mendelsohn, 2003).

Because in most cases erectile dysfunction is due to situational factors, the problem is usually self-correcting. However, when it occurs more than occasionally or—as happens in rare cases—every time a male hopes to achieve an erection, it is a problem that requires treatment. Treatment may involve drugs such as Viagra and psychological counseling.

It is important for adolescents who experience erectile dysfunction to seek out legitimate medical advice. Despite the thousands of Web sites that offer to sell drugs to enhance sexual functioning, most are illegitimate and provide counterfeit or inactive substances.

- *Female orgasmic disorder. Female orgasmic disorder* is a lack of orgasm in a woman. In primary orgasmic dysfunction, a woman has never experienced orgasm. In secondary orgasmic dysfunction, a woman has had an orgasm at some point but no longer does, or does so only under certain conditions, such as masturbation but not during sexual intercourse.

   There is some lack of clarity in the definition of female orgasmic disorder. For example, it is not clear that the lack of an orgasm during sexual intercourse qualifies as a disorder because many women routinely experience orgasms not during intercourse but only through manual stimulation by their partner. Suggesting that an orgasm "counts" only if it occurs during intercourse is quite restrictive, and some sex experts are reluctant to label the lack of an orgasm during intercourse as a disorder (Hyde & DeLameter, 2007).

It is important to keep in mind that all the sexual difficulties we've considered occur at one point or another in the lives of most adolescents who are actively engaged in sex with a partner. It is only when they are persistent and cause anxiety that they become problematic.

Sexually Transmitted Infection (STI): A Risk of Sexual Activity

For Caleb Schwartz, the news could not have been better: the presence of the virus that causes AIDS had dropped to undetectable levels. Only a year earlier, he had been deathly ill with AIDS-related illnesses, suffering from meningitis, an acute brain inflammation. But with the addition of a third drug to the two he was already taking, Schwartz's health turned completely around. As the amount of virus in the blood shrank, he began to feel both physically and psychologically terrific. Although costing thousands of dollars a year, the combination of three drugs is permitting him to think what had once been unthinkable: that he might be able to beat the virus.

On the other side of the globe, the situation was considerably more grim. After testing positive for the virus in 1992, Rosemary Omuga, a mother of four living in Nairobi, Kenya, lost her job and her home. Now she earns just enough to feed her children and pay the $12 a month rent for a tin-roof shack. Occasionally she scrapes together enough funds to pay for medicine which helps the symptoms of her disease. As to paying for medicines that might actually reduce the potency of the virus, that remains a dim dream. "We are dying because we don't have medicine," she says. "I heard that there are new treatments. But I cannot afford them." (Purvis, 2001, p. 76; Lacayo, 1997)

AIDS. *Acquired immunodeficiency syndrome,* or *AIDS,* is one of the leading causes of death among young people. AIDS has no cure, and although it can be treatable with a "cocktail" of powerful drugs, the death toll from the disease is significant.

Because AIDS is spread primarily through sexual contact, it is classified as a **sexually transmitted infection (STI)**. Although it began as a problem that primarily affected homosexuals, it has spread to other populations, including heterosexuals and intravenous drug users. Minorities have been particularly hard hit: African Americans and Hispanics account for some

sexually transmitted infection (STI) an infection that is spread primarily through sexual contact

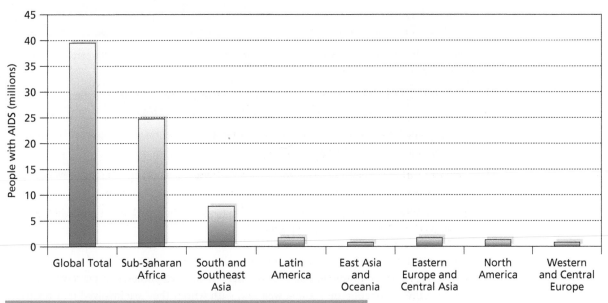

▲ **FIGURE 9-7**

The number of people carrying the AIDS virus varies substantially by geographic region. Most of the afflicted people are in Africa and South Asia.

(*Source:* UNAIDS & World Health Organization, 2006.)

40% of AIDS cases, although they make up only 18% of the population. Already, 16 million people have died due to AIDS, and the number of people living with the disease has reached 34 million worldwide (see Figure 9-7).

It is no secret how AIDS is transmitted—through the exchange of bodily fluids, including semen and blood. Changes in sexual practices have begun to make a difference in transmission levels. The use of condoms during sexual intercourse has increased, and people are less likely to engage in casual sex with new acquaintances (Everett et al., 2000; Hoppe, 2004).

But the temptation to think that "It can't hurt this one time," is always there. The use of safer sex practices is far from universal. As we discussed earlier in the chapter, teens are prone to feel invulnerable and are therefore more likely to engage in risky behavior, believing their chances

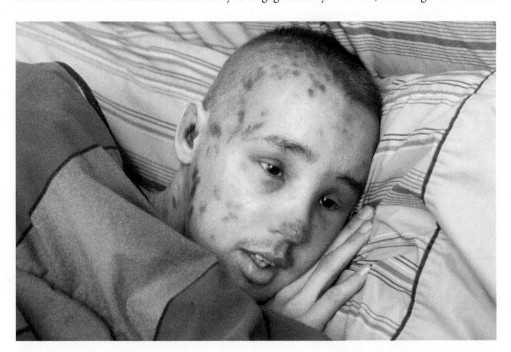

◀ AIDS remains a significant problem across the globe for adolescents.

TABLE 9-1   Safer Sex: Preventing the Transmission of AIDS

Health psychologists and educators have devised several guidelines to help prevent the spread of AIDS. Among them are the following:

• **Use condoms.** The use of condoms greatly reduces the risk of transmission of the virus that produces AIDS, which occurs through exposure to bodily fluids such as semen or blood.

• **Avoid high-risk behaviors.** Such practices as unprotected anal intercourse or sharing needles used for injecting drugs greatly increase the risk of AIDS.

• **Know your partner's sexual history.** Knowing your partner's sexual history can help you to evaluate the risks of sexual contact.

• **Consider abstinence.** Although not always a practical alternative, the only certain way of avoiding AIDS is to refrain from sexual activity altogether.

of contracting AIDS are minimal. This is particularly true when adolescents perceive that their partner is "safe"—someone they know well and with whom they are involved in a relatively long-term relationship (Raffaelli & Crockett, 2003; Tinsley, Lees, & Sumartojo, 2004).

Unfortunately, unless an individual knows the complete sexual history and HIV status of a partner, unprotected sex remains risky business. And learning a partner's complete sexual history is difficult. Not only is it embarrassing to ask, partners may not be accurate reporters, whether from ignorance of their own exposure, embarrassment, a sense of privacy, or simply forgetfulness.

Short of abstinence, there is no certain way to avoid AIDS. But there are things you can do to make sex safer; these are listed in Table 9-1.

Other Sexually Transmitted Infections.   Although AIDS is the deadliest of sexually transmitted diseases, a number of other STIs are far more common (see Figure 9-8). In fact, one out

▼ **FIGURE 9-8**

Aside from AIDS, these are the most common sexually transmitted diseases (STDs) among adolescents.

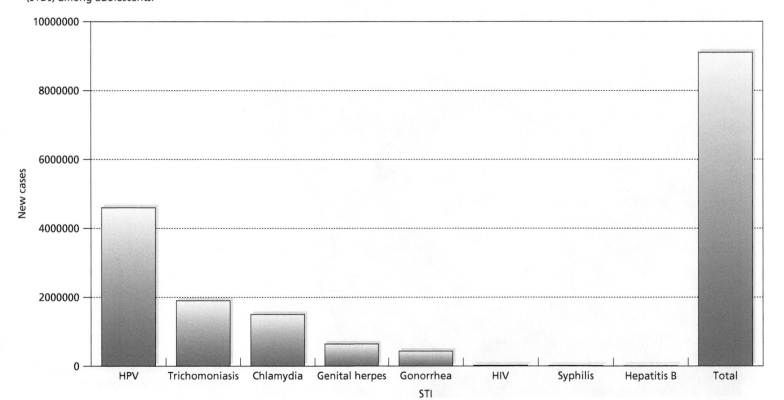

of four adolescents contracts an STI before graduating from high school. Overall, around 2.5 million teenagers contract an STI, such as the ones listed here, each year (Leary, 1996; Weinstock, Berman, & Cates, 2004).

Chlamydia, a bacterial disease, is the most common STI. Initially it has few symptoms, but later it causes burning urination and a discharge from the penis or vagina. It can lead to pelvic inflammation and even to sterility. Chlamydial infections can be treated successfully with antibiotics. Too often, adolescents are not aware of chlamydia, and those who have heard of it may be unaware of the serious problems it causes (Nockels & Oakshott, 1999; Favers et al., 2003).

Another common STI is *genital herpes,* a virus not unlike the cold sores that sometimes appear around the mouth. The first symptoms of herpes are often small blisters or sores around the genitals, which may break open and become quite painful. Although the sores may heal after a few weeks, the disease often recurs after an interval, and the cycle repeats itself. When the sores reappear, the disease, for which there is no cure, is contagious.

Several other STIs are frequent among adolescents. *Genital warts,* caused by *human papilloma virus,* (HPV) are small, lumpy warts that form on or near the penis or vagina that look like small cauliflower bulbs. *Trichomoniasis,* an infection in the vagina or penis, is caused by a parasite. Initially without symptoms, it can eventually cause a painful discharge. *Gonorrhea* and *syphilis* are the STIs that have been recognized for the longest time; cases were recorded by ancient historians. Until the advent of antibiotics, both diseases were deadly; today both can be treated quite effectively.

Contracting an STI is not only an immediate problem during adolescence, but could become a problem later in life, too. Some diseases increase the chances of future infertility and cancer. (For more on STIs and their prevention, see the Career Choices box).

Sexual Harassment

"A girl pulled down my shorts, exposing my boxers, and then kissed me." (Eighth-grade boy)
"A girl smacked my butt." (Ninth-grade boy)
"Someone made a motion like they were masturbating." (Eighth-grade girl)
"This girl I know started a rumor that I slept with this guy while he was dating my friend." *(10th-grade girl)*
"Someone drew a penis on my notebook" (11th-grade girl). (AAUW, 2001, p. 24)

As these comments suggest, **sexual harassment**, defined as unwanted sexual attention, the creation of a hostile or abusive environment, or explicit coercion to engage in unwanted sexual activity, is alive and well in U.S. schools. Furthermore, it's a common phenomenon faced by both male and female adolescents.

According to the results of one survey, 81% of middle and high school students reported receiving some form of sexual harassment in school, and 6 in 10 experienced physical sexual harassment at some point in their school lives (see Figure 9-9 on page 305). Around a third of students say they are afraid of being sexually harassed, with girls two times as likely to report concern about the problem. Furthermore, it is a problem that extends into college. For example, almost a third of the female graduates of one large California university reported experiencing some form of harassment (Fitzgeral, 2003; AAUW, 2001).

Sexual harassment often has less to do with sex than with power—similar to the motivation behind rape, as we'll see later. Often the individual who engages in sexual harassment is less concerned with receiving sexual favors than with showing power over the recipient (Paludi, 1996; O'Donohue, 1997).

Victims of sexual harassment experience a variety of emotions. Typically they feel shame and embarrassment. The harassment also may produce a sense of helplessness and powerlessness. Victims are less likely to speak up in class and more likely to have trouble paying attention, and some try to avoid school altogether (AAUW, 2001).

sexual harassment unwanted sexual attention, the creation of a hostile or abusive environment, or explicit coercion to engage in unwanted sexual activity

CAREER CHOICES

Sandra Caron, Sex Educator

Name: Sandra L. Caron, PhD

Education: BS Health and Family Life, University of Maine; MS Human Development, University of Maine; PhD, Human Development/Family Studies, Syracuse University

Position: Professor of Family Relations/ Human Sexuality, University of Maine

Home: Orono, ME

DEALING WITH THE physical, emotional, and social changes related to sexuality represents some of the most important challenges faced by adolescents. However, although sexuality is a topic to which teenagers are repeatedly exposed in the media, they rarely receive accurate information.

According to Sandra Caron, professor of family relations and human sexuality and a frequent sex education lecturer, the average adolescent needs to understand more about sex.

"The fact is that many young people know very little about their own sexuality," she said. "Some are embarrassed at their ignorance and fear ridicule for not knowing more."

One of the main aspects of sex education that Caron feels is most important is teaching about relationships.

"We often emphasis the three traditional R's, but rarely consider the fourth, relationships," Caron noted. "We seem to spend very little time explaining relationships and getting into the psychology of relationships.

"It's important to teach what it means to connect with another human being and what it means to be in a loving relationship, to have mutual respect, and understand what it means."

Being in the information age may be helpful in other areas of life, but according to Caron, when it comes to sexuality, the media only add to confusion.

"Take body image, for example. No one has a perfect body, but unfortunately the media are constantly telling us what's wrong with the way we look," she explained.

"The irony with sex education is that we live in a culture where we have considerable information about many other topics. But while there is much about sex in the media, it often is not real or accurate information. The emphasis should be on trust, honesty, and committed relationships, rather than on body parts."

Thinking of becoming a sex educator?

Sex educators instruct adolescents (and adults) on a variety of topics related to healthy human sexuality. They help adolescents understand their changing bodies and address their emerging sexual feelings. Sex educators teach adolescents about reproductive anatomy, sexual practices, pregnancy and childbearing, methods of birth control, sexually transmitted diseases and their prevention, and having healthy sexual relationships.

There is no single path to a career as a sex educator. Most sex educators first earned advanced degrees in related fields such as education, psychology, counseling, social work, health, or medicine. They then received specialized training and certification in human sexuality and sex education. Such training and certification is available from the American Association of Sex Educators, Counselors, and Therapists, although service agencies in the field of human sexuality (such as the Planned Parenthood League of Massachusetts) may offer training programs of their own. ■

Rape

Whether it occurs in the context of a date or is committed by strangers, there can be no greater violation of an adolescent than rape. **Rape** occurs when one person forces another person to submit to sexual activity such as intercourse or oral–genital sex. Although it most frequently applies to a male forcing a female, rape occurs when members of either sex are forced into sexual activities without their consent.

If you think of rape as a rare crime, and if you believe it is most often committed by strangers, you are wrong on both counts. Rape occurs far more frequently than most people believe, and it is committed more often by an acquaintance of the victim than by a stranger. Although it is difficult to find fully reliable statistics—many rapes go unreported—almost 10% of 14- to 18-year-old girls said they had been forced into sexual activity by a date, and in more than 50% of those cases the incident had been accompanied by hitting, slapping, or shoving. For some pop-

rape one person forcing another person to submit to sexual activity such as intercourse or oral–genital sex

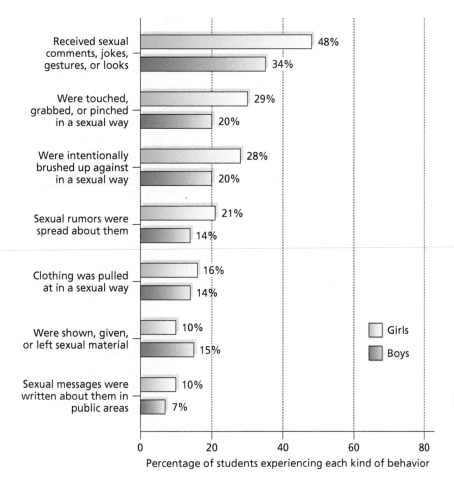

◄ FIGURE 9-9

A significant number of adolescents report experiencing unwelcomed sexual attention at school.

(*Source:* American Association of University Women, 2001.)

ulations of adolescent girls, such as female street youth, almost two thirds report being raped. Overall, a woman has a 14 to 25% chance of being a victim of rape during her lifetime (Rickert & Weinmann, 1998; Silverman, 2001; Ackard & Neumark-Sztainer, 2002).

One national survey found that one out of eight female college students reported being raped. Among those women, about half said the rapists were first dates, casual dates, or romantic acquaintances—a phenomenon called **date rape** (Koss, 1993).

Although it might seem that the predominant motivation behind rape is sexual gratification, most rapists have other motivations. Most frequently, rapists use sex as a way of exerting power and control over the victim. The pleasure in the rape comes from forcing another person to be submissive, rather than from the sex itself (Zurbriggen, 2000; Gowaty, 2003).

In other cases, rape is a crime of anger. Sex is used as a way for a male rapist to act out rage toward women in general. Such rapes often include physical violence or degrading acts.

Finally, some rapes occur as a result of drastically discordant perceptions about sex. In some cases, males and females have different views of what is sexually permissible. Some males hold the belief—completely groundless—that males should be seeking sex insistently, and that sexual aggression is acceptable. In this mistaken view, sex is a war, with winners and losers, and violence and intimidation are among the ways that the goal of sexual intercourse can be attained (Mosher & Anderson, 1986; Hamilton & Yee, 1990). There is also the erroneous and harmful societal belief that a woman who says "no" to sex really doesn't mean it. This can easily result in misinterpretations that ultimately lead to rape.

It is unfortunately possible for men and women to be engaged in a shared social situation and yet to have completely different perceptions of the nature of the situation and the cues associated with it (Muehlenhard & Hollabaugh, 1988; Anderson, Cooper, & Okamura, 1997). For instance, consider the following descriptions:

date rape rape in which the rapist is either a date or a romantic acquaintance

Bob: *Patty and I were in the same statistics class together. She usually sat near me and was always very friendly. I liked her and thought maybe she liked me, too. Last Thursday I decided to find out. After class I suggested that she come to my place to study for midterms together. She agreed immediately, which was a good sign. That night everything seemed to go perfectly. We studied for a while and then took a break. I could tell that she liked me, and I was attracted to her. I was getting excited. I started kissing her. I could tell that she really liked it. We started touching each other and it felt really good. All of a sudden she pulled away and said "Stop." I figured she didn't want me to think that she was "easy" or "loose." A lot of girls think they have to say "no" at first. I knew once I showed her what a good time she could have, and that I would respect her in the morning, it would be OK. I just ignored her protests and eventually she stopped struggling. I think she liked it but afterwards she acted bummed out and cold. Who knows what her problem was?*

■ ■ ■

Patty: *I knew Bob from my statistics class. He's cute and we are both good at statistics, so when a tough midterm was scheduled, I was glad that he suggested we study together. It never occurred to me that it was anything except a study date. That night everything went fine at first, we got a lot of studying done in a short amount of time, so when he suggested we take a break I thought we deserved it. Well, all of a sudden he started acting really romantic and started kissing me. I liked the kissing but then he started touching me below the waist. I pulled away and tried to stop him but he didn't listen. After a while I stopped struggling; he was hurting me and I was scared. He was so much bigger and stronger than me. I couldn't believe it was happening to me. I didn't know what to do. He actually forced me to have sex with him. I guess looking back on it I should have screamed or done something besides trying to reason with him but it was so unexpected. I couldn't believe it was happening. I still can't believe it did.*

The view that sexual coercion is acceptable, although it is an unjustified opinion, is surprisingly common. For example, high school students in one study were asked to indicate under what circumstances it was permissible for a man to hold a woman down and force sexual intercourse. Only 44% of females and 24% of males said that forced sex was never permissible; the rest said that some conditions warranted rape (Mahoney, 1983; White & Humphrey, 1990).

Whatever the cause of date rape, it has severe, and often lingering, negative consequences. Not only does it result in a loss of trust, but it can also disrupt future intimate relationships. Victims report shock, anxiety, and fearfulness, in some cases lasting for years. However, quick psychological intervention, such as is provided by rape crisis centers, may diminish the long-term reactions to rape (Monnier et al., 2002; Zaslow, 2003).

Avoiding Date Rape.   Although there is no foolproof way to prevent date rape, several guidelines, developed by university counseling centers, health services, and women's and men's groups, may help minimize the risk (American College Health Association, 1989; Jackson, 1996; Shultz, Scherman, & Marshall, 2000). Among them are the following:

- Set clear sexual limits. Both parties should clearly articulate what their sexual limits are, and they should do so early in the relationship.

- Do not give mixed messages. "No" should always mean "no." If someone means "yes," they should say "yes."

- Be assertive if someone is pressuring you. Politeness is not called for in such a situation; directness is. Passivity may be seen as a sign of assent.

- Be wary of risky situations. Others may make interpretations about dress and behavior that may be inaccurate. Remember that not everyone shares your own sexual standards.

- Remember that alcohol and drugs are often associated with date rape.
- Trust your instincts. If a situation seems risky or dangerous, leave or confront your date.

Review and Apply

Review

1. Although sexual activity develops normally in most cases, adolescents can experience some difficulties as they explore their sexuality.

2. Premature ejaculation, erectile dysfunction, and female orgasmic disorder are common difficulties.

3. Among prevalent sexually transmitted infections are AIDS, chlamydia, genital herpes, genital warts, trichomoniasis, gonorrhea, and syphilis.

4. Sexual harassment, a frequent problem for both male and female adolescents, is usually motivated by the desire to demonstrate power over another person.

5. Rapes are surprisingly common. When it occurs during first dates, casual dates, or between romantic acquaintances, it is known as date rape.

Apply

1. What sorts of interventions and programs at the high school level would help to prevent the misunderstandings between acquaintances that often lead to date rape?

2. *From the perspective of an educator:* What sort of sexual harassment policy do you think makes sense in high school, given that adolescents are overtly engaged in sexual experimentation, intimacy development, and flirting? Is "zero tolerance" feasible? Is it possible to be too "politically correct"?

EPILOGUE

In this chapter we took a close look at adolescent sexuality. We reviewed the biology of sex and examined the ways in which adolescents experience sexual activities, both alone and with partners. One issue on which we focused is sexual orientation, which is a key concern during adolescence and is wrapped up in controversy.

We turned to an examination of pregnancy and contraception, discussing both the causes and consequences of teenage pregnancy. We looked at pregnancy prevention programs and at the choices that adolescents face when pregnancy occurs.

Finally we discussed some of the issues and difficulties that adolescents can experience as they engage in sexual activities. We looked at sexual disorders, sexually transmitted infections, sexual harassment, and rape.

Before we move to the next chapter, recall the experience of Lucian Schulte, who felt guilty about his first sexual encounter and resolved to remain celibate until marriage. Consider the following questions.

1. What do you think motivated Lucian to experiment with sex despite his desire to wait until marriage?

2. Lucian says his first sexual experience turned out differently from what he had expected. What consequences did Lucian fail to take into account?

3. What effect do you think Lucian's religious upbringing, his parents' values, and his abstinence classes had on his sexual activity?

4. What tentative conclusions can you draw about how Lucian's personality relates to his notions about sexuality? How typical does he seem to be?

SUMMARY

REVIEW

- **What sexual activities are common among adolescents?** *(p. 281)*

  1. The first sexual act in which adolescents engage is often masturbation, which is now perceived as normal rather than abnormal or shameful.

  2. As adolescence proceeds, sexual activities begin to involve partners, following a culturally influenced sexual script that determines the milestones of the typical sexual progression.

  3. Societal norms about sex change over time, with "permissiveness with affection" and sometimes "friends with benefits" largely displacing the double standard that prevailed about 50 years ago in the United States.

- **Why are there different sexual orientations, and what determines one's orientation?** *(p. 284)*

  4. The most common sexual orientation among adolescents is heterosexuality, with a smaller number of adolescents having homosexual or bisexual orientations.

  5. Homosexuality and heterosexuality, rather than being distinct sexual orientations, are regarded by some researchers as a continuum along which people experience their individual sexuality, which may change over time.

  6. The factors that cause individuals to develop as heterosexual, homosexual, or bisexual are not completely understood, but genetic and biological factors play an important role, most likely in combination with physiological and environmental factors.

  7. Gay and lesbian adolescents face challenges in a society that continues to be prejudiced against homosexuality, including the challenge of informing their parents of their orientation.

- **What are the issues associated with adolescent pregnancy, and how can it be prevented?** *(p. 290)*

  8. Adolescents who do not choose abstinence can learn to prevent pregnancy by informing themselves about their contraceptive options.

  9. Teenage pregnancy, which is unusually prevalent in the United States, can lead to a cycle of poverty and can restrict educational and employment options.

  10. Adolescents who become pregnant face a series of decisions about the pregnancy that their cognitive abilities are only beginning to be able to process. Family and societal supports are needed to help make sound decisions.

  11. Among the choices that adolescents may consider are abortion and adoption—both of which are serious decisions not easily made or experienced.

12. The most promising programs for reducing adolescent pregnancy use an approach that combines the encouragement of abstinence with realistic information on contraceptive use.

● **What sorts of difficulties may adolescents encounter as they negotiate their sexuality?** *(p. 299)*

13. Although most adolescents experience little difficulty as they engage in sexual activity, the problems that may occur take on added significance because sexuality is an important aspect of self.

14. Some adolescents may experience premature ejaculation, erectile dysfunction, and difficulties with orgasm.

15. Sexually transmitted infections (STIs) include AIDS, chlamydia, trichomoniasis, gonorrhea, and syphilis.

● **Why are sexual harassment and rape particular threats during adolescence?** *(p. 303)*

16. Sexual harassment, a phenomenon faced by male and female adolescents, continues to be a problem in high schools and can have long-term effects.

17. Rape is the most serious sexual danger faced by adolescents, and its occurrence is not rare. Typically it is based on a desire for power rather than sex.

18. Rape is often committed by acquaintances rather than strangers—a phenomenon known as date rape.

19. Clear limits, unambiguous messages, assertiveness, and the avoidance of risky situations are ways to minimize date rape.

KEY TERMS AND CONCEPTS

masturbation (p. 281)
sexually transmitted
  infection (STI) (p. 300)

sexual harassment (p. 303)
rape (p. 304)

date rape (p. 305)

Schooling, Education, and Society

CHAPTER OUTLINE

PROLOGUE Middle School Days

I T'S **10 A.M. ON A** bright May day, and the arts wing at Gustav A. Fritsche Middle School in Milwaukee, Wisconsin, is hopping. In a band room, 21 members of the jazz ensemble are rehearsing *Soul Bossa Nova* with plenty of heart and impressive intonation, in preparation for a concert downtown. In another room, woodblocks, timpani and bells are whipping up a rhythmic frenzy as the 75-member Fritsche Philharmonic Orchestra tackles Elliott Del Borgo's *Aboriginal Rituals.* In an art room, eighth graders are shaping clay vessels to be baked in the school kiln. Down the hall, students are dabbing acrylic paints on canvas to create vivid still lifes à la Vincent van Gogh. At 10:49, when the 82-minute arts period ends, kids of all sizes, colors and sartorial stripes pour out of the classrooms, jostling and joking, filling the hallway with the buzz of pubescent energy. Then it's off to language arts, math, social studies and the array of other subjects at this sprawling arena for adolescents. (Wallis, 2006, p. 48) ■

th!nk ABOUT THIS

SOUNDS LIKE AN ideal place to go to school, doesn't it? In fact, for many younger adolescents, middle school offers an excellent educational experience, permitting students to expand their horizons both intellectually and socially.

But for other adolescents, the picture is not so pretty. Some become overwhelmed by the choices they face, and others get lost—figuratively and sometimes even literally—in schools that most often are much larger than the cozier elementary schools in which they were educated when they were younger.

In this chapter, we consider the education of adolescents. Because so much of the average adolescent's day is spent in school—in classes, in extracurricular activities, or in social contexts such as the lunchroom—the educational system has a significant impact on the lives of adolescents. In fact, the success of adolescents' school experiences will last a lifetime, influencing their aspirations, their career success, their degree of civic engagement, and ultimately their ability to navigate the complexities of society.

We begin the chapter examining how the structure of schooling, including the configuration of grades in particular schools, affects adolescents' educational experience. We look at the success of middle schools in helping adolescents transition from elementary to secondary education. We also consider bilingual and multicultural education, as well as the effectiveness of alternatives to traditional education such as home schooling.

Next, we turn to the factors that affect individual student achievement. We consider how socioeconomic status, ethnicity, race, and gender are related to school performance. We examine the achievement testing movement, as well as the factors that lead some adolescents to drop out of school. We also look at the education of adolescents with special needs.

Finally, we examine the pursuit of higher education. We talk about who goes to college—and who doesn't. We also look at how gender affects the way students are treated in class and how students can overcome the gender and racial barriers they encounter. ■

After reading this chapter,

YOU WILL BE ABLE TO
ANSWER THESE QUESTIONS:

- What models of schooling are used with adolescents, and what are their effects?
- What factors have the most influence on school performance?
- What approaches are used for educating adolescents with special needs?
- What factors affect college attendance and performance by women and minorities?

The Impact of Schools on Adolescents: The Structure of Education

I LOVE MIDDLE SCHOOL! none of my old friends are really in my classes though (ok I have some in gym and Steph in get the facs but that's only like 1 class per person) but Joe just happened to be in 4 of my classes so I spend 5 periods of every day with him, sitting by him in 3 of them. he's gotten nicer though, kinda. anyway I LOVE MIDDLE SCHOOL!! it's the greatest. and plus there's Vivi who is sick right now but I have my last 3 periods with her and Morgan . . . I love Latin too it's so much fun and I love my teacher Mrs. Whittaker. She's the best.

■ ■ ■

From 4th grade till the summer before 6th grade I was depressed. It was in 6th grade that I decided that I needed to live. I figured that since I was moving to middle school I might be able to sort of start over. However that was not the case. My brothers had by this point stopped messing with me for the most part. But school was horrible I was the kid that everyone picked on. that lasted for 2 years until I realized that if I stopped reacting to being made fun of people stopped making fun of me. So throughout middle school I was a loner. I had a lot of people who would claim to be my friends but they would still make fun of me so I became a loner.

If nothing else, middle school evokes strong feelings on the part of adolescents, as these two reactions illustrate. That's hardly surprising, given that the transition from elementary school to middle school comes at time when students are changing radically along a variety of dimensions.

The Transition from Elementary School

The transition from elementary school into secondary education is a normative transition, meaning it is a part of the life of almost all adolescents in the United States. However, the fact that nearly everyone is doing it doesn't make it easy. The transition can be particularly difficult because of the physical, intellectual, and social changes that are occurring at about the same time.

After leaving elementary school, most students enter a *middle school,* which typically comprises grades 6 to 8 (see Figure 10-1). At the same time, most adolescents are beginning puberty and coming to grips with the changes taking place in their bodies. Furthermore, their thinking is becoming more sophisticated, and their relationships with their family and friends are becoming far more complicated than ever before.

For most adolescents, middle schools provide a very different educational structure from the one they grew accustomed to in elementary school. Rather than spending the day in a self-contained classroom, students move from one class to another. Not only must they adapt to the demands of different teachers, but also their classmates in each course may be different every class period. Those classmates may be more heterogeneous and diverse than those they encountered in their elementary schools.

Furthermore, because they are the youngest and least experienced, students in middle school enter an environment in which they suddenly find themselves at the bottom of the status hierarchy. Coming from elementary schools in which they were at the top of that status hierarchy (and at which they were physically and cognitively so different from the kindergarteners and first graders who occupied the bottom of the hierarchy), students can find the middle school experience alarming and sometimes damaging.

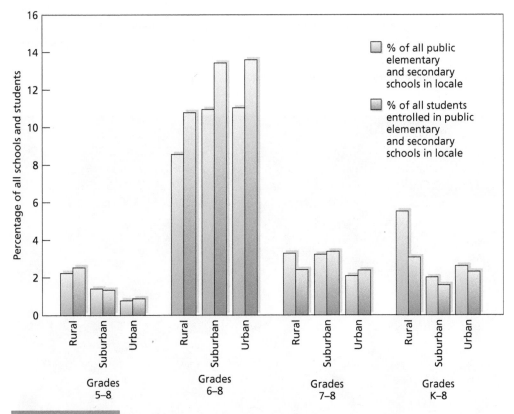

▲ **FIGURE 10-1**

Comparison of different middle school configurations. The majority of middle schools are comprised of grades 6 to 8, particularly in suburban and urban locations.

(*Source:* Juvonen, et al., 2004.)

In addition, middle schools are typically considerably larger than elementary schools. This factor alone makes the transition to middle school more difficult. A significant amount of research demonstrates quite clearly that students do better, both academically and psychologically, in smaller, less-bureaucratic educational settings (Lee & Burkam, 2003; Ready, Lee, & Welner, 2004).

To understand the nature and consequences of the transition from elementary school to middle school, we first need some background information on how middle schools came into being in the first place. A little bit of history can help us understand how we arrived at what is now the typical middle school configuration (Juvonen et al., 2004).

The Middle School Movement

In the early 1900s, students typically proceeded through the two main types of schools: primary school that went from grade 1 to grade 8 and high school that comprised 9th through 12th grades. However, because of pressures due to increased immigration, greater industrialization, and concerns that students were not starting college preparation early enough, the educational establishment began to argue for earlier and more rigorous training during what had been the final years of elementary schooling. These concerns led to the development of what was to become the dominant approach: the establishment of junior high schools encompassing grades 7 and 8.

In most cases, junior high schools took their names quite literally: They were *junior* high schools, mimicking the structure and subject matter—and often the rigidity—of their senior counterparts. In other words, they did very much what high schools did, with little regard for the developmental status of the students.

Almost half a century later, in the mid-1900s, dissatisfaction with the junior high school model began to increase. Educators began to argue that the developmental stage of early adolescence required a different form of education from that supplied to older adolescents. There was also a practical reason for the establishment of middle schools instead of junior high schools: Changing birthrates led to new enrollment patterns, with elementary school enrollments growing and secondary school enrollments declining.

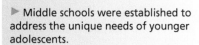

► Middle schools were established to address the unique needs of younger adolescents.

Taken together, these factors led to the establishment of middle schools encompassing grades 6 through 8. This trend began in the 1960s and rapidly escalated in the following decades. The widespread introduction of middle schools was driven largely by a recognition of the unique educational requirements of early adolescence, as well as the sense that the transition from elementary school into subsequent stages of education was particularly precarious for adolescents. (Table 10-1 summarizes the major aspects of the transitions faced by students in middle school.)

According to *Great Transitions*, an influential report by the Carnegie Council on Adolescent Development (1995), eight principles underlie good education for adolescents in middle schools:

- Create learning communities to make larger schools more manageable and to promote teacher–student and student–student relationships.

- Identify and teach a common core of knowledge, helping students to make the connections between different disciplines.

- Provide opportunities for all students to succeed by using cooperative learning techniques. In cooperative learning, students work together to achieve a common goal. By working cooperatively, students benefit from the insights of others, and if they get off on the wrong track, they may be brought back to the correct course by others in their group (Slavin, 1995; Karpov & Haywood, 1998).

- Prepare teachers better for middle school instruction. Teachers need to understand adolescent development and should be trained to work with diverse populations of students.

- Support academic instruction by providing programs to address adolescents' health and fitness needs.

- Involve parents and families in the education of adolescents.

- Give teachers and principals the ability to make changes in curriculum and to use innovative teaching techniques, rather than holding them rigidly to a particular way of teaching.

- Connect education more effectively with the community by providing *full-service schools* that offer youth social and health services, staffed by outside agencies.

TABLE 10-1 The Transition from Elementary School to Middle School		
	Elementary School	**Middle School**
Environmental changes	Small schools	Large schools
	Oldest in the school	Youngest in the school
	One or two teachers, close relationship	Many teachers, distant relationships
	Same classroom with same classmates	Changing classrooms from one period to another
Changes in teaching practices	Smaller classes with opportunities for decision making	Greater emphasis on teacher control and discipline: fewer decision-making opportunities for students
	Small group and individual instruction	Whole-class instruction
	Mix of abilities in each class	Increased between-class ability grouping
	Learning opportunities that demand higher-order cognitive processes	Less cognitively demanding tasks (for example, drill), yet stricter evaluation criteria

Sources: Eccles and Midgley (1989) and Eccles, Lord, and Midgley (1991).

In short, proponents of middle school suggested that schools needed to go beyond the subject-matter curriculum and engage students socially and emotionally, addressing the needs of the "whole child." In this view, schools were expected to foster close teacher–student relationships, making adolescents feel that teachers were both supporters and advocates for them. Middle school proponents also suggested that teachers should work in teams, integrating different disciplines so that students could see the connections between subject areas and learn to integrate the different information.

In addition, middle school advocates promoted an emphasis on discovery learning. In discovery learning, students are given the opportunity to participate in hands-on learning experiences, identifying principles on their own through experimentation. In this view, traditional lecturing is seen as less effective than working out ideas on one's own.

In short, middle schools were seen as the best way to take into account adolescents' developmental stage. But have the ambitious goals that led to the establishment of the middle school model been realized? Are students really better off than they would have been in school configurations more similar to the ones that middle schools replaced? For proponents of middle schools, the research findings are not comforting.

Research On the Success of Middle Schools: A Mixed Picture

Everyone agrees that some middle schools are successful in supporting their students' socioemotional growth, creating an environment that encourages learning, and optimizing student achievement. Furthermore, schools that have adopted the *Great Transitions* recommendations have seen improvements, including some significant gains in reading, math, and science scores (Jackson, 1997; Manzo, 2003).

On the other hand, the overall record of middle schools has been harshly criticized. According to a comprehensive report by the Rand Corporation, middle schools have failed in several ways (Juvonen et al., 2004):

- Over half of eighth graders do not achieve proficiency in reading, math, and science according to national standards.

- In comparison to their peers in other countries, eighth graders rank in 12th place academically, which places them below average. In some cases, students from the United States who did better than their international peers in elementary school actually declined in rank when they entered middle school. For instance, in fourth grade, U.S. students are average in math and science compared to their international peers; 4 years later, when they enter eighth grade, they score below the international average.

- The proportion of middle school students who suffer from emotional problems is higher for students in the United States than for students in all 11 of the other countries examined by the World Health Organization. U.S. middle school students exhibit higher rates of depression, a greater degree of disengagement with school, and a greater desire to drop out of school than students their age in other countries.

- Even when middle school students report feeling connected to their peers and their school, this does not lead to greater academic achievement. In fact, the link between social-emotional climate and academic success is weak at best, according to carefully conducted research (Williamson & Johnston, 1999).

Although such findings suggest that middle schools have not been up to the task of educating young adolescents, it's important to keep in mind that the findings don't necessarily mean that students in middle schools fare worse than students in other school configurations. Only a limited number of studies compare outcomes in schools with different grade configurations. Although some evidence suggests that students in some traditional configurations, such as the kindergarten-through-eighth-grade pattern, may outperform students in elementary/middle schools, the data are far from conclusive (Yecke, 2005).

Furthermore, in many cases, the philosophy behind the middle school movement—such as a focus on discovery learning—never was fully implemented. In fact, many school districts replaced large junior high schools with large middle schools and otherwise made only minimal changes, which was hardly a fair test of the middle school philosophy (Roeser, Eccles, & Sameroff, 2000; Wigfield & Eccles, 2002; Wallis, 2006).

In any event, the lack of unequivocal research support for the middle school idea has led a number of school systems to return to more traditional school configurations. For example, in the city of Milwaukee, Wisconsin, the number of kindergarten-to-eighth-grade schools has quadrupled since 2001, while the number of middle schools has declined by a third. Although partly due to enrollment issues, the major reason for the change is a shift in educational philosophy favoring more traditional school structures.

It's too early to state unequivocally whether middle schools have or have not been successful in meeting the needs of young adolescents. What is clear is that more work is needed if we are to have any hope of identifying and implementing the optimal educational experience for students—whether their schools are configured as middle schools, junior high schools, the more traditional kindergarten-to-eighth grade schools, or some other pattern.

Although decisions about the optimal configuration of schools are of critical importance, other educational issues also have a major impact on adolescents' educational success. As we discuss next, one question that is of particular importance is bilingual and multicultural education—an issue that has an impact not only on students who enter U.S. schools speaking a language other than English, but on every student.

Adolescent
DIVERSITY   Multicultural Education

The students came into Room 42 after lunch today with all kinds of questions about their upcoming field trip to Boyne River. They wanted to know when they would be leaving, when they would be returning, what they should bring, whether it would be cold at Boyne River, what they would eat, where they would sleep, and so on. They seemed very excited about the trip.

William [their middle school teacher] answered their questions . . . [but] when he asked for a show of hands of students from those who would be participating, I was surprised to see that many students did not put their hands up. Sahra, who was sitting directly in front of William, did not put her hand up.

"My father won't let me go" Sahra said. She explained that she could not go on field trips where they would be spending the night. Sahra's family is South Asian and her parents, especially her father, are very strict about the kinds of school activities they allow her to take part in.

"Do you want me to talk to him?" William asked her. "You should be able to go."

I asked some of the students sitting near me whether they would be going on the field trip.

"It's against my religion for girls to go out" Zeynab said.

"I can't. I need to go with my father to the hospital, to help translate for him."

"I need to pick my sister up from school and get my brother from daycare—my parents have to work."

"I work at my family's tea store, and sometimes I need to help them [i.e. my parents] with the forms." (Chan, 2006, p. 161)

FOR TEACHERS IN this eighth-grade classroom, composed of students whose families represent a variety of cultures, arranging a field trip is a complicated process.

Since the earliest period of formal education, classrooms have been populated by individuals from a broad range of backgrounds and experiences. Yet it is only relatively recently that variations in student backgrounds have been viewed as one of the major challenges—and opportunities—that educators face.

In fact, the diversity of background and experience in the classroom relates to a fundamental objective of education, which is to provide a formal mechanism to transmit the information a society deems important. As the famous anthropologist Margaret Mead (1942) once said, "In its broadest sense, education is the cultural process, the way in which each newborn human infant, born with a potentiality for learning greater than that of any other mammal, is transformed into a full member of a specific human society, sharing with the other members of a specific human culture" (p. 633).

Culture, then, can be thought of as a set of behaviors, beliefs, values, and expectations shared by members of a particular society. But although culture is often thought of in a relatively broad context (as in "Western culture" or "Asian culture"), it is also possible to focus on particular *subcultural* groups within a larger, more encompassing culture. For example, we can consider particular racial, ethnic, religious, socioeconomic, or even gender groups in the United States as manifesting characteristics of a subculture.

Membership in a cultural or subcultural group might be of only passing interest to educators were it not for the fact that students' cultural backgrounds have a substantial impact on the way that they—and their peers—are educated. In fact, in recent years, a considerable amount of thought has gone into establishing **multicultural education,** a form of education in which the goal is to help minority students develop competence in the culture of the majority group while maintaining positive group identities that build on their original cultures (Nieto, 2005).

multicultural education a form of education in which the goal is to help minority students develop competence in the culture of the majority group while maintaining positive group identities that build on their original cultures

cultural assimilation model an approach in which the goal of education was to assimilate individual cultural identities into a unique, unified American culture

pluralistic society model the concept in which American society is made up of diverse, coequal cultural groups that should preserve their individual cultural features.

Cultural Assimilation or Pluralistic Society? Multicultural education developed in part as a reaction to a **cultural assimilation model,** in which the goal of education was to assimilate individual cultural identities into a unique, unified American culture. In practical terms, this meant, for example, that students who did not speak English were discouraged from speaking their native tongues and were totally immersed in English.

In the early 1970s, however, educators and members of minority groups began to suggest that the cultural assimilation model ought to be replaced by a **pluralistic society model.** According to this conception, American society is made up of diverse, coequal cultural groups that should preserve their individual cultural features.

The pluralistic society model grew in part from the belief that teachers, by discouraging students' use of their native tongues, denigrated their cultural heritages and lowered their self-esteem. Furthermore, because instructional materials inevitably feature culture-specific events and understandings, adolescents who were denied access to their own cultural materials might never be exposed to important aspects of their backgrounds. For example, English-language texts rarely present some of the great themes that appear throughout Spanish literature and history (such as the search for the Fountain of Youth and the Don Juan legend). Hispanic students immersed in such English-language texts might never come to understand important components of their own heritage.

Ultimately, educators began to argue that the presence of students representing diverse cultures enriched and broadened the educational experience of all students. Pupils and teachers exposed to people from different backgrounds could better understand the world and gain greater sensitivity to the values and needs of others (Gurin, Nagda, & Lopez, 2004; Zirkel & Cantor, 2004).

Today, most educators agree that the pluralistic society model is the most valid one for schooling and that minority students should be encouraged to develop a **bicultural identity.** They recommend that school systems encourage adolescents to maintain their original cultural identities while they integrate themselves into the dominant culture. This view suggests that an individual can live as a member of two cultures, with two cultural identities, without having to choose one over the other. As we see next, the issue is particularly acute for students who enter school not speaking English (Lu, 2001; Oyserman et al., 2003; Vyas, 2004).

Bilingual Education

Adolescents who enter school with little or no English proficiency must learn both the standard curriculum and the language in which that curriculum is taught. Known as *English language learners (ELL),* these adolescents face special challenges. Their lack of English language skills may significantly slow their academic progress and isolate them from other adolescents. In addition, their specific cultural background may lead ELLs to understand the educational process differently. For example, in some cultures it is considered disrespectful to ask teachers questions about material they are presenting (Klingner & Artiles, 2006; Stipek & Hakuta, 2007).

One approach to educating students who don't at first speak English is *bilingual education,* in which adolescents are initially taught in their native language, while at the same time learning English. With bilingual instruction, students are able to develop a strong foundation in basic subject areas using their native language. The ultimate goal of most bilingual education programs is to gradually shift instruction into English.

An alternative approach is to immerse students in English, teaching solely in that language. To proponents of this approach, initially teaching students in a language other than English hinders students' efforts to learn English and slows their integration into society.

▲ Most educators believe that a bicultural identity is advantageous.

The two quite different approaches have been highly politicized, with some politicians arguing in favor of "English-only" laws, while others urge school systems to respect the challenges faced by students who do not speak English by offering some instruction in their native language. Still, the psychological research is clear in suggesting that knowing more than one language offers several cognitive advantages. Because they have a wider range of linguistic possibilities to choose from as they assess a situation, speakers of two languages show greater cognitive flexibility. They can solve problems with increased creativity and versatility. Furthermore, learning in one's native tongue is associated with higher self-esteem in minority students (Romaine, 1994; Wright & Taylor, 1995; Barker, Giles, & Noels, 2001; Zehr, 2006).

Bilingual students often have greater metalinguistic awareness, understanding the rules of language more explicitly than students who speak only one language. Bilingual students even may score higher on tests of intelligence, according to some research. For example, one survey of French- and English-speaking students in Canada found that bilingual students scored significantly higher on both verbal and nonverbal tests of intelligence than those who spoke only one language (Lambert & Peal, 1972; Bochner, 1996; Crutchley, 2003; Swanson, Saez, & Gerber, 2004).

Finally, because many linguists contend that universal processes underlie language acquisition, instruction in a native language may enhance instruction in a second language. In fact, most educators believe that second-language learning should be a regular part of schooling for *all* adolescents (Perozzi & Sanchez, 1992; Yelland, Pollard, & Mercuri, 1993; Kecskes & Papp, 2000; Bialystok, McBride-Chang, & Luk, 2005).

bicultural identity a dual identity in which adolescents maintain their original cultural identities while also integrating themselves into the dominant culture

Home Schooling: An Alternative to Traditional Schools

Amanda Crosswhite is part of a school of 1,702 students. But when she goes to class, it's one-on-one with her mother.

Sharon Crosswhite has been home-schooling Amanda, 9, for three years and her son, Adam, 17, for two years.

"I had always wanted to try this experience," said Sharon Crosswhite, 48. "I was just getting a little disillusioned with the public school . . . ."

[Adam,] a high school senior, ... takes classes at Palomar College in San Marcos while continuing with high school subjects taught by his mother.

"He wasn't doing all that great in high school," Crosswhite said, adding it was Adam's choice to be home-schooled. "He's done a real turnaround. I think a big part of that is because I know what the assignments are." (Lepper, 2006, p. NC-8)

For students like the Crosswhite siblings, there is no distinction between their living room and classroom, because they are among the close to one million students who are homeschooled. **Home schooling** is a major educational phenomenon in which students are taught not by teachers in schools, but by their parents in their own homes.

There are a number of reasons why parents may choose to school their adolescents at home. Some parents feel their children will thrive with the one-to-one attention that homeschooling can bring, whereas they might get lost in a larger public school. Other parents are dissatisfied with the nature of the instruction and the quality of the teachers in their public schools and feel that they can do a better job teaching their children. And some parents engage in homeschooling for religious reasons, wishing to impart particular religious beliefs and practices that would not be provided in a public school and hoping to avoid exposing their children to values and aspects of the popular culture with which they disagree (Bauman, 2001; Dennis, 2004).

Homeschooling clearly works, in the sense that adolescents who have been homeschooled score generally as well on standardized tests as students who have been educated traditionally. In addition, their acceptance rate into colleges appears to be no different from that of traditionally schooled students (Lattibeaudiere, 2000; Lauricella, 2001; Lines, 2001).

However, the apparent academic success of adolescents schooled at home does not mean that homeschooling, per se, is effective because parents who choose to homeschool their children may be more affluent or have the kind of well-structured family situation in which children would succeed no matter what kind of schooling they had. In contrast, parents in dysfunctional and disorganized families are unlikely to have the motivation or interest to homeschool their children. For adolescents from families like these, the demands and structure of a formal school are probably a good thing.

Critics of homeschooling argue that it has considerable drawbacks. For example, the social interaction with groups of adolescents that is inherent in classrooms in traditional schools is largely missing for homeschooled students. Learning in an at-home environment, while perhaps strengthening family ties, hardly provides an environment that reflects the diversity of U.S. society. Furthermore, even the best-equipped home is unlikely to have the sophisticated science materials and educational technology that are available at many schools. Finally, most parents do not have the preparation of well-trained teachers, and their teaching methods may be unsophisticated. Although parents may be successful in teaching subject areas in which their child is already interested, they may have more difficulty teaching subjects that their child seeks to avoid (Murray, 1996; Sharp, 1997; Cai, Reeve, & Robinson, 2002).

Because homeschooling is relatively new, few controlled experiments have been conducted to examine its effectiveness. More research is needed to clarify how and when home schooling is an effective way to educate adolescents.

homeschooling a major educational phenomenon in which students are taught not by teachers in schools, but by their parents in their own homes

BECOMING AN INFORMED CONSUMER OF ADOLESCENT SCIENCE

Smoothing Adolescents' Transition to Middle School

MAKING THE TRANSITION from elementary school to middle school can be difficult. But there are several steps that parents, educators, and other adults can take to facilitate the change. Among them are the following (Elias, 2001; National Middle School Association/National Association of Elementary School Principals, 2002):

- Familiarize students with the new school before the first day. If the school does not provide a visitation day, arrange for a tour of the school. Get a map and review it (one of the greatest fears expressed by new middle school students is getting lost in the school and not being able to find their lockers and classrooms).

- Learn as much as possible about school rules, schedules, and available counseling support.

- Meet with middle school guidance counselors to help students choose the optimal combination of courses. Encourage students to choose a combination of harder and easier courses.

- Teach students basic time management skills. Provide students with calendars so they can write in due dates for homework and tests.

- Be attentive to signs of depression and anxiety, and seek out help for adolescents who need it.

Review and Apply

Review

1. Handling the transition from elementary to secondary school is especially difficult for young adolescents because of the other developmental issues that they face at around the same time.

2. Middle schools arose in response to the perceived failure of other school configurations to deal simultaneously with the educational and developmental needs of early adolescents.

3. Multicultural education is an attempt to acknowledge the heritages and languages of students from diverse cultural backgrounds while providing instruction that reflects the surrounding culture of the United States.

4. Bilingual education has become politically controversial, but it appears to offer solid benefits to students by supporting their learning of English while at the same time enabling them to achieve their other academic requirements.

5. In recent years, homeschooling has emerged as a way for parents who choose it to educate their children at home while meeting district and state educational requirements.

Apply

1. What advantages do you think students who are bilingual might have in today's world? How would you design a research study to demonstrate such advantages?

2. In terms of the development of identity and intimacy, what advantages and disadvantages would you predict for homeschooled adolescents?

School Performance

Yay! I did my homework! *I'm so proud of myself. Math, English, history. Whoo. . . . It wasn't really hard but it was a lot. I have my high school orientation next week! And we're having the assembly maybe Friday or next week. I'm so nervous! HIGH SCHOOL! Ahhhh. . . . (breathe). . . . OMG. Can you say scary? How short life is! I'm going to miss my middle school. It was nice. It was cramped but nice. But it's so scary how the time has gone by so quickly. I have to bring my grades up to A's or I won't get in the good classes next year in high school! That would suck to be in the dumb classes. But I'm doing my homework. So that's a start.*

Like this student, adolescents spend a considerable amount of time and energy working through concerns about their education. They worry about homework, the transition from middle to high school, grades, getting into the right classes, and a host of other issues.

Even knowing how one stands academically is not easy to accomplish, in part because there are few totally reliable measures of academic success. For example, consider grades. Grades awarded to high school students have shifted upward in the last decade. The mean grade point average for college-bound seniors was 3.3 (out of a possible 4.0), compared with 3.1 a decade ago. More than 40% of seniors reported average grades of A+, A, or A– (College Board, 2005).

At the same time, though, independent measures of achievement, such as SAT scores, have not risen. Consequently, a more likely explanation for the higher grades is the phenomenon of grade inflation. According to this view, it is not that students have changed. Instead, instructors have become more lenient and are awarding higher grades for the same level of performance (Cardman, 2004).

Further evidence for grade inflation comes from the relatively poor achievement of students in the United States when compared to students in other countries. For instance, students in the United States score lower on standardized math and science tests when compared to students in other industrialized countries (see Figure 10-2; OECD, 2005).

There is no single reason for this gap in the educational achievement of U.S. students, but a combination of factors, such as less time spent in classes and less-intensive instruction, are at work. Furthermore, the broad diversity of the U.S. school population may affect performance relative to that of other countries, where the population attending school is more homogeneous and affluent (Stedman, 1997; Schemo, 2001).

The poorer accomplishments of U.S. students is also reflected in high school graduation rates. Although it once stood first in the percentage of the population graduating from high school, the United States has dropped to 24th among industrialized countries. Only 78% of U.S. high school students graduate—a rate considerably lower than that of other developed countries (OECD, 1998; Organization for Economic Cooperation and Development, 2001).

Socioeconomic Status and School Performance: Individual Differences in Achievement

All students are entitled to the same opportunity in the classroom, but it is very clear that certain groups have greater educational advantages than others. One of the most telling indicators of this reality is the relationship between educational achievement and socioeconomic status (SES).

Middle- and high-SES students, on average, earn higher grades, score higher on standardized tests of achievement, and complete more years of schooling than students from lower-SES homes. Of course, this disparity does not start in adolescence; the same findings hold for children in lower grades. However, by the time students are in high school, the effects of socioeconomic status become even more pronounced.

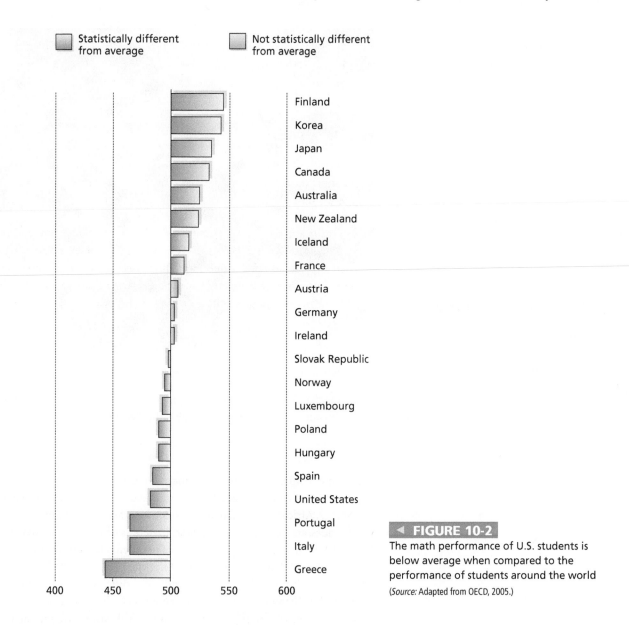

Statistically different from average   Not statistically different from average

Finland
Korea
Japan
Canada
Australia
New Zealand
Iceland
France
Austria
Germany
Ireland
Slovak Republic
Norway
Luxembourg
Poland
Hungary
Spain
United States
Portugal
Italy
Greece

400   450   500   550   600

◀ **FIGURE 10-2**

The math performance of U.S. students is below average when compared to the performance of students around the world

(*Source:* Adapted from OECD, 2005.)

Why do students from middle- and high-SES homes show greater academic success? There are several reasons. For one thing, adolescents living in poverty lack many of the advantages enjoyed by other adolescents. Their nutrition and health may be less adequate. Often living in crowded conditions and attending inadequate schools, they may have few places to do homework. Their homes may lack the books and computers commonplace in more economically advantaged households.

Furthermore, poor adolescents may lack *self-efficacy,* which—as we first discussed in Chapter 5—is the learned expectation that one is capable of carrying out a behavior or producing a desired outcome in a particular situation. Adolescents high in self-efficacy exert greater effort and show greater persistence when faced with challenging tasks. The result is to increase their likelihood of academic success (Adams & Singh, 1998; Bowen & Bowen, 1999; Prater, 2002; DuBois et al., 2003).

For all these reasons, students from impoverished backgrounds may be at a disadvantage from the day they begin their schooling. As they grow older, their school performance may continue to lag, and in fact their disadvantage may snowball. Because later school success builds heavily on basic skills presumably learned early in school, children who experience early

► Students from middle- and high-socioeconomic status families have greater academic success.

problems may find themselves falling increasingly behind the academic eight ball as adolescents (Huston, 1991; Phillips et al., 1994; Biddle, 2001).

Ethnic and Racial Differences in School Achievement

Achievement differences between ethnic and racial groups are significant, and they paint a troubling picture of American education. For instance, data on school achievement indicate that, on average, African-American and Hispanic students tend to perform at lower levels, receive lower grades, and score lower on standardized tests of achievement than Caucasian students (see Figure 10-3). In contrast, Asian American students tend to receive higher grades than Caucasian students (National Center for Educational Statistics, 2003).

What is the source of such ethnic and racial differences in academic achievement? Clearly, much of the difference is due to socioeconomic factors: Because more African-American and Hispanic families live in poverty, their economic disadvantage may be reflected in their school performance. In fact, when we take socioeconomic levels into account by comparing different ethnic and racial groups at the same socioeconomic level, achievement differences diminish. But they do not vanish (Luster & McAdoo, 1994; Meece & Kurtz-Costes, 2001; Cokley, 2003).

Anthropologist John Ogbu (1988, 1992) argued that members of certain minority groups may perceive school success as relatively unimportant. They may believe that societal prejudice in the workplace will dictate that they will not succeed, no matter how much effort they expend. The conclusion is that hard work in school will have no eventual payoff.

Ogbu suggested that members of minority groups who enter a new culture voluntarily are more likely to be successful in school than those who are brought into a new culture against their will. For instance, he noted that Korean children who are the sons and daughters of voluntary immigrants to the United States tend to be, on average, quite successful in school. On the other hand, Korean children in Japan, whose parents were forced to immigrate during World War II and work as forced laborers, tend to do relatively poorly in school. The reason for the disparity? The process of involuntary immigration apparently leaves lasting scars, reducing the motivation to succeed in subsequent generations. Ogbu suggested that in the United States, the involuntary immigration, as slaves, of the ancestors of many African-American students might be related to their motivation to succeed (Ogbu, 1992; Gallagher, 1994).

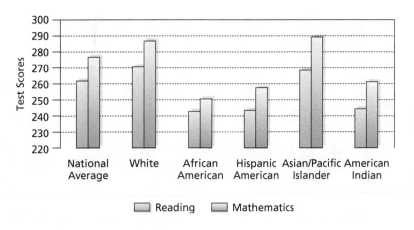

◄ **FIGURE10-**

Racial discrepancies between groups are apparent on a national test of reading and math achievement administered to a sample of 150,000 eight-graders

(Source National Assessment of Educational Progress, NAEP, 2003.)

Attributions and Beliefs about Academic Success. Another factor in the differential success of various ethnic and racial group members has to do with academic *attributions*—their explanations of the reasons behind academic success. Students from many Asian cultures tend to view achievement as the consequence of temporary situational factors, such as how hard they work. In contrast, African-American students are more apt to view success as the result of external causes over which they have no control, such as luck or societal biases. Students who subscribe to the belief that effort will lead to success, and then expend that effort, are more likely to do better in school than students who believe that effort makes less of a difference (Stevenson, Chen, & Lee, 1992; Fuligni, 1998; Saunders, Davis, & Williams, 2004).

Adolescents' beliefs about the consequences of not doing well in school may also contribute to racial and ethnic differences in school performance. Specifically, it may be that African-American and Hispanic students tend to believe that they can succeed *despite* poor school performance. This belief in their eventual success no matter how poorly they do in school may cause them to put less effort into their studies.

In contrast, Asian-American students tend to believe that if they do not do well in school, they are unlikely to get good jobs and be successful. The Asian view, which stems in part from ancient Confucian writings, tends to accentuate the necessity of hard work and perseverance.

◄ Beliefs about the consequences of academic status contribute to students' school performance.

▶ This cartoon reflects the reality that Asian students' attributions regarding the causes of success may lead to better academic performance.

Ultimately, Asian Americans are motivated to work hard in school by a fear of the consequences of poor academic performance (Steinberg, Dornbusch, & Brown, 1992).

This cultural difference in attributional styles is displayed in several ways. For instance, surveys show that mothers, teachers, and students in Japan and Taiwan all believe strongly that students in a typical class tend to have the same amount of ability. In contrast, mothers, teachers, and students in the United States are apt to disagree, arguing that there are significant differences in ability among the various students (see Figure 10-4).

It is easy to imagine how such different attributional styles can influence academic success. If, as in the United States, adolescents seem to believe that ability is fixed and locked in, poor academic performance will be greeted with a sense of failure and reduced motivation to work harder to overcome it. In contrast, Japanese adolescents are apt to see failure as a temporary setback due to their lack of hard work. After making such an attribution, they are more apt to expend increased effort on future academic activities.

According to some developmentalists, these different attributional orientations may explain the fact that Asian students frequently outperform American students in international comparisons of student achievement (Linn, 1997; Wheeler, 1998). Because Asian students tend to assume that academic success results from hard work, they may put greater effort into their schoolwork than American students, who believe that their inherent ability determines their performance. These arguments suggest that the attributional style of adolescents in the United States might well be maladaptive. They also argue that the attributional styles taught to children by their parents may have a significant effect on their future success (Eaton & Dembo, 1997; Little & Lopez, 1997; Little, Miyashita, & Karasawa, 2003).

On the other hand, holding an attributional style that attributes success primarily to hard work may have a less beneficial side, as we consider next when we discuss the potential costs of pushing adolescents too hard.

▶ FIGURE 10-4

Responding using a 7-point scale, where 1 indicated "strongly disagree" and 7 indicated "strongly agree," U.S. mothers were less apt to believe that all children have the same degree of underlying, innate ability compared with their Japanese and Taiwanese counterparts.

(*Source:* Stevenson & Lee, 1990.)

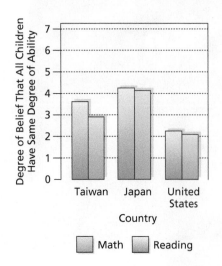

Are There Psychological Costs to Academic Achievement? It Depends on Your Culture.

On a brisk Saturday morning, while most of their friends were relaxing at home, 16-year-old Jerry Lee and eight other Asian teenagers huddled over their notebooks and calculators for a full day of math and English lessons.

During the week, they all attend public schools in the city. But every Saturday, they go to a Korean hag-won, or cram school, in Flushing to spend up to seven hours immersed in the finer points of linear algebra or Raymond Chandler.

"I complain, but my mom says I have to go," said Jerry, a Stuyvesant High School student from Sunnyside, Queens, who has already scored a 1520 on the Scholastic Assessment Test for college, but is shooting for a perfect 1600. "It's like a habit now." (Dunn, 1995, p. 1)

Long a tradition in Korea, Japan, and China, cram schools have begun to spring up in the United States as Asian parents, committed to the success of their children, demand them in increasing numbers.

Cram schools are a fixture in Asian society, where competition for success begins as young as age 4 or 5. By the time children reach adolescence, competition to attend prestigious schools has reached fever pitch. Some high-school-age students spend hours every day after school and on weekends in instruction that goes beyond what is covered in public schooling.

Being pushed to attend cram school is one type of intense pressure under which Asian children are often placed. In fact, although the scholastic performance of adolescents in Asia typically exceeds that of adolescents in the United States, critics suggest that such success comes at the price of increased stress, psychological burdens, and depression (e.g., Holman, 1991; Watanabe, 1992).

Not so—at least according to recent research that casts doubt on the critics' contentions. Developmental psychologist David Crystal and his colleagues examined psychological adjustment in a group of 11th-grade students in the United States, China, and Japan. Compared with the U.S. students, the Asian students reported that their parents held higher expectations for their academic achievement and were less satisfied with their academic success (Crystal et al., 1994).

Despite the higher parental pressure, both Japanese and Chinese students experienced lower levels of stress than their U.S. counterparts. As can be seen in Figure 10-5, more than 75% of U.S. students said they felt stress once a week or almost every day. In comparison, 50% or fewer of Japanese and Chinese students reported such frequent stress.

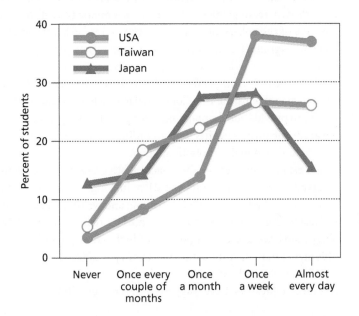

◄ **FIGURE 10-5**

According to one study, Asian students despite attending cram schools and higher parental pressure, feel less stress than their American peers.

(*Source:* Crystal, et al., 1994.)

Furthermore, Japanese students were less depressed and in general had lower academic anxiety than their American counterparts. Chinese students, too, reported lower levels of anxiety regarding academic performance than U.S. students, although they did suffer somewhat more often from depression and health-related problems than U.S. and Japanese students.

Why should American students experience greater stress and anxiety than Asian students, who are subject to significantly greater demands from their parents? One explanation may be that students in the United States view academics as only one of many spheres in which they need to achieve. As we discussed in the two previous chapters, social relationships play a major role in U.S. adolescents' lives. In addition, many adolescents experience pressures about dating or part-time jobs. Consequently, pressures and competition between academic and social pursuits may contribute to U.S. students' high levels of stress.

In contrast, Asian students perceive that the major task they face during adolescence is achieving high levels of academic success. Other demands are clearly secondary. As a consequence, they may be more focused on the pursuit of academic excellence and feel less conflict from competing demands.

Although the full explanation for these findings remains to be discovered, one lesson is clear: High academic achievement of the sort attained by students in Japan and China does not necessarily come at the expense of psychological adjustment.

The Special Problems of Boys

Spend a few minutes on the phone with Danny Frankhuizen and you come away thinking, "What a nice boy." He's thoughtful, articulate, bright. He has a good relationship with his mom, goes to church every Sunday, loves the rock band Phish and spends hours each day practicing his guitar. But once he's inside his large public Salt Lake City high school, everything seems to go wrong. He's 16, but he can't stay organized. He finishes his homework and then can't find it in his backpack. He loses focus in class, and his teachers, with 40 kids to wrangle, aren't much help. "If I miss a concept, they tell me, 'Figure it out yourself,'" says Danny. Last year Danny's grades dropped from B's to D's and F's. (Tyre, 2006, p. 44)

How did Danny end up in this position? It's a question that educators increasingly have begun to ask about many boys like Danny, boys who take an educational tailspin during adolescence.

According to many measures, adolescent boys are falling behind the progress of girls. Boys are twice as likely to be placed in special education classes. The proportion of boys who say they don't like school has increased by 71% since 1980. Even in college, the gender gap favoring girls is increasing: Males now make up a minority of students enrolled in college, composing 44% of the college population, compared to 56% for females. Overall, the percentage of male undergraduates has declined by a quarter between 1970 and 2000.

The educational difficulties faced by males were not always as problematic as they are currently. In the 1970s, the gender gap favored boys, who outperformed girls educationally. To address such problems, the U.S. Congress passed a federal law in 1972 referred to as Title IX, which sought to provide equal opportunity for girls. In many ways, the law was successful, encouraging academic success in girls. But, according to some educators, it created school environments that discouraged male scholastic success.

For example, by the time they reach eighth grade, girls' scores are 11 points higher than boys' on standardized reading tests and 21 points higher on standardized writing tests. The gap is even larger in high school in both reading and writing, as well as on other measures of success. For instance, girls are more than one third more likely to take Advanced Placement honors biology than boys, and the proportion of high school girls who are planning to go to college is a fifth higher than the proportion of boys (Tyre, 2006).

What explains the decline in male performance? Although no definitive explanation has emerged, educators have suggested several possibilities. One is that as the amount of accountability has increased, with more standardized testing and curriculum requirements being mandated by states and even the federal government, schools have become more rigid. Curriculum reforms have cut back on physical education and sports, and the lack of physical outlets may impact boys more negatively than girls.

In addition, girls' earlier physical maturation at the start of adolescence may also be linked to earlier cognitive maturation. For example, the prefrontal cortex in the brain, which is involved in intellectual activity and impulse control, develops its maximum thickness at around age 11 in girls—18 months earlier than in boys. In addition, the brain activation involved in the perception of facial expressions comes to resemble adult perception earlier in girls than boys, suggesting that boys' brain development lags behind girls' brain development (Giedd, 2004; Killgore & Yurgelun-Todd, 2004; Shaw et al., 2006).

For some male adolescents, the lack of male figures in the home may also be related to school difficulties. The lack of a stable role model for the 40% of boys who are being raised without a father in the home—and the percent is even higher for adolescents of color—puts them at risk not only for educational failure but for other antisocial behavior as well (Tremblay, Tremblay, & Saucier, 2004).

Although it is clear that adolescent boys are falling behind girls in at least some educational domains, the extent of the problem has not been precisely determined. Furthermore, as we will consider later in the chapter, sexism directed at girls is still a source of considerable difficulty. Clearly, efforts are needed to increase the educational opportunities for both boys and girls to allow them to reach their potential. (For further discussion of educators' efforts to permit all adolescents to reach their potential, see the *Transitions* box.)

Expectation Effects: How Teachers' Expectancies Influence their Students

Suppose you were a middle school teacher and were told that certain students in your class were expected to bloom intellectually in the coming year. Would you treat them differently from the students who were not so designated?

◀ Adolescent boys are more likely than girls to underachieve educationally.

Transitions

Achievement Testing: Will No Child Be Left Behind?

A student was shot dead by a classmate during lunch period outside Frank W. Ballou Senior High. It didn't come as much of a surprise to anyone at the school, in this city's most crime-infested ward. Just during the current school year, one boy was hacked by a student with an ax, a girl was badly wounded in a knife fight with another female student, five fires were set by arsonists, and an unidentified body was dumped next to the parking lot. (Suskind, 1994, p. 1; Suskind, 1999)

Can schools like this be turned around and made to provide not only a safe environment but also a setting that provides an excellent education for every student? Most definitely, according to the thinking behind the passage of the No Child Left Behind Act, a comprehensive law designed to improve school performance across the United States.

The No Child Left Behind Act, passed by Congress in 2002, requires that every one of the 50 U.S. states design and administer achievement tests that students must pass to graduate from high school. In addition, schools themselves have to be graded so that the public is aware of which schools have the best (and worst) test results (Bourque, 2005; Jehlen & Winans, 2005).

The basic idea behind mandatory testing programs like the No Child Left Behind Act is to ensure that students graduate with a minimum level of proficiency. Proponents suggest that students—and teachers—will be motivated by the tests and that overall educational standards will be raised.

In addition, schools that are successful will attract more students (and funding), while nonperforming schools will either improve or, essentially, be driven out of business and shut down due to a loss of accreditation. The law allows parents to transfer their children to more effective public schools if their local school is not doing a good job (Moores, 2004; Lewis & Haug, 2005; Phelps, 2005).

Critics of the Act (and other forms of mandatory standardized testing) argue that a number of unintended negative consequences will result from implementation of the law. To ensure that the maximum numbers of students pass the tests, they suggest, instructors will "teach to the test," meaning that they will focus on the content of the tests to the exclusion of material that is not tested. Approaches to teaching designed to foster creativity and critical thinking may be discouraged by an emphasis on testing, in this view (Costigan & Crocco, 2004; McMillian, 2004; Thurlow et al., 2005).

In addition, mandatory high-stakes tests raise the anxiety level for students, potentially leading to poor performance, and students who might have performed well throughout their schooling face the possibility of not graduating if they do poorly on the test. Moreover, because students from lower socioeconomic and ethnic and racial minority backgrounds and those with special needs fail tests disproportionably, critics have argued that mandatory testing programs may be inherently biased (Samuels, 2005).

Although the No Child Left Behind Act has been controversial from the time of its passage, one part of the law has received nearly universal approval. Specifically, the law provides funding to help determine which educational practices and programs have been proven to be effective based on scientific research. Although there is disagreement over what constitutes "proof" of best educational practices, developmental and educational researchers have welcomed the emphasis on research (Chatterji, 2004).

It is too early to tell whether the No Child Left Behind Act will be successful in achieving its goals. It is clear that it is having a significant impact on education as schools respond to its requirements.

- Do you think it is fair for schools and teachers to be judged based on the way their students perform on standardized tests? Is there a better way to judge school and teacher performance?

- Do you agree that it is always a bad thing to "teach to the test"? What have teachers "taught to" in the past?

You probably would, according to the results of a classic but controversial study. Teachers do, in fact, treat students for whom they have expectations of improvement differently from those for whom they have no such expectations (Rosenthal & Jacobson, 1968). In the experiment, school teachers were told at the beginning of a new school year that based on test results, five students in their classes would be likely to "bloom" in the upcoming year. In reality, however, the information was bogus: The names of the students had been picked at random, although the teachers didn't know that. At the end of the year, the students completed an intelligence test that was identical to one taken a year earlier. The results showed that clear differences existed in the intellectual growth of the so-called bloomers, compared with that of the other members of their classes. Those randomly designated as likely to make significant gains did, in fact, improve more than the other students.

When the findings of the experiment, reported in a book titled *Pygmalion in the Classroom,* were published, they caused an immediate stir among educators—and in the public at large. The reason for this furor was the implication of the results: If merely holding high expectations is sufficient to bring about gains in achievement, wouldn't holding low expectations lead to slowed achievement? And because teachers may sometimes hold low expectations for adolescents from lower socioeconomic and minority backgrounds, did this mean that students from such backgrounds were destined to show low achievement throughout their educational careers?

Although the original experiment has been criticized on methodological and statistical grounds (Wineburg, 1987), enough subsequent evidence has been amassed to make it clear that the expectations of teachers are communicated to their students and can in fact bring about the expected performance. The phenomenon has come to be called the **teacher expectancy effect**—the cycle of behavior in which a teacher transmits an expectation about a student and thereby actually brings about the expected behavior (Rosenthal, 2002; see Figure 10-6).

The teacher expectancy effect can be viewed as a special case of a broader concept known as the *self-fulfilling prophecy,* in which a person's expectation is capable of bringing about an outcome. For instance, physicians have long known that providing patients with placebos (pills with no active ingredients) can sometimes "cure" them simply because the patients expect the medicine to work.

In the case of teacher expectancy effects, the basic explanation seems to be that teachers, after forming an initial expectation about a student's ability—often based inappropriately on

teacher expectancy effect   the cycle of behavior in which a teacher transmits an expectation about a student and thereby actually brings about the expected behavior

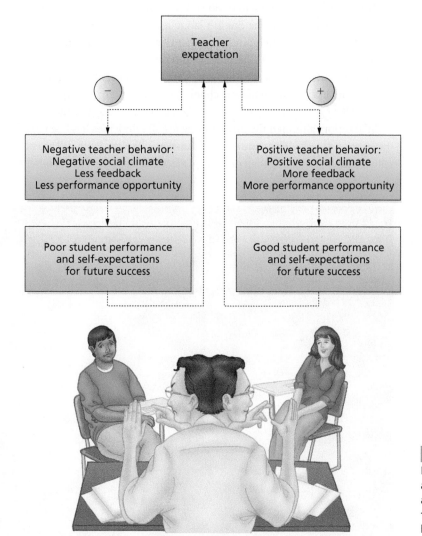

◀ **FIGURE 10-6**

Positive or negative teachers' expectations about their students can actually bring about positive or negative performance from the students. Is there a relationship between this and self-esteem?

such factors as previous school records, physical appearance, gender, or even race—transmit their expectation to the child through a complex series of verbal and nonverbal cues. These communicated expectations in turn indicate to the student what behavior is appropriate, and the student what behavior is appropriate, and the student behaves accordingly (Rosenthal, 2002; Carpenter, et al. 2004; Gewertz, 2005).

Dropping Out of School

Shawn Sturgill, 18, had a clique of his own at Shelbyville High, a dozen or so friends who sat at the same long bench in the hallway outside the cafeteria. They were, Shawn says, an average crowd. Not too rich, not too poor; not bookish, but not slow. They rarely got into trouble. Mainly they sat around and talked about Camaros and the Indianapolis Colts.

These days the bench is mostly empty. Of his dozen friends, Shawn says just one or two are still at Shelbyville High. If some cliques are defined by a common sport or a shared obsession with Yu-Gi-Oh! Cards, Shawn's friends ended up being defined by their mutual destiny: nearly all of them became high school dropouts. (Thornburgh, 2006, p. 32)

Shawn and his friends are hardly alone: Although most students complete high school, nearly one out of three public high school students drops out without graduating. The consequences of dropping out are severe. High school dropouts earn 42% less than high school graduates, and the unemployment rate for dropouts is 50%.

Adolescents who leave school do so for a variety of reasons. Some leave because of pregnancy or problems with the English language. Some leave for economic reasons, needing to support themselves or their families. Others leave because they are academically or socially disengaged (Croninger & Lee, 2001; Lee & Burkam, 2003).

Dropout rates differ according to gender and ethnicity (see Figure 10-7). Males are considerably more likely to drop out of school than females. For example, in the high school class of 2003, 72% of girls but only 65% of boys earned diplomas (Greene & Winters, 2006).

In addition, although the dropout rate for all ethnicities has been declining somewhat over the last two decades, Hispanic and African-American students still are more likely to leave high school before graduating than non-Hispanic white students. On the other hand, not all minority

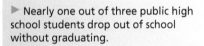

▶ Nearly one out of three public high school students drop out of school without graduating.

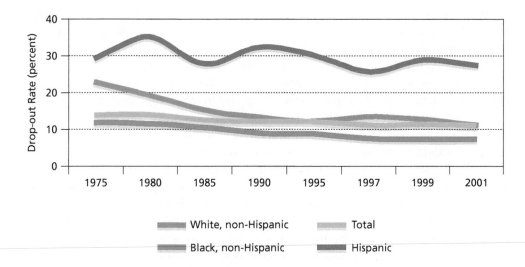

Despite the fact that dropout rates have been falling for all ethnic groups, Hispanic and African-American students are still more likely not to graduate.

(*Source:* National Center for Education Statistics, 2003).

groups show such pronounced dropout rates: Asians, for instance, drop out at rates close to those of Caucasians (National Center for Educational Statistics, 2003).

Poverty plays a large role in determining whether a student completes high school. Students from lower-income households are three times more likely to drop out than students from middle- and upper-income households. Because economic success is so dependent on education, dropping out often perpetuates a cycle of poverty (National Center for Education Statistics, 2002).

Educating Adolescents with Special Needs

When Mindie was born, physicians said she would always be hopelessly retarded, that she would never sit up, never walk, never speak. "She will never know you're her mother," they told 25-year-old Diane Crutcher. "Tell relatives your baby is dead."

Today, the child who would never sit up is a lively seventh-grader. The child who would never talk or know her own mother told a symposium of physicians she was "glad Mom and Dad gave me a chance." (Turkington, 1987, p. 42)

Although the experts were right about Mindie's level of intelligence—she does have mental retardation, scoring well below normal on IQ tests—they were clearly wrong about its significance to Mindie's life. Like millions of others with mental retardation, Mindie is attending school and is experiencing a full, rich life.

Below the Norm: Mental Retardation. Approximately 1 to 3% of the school-age population is considered mentally retarded. Estimates vary because the most widely accepted definition of mental retardation is one that leaves a great deal of room for interpretation. According to the American Association on Mental Retardation, **mental retardation** refers to disability characterized by significant limitations both in intellectual functioning and in adaptive behavior involving conceptual, social, and practical adaptive skills (AAMR, 2002).

Although limitations in intellectual functioning can be measured in a relatively straightforward manner using standard IQ tests, it is more difficult to determine how to gauge limitations in adaptive behavior. Ultimately, this imprecision leads to a lack of uniformity in the ways experts apply the label of "mental retardation." Furthermore, it has resulted in significant variation in the abilities of people who are categorized as mentally retarded. Accordingly, mentally retarded people range from those who can be taught to work and function with little special attention to those who are virtually untrainable and who never develop speech or such basic motor skills as crawling or walking.

In addition, even when objective measures such as IQ tests are used to identify mentally retarded individuals, discrimination may occur against adolescents from ethnically diverse

mental retardation a disability characterized by significant limitations both in intellectual functioning and in adaptive behavior involving conceptual, social, and practical adaptive skills

backgrounds. Most traditional intelligence tests are standardized using white, English-speaking, middle-class populations. As a result, adolescents from different cultural backgrounds may perform poorly on the tests not because they are retarded but because the tests use questions that are culturally biased in favor of majority group members.

In fact, one classic study found that in one California school district, Mexican American students were 10 times more likely than whites to be placed in special education classes (Mercer, 1973). More recent findings show that nationally, twice as many African-American students as white students are classified as mildly retarded, a difference that experts attribute primarily to cultural bias and poverty (Reschly, 1996; Ferri & Connor, 2005).

Degrees of retardation. The vast majority of the mentally retarded—some 90%—have relatively minor levels of deficits. Classified with **mild retardation,** they score in the range of 50 or 55 to 70 on IQ tests. (The average IQ score is set at 100, with approximately two thirds of the population scoring between 85 and 115.) Typically, the retardation of people with mild retardation is not even identified before they reach school, although their early development is often slower than average. Once they enter elementary school, their retardation and their need for special attention usually become apparent. With appropriate training, these students can ultimately reach a third- to sixth-grade educational level, and although they cannot carry out complex intellectual tasks, they are able to hold jobs and function independently and successfully.

Intellectual and adaptive limitations become more apparent, however, at more extreme levels of mental retardation. People whose IQ scores range from around 35 or 40 to 50 or 55 are classified as having **moderate retardation.** Accounting for 5 to 10% of those classified as mentally retarded, persons with moderate retardation display distinctive behavior early in their lives. They are slow to develop language skills, and their motor development is also affected. Regular schooling is usually not effective in training people with moderate retardation to acquire academic skills because generally they are unable to progress beyond the second-grade level. Still, they are capable of learning occupational and social skills, and they can learn to travel independently to familiar places. Typically, they require moderate levels of supervision.

At the most significant levels of retardation—in individuals with **severe retardation** (IQs ranging from around 20 or 25 to 35 or 40) and **profound retardation** (IQs below 20 or 25)—the ability to function is severely limited. Usually, such people produce little or no speech, have poor motor control, and may need 24-hour nursing care. At the same time, though, some people with severe retardation are capable of learning basic self-care skills, such as dressing and eating, and they may even develop the potential to become partially independent as adults. Still, the need for relatively high levels of care continues throughout the life span, and most severely and profoundly retarded people are institutionalized for the majority of their lives.

Mainstreaming and Full Inclusion of Adolescents with Special Needs. Are exceptional students best served by providing specialized services that separate them from their peers who do not have special needs, or do they benefit more from being integrated with their peers to the fullest extent?

If you had asked that question three decades ago, the answer would have been simple: Exceptional adolescents were assumed to do best when removed from their regular classes and placed in a class taught by a special-needs teacher. Such classes often accommodated a hodge-podge of afflictions (emotional difficulties, severe reading problems, and physical disabilities such as multiple sclerosis). In addition, they kept students segregated from the regular educational process.

However, that changed when Congress passed Public Law 94-142, the Education for All Handicapped Children Act, in the mid-1970s. The intent of the law was to ensure that students with special needs received a full education in the **least restrictive environment,** the setting most similar to that of students without special needs (Handwerk, 2002; Swain, 2004).

mild retardation retardation in which IQ scores fall in the range of 50 or 55 to 70

moderate retardation retardation in which IQ scores fall in the range of 35 or 40 to 50 or 55

severe retardation retardation in which IQ scores fall in the range of 20 or 25 to 35 or 40

profound retardation retardation in which IQ scores fall below 20 or 25

least restrictive environment the setting most similar to that of students without special needs

◀ In mainstreaming, students with special needs are integrated as much as possible into traditional classes, but are also provided with additional educational experiences.

In practice, the law has meant that students with special needs must be integrated into regular classrooms and regular activities to the greatest extent possible, as long as doing so is educationally beneficial. Students are to be isolated from the regular classroom only for subjects that are specifically affected by their exceptionality; for all other subjects, they are to be taught with nonexceptional students in regular classrooms. Of course, some students with severe handicaps still need a mostly or entirely separate education, depending on the extent of their condition. But the goal of the law is to integrate exceptional students and typical students to the fullest extent possible (Burns, 2003).

This educational approach to special education, designed to end the segregation of exceptional students as much as possible, has come to be called mainstreaming. In **mainstreaming,** exceptional adolescents are integrated as much as possible into the traditional educational system and are provided with a broad range of educational alternatives.

Mainstreaming was meant to provide a mechanism to equalize the opportunities available to all adolescents. The ultimate objective of mainstreaming was to ensure that all persons, regardless of ability or disability, had—to the greatest extent possible—opportunities to choose their goals on the basis of a full education, enabling them to obtain a fair share of life's rewards (Burns, 2003).

To some extent, the benefits extolled by proponents of mainstreaming have been realized. However, classroom teachers must receive substantial support for mainstreaming to be effective. It is not easy to teach a class in which students' abilities vary greatly. Furthermore, providing the necessary support for students with special needs is expensive, and sometimes budgetary tensions exist that pit parents of children with special needs against parents of nonexceptional children (Daly & Feldman, 1994; Jones-Harden 2004; Waite, Bromfield, & McShane, 2005).

The benefits of mainstreaming have led some professionals to promote an alternative educational model known as full inclusion. **Full inclusion** is the integration of all students, even those with the most severe disabilities, into regular classes. In such a system, separate special education programs would cease to operate. Full inclusion is controversial, and it remains to be seen how widespread the practice will become. (For more on special education instruction, see the *Career Choices* box (Hocutt, 1996; Kavale & Forness, 2000; Jacobson, Foxx, & Mulick, 2005).

mainstreaming an educational approach to special education in which exceptional adolescents are integrated as much as possible into the traditional education system and are provided with a broad range of educational alternatives

full inclusion the integration of all students, even those with the most severe disabilities, into regular classes

CAREER CHOICES

Special Education Teacher

Name: Sarah Milford Barnes

Education: BA, elementary education, Kutztown University, Kutztown, Pennsylvania; M.Ed, Lesley College, Cambridge, Massachusetts

Position: Special Education Teacher

Home: Nashua, NH

AMONG THE GREATEST challenges facing special educators is to deal effectively with students with dyslexia, according to special education teacher Sarah Barnes, a specialist in the disorder. Dyslexia represents a complex and often puzzling combination of characteristics.

"A student with dyslexia by definition is one who generally has an above-average IQ, but who is, for neurological reasons, unable to read," she said. "The student has a difficult time sequencing symbols associated with sounds. As a result, I teach students with dyslexia by breaking down the language into its simplest form and then build it up again."

One technique used by Barnes is the Orton-Gillingham multisensory method, an approach that helps teach the phonetic structure of language to students with dyslexia.

"One part of the method is teaching the six types of syllables, including closed syllables that always end in a consonant, and open syllables that always end in a vowel," she explained. "The student needs to learn to sequence the sounds of each syllable type and then use that to build on the real words.

"Building on the words is a way in which dyslexic students can crack the code of language," Barnes added. "But there is no quick fix.

It generally takes a couple of years of intensive instruction to be successful."

Although the challenges are many for a special education teacher, Barnes says she finds it rewarding in many ways.

"The special education teacher enters the profession with abundant anticipation to make a positive difference in the lives of the most needy students," she said. "The profession continues to be an honorable one. Students always learn, and their good humor adds to the quality of my life."

Thinking of becoming a special education teacher?

Teaching special education can be a highly rewarding career for individuals who are interested in helping adolescents with special needs reach their full potential. Special education instructors may teach classes with students with a variety of special needs, or they may work one-on-one with students to focus on particular areas in which they need instruction.

Special education teachers require patience and the ability to motivate students. They also need considerable knowledge of a wide variety of conditions that produce learning difficulties and awareness of alternative teaching strategies.

Special education teachers typically hold at least a bachelor's degree in special education, which requires in-classroom experience in special education. They also need to be certified to teach in their state. Many special education teachers also hold master's degrees. Because of shortages of special educators, some states provide alternative routes to licensure for people with degrees in other fields.

Above the Norm: The Gifted and Talented

Most aspiring college students wait until they are in high school to take the SAT test, but when Vino Vasudevan took them, she was only 13. Vino, a middle-school student in Lake Oswego, Oregon, at the time, was encouraged to take the test as part of the annual Johns Hopkins University search to identify gifted children. "It wasn't supereasy and it wasn't superhard," she says of the exam. "I felt like I had done okay" (Fields-Meyer, 1999, p. 63).

When her parents received her scores, friends had to tell them the significance of the results. Vino, who had come to the United States as an infant when her parents immigrated from India, had achieved perfect 800 math and 800 verbal scores, a rarity even among high school students.

gifted and talented children who give evidence of high performance capability in areas such as intellectual, creative, artistic, leadership capacity, or specific academic fields

Which students are considered to be **gifted and talented**? Although students like Vino Vasudevan clearly fit the category, little agreement exists among researchers on a single definition. However, the federal government considers the term *gifted* to include "children who give evidence of high performance capability in areas such as intellectual, creative, artistic, leadership capacity, or specific academic fields, and who require services or activities not ordinarily provided by the school in order to fully develop such capabilities" (Sec 582, P.L. 97-35). Intellectual capabilities, then, represent only one type of exceptionality; unusual potential in areas outside the academic realm are also included in the concept. Gifted and talented students have so much potential that they, no less than students with low IQs, warrant special concern—although special school programs for them are often the first to be dropped when school systems face budgetary problems (Winner, 1997; Robinson, Zigler, & Gallagher, 2000; Pfeiffer & Stocking, 2000; Schemo, 2004).

Despite the stereotypic description of the gifted—particularly those with exceptionally high intelligence—as "unsociable," "poorly adjusted," and "neurotic," most research suggests that highly intelligent people tend to be outgoing, well adjusted, and popular (Field et al., 1998; Howe, 2004).

For instance, one landmark, long-term study of 1,500 gifted students, which began in the 1920s, found that not only were the gifted smarter than average, but they were also healthier, better coordinated, and psychologically better adjusted than their less-intelligent classmates. Furthermore, their lives played out in ways that most people would envy. The subjects received more awards and distinctions, earned more money, and made many more contributions in art and literature than the average person. For instance, by the time they had reached the age of 40, they had collectively produced more than 90 books, 375 plays and short stories, and 2,000 articles, and they had registered more than 200 patents. Perhaps not surprisingly, they reported greater satisfaction with their lives than the nongifted (Terman & Oden, 1959; Sears, 1977; Shurkin, 1992; Reis & Renzulli, 2004).

▲ Gifted adolescents are generally outgoing, well adjusted, and popular

Yet, being gifted and talented is no guarantee of success in school, as we can see if we consider the particular components of the category. For example, the verbal abilities that allow the eloquent expression of ideas and feelings can equally permit the expression of glib and persuasive statements that happen to be inaccurate. Furthermore, teachers may sometimes misinterpret the humor, novelty, and creativity of unusually gifted students, regarding their intellectual fervor as disruptive or inappropriate. And peers are not always sympathetic: Some very bright students try to hide their intelligence in an effort to fit in better with other students (Swiatek, 2002).

Educating the Gifted and Talented. Educators have devised two approaches to teaching the gifted and talented: acceleration and enrichment. **Acceleration** allows gifted students to move ahead at their own pace, even if this means skipping to higher grade levels. The materials that students receive under acceleration programs are not necessarily different from those that other students receive; they simply are provided at a faster pace than for the average student (Passow, 1996; Algozzine & Ysseldyke, 2006).

An alternative approach is **enrichment,** through which students are kept at grade level but are enrolled in special programs and given individual activities to allow greater depth of study on a given topic. In enrichment, the material provided to gifted students differs not only in the timing of its presentation, but in its sophistication as well. Thus, enrichment materials are designed to provide an intellectual challenge to the gifted student, encouraging higher-order thinking (Worrell, Szarko, & Gabelko, 2001; Rotigel, 2003; Callahan & Kyburg, 2005).

acceleration an educational approach that allows gifted students to move ahead at their own pace, even if this means skipping to higher grade levels

enrichment an alternative approach to acceleration through which students are kept at grade level but are enrolled in special programs and given individual activities to allow greater depth of study on a given topic

Acceleration programs can be remarkably effective. Most studies have shown that gifted students who begin school even considerably earlier than their age-mates do as well as or better than those who begin at the traditional age. One of the best illustrations of the benefits of acceleration is the "Study of Mathematically Precocious Youth," an ongoing program at Vanderbilt University. In this program, seventh- and eighth-graders who have unusual abilities in mathematics participate in a variety of special classes and workshops. The results have been nothing short of sensational, with students successfully completing college courses and sometimes even enrolling in college early. Some students have even graduated from college before the age of 18 (Lubinski & Benbow, 2001; Webb, Lubinski, & Benbow, 2002).

Review and Apply

Review

1. Performance in school depends on a number of factors, including socioeconomic status, race/ethnicity, the attributions that parents and students associate with school success, and the expectations that teachers have regarding the abilities of their students.

2. Gender also affects performance, with the performance of boys presenting particular challenges.

3. Much recent activity intended to improve U.S. schooling has focused on standardized testing of students in the key academic areas, especially testing under the No Child Left Behind Act.

4. Students with special needs represent a significant proportion of the school-age population and, since the passage of PL 94-142 in the mid-1970s, are often included in regular classrooms.

5. Gifted and talented students are sometimes given special educational opportunities under either acceleration or enrichment approaches.

Apply

1. How might attribution patterns that contribute to underperformance and a lack of effort be changed? Does popular culture add to the impression that success and failure are attributable to external factors over which students have no control?

2. Have Title IX and other programs intended to improve educational access for females gone too far? Should there now be a similar emphasis on improving education for males, or should all gender-based efforts be eliminated?

Beyond High School: The Pursuit of Higher Education

F or Enrico Vasquez, there was never any doubt: He was headed for college. Enrico, the son of a wealthy Cuban immigrant who had made a fortune in the medical supply business after fleeing Cuba 5 years before Enrico's birth, has had the importance of education constantly drummed into him by his family. In fact, the question was never whether he would go to college but what college he would be able to get into. As a consequence, Enrico found high school to be a pressure cooker: Every grade and extracurricular activity was evaluated in terms of its helping or hindering his chances of admission to a good college.

■ ■ ■

Armando Williams's letter of acceptance to Dallas County Community College is framed on the wall of his mother's apartment. To her, the letter represents nothing short of a miracle, an answer to her prayers. Growing up in a neighborhood infamous for its drugs and drive-by shootings, Armando had always been a hard worker and a "good boy," in his mother's view. But when he was growing up, she never even entertained the possibility of his making it to college. To see him reach this stage in his education fills her with joy.

Whether a student's enrollment seems almost inevitable or signifies a triumph over the odds, attending college is a significant accomplishment. Although students already enrolled may feel that college attendance is nearly universal, this is not the case at all: Nationwide, only a minority of high school graduates enter college.

Furthermore, even for students for whom college was an inevitability, getting admitted to college may become a process that produces significant stress. Students who apply to colleges that accept only a small proportion of applicants may experience considerable anxiety as they await notification of which colleges will accept them. This stress, some of which is self-generated and some of which comes from family and peer pressure, can make the senior year of high school quite trying, as these blog excerpts suggest:

Desperately need help choosing college!!! Need advice please read!!! Can't sleep!!

Thank you O powerful (and treacherous) college gods for nothing but my current state of depression and anxiousness.

In this final part of the chapter, we'll consider who goes to college and discuss some of the issues that relate to college attendance.

Who Goes to College?

As in the U.S. population as a whole, U.S. college students are primarily white and middle class. Although nearly 69% of white high school graduates enter college, only 61% of African-American and 47% of Hispanic graduates do so (see Figure 10-8). Even more striking, although the absolute number of minority students enrolled in college has increased, the overall *proportion* of the minority population that does enter college has *decreased* over the past decade—a decline that most education experts attribute to changes in the availability of financial aid (U.S. Bureau of the Census, 1998, 2000).

Furthermore, the proportion of students who enter college but ultimately never graduate is substantial. Only around 40% of those who start college finish 4 years later with a degree. Although about half of those who don't receive a degree in four years eventually do finish, the other

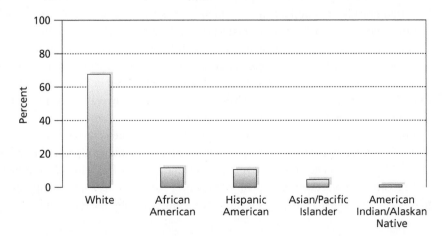

◀ **FIGURE 10-8**

The proportion of African Americans and Hispanics who enter college after graduating from high school is lower than the proportion of whites.

(*Source: The Condition of Education 2004*, National Center for Education Statistics, 2004).

half never obtain a college degree. For minorities, the picture is even worse: The national dropout rate for African-American college students stands at 70% (Minorities in Higher Education, 1995; American College Testing Program, 2001).

These observations notwithstanding, the number of students traditionally classified as "minorities" attending college is rising dramatically, and ethnic and racial minorities make up an increasingly larger proportion of the college population. Already at some colleges, such as the University of California at Berkeley, whites have shifted from the majority to the minority, as diversity among the students has increased significantly. These trends, reflecting changes in the racial and ethnic composition of the United States, are significant because higher education remains an important way for families to improve their economic well-being.

Gender in the Classroom

I registered for a calculus course my first year at DePauw. Even twenty years ago I was not timid, so on the very first day I raised my hand and asked a question. I still have a vivid memory of the professor rolling his eyes, hitting his head with his hand in frustration, and announcing to everyone, "Why do they expect me to teach calculus to girls?" I never asked another question. Several weeks later I went to a football game, but I had forgotten to bring my ID. My calculus professor was at the gate checking IDs, so I went up to him and said, "I forgot my ID but you know me, I'm in your class." He looked right at me and said, "I don't remember you in my class." I couldn't believe that someone who changed my life and whom I remember to this day didn't even recognize me. (Sadker & Sadker, 1994, p. 162)

Although such incidents of blatant sexism are less likely to occur today, prejudice and discrimination directed at women are still a fact of college life. For instance, the next time you are in class, consider the gender of your classmates and the subject matter of the class. Although men and women attend college in roughly equal numbers, there is significant variation in the classes they take. Classes in education and the social sciences, for instance, typically have a larger proportion of women than men; and classes in engineering, the physical sciences, and mathematics tend to have more men than women.

The gender gap is also apparent when we look at college instructors. Although the number of female faculty members has increased, there is still evidence of discrimination. For example, the more prestigious the institution, the smaller the proportion of women who have attained the highest rank. The situation is even more pronounced in the fields of math, science, and engineering, where women are significantly underrepresented (Wilson, 2004).

The persistent differences in gender distribution across subject areas likely reflect the powerful influence of gender stereotypes that operate throughout the world of education and beyond. For instance, when women in their first year of college are asked to name a likely career choice, they are much less apt to choose careers that have traditionally been dominated by men, such as engineering or computer programming, and more likely to choose professions that have traditionally been populated by women, such as nursing and social work (Glick, Zion, & Nelson, 1988; Cooperative Institutional Research Program, 1990; Avalon, 2003).

Male and female college students also have different expectations regarding their areas of competence. For instance, one survey asked first-year college students whether they were above or below average on a variety of traits and abilities. As can be seen in Figure 10-9, men were more likely than women to think of themselves as above average in overall academic and mathematical ability, competitiveness, and emotional health.

Both male and female college professors treat men and women differently in their classes, even though the different treatment is largely unintentional, and often the professors are unaware of their actions. For instance, professors call on men in class more frequently than women, and they make more eye contact with men than with women. Furthermore, male students are more likely to receive extra help from their professors than women. Finally, the male students often receive

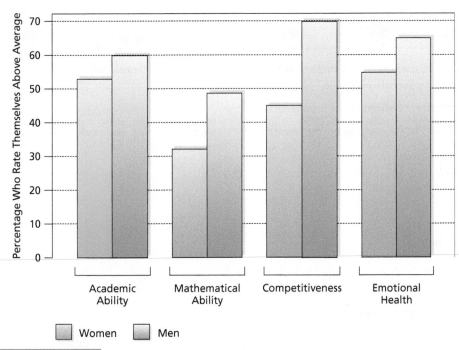

▲ FIGURE 10-9

During their first year of college, men are more likely than women to view themselves as above average in areas relevant to academic success.

(*Source:* Sax et al., 2000).

more positive reinforcement for their comments than female students—exemplified by the startling illustration in Table 10-2 (American Association of University Women, 1992; Epperson, 1988; Sadker & Sadker, 1994, 2005).

The different treatment of men and women in the classroom has led some educators to argue in favor of single-sex education for women. They point to evidence that the rate of participation and ultimately the success of women in the sciences is greater for graduates of women's colleges than for graduates of coeducational institutions. Furthermore, some research suggests that women who attend same-sex colleges may show higher self-esteem than those attending coeducational colleges, although the evidence is not entirely consistent on this count (Mael, 1998; Sax, 2005).

Why might women do better in single-sex environments? One reason is that they receive more attention than they would in coeducational settings, where professors are affected, however inadvertently, by societal biases. In addition, women's colleges tend to have more female professors than coeducational institutions, and they thereby provide more role models for women. Finally, women attending women's colleges may receive more encouragement for participation in nontraditional subjects such as mathematics and science than those in coeducational colleges (Robinson & Gillibrand, 2004).

Overcoming Gender and Racial Barriers to Achievement

In her 10th-grade math class, Frankie Teague dimmed the lights, switched on soothing music and handed each student a white board and a marker. Then, she projected an arithmetic problem onto a screen at the front of the room.

"As soon as you get the answer, hold up your board," she said, setting off a round of squeaky scribbling. The simple step of having students hold up their work, instead of raising their

TABLE 10-2	Gender Bias in the Classroom

The course on the U.S. Constitution is required for graduation, and more than 50 students, approximately half male and half female, file in. The professor begins by asking if there are questions on next week's midterm. Several hands go up.

BERNIE: Do you have to memorize names and dates in the book? Or will the test be more general?

PROFESSOR: You do have to know those critical dates and people. Not every one but the important ones. If I were you, Bernie, I would spend time learning them. Ellen?

ELLEN: What kind of short-answer questions will there be?

PROFESSOR: All multiple choice.

ELLEN: Will we have the whole class time?

PROFESSOR: Yes, we'll have the whole class time. Anyone else?

BEN (calling out): Will there be an extra-credit question?

PROFESSOR: I hadn't planned on it. What do you think?

BEN: I really like them. They take some of the pressure off. You can also see who is doing extra work.

PROFESSOR: I'll take it under advisement, Charles?

CHARLES: How much of our final grade is this?

PROFESSOR: The midterm is 25 percent. But remember, class participation counts as well. Why don't we begin?

The professor lectures on the Constitution for twenty minutes before he asks a question about the electoral college. The electoral college is not as hot a topic as the midterm, so only four hands are raised. The professor calls on Ben.

BEN: The electoral college was created because there was a lack of faith in the people. Rather than have them vote for the president, they voted for the electors.

PROFESSOR: I like the way you think. (He smiles at Ben, and Ben smiles back.) Who could vote? (Five hands go up, five out of fifty.) Angie?

ANGIE: I don't know if this is right, but I thought only men could vote.

BEN (calling out): That was a great idea. We began going downhill when we let women vote. (Angie looks surprised but says nothing. Some of the students laugh, and so does the professor. He calls on Barbara.)

BARBARA: I think you had to be pretty wealthy, own property—

JOSH (not waiting for Barbara to finish, calls out): That's right. There was a distrust of the poor, who could upset the democracy. But if you had property, if you had something at stake, you could be trusted not to do something wild. Only property owners could be trusted.

PROFESSOR: Nice job, Josh. But why do we still have electors today? Mike?

MIKE: Tradition, I guess.

PROFESSOR: Do you think it's tradition? If you walked down the street and asked people their views of the electoral college, what would they say?

MIKE: Probably they'd be clueless. Maybe they would think that it elects the Pope. People don't know how it works.

PROFESSOR: Good, Mike. Judy, do you want to say something? (Judy's hand is at "half-mast," raised but just barely. When the professor calls her name, she looks a bit startled.)

JUDY (speaking very softly): Maybe we would need a whole new constitutional convention to change it. And once they get together to change that, they could change anything. That frightens people, doesn't it? (As Judy speaks, a number of students fidget, pass notes, and leaf through their books; a few even begin to whisper.)

(*Source:* Sadker & Sadker, 1994)

hands or shouting out the answer, gives a leg up to a group of pupils who have long lagged in math classes—girls. (Whalen & Begley, 2005, p. A1)

This simple innovation is part of a large-scale, and ultimately successful, effort in England to improve the teaching of math. Although meant to benefit all students, it has had an unintended result: erasing a gender gap that favored boys over girls in math performance.

As illustrated in Figure 10-10, the introduction of the new math curriculum in the late 1980s brought about a rise in overall math exam scores. But the rise was more pronounced for girls, and today girls outperform boys on some standardized math tests.

What changes in the curriculum led to the improvement in performance? Teachers were taught to be on the alert for gender stereotyping in their courses, and they were encouraged to include girls in discussions more vigorously. In addition, gender stereotypes were removed from textbooks. Classrooms were made "safer" for girls by discouraging students from shouting out answers and by encouraging girls more directly to participate. Tests were changed, too, to give partial credit when students write out their thinking—something that benefited girls, who tend to be more methodical when working on test items.

Academic Performance and Stereotype Threat.   Research on gender stereotypes suggests that the curricular changes adopted in England are moving in the right direction. For instance, consider this fact: When women take college classes in math, science, and engineering, they are more likely to do poorly than men who enter college with the same level of preparation and identical SAT scores. Strangely, however, this phenomenon does not hold true for other areas of the curriculum, where men and women perform at similar levels.

According to psychologist Claude Steele, the reason has to do with women's acceptance of society's stereotypes about achievement in particular domains. Steele suggested that women are no strangers to society's dominant view that some subjects are more appropriate areas of study for women than are others. In fact, the pervasiveness of the stereotype makes women who attempt to achieve in traditionally "inappropriate" fields highly vulnerable (Steele, 1997; Suzuki & Aronson, 2005).

Specifically, because of the strength and pervasiveness of such stereotypes, the performance of women seeking to achieve in nontraditional fields may be hindered as they are distracted by worries about the failure that society predicts for them. In some cases, a woman may decide that

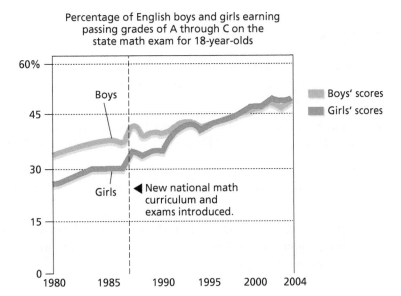

Percentage of English boys and girls earning passing grades of A through C on the state math exam for 18-year-olds

◀ **FIGURE 10-10**

Following the introduction of a new math curriculum and exams in England, the performance of girls and boys began to converge.

(*Source:* Department for Education and Skills, England, 2004.)

failure in a male-dominated field, because it would confirm societal stereotypes, would be so unpalatable that the struggle to succeed is not worth the effort. In that instance, the woman may not even try very hard.

But there is a bright side to Steele's analysis: If women can be convinced that societal stereotypes regarding achievement are invalid, their performance might well improve. And in fact, this is just what Steele found in a series of experiments he conducted at the University of Michigan and Stanford University (Steele, 1994).

In one study, male and female college students were told they would be taking two math tests: one in which there were gender differences—men supposedly performed better than women—and a second in which there were no gender differences. In reality, the tests were entirely similar, drawn from the same pool of difficult items. The reasoning behind the experimental manipulation was that women would be vulnerable to societal stereotypes on a test that they thought supported those stereotypes but would not be vulnerable on a test supposedly lacking gender differences.

The results fully supported Steele's reasoning. When the women were told there were gender differences in the test, they greatly underperformed the men. But when they were told there were no gender differences, they performed virtually the same as the men.

In short, the evidence from this study and others clearly suggests that women are vulnerable to expectations regarding their future success, whether the expectations come from societal stereotypes or from information about the prior performance of women on similar tasks. More encouraging, the evidence suggests that if women can be convinced that other women have been successful in given domains, they may overcome even long-standing societal stereotypes (Croizet et al., 2004; Davies, Spencer, & Steele, 2005).

We should also keep in mind that women are not the only group susceptible to society's stereotyping. Members of minority groups, such as African Americans and Hispanic Americans, are also vulnerable to stereotypes about academic success. In fact, Steele suggests that African Americans may "disidentify" with academic success by putting forth less effort on academic tasks and generally downgrading the importance of academic achievement. Ultimately, such disidentification may act as a self-fulfilling prophecy, increasing the chances of academic failure (Perry, Steele, & Hilliard, 2003; Ryan & Ryan, 2005).

Review and Apply

Review

1. African-American and Hispanic high school graduates enroll in colleges in lower proportions than white high school graduates, a situation attributable in part to declining financial aid for college attendance.

2. Overall, however, the number of students from minority groups attending college is on the rise, and their proportions within the college population are growing.

3. There are significant gender differences in collegiate education, which affect course and major selections, treatment in class, and expectations for success, especially in science and math.

4. The phenomenon of stereotype threat—by which societal stereotypes influence individuals' attitudes, expectations, and performance—negatively affects women and members of minority groups attending college.

Apply

1. Are male and female college students still treated differently by professors? If so, how can this situation be changed at the campus level?

2. If there is a stereotype threat to students expected to perform poorly in college, is there a "stereotype boost" for students from groups expected to perform well? If so, is this a good or a bad thing?

EPILOGUE

In this chapter we considered education during adolescence, from middle school to college. We began by discussing the history and justification of the middle school movement and examining the outcomes of this approach to early adolescent education. We also looked at several ways in which schools deal with diversity and multiculturalism, and we examined the recent phenomenon of homeschooling. Next we discussed some of the factors that affect school performance and academic success, considering both external factors such as socioeconomic status and internal factors such as teacher expectancies. We also looked at how adolescents with special needs are educated in public schools. We finished the chapter by moving on to college, where we looked at factors that influence college attendance and success. We found that racial and gender barriers continue to be a reality, despite recent improvements.

Before we proceed to the next chapter, recall the bustling environment at Fritsche Middle School that we discussed in the Prologue. Consider the following questions.

1. Do the factors that caused educators decades ago to create middle schools as a way to separate young adolescents from older and younger students still exist? Have they changed in any way? Is middle school still a good idea?

2. What aspects of early adolescent development are apparent in the description of a day at the Fritsche Middle School? How might these adolescents be different in two or three years when they reach later adolescence?

3. If you ran this middle school, would you try to ensure that students with special needs participated in the range of activities described? How would you do this?

4. Some educators, politicians, and parents believe that middle school (and high school) should focus more on core academic subjects than on the diffuse variety of arts and music courses described in the prologue. What do you think of this idea?

SUMMARY

REVIEW

● **What models of schooling are used with adolescents, and what are their effects?**
(p. 313)

1. Adolescents must deal with the transition from elementary school to some form of secondary school, which is particularly challenging because they have to manage a range of developmental changes at around the same time.

2. The typical postelementary level of schooling is the middle school, which was created to take account of adolescents' developmental needs while also meeting their educational needs. It has had mixed success doing this.

3. Multicultural education is based on the understanding that U.S. society is pluralistic, consisting of diverse cultural groups with traditions and heritages that merit respect.

4. Bilingual education has been shown to have positive effects for those who are learning to speak English as well as those for whom English is the first language.

5. Homeschooling is a recent development chosen by parents and children who believe that the home environment provides a superior academic education and a more supportive framework for developing values.

● **What factors have the most influence on school performance?** *(p. 332)*

6. Many factors beyond simple ability and instructional quality influence student academic performance, including socioeconomic status (and the related factors of race and ethnicity), gender, and teacher expectations.

7. The attributions that students apply to academic success also influence school performance, especially whether the students attribute success and failure to internal, changeable factors (such as effort) or external, unchangeable factors (such as bias).

8. Supporters of standardized testing argue that testing can positively influence education by identifying low-performing schools and teachers.

● **What approaches are used for educating adolescents with special needs?** *(p. 333)*

9. Students with special needs can benefit from schooling beyond levels expected several decades ago.

10. Mainstreaming and inclusion programs aim to provide for students with special needs an education in the least restrictive environment, which frequently means the regular school classroom.

11. Gifted and talented students can benefit from special programs taking either an acceleration or an enrichment approach.

● **What factors affect college attendance and performance by women and minorities?** *(p. 339)*

12. Despite a rise in the proportion of the college population represented by minority students, fewer African-American and Hispanic high school graduates enroll in and graduate from college than white high school graduates.

13. Even though women represent a majority of the students in colleges nationwide, gender stereotyping remains a persistent problem that affects choice of classes, treatment by professors, and student expectations for success.

14. Stereotype threat affects women and members of minority groups in college by negatively influencing expectations for success, especially in nontraditional fields.

KEY TERMS AND CONCEPTS

multicultural education (p. 318)

cultural assimilation model (p. 318)

pluralistic society model (p. 318)

bicultural identity (p. 319)

home schooling (p. 320)

teacher expectancy effect (p. 331)

mental retardation (p. 333)

mild retardation (p. 334)

moderate retardation (p. 334)

severe retardation (p. 334)

profound retardation (p. 334)

least restrictive environment (p. 334)

mainstreaming (p. 335)

full inclusion (p. 335)

gifted and talented (p. 336)

acceleration (p. 337)

enrichment (p. 337)

11 Work and Leisure

CHAPTER OUTLINE

PROLOGUE

I T'S 9:30 P.M., AND Stephen and Georgina Cox know exactly where their children are. Well, their bodies, at least. Piers, 14, is holed up in his bedroom—eyes fixed on his computer screen—where he has been logged onto a MySpace chat room and AOL Instant Messenger (IM) for the past three hours. His twin sister Bronte is planted in the living room, having commandeered her dad's iMac—as usual. She, too, is busily IMing, while chatting on her cell phone and chipping away at homework. . . .

Zooming in on Piers' screen gives a pretty good indication of what's on his hyperkinetic mind. O.K., there's a Google Images window open, where he's chasing down pictures of Keira Knightley. Good ones get added to a snazzy Windows Media Player slide show that serves as his personal e-shrine to the actress. Several IM windows are also open, revealing such penetrating conversations as this one with a MySpace pal:

MySpacer: suuuuuup (Translation: What's up?)

Piers: wat up dude.

MySpacer: nmu (Not much. You?)

Piers: same

Naturally, iTunes is open, and Piers is blasting a mix of Queen, AC/DC, classic rock and hip-hop. Somewhere on the screen there's a Word file, in which Piers is writing an essay for English class. "I usually finish my homework at school," he explains to a visitor, "but if not, I pop a book open on my lap in my room, and while the computer is loading, I'll do a problem or write a sentence. Then, while mail is loading, I do more. I get it done a little bit at a time." (Wallis, 2006, pp. 49–50) ■

 ABOUT THIS

EXCEPT FOR THEIR occasional attention to their homework, multitasking twins Piers and Bronte Cox are passing their evening in activities that didn't even exist a decade ago. The MySpace chat room, Instant Messenger, Windows Media Player, and iTunes are each thoroughly 21st-century pastimes.

Yet their juggling of schoolwork and leisure activities is hardly unique to this era. One of the important challenges adolescents consistently face is meeting the multiple demands on their time, whether stemming from school, their choices of leisure activities, or employers.

In this chapter, we consider leisure and work. We begin by looking at how adolescents spend their time, both in the United States and in other cultures. We pay special attention to the media, because so much of adolescents' leisure time is spent virtually interacting with the world by using computers, watching television, and even playing video games.

Next we turn to a discussion of adolescents who work for pay. We consider the pros and cons of working while attending school, and we look at youth who enter the workforce full time during adolescence. We also address the question of whether involvement in work builds character.

Finally, we discuss how adolescents identify the career path they wish to follow. We look at various perspectives on career development, as well as how socioeconomic status, gender, race, and ethnicity affect job choices and aspirations. ■

After reading this chapter,

YOU WILL BE ABLE TO
ANSWER THESE QUESTIONS:

- What do adolescents in the United States and other cultures do with their time?
- How has increased access to media and technology affected adolescents' lives?
- What are the effects of working while attending school?
- Are schools doing enough to prepare adolescents for the workforce?
- What factors influence an adolescent's choice of a career?

Time and Leisure

For fun I like doing things outside, like playing sports. I played football for my high school and I also did a lot of drama classes. I was in chorus. I love acting and singing and pretty much being on stage. I love hanging out with friends and going to parties and cookouts or camping—anything to do with a lot of people . . . So anything fun that can make me laugh or make someone around me laugh I like. I also love going to the movies or out to eat.

The leisure time of this highly social adolescent is filled with a swirl of group activities. For others, leisure time is occupied by more solitary interests, with more hours spent in front of a computer screen than in the presence of other people. For still others, especially the many adolescents who are employed, leisure time is a rare commodity.

Whatever they choose to do, most adolescents have a considerable amount of time outside of school that they get to carve up as they like. In fact, although they may think of their time as being consumed by school and homework, adolescents actually spend only a minority of their waking hours in education-related activities.

What *are* adolescents doing with their time? Surprisingly, it's a question that has been addressed systematically only recently, because most adolescent specialists assumed that schooling was the predominant influence on adolescent development. But it's becoming increasingly clear that we need to better understand how adolescents spend their non-school-related time to get a complete picture of the major influences on adolescent development. To do that, adolescent scientists have used a variety of techniques designed to understand just what adolescents are doing.

Spending Time

It's not easy to know with precision what adolescents are doing. The easiest technique—simply asking them what they've been doing—is not always the most precise. Consider, for example, how you would respond if you were asked to pinpoint to the minute what you did yesterday. Although you might be able to broadly define your activities, many of the details would probably be lost. (For instance, just how often and how long did you spend checking your e-mail throughout the day?)

To overcome the problem, social scientists have devised methodologies that go beyond mere questionnaires. For example, one increasingly common technique is the Experience Sampling Method in which study participants wear an alarm watch that is remotely signaled to sound once every two hours during participants' waking hours. When the alarm sounds, participants complete a self-report form that asks what they are doing, the situation, and their emotional state. Because the Experience Sampling Method relies less on memory and more on immediate self-report, it has proven a reliable measure of how adolescents use their time (Csikszentmihalyi & Larson, 1992; Chen, 2006; Green et al., 2006).

Using the Experience Sampling Method, researchers have found that suburban, middle-class white adolescents spend, on average, almost half their time in leisure activities. Furthermore, some 29% is spent in "productive" activities such as school, homework, and paid work. Another quarter or so is spent on "maintenance" activities such as eating, transportation, chores and errands, and personal maintenance such as personal hygiene (Larson et al., 2001; see Figure 11-1).

On the other hand, there are significant racial and cultural differences and individual differences. For example, compared to their white suburban counterparts, poor African-American adolescents living in urban areas spend somewhat less time on productive activities and somewhat more on leisure activities, especially viewing television (18%, compared with 13% of the white sample) (Larson et al., 2001).

Furthermore, adolescents fall into several broad categories in terms of time use relating to the specific activities in which they participate. More than half are quite busy, spending significant amounts of time on homework, extracurricular activities, time with friends after school and on weekends, chores, and sometimes paid work. On the other hand, around a third of adolescents spend time on only one or just a few activities, such as primarily engaging in paid employment, with little or no engagement in extracurricular activities. Another group spends most of their time hanging out with friends, and neither work nor participate in extracurricular activities (Shanahan & Flaherty, 2001).

In addition, some adolescents' time investments change according to their age. For instance, as they become older, they are more likely to spend a greater proportion of their time working. On the other hand, individuals who were highly involved in many activities as younger adolescents usually remain busy throughout adolescence. Similarly, those who were less busy and were

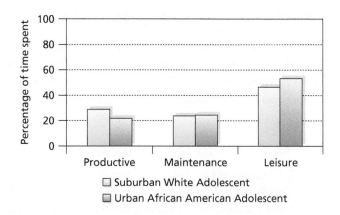

◄ FIGURE 11-1

According to the Experience Sampling Method, suburban middle-class white adolescents differ from poor African Americans in terms of how they spend their time.

(*Source:* Larson et al., 2001, Table 2.)

involved in a small number of domains continue to be involved in only a few domains. But the less-busy adolescents often shift their interests over the course of adolescence (Shanahan & Flaherty, 2001).

The overall degree of time use is related to adolescent success. Busier adolescents tend to be more successful academically. They have higher grades and are better adjusted than those who are committed to fewer tasks. Busier adolescents are particularly better off than adolescents who spend minimal time in academic-related pursuits and more time in work (Shanahan & Flaherty, 2001; Mortimer, 2003).

The findings from research using both the Experience Sampling Method and questionnaire studies show that adolescents' use of time is not a zero-sum situation in which participation in one domain displaces participation in another domain. Instead, some adolescents are very busy, and others are not. Furthermore, some adolescents are carrying out multiple tasks simultaneously. Indeed, popular wisdom suggests that adolescents are particularly accomplished multitaskers. Is that true?

Shifting Attention: This is Your Brain on Multitasking

When an adolescent like Piers Cox, described in the chapter Prologue, is simultaneously using Instant Messaging, listening to iTunes, and writing a paper for class, is there a particular part of the brain that permits him to multitask in this way? More broadly, are adolescents, more than adults, adept at multitasking?

The answer to both questions is no. No one's brain—even one belonging to the most practiced multitasking adolescent—is designed to allow for the simultaneous processing of information in multiple channels. Instead, the brain switches back and forth between different media sources, prioritizing the information that is of greatest interest and importance. Although some highly routine tasks can be done simultaneously—like chewing gum and walking—most tasks are performed sequentially. Solving calculus problems while reading a history book, or even talking on a cell phone while driving, can be challenging propositions (Rosen et al., 2003).

According to functional magnetic resonance imaging (fMRI) studies, the brain's anterior prefrontal cortex is responsible for switching attention from one task to another (see Figure 11-2). One part in particular permits adolescents (as well as the rest of us) to return to tasks that they have already started and take up where they left off. The prefrontal cortex is one of the last areas of the brain to mature, suggesting that younger adolescents may be less efficient at multitasking than older ones (Koechlin et al., 1999; Wallis, 2006).

However, even the most adept multitaskers are limited by the hardwired nature of the brain in their efforts to switch among different activities. The more tasks that individuals seek to accomplish, the greater the difficulties they encounter. Not only do errors increase, but also efficiency plummets. Consequently, it takes longer to complete tasks when alternating between them than when doing them sequentially (Rubenstein, Meyer, & Evans, 2001; Meyer et al., 2002; Luria & Meiran, 2005).

In short, despite popular wisdom that contemporary adolescents are particularly proficient at multitasking, there's no evidence showing that they do it better than adults. They may multitask more frequently, but they suffer from the same limitations as older people. The brain simply does not have the wiring to allow great success at multitasking.

Cross-Cultural Differences in Time Use

Significant differences in adolescents' use of time emerge when we look across different cultures. This is hardly surprising, given cross-cultural differences in educational systems and in the likelihood that a student will be working full time during adolescence.

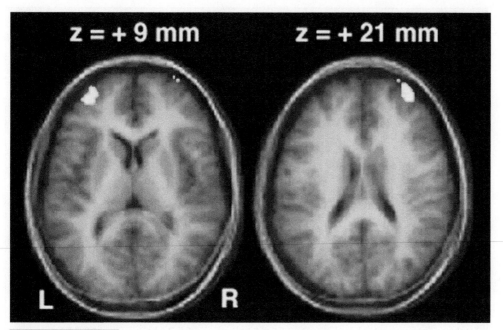

Two regions, located symmetrically, in these right and left brain scans show the switching of attention from one task to another.
(*Source*: Koechlin et al., 1999.)

In general, adolescents in nonindustrial, developing societies are more likely to be involved in a substantial amount of household labor than those in developed societies. Furthermore, they are likely to have less free time.

Moreover, adolescents in East Asian postindustrial societies shift the time gained from not working to academic pursuits, whereas adolescents in North America shift their freed-up time to leisure activities. Overall, adolescents in the United States spend 40 to 50% of their time during the school year on discretionary activities, compared with 25 to 35% in East Asia and 35 to 45% in European countries (Larson & Verma, 1999; see Table 11-1).

The greater amount of flexible time at the disposal of U.S. adolescents is not necessarily conducive to optimal development. Because discretionary activities often include high levels of television viewing and other media use—which, as we discuss later, may produce some significantly undesirable consequences—having more spare time is not necessarily advantageous.

We'll begin our consideration of how adolescents use their time by focusing on the impact of various types of media, which have significant consequences on teenagers. Later we'll look at after-school employment, another large consumer of adolescents' time.

Media and Technology Use by Adolescents

Dominique Jones, 12, of Los Angeles, likes to IM her friends before school to find out what they plan to wear. "You'll get IMs back that say things like 'Oh, my God, I'm wearing the same shoes!' After school we talk about what happened that day, what outfits we want to wear the next day."
(Wallis, 2006, p. 55)

Instant Messaging (IMing) is only one of the enormous variety of media and technologies available to adolescents, ranging from more traditional sorts, such as radio and television, to newer forms, such as Instant Messaging, cell phones, and MP3 players. And adolescents make use of them—to a staggering degree.

According to a comprehensive survey using a sample of boys and girls 8 to 18 years old conducted by the Kaiser Family Foundation (a well-respected think tank), young people spend an average of 6.5 hours a day with media. Furthermore, because around a quarter of the time they

	Nonindustrial, unschooled population	Postindustrial, schooled population		
Activity		**North America**	**Europe**	**East Asia**
Household labor	5–9 hr	20–40 min	20–40 min	10–20 min
Paid labor	0.5–8 hr	40–60 min	10–20 min	0–10 min
Schoolwork	—	3.0–4.5 hr	4.0–5.5 hr	5.5–7.5 hr
Total work time	6–9 hr	4–6 hr	4.5–6.5 hr	6–8 hr
TV viewing	*insufficient data*	1.5–2.5 hr	1.5–2.5 hr	1.5–2.5 hr
Talking	*insufficient data*	2–3 hr	*insufficient data*	45–60 min
Sports	*insufficient data*	30–60 min	20–80 min	0–20 min
Other active structured leisure activities	*insufficient data*	10–20 min	10–20 min	0–10 min
Total free time	4–7 hr	6.5–8.0 hr	5.5–7.5 hr	4.0–5.5 hr

TABLE 11-1 Estimates of the Time That Adolescents Spend in Activities Per Day

Note. Estimates are averaged across a 7-day week, including weekdays and weekends.

are using more than one form of medium simultaneously, they are actually being exposed to the equivalent of eight-and-a-half hours per day (Rideout, Roberts, & Foehr, 2005; see Figure 11-3).

In fact, these figures probably underestimate media use by teenagers for at least two reasons. First, the sample included preteens, many of whom likely have less opportunity and access to media than do older youth. Second, the survey was conducted in 2003 and 2004, meaning that some technologies, such as Instant Messaging, were not as widespread as they are now. It seems reasonable, then, that media use is even more extensive than initially found in the survey.

These varied media play a number of significant functions in adolescents' lives. Not only do media provide entertainment and information, but they also help adolescents cope with the stress of everyday life. Losing oneself in a television show or CD can be a way of escaping from one's current problems.

In addition, the media provide models and a sense of norms that are operating among other adolescents. Teenagers watching MTV's popular music program *Total Request Live* not only are exposed to major musical artists, but they can also view how their peers in the audience look, dress, and behave (Arnett, 1995; Head, 2005).

Clearly, the media play a number of roles in adolescents' lives. Let's look at some of the specific types of media to which teenagers are exposed and consider their consequences.

Viewing Television. Despite the proliferation of new technologies, television viewing remains the most frequent activity. Although figures on actual exposure to television vary significantly depending on how viewing is assessed, television use is substantial, averaging around 3 hours a day. There is some change with age, though: Older adolescents watch somewhat less television than younger adolescents, in part because older adolescents begin to have more time-consuming responsibilities, such as homework and work. In addition, older adolescents have greater mobility, permitting them to leave home to participate in other activities more easily (Roberts, Henriksen, & Foehr, 2004).

It's certainly easy for adolescents to watch television, given that two thirds of U.S. 8- to 18-year-olds have television sets in their bedrooms. But not all of that viewing is particularly

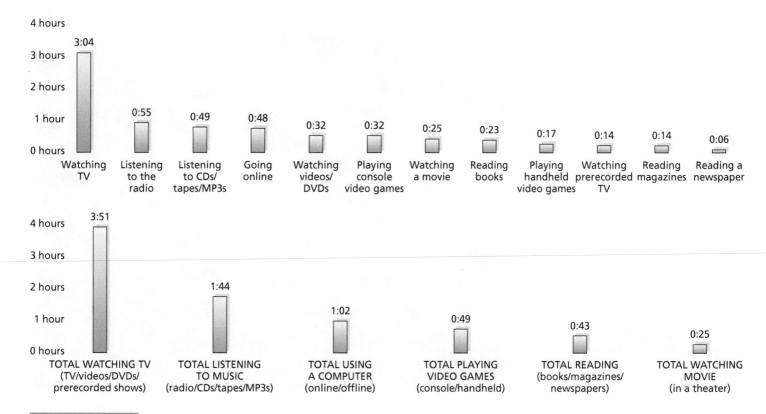

Time Spent with Media in a Typical Day   One comprehensive study by the Kaiser Family Foundation has shown that young people spend more than 6.5 hours a day interacting with various media.

(*Source:* Rideout et al., 2005).

attentive. Sometimes adolescents leave the television on and only monitor what is going on, rather than paying careful attention (Comstock & Scharrer, 1999; Rideout, Roberts, & Foehr, 2005).

When they do pay attention to what they are watching, though, they are affected by their viewing in significant ways. For instance, television provides information about appropriateness of body image. In many ways, the television-based view of women's bodies is idealized in a way that barely approaches reality. Women with large breasts, small waists, and slender legs are represented as an ideal. Yet few adolescents (or anyone else) can achieve such a standard. Ultimately, the more adolescents watch television and are exposed to these idealized body images, the more negative is their own body image (Anderson et al., 2001; Clay, Vignoles, & Dittmar, 2005; Ward & Friedman, 2006).

Television also may have an impact on the physical well-being of adolescents. For instance, according to the results of one survey, teenagers with the greatest number of electronic devices were twice as likely to fall asleep in school, suggesting that the availability of the equipment reduced the number of hours the most technologically well-equipped adolescents were sleeping. In addition, obesity has been linked to the level of television viewing: More hours spent viewing are associated with higher levels of adolescent obesity—largely due to the sedentary nature of television (Hancox, Milne, & Poulton, 2004; Lawlor et al., 2005; National Sleep Foundation, 2006).

But television's greatest consequence may be related to its presentation of a violent, aggressive world. Assessing how exposure to such media violence affects adolescent viewers is a major—and difficult—issue.

Media aggression: Visions of violence.   On a typical Sunday in a typical U.S. city, a person who wants to watch a movie on TV can choose from the following selection:

▶ The extent of violence on television is staggering. By the end of adolescence, the average viewer will have seen 200,000 violent acts on television.

Mean Creek.   Boys plan an elaborate revenge on a bully.

Kill Bill: Vol. 2.   An assassin confronts her former boss and his gang.

Tombstone.   Wyatt Earp and Doc Holliday battle the Clanton gang.

The Omen.   An ambassador discovers that his son may be the Antichrist.

Cross of Iron.   Soldiers endure brutal warfare on the Russian front. (*TV Week*, 2006)

This sampling offers a telling commentary on the state of the airwaves in the United States. It is hard for people to insulate themselves from aggression, whether real or fictitious. Whether aggression is viewed through the lens of the media or is observed in real-life situations (as in cases of family violence), exposure to aggression has a profound impact on people's lives.

By the time the average person in the United States reaches adolescence, he or she will have viewed more than 8,000 murders and over 100,000 additional acts of violence. By the end of adolescence, each person will have watched some 200,000 violent acts on television. Almost two thirds of prime-time fictional dramas involve violence. Even Saturday morning cartoon shows contain lengthy sequences of aggression. In fact, in an average hour, programs geared to nonadults contain more than twice as many violent incidents as other types of programs (see Figure 11-4). Movies, too, contain significant amounts of violence (Huston et al., 1992; AAP Committee on Communications, 1995; Fabrikant, 1996; Wilson et al., 2002; Anderson et al., 2003).

This high level of violence clearly has the potential to produce a significant effect on the actual aggression of adolescents, and laboratory experiments are clear in showing the consequences of observed violence. For example, in one study, college students watched a feature film each day for 4 consecutive days, supposedly to provide ratings of the entertainment value of the films (Weaver & Zillman, 1999).

Half the participants saw films that contained needless violence (for example, *Death Warrant*). The other participants in the study watched nonviolent films. On the fifth day, all participants returned, supposedly to participate in an entirely different study on emotion

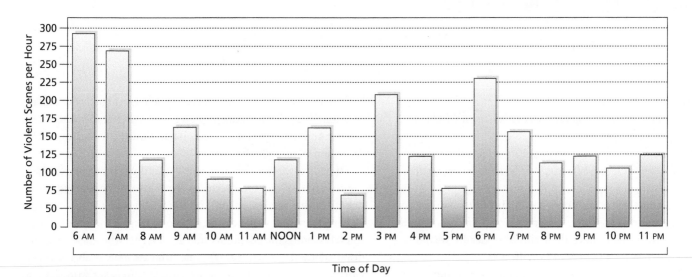

▲ **FIGURE 11-4**

Acts of violence were found during every time period in one study of network broadcasts in a 24-hour period in Washington, DC. From the perspective of an educator, do you think violence on TV should be regulated? Why or why not?

(*Source:* Center for Media and Public Affairs, 1995).

recognition. During the course of the study, a research assistant behaved abusively toward the participants. Later, they were given the opportunity to harm the research assistant. The results were clear: Consistent with other research, participants who had viewed the films with violence were more apt to try to harm the research assistant who had been abusive to them.

Of course, it's one thing to demonstrate the link between observation of violence and later actual aggression in a laboratory setting, and quite another to demonstrate that link in the real world. Although it is clear that laboratory observation of aggression on television leads to higher levels of aggression, evidence showing that real-world viewing of aggression is associated with subsequent aggressive behavior is correlational. (Think, for a moment, of what would be required to conduct a true experiment investigating adolescents' viewing habits. We would have to control the television viewing of a group of adolescents in their homes for extended periods, exposing some to a steady diet of violent shows and others to nonviolent ones—a procedure that most adolescents would not agree to.)

However, despite the fact that the results are primarily correlational, the overwhelming weight of research evidence is clear in suggesting that observation of televised aggression does lead to subsequent aggression. Longitudinal studies have found that preferences for violent television shows at age 8 are related to the seriousness of criminal convictions by age 30. Other evidence supports the notion that observation of media violence can lead to a greater readiness to act aggressively, bullying, and an insensitivity to the suffering of victims of violence (Johnson et al., 2002; Huesmann, Moise-Titus, & Podolski, 2003; Anderson et al., 2003; Slater, Henry, & Swaim, 2003); see also the *Transitions* box on page 358.

There are several reasons why media violence, like that found on television and in movies, may contribute to real-life aggressive behavior. For one thing, observing violence continually may lower inhibitions against acting aggressively. Aggression may be seen as a reasonable response to frustration, and it is more likely that violence will be viewed as socially acceptable. In short, adolescents may use television plots as "scripts" for aggressive behavior. After such as script is learned, it may be recalled in some future situation, providing a guide for behavior.

In addition, exposure to a continual diet of media violence may distort adolescents' understanding of the behavior of others. If this happens, the violence-exposed adolescents may be predisposed to view even nonaggressive acts by others as aggressive. In addition, viewing substantial

Transiti⬤ns

Playing Video Games: Does Virtual Aggression Lead to Actual Aggression?

See a car you want? Steal it.

A police officer tries to stop you? Shoot him with a Glock submachine gun, or cut off his head.

Don't like the look of a woman on the street? Knock her down and stomp on her. Or maybe it would be better to set her on fire.

Such gruesome behavior is only a sampling of the violent possibilities found in the computer game *Grand Theft Auto*. In the game, players—who have their choice of deadly weapons—can repeatedly commit a variety of horrific acts.

Grand Theft Auto is just one of many highly realistic and very involving violent video games that are favorites of adolescents. Some 80% of the most popular video games include violence or aggressiveness as a major theme. *Grand Theft Auto* alone has been purchased by more than 35 million consumers, many, if not most, of them adolescents. In fact, two thirds of all adolescents in grades 7 through 12, including 77% of the boys in this age group, have played *Grand Theft Auto* at least once (Bradley, 2005; Rideout, Roberts, & Foehr, 2005).

Does playing violent video games such as *Grand Theft Auto* cause any ill effects? Research increasingly suggests it does. According to a growing body of research by psychologists, playing violent video games is associated with later aggressive behavior. For example, in one study, students who played violent video games on a regular basis were more likely to be involved in delinquent behavior and aggression. In addition, frequent players had lower academic achievement (Anderson & Dill, 2000; Bartholow & Anderson, 2002; Anderson et al., 2004).

Of course, we face the same chicken-and-egg question regarding the research linking long-term violent video game use and subsequent real-life aggression. As with the findings on the link between viewing television violence and subsequent aggression, we can't absolutely dismiss the possibility that adolescents who are already predisposed toward violence are the ones who are more drawn to violent video games and use them more frequently. In other words, it may be the interest in violence that causes violent video game use, rather than the video games causing the interest in violence.

Still, the research findings on video game violence are quite consistent with findings on the consequences of simply viewing violent television shows, which show a link between the observation of aggressive programming and the actual enactment of aggression. Moreover, the effects of playing video games may be even stronger than the consequences of merely watching aggressive television programs, because video games actually teach the motor skills involved in aggression. By actually firing virtual weapons at people and objects on the screen, game players may be perfecting the skills that would make them more effective at using actual weapons (Cooper & Mackie, 1986; Cohen, 1996; Griffiths, 1997).

▶ A growing body of research suggests that playing violent video games such as Grand Theft Auto is associated with later violence.

Brain imaging studies also suggest that playing violent video games is a particularly involving activity that produces significant neurological arousal. For example, in one study, participants played a violent video game while undergoing a functional magnetic resonance imaging (fMRI) brain scan. Examination of the scans (see Figure 11-5) showed that virtual violence produced activation effects on the anterior cingulate cortex and the amygdala—reactions associated with the experience of actual violence (Weber, Ritterfield, & Mathiak, 2006).

- It seems that every generation of violent games is more violent and realistic than its predecessor. How would you examine the effects of steadily increasing levels of violence in games on actual levels of violence in U.S. society. What variables and outcomes would you look for?

- *From the perspective of a politician:* If a link between violent games and aggressive behavior is established, should society attempt to ban or limit such games? Are the current age ratings on video games adequate? Why or why not?

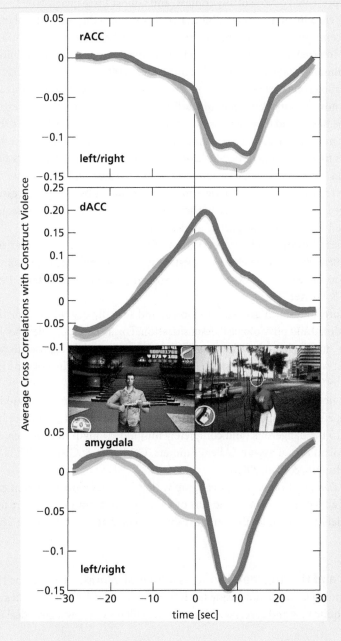

◄ **FIGURE 11-5**

According to brain scans conducted while participants were playing violent video games, it was found that virtual violence produced similar effects on the anterior cingulate cortex and the amygdala as did actual violence.

(*Source:* Weber, René et al.; 2006.)

amounts of aggression may leave adolescents desensitized to violence. What previously would have repelled them now leads to little emotional response—or, in the worst case, a positive response. Their sense of the pain and suffering brought about by aggression may be lost (Bushman & Anderson 2002; Anderson, Carnagey, & Eubanks, 2003; Huesmann et al., 2003; Funk, 2005).

Sex and the Media. Sex, like aggression, is commonplace in the media. Surveys find that more than half of representative samples of television shows contain sexual content, and two thirds of prime-time shows contain sexual scenes, at the rate of more than three per hour. Shows aimed at adolescents, such as *The O.C.*, contain significant amounts of sexual activity. Furthermore, the amount of sexual behavior depicted on television is increasing (see Figure 11-6; Kunkel et al., 1999; Farrar et al., 2003).

The Internet provides even more sexual content, presenting—in ways that could not be more graphic—virtually unlimited amounts of sexual content. Furthermore, sexual content on the Web is often presented devoid of any context, and almost three quarters of 15- to 17-year-olds report having encountered pornographic material even when they weren't looking for it. Because many adolescents get inadequate information about sex from their parents and schools, television and the Internet are a significant (and sometimes primary) source of information about sexuality (Zillmann, 2000; Kaiser Family Foundation, 2001).

What are adolescents learning about sex from the media, and how does this affect them? We don't really know for sure. A number of studies have looked at the effects of exposure to sexual material in the media, and they have produced mixed results. Some studies have shown that those who watched more sexual content were more likely to have more sex, whereas others have found that exposure to sexual content had little or no effect (Roberts, Henriksen, & Foehr, 2004).

In addition, we have the same issues in pinpointing cause and effect as we do with understanding the relationship between viewing violence and subsequent aggression in viewers. Specifically, it is not apparent if viewing sexual content is a cause or a consequence of higher levels of sexual behavior on the part of adolescents.

What is clear, however, is that observation of pornography that links sex with violence *is* detrimental. Research evidence clearly suggests that pornographic depictions of violence against women lead to increased aggression against women (Donnerstein & Linz, 1998; Malamuth, 1998; Carter & Weaver, 2003).

Furthermore, long-term exposure to violent and sexually degrading depictions of women leads to emotional and physiological desensitization. For instance, people who view R-rated violent "slasher" movies later show less anxiety and depression when exposed to depictions of violence against women and demonstrate less sympathy toward victims of rape (Donnerstein & Malamuth, 1997; Malamuth, Addison, & Koss, 2000).

Similarly, viewing films containing sexual violence against women leads to inaccurate attitudes and beliefs about rape. For instance, men exposed to violent pornography are more apt to subscribe to the dangerous (and completely misguided) myth that women enjoy being the victims of violent sexual assault (Allen, Emmers, Gebhardt, & Giery, 1995; Greenfield, 2004; Malamuth, Huppin, & Paul, 2005).

It is clear, then, that observing pornography that includes violent content can increase the likelihood of actual aggression on the part of viewers. Furthermore, exposure to such material produces beliefs and attitudes that support the concept that sexual violence against women is permissible.

Computers and the Internet: Living in a Virtual World. Despite the fact that adolescents are spending far more time using the Internet than they did a few decades ago—when the Internet was quite new and access was limited—we still don't know a great deal about its effects

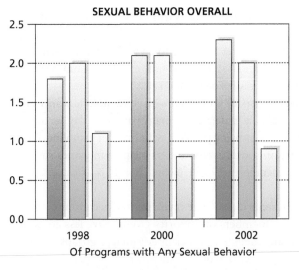

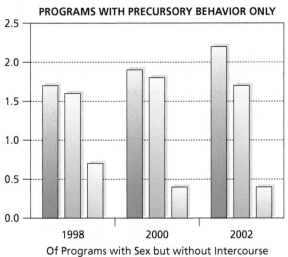

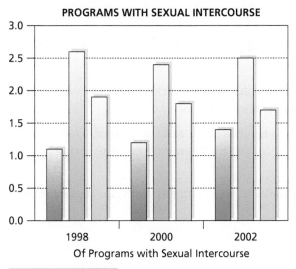

▲ **FIGURE 11-6**

The amount of sexual behavior depicted on television has been steadily increasing over the years, which explains why shows aimed at adolescents contain significant amounts of sexual activity.

(*Source:* Farrar et al., 2003).

on adolescent development. Surveys are only recently telling us what, at least generally, adolescents are doing when they are online.

Most of the time, adolescents are visiting Web sites that have to do with entertainment and sports. Older adolescents also spend more substantial amounts of time on relationship-oriented sites like *MySpace.com* and *Facebook.com* (Roberts & Foehr, 2003).

On the other hand, although fears that cyberspace is overrun with child molesters are exaggerated, it is true that the Internet makes available material that many parents and other adults find highly objectionable. In addition, there is a growing problem with Internet gambling. High school and college students can easily bet on sports events and participate in games such as poker on the Web using credit cards (Staudenmeier, 1999; Dowling, Smith, & Thomas, 2005; Winters et al., 2005).

The growing use of computers also presents a challenge involving socioeconomic status, race, and ethnicity. Poorer adolescents and members of minority groups have less access to computers than more affluent adolescents and members of socially advantaged groups—a phenomenon known as the *digital divide*. For example, 77% of African-American students reported using a personal computer frequently, compared with 87% of white students and 81% of Hispanic/Latino students. Asian-American students had the highest rates of computer use, at 91% (Sax et al., 2004; Fetterman, 2005).

Differences in socioeconomic status also affect computer access across different countries. For example, adolescents in developing countries have less access to the Internet than those in industrialized countries. On the other hand, as computers become less expensive, their availability is becoming more common, opening up opportunities for cultural exchange among adolescents worldwide (Anderson, 2002, 2003).

Review and Apply

Review

1. Adolescents spend almost half their time on leisure activities, with the rest divided between productive activities and maintenance activities.

2. Adolescents can be categorized into two broad groups: busier and less busy, with busier adolescents tending to be more successful academically.

3. True multitasking is no more possible for adolescents than for adults, although adolescents seem to prefer switching among a large number of activities.

4. Adolescents have access to an enormous range of media and technologies, which can enhance entertainment and ease stress, but can also enable excessive exposure to violence and sexual content.

5. Correlational studies have established links between playing violent video games and performing aggressive acts.

Apply

1. Do you think adolescents' increased access to technology and media simply continues a trend that began with radio and television, or is the abundance of new technologies likely to have significant psychological and societal effects? Why?

2. In addition to the "digital divide" between more- and less-affluent adolescents, is there also a digital divide between adolescents and their parents? What effects is this likely to have?

Work: Students on the Job

L   ike many American teenagers, Julissa Vargas, 17, has a minimum-wage job in the fast-food industry—but hers has an unusual geographic reach.

"Would you like your Coke and orange juice medium or large?" Ms. Vargas said into her headset to an unseen woman who was ordering breakfast from a drive-through line. She did not neglect the small details—"You Must Ask for Condiments," a sign next to her computer terminal instructs—and wished the woman a wonderful day.

What made the $12.08 transaction remarkable was that the customer was not just outside Ms. Vargas's workplace here on California's central coast. She was at a McDonald's in Honolulu. And within a two-minute span Ms. Vargas had also taken orders from drive-through windows in Gulfport, Mississippi, and Gillette, Wyoming.

Ms. Vargas works not in a restaurant but in a busy call center. . . . She and as many as 35 others take orders remotely from 40 McDonald's outlets around the country. The orders are then sent back to the restaurants by Internet, to be filled a few yards from where they were placed. (Richtel, 2006, p. A1)

Although Julissa Vargas's job may employ some high-tech wizardry (including constant electronic monitoring of how fast she enters orders into her computer), the fact that she has a job in the first place is hardly remarkable. For many high school students, school is sandwiched between one or more part-time jobs.

In fact, most 16- and 17-year-olds work at some sort of job at least occasionally, and 38% of 15-year-olds have regular employment during the school year. By the time they graduate from high school, nearly 80% of adolescents will have held some job (Employment Policies Institute, 2000; National Center for Education Statistics, 2001).

By the time they reach college, even more adolescents are working. Almost three quarters of full-time college students work at least a few hours a week. Many work even more. For example, nearly half of all students work 25 hours or more a week, and 20% work full time. In addition, nearly half of high school graduates don't go on to college and instead enter the workforce immediately on graduation (King & Bannon, 2002; Ramachandran, 2006).

Work, then, is a common part of adolescent life, regardless of whether adolescents are enrolled in school or not. However, it wasn't always that way. Until relatively recently, work and school were mutually exclusive, as we see when we consider the history of how work and education relate to one another.

Work and Education: The Historical Background

Although it may seem as if working while attending school is a normal part of adolescent life, historically it is a relatively recent phenomenon. For most of the 20th century, the pattern of adolescents simultaneously attending school and spending part of their time in paid employment was rare.

In the early 1900s, when the typical student did not proceed beyond the eighth grade, most adolescents were working in full-time jobs by the time they were 15 years old. Only a minority attended postprimary school, and because these students came from affluent families, it was unusual for a high school student to work (Webb, 2005).

Things changed in the second half of the twentieth century as high school attendance became more nearly universal. As the proportion of less-affluent students attending high school rose, part-time work became more common. Supporting this trend was the emergence of jobs that were suitable for relatively unskilled labor, such as service jobs in fast-food restaurants and retail chains. For such jobs, high school students were ideal, because they accepted low wages and didn't require expensive benefits such as health care.

Today, working during high school has become so commonplace that it is, in many ways, a normative experience, shared by most adolescents. About half of employed adolescents work in the retail sector (in department and grocery stores, restaurants, and other stores), and a quarter work in the service sector (in recreation, health services, and private households). The most common job is cashier (Staff, Mortimer, & Uggen, 2004).

Furthermore, although previously it was less-affluent adolescents who worked, today the opposite is true: High schoolers who work are more likely to come from middle- and upper-class homes than from lower socioeconomic classes. Furthermore, white adolescents are more likely to work than nonwhite adolescents (Steinberg & Cauffman, 1995; Steinberg & Avenevoli, 1998).

The same explanation may account for both phenomena. It's often easier for affluent (and white) students to get jobs because of where the jobs are located. Many of the jobs most suitable for high school students are located in malls or other areas in the suburbs, where more affluent adolescents reside. In addition, such jobs may be difficult to reach without an automobile, putting them out of reach for poorer adolescents who live in urban areas.

Furthermore, for many adolescents, work is less of a necessity and more of a choice. Let's examine why adolescents work and the outcomes of adolescent work.

The Pros and Cons of Work

Why do so many adolescents work? The most obvious answer is money. Some adolescents—particularly the less-affluent ones—must work to help support themselves and their families. Moreover, many college students couldn't afford the steep costs of higher education without working.

In addition, quite apart from the *need* for money to purchase necessities, many adolescents work for the luxuries that their wages can buy. A significant number of adolescents work to afford what they regard as critical niceties of life, such as buying clothes, purchasing an iPod, or paying for cell phone and text messaging services for which their parents either can't or won't pay.

Working offers several potential advantages. In addition to providing funds for recreational activities and (sometimes) necessities, holding a job helps adolescents learn responsibility, gives

▶ In the early 1900s, most adolescents were working full-time jobs by the time they were 15 years old.

◀ Even relatively unskilled jobs can help adolescents develop good work habits and learn workplace skills.

practice with the ability to handle money, and can help teach workplace skills. Adolescents also can develop good work habits that may help them do better academically. Finally, participation in jobs and paid internships can help adolescents understand the nature of work in specific employment settings.

On the other hand, surveys of students show that these potential benefits often are not achieved. Many jobs that are available to high school students are high on drudgery and low on transferable skills. For example, sometimes the only jobs that are available are low-paying positions that do not require high-level skills or training and do not lead to higher-level work. Typical student jobs are serving food in fast-food restaurants, landscaping, and working as video store clerks.

Furthermore, because part-time work takes place after school, employment may prevent students from participating in extracurricular activities such as sports. Because organized activities have been shown to enhance adolescent development, the inability to participate is a downside of work (Danish, Taylor, & Fazio, 2006).

In addition, as their ability to participate in positive, structured extracurricular activities decreases, adolescents' participation in unsupervised, unstructured, and potentially inappropriate activities may rise. This is especially true for adolescents who spend the most time at work; compared to adolescents who work less, they are more likely to spend time in bars, attend parties, and cruise around in cars. The time spent in such activities can lead to participation in deviant behaviors, such as high alcohol and drug use. In fact, there is a link between the number of hours worked, on the one hand, and delinquency and drug and alcohol use on the other, with more hours of work associated with more negative behaviors (Safron, Schulenberg, & Bachman, 2001; Bachman et al., 2003).

The Link between Work and Academic Performance. Perhaps the most troubling consequence of high school employment is that school performance is negatively related to the number of hours a student works: generally, the more hours on the job, the lower a student's grades (see Figure 11-7). In addition, some research suggests that students who work many hours are more likely to drop out of school than those who work fewer hours. One reason for the negative impact of work is that there are only 24 hours in each day, and with fewer hours to study, students are unable to devote enough time to academics (Warren & Lee, 2003).

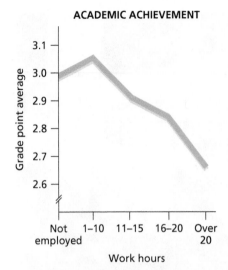

ACADEMIC ACHIEVEMENT

(y-axis: Grade point average, values 2.6, 2.7, 2.8, 2.9, 3.0, 3.1)

(x-axis: Work hours — Not employed, 1–10, 11–15, 16–20, Over 20)

► **FIGURE 11-7**

School performance declines as students put in more hours of employment during a school week. Some research indicates that students who work many hours are more likely to drop out.

(*Source:* Steinberg & Dornbusch, 1992, p. 308).

The impact of work on academic performance takes many forms. Because students have fewer after-school hours, they can devote less time to their homework and to studying for tests. School projects may take a backseat to immediate work pressures. In addition, working students have less time to consult with teachers or get extra help if they are having academic problems (Staff, Mortimer, & Uggen, 2004).

But the negative impact of work may go beyond the sheer number of hours that are spent in the workplace and away from schoolwork. It also is possible that students who work a greater number of hours are more psychologically invested in their work than in high school—an explanation called the primary orientation model. According to the **primary orientation model,** adolescents usually focus their attention mainly either on school or work, but not both. If their primary focus is on work, they have more motivation to do well in the workplace; however, as a consequence, they have less motivation to do well academically, and their grades may suffer as a result of their attention to their jobs (Warren, 2002; Warren & Lee, 2003; Warren, Lee, & Cataldi, 2004).

A premature focus on work also may cause some adolescents to experience a phenomenon known as pseudomaturity. **Pseudomaturity** involves an unusually early entry into adult roles before an adolescent is ready developmentally to assume them. Some adolescents, particularly those who do not have strong ties to school or their peers, may see early entry into adulthood as a desirable escape from their current roles, and this may provide them with great satisfaction. In such cases, working many hours at a job may be a way for such adolescents to escape from current sources of stress. In other situations, however, socioeconomic pressures force adolescents into pseudomaturity (Staff, Mortimer, & Uggen, 2004).

In either case, adolescents who experience pseudomaturity may miss important developmental milestones that typically occur during adolescence. They may lose the opportunity to explore different interests. Furthermore, adolescents may be prematurely thrust into situations for which they have few or no coping skills because of their lack of experience (Newcomb, 1996; Locke & Newcomb, 2004).

Ultimately, the consequences of working on adolescents are quite varied. Work is neither good nor bad in itself. What matters is both the quality and quantity of the work experience, as well as the particular individuals involved. For some adolescents, particularly those who work a limited number of hours each work, the advantages of working can be substantial. On the other hand, for those who work long hours, employment is likely to hinder academic performance (Vondracek & Porfeli, 2006).

In fact, in the case of college students, some educational experts recommend limiting the number of hours that students work, even if it means taking out substantial loans to pay for

primary orientation model   a situation in which adolescents usually focus their attention mainly either on school or work, but not both.

pseudomaturity   a period of adolescent development that involves an unusually early entry into adult roles before an adolescent is ready developmentally to assume them.

college costs. Ultimately, students who work less (and instead use loans to pay for tuition and living expenses) are more likely to be academically successful than those who work part time to cover their expenses. This is one case in which loans ultimately pay off (King, 2005).

Adolescent
DIVERSITY   Cross-Cultural Adolescent Work Practices

FOR MANY ADOLESCENTS living outside the United States, work is the primary activity. In the most traditional, nonindustrialized countries, where formal schooling is not the norm, children are trained by their parents and other adults to participate in adult work at an early age. In farming communities, adolescents participate in farming with the adults; where hunting is the major activity, adolescents work alongside adults as they hunt. In an important sense, there is no separate workplace, and schooling consists of teaching children how to participate in the activities that allow the family to subsist.

In developing countries, where poverty is extensive, adolescents typically leave school around the age of 15 or 16—much earlier than in the United States—and begin full-time employment. When they start working, they typically work with their families in jobs they expect to keep for the rest of their lives. In addition, there is a gender difference: Boys are more likely to participate in paid employment, whereas girls are more likely to stay at home and provide unpaid domestic help to the family (Verma & Larson, 2003).

Although in many ways other affluent, industrialized countries share similar educational patterns to that of the United States—in which students are expected to continue formal education until around age 18—the patterns of adolescent work are actually quite different. In most industrialized countries other than the United States, it is unusual for adolescents to work. For example, in Japan and Taiwan, only about a quarter of adolescents engage in part-time work. Adolescent paid employment in Europe is very rare, and the few youth who do work usually have informal jobs such as garden work or babysitting, and they spend only a few hours each week at such jobs (Nishino & Larson, 2003).

Several factors explain why European adolescents work so little in comparison to adolescents in the United States. One factor is that not only do European schools often require more homework than those in the United States, but also school hours are different in Europe, with classes often extending into the late afternoon. Because retail stores are less likely to be open in the evenings, there is simply less opportunity to hold down a job. In addition, there are fewer establishments of the sort that hire adolescents in the United States, such as fast-food restaurants. Finally, there also is a sense of shame attached to adolescent work. Rather than viewing teenage work in positive terms, Europeans are more likely to view adolescents who hold down jobs as doing so because they are poor (Flammer & Schaffner, 2003; Verma & Larson, 2003).

Although it is relatively rare for European adolescents to work while in school, they are much more likely than their counterparts in the United States to participate in formal apprenticeships. These apprenticeships train students for specific positions as carpenters, electricians, and the like, and they are seen, in part, as an extension of formal schooling. The apprenticeships provide skills that will be used professionally later in life. In contrast, jobs for adolescents in the United States are not considered important in terms of adolescents' later careers, but are merely viewed as a way to earn money in the short term (Hamilton & Hamilton, 2004).

Job Training for Adolescents Entering the Workforce

Every day, after a morning of classes at Wheaton High School, David Gonzales, a dark-haired, slightly scruffy senior, headed to Thomas Edison High School of Technology. There he donned a tool belt and goggles and went to work as part of a team of student builders who have been constructing a 2,252-square-foot home in Silver Spring since October.

Others might have chafed at the heavy lifting and chilly weather—not to mention the splinters and the potential for puncture wounds—but the 18-year-old was fully aware of the benefits of being able to hammer a nail into a two-by-four.

Last summer, while other teenagers were flipping burgers for minimum wage, Gonzales picked up $1,600 a month using the carpentry skills he had learned at Edison. (Aratani, 2006, p. C11)

The innovative program that is training David Gonzales represents an important approach for preparing adolescents who plan to enter the workforce on high school graduation. And it's also surprisingly rare.

Despite the fact that almost half of U.S. high school graduates enter the workforce directly on graduation, public schooling has not traditionally focused on offering training for specific jobs or even providing much in the way of career counseling. The philosophy of most schools is that training in basic skills—reading, writing, and math—is more important than preparation in job skills. Consequently, far more resources are invested in programs for students who plan to attend college than for students who are entering the workforce when they leave school.

The result of this orientation is that many students leave school (either because they drop out or graduate) ill-suited for the workforce. Whereas school provides a routine and highly secure environment for students, the workplace is less predictable and far less secure. Furthermore, good-paying jobs require specific skills that most often are not taught as part of the standard high school curriculum. Consequently, many adolescents are unprepared for the challenges that work presents (Rasheed, McWhirter, & Chronister, 2005).

There are some exceptions. For example, *career and technical education programs*—formerly called vocational education—are designed to provide specific skills in careers such as automotive technology, data entry, and the allied health professions. Students not only are trained in classrooms, but also many programs offer internships at workplace sites. Students who complete career and technical education programs usually find jobs after graduation, and their salaries are higher than those of individuals without such training. In addition, students are more motivated, and their graduation rates are higher and dropout rates lower than for nonparticipants (Lever et al., 2004; Beekhoven & Dekkers, 2005; Lash, 2006).

▶ Career and technical education programs provide skills to high school students that can be used in specific professions upon graduation.

Although many, if not most, students gain marketable skills from career and technical education programs, the programs have been criticized on a number of grounds. First, some educators point to them as dumping grounds for less academically inclined students or those who are disruptive and have discipline problems. Because of this, participation in career and technical education can carry something of a stigma.

In addition, because adolescents are forced to make major career decisions very early in life—in some cases as early as eighth or ninth grade—some may make choices that are not optimal or just plain wrong. Pushing students to make career decisions prematurely may place them on a career track for which they are ill-suited, and revising their decision may be difficult once they have started along their chosen path.

Furthermore, once students are in a career and technical education program, they may not be taking courses that would prepare them for college-level work. Because they may not have taken any college-preparation courses by the time they graduate from high school, they will find it difficult to enroll in college if their aspirations later change. In a sense, their choice of a career and technical education program prevents them from going to college—which ultimately means that they are relegated to relatively low-status, low-paying jobs that don't require a college degree.

On the other hand, as the requirements of even blue-collar jobs become more complex, higher-level skills are needed. For example, to become a steamfitter, applicants must pass an exam containing 50 math problems, and cosmetologists must know some chemistry. In fact, a quarter of students in career and technical education take trigonometry or higher-level math (Aratani, 2006).

Perhaps the biggest concern about career and technical education programs is whether they do an adequate job. Are adolescents who participate in career and technical education programs trained sufficiently to get good jobs on graduation?

For the most part, the answer is yes, although with some qualification. For adolescents who work in the field for which they are trained, the results are quite positive. They are more likely to get a job and to make more money in the field compared with those who have not been trained. In fact, the more career and technical education courses they take, the more they earn. Specifically, 7 years after high school graduation, students earn almost 2% more for each extra high school occupational course they take (Policy and Program Studies Service, 2004).

But it is not only career and technical education courses that matter. The most successful students are those who have combined vocational training with strong academic courses. Furthermore, the greatest success comes to those who continue their training, getting either an associate's or bachelor's college degree.

In short, career and technical education can be quite successful in producing well-trained, productive workers in specific fields. They are less successful for students who get jobs in fields other than the ones in which they were trained, in part because the skills they teach are typically quite specific to a particular field. The challenge for career and technical education is to teach skills that can transfer across different fields, particularly because—as we will discuss later in the chapter—most workers will change careers several times during their lifetimes.

The Elusive Link between Work and Character

Paid employment builds character, teaches responsibility, and otherwise makes adolescents better prepared for adulthood. At least that's the argument put forward by proponents of work, who see the activity as an important passage in adolescent development.

However, it's been difficult to prove the point. Although people looking back on their work experiences say that they helped build character and taught them responsibility, supportive evidence from adolescents who are objectively assessed while they are currently at work has been harder to find. In fact, adolescents who work a great deal—more than 20 hours a week—may develop a cynical view of the workplace and are more likely to hold less ethical views of business.

At the same time, they do have greater knowledge about the world of business, money, and consumers (Steinberg et al., 1982; Mortimer, 2003).

One reason that work may not produce positive outcomes in terms of building character is the type of motivation that underlies the decision to work. For many adolescents, work is seen as a necessary evil, simply to earn money. The work itself is not an activity that is of much interest. That's not surprising, given that the only jobs for which many adolescents are qualified are menial, unskilled, or tedious. Their jobs often require little responsibility and they are closely supervised by adults, giving them little chance to show initiative.

In such a situation, the adolescent's work is based primarily on *extrinsic motivation,* which is motivation that causes individuals to participate in activities for the tangible rewards they receive. In contrast, *intrinsic motivation* is motivation that causes people to participate in activities for their own enjoyment, not for the reward the activities bring them. If work was seen purely as a means to an end (as in extrinsic motivation), it may be less likely to produce positive benefits than if the work itself is seen as meaningful (as in intrinsic motivation) (Twenge, 2006).

On the other hand, adolescents who work do have the opportunity to develop close, meaningful relationships with adults other than their parents. In turn, this may help reduce stress they experience with their parents. Furthermore, moderate amounts of work may increase adolescents' confidence, and their time management skills may improve (Mortimer, 2003).

Ultimately, whether paid employment enhances character development and teaches responsibility depends on the nature of the job, the specific personality characteristics of the adolescent on the job, and the motivation that underlies the decision to work. Jobs that are intrinsically interesting and that permit employees to exercise some degree of independence and autonomy are likely to produce positive results, with adolescents feeling good about themselves and their abilities—ultimately leading to positive psychological outcomes. In contrast, jobs that are uninteresting, stressful, or tedious and jobs that require few skills may do little to improve the psychological well-being of adolescents. In fact, if the nature of the job is sufficiently dreary, adolescents may be harmed by their participation in the workplace (Mortimer, 2003).

Review and Apply

Review

1. Most adolescents spend some time working at part-time jobs while attending school, a trend that represents a significant change in U.S. society over the past 60 years.

2. The main reason that adolescents work during school is to earn money—to support either themselves and their families or to purchase desirable goods.

3. Working can help adolescents learn responsibility, money management, workplace skills, and good work habits, but few jobs available to students offer more than drudgery.

4. School performance is typically negatively affected if adolescents spend a large number of hours working, and adolescents who work long hours may miss important steps in their development.

5. In general, high schools do not do a good job preparing graduates to enter the workforce directly after graduation, although some career and technical education programs are successful at preparing students for specific careers.

Apply

1. Should typical employers of students work harder to make their jobs more advanced, challenging, and interesting, or is the current system fine as it is? Does the primary orientation model suggest a way of looking at this issue?

2. *From the perspective of an educator:* All things considered, do you think that high schools that offer career and technical education programs for students who have no current plans to attend college are helping or hurting their students? Should all students be prepared for college? Why or why not?

Picking an Occupation: Choosing Life's Work

I *would love to just go off and do my own thing, pursue my own interests and my own education. But I want to be a teacher someday, and I want to be recognized by this society as a legitimate teacher. And unfortunately, the Academy (accredited schools and universities) has a monopoly on legitimate education in our society. In other words, if you really want to teach, you have to have a degree from an accredited university or else you're just some New Age quack. So do I try to work within the system, get a PhD so I can start my own school? Or break away and try to forge my own path, creating a new standard of legitimacy? This is enough to drive any undergraduate nuts. Especially while I'm working on three research papers at the same time with a bad cold.*

For most adolescents, choosing a professional goal—and finding the best way to achieve that goal—is not simple. Some people know from childhood that they want to be teachers or physicians or actors or go into business, and they follow direct paths toward that goal. For others, the choice of a career is very much a matter of chance, of watching something on television or scrolling through monster.com and seeing what's available.

Regardless of how a career is chosen, it is unlikely to be the only career that people will have during the course of the lifetime. As technology rapidly alters the nature of work and globalization alters the economic outlook, changing careers at least once, and sometimes several times, is likely to be the norm in the 21st century. Consequently, adolescents no longer choose *a* career. Instead, they are at the start of what may be a lifelong decision-making process (Vondracek & Porfeli, 2006).

Perspectives on Career Development

In considering how adolescents choose career paths, researchers have developed a variety of perspectives. The three major ones are Ginzberg's three developmental periods, Holland's personality types, and Super's self-concept approach.

Ginzberg's Three Developmental Periods. According to Eli Ginzberg (1972), people generally move through several stages in choosing a career. In the **fantasy period,** which lasts until around age 11, career choices are made—and discarded—without regard to skills, abilities, or available job opportunities. Instead, choices are based solely on what sounds appealing. Thus a child may decide that she wants to be a veterinarian, despite the fact that she is allergic to dogs and cats.

People begin to take practical considerations into account during the tentative period, which spans adolescence. During the **tentative period,** people begin to think in pragmatic terms about the requirements of various jobs and how their own abilities might fit with those requirements. They also consider their personal values and goals, exploring how well a particular occupation might satisfy them. Finally, in early adulthood, people enter the **realistic period,** in which they explore specific career options either through actual experience on the job or through training for a profession. They begin to narrow their choices to a few alternative careers and eventually make a commitment to a particular one.

Ginzberg's perspective has been criticized on several grounds. For one thing, it seems to emphasize middle- and upper-middle-class career patterns and is a less adequate description of the

fantasy period according to Ginzberg the period of life when career choices are made—and discarded—without regard to skills, abilities, or available job opportunities.

tentative period the second stage of Ginzberg's theory, which spans adolescence, in which people begin to think in pragmatic terms about the requirements of various jobs and how their own abilities might fit with those requirements.

realistic period the third and final stage of Ginzberg's three developmental periods in which people explore specific career options, either through actual experience on the job or through training for a profession.

career-related behavior of individuals of lower socioeconomic status. Specifically, many poor adolescents have far fewer options than adolescents who are more affluent.

In addition, the ages at which the stages supposedly occur are too rigid. Some adolescents still behave as if they were in the fantasy period, which is supposedly over by age 11. Many adolescents have unrealistic views of the type of job to which they aspire. They want work that is high paying, is fulfilling, helps others, and provides lots of vacation time (who wouldn't?), but they don't realize that such jobs are rare, if they exist at all. These unrealistic expectations ultimately may cause such individuals to be disappointed when they actually enter the workforce (Schneider & Stevenson, 2000).

Holland's Six Personality Types.   Although the three stages described by Ginzberg make intuitive sense, the stage approach oversimplifies the process of choosing a career. Consequently, some researchers suggest that it is more fruitful to examine the match between job seekers' personality types and the requirements of particular careers. For example, according to researcher John Holland (1973, 1987; Gottfredson & Holland, 1990), certain personality types match particularly well with certain careers. Specifically, he suggested that six personality types are important in career choice:

- *Realistic:* These people are down-to-earth, practical problem solvers who are physically strong, but their social skills are mediocre. They make good farmers, laborers, and truck drivers.

- *Intellectual:* Intellectual types are oriented toward the theoretical and the abstract. Although not particularly good with people, they are well suited to careers in math and science.

- *Social:* The traits associated with the social personality type are related to verbal skills and interpersonal relations. Social types are good at working with people and consequently make good salespersons, teachers, and counselors.

- *Conventional:* Conventional individuals prefer highly structured tasks. They make good clerks, secretaries, and bank tellers.

- *Enterprising:* These individuals are risk takers and take-charge types. They are leaders and may be particularly effective as managers or politicians.

- *Artistic:* Artistic types use art to express themselves, and they often prefer the world of art to interactions with people. They are best suited to occupations involving art.

Of course, not everyone fits neatly into one particular personality type. Furthermore, there are certainly exceptions to the typology, with jobs being held successfully by people who don't have the predicted personality. Still, the theory forms the foundation of several instruments designed to assess the occupational options for which a given person is particularly suited (Randahl, 1991).

Super's Career Self-Concept Perspective.   When an adolescent with a part-time job identifies herself by saying, "I'm a gardener" or "I'm a supermarket cashier," she is beginning to build a career self-concept. A **career self-concept** is a sense of oneself viewed through the context of work.

According to Donald Super, the career self-concept frames the choices and decisions that adolescents make regarding career issues. As adolescents build their career self-concepts, they pass through a series of stages that ultimately lead to specific career choices (Super, 1990; Freeman, 1993).

In this view, adolescents first begin to think about careers between the ages of 14 and 18 as they proceed through the crystallization stage. In the *crystallization stage,* adolescents think of careers that are consistent with their global self-concept, using their current strengths and interests to guide their thinking. For example, an adolescent who enjoys service learning activities

career self-concept   a sense of oneself viewed through the context of work.

might begin to consider helping professions as a possible future career. Similarly, a particularly sociable adolescent might begin thinking that she wants to work in sales.

In the next period, they enter the *specification stage.* During this period, which extends from around age 18 to 22—generally comprising the college years—adolescents and young adults realize the importance of becoming more specific in their career interests. Not only do they actively seek information about potential careers but they also begin to choose courses and get training related to their career possibilities. Their interests also become more precise as they focus less on broad occupational categories (e.g., health-care provider) and more on specific professions (e.g., nurse practitioner or physical therapist).

The next period following specification is the *implementation stage.* In this stage, which generally occurs around ages 22 to 24, people actually seek out work in their chosen profession and begin their careers. Later, as they become familiar with their jobs and settle into their careers, they enter the *stabilization stage,* which lasts from around ages 25 to 35. Finally, they move into the *consolidation stage,* in which they are established and try to advance to other, higher-status positions.

Although Super's stages certainly describe a reasonable sequence that many people follow, critics have complained that his description of the stages and the sequence they follow is not necessarily universal. Many people do not follow alternative routes, particularly in terms of moving in and out of different careers over the course of their lifetimes. Furthermore, the ages associated with the stages should not be viewed as fixed, but as varying according to the specific individual involved.

Still, Super's career self-concept perspective has been influential. It also led to the development of the Career Development Inventory, which adolescents can take to further their own career exploration (Patton & Creed, 2001).

Limitations of Career Development Theories.   We've considered three major perspectives on career development: Ginzberg's three developmental periods, Holland's personality types, and Super's career self-concept perspective. Each provides a different account of how adolescents choose a career, and—although there is some overlap—they differ in terms of the number of stages and the degree to which personality traits are deemed important.

Despite their differences, all three place particular emphasis on career decision making that takes place during adolescence. To many critics, this emphasis is misplaced. They note that interests and competencies are at least potentially changeable during adolescence (as well as in adulthood). Even some personality traits may change over the course of development. For example, the nature of a job itself can influence personality development. Thus, rather than personality affecting job selection, the opposite can be true: Job selection can influence personality. Ultimately, then, limitations are inevitable in any theories that emphasize career choices that are made during adolescence, a period of considerable cognitive and social-emotional change (Mullis, Mullis, & Gerwels, 1998; Low et al., 2005).

There's another drawback to career development theories. Adolescents' choices of career paths are not only influenced by their interests and personalities, but also by what they (and others in society) perceive as appropriate (Johnson & Stokes, 2002).

For example, significant parental and even societal pressures push adolescents from upper socioeconomic status backgrounds to choose an "acceptable" profession—law or business, for instance—over blue-collar, lower-status jobs, regardless of the adolescent's interests. An adolescent from a wealthy family who chooses to be a truck driver may face considerable pressure. Conversely, even the most capable and most motivated adolescent who is deeply interested in the law may be unable to consider the profession if she is unable to afford the cost of law school.

In short, interests, abilities, and personality traits are only part of the story when it comes to understanding career choices and development. Let's consider several additional important factors, including socioeconomic status, gender, and race. (To learn about career choice from the perspective of a career counselor, see the *Career Choices* box.)

CAREER CHOICES

Career Counselor

Name: Greg Borgstede

Education: BS, Anthropology, Florida State University, Tallahassee, Florida; PhD, Anthropology, University of Pennsylvania

Position: Career Counselor, Career Services—University of Pennsylvania

Home: Philadelphia, PA

Although many students begin college with some idea of what they want to pursue for a career, quite a few don't give it much thought until they get close to graduation. And even then their thinking about what path to follow is often vague and unfocused, according to career counselor Greg Borgstede.

"A lot of students get ideas from three areas: parents, peers, and their educational experiences," Borgstede explained. "For example, they may get ideas from their teachers in high school, or because of a good psychology professor, they may decide to pursue a career in psychology."

"With sophomores and freshman, I typically have a conversation with them on what they are interested in, what they are majoring in, and what they see down the road. Then I try to give them the tools to explore different options," he added.

It is common for college students to feel they need to pursue a career connected to their major. Borgstede says that's fine, but students should also look at all their options.

"I help students weed through the extraneous material out there," he explained. "I'm big on having students explore on their own. Our goal is to give students choices and let them see there are a lot of options, but not so many that they are overwhelmed."

In addition to current students, many career counselors also see alumni at later points in their life who wish to make a career change. In this case, counselors take a different approach.

"In some cases it is difficult to demonstrate that they have transferable skills," said Borgstede. "They need to have positive evaluations and understand they do have skills that can be useful in the next job search.

"This is often a difficult area with someone changing careers," Borgstede said. "They can take their skills with them, but they may have to move down the ladder a bit, rather than moving laterally."

Thinking of working in the career counselor field?

Career counseling is a growing field. Career counselors help identify a range of appropriate careers for clients. Most have a masters degree in counseling, psychology, or another mental health-related field. They must know what skills are required in various professions, and they help clients understand how their own strengths and personality traits will mesh with the requirements of the profession. ■

Career Choices and Socioeconomic Status, Gender, and Race and Ethnicity

Whereas traditional approaches to career development have focused on adolescents' personalities or on the stages they pass through in decision making, new approaches have acknowledged the unique role played by social factors in determining which careers are chosen and how the choice is made. After all, adolescents, like all members of society, are affected by the social climate and the norms and values of the family and society in which they are raised. Let's start by looking at one of the most powerful social factors affecting career choices: socioeconomic status.

Socioeconomic Status and Career Choices.   As it does in many other domains, socioeconomic status plays a significant role in determining adolescent career choice. Although there is significant *upward mobility* in job status in the United States (meaning that most adolescents end up in jobs that are at a higher occupational level than those of their parents), much of the mobility is relatively minor. In other words, even though the majority of adolescents will eventually work in jobs that are superior to those held by their parents, the jobs usually are not that much better in terms of status and wages. For example, an adolescent whose father is a laborer may become a medical technician but is much less likely to become a physician (Ali, McWhirter, & Chronister, 2005; Schaefer, 2005).

◀ Most adolescents end up in jobs that are of higher status than those of their parents.

Part of the importance of socioeconomic status in determining career choice is the strong link between socioeconomic status and education. Because lower-class adolescents are more likely to have fewer years of education under their belts than middle-class adolescents before entering the workforce, lower-class youth are more likely to start out—and remain—in lower-status, lower-paying jobs. In addition, parents of middle- and upper-class adolescents tend to instill higher levels of achievement motivation in their children than parents in lower-class households. In families in which there is significant economic stress, parents are less likely to encourage independence and autonomy (key factors in high-status jobs), in part because the parents themselves probably experience relatively little independence and autonomy in their own lives (Kohn, 1977; Robbins et al., 2004; Turner & Lapin, 2005).

Finally, changes in socioeconomic status brought about by upward mobility are much more common for males than females, and male and female adolescents' career choices reflect this fact. Although their motivation to work is similar, adolescent females are more apt to limit their aspirations and career choices to those that society deems appropriate for women, ultimately yielding them less change in socioeconomic status. Furthermore, as we discuss next, women's employment opportunities are more limited than those of males (Greene & DeBacker, 2004).

Gender and Career Choices: Women's Work

WANTED: Full-time employee for small family firm. DUTIES: Including but not limited to general cleaning, cooking, gardening, laundry, ironing and mending, purchasing, bookkeeping and money management. Child care may also be required. HOURS: Avg. 55/wk but

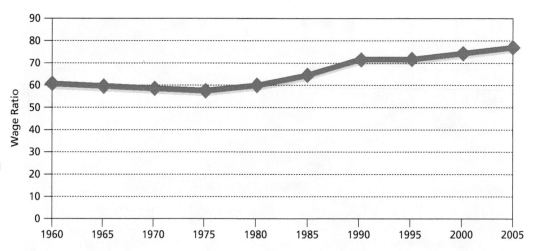

▶ **FIGURE 11-8**

Women's weekly earnings as a percentage of men's has increased since 1979 but is still slightly more than 75% and has remained steady in recent years.

(*Source:* U.S. Census Bureau, (2006). Woman's Earnings as a Percentage of Men's Earnings: 1960 to 2005. "Historical Income Tables—People" Table P-40.)

standby duty required 24 hours/day, 7 days/wk. Extra workload on holidays. SALARY AND BENEFITS: No salary, but food, clothing, and shelter provided at employer's discretion; job security and benefits depend on continued good will of employer. No vacation. No retirement plan. No opportunities for advancement. REQUIREMENTS: No previous experience necessary, can learn on the job. Only women need apply. (Unger & Crawford, 1992, p. 446)

Just three decades ago, many female adolescents assumed that this admittedly exaggerated job description matched the work for which they were best suited and to which they aspired: housewife. Even those female adolescents who wished to seek work outside the home were limited to certain professions. For instance, until the 1960s, employment ads in newspapers throughout the United States were almost always divided into two sections: "Help Wanted: Male" and "Help Wanted: Female." The men's job listings encompassed such professions as police officer, construction worker, and legal counsel; the women's listings were for secretaries, teachers, cashiers, and librarians.

The breakdown of jobs deemed appropriate for men and women reflected society's traditional view of what the two genders were best suited for. Traditionally, women were considered most appropriate for **communal professions,** occupations associated with relationships. In contrast, men were perceived as best suited for **agentic professions.** Agentic professions are associated with getting things accomplished. It is probably no coincidence that communal professions typically have lower status and lower salaries than agentic professions (Eagly & Steffen, 1986; Eagly, Beall, & Sternberg, 2004; Diekman et al., 2005).

Although discrimination based on gender is far less blatant today than it was several decades ago—it is now illegal, for instance, to advertise a position specifically for a man or a woman—remnants of traditional gender role prejudice persist. One reflection of this is illustrated by the discrepancy between women's and men's salaries. As shown in Figure 11-8, in 97% of the occupations for which data have been collected, women's weekly earnings are less than men's. On average, women earn 76 cents for every dollar that men earn. Moreover, women who are members of minority groups do even worse: African-American women earn 65 cents for every dollar men make, while for Hispanic women the figure is 54 cents (U.S. Bureau of the Census, 2004).

Nevertheless, despite status and pay that are often lower than men's, more women are working outside the home than ever before. Between 1950 and 2000, the percentage of the female population aged 16 and over in the U.S. labor force overall increased from around 35% to 60%. Today, women make up around 46% of the workforce. Almost all women expect to earn a living, and almost all do at some point in their lives. Furthermore, in about one half of U.S. households, women earn about as much as their husbands (Lewin, 1995; Women's Bureau, 2002).

communal professions occupations associated with relationships.

agentic professions occupations associated with getting things accomplished.

In addition, opportunities for women are in many ways considerably greater today than they were in earlier years. Women are more likely to be physicians, lawyers, insurance agents, and bus drivers than they were in the past. However, within specific job categories, sex discrimination still occurs. For example, female bus drivers are more apt to have part-time school bus routes, while men hold better paying full-time routes in cities. Similarly, female pharmacists are more likely to work in hospitals, while men work in higher paying jobs in retail stores (Crawford & Unger, 2004).

In fact, there is considerable occupational segregation in which women continue to work at jobs that have been traditionally held by women (see Figure 11-9). For example, 98% of all secretaries and dental assistants are female. (Ask yourself: What was the gender of the person who cleaned your teeth the last time you visited the dentist?) Employment in sex-typed occupations typically results in women playing service roles analogous to the traditional gender roles in which women served their husbands (Schaefer, 2005).

Even women and minorities in high-status, visible professional roles often hit what has come to be called the glass ceiling. The *glass ceiling* is an invisible barrier in an organization that prevents individuals from being promoted beyond a certain level because of discrimination. It operates subtly, and the people responsible for keeping the glass ceiling in place may not even be aware of how their actions perpetuate discrimination against women and minorities. For instance, a male supervisor in the oil exploration business may conclude that a particular task is "too dangerous" for a female employee. As a consequence of his decision, he may be preventing female candidates for the job from obtaining the experience they need to get promoted (Reid, Miller, & Kerr, 2004; Stroh, Langlands, & Simpson, 2004; Probert, 2005).

The Influence of Race and Ethnicity on Career Choices. Adolescents who are members of a group that has been traditionally discriminated against in U.S. society face a number of significant challenges as they make occupational decisions. Because of the level of prejudice in society, they may have experienced less success educationally, and the lower income level of their families restricts the opportunities available to them compared to those of racial and ethnic majorities. Furthermore, they may have less information about various career paths available to them.

As a consequence, members of minority groups may hold lower occupational aspirations, and even when they have similar career aspirations to those of majority adolescents, minority

Underrepresented		Overrepresented	
Firefighters	3%	High school teachers	59%
Airline pilots	4	Social workers	72
Engineers	10	Cashiers	77
Police	14	File clerks	82
Clergy	15	Elementary teachers	83
Dentists	20	Librarians	86
Computer systems analysts	27	Registered nurses	93
Lawyers	29	Child care workers	97
Physicians	29	Receptionists	97
Mail carriers	31	Secretaries	98
College teachers	43	Dental hygienists	98

◄ **FIGURE 11-9**

Although strides have been made with women joining professions that were formerly male-dominated, there still remains a considerable amount of occupational segregation. This figure shows survey results illustrating professions in which women are under- and over-represented.

(*Source:* Schaeffer, 2005, p. 294).

adolescents have lower expectations about the likelihood that they will achieve their goals. In part, their attitude reflects the reality that occupational opportunities and upward mobility are more restricted for them. African Americans, in particular, experience less professional upward mobility than members of other minority groups (Arbona, 2005; Fouad & Byars-Winston, 2005).

It's important to keep in mind that there are significant differences between different minority groups and their career choices. For example, Asian adolescents are more likely to aspire to careers in science and math, and in fact the proportion of Asian scientists and mathematicians is far greater than the proportion of Asians in the general population. On the other hand, Asians are underrepresented in professional fields such as the law. Such differences may be due to the presence or absence of role models in particular fields, as well as the influence of parental pressure, which may be particularly strong among Asian adolescents (Leung, Ivey, & Suzuki, 1994; Fouad & Byars-Winston, 2005).

BECOMING AN INFORMED CONSUMER OF ADOLESCENT SCIENCE

Choosing a Career

ONE OF THE GREATEST challenges that people face in late adolescence is making a decision that may have lifelong implications: the choice of a career. Although there is no single correct choice—most people can be happy in any of several different jobs, and the reality is that they will change jobs and occupations several times in their lives—the options can be daunting. Here are some guidelines for adolescents coming to grips with the question of which occupational path to follow:

- Systematically evaluate a variety of choices. Libraries and the Internet contain a wealth of information about potential career paths, and most colleges and universities have career centers that can provide occupational data and guidance.

- Know yourself. Evaluate your strengths and weaknesses, perhaps by completing a questionnaire at a college career center that can provide insight into your interests, skills, and values.

- Create a "balance sheet" listing the potential gains and losses that you will incur from a particular profession. First, list the gains and losses that you will experience directly, and then list the gains and losses for others. Next, write down the projected social approval or disapproval you are likely to receive from others. By systematically evaluating a set of potential careers according to each of these criteria, you will be in a better position to compare different possibilities.

- "Try out" different careers through paid or unpaid internships. By experiencing a job firsthand, interns are able to get a better sense of what an occupation is truly like.

- Remember that if you make a mistake, you can change careers. In fact, people today increasingly change careers in early adulthood or even beyond. No one should feel locked into a decision made earlier in life.

As we've seen throughout this book, people develop substantially as they age, and this development continues beyond adolescence to cover the entire life span. It is reasonable to expect that shifting values, interests, abilities, and life circumstances might make a different career more appropriate later in life than the one chosen in late adolescence. ■

Review and Apply

Review

1. The major career development perspectives are Ginzberg's three developmental periods, Holland's personality types, and Super's self-concept approach.

2. All three perspectives focus excessively on decision making during adolescence, when in fact changes during and beyond adolescence can affect people's career choices.

3. Socioeconomic status plays a significant role in career decisions, limiting the amount of upward mobility that is typically achieved by successive generations.

4. Despite great gains in entering and advancing in the workforce, women continue to be limited in their career progression by the "glass ceiling."

5. Race and ethnicity also influence career choice because adolescents from groups that have experienced discrimination start with restricted opportunities and lower occupational expectations.

Apply

1. Can you think of other personality types that might influence career choice beyond the six identified by Holland?

2. If women are regarded as suitable for communal professions and men for agentic professions, is it possible that a "communally agentic" orientation would be successful in a leadership position in a major business? How would this work?

EPILOGUE

In this chapter, we looked at how adolescents spend their time. We discovered that they spend a great deal of time on leisure activities, especially since advances in media and technology have expanded their after-hours opportunities. We noted that the increased use of media and technology has its own intrinsic dangers related to sex and violence.

Next we considered the value of work in the lives of adolescents, because so many U.S. teenagers have part-time jobs in addition to their school attendance. We found that working after school can provide both benefits and challenges. Turning to work immediately after graduation, we looked at the general inadequacy of programs designed to prepare students for careers after high school.

Finally we discussed how adolescents explore career opportunities. We looked at several formal theories about career decision making, finding each less than complete. We also discussed the effects of socioeconomic status, race and ethnicity, and gender on career opportunities and choices.

Before we proceed to the next chapter, recall the busy multimedia lives of the twins Piers and Bronte Cox, whom we met in the chapter Prologue. Consider the following questions.

1. What function do IMing and chatting on MySpace seem to serve in Piers's life? Do they increase interpersonal contact or merely give the appearance of doing so?

2. Which elements of the twins' multitasking do you think are cooperative (i.e., truly capable of being performed simultaneously without quality loss) and which are competitive (i.e., likely to interfere with each other)?

•. Should schools discourage adolescents from multitasking, should they teach adolescents the most effective ways to do it, or should they just back off?

•. Do you think that the studying style depicted in the Prologue will become the dominant working style when today's adolescents find jobs? Will the workplace adapt to this sort of multitasking, or will multitasking yield to a more focused work style?

SUMMARY

REVIEW

● **What do adolescents in the United States and other cultures do with their time?** *(p. 351)*

1. Although there are cultural, racial, and individual differences in the use of time, typical U.S. adolescents spend almost half their time in leisure activities, with the rest divided between productive and maintenance activities.

2. Adolescents can be categorized as being more or less busy, with the busier adolescents experiencing the greater amount of academic success.

3. Although true multitasking is no more possible for adolescents than for adults, adolescents favor a style that involves the near-simultaneous performance of a great number of tasks and activities.

4. Cross-cultural studies reveal that adolescents in developing societies have less free time and devote more time to household labor.

● **How has increased access to media and technology affected adolescents' lives?** *(p. 353)*

5. New technologies and media have found ready consumers in adolescents, who use media for entertainment, coping with stress, and developing a sense of the norms that apply to their age group.

6. Television viewing is the activity in which adolescents engage most frequently, which raises questions about the effects of television on attitudes toward sex, body image, and violence, as well as on sleeping habits and obesity.

7. Video games occupy an increasing amount of adolescents' (especially male adolescents') time, and the prevalence of extreme violence in many games has been linked with a tendency to perform aggressive acts.

8. The Internet can provide adolescents with a powerful resource but can also present dangers. Access to the Internet is unequal, with the "digital divide" favoring more affluent adolescents.

● **What are the effects of working while attending school?** *(p. 363)*

9. In the United States, unlike in other developed countries, it is considered normal for adolescents to hold part-time jobs while attending school.

10. Jobs provide adolescents with additional money for necessities or luxuries and can help them learn responsibility, money management, work habits, and workplace skills.

11. Jobs involving long hours can interfere with academic success and extracurricular activities.

● **Are schools doing enough to prepare adolescents for the workforce?** *(p. 367)*

12. Traditional public schooling has not focused on preparing students for jobs directly after graduation, focusing instead on college preparation.

13. Career and technical education programs provide particular skills suitable for certain careers, at which they are generally successful, but they are less successful at preparing students for a range of potential occupations and enabling them to return to college later in life.

14. The idea that work "builds character" is largely a myth because the kinds of jobs that adolescents get tend to be dead-end jobs that discourage initiative and advancement.

● **What factors influence an adolescent's choice of a career?** *(p. 371)*

15. Ginzberg identified three developmental periods through which adolescents pass on the way to a career decision, while Holland focused on six key personality types, and Super studied five stages of career self-concept.

16. Socioeconomic status, gender, and race and ethnicity all play a large role in determining which careers are considered realistic and which jobs are sought and found.

17. Despite gains in achieving equality, women and minorities still face limits and barriers to entering and advancing in top-level professions.

KEY TERMS AND CONCEPTS

primary orientation model (p. 366)

pseudomaturity (p. 366)

fantasy period (p. 367)

tentative period (p. 371)

realistic period (p. 371)

career self-concept (p. 372)

communal professions (p. 376)

agentic professions (p. 376)

12 Culture and Diversity

CHAPTER OUTLINE

PROLOGUE

O N A RECENT TUESDAY, three Jewish teenagers—one each from the Orthodox, Conservative and Reform branches of the faith—stood in front of a class of 25 Catholic teenagers and answered questions as part of a program called Student-to-Student.

The program was set up by St. Louis' Jewish Community Relations Council to prevent prejudice before it has a chance to take root in non-Jewish teens who otherwise might not have any personal contact with Jewish youths.

At John F. Kennedy Catholic High School, Ben Goldberg, a 17-year-old senior at Block Yeshiva High School in University City, was participating in his ninth presentation. Ben was representing Orthodox Judaism in the group of three presenting in Kennedy's World Religions class. . . .

The presenters used props to get the Catholic teenagers involved, passing around everything from a Torah written in Hebrew to challah bread. . . . Along the way, they talked about Jewish holidays, the Hebrew language, Jewish dietary laws and conscription in the Israeli military.

The questions came slowly at first, but in the second part of the hour, they came tumbling out:

"Will you raise your kids in the same branch of Judaism you grew up in?"

"How do you go about becoming a rabbi?"

"Can you eat chicken?" (Townsend, 2005, p. C1) ■

th!nk ABOUT THIS

IT IS THROUGH small steps like these that the gulf between adolescents of different backgrounds can be broken down. Culture affects issues big and small, and it colors the way that adolescents view the world and interact with one another.

In this chapter we look at culture and diversity. We begin by considering the ways in which culture affects virtually everything that adolescents do, as well as addressing the question of whether adolescents are members of their own distinct culture. We also look at how members of different cultures relate to one another and how adolescents develop an ethnic identity.

We next turn to the diversity of adolescence. We look at the characteristics of different ethnic minority adolescents, as well as considering the impact of socioeconomic status and poverty on adolescent development.

Finally, we examine prejudice and discrimination. We consider how stereotypes distort the way in which adolescents view members of groups other than their own. We pay special attention to the most common types of discrimination—those involving sexism and racism. ■

- In what ways are adolescents affected by culture and ethnicity?
- What are the major racial and ethnic minority groups to which adolescents belong?
- How is socioeconomic status related to race and ethnicity?
- How do prejudice, stereotypes, and discrimination work together?
- How are the lives of adolescents affected by sexism and racism?

Culture and Adolescence

grew up in the bosom of suburbia surrounded by Beckys and Suzies and Mollys, not a Shaniqua, LaTonya, or Dawnisha in sight. Becky and Suzie played jump rope, not double Dutch. Becky and Suzie had posters of Dylan McKay on their walls, not K-Ci and JoJo. Becky and Suzie watched Dance Party USA, not Soul Train. . . . I never felt comfortable around other black children, often being ostracized for the music I listened to and the ability to properly conjugate my verbs. . . . It wasn't that I didn't realize that I was black. From an early age, I knew that my hair didn't blow in the wind and my skin didn't turn red and peel on a blistering July day. Plus, there was always some obnoxious kid in my class to call me Cocoa Puff or Tar Baby, in case I forgot that I was many shades darker than everyone else. . . .

In junior high school, all of the black students peppered throughout the district converged in one building. Instead of being the only, I was now one of thirty, which was an exponential increase.

By the time I reached high school, my friends were an even mix. I spent just as much time with the AquaNet Addict (white girl) as I did with Stumpy (black girl). The objects of my affection were equally diverse, ranging from a Kurt Cobain (I really loved him) look-alike to a Larenz Tate knockoff. Gradually, the scales began to tip and by 12th grade I was gravitating towards all things black. The ease with which I once related to white people shifted, and I found myself more at ease roaming city streets than I was walking through the halls of my school. I craved contact with people who looked like me.

As this blog excerpt exemplifies, an essential part of how adolescents define themselves relates to their cultural background. Whether it involves race, ethnicity, gender, socioeconomic status, or a host of other factors, that cultural background plays a central role in determining who they are, how they view themselves, and how others treat them.

Culture is a set of traditions, behaviors, beliefs, values, attitudes, and expectations shared by members of a particular society. It comprises the ideas, beliefs, customs, values, language, and artifacts (for example, iPods, comic books, backpacks, DVDs, and highlighters) of a particular group of individuals (Betancourt & Lopez, 1993; Ponterotto, Gretchen, & Utsey, 2004).

Culture is so much a part of adolescents' daily lives that most are not even aware of the degree to which it influences and even helps define them. Sharing a culture simplifies life for adolescents, because it helps them to navigate their day-to-day activities in very basic ways.

Because of their knowledge of their own culture, adolescents understand what clothes are appropriate to wear, are guided in their choice of what foods to choose and what to avoid, and know which sexual practices are likely to be acceptable on a date (kissing) and which are not (forced sexual intercourse). Such knowledge reflects basic cultural beliefs and values.

We can look at culture on various levels. At the broadest level, we all belong to the human culture, sharing certain customs that are brought about by particular biological necessities

culture a set of traditions, behaviors, beliefs, values, attitudes, and expectations shared by members of a particular society.

(sleeping every night or eating at various times during the day rather than once every few days, for example). All humans use language, which is a defining characteristic of human culture. Furthermore, there are other cultural universals such as cooking and funeral ceremonies that, although practiced in different ways, are found in every culture.

But we also belong to various cultures that are more limited. Although culture is often thought of in a relatively broad context (as in "Western culture" or "Asian culture"), it is also possible to focus on particular *subcultural* groups within a larger, more encompassing culture. For example, we can consider particular racial, ethnic, religious, socioeconomic, or even gender groups within the United States as manifesting characteristics of a subculture. Similarly, many Texans consider themselves to be part of a particular culture. Culture can also be broken down along racial and ethnic lines. Consequently, Asian Americans or Irish Americans may look at themselves as part of a culture.

Adolescent Culture

Is adolescence a separate culture? In some important ways, it is. Adolescents have specific norms, beliefs and values, and traditions. Their use of language, too, may differ from that of the broader array of English speakers. For instance, when adolescents discuss "weed," they are more likely to be speaking of marijuana than their parents, who are more apt to think of "weed" in the context of lawn care.

But adolescence is hardly a single, homogeneous culture. As with the larger society in the United States, the individuals who compose the class of adolescents also belong to particular racial and ethnic groups, and they represent the spectrum of socioeconomic statuses. Consequently, the same divisions that distinguish members of the larger society also operate among adolescents, paving the way for cultural confusions and disagreements.

It's only relatively recently that adolescent scientists have begun to focus on culture. For most of the 20th century, the study of adolescence was focused on a relatively homogeneous population, one that was white, middle-class, American, and largely male (Swanson et al., 2003; Spencer, 2005).

Today, however, adolescence is viewed through a considerably broader lens. The United States has become a more diverse culture, as we discussed in Chapter 1. Furthermore, globalization, the integration of cultures, social movements, and financial markets around the world, has become increasingly common across a variety of dimensions, exposing adolescents to individuals with cultural backgrounds different from their own. Ultimately, it is clear that a full understanding of adolescence cannot be achieved without taking culture into account.

Acculturation: When Cultures Collide

Let's begin our look at culture by considering the reactions of adolescents when they encounter for sustained periods individuals from cultures other than their own, and how that may change them—a process called acculturation. **Acculturation** refers to the changes and adjustments that occur when groups of different people come into sustained firsthand contact.

The process of acculturation is particularly significant for adolescents belonging to racial and ethnic minorities. They are faced with reconciling the demands of their own culture with those of the dominant culture. The issue of acculturation is particularly acute for adolescents who enter a new culture through immigration, an experience that typically involves leaving their native country and suddenly finding themselves in an entirely new culture. However, even racial and ethnic minority youth who are raised their entire lives in the United States face pressures in reacting to their status as a subset of individuals living within a society in which they are a cultural minority.

acculturation the changes and adjustments that occur when groups of different people come into sustained firsthand contact.

A

B

▲ The cultural background of adolescents determines much about who they are.

The process of acculturation can produce one of four outcomes, depending on both the degree of identification with one's own culture and the strength of identification with the majority culture (illustrated in Figure 12-1):

- *Integration: Identifying with multiple cultures.* **Integration** is the process in which adolescents maintain their own culture while simultaneously seeking to adapt and incorporate the majority culture. By embracing the dominant culture, adolescents are able to feel more secure and assimilated. Adolescents who employ integration often have a *bicultural identity* in which they see themselves as part of, and comfortable with, two different cultures.

- *Assimilation: Identifying with the majority culture.* **Assimilation** occurs when an adolescent begins to identify with the mainstream culture and rejects the minority culture. Assimilated adolescents not only may adopt the values and beliefs of the majority, but also, because they are only relatively weakly identified with their own culture, may reject the values and beliefs of their own culture (Unger et al., 2006).

- *Separation: Identifying with the minority culture and rejecting the majority culture.* **Separation** occurs when adolescents identify with the ethnic minority culture to which they belong while rejecting or rebuffing the majority culture. Separation sometimes occurs with new immigrants, who may have difficulty with integrating into their new society because of a lack of understanding of the dominant culture. Often, they eventually take on the norms and values of the dominant culture. But the process of acculturation can be slow and painful, producing anxiety and depression (Kim et al., 2005; Sawrikar & Hunt, 2005).

  Separation may also occur voluntarily, as a political act. Some adolescents may wish to accentuate their racial or ethnic identity by actively separating themselves, both psychologically and physically, from members of the dominant culture. This strategy of separation, which can be used to bolster group identity, can have positive psychological benefits (Sue & Chu, 2003; Phinney, 2005).

- *Marginalization: Nonidentification with minority or majority cultures.* **Marginalization** occurs when adolescents identify neither with their minority culture nor with the majority culture. Marginalized adolescents may feel isolated from both their own cultural group and from members of the majority culture, either because they have tried to connect and failed, or sometimes because they are rejected for personal reasons by others. Ultimately, they lack a clear cultural identity, and they typically feel isolated and alienated from society (Kosic, 2004; Arredondo et al., 2006).

The particular type of identification found in racial and ethnic minorities has significant implications for their well-being. Some of the outcomes—like assimilation, integration, and occasionally even separation—can produce important psychological benefits.

integration the process in which adolescents maintain their own culture while simultaneously seeking to adapt and incorporate the majority culture.

assimilation the process in which an adolescent begins to identify with the mainstream culture and rejects the minority culture.

separation the process in which adolescents identify with the ethnic minority culture to which they belong while rejecting or rebuffing the majority culture.

marginalization the process that occurs when adolescents identify neither with their minority culture nor with the majority culture.

Identification with one's own culture

Identification with Majority Culture	STRONG	WEAK
STRONG	INTEGRATION	ASSIMILATION
WEAK	SEPARATION	MARGINALIZATION

◄ **FIGURE 12-1**

Depending on both the degree of identification with one's own culture and the strength of identification with the majority culture, the process of acculturation can produce one of the four outcomes shown here.

(*Source:* Phinney, 1990.)

On the other hand, strongly identifying with the majority culture may be seen negatively by one's minority peers. For example, although integration of majority and minority identities would seem to bring the benefits of belonging to both cultures, this may not always be true. Thus, blacks who seek to integrate the majority culture into their lives may be derided for trying to "act white" (i.e., trying to act like something they are not).

Similarly, it can be stressful for members of nondominant cultures to try to integrate themselves into the majority culture if the majority culture resists their efforts. Minority youth who are prevented from fully participating in the majority culture because of prejudice and discrimination may suffer psychological harm as a result (Schwartz, Montgomery, & Briones, 2006).

For some minority-culture adolescents, the most successful approach may be to be highly adaptive, switching back and forth between the majority and minority cultures depending on the specific situation—a process called *code switching.* In some cases, minority youth are so adept at code switching that they use different vocabulary and styles of speech depending on the group with which they are interacting (Cashman, 2005).

Developing an Ethnic Identity

Think of how you would briefly describe yourself to someone who had never met you. Would you include your ethnic background? The country from which your ancestors emigrated?

If you are a member of a minority ethnic or racial group or a recent immigrant, it is highly likely your description would prominently include that fact: "I'm a Korean American," "I'm Black," or "I'm a Serb." But if you are a member of a group that is dominant in society or statistically in the majority, it might not even occur to you to say, for example, "I'm white."

The difference between the two responses reflects differences in ethnic identity and its salience in everyday life. **Ethnic identity** refers to how members of ethnic, racial, and cultural minorities view themselves, both as members of their own group and in terms of their relationships with other groups. Ethnic identity relates to the part of adolescents' self-concept that is derived from their awareness and knowledge that they are members of a distinct social group (Umaña-Taylor, Bhanot, & Shin, 2006).

According to psychologist Jean Phinney, ethnic identity develops in several stages. The first stage is *unexamined ethnic identity,* which is characterized by a lack of consideration or exploration of one's ethnicity, as well as acceptance of the norms, beliefs, and attitudes of the dominant culture. In this stage, adolescents might not even think about ethnicity nor consider its impact on their lives. If they do think about their ethnicity, they may be embarrassed by it or reject it, believing that the dominant culture is superior (Phinney, 2003, 2006).

Although some adolescents don't move beyond an unexamined ethnic identity, most reach the next stage, ethnic identity search. In *ethnic identity search,* adolescents experience some sort of crisis that makes them become aware of ethnicity as a significant factor in their lives. It may be a shocking news event, such as a racially motivated killing, or they may be denied a job and suspect it's because of their race. In other cases, they may more gradually become aware that they are being treated differently by others because of their ethnicity.

Whatever the cause, adolescents who enter the ethnic identity search phase become motivated to obtain a deeper understanding of their cultural identity. They may read books, attend ethnic celebrations and events, or—if their ethnic identity is tied to a religious group, such as Irish Catholics—may begin to attend religious services.

The ethnic identity search may produce resentment toward dominant groups in society. As they learn more about the consequences of prejudice and discrimination, adolescents may come to believe that the majority should make amends for its discriminatory behavior.

Finally, the last stage of ethnic identity development is *achieved ethnic identity,* in which adolescents fully embrace their ethnic identity. People in this stage develop a clear sense of themselves as members of an ethnic minority and realize that this has become part of the way that

ethnic identity how members of ethnic, racial, and cultural minorities view themselves, both as members of their own group and in terms of their relationships with other groups.

they view themselves. Their membership is viewed with pride, and they have a sense of belonging to others who share their ethnic identity.

Whereas adolescents earlier may have experienced resentment or hostility regarding their ethnicity, directed either toward members of majority groups, others of their own ethnicity, or even themselves, they may feel more secure and optimistic after reaching the achieved ethnic identity stage. Furthermore, earlier feelings that they had two separate identities—one that identified with the majority culture and one that identified with their ethnic culture—are replaced with a more unified ethnic identity that draws on both parts of who they are (Shih & Sanchez, 2005).

Achieving Ethnic Identity. It's important to note that the stages of ethnic identity do not unfold according to any particular timetable. Some people may reach the achieved ethnic identity stage while still in adolescence, whereas for others it may occur later. Generally, the extent of identification with one's ethnicity increases with age.

Furthermore, some individuals may never enter the achieved ethnic identity stage or even the ethnic identity search stage at all. In such cases, ethnic identity is not perceived as part of the core of the individual. The danger is that an adolescent will be treated (and sometimes discriminated against) by others due to his or her membership in an ethnic or racial group. Such treatment may be confusing at best and psychologically damaging at worst (Yasui, Dorham, & Dishion, 2004).

Ultimately, the nature and strength of adolescents' ethnic identities are determined both by parental socialization and by the particular experiences that an individual encounters. For example, ethnic minority parents teach their children, both explicitly and implicitly, about their own culture and about the dominant culture of the society in which they live. In addition, they may explicitly teach adolescents how to deal with the prejudice and discrimination that they are likely to encounter.

Finally, as we suggested earlier, ethnic identity is likely to be strongest for members of minority groups and weakest for members of the dominant societal group (which, in U.S. society, is whites). The reason: Members of the dominant group simply don't have to think as much about their ethnicity, given that they are not subject to the discrimination and prejudice experienced by members of ethnic minority groups. In contrast, members of minority groups expend more time and effort thinking not only about their own ethnicity but also about the majority group. For ethnic minority group members, ethnicity becomes more of a part of who they are (Fiske, 2001; Guinote & Fiske, 2003).

On the other hand, the fact that whites generally have less-pronounced ethnic identities does not mean that ethnicity plays no role in their lives. Being a member of a particular nonracial ethnic or religious group (Italian, Jewish, or Irish, for example) may be a significant source of pride and may be perceived as a central part of identity. Furthermore, when whites find themselves in settings in which they are in the minority, their sense of racial identity may become magnified (Roberts et al., 1999; Romero & Roberts, 2003).

The Ethnic Identity of Immigrants. Immigration to the United States has risen significantly in the last 30 years. More than 13 million youth in the United States are either foreign born or the children of immigrants—some one fifth of the total population of children and adolescents.

What is the nature of the ethnic identity of immigrant youth? Although there's not a great deal of research on the topic, one surprising finding has emerged: Ethnic minority adolescents who are foreign born often show greater identification with the dominant culture in the United States than native-born ethnic minority youth. Furthermore, immigrant youth, overall, tend to be well adjusted. For example, they have equal or better grades in school than children whose parents were born in the United States. Psychologically, they also do quite well, showing levels of self-esteem similar to those of nonimmigrant children. They also are less likely to be involved

Transiti⊙ns

When a School Transition Fosters Ethnic Identity Development

Phinney's stage theory of ethnic identity development helps to explain how adolescents come to view themselves as members of their ethnic groups. They start out with a lack of interest in the meaning of their ethnicity, or even with a sense of detachment from it. In time, they become motivated to explore their ethnic identity, a process that ideally ends with them embracing and taking pride in their ethnicity.

Many different kinds of events or experiences may motivate adolescents to begin an active exploration of the meaning of their ethnicity. These may include suddenly encountering prejudice or gradually awakening to being treated differently from others (Cross, 1995). Some research evidence suggests that important role changes, such as the transition to senior year in high school, can also induce adolescents to examine more carefully what it means to be a member of their ethnic group (French et al., 2000). An important implication of this finding is that normal school transitions, at least under certain circumstances, may foster the development of students' ethnic identities.

Exploring the impact of school transitions was part of the focus of psychologist Sabine French and her colleagues' research on ethnic identity development in adolescence (French et al., 2006). They examined changes in ethnic identity over time in groups of early and middle adolescents who were enrolled in predominantly African-American, Hispanic, or white schools. Participants were selected who were in the last grade prior to the transition into junior high or into senior high school, and their level of ethnic identity development was measured with a questionnaire that consisted of two components. One component measured the adolescents' degree of group esteem, or how they felt about being a member of their ethnic group, and the other component measured their degree of exploration, or how much they were trying to learn more about their ethnic group. The students then completed this same questionnaire two additional times: once around the time of their school transition (1 year later) and again during the following year (2 years later).

The researchers found different results for the different components of ethnic identity. While group esteem rose over time for both the early and middle adolescent groups, exploration rose only for the middle adolescents. Early adolescents may become more favorably inclined toward their ethnic group as a result of peer and family influence, but exploration of the deeper meaning of their ethnicity and achievement of a sense of ethnic identity seem to come later in adolescence.

But something else interesting was occurring in this study: The elementary and junior high schools were ethnically homogeneous (that is, predominantly African American, Hispanic, or white) but the senior high schools were much more ethnically diverse. The transition experiences of the two groups of adolescents were therefore different. Early adolescents were transitioning into new school environments that were much like their previous school environments, but middle adolescents were encountering a sudden change in the ethnic composition of their new schools. French and her colleagues interpreted the increase in exploration for the middle adolescents as an indication that encountering ethnic diversity—and perhaps increased personal and institutional prejudice to go along with it—helped to trigger their exploration of their ethnic identities.

- What are the benefits and drawbacks of attending a racially homogeneous school?

- Why is it important for people to explore the meaning of their ethnicity to develop an ethnic identity?

in antisocial behavior such as drug use. On the downside, they do report feeling less popular and less in control of their lives (Kao, 2000; Kulis, Marsiglia, & Hurdle, 2003; Fuligni, Witkow, & Garcia, 2005).

One explanation for greater identification with the majority culture by minority adolescents whose parents are immigrants is that they come to the United States with especially idealistic attitudes about the nature of society. They come seeking a better life for themselves, and they support the view of America as a "melting pot" where all are welcome. Such positive attitudes may motivate newly arrived immigrants to identify strongly with the dominant culture. These positive attitudes may not last forever, however. Later, after facing prejudice and discrimination because of their minority status, they may become more cynical and discouraged. This can lead them to be more inclined to distance themselves from mainstream society.

The better adjustment of immigrant youth may also be explained by the relatively higher educational and often socioeconomic status of families that choose to emigrate to the United States. Despite stereotypes that immigrant families come from lower social classes, many in fact are well educated and come to the United States seeking greater opportunities. Furthermore, even the immigrant youth who are not financially well off are often more highly motivated to succeed and place greater value on education than children in nonimmigrant families. In addition, many immigrants come from societies that emphasize collectivism, and consequently their children may feel more of a sense of family obligation and duty to succeed. Finally, their country of origin may give some immigrant youth a strong enough cultural identity to prevent them from adopting undesirable "American" behaviors, such as materialism or selfishness (Fuligni, Tseng, & Lam, 1999; Fuligni & Yoshikawa, 2003; Fuligni, 2005).

Ethnic identity also varies according to how long an immigrant family has been in its new home. First-generation immigrants initially may be more invested in maintaining the culture of their country of origin because it is so much a part of them, particularly if they live in a neighborhood with other recent immigrants. By the second generation, immigrants are more likely to have a strong bicultural identity in which they view themselves as both American and members of their family's culture of origin. In the third generation, the ethnic identity of immigrants may be less pronounced, and they may feel more or less completely integrated into American society. However, there are significant individual differences. Part of ethnic identification is based on racial factors; if the immigrant family is from a European country of origin, it is much easier for it to assimilate into society because its ethnic background is less apparent. In contrast, non-Europeans, who are more easily identifiable as members of an ethnic or racial minority, are more likely to maintain their ethnic identity (Phinney, 2003).

▲ First-generation immigrants often seek to maintain the culture of their country of origin. Later generations become increasingly assimilated.

Review and Apply

Review

1. Culture influences and defines adolescents to a significant extent.

2. Acculturation into a new culture can produce one of four outcomes: integration, assimilation, separation, or marginalization.

3. Developing an ethnic identity, which is especially important to members of ethnic, racial, and cultural minorities, proceeds in stages from unexamined ethnic identity, through ethnic identity search, to achieved ethnic identity.

4. In general, foreign-born youth and the children of immigrants identify with their adopted country's dominant culture more strongly than do native-born ethnic minority youth.

5. The cultural identity of immigrant youth typically declines in strength the longer their family has been in its new home.

Apply

1. Immigrants undergo a process of assimilation with the dominant culture over time. Do adolescents experience a similar process as they age and assume adult roles in society?

2. The United States has been called a "nation of immigrants," and yet feelings toward new immigrants are often negative. How might the phenomenon of cultural identity help to explain this?

The Diversity of Adolescence

A small, troubled high school in East Harlem seemed an unlikely place to find students for a nationwide robot-building contest, but when a neighborhood after-school program started a team last winter, 19 students signed up. One was Amadou Ly, a senior who had been fending for himself since he was 14.

The project had only one computer and no real workspace. Engineering advice came from an elevator mechanic and a machinist's son without a college degree. But in an upset that astonished its sponsors, the rookie team from East Harlem won the regional competition last month, beating rivals from elite schools like Stuyvesant in Manhattan and the Bronx High School of Science for a chance to compete in the national robotics finals in Atlanta that begins tomorrow.

Yet for Amadou, who helps operate the robot the team built, success has come at a price. As the group prepared for the flight to Atlanta today, he was forced to reveal his secret: He is an illegal immigrant from Senegal, with no ID to allow him to board a plane. Left here long ago by his mother, he has no way to attend the college that has accepted him, and only a slim chance to win his two-year court battle against deportation. (Bernstein, 2006, p. A1)

For Amadou Ly, who labored for weeks with his teammates to build an entry to the robotics competition, attending high school in the United States is a dream come true. He arrived with his mother from Senegal when he was 13 years old. His mother, who knew no English, overstayed her tourist visa to enroll Ly in school. She returned to Senegal a year later, leaving Ly with a Senegalese acquaintance. Ly hopes to attend college, studying math and computer science—assuming he isn't deported from the United States due to his status as an illegal immigrant.

Immigration: Building Diversity

Ly's story is less unusual than you might think. In the aftermath of the terrorist attacks on the World Trade Center and Pentagon in 2001, the treatment of both legal and illegal immigrants has become a vexing political issue, not only in the United States, but also worldwide, where some 2 to 4 million people leave one country and move to another each year.

In fact, though, immigration has consistently been a difficult issue. Even in the United States, a country with a long and honored tradition of immigration, deciding who should be allowed to enter the country has been a divisive political issue. Furthermore, immigration policies designed to exclude members of certain groups have reflected the prejudices of particular eras. For example, in the 1920s, people from western European countries were given preference in immigration to the United States, thereby excluding those from eastern Europe, Africa, and Asia.

One reason that immigration represents such a difficult issue is that it involves basic issues of race and ethnicity, which are thorny concepts in our society. Although U.S. society holds equality as a core value, the reality of life for many members of racial and ethnic minorities is that they consistently face prejudice and discrimination. Addressing and rectifying these inequalities is one of the greatest challenges facing U.S. society today.

Understanding the role that race and ethnicity play in adolescents' lives is hampered by difficulties in finding a common vocabulary. For example, the terms *race* and *ethnic group* are often used in inappropriate ways. *Race* is a biological concept, which should be used to refer to classifications based on physical and structural characteristics of species. In contrast, *ethnic group* and *ethnicity* are broader terms, referring to cultural background, nationality, religion, and language.

The concept of race has proved particularly problematic. Although it formally refers to biological factors, race has taken on substantially more meanings—many of them inappropriate—that range from skin color to religion to culture. Moreover, the concept of race is exceedingly imprecise; depending on how it is defined, there are between 3 and 300 races, and no race is biologically pure. Furthermore, the fact that 99.9% of humans' genetic makeup is identical in all humans makes the question of race seem comparatively insignificant, at least from a biological vantage point (Angier, 2000; Carpenter, 2000; Bamshad & Olson, 2003).

In addition, there is little agreement about which names best reflect different races and ethnic groups. Should the term *African American*—which has geographical and cultural implications—be preferred over black, which focuses primarily on skin color? Is *Native American* preferable to *Indian*? Is *Hispanic* more appropriate than *Latino*? And how can researchers accurately categorize people with multiethnic backgrounds? The choice of category has important implications for the validity and usefulness of research. The choice even has political implications. For example, the decision to permit people to identify themselves as "multiracial" on U.S. government forms and in the 2000 U.S. Census was highly controversial (Perlmann & Waters, 2002; Wang, Baillargeon & Paterson, 2005).

Even the term minority group to refer to racial and ethnic groups is contentious, in part for political reasons and also because it is sometimes inaccurate. For example, in some cities in the United States, groups that are typically referred to as "minorities" are actually numerically the majority, such as Hispanics in Miami, Florida. Consequently, it is often more accurate—if also more awkward—to refer to "historically discriminated-against groups" than "minority groups." It is also possible to use the term *minority group* as a shorthand for groups whose members have significantly less power, control, and influence over their own lives than do members of a dominant group—which is the way the term is used in this book.

To compound the difficulties we face in understanding the role of race and ethnicity, some research on the topics has made the mistake of overlooking the importance of socioeconomic status. Because ethnic and racial minorities are found disproportionately in lower socioeconomic levels, sometimes what appears to be an ethnic or racial difference is really a difference in socioeconomic status.

Racial and Ethnic Minority Adolescents: Who Are They?

Regardless of what labels are used, as the proportion of racial and ethnic minority adolescents in U.S. society continues to increase, it becomes crucial to take the complex issues associated with human diversity into account to fully understand adolescence. However, as we consider next the main ethnic and racial minority groups, considerable diversity lies within each group. None of the groups is homogeneous, and it is essential to keep in mind that behind every generalization lies a range of individual adolescents (Olson, 2003; Bamshad et al., 2003; Quintana, 2004).

African Americans. African-American adolescents sometimes find themselves in an ironic position. They are members of what is the most visible of racial and ethnic minority groups in the United States. But at the same time, as writer Ralph Ellison wrote in his famous novel *Invisible Man,* African Americans are the most invisible group—invisible in the sense of often being overlooked and consigned to lower-status living conditions and jobs (Schaefer, 2005).

Although other subordinate groups in U.S. society have been relatively poor, most African-American adolescents and their families face the added burden of having ancestors who were slaves. Unable to amass wealth or property, African-American slaves could not improve their own economic situation, nor that of their families, regardless of how hard they worked. Furthermore, as we discussed in Chapter 10, anthropologist John Ogbu has noted that members of minority groups who enter a new culture involuntarily are less likely to experience success than those who emigrate voluntarily. Involuntary immigration leaves lasting wounds, diminishing the capability to succeed in subsequent generations (Ogbu, 1992; Gallagher, 1994).

On the other hand, it is a mistake to draw a portrait of African-American adolescents that depicts impoverished youth living on the margins of society. Nothing could be further from the truth. Most African-American adolescents are in school, do not live in poverty, don't take drugs, and have stability in their home lives. They don't live in urban ghettos, and they are not involved

► Members of racial and ethnic minorities may face considerable prejudice and discrimination despite substantial personal achievement.

in criminal activities. In short, despite having to overcome discrimination and prejudice that the majority of adolescents do not encounter (and have a hard time comprehending), most African-American adolescents lead stable, productive lives, experiencing a rich family and cultural life.

Still, prejudice and discrimination are a fact of life for even well-educated, affluent African Americans. African Americans face discrimination when looking for jobs, seeking housing, or even hailing a cab in U.S. cities. The median household income of African-American households is only 60% that of Whites. In many professions, African Americans are underrepresented. For example, only 7% of physicians, scientists, lawyers, and engineers are African American. Although the number of African Americans holding elective office increased substantially between 1970 and 2000, African Americans remain underrepresented (Bureau of the Census, 2002; Schaefer, 2005).

Native Americans.   Native Americans have not had an easy time in the United States. From the day Europeans arrived on the shores of North America, Native Americans have had to struggle to maintain their culture in the face of relentless pressure from more technologically developed societies that felt it was their "destiny" to occupy Indian lands. By the end of the 1800s, the Indian population was drastically reduced from its former numbers. Native Americans had been relegated to reservations or dispersed, and schools set up by the U.S. government were forbidden to teach about Native American culture.

Although educating Native Americans about their own cultural practices is no longer prohibited in their schools, Native American adolescents continue to suffer from the significant discrimination they faced, which historically took the form of efforts to eliminate not only Native American cultures but also Native Americans themselves. As a consequence of this discrimination, Native Americans face substantial social ills. Native Americans experience a high rate of poverty and poor health, including high levels of alcoholism and other substance abuse. In addition, their school dropout rate is among the highest of any racial or ethnic group, as is the suicide rate (Wilkins, 2006).

The problems seen in Native American adolescents are reflected in a level of self-esteem that is lower than in any other minority group in the United States. Furthermore, they often have problems in developing a stable identity. Native American adolescents find it difficult to resolve their rich cultural background with the high degree of repression faced by their ancestors and the prejudice they encounter today (Martinez & Dukes, 1997; Robertson, 2001; Oyserman & Fryberg, 2006).

Asian Americans. Asian-American adolescents are sometimes described as members of the *model minority.* The term is meant to be a compliment, suggesting that Asian Americans, unlike other minorities, have successfully overcome prejudice and discrimination to achieve significant accomplishments. However, the term is in fact stereotypical, demeaning to other minority groups, and ultimately not terribly accurate (Kawai, 2005).

Specifically, the use of the term *model minority* suggests that although Asian Americans somehow have been able to achieve success, other groups are less capable of becoming successful—an example of "blaming the victim" for being unable to overcome prejudice and discrimination. Moreover, there is great diversity among Asian-American adolescents. Asian Americans come from a variety of different countries (China, Vietnam, Japan, Cambodia, and Korea, among others), some of which share relatively little cultural commonality. Although some Asian Americans are wealthy, many are poor; although some do particularly well in school, others don't; some fit in socially, but others are antisocial gang members (Thao, 2005; Tsunokai, 2005; Wong & Halgin, 2006).

Furthermore, although Asian Americans complete more years of schooling than members of other racial and ethnic groups (see Table 12-1), their median household income is only slightly higher than that of whites. Furthermore, proportionally, more Asian families are living in poverty than white families.

As a group, Asian-American adolescents typically have strong family ties. As we first discussed in Chapter 5, Asian cultures largely follow a collectivistic philosophy, meaning that the well-being of the group is viewed as more important than that of the individual. In contrast to the strong belief in individualism among people in Western cultures, people in collectivistic cultures emphasize the importance of achieving not for individual rewards but to make a collective contribution to group achievement. In this context, adolescents are rewarded for good academic performance because academic success reflects positively on the family group (Fiske et al., 1998; Hoppe-Graffe & Kim, 2005; Yamaguchi et al., 2005).

The emphasis on education may also reflect the continuing cultural influence of Confucianism. The ancient Chinese philosopher Confucius emphasized the importance of discipline, respect for authority, and family honor—values that remain bedrocks of Asian culture. These

TABLE 12-1 Relative Economic Positions of Various Racial and Ethnic Groups					
Characteristic	Whites	African Americans	Native Americans	Asian Americans	Hispanic
Four-year college education, people 25 and over (2002)	27.3%	17.5%	11.5%	43.8%	11.2%
Median household income (2001)	$46,305	$29,470	$32,116	$53,635	$33,564
Unemployment rate (2003)	5.5%	11.1%	—	5.9%	8.2%
People below the poverty line (2001)	7.8%	22.7%	25.7%	10.2%	21.4%

Notes: Data on Whites, where available are for White non-Hispanics. On reservations, estimated median family income for Native Americans is $18,063. Educational and poverty data for Native Americans are for 2000 and 1999, respectively. Unemployment rate for Asian Americans by author.
(*Source:* Schaefer, 2005, pg 266).

values lead to a number of concrete parenting practices that result in higher academic achievement, such as strict parental control of adolescents' after-school hours, emphasis on the importance of self-sacrifice, and strong pressure to succeed, coupled with high expectations (Pong, Hao, & Gardner, 2005; Sy & Schulenberg, 2005; Zhou & Kim, 2006).

Hispanic Americans.   Like Asian Americans, Hispanic Americans represent a diverse lot. Comprising mainly Mexican Americans, this group also includes immigrants from Central and South America, Puerto Rico, and Cuba. The common thread among Hispanics is their Spanish origin and culture, exemplified by the use of the Spanish language by a significant number of Hispanics.

Hispanics represent the largest and one of the fastest-growing minority groups in the United States. There is great socioeconomic diversity among Hispanics, whose median household income is significantly lower than that of whites.

Family and religious values are particularly important to Hispanics, most of whom are Catholic. Families are quite influential in the lives of adolescents, with fathers, in particular, acting as strong disciplinarians. The Catholic Church is also an essential part of many Hispanic families. Ironically, the centrality of Catholicism among Mexican Americans has sometimes acted to increase the barriers that divide them and their largely Protestant neighbors in the southwestern United States (Schaefer, 2005).

As we discussed in Chapter 10, many Hispanic students enter school speaking only Spanish, and the strategies for teaching them English have been controversial. Also controversial is the extent of Spanish being used outside the classroom in areas of the United States with high Hispanic populations, such as the Southwest and Florida, as well as the presence of tens of thousands of immigrants from Mexico who have entered the country illegally (Abraham & Cramer, 2006).

For adolescents who are the children of illegal immigrants, the lack of official documentation can lead to difficult situations (similar to the situation faced by Amadou Ly, described at the beginning of this part of the chapter). For instance, some states require adolescents whose parents are illegal immigrants to pay out-of-state tuition at state colleges, effectively barring them from college attendance. In some cases adolescents affected by such policies have lived virtually their entire lives in the United States.

The educational and socioeconomic barriers faced by many Hispanic adolescents are reflected in the fact that Hispanics have one of the lowest average levels of educational attainment of any minority group. Furthermore, employment rates and the proportion of Hispanic professionals trail those of whites.

Poor Adolescents: The Impact of Socioeconomic Status and Poverty on Adolescents

One of the greatest cultural divides between adolescents relates to their socioeconomic status. It is not a trivial problem that affects only a small part of the population: Some 15% of adolescents in the United States are living in poverty (with income levels below $19,000/year for a family of 4), and 35% live in low-income households. Furthermore, although the number of youth living in low-income households began to decline in the early 1990s, it has been on the rise since 2000. The discrepancy between the rich and the poor also is growing (National Center for Children in Poverty, 2006).

Members of minority groups are proportionately more likely to be living in poverty than non-minority-group members (see Figure 12-2). However, although Latino and black children and adolescents are disproportionately from low-income households, whites are the largest group of low-income individuals. More than half of the children of immigrant parents live in low-income families.

Poverty expands well beyond the stereotyped view of poor minority youth living in cities. Adolescents living in poverty are found throughout the United States in both urban and rural

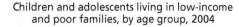

Children and adolescents living in low-income
and poor families, by age group, 2004

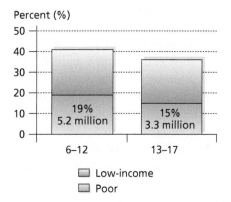

Percent (%)

	6–12	13–17
	19% 5.2 million	15% 3.3 million

☐ Low-income
☐ Poor

◀ **FIGURE 12-2**
Socioeconomic status is one of the greatest
cultural divides between adolescents.
According to the National Center for
Children in Poverty, members of minority
groups are proportionately more likely to
be living in poverty than non-minority-
group members.
(*Source:* National Center for Children in Poverty, 2006).

areas. According to Nobel winner Robert Solow, the cost of child poverty in the United States runs between $36 billion and $177 billion each year.

Poverty affects adolescents in a number of ways. In some households, there is not enough food, and adolescents go to school and to bed hungry. Because many poor households lack health insurance, adolescents living in poverty are unable to afford good medical care, and minor illnesses, left untreated, become major ones. The greater the degree of poverty, the higher the health risks.

As we've discussed in many of the previous chapters, the impact of poverty on adolescent development is profound. It impedes adolescents' ability to learn and can slow their cognitive development, making academic success less likely. In addition, poverty is associated with behavioral and emotional difficulties. Adolescents living in persistent poverty are less well adjusted and have more conduct problems, in part because their parents' emotional well-being is reduced, making them less-successful caregivers (Maughan, 2001; Smokowski et al., 2004; Gutman, McLoyd, & Tokoyawa, 2005)

Poverty, of course, is not an insoluble problem, and solutions should be within the means of as affluent a country as the United States. However, the rate of poverty in the United States is actually higher than in many other industrialized countries. Why? The answer has a good

◀ Adolescents living in poverty are at
greater risk for behavioral and emotional
problems.

deal to do with aggressive antipoverty measures adopted by other nations. Compared with the United States, public assistance levels for poor families are often higher, health-care benefits are better, and governments have more programs to help those living in poverty (Smeeding, Danziger, & Rainwater, 1995).

The lower poverty rates in countries other than the United States offer a ray of hope even to poor people in this country, suggesting that the rate can be reduced. One route is clearly educational, for the higher the parental educational level, the less the chance of a child being raised in poverty. For example, only 11% of children living in poverty had at least one parent who had achieved an educational level beyond high school. In contrast, an astonishing 89% of children whose more educated parent did not graduate from high school lived in poverty (National Center for Children in Poverty, 1996).

Another route is through improvements in government programs and benefits targeted to the poor. Although current political trends and the 1996 federal welfare reform laws have been interpreted as moving the United States further from the goal of reducing poverty, some government programs on the state and local levels have been successful in breaking the bonds of poverty. Ultimately, improvements in income levels will produce substantial benefits, not just for the poor, but for all children and for society in general (Huston, Coll, & McLoyd, 1994; Rickel & Becker, 1997; Takanishi, Hamburg, & Jacobs, 1997).

Review and Apply

Review

1. Adolescents from other countries often face challenges in the United States stemming from political controversy surrounding the issue of immigration.

2. In the United States, the major groups of minority adolescents are African Americans, Native Americans, Asian Americans, and Hispanic Americans, each of which actually comprises many separate ethnic groups.

3. Minority adolescents are more likely to live in poverty than nonminority adolescents, with all the disadvantages and challenges that poverty brings.

4. Poverty rates in the United States are higher than in many other industrialized countries, largely because policy makers have not supported aggressive antipoverty programs.

Apply

1. If the lives of most African-American adolescents are stable and productive, why does the stereotype of ghettoized, impoverished young blacks remain so dominant?

2. Do you think Hispanics of Mexican descent living in California have more in common with their white neighbors or with Hispanics of Puerto Rican descent living in New York? Does your answer change depending on how long each group has been in the United States?

Prejudice and Discrimination

*W*hen I was 17, I wanted to be "authentic" too. I was a white, suburban, middle class kid and I wanted to be tough, street-smart and sexy. I wanted to be cool. Part of being cool was being, well—black.

And since I had no hope of changing my skin color it meant listening to black music, reading black authors, and feeling, at least, a sense of solidarity with an oppressed and talented people.

But in fact I had very little contact with actual black people.

■ ■ ■

Black and white kids did not play together in the schoolyard, and the black kids ate together in the cafeteria. We didn't socialize at all outside of school. This continued into high school and the only chance you might have to socialize with black people was in team sports. Even then, contact was largely limited to team activities. I did not know why this was so, and I never questioned it. It was just the way things were.

■ ■ ■

Ethnicity = individualism = self-segregation?

Black kids huddling in the cafeteria, all dressing alike.... Third generation Asian-American kids still speaking their parents' native tongue w/ friends.... Arabic kids dating only Arabic girls.

Is cultural pride segregating American kids today?

■ ■ ■

Stepping into the cafeteria, there was somewhat of a racial divide. White kids in this corner, black kids over there, Mexican kids there, etc. So if the dream is still alive, why do these things exist?

Navigating racial, ethnic, and other cultural differences is among the most difficult challenges that adolescents face, as these blog excerpts imply. Learning how to accept and interact with individuals who are different in important ways from oneself represents an important developmental task for adolescents.

For some, the challenge is too great, and adolescents' prejudiced attitudes and stereotypes guide their behavior. In this final part of the chapter, we examine the basic concepts of prejudice, stereotypes, and discrimination.

Prejudice, Stereotypes, and Discrimination: The Foundations of Hate

Prejudice refers to the negative (or positive) evaluations or judgments of members of a group that are based primarily on group membership, and not necessarily on the particular characteristics of individuals. For example, gender prejudice occurs when an adolescent is evaluated on the basis of being a male or female and not because of his or her own specific characteristics or abilities.

Although prejudice is generally thought of as a negative evaluation of group members, it can also be positive: As we'll see, at the same time adolescents dislike members of groups to which they don't belong, they may also positively evaluate members of their own group. In both cases, the assessment is unrelated to qualities of particular individuals; rather, it is due simply to membership in the specific group to which the individuals belong.

The mental framework that maintains prejudice is a stereotype. A **stereotype** is a set of beliefs and expectations about members of a group that are held simply because of their membership in the group. Stereotypes are oversimplifications that people employ in an effort to make sense of the complex social environment in which they live. They determine how information is interpreted, so that even when adolescents are exposed to evidence contrary to their stereotypes, they may interpret the information in a way that supports their prejudice (Aronson & Steele, 2005; Dovidio, Glick, & Rudman, 2005; Judd & Park, 2005).

Ultimately, prejudice and stereotypes can lead to **discrimination,** the negative (or sometimes positive) actions taken toward members of a particular group because of their membership in

prejudice   the negative (or positive) evaluations or judgments of members of a group that are based primarily on group membership, and not necessarily on the particular characteristics of individuals.

stereotype   a set of beliefs and expectations about members of a group that are held simply because of their membership in the group.

discrimination   the negative (or sometimes positive) actions taken toward members of a particular group because of their membership in the group.

▲ Prejudice and stereotypes are learned during childhood.

the group. Although prejudice and discrimination often go hand in hand, one may be present without the other.

In the most extreme case, people's biases lead them to engage in self-fulfilling prophecies. *Self-fulfilling prophecies* reflect the tendency of people to act in ways that are consistent with their expectations, beliefs, or cognitions about an event or behavior, thereby increasing the likelihood that the event or behavior will occur. Consequently, if an adolescent thinks that members of a certain group are lazy, he or she may act in a way that actually elicits laziness from the members of that group.

The Roots of Prejudice

Female. African American. Islamic fundamentalist. Gay.

Quick: What images first come to mind when you read or hear each of these words? For most people, encountering a description of a person that includes such a label is enough to summon a rich network of impressions, memories, and probably even predictions of how that person will behave in a given situation. The presence of such connections suggests that we are all susceptible to prejudice.

But where does prejudice originate? There are several sources.

Social Learning Explanations: The School of Stereotyping. Adolescents are not born feeling prejudice and showing discrimination to members of different religions, ethnic groups, or races. It is something that is taught to them, in much the same way that they learn that $2 + 2 = 4$.

The *social learning view* suggests that people develop prejudice and stereotypes about members of various groups in the same way they learn other attitudes, beliefs, and values. For instance, one important source of information for children regarding stereotypes and prejudice is the behavior and teaching of parents, other adults, and peers. Through direct reinforcement, and through observation of the reinforcement given to others, people learn about members of other groups. Such learning begins at an early age: By the time they are preschoolers, children are able to distinguish between African Americans and whites, and even at that age they can possess preferential feelings for members of their own group over others (Ramsey & Myers, 1990; Cossman, 2004).

Children are not the only ones who learn stereotypes and prejudice from others. Although significant improvements have been made in the past decade, television and other media often portray minority group members in shallow, stereotyped ways. For instance, portrayals of African Americans perpetuate some of society's most distasteful stereotypes, with many African-American males being portrayed as sexually obsessed, shiftless, and speaking primarily in jive. Other groups are stereotyped in the media in equally derogatory ways, such as Godfather-like Italian mobsters, greedy Jewish bankers, and Hispanics in criminal or menial jobs (Mok, 1998; Alexander, Brewer, & Livingston, 2005; Jost & Hamilton, 2005).

Social Identity Theory: The Self-Esteem of Group Membership. Think about your ethnic or religious identity for a moment. Are you proud of it? Does it make you feel good to be part of the group? Would you feel threatened if your group were criticized or attacked?

Most adolescents feel pride in the groups to which they belong. But this pride has a downside: It can lead to prejudice and discrimination. According to **social identity theory,** adolescents use group membership as a source of pride and self-worth. However, to feel such pride, they must assume that their group is, in fact, superior to others. As a result, their quest for a positive social identity leads them to inflate the positive aspects of groups to which they belong and belittle groups to which they do not belong (Abrams & Hogg, 1999; Tajfel, 2001; Tajfel & Turner, 2004).

Certainly, there is ample evidence that members of various cultural groups tend to see their own groups in more positive terms than others. For instance, one cross-cultural investigation

social identity theory the theory that adolescents use group membership as a source of pride and self-worth.

that examined 17 different societies found that, universally, people rated the group to which they belonged as more peace loving, virtuous, and obedient than other groups (LeVine & Campbell, 1972). Even countries in which national pride is relatively lower than that of other countries still are viewed quite positively by their citizens (see Table 12-2).

Of course, not all groups allow us to achieve the same sense of self-worth as others. It is important for groups to be small enough so that people can feel somewhat unique and special. In fact, minority group membership sometimes produces stronger feelings of social identity than majority group membership. Minority group leaders of the past who used slogans such as "Black is Beautiful" and "Gay Pride" reflected an awareness of the importance of instilling group pride. Research has supported this strategy: Ethnic group membership can be an important source of psychological support, particularly for minority group members (Mossakowski, 2003; González & Gándara, 2005).

TABLE 12-2 National Pride by Countries					
NATIONAL PRIDE IN SPECIFIC ACHIEVEMENTS			**GENERAL NATIONAL PRIDE**		
Rank	Country	Score	Rank	Country	Score
1	Ireland	39.3	1	Austria	17.6
2	United States	38.5	2	United States	17.2
3	Canada	37.5	3	Bulgaria	17.0
4	Austria	36.5	4	Hungary	16.7
5	New Zealand	36.4	5	Canada	16.6
6	Norway	35.2	6	The Philippines	16.5
7	Great Britain	34.7	7	New Zealand	16.4
8	The Netherlands	34.6	8	Japan	16.4
9	Japan	34.5	9	Ireland	16.3
10	Spain	33.1	10	Spain	16.0
11	The Philippines	32.4	11	Slovenia	16.0
12	Germany (West)	32.2	12	Norway	15.8
13	Sweden	31.6	13	Poland	15.8
14	Bulgaria	31.4	14	Great Britain	15.4
15	Germany (East)	31.0	15	Russia	15.3
16	Slovenia	30.9	16	The Netherlands	14.5
17	Italy	30.5	17	Sweden	14.4
18	Czech Republic	29.5	18	Czech Republic	14.3
19	Hungary	28.4	19	Italy	14.1
20	Slovakia	28.2	20	Latvia	13.9
21	Poland	28.2	21	Germany (West)	13.7
22	Russia	28.0	22	Germany (East)	13.6
23	Latvia	27.8	23	Slovakia	13.5

Source: GSS News, 1998.

Overall, membership in a group provides people with a sense of personal identity and self-esteem. When a group is successful, self-esteem can rise; conversely, when self-esteem is threatened, people feel enhanced attraction to their own group and increased hostility toward members of other groups (Swann & Wyer, 1997; Branscombe, Ellemers, Spears, & Doosje, 1999; Garcia et al., 2005).

However, the use of group membership as a source of pride can lead to unfortunate consequences. For instance, in an effort to raise their own self-esteem, adolescents may come to think that their own group (known as the *ingroup*) is superior to groups to which they do not belong (the *outgroup*). Consequently, they inflate the positive aspects of the ingroup and, at the same time, devalue outgroups and their members. Eventually they come to see members of outgroups as inferior to members of their ingroup. The ultimate result is prejudice toward members of groups of which they are not a part (Tajfel & Turner, 2004; Brown, Bradley, & Lang, 2006; Lam et al., 2006).

As we first noted in Chapter 7, the belittling of the outgroup leads adolescents to another sort of bias, called the outgroup homogeneity bias, which is the perception that there is less variability among the members of outgroups than within one's own ingroup. They assume that members of other groups are fairly similar to one another. In contrast, they are acutely sensitive to differences among members of their own groups (Linville & Fischer, 1998; Eckes, Trautner, & Behrendt, 2005; Judd et al., 2005).

Why do adolescents assume that the outgroup is homogeneous? One reason is that they have less complex conceptualizations of outgroup members. White adolescents asked to describe African Americans tend to use fewer descriptive dimensions, just as adolescents have more general and incomplete views of older people than they do of persons of their own age. In contrast, people tend to have considerably more differentiated views of members of their own group. To a Latino adolescent, all Latinos don't seem similar; to a white adolescent, all whites don't appear to act alike (Judd, Ryan, & Park, 1991; Robbins & Krueger, 2005; Corenblum & Meissner, 2006).

Adolescents are particularly susceptible to such assumptions when they have relatively little contact with members of outgroups. But even in situations in which they have substantial contact with members of an outgroup, adolescents may harbor significant prejudice. A case in point is prejudice based on gender, as we see next.

Sexism: Prejudice and Gender

The words, "It's a boy" or "It's a girl" are almost always the initial words spoken in delivery rooms everywhere upon the emergence of an infant into the world. And as soon as the gender of the child becomes known, other things quickly unfold: Girls are wrapped in pink, boys in blue; girls and boys are dressed in different styles of clothing; and members of the two genders receive different toys. From the moment of birth, boys and girls are treated quite differently, and those differences persist into adolescence and beyond (Fogel, Toda, & Kawai, 1988; Grieshaber, 1998; Goodheart, 2006).

The difference in the way boys and girls are treated is a result of **gender roles,** the set of expectations, defined by society, that indicate what is appropriate behavior for males and females. These gender roles have a profound effect not only on how males and females are treated by others, but also on how they themselves behave.

Because gender roles differ between men and women, they can produce *stereotyping*, judgments about individual members of a group on the basis of their membership in that group. Stereotypes about gender roles are reflected in **sexism,** negative attitudes and behavior toward a person that are based on that person's gender.

In Western societies, stereotypes about males and females fall into consistent, well-established patterns that occur regardless of age, socioeconomic status, or social and educational background. Specifically, females are seen as having traits involving warmth and expressiveness, such as being gentle or aware of others' feelings. In contrast, men tend to be seen as having

gender roles the set of expectations, defined by society, that indicate what is appropriate behavior for males and females.

sexism negative attitudes and behavior toward a person that are based on that person's gender.

traits involving competence, such as independence and competitiveness. The problem is not so much that there is a difference in stereotypes, but that such differences in perception favor males over females because Western societies traditionally hold competence in higher esteem than warmth and expressivity (Fiske, Cuddy, & Glick, 2002; Anderson & Smith, 2005; Crawford & Kaufman, 2006; Harway & Nutt, 2006).

Such differences are not only a phenomenon pertaining to Western societies; they also hold true across cultures. For instance, one 25-nation study found that certain adjectives used to describe men and women were similar across cultures: Women were seen as sentimental, submissive, and superstitious, while men were viewed as adventurous, forceful, and independent. Generally, men were seen as having higher status than women (see Table 12-3; Williams & Best, 1990; Lips, 2003).

Gender stereotypes like these matter. They shape beliefs and expectations about how boys and girls should behave during adolescence and later in life. In turn, these rigid expectations keep inequalities between the sexes alive by putting pressure on adolescents to fulfill societal

TABLE 12-3 Descriptive Adjectives for Men and Women

Items Associated with Males		Items Associated with Females
Active	Initiative	Affected
Adventurous	Inventive	Affectionate
Aggressive	Lazy	Attractive
Ambitious	Logical	Charming
Arrogant	Loud	Curious
Assertive	Masculine	Dependent
Autocratic	Opportunistic	Dreamy
Clear-thinking	Progressive	Emotional
Coarse	Rational	Fearful
Courageous	Realistic	Feminine
Cruel	Reckless	Gentle
Daring	Robust	Mild
Determined	Rude	Sensitive
Disorderly	Self-confident	Sentimental
Dominant	Serious	Sexy
Egotistical	Severe	Softhearted
Energetic	Stern	Submissive
Enterprising	Stolid	Superstitious
Forceful	Strong	Talkative
Hardheaded	Unemotional	Weak
Hardhearted	Wise	
Independent		

(*Source:* Williams & Best, 1990)

stereotypes. They also lead adolescents to behave in accordance with the stereotypes rather than in accordance with their own abilities (Lips, 2003; Alley & Hicks, 2005).

Gender stereotyping is particularly pronounced during adolescence. Adolescents often hold rigid views about what is appropriate behavior for males and females, and those who deviate from the norm face particularly harsh reactions from their peers. In turn, these negative reactions can produce declines in self-esteem for those who violate the implicit rules of conduct for females and males (Abrahams & Ahlbrand, 2002; Alley & Hicks, 2005).

We've already seen in earlier chapters how gender stereotypes play out. For instance, girls and boys are treated differently in the classroom (Chapter 10), and professional opportunities for women are more limited than those for men (Chapter 11). But men are not always the beneficiaries of society's gender stereotypes. For example, adolescent males may view the appearance of sensitivity as somehow inappropriate and hide their emotions and vulnerabilities, hampering their relationships with others. Later, when they become parents, they may feel that their wives are better suited to raising their children, subsequently missing out on the joys of child rearing (Crawford & Unger, 2004.

In addition, stereotypes for males are sometimes more rigid and confining than those for females. A male adolescent who acts in what is seen as a "feminine" manner is likely to face more social disapproval than a female who acts in what is seen as a "masculine" manner (Alfieri, Ruble, & Higgins, 1996; Best, 2004; Trautner et al., 2005).

Benevolent Sexism: When Being Nice is Not So Nice.   Although some cases of unequal treatment of women represent *hostile sexism* in which people treat women in a way that is overtly harmful, in other cases women are the victims of benevolent sexism. *Benevolent sexism* is a form of sexism in which women are placed in stereotyped and restrictive roles that appear, on the surface, to be positive.

Benevolent sexism even seems, at first, to be beneficial to women. For instance, a male college professor may compliment a female student on her good looks or offer to give her an easier research project so she won't have to work so hard. Although the professor may feel that he is merely being thoughtful, in fact he may be making the woman feel that she is not taken seriously, thereby undermining her view of her competence. In short, benevolent sexism can be just as harmful as hostile sexism (Glick et al., 2000).

▶ Gender stereotypes may limit the choice of activities that men (and women) feel are appropriate.

Sources of Gender Stereotypes. How do gender stereotypes arise in the first place, and why are they so powerful during adolescence? Developmentalists have proposed several explanations.

Biological perspectives on gender. Some sources of gender-related behavior seem to be related to biological factors. For example, hormones appear to affect gender-based behaviors. Girls exposed to unusually high levels of *androgens* (male hormones) prenatally are more likely to display behaviors associated with male stereotypes than are their sisters who were not exposed to androgens (Hines et al., 2002; Servin, Nordenstroem, & Larsson, 2003; Dluzen, 2005; Iervolino et al., 2005).

In addition, androgen-exposed girls preferred boys as friends and spent more time during childhood than other girls in activities associated with the male role. Similarly, boys exposed prenatally to atypically high levels of female hormones are apt to display more behaviors that are stereotypically female than is usual (Hines & Kaufman, 1994; Berenbaum, 1999; Servin et al., 2003).

Moreover, some research suggests that biological differences exist in the structure of female and male brains. For instance, part of the *corpus callosum,* the bundle of nerves that connects the hemispheres of the brain, is proportionally larger in women than in men. To some theoreticians, evidence such as this suggests that gender differences may be produced by biological factors like hormones (Benbow, Lubinski, & Hyde, 1997; Westerhausen et al., 2004; Shin et al., 2005).

Before accepting such contentions, however, it is important to note that alternative explanations abound. For example, it may be that the corpus callosum is proportionally larger in women as a result of certain kinds of experiences that influence brain growth in particular ways. For instance, because girls are spoken to more than boys as infants, this difference in behavior might produce differences in brain development. If this is true, environmental experience produces biological change—and not the other way around.

Other scientists see gender differences as serving the biological goal of survival of the species through reproduction. Basing their work on an evolutionary approach, these theorists suggest that our male ancestors who showed more stereotypically masculine qualities, such as forcefulness and competitiveness, may have been able to attract females who were able to provide them with hardy offspring. Females who excelled at stereotypically feminine tasks, such as nurturing, may have been valuable partners because they could increase the likelihood that children would survive the dangers of childhood (Geary, 1998; Firestone, Firestone, & Catlett, 2006).

As in other domains that involve the interaction of inherited biological characteristics and environmental influences, it is difficult to attribute behavioral characteristics unambiguously to biological factors. Because of this problem, we must consider other explanations for gender differences.

Psychoanalytic Perspectives. You may recall from Chapter 1 that Freud's psychoanalytic theory suggests that we move through a series of stages related to biological urges. To Freud, the preschool years encompass the phallic stage, in which the focus of a child's pleasure relates to genital sexuality.

Freud argued that the end of the phallic stage is marked by an important turning point in development: the Oedipal conflict. According to Freud, the *Oedipal conflict* occurs at around the age of 5, when the anatomical differences between males and females become particularly evident. Boys begin to develop sexual interests in their mothers, viewing their fathers as rivals.

As a consequence, boys conceive a desire to kill their fathers—just as Oedipus did in the ancient Greek tragedy. However, because they view their fathers as all-powerful, boys develop a fear of retaliation, which takes the form of castration anxiety. To overcome this fear, boys repress their desires for their mothers and instead begin to identify with their fathers, attempting to be as similar to them as possible. **Identification** is the process in which children attempt to be similar to their same-sex parent, incorporating the parent's attitudes and values.

identification the process in which children attempt to be similar to their same-sex parent, incorporating the parent's attitudes and values.

Girls, according to Freud, go through a different process. They begin to feel sexual attraction toward their fathers and experience *penis envy*—a view that not unexpectedly has led to accusations that Freud viewed women as inferior to men. In order to resolve their penis envy, girls ultimately identify with their mothers, attempting to be as similar to them as possible.

In the cases of both boys and girls, the ultimate result of identifying with the same-sex parent is that the children adopt their parents' gender attitudes and values. In this way, said Freud, society's expectations about the ways females and males "ought" to behave are perpetuated into new generations.

You may find it difficult to accept Freud's elaborate explanation of gender differences. So do many adolescent scientists, who believe that gender development is best explained by other mechanisms. In part, they base their criticisms of Freud on the lack of scientific support for his theories.

For example, children learn gender stereotypes much earlier than the age of 5. Furthermore, this learning occurs even in single-parent households. Although research supports some aspects of psychoanalytic theory—such as findings indicating that preschool-age children whose same-sex parents support sex-stereotyped behavior tend to demonstrate that behavior also—simpler processes can account for such phenomena. Consequently, many developmentalists have searched for explanations of gender differences other than Freud's (Martin & Ruble, 2004).

Social Learning Approaches. As their name implies, social learning approaches see children as learning gender-related behavior and expectations by observing others. Adolescents are keen observers of the behavior of their parents, teachers, siblings, and peers. A little boy sees the glory of a major league baseball player and becomes interested in sports. A middle-school girl watches her high school neighbor practicing cheerleading moves and begins to try them herself. The observation of the rewards that these others attain for acting in a way that is consistent with gender stereotypes leads observers to conform to such behavior themselves (Rust et al., 2000).

Books and the media, and in particular television and video games, also play a role in perpetuating traditional views of gender-related behavior. Analyses of the most popular television shows, for example, find that male characters outnumber female characters 2 to 1. Furthermore, females are more apt to appear with males, whereas female–female relationships are relatively uncommon (Calvert, Kotler, & Zehnder, 2003).

Television also presents men and women in traditional gender roles. Television shows typically define female characters in terms of their relationships with males. Females are more likely to appear as victims than males (Wright et al., 1995; Turner-Bowker, 1996). They are less likely to be presented as productive or as decision makers and more likely to be portrayed as interested in romance, their homes, and their families. Such models, according to social learning theory, are apt to have a powerful influence on observers' definitions of appropriate behavior (VandeBerg & Streckfuss, 1992; Browne, 1998; Nathanson, Wilson, & McGee, 2002).

Popular magazines for adolescents also perpetuate and teach gender stereotypes. For example, an analysis of the articles in Seventeen, a monthly magazine targeted toward teenage girls, found that over 60% of the articles in every issue were devoted to the topics of fashion, beauty, food, and decorating. The fiction showed women and men in gender-traditional professional roles, and the emphasis was often on finding a boyfriend or husband. For example, in one case, a high school sophomore suddenly finds a boyfriend, and announces with elation, "Now I was someone with a future. . . . Until now I'd been a kid, stumbling along. . . . A few weeks ago I'd been a zero and now I had a boyfriend!" (Pierce, 1993, p. 64).

In some cases, the learning of social roles does not involve models, but occurs more directly. For example, a father may tell his adolescent son to "act like a man"—which may mean to avoid showing emotion or to act tough and stoic. In contrast, girls are encouraged to behave politely and courteously—traits associated with society's traditional stereotypes of women. Such direct training sends a clear message about the behavior expected of male and female adolescents (Witt, 1997; Leaper, 2002).

Cognitive approaches. In the view of some theorists, as part of their motivation to form a clear sense of identity, adolescents establish a *gender identity,* a perception of themselves as male or female. As they develop this gender identity, they build a **gender schema,** a mental framework that organizes information relevant to gender.

Gender schemas are particularly powerful, as sex represents one of the most salient and potent social categories that adolescents employ. Having been learned early in life, gender schemas provide a lens through which adolescents view their peers and themselves. For example, a male adolescent who is urged to take a cooking class may refuse not because he doesn't actually like cooking, but because the activity is incompatible with his gender schema (Bem, 1998; Martin, 2000; Barberá, 2003; Martin & Ruble, 2004).

How do we discourage people from using gender schemas to evaluate others and themselves? According to psychologist Sandra Bem (1998), one way is to encourage adolescents to be androgynous, a state in which gender roles encompass characteristics thought typical of both sexes. For instance, androgynous males may sometimes be assertive and pushy (typically thought of as male-appropriate traits), but they may also behave with warmth and tenderness (typically seen as female-appropriate traits).

Similarly, androgynous females may behave with empathy and tenderness but also may be competitive, aggressive, and independent. The key point is that androgynous people do not react to individual situations on the basis of traditional expectations about what constitutes masculine or feminine behavior. Instead, they draw on both sets of characteristics, behaving in ways that are appropriate for given situations.

The idea of the androgynous adolescent does not mean that boys and girls should be expected to behave in exactly the same way, nor that the differences between the sexes, of which there are many, should be altogether minimized or ignored. Similarly, it does not imply that the use of gender schemas necessarily leads to sexism. What the concept does suggest is that rather than acting in ways that society deems appropriate for male and female adolescents, adolescents should behave in a human way, based on freely made choices.

▲ The media perpetuate specific views relating to gender.

Adolescent
DIVERSITY   Sexual Minority Adolescents and Sexual Prejudice

G AY, LESBIAN, AND BISEXUAL adolescents have long been stigmatized in the United States, and although attitudes toward these groups have been improving in recent years, sexual prejudice remains strong. For example, overt expressions of sexual prejudice are commonplace among adolescents, who tend to use antigay slurs frequently and with little regard for their hurtfulness. This practice begins early in adolescence, and it often seems to represent a way for adolescent boys and girls to express their own masculinity or femininity and to assert their heterosexual identities. Adolescents may subtly use antigay language in this

gender schema   a mental framework that organizes information relevant to gender.

way, even when they try to appear overtly tolerant and unprejudiced (Herek, 2000; Renold, 2002; Korobov, 2004; Pascoe, 2005).

This open atmosphere of sexual prejudice stigmatizes gay, lesbian, and bisexual adolescents, creating a sense of alienation and damaging their self-esteem. Antigay bullying at school can also have long-term harmful effects for these adolescents, including posttraumatic stress, depression, and alcohol or substance abuse (Savin-Williams, 1990; Rivers, 2004).

Certain themes that devalue nonheterosexuality are prevalent in the sexual prejudice that sexual-minority adolescents encounter. These themes include beliefs that homosexuality is evil, immoral, unnatural, a temporary phase, or an illness (Hillier & Harrison, 2004).

Chronic reminders of these beliefs are anxiety provoking to sexual-minority adolescents, who may worry that they will disappoint their parents or be rejected by them or that they will be abused by or alienated from their peers if their nonheterosexuality is discovered. Shame and despair are the unsurprising consequences for many of these adolescents.

But not every outcome is negative. Many adolescents become psychologically resilient by challenging these beliefs. For example, resilient adolescents may dismiss these messages as stemming from ignorance, or they might decide that it's the people who express sexual prejudice who have the real problem.

A common theme to these resistance strategies used by sexual-minority adolescents is the reassessment of the standard by which they have been judged. Most basically, these resilient adolescents believe that their sexual feelings are normal and strive to have them recognized as such (Hillier & Harrison, 2004).

Racism: Hatred in Color

Despite enormous strides in the civil rights arena, including the end to legal segregation in the United States, African Americans still fall behind whites on many crucial measures of economic and social success. The proportion of African Americans who have completed college is half that of whites; the African-American unemployment rate is more than double that of whites; and the proportion of African Americans who live below poverty levels is three times greater than that of whites (Bureau of the Census, 2005).

Curiously, such grim social and economic facts fly in the face of data regarding white society's stated views about African Americans, which, at least on the surface, have become considerably more positive over the years. For example, studies of stereotypes begun in the 1930s and followed up through subsequent decades show that many of the more blatant negative views about African Americans, which people admitted freely in the first half of this century, have been moderated. In general, when directly asked, fewer people feel that African Americans as a group harbor such negative traits as "laziness" or "ignorance"—stereotypes that were believed and openly acknowledged as recently as the 1950s (Katz & Brayly, 1933; Karlins, Coffman, & Walters, 1969; Dovidio & Gaertner, 1986).

Modern Racism.   But has the white majority, by and large, really become less prejudiced? Some psychologists suggest that despite the apparent reduction of visible stereotyping of African Americans and other racial minorities, a new kind of racism has taken its place, called modern racism. **Modern racism** is a subtle form of prejudice in which adolescents appear, on the surface, not to harbor prejudice, while actually holding racist attitudes. According to this view, if we scratch the apparently nonracist surface of many adolescents, we will find bigotry lurking beneath (Gaertner & Dovidio, 1986; McConahay, 1986; Dovidio & Gaertner, 1991).

Modern racism arises because adolescents often embrace competing beliefs and values. They want to see themselves as part of the mainstream of society and as fair, humanitarian, and

modern racism a subtle form of prejudice in which adolescents appear, on the surface, not to harbor prejudice, while actually holding racist attitudes.

CAREER CHOICES

Diversity Counselor

Name: Maria Lopez-Strong

Education: BS, Human Development, Texas Tech University, Lubbock, Texas; MA, Interdisciplinary program in Educational Psychology, Bilingual Education, Communications Studies, Sociology, Texas Tech University, Lubbock Texas.

Position: Diversity Coordinator, South Plains College, Levelland, Texas

Home: Lubbock, Texas

WITH CENSUS PROJECTIONS showing the ethnic mix of the United States changing dramatically over the next 100 years, many college campuses are working not only toward establishing greater student diversity but also preparing students for a more diverse future in the workforce.

For South Plains College, a small community college in the northwest area of Texas, diversity is an important issue, according to Maria Lopez-Strong, diversity coordinator for the 9,300-student school.

"In Texas, the Hispanic population is growing at such a rapid rate that the state has to make significant adjustments," she said. "We have to be prepared to educate students with non-English-speaking backgrounds. We have to look into the future to make sure we have a workforce that can sustain itself in a diverse environment—not just in Texas, but all over America."

Because more than half of the student body at South Plains College is the first in their families to attend college, the two-year institution offers a variety of programs to help students make the transition into college.

"Many of our students come from rural areas and many are from Hispanic backgrounds, and they may not have been exposed to other cultures and backgrounds," said Lopez-Strong, who is also advisor to the school's Hispanic and Black student organizations. "One

course we offer that many students take is American Minority Studies. It covers the historical, economic, social, and cultural developments of all American minorities."

In addition, South Plains College presents numerous diversity events and lectures throughout the year coordinated by Lopez-Strong.

"One of our more interesting ones was a "Year of the Dog Mixer," in which one of our professors from China offered an explanation of what "Year of the Dog" means and discussed what it was like to live in China," she explained. "Students were able to see through his eyes what China is and what his culture is like. I think it is important to show students your own perspective on your culture, letting them see it through your eyes.

"We have to understand that we are not all going to look like and think like each other," she added.

Thinking of becoming a diversity counselor?

The job of diversity counseling is becoming increasingly important as the population becomes more diverse. They help promote diversity in educational institutions and the workplace by conducting workshops and programs designed to sensitize individuals to diversity issues, including the development of policies for dealing with harassment, discrimination, and bullying. In addition, diversity counselors may provide support to victims of prejudice and discrimination and may engage in conflict resolution activities.

Diversity counselors often have a master's or doctorate in some counseling-related field. They may also have degrees in psychology, social justice, women's studies, ethnic studies, or education. Diversity counselors need to be fair, open-minded, and able to consider multiple viewpoints simultaneously. ■

egalitarian individuals (Katz & Hass, 1988). At the same time, though, they may still hold somewhat negative views of members of groups other than their own (Biernat et al., 1996). In most cases, they keep their prejudice under wraps, but when placed in situations in which they are given social support for racism, they are willing to express, and sometimes act on, their unfavorable opinions (Schnake & Ruscher, 1998).

For instance, most people avoid publicly endorsing overtly racist statements because of social pressures against such behavior. But when more subtle measurement techniques are used, it becomes clear that many negative stereotypes of African Americans and members of other racial groups remain in force (McConahay, Hardee, & Batts, 1981; Pettigrew, 1989; Pfiefer & Ogloff, 1991; Fazio et al., 1995).

For example, when an ethnically diverse group of college students in one study were asked to list the first 10 adjectives that came to mind when they thought of members of various racial and ethnic groups, the lists reflected traditional stereotypes. For instance, African-American males were seen as "antagonistic" and "athletic," whereas Mexican-American males were seen as "lower class." In contrast, Anglo-American and Asian-American males were viewed more positively, although no group was viewed as possessing uniformly positive traits (Niemann et al., 1994). (For a profession involved in facilitating diversity, see the Career Choices box on page 409.)

BECOMING AN INFORMED CONSUMER OF ADOLESCENT SCIENCE

Taking a Stand Against Prejudice

TEACHERS AND ADMINISTRATORS can use a number of strategies to combat prejudice in schools and create an atmosphere of respect and tolerance. But combating prejudice is everyone's responsibility, and adolescents can do much to get actively involved in responding to hatred in their schools and communities. The Southern Poverty Law Center (2005) has put together a list of strategies for getting started:

- Act. The first step to combating hatred is being willing to take responsibility for doing something about it. Standing by and doing nothing sends a message to the perpetrators, the victims, and the community that prejudice is acceptable. Apathy encourages more hatred.

- Unite. Get others involved in direct action, too. These could be family and friends, neighbors, church and civic group members, or teachers and administrators. Ways to get others involved range from informal discussions to writing letters to the editor of a local newspaper to organizing a community rally or event.

- Support the victims. Being a victim of prejudice can be a traumatic experience. Victims may feel frightened, intimidated, or alienated. Giving them your support and encouragement shows them that they are valued members of the community and that they are not alone. Even a kind word or a simple gesture can make a difference.

- Speak up. Prejudice has a voice; tolerance needs to have a voice as well. Condemning hateful messages is a good start, but letting others know that you actively value diversity is important, too. Create an atmosphere of tolerance by communicating your values.

- Hold leaders accountable. Adolescents can do a lot to combat prejudice, but people in leadership positions enjoy special influence. The way that teachers, administrators, and other people in leadership roles respond to incidents of prejudice sends a strong message to others in the community. Quick, decisive action shows that prejudice is unacceptable; slow, uninspired action—or inaction—appears to condone it. Make sure that leaders know you expect them to respond decisively.

- Examine your own prejudices. Even tolerant people can harbor some prejudices. Are there any social groups you disparage, or just don't know much about? Do you include people who are different from you in your circle of friends and in your group activities? Be continually on the lookout for ways to learn about different cultures and ethnicities and to build bridges across racial and ethnic divides.

Review and Apply

Review

1. Adolescents must deal with prejudices (judgments of members of groups), stereotypes (beliefs and expectations about members of groups), and outright discrimination (actions taken toward members of groups).

2. The social learning view suggests that people learn prejudice the same way they learn other attitudes, beliefs, and values: from other people.

3. According to social identity theory, adolescents use group membership as a source of pride, dividing people into the ingroup and the outgroup, which is assumed to be inferior.

4. Different gender roles cause boys and girls to be treated differently from birth, which leads to sexism.

5. Overt racism has greatly diminished in recent decades, but modern racism—in which individuals secretly hold racist attitudes while professing to be nonracist—persists.

Apply

1. As overt sexism is reduced in coming decades, do you think that "modern sexism" will take its place? How will it be manifested?

2. *From the perspective of an educator:* Do you see any signs that an androgynous gender schema is gaining acceptance and adoption in U.S. society? How might such a schema be encouraged and strengthened?

EPILOGUE

In this chapter we took a close look at culture, examining how culture affects the everyday lives of adolescents and weighing the question of whether adolescence is itself a culture. Next we considered diversity, beginning with a look at the phenomenon of immigration and examining more closely the ethnic and racial makeup of the U.S. adolescent population. We also saw how poverty and socioeconomic status interact with race and ethnicity and affect adolescents' lives. Finally, we turned to prejudice, stereotypes, and discrimination and explored how these phenomena act in concert to negatively affect the lives of adolescents.

Before we move to the next chapter, take a look back to the Prologue of this chapter, about the three Jewish students taking part in the Student-to-Student program. Consider the following questions.

1. How might these three students sharing their beliefs with non-Jewish students be fostering their own development by working with others of different faiths?

2. Do you think the teaming of members of three quite different branches of Judaism was intentional? What might these three adolescents be learning about one another?

3. How is the question about eating chicken different from the other two questions quoted at the end of the Prologue?

4. How effective do you think the Student-to-Student program might be in reducing prejudice against Jewish adolescents?

SUMMARY

- **In what ways are adolescents affected by culture and ethnicity?** *(p. 384)*

  1. Culture helps adolescents define themselves and make decisions ranging from what clothes to wear to what sexual practices are appropriate.

  2. Adolescence is partly a culture of its own, with specific norms, beliefs, values, traditions, and vocabulary, but the universality of "adolescent culture" should not be overestimated.

  3. Acculturation is the process by which an individual of a different culture adjusts to a new culture and may produce integration, assimilation, separation, or marginalization.

  4. It is especially important for members of minority cultures to develop an ethnic identity, a view of themselves as members of both a minority culture and a new culture.

- **What are the major racial and ethnic minority groups to which adolescents belong?** *(p. 393)*

  5. Adolescents are a diverse group, with many coming from other countries or having parents who immigrated to the United States.

  6. Immigrant adolescents face particular challenges that are complicated by political controversies that surround them.

  7. Hispanics, African Americans, Asian Americans, and Native Americans are the most prevalent adolescent minority groups.

- **How is socioeconomic status related to race and ethnicity?** *(p. 396)*

  8. Many of the problems faced by minority adolescents are more closely linked to socioeconomic status than to ethnicity or race.

  9. Half of adolescents in the United States live in poverty or in low-income households, and members of minority groups are disproportionately represented in these households.

- **How do prejudice, stereotypes, and discrimination work together?** *(p. 399)*

  10. Evaluations of individuals on the basis of their membership in a group are reinforced by the existence of stereotypes, which are beliefs and expectations about group members.

  11. Prejudice and stereotypes can lead to discrimination, actions taken toward group members because of their membership in the group.

- **How are the lives of adolescents affected by sexism and racism?** *(p. 402)*

  12. Adolescents use group membership as a source of pride and self-worth, but the danger is that they will conclude that their group is better than others.

  13. The gender roles assigned to individuals at birth not only determine how society will regard them, but also affect how they themselves think and behave.

  14. Gender stereotyping is particularly prevalent during adolescence, a time when adolescents are working out their own gender identity and often hold rigid views of appropriate and inappropriate behavior for males and females.

  15. Because different races and ethnicities are educated in the same setting, adolescents have learned to show more positive views of other-race individuals.

16. As overt racism has gone underground, modern racism, in which surface nonracist views mask underlying racist attitudes, has become a common stance.

KEY TERMS AND CONCEPTS

culture (p. 384)

acculturation (p. 385)

integration (p. 387)

assimilation (p. 387)

separation (p. 387)

marginalization (p. 387)

ethnic identity (p. 388)

prejudice (p. 399)

stereotype (p. 399)

discrimination (p. 399)

social identity theory
    (p. 400)

gender roles (p. 402)

sexism (p. 402)

identification (p. 405)

gender schema (p. 407)

modern racism (p. 408)

13 Adolescent Problems

CHAPTER OUTLINE

PROLOGUE

MATTHEW PEARLSTONE, 19, was smart, genius-smart—a teen who glided through Ladue Horton Watkins High and into the Ivy League with near-perfect grades and a star SAT score, a super-achiever who played water polo, ran marathons and had plenty of friends.

But Matthew also liked to drink. He was well-versed in the dangers of alcohol. He clearly did not drink thoughtlessly; he intellectualized it. In dozens of online messages that delved into his drinking habits, he defended and defined them. . . .

Matthew advocated his version of responsible use of alcohol. That meant not drinking and driving. It meant knowing your limits. But it also meant finding your limits. . . . In another post, Matthew argued the relative risks of drinking.

"Alcohol-related injuries (falls, etc.) are possible, but again serious ones (more than scrapes or minor bruises) are rare relative to the amount of drunken stupidity in the world," he wrote. . . . "I can tell you, both statistically and anecdotally, that it is very rare and comparatively hard for someone to drink themselves to death. . . . I don't take blind risks, and I'm fully aware of the risks I take with drinking."

Just two months after he wrote those words, Matthew went to visit with a friend at the University of Virginia. It was supposed to be a brief stop, in and out, then back to spend the rest of spring break at home. Matthew went out partying and ended the night asleep in a dorm room. The next morning, he couldn't be roused.

Matthew Pearlstone, a 19-year-old freshman at Cornell University, had died from accidental alcohol poisoning. (Frankel, 2006, p. A1) ■

th!nk ABOUT THIS

PEARLSTONE'S DEATH IS an extreme, but not so rare, example of the potential problems in adolescence. Despite their increasing cognitive abilities, adolescents may not appreciate the dangers posed by behavior that may be seen as common.

In this chapter, we focus on the major problems that adolescents face, many of which are unique to the period. We begin by attempting to distinguish the difference between real problems and the kind of experimentation with a variety of behaviors that characterize adolescence.

We then look at specific problems that are focused outward, toward others. We consider juvenile delinquency, as well as substance use and abuse among adolescents. We also focus on children who leave home, either voluntarily or because they have been rejected by their families.

Finally, we examine physical and psychological problems that are turned inward and primarily affect only the adolescent in question. For example, we look at depression and suicide in adolescents, examining their prevalence and origins. We also look at the victimization of adolescents, which may take the form of physical, sexual, or psychological abuse. ■

- **What are the major types of problems adolescents encounter?**

- **What are some of the underlying causes of the externalizing difficulties of adolescence?**

- **What externalizing problems do adolescents face at school, in their neighborhoods, and at home?**

- **What are the major internalizing problems of adolescence?**

- **What are the typical kinds of adolescent abuse?**

Categorizing Adolescent Difficulties

Yevonda Graham's childhood memories are mostly the stuff of nightmares. In and out of 36 foster homes, Vonda, now 22, says she was sexually abused by relatives, molested by a foster parent and raped as a teenager. By the time she got to the home of Dale Graham and Karla Groschelle in Whitley City, Ky., at 17, she had been in eight hospitals and three group homes and had just run away from her last foster home. [She arrived] at the couple's house for what she expected to be yet another short-term placement. . .

Instead she found that for the first time in her peripatetic life, she felt at home. Karla and Dale "didn't seem fake," she says. "Usually when I'd act up, my [other] foster parents would just send me away, but they didn't. They stuck in there with me...." In fact, for the first several months, things went so well that one evening Vonda sat Karla and Dale down in the living room and asked whether they would adopt her even though she was about to turn 18. "I wanted a place to always come home to," she says. . . . (Hamilton, 2006, p. 63)

It would be nice to be able to say there's a happy ending to this story, but the reality is otherwise. During her adolescence, Yevonda was diagnosed with bipolar disorder, explaining her periods of depression. Although physicians prescribed drugs to treat the disorder, she stopped taking them, and then got hooked on the painkiller Oxycontin. Although she agreed to enter a rehab program, she checked out only three hours after her arrival. She has been repeatedly jailed for such offenses as public intoxication and stealing money to pay for drugs.

The combination of problems faced by Yevonda was overwhelming. Fortunately, though, most young people pass through adolescence with less-serious kinds of problems. Nevertheless, the problems they do have can leave a lasting impact on their lives.

The problems of adolescents fall into two broad categories: internalizing and externalizing. **Internalizing disorders** are physical and psychological problems that are turned inward and primarily affect only the adolescent in question; they include such problems as depression, anxiety, and phobias. In contrast, **externalizing disorders** are problems that are directed outward, towards others, and typically are displayed as behavioral problems. For example, externalizing disorders include aggression, fighting, destructiveness, truancy, and other conduct disorders in which adolescents act out their problems.

Some adolescent problems don't fit neatly into either of these two categories. Take drug abuse, for example. Traditionally, substance abuse, such as underage drinking, has been seen as an externalizing disorder (and that's the way we'll consider it later in the chapter). The rationale for categorizing substance abuse as an externalizing disorder is that it is often most obvious when occurring in adolescents who are acting out in additional ways, such as in a group of drunken adolescents at a bar. However, it's also reasonable to look at substance abuse as a symptom of depression or as a strategy used to reduce anxiety. In such cases, it is fair to see it as a sign of an internalizing problem. In short, some problems are simultaneously internalizing and externalizing disorders.

internalizing disorders physical and psychological problems that are turned inward and primarily affect only the adolescent in question; they include such problems as depression, anxiety, and phobias.

externalizing disorders problems that are directed outward, toward others, and typically are displayed as behavioral problems.

Distinguishing Problems from Experimentation

There's another complication to categorizing adolescent problems: distinguishing between when a problem behavior is a sign of an actual disorder and when it is simply a case of adolescents' typical desire to try things out for themselves. The problem behaviors of the vast majority of adolescents are not enduring but are rather a sign of adolescent experimentation or an example of succumbing to peer pressure. For example, most youth break the law in some way during adolescence. Typically, though, the infractions are minor (as are the offenses of most adults who engage in lawbreaking by, for instance, speeding). Such law-breaking on the part of adolescents does not lead to a lifetime of criminal activity.

Similarly, at some point before they graduate from high school, most adolescents drink so much that they become drunk at least once. However, this does not mean that they are destined to become alcoholics. As we've seen throughout this book, adolescence is a time of experimentation, and it is quite normal for teenagers to engage in a variety of risky behaviors that they may never again engage in for the remainder of their lives. In fact, the prevalence of illegal activities rises dramatically at the start of adolescence, peaks at around age 15 or 16, and then declines significantly in early adulthood until it plateaus at around age 30 (Capaldi & Shortt, 2006).

We also need to differentiate problems that are unique to the period of adolescence—beginning and ending in that period—from those that begin in adolescence and continue through the life span. Many of the problem behaviors that we see in adolescents are short-lived, and they do not affect individuals beyond the period of adolescence. For example, the incidence of delinquency is higher in adolescence than later in life, meaning that most adolescent delinquents do not go on to a life of criminality but instead grow up to be law-abiding adults. Many problems we see in adolescents thus are temporary.

Finally, it's important to realize that many individuals who display problems during adolescence had those same problems before they reached that age. Consequently, in addressing adolescent problems, it is crucial to distinguish those that begin in adolescence and those that have their origins in childhood.

▲ Internalizing disorders, such as depression and anxiety, are focused inward and typically only affect the individual adolescent.

The Origin of Problems

Although every adolescent's problems are unique in some ways, there are several broad approaches to considering the origins of adolescent difficulties, particularly with respect to externalizing disorders. Not only do these approaches seek to explain why particular problems arise in the first place, but they also suggest reasons why various difficulties very often are found to be **comorbid,** or to co-occur, in the same adolescent. For instance, adolescent drug abuse is associated with delinquency, dropping out of school, and early initiation of sexual behavior. Similarly, early sexual intercourse is associated with juvenile delinquency (see Figure 13-1; Zweig, Lindberg, & McGinley, 2001; Capaldi & Shortt, 2006).

Comorbidity of Externalizing Disorders.   Several theories seek to explain the comorbidity of externalizing disorders. In one view, externalizing problems arise during adolescence because of unconventionality in an adolescent's personality and the environment in which he or she lives. Specifically, adolescents with unconventional personalities are not closely tied to the norms of society, and they are accepting of deviance. When unconventional adolescents are put in environments in which others are equally unconventional, they are likely to engage in high levels of risk-taking behavior across several domains, including substance abuse and delinquent

comorbid   a situation in which various difficulties co-occur in the same adolescent.

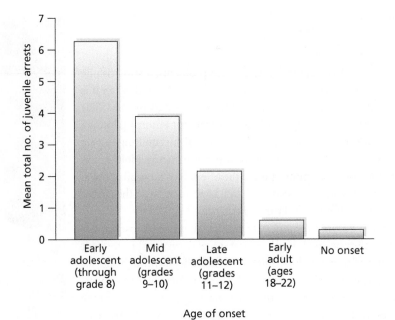

▶ **FIGURE 13-1**

This example of comorbidity shows a greater increase in delinquency when the adolescent is involved in early sexual intercourse.

(*Source:* Capaldi & Shortt, 2006.)

behavior, thereby explaining the comorbidity of externalizing problems (Jessor, Donovan, & Costa, 1996; Costa, Jessor, & Turbin, 2005).

Family influences may also help explain the comorbidity of externalizing factors. For instance, genetic factors have been shown to be related to externalizing behaviors, and siblings of adolescents with externalizing disorders are at higher risk for displaying similar behavior (Haberstick, Young, & Hewitt, 2005).

Another explanation of the comorbidity of externalizing disorders is that adolescents with externalizing disorders are more likely to seek out environments that support their risk-taking tendencies, or that their risk-taking tendencies may lead them to restrict their environments in some ways. For example, adolescents who, because of their poor academic efforts, do not graduate from high school limit themselves to employment environments in which other employees also may have experienced limited academic success. Those employees may encourage the risk-taking behaviors of one another. In a sense, then, those with externalizing disorders are more likely to find themselves in environments with similar others (Capaldi & Shortt, 2006).

Rather than seeing externalizing disorders as triggered by a personality trait such as unconventionality, an alternative explanation for the co-occurrence of externalizing disorders argues that once an adolescent displays a particular externalizing problem, the problem itself can lead to other problems. For instance, an adolescent who has a drug abuse problem may become delinquent as a result of wishing to purchase more drugs. In this view, there is no underlying trait that is causing both drug abuse *and* delinquency; instead, the externalizing drug abuse problem leads to another externalizing problem—delinquency (Yamaguchi & Kandel, 1987; Chen & Kandel, 2002).

Finally, the *social control perspective* suggests an alternative explanation for the origin and co-occurrence of externalizing problems. Rather than the problem being due to some kind of personality characteristic of an adolescent, the social control perspective argues that adolescents learn to conform to society's norms. Those adolescents with weaker ties to societal institutions such as family, school, the media, or religious institutions are more likely to behave in unconventional ways and to display externalizing problems. In this view, the behavior of adolescents with multiple externalizing problems is not so much the result of the adolescents picking up some personality characteristic or flaw as it is an outcome of their failing to learn appropriate methods of self-control and self-regulation (Hirschi, 2004; Bernburg & Thorlindsson, 2005; Brown et al., 2005; Miner & Munns, 2005).

Comorbidity of Internalizing Problems. In the same way that many externalizing disorders co-occur in the same adolescent, internalizing problems also often cluster together within the same individual. For example, between half and two thirds of adolescents who experience significant depression have at least one additional condition. Anxiety, too, often co-occurs with other problems. In many cases, childhood anxiety disorders are likely to precede depression during adolescence (Graber, 2004).

One reason for the comorbidity of internalizing problems is that multiple problems may be caused by the same underlying psychological syndrome. In other words, it is possible that both, say, depression and anxiety displayed by an adolescent are caused by a similar core psychological disorder (Krueger et al., 1998; Krueger, Caspi, & Moffitt, 2000).

Specifically, some psychologists believe that *negative affectivity*—a syndrome in which an adolescent becomes upset or distressed easily—may predispose adolescents to internalize problems. For example, negative affectivity is linked to depression, anxiety, and a number of other internalizing symptoms (Anthony et al., 2002; Craske, 2003; Lonigan, Phillips, & Hooe, 2003).

In the remainder of the chapter, we'll address several of the major problems to which adolescents are susceptible. As we consider them, it is important to reiterate that the problems we're discussing don't always fall neatly into internalizing or externalizing categories, and that many contain elements of both.

Review and Apply

Review

1. There are two main categories of problems faced by adolescents: internalizing disorders and externalizing disorders.

2. Categorizing adolescent disorders is complicated by the fact that adolescence is a time of experimentation, and some seemingly antisocial behaviors are nothing more than experiments.

3. Some adolescent disorders (particularly externalizing disorders) are comorbid—occurring in connection with other disorders.

4. Various reasons have been suggested for this comorbidity, including the grouping of unconventional adolescents on the basis of likes and dislikes and adolescents' failure to learn appropriate self-control.

5. Like externalizing problems, internalizing disorders often occur together in the same individual.

Apply

1. How might a parent be able to distinguish between adolescent experimentation involving illegal activities from a true problem?

2. Do you think that modern technology is increasing or decreasing the occurrence of externalizing disorders? Internalizing disorders? Why?

Externalizing Difficulties

10th grade, first year of real high school, I . . . started going a little crazy that year . . . I ran away from home and joined a street gang, complete with initiation rituals consisting of committing a major felony and being violently beaten down by every other gang member present at the time . . . spent the next several months burglarizing houses, stealing cars, breaking the coin boxes off of payphones, robbing people, partying like a rock star, getting arrested, running from cops, etc . . . then, in one week, everything fell [apart] . . . first one of the more corrupt local cops set his K-9 on me and didn't call him off, forcing me to jump from a bridge into a slough filled mostly with polluted muck, . . . somehow this struck me as worse than getting arrested or beaten up . . . then one of my buddies got murdered in a dispute with a rival gang, shot right in the face . . . he would be the first of too many friends to meet a violent end.

Clearly, this represents an extreme case; most adolescents' lives include far less criminality and violence than the one described. In fact, adolescents are considerably more likely to be victims of crime, rather than perpetrators. Still, a small but significant minority of adolescents do experience externalizing problems—difficulties that are directed outwardly, toward others. As we'll discuss, externalizing problems include juvenile delinquency, violence, substance abuse, and running away from home.

Juvenile Delinquency

Adolescents, along with young adults, are more likely to commit crimes than any other age group. This is a misleading statistic in some respects: Because certain behaviors (such as drinking) are illegal for adolescents but not for older individuals, it is rather easy for adolescents to break the law by doing something that, were they a few years older, would be legal. But even when such crimes are disregarded, adolescents are disproportionately involved in violent crimes such as murder, assaults, and rape and in property crimes involving theft, robbery, and arson.

Although the number of violent crimes committed by U.S. adolescents over the past decade has shown a decline of 40%, probably due to the strength of the economy, delinquency among some teenagers remains a significant problem. Overall, 16% of all arrests for serious crimes involved a person under the age of 18. Older adolescents and young adults between the ages of 18 to 25 are even more likely to be arrested (Snyder & Sickmund, 2006).

Boys are far more likely to be involved in delinquency than girls. Compared to girls, from three to eight times as many boys are involved in serious crimes. In part, this reflects the higher levels of aggression that we see in boys from the time of childhood.

There are also significant differences in delinquency between majority and minority youth, at least in terms of arrest records. Adolescents of ethnic and racial minorities are more likely to have criminal records than whites, a phenomenon known as *disproportionate minority contact.* In addition, poor adolescents are more likely to have arrest records than more affluent adolescents (Snyder & Sickmund, 2006).

But arrests are not the same as actual delinquent acts. When we look at self-reports of criminal activity, the differences shrink. The reason is that affluent and white adolescents who are involved in delinquency sometimes get treated more leniently by the criminal justice system. Their parents are more likely to have the resources to work out deals with police and prosecutors that avoid or expunge arrest records. In contrast, poor, ethnic minority youth are less equipped to deal with the criminal justice system, and consequently they are more likely to be arrested, charged, and receive punishment than their more-affluent peers.

Reasons for Delinquency.   Why do adolescents become involved in criminal activity? Some offenders, known as **undersocialized delinquents,** are adolescents who are raised with little discipline or with harsh, uncaring parental supervision. Although they are influenced by their peers, these children have not been socialized appropriately by their parents and have not been taught standards of conduct to regulate their own behavior. Undersocialized delinquents typically begin criminal activities at an early age, well before the onset of adolescence.

undersocialized delinquents   adolescents who are raised with little discipline or with harsh, uncaring parental supervision.

Undersocialized delinquents share several characteristics. They tend to be relatively aggressive and violent fairly early in life, characteristics that lead to rejection by peers and academic failure. They also are more likely to have been diagnosed with attention deficit disorder as children, and they tend to be less intelligent than average (Henry et al., 1996; Silverthorn & Frick, 1999; Rutter, 2003).

Undersocialized delinquents often suffer from psychological difficulties, and as adults they fit a psychological pattern called antisocial personality disorder. They are relatively unlikely to be successfully rehabilitated, and many undersocialized delinquents live on the margins of society throughout their lives (Rönkä & Pulkkinen, 1995; Lynam, 1996; Frick, 2003).

Socialized delinquents constitute a larger group of adolescent offenders. **Socialized delinquents** know and subscribe to the norms of society; they are fairly normal psychologically. For them, transgressions committed during adolescence do not lead to a life of crime. Instead, most socialized delinquents pass through a period during adolescence when they engage in some petty crimes (such as shoplifting), but they do not continue lawbreaking into adulthood.

Socialized delinquents are typically highly influenced by their peers, and their delinquency often occurs in groups. In addition, some research suggests that parents of socialized delinquents supervise their children's behavior less closely than other parents. But like other aspects of adolescent behavior, these minor delinquencies are often a result of giving in to group pressure or seeking to establish one's identity as an adult (Dornbusch et al., 1985; Windle, 1994; Fletcher et al., 1995; Thornberry & Krohn, 1997).

Paths to Adolescent Delinquency. There are two main routes to delinquency, one of which starts quite early in life and the other begins later. It turns out that the timing of onset has a great deal to do with the persistence of the delinquency.

Although both early-onset and late-onset types engage in similarly serious offenses during adolescence, *early-onset delinquency* is more likely to persist well beyond adolescence and set the stage for a lifetime of crime and violence. In contrast, *late-onset delinquency* is more likely to be a temporary phenomenon of adolescence (Granic & Patterson, 2006).

Early-onset delinquency, in fact, begins very early in life. As early as the age of two, early-onset delinquents have a difficult temperament and personality. They are physically aggressive, display negative emotions, and are prone to outbursts. They have considerable difficulty with self-regulation, being unable to control themselves when they are frustrated. They often have cognitive difficulties. Not only are they often of low intelligence, but some experience attention-deficit hyperactivity disorder (ADHD), a psychological disorder characterized by inattention, impulsiveness, a low tolerance for frustration, and generally a great deal of inappropriate activity.

In early-onset delinquency, poor parenting compounds children's behavioral problems. There is often a high degree of parental conflict, and parents may use lax and inconsistent parenting. As a consequence, their children become hostile and defiant, and their aggression persists. By the time they reach middle childhood, their difficult behavior often leads them to do poorly in school and to be avoided by most of their peers. In turn, this makes it more likely that they will seek out the company of other deviant peers, and they become psychologically and socially committed to deviant peer groups (see Figure 13-2 for a summary of these steps; Patterson, DeBaryshe, & Ramsey, 1989; DeBaryshe, Patterson, & Capaldi, 1993; Dishion & Patterson, 2006).

Ultimately, the result of this early-onset pattern is delinquency during adolescence. Furthermore, the delinquent behavior persists into adulthood. Compared to late-onset delinquents, early-onset delinquents have higher levels of unemployment, substance abuse, and marital difficulties as adults. Ultimately, they are more likely to engage in criminal activities and be arrested as adults.

▲ Although socialized delinquents may commit petty crimes, such as defacing property with graffiti, they typically do not continued lawbreaking into adulthood.

socialized delinquents adolescents who know and subscribe to the norms of society; they are fairly normal psychologically.

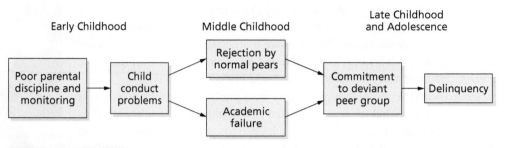

Early Childhood   Middle Childhood   Late Childhood and Adolescence

▲ **FIGURE 13-2**

The first step in early-onset delinquency can be traced to poor parental discipline and monitoring that can compound a child's behavioral problems and affect later development.

(*Source:* Patterson, DeBaryshe, & Ramsey, 1989.)

In contrast, late-onset delinquents typically don't begin to display delinquency until the start of puberty, but their level of delinquency escalates to the same level as that of the early-onset group. Although the parenting they experience during adolescence may decline—as their parents seek to deal with the unaccustomed behavior of their children—usually they have not experienced a previous history of poor parenting. In addition, they have not been temperamentally difficult early on, don't have the cognitive deficits of the early-onset group, and haven't previously displayed high levels of aggressiveness or lack of self-regulation.

Although some late-onset adolescents do continue to behave antisocially past adolescence, most don't. Instead, as they become older, they become better integrated into society. With age, they obtain more privileges of adulthood, and the social skills they learned prior to adolescence allow them to more effectively navigate the social world. Ultimately, their delinquency ends (Loeber, Lacourse, & Homish, 2005)

It's important to keep in mind that most of the work on early- and late-onset delinquency has focused on boys. The findings are less clear for girls, largely because girls are less apt to display more violent forms of delinquency during adolescence than boys (Pepler et al., 2005).

School Violence

Columbine . . . Jonesboro . . . West Paducah. You may remember the names of these places where school violence occurred, and you may conclude—like many Americans—that schools are particularly dangerous places.

However, the reality of school violence is different. Despite the public perception that school violence is on the upswing, there has in fact been an overall decline in violence. Even in the year of the Columbine shooting, the number of deaths in school-related incidents dropped 40% from the previous year. School is actually one of the safest places for adolescents (Spencer, 2001).

The likelihood of injury from a school shooting is tiny (a student has about a one in a million chance of being killed in school). Nonetheless, parents and their children still worry about safety issues. Is it possible to identify beforehand students who pose a threat? It turns out that some students are prone to violence; for instance, the FBI has identified several characteristics of individuals who are at risk for carrying out violence in schools. They include a low tolerance for frustration, poor coping skills, a lack of resiliency, failed love relationships, resentment over perceived injustices, depression, self-centeredness, and alienation (O'Toole, 2000).

Furthermore, school shootings are rarely spontaneous. Attackers typically make plans, plotting out beforehand whom they wish to harm. Not only do they usually tell someone about their plans, but also they often are encouraged by others. In almost half the cases of school shootings, attackers were influenced or encouraged to act by friends or fellow students. They also have easy access to guns. In around two thirds of school shootings, the attackers used guns from their own home or that of a relative (U.S. Secret Service, 2002).

According to psychologist Elliot Aronson, students who carry out violence in schools frequently were the targets of bullying or have been rejected in some way. He notes that there are tremendous status differences in schools, and students who have been taunted and humiliated by students of higher status (or by their parents or other adults) may lash out in frustration (Aronson, 2000).

To respond to the potential of violence, many schools have instituted programs designed to prevent aggression among students. One of the most prominent is *Second Step*, which is designed to teach children to recognize and understand their feelings, experience empathy for others, make effective choices, and keep anger from escalating into violence. Carefully conducted studies have supported the program, finding improvements in students' social skills and a reduction in aggressive acts (Van Schoiack-Edstrom, Frey, & Beland, 2002; McMahon & Washburn, 2003).

Other school programs that involve cooperative learning, peer mediation, and communication skills training appear to be helpful. In addition, teaching students, parents, and educators to take threats seriously is important; many students who become violent threaten to commit violence before they actually engage in violent acts. Ultimately, schools need to be places where students feel comfortable discussing their feelings and problems, rather than sources of alienation and rejection (Aronson, 2000; Spencer, 2001).

Substance Use and Abuse in Adolescence

Like most parents, I had thought of drug use as something you worried about when your kids got to high school. Now I know that, on the average, kids begin using drugs at 11 or 12, but at the time that never crossed our minds. Ryan had just begun attending mixed parties. He was playing Little League. In the eighth grade, Ryan started getting into a little trouble—one time he and another fellow stole a fire extinguisher, but we thought it was just a prank. Then his grades began to deteriorate. He began sneaking out at night. He would become belligerent at the drop of a hat, then sunny and nice again. . . .

It wasn't until Ryan fell apart at 14 that we started thinking about drugs. He had just begun McLean High School, and to him, it was like going to drug camp every day. Back then, everything was so available. He began cutting classes, a common tip-off, but we didn't hear from the school until he was flunking everything. It turned out that he was going to school for the first period, getting checked in, then leaving and smoking marijuana all day. (Shafer, 1990, p. 82)

Ryan's parents learned that marijuana was not the only drug Ryan was using. As his friends later admitted, Ryan was what they called a "garbage head." He would try anything. Despite efforts to curb his use of drugs, he never succeeded in stopping. He died at the age of 16, hit by a passing car after wandering into the street during an episode of drug use.

Few cases of adolescent drug use produce such extreme results, but the use of drugs, as well as other kinds of substance use and abuse, is one of several kinds of threats to health during adolescence—otherwise one of the healthiest periods of life. Although the extent of risky behavior is difficult to gauge, preventable problems such as drug, alcohol, and tobacco use, as well as sexually transmitted diseases, represent serious threats to adolescents' health and well-being.

Illegal Drugs. How common is illegal drug use during adolescence? Very. For instance, the most recent annual survey of nearly 50,000 U.S. students shows that almost 50% of high school seniors and a fifth of eighth-graders report having used some illegal drug at least once during their lifetime. The most widely used illegal drug is marijuana, although 19% of 12th graders report having used some other illicit drug (such as hallucinogens, cocaine, Ecstasy, or inhalants).

Although the data on drug use still represents substantial adolescent involvement, overall there has been a general reduction in illegal drug use extending from the mid-1990s. Some drug usage, such as the use of *LSD* and *ecstasy*, has declined significantly (Johnston, Bachman, & O'Malley, 2006; see Figure 13-3).

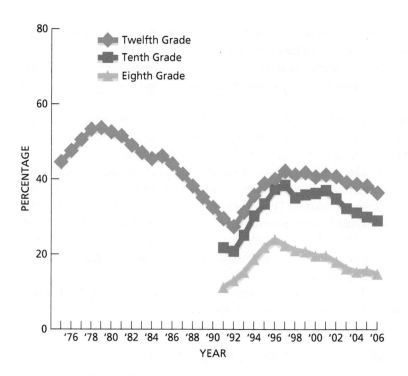

The use of marijuana has steadily declined over the past 5 years, but surveys have found that drug use among adolescents is still substantial.

(*Source:* Monitoring the Future: National Results on Adolescent Drug Use. Overview of Key Findings, 2006.)

Adolescents have a variety of reasons for using drugs. Some use them for the pleasurable experience drugs supposedly provide. Others use them to try to escape, however temporarily, from the pressures of everyday life. Some adolescents try drugs simply for the thrill of doing something illegal. The alleged drug use of high-profile entertainment figures such as Snoop Dog may also contribute. Finally, peer pressure plays a role: Adolescents, as we discussed in Chapter 7, are particularly susceptible to the perceived standards of their peer groups (Jenkins, 1996; Bogenschneider et al., 1998; Urberg, Luo, & Pilgrim, 2003).

The use of illegal drugs is dangerous in several respects. For instance, some drugs are addictive. **Addictive drugs** are drugs that produce a biological or psychological dependence in users, leading to increasingly powerful cravings for them.

When drugs produce a biological addiction, their presence in the body becomes so common that the body is unable to function in their absence. Furthermore, addiction causes actual physical—and potentially lingering—changes in the nervous system. In such cases, drug intake no longer may provide a "high," but may be necessary simply to maintain the perception of everyday normality (Cami & Farré, 2003; Munzar, Cami, & Farré, 2003).

In addition to physical addiction, drugs also can produce psychological addiction. In such cases, people grow to depend on drugs to cope with the everyday stress of life. If drugs are used as an escape, they may prevent adolescents from confronting—and potentially solving—the problems that led them to drug use in the first place. Finally, drugs may be dangerous because even casual users of less-hazardous drugs can escalate to more dangerous forms of substance abuse (Toch, 1995; Segal & Stewart, 1996).

Alcohol: Use and Abuse. Three quarters of college students have something in common: They've consumed at least one alcoholic drink during the last 30 days. More than 40% say they've had five or more drinks within the past 2 weeks, and some 16% drink 16 or more drinks per week. High school students, too, are drinkers: some three quarters of high school seniors report having had an alcoholic drink in the last year, and in some subgroups—such as male athletes—the proportion of drinkers is even higher. Six percent of eighth graders and 30% of 12th graders report being drunk at least once in the past month (Johnston, O'Malley, & Bachman, 2006).

Binge drinking is a particular problem on college campuses. Binge drinking is defined for men as drinking five or more drinks in one sitting; for women, who tend to weigh less and whose

addictive drugs drugs that produce a biological or psychological dependence in users, leading to increasingly powerful cravings for them.

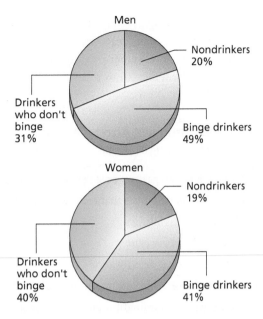

Men

Nondrinkers
20%

Drinkers
who don't
binge
31%

Binge drinkers
49%

Women

Nondrinkers
19%

Drinkers
who don't
binge
40%

Binge drinkers
41%

◀ **FIGURE13-**

For women, binge drinking was defined as consuming four or more drinks in one sitting; for men, the total was five or more. (Source Wechsler et al., 2003).

bodies absorb alcohol less efficiently, binge drinking is defined as four drinks in one sitting. Surveys find that almost half of male college students and over 41% of female college students say they participated in binge drinking during the previous 2 weeks (see Figure 13-4).

Binge drinking affects even those who don't drink or drink very little. Two thirds of lighter drinkers report that they have been disturbed by drunken students while sleeping or studying. Around a third have been insulted or humiliated by a drunken student, and 25% of women say they have been the target of an unwanted sexual advance by a drunk classmate (Wechsler et al., 2000, 2003).

Why do adolescents start to drink? There are many reasons. For some—especially male athletes, whose rate of drinking tends to be higher than that of the general adolescent population—drinking is seen as a way of proving they can drink as much as anybody. Others drink for the same reason that some use drugs: It releases inhibitions and tension and reduces stress. Many begin because the conspicuous examples of drunkenness strewn around campus convince them that everyone is drinking heavily, something known as the *false consensus effect* (Pavis, Cunningham-Burley, & Amos, 1997; Nelson & Wechsler, 2003; Weitzman, Nelson, & Wechsler, 2003).

For some adolescents, alcohol use becomes a habit that cannot be controlled. **Alcoholics**, those with alcohol problems, learn to depend on alcohol and are unable to control their drinking. They also become increasingly able to tolerate alcohol and therefore need to drink ever-larger amounts of liquor to bring about the positive effects they crave. Some drink throughout the day, while others go on binges in which they consume huge quantities of alcohol.

The reasons that some adolescents—or people of all ages, for that matter—become alcoholics are not fully known. Genetics plays a role: Alcoholism runs in families. Furthermore, alcoholism may be triggered by efforts to deal with the stress that can be caused by having an alcoholic parent or family member or by other family stressors (Bushman, 1993; Boyd, Howard, & Zucker, 1995; Berenson, 2005).

Alcoholism is also related to the alcohol use by peers and peer pressure. Delinquency and other forms of substance abuse also are related to alcoholism. Finally, certain personality traits are associated with the development of alcoholism. For example, lower constraint of impulses and higher negative emotionality are related to adolescent alcoholism (Barnow et al., 2004; Elkins et al., 2006).

▲ Binge drinking is a serious problem among adolescents.

alcoholic   persons with alcohol problems who have learned to depend on alcohol and are unable to control their drinking.

Of course, the origins of an adolescent's problems with alcohol or drugs are less important than getting help. Parents, teachers, and friends can provide the help a teen needs to address the problem—if they realize there is a problem. How can concerned friends and family members tell if an adolescent they know is having difficulties with alcohol or drugs? Some of the telltale signs are described next.

Identifying Drug and Alcohol Abuse.   Although it is not always easy to determine if an adolescent has a drug or alcohol abuse problem, there are some signals. Among them:

- Drug-related magazines or slogans on clothing
- Conversation and jokes that are preoccupied with drugs
- Hostility discussing drugs
- Collection of beer cans
- Signs of physical deterioration
- Memory lapses, short attention span, difficulty concentrating
- Poor physical coordination, slurred or incoherent speech
- Unhealthy appearance, indifference to hygiene and grooming
- Bloodshot eyes, dilated pupils
- Dramatic changes in school performance
- Marked downturn in grades—not just from Cs to Fs, but from As to Bs and Cs; assignments not completed
- Increased absenteeism or tardiness
- Changes in behavior
- Chronic dishonesty (lying, stealing, cheating), trouble with the police
- Changes in friends, evasiveness in talking about new ones
- Possession of large amounts of money
- Increasing and inappropriate anger, hostility, irritability, secretiveness
- Reduced motivation, energy, self-discipline, self-esteem
- Diminished interest in extracurricular activities and hobbies (Adapted from Franck & Brownstone, 1991, pp. 593–594)

If an adolescent—or anyone else—fits any of these descriptors, help is probably needed. A good place to start is a national hotline run by the National Institute on Drug Abuse at (800) 662-4357 or its Web site at www.nida.nih.gov. In addition, those who need advice can find a local listing for Alcoholics Anonymous in the telephone book. (For more on dealing with alcohol and drug programs, see the *Career Choices* box.)

Tobacco: The Dangers of Smoking.   Most adolescents are well aware of the dangers of smoking, but many still indulge in it. Recent figures show that, overall, a smaller proportion of adolescents smoke than in prior decades, but the numbers remain substantial, and within certain groups the numbers are increasing. Smoking is on the rise among girls, and in several countries, including Austria, Norway, and Sweden, the proportion of girls who smoke is higher than the proportion of boys. There are racial differences, as well: White children and children in lower socioeconomic status households are more likely to experiment with cigarettes and to start smoking earlier than African-American children and children living in higher socioeconomic status households. Also, significantly more white males of high school age smoke than do African-American males in high school, although the differences have narrowed in recent years (Harrell et al., 1998; Stolberg, 1998; Baker, Brandon, & Chassin, 2004).

CAREER CHOICES

Substance Abuse Counselor

Name: Martha Cristo

Education: BA, psychology, California State University, Los Angeles; MA, clinical psychology, California School of Professional Psychology, Los Angeles; PhD, California School of Professional Psychology, Los Angeles

Position: Acting clinical director, Institute for Women's Health, Bienvenidos Family Services, Los Angeles, California

Home: Pasadena, California

WHAT IS TYPICALLY one of the healthiest periods of life can also be one in which adolescents become involved in substance abuse, a potentially life-threatening activity. Cases of adolescent substance abuse typically require considerable intervention, a circumstance that is very familiar to Martha Cristo, a substance abuse counselor in Los Angeles.

"The primary drug of choice among the adolescents we see is marijuana, and more than likely they have used other substances as well," she noted. "In this community, the onset of drug use is 10 to 11 years of age."

By the time they arrive at Bienvenidos Family Services, adolescents' addiction is in an advanced stage, according to Cristo, and only 5% come voluntarily. The rest are referred by schools, the courts, or the Department of Family Services.

"They are not doing well at all. Their addiction affects their relationship with family, school and peers," she noted. "Furthermore, for this population, there is often intergenerational substance abuse, so parents are not a resource for support."

Working in a community that is predominately first- to third-generation Hispanic, Cristo says the programs she offers deal both with prevention and treatment. They typically begin with a thorough clinical assessment as well as drug history.

"Using a cognitive behavioral approach, clients attend a comprehensive and rigorous six-month program which is broken down into 96 sessions," she explained. "Upon first entering the program we found that drug education and an interactive group modality works well. The clinic also provides psychoeducational programs that involve drug education and coping with family trauma. In addition, programs such as *Joven Noble* (Young Noble Men) that relate to the Latino culture provide a measure of empowerment for teenage males.

"Following the six month program, participants are then enrolled in an expanded after-care ancillary program and receive continued mental health treatment," Cristo added. "We first try to stabilize the substance abuse and then stabilize the consequences of the substance abuse."

Thinking of becoming a substance abuse counselor?

Substance abuse counselors help adolescents who have problems with alcohol or drug use. They provide support and counseling to individuals, families, or groups; one of their goals is to help people to see the behavioral patterns related to their addiction. They also give support and advice to family members and friends of substance abusers, and they conduct preventive programs designed to discourage adolescents from becoming involved with drugs or alcohol in the first place.

Preparation for a career as a substance abuse counselor requires at least a master's degree in counseling, which includes many hours of coursework, practical training, and a supervised internship. Licensing and continuing education are requirements for substance abuse counselors in almost all states. Some counselors pursue national certification from the National Board for Certified Counselors, which has rigorous requirements, including professional endorsements and an exam. Such certification is not necessary, but it provides an additional credential that can enhance employment prospects.

Smoking is becoming a habit that is harder and harder to maintain. There are growing social sanctions against it. It's becoming more difficult to find a comfortable place to smoke as more places, including schools and places of business, have become "smoke free." Even so, a good number of adolescents still smoke, despite knowing the dangers of smoking and of second-hand smoke. Why, then, do adolescents begin to smoke and maintain the habit? Advertisements for cigarettes depict attractive individuals smoking, and clever ads, such as the highly successful "Joe Camel" series, make an effective pitch to young males, drawing a connection between smoking and being cool. In fact, before Joe Camel commercials were withdrawn from use, children as young as six could identify Joe Camel as readily as Mickey Mouse (Bartecchi, MacKenzie, & Schrier, 1995; Urberg, Degirmencioglu, & Pilgrim, 1997; Wills, Resko, & Ainette, 2004).

Cigarettes are also very addicting. Nicotine, the active chemical ingredient of cigarettes, can produce biological and psychological dependency very quickly. Although one or two cigarettes

▶ U.S. tobacco companies aggressively promote smoking in developing countries.

generally do not produce a lifelong smoker, it takes only a little more to start the habit. In fact, people who smoke as few as 10 cigarettes early in their lives stand an 80% chance of becoming habitual smokers (Salber, Freeman, & Abelin, 1968; Bowen et al., 1991; Stacy et al., 1992).

Smoking produces a pleasant emotional state that smokers seek to maintain. Seeing parents and peers smoking increases the chances that an adolescent will take up the habit. Finally, smoking is sometimes viewed as an adolescent rite of passage, a sign of growing up. (Botvin, et al., 1994; Webster, Hunter, & Keats, 1994; Kodl & Mermelstein, 2004).

Selling Death: Pushing Smoking to the Less Advantaged.

In Dresden, Germany, three women in miniskirts offer passers-by a pack of Lucky Strikes and a leaflet that reads "You just got hold of a nice piece of America." Says a local doctor, "Adolescents time and again receive cigarettes at such promotions."

A Jeep decorated with the Camel logo pulls up to a high school in Buenos Aires. A woman begins handing out free cigarettes to 15- and 16-year-olds during their lunch recess.

At a video arcade in Taipei, free American cigarettes are strewn atop each game. At a disco filled with high school students, free packs of Salems are on each table. (Ecenbarger, 1993, p. 50)

If you are a cigarette manufacturer and you find that the number of people using your product is declining, what do you do? U.S. companies have sought to carve out new markets by turning to the least-advantaged groups of people, both at home and abroad. For instance, in the early 1990s the R. J. Reynolds tobacco company designed a new brand of cigarettes it named "Uptown." The advertising used to herald its arrival made clear who the target was: African Americans living in urban areas (Quinn, 1990). Because of subsequent protests, the tobacco company withdrew "Uptown" from the market.

In addition to seeking new converts in the United States, tobacco companies aggressively recruit adolescent smokers abroad. In many developing countries the number of smokers is still low. Tobacco companies are seeking to increase this number through marketing strategies designed to hook adolescents on the habit by means of free samples. In addition, in countries where American culture and products are held in high esteem, advertising suggests that the use of cigarettes is an American—and consequently prestigious—habit (Sesser, 1993).

The strategy is effective. For instance, in some Latin American cities as many as 50% of teenagers smoke. According to the World Health Organization, smoking will prematurely kill some 200 million of the world's children and adolescents, and overall, 10% of the world's population will die because of smoking (Ecenbarger, 1993).

BECOMING AN INFORMED CONSUMER OF ADOLESCENT SCIENCE

Quitting Smoking Before It Becomes a Lifelong Habit

SMOKING IS ONE of the most difficult habits to break. The best practice is to never start smoking in the first place; most adolescents who don't try smoking before adulthood rarely ever begin smoking later. But adolescents who do begin to smoke face a difficult path. Even though most who start smoking expect to stop again within a few years, the vast majority of them don't.

If you've started smoking and want to quit, the U.S. Department of Health and Human Services (1996) offers the following advice:

- Get ready. Pick a date on which you'll quit for good. The night before, get rid of all your smoking materials—cigarettes, lighters, ashtrays, and so forth. Don't just hide them, destroy them.

- Get support from others. Tell your roommate, your friends, and your family that you're quitting, and what your quit date is. Ask them to keep cigarettes away from you, and to keep you away from cigarettes. Join a support group for people who are quitting smoking, and even consider seeing a counselor for added support—check with the health office at your school for references.

- Learn new behaviors. Change the daily routines that you associate with smoking. For example, if you usually smoke after a meal, go for a walk instead. Shake up your other routines, too—walk to class a different way, eat meals at different times, spend time with different friends—so that you're exposed to fewer smoking cues. Avoid people who smoke and situations where you were particularly likely to smoke.

- Use relaxation strategies. Try new methods of relaxing and reducing your stress—take a walk, ride a bike, call a friend, or take a long bath. Use these strategies to relax yourself when you get the urge to smoke. Remember, the urge will eventually pass whether you smoke or not; choose to do something other than smoking until it does.

- Get and use medications to help you quit. A number of medications are available to help you stop smoking—using any one of them will double your chances of quitting successfully. These include nicotine patches and gums, which are available over the counter, as well as nicotine inhalers and nasal sprays and a nonnicotine pill, all of which require prescriptions. Your physician can help you decide which medication is best for you and advise you on using it correctly.

- Don't get discouraged by relapses. Many people who successfully quit smoking must make several attempts at it. Relapses happen—don't think of them as failures, but as learning opportunities. The next time you attempt to quit, you'll know what made you relapse before, and you'll be better able to avoid it. Like anything else, quitting smoking takes practice. ■

Runaways and Throwaways: Leaving Home

Each year, some half million adolescents abruptly leave their homes, not because they are moving on to a new, planned future but because they are either running away or their parents have thrown them out. For some, running away is a short-term solution to an immediate problem; for others, it represents a desperate need to leave problems for which there appears no other way out. And some adolescents leave because they are told, either explicitly or implicitly, that they must leave home (Hammer et al., 2004; Gullotta, 2006).

Runaway Adolescents. *Runaways* leave home voluntarily for at least one night, without parental permission. In most households where adolescents run away, there is considerable conflict, not only between parents and their children, but between parents themselves. Runaways often are the victims of sexual or physical abuse.

There are several perspectives on the causes of running away from home. According to *strain theory,* runaways become alienated from their families. In this view, adolescents are unable to obtain a sense of psychological support from their immediate family members, and sometimes they lack support from peers or school. In such cases, the decision to run away is often impulsive (Adams & Adams, 1987; Thompson, Zittel-Palamara, & Maccio, 2004).

Other explanations for running away are based on *social control theory,* which suggests that adolescents who run away have not internalized appropriate values and norms. Running away is viewed as an act of deviance and is likely to be associated with other deviant behaviors such as criminal behavior or juvenile delinquency (Gullotta, 2006).

Running away is usually associated with severe emotional problems. Runaways often have low self-esteem and are anxious, depressed, and hostile. They are at heightened risk for suicide, particularly those who have suffered from physical abuse from their parents (Chun & Springer, 2005).

On the other hand, not all runaways are psychologically disordered. Some leave home because of a temporary conflict. For those adolescents, leaving home is not seen as a permanent state. Instead, for many runaways leaving home is the unplanned outcome of an argument; these adolescents typically stay close to home, moving temporarily to the home of a friend or relative. Some runaways leave home out of a romantic sense of adventure, seeing themselves as modern-day Huck Finns. In such cases, the psychological consequences of running away are less severe. Parents often know where their children have run away to, and adolescents often return home relatively soon after leaving (Gullotta, Adams, & Markstrom, 2000; Gullottta, 2006).

Throwaway Adolescents. Among the most devastating cases are those of throwaway adolescents. *Throwaways* are youth who do not leave home willingly, but are forced to leave because of the behavior of their parents or guardians. In some cases, throwaways are explicitly told to leave home. In other cases, their parents make the situation so difficult for adolescents that they feel they have no other choice than to leave (Thompson, Safyer, & Pollio, 2001).

In some throwaway cases, parents may be physically or sexually abusive. The discovery of incest between one parent and an adolescent, or between siblings, can lead to a throwaway situation. In other cases, parents reject children because of the adolescent's use of drugs or refusal to follow treatment for drug abuse. In some situations, an adolescent's behavioral problems are so difficult to handle that parents essentially give up on parenting and order their child to leave home (Ringwalt, Greene, & Robertson, 1998; Whitbeck et al., 2001).

Sometimes throwaways leave home because their parents provide them with little or no support. The parents may abuse alcohol or drugs themselves, they may provide no emotional encouragement, or they may be psychologically abusive.

Throwaway adolescents, who make up perhaps 20% of the total population of runaways, are the most needy of runaway adolescents. They are the most likely to become homeless and to be victimized by sexual predators, and they are more likely to engage in high-risk sexual behavior. They also have the highest levels of suicidal thoughts.

Although runaway and throwaway adolescents are in desperate need of support, there is insufficient help available. Although in recent years temporary shelters for runaways and national telephone hotlines such as the one supported by the National Center for Missing and Exploited Children (call 1-800–THE–LOST) have been established, they are insufficient to meet the needs of runaway children.

Review and Apply

Review

1. Adolescents face several kinds of externalizing problems, including juvenile delinquency, school violence, and substance use and abuse.

2. Some adolescents are undersocialized delinquents reared with little discipline or with uncaring supervision, while others are socialized delinquents who pass through a delinquency phase, which they abandon when they reach adulthood.

3. School violence receives a lot of attention from the media, but a school is in fact a safer environment for adolescents than any other.

4. The use of illegal drugs, alcohol, and tobacco is common among adolescents, typically producing physical or psychological addiction.

5. Some adolescents leave home abruptly during the period—some as runaways and others as throwaways.

Apply

1. Because smoking still is attached to an image of "coolness," some people advocate a ban on smoking in movies, videos, and other forms of popular entertainment. Is this a good idea? Why or why not?

2. In what areas of an adolescent's life other than the use of alcohol does the false consensus effect play a role? What is an effective way to reveal it as false?

Internalizing Problems in Adolescence

*B*rianne Camilleri had it all: *Two involved parents, a caring older brother and a comfortable home near Boston. But that didn't stop the overwhelming sense of hopelessness that enveloped her in ninth grade. "It was like a cloud that followed me everywhere," she says. "I couldn't get away from it."*

Brianne started drinking and experimenting with drugs. One Sunday she was caught shoplifting at a local store and her mother, Linda, drove her home in what Brianne describes as a "piercing silence." With the clouds in her head so dark she believed she would never see light again, Brianne went straight for the bathroom and swallowed every Tylenol and Advil she found—a total of 74 pills. She was only 14, and she wanted to die. (Wingert & Kantrowitz, 2002, p. 54)

Although by far the majority of teenagers weather the search for identity—as well as the other challenges presented by adolescence—without major psychological difficulties, some find the period particularly stressful. Some, in fact, develop severe psychological problems.

In the final part of this chapter we'll focus on internalizing difficulties, those physical and psychological problems that are turned inward and primarily affect the adolescent in question. We'll focus on the most serious of problems: adolescent depression, suicide, and reactions to physical and psychological abuse.

Adolescent Depression

The worst night of my life I envisioned my own funeral, my death by suicide. I curled up in a tight ball, paralyzed by my imagination. Scene after self-destructive scene reeled through my consciousness. My parents were the only people who cried at the service.

Although I crashed that one night, I had been falling for months. Since the end of my tenth-grade year, self-judgment had tugged at the upturned corners of my lips—that's why my smile looked forced, and my bottom lip often quivered. I didn't like myself. I only saw my weaknesses. I heard only the abrasive tone of self-criticism.

I understand depression. I deeply wish I didn't.

No one is immune to periods of sadness and bad moods, and adolescents are no exception. The end of a relationship, failure at an important task, the death of a loved one—all may produce profound feelings of sadness, loss, and grief. In situations such as these, depression is a fairly typical reaction.

How common are feelings of depression in adolescence? More than a quarter of adolescents report feeling so sad or hopeless for two or more weeks in a row that they stop doing their normal activities. Almost two thirds of teenagers say they have experienced such feelings at one time or another. On the other hand, only a small minority of adolescents—some 3%—experience *major depression,* a full-blown psychological disorder in which depression is severe and lingers for long periods (Cicchetti & Toth, 1998; Grunbaum, et al. 2001; Galambos, Leadbeater, & Barker, 2004).

Gender, ethnic, and racial differences also are found in depression rates. As is the case among adults, adolescent girls, on average, experience depression more often than boys. Some studies have found that African-American adolescents have higher rates of depression than white adolescents, although not all research supports this conclusion. Native Americans, too, have higher rates of depression (Stice, Presnell, & Bearman, 2001; Jacques & Mash, 2004; Hightower, 2005).

▶ Although feelings of depression are common during adolescence, only a few suffer from major depression, a serious psychological disorder.

In cases of severe, long-term depression, biological factors are often involved. Although some adolescents seem to be genetically predisposed to experience depression, environmental and social factors relating to the extraordinary changes in the social lives of adolescents are also important influences. An adolescent who experiences the death of a loved one, for example, or one who grows up with an alcoholic or depressed parent, is at higher risk for depression. In addition, being unpopular, having few close friends, and experiencing rejection are associated with adolescent depression (Lau & Kwok, 2000; Goldsmith et al., 2002; Eley, Liang, & Plomin, 2004).

One of the most puzzling questions about depression is why its incidence is higher among girls than boys. There is little evidence that it is linked to hormone differences or a particular gene. Instead, some psychologists speculate that stress is more pronounced for girls than for boys in adolescence due to the many, sometimes conflicting demands of the traditional female gender role. For example, adolescent girls may be more worried than boys both about doing well in school and about being popular. If they believe that academic success undermines their popularity, they are placed in a difficult bind that can leave them feeling helpless. Added to this is the fact that traditional gender roles still give higher status to men than to women (Nolen-Hoeksema, 2003; Gilbert, 2004).

Girls' generally higher levels of depression during adolescence also may reflect gender differences in ways of coping with stress, rather than gender differences in mood. Girls may be more apt than boys to react to stress by turning inward, thereby experiencing a sense of helplessness and hopelessness. In contrast, boys more often react by externalizing the stress and acting more impulsively or aggressively or by turning to drugs and alcohol (Hankin & Abramson, 2001; Winstead & Sanchez, 2005).

Treating Depression. Because depression typically first becomes a significant problem in adolescence, a number of treatment techniques have been developed to reduce the likelihood that it will grow into more severe forms of the disorder. For instance, in one study, adolescents who were at high risk for developing major depression because they already showed mild or moderate symptoms participated in 15 sessions of group therapy. Meeting after school, psychologists taught them strategies for overcoming negative thinking as well as ways of dealing with stress (Clarke et al., 1995).

After participation in the therapy, the adolescents were followed for 18 months. Compared with adolescents who did not participate in the therapy, participants showed a marked decline in the number of depressive symptoms over the course of therapy. Even more remarkable, participation in therapy reduced the likelihood of developing major depression over the next 18 months, compared to the no-therapy group, as can be seen in Figure 13-5.

Therapy may also involve drugs, although their use is controversial. Advocates for the use of antidepressants such as Prozac, Zoloft, Paxil, and Wellbutrin for adolescents suggest that depression can be treated quite successfully using drug therapies. In many cases, more traditional nondrug therapies that largely employ verbal methods simply are ineffective. In such cases, drugs can provide the only available form of relief. Furthermore, several clinical tests have shown that the drugs, in combination with traditional talk psychotherapy, are effective with children and adolescents (Emslie et al., 1997; Garland, 2004; March, Brian, & Kremer, 2006).

Critics, however, contend that there is little evidence for the long-term effectiveness of antidepressants with children. Even worse, no one knows what are the consequences of the use of antidepressants on the developing brains of adolescents, nor the long-term consequences more generally. Furthermore, relatively little is known about the correct dosages to use with adolescents, whose rapid physical growth makes it difficult to fix on a dosage that is both effective and safe. Furthermore, some observers suggest that the use of drugs that affect adolescents' moods may encourage the use of illegal drugs (Strauch, 1997; Goode, 2004; Andersen, & Navalta, 2004; Couzin, 2004).

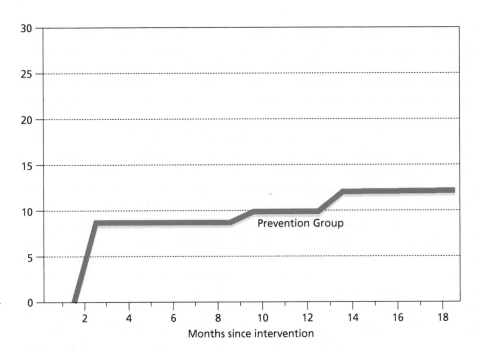

▶ **FIGURE 13-5**

Intervention providing group therapy has shown to be very beneficial for adolescents who were at high risk for developing major depression.

(*Source:* Clarke et al., 1995.)

Finally, there is some evidence linking the use of antidepressant medication with an increase in suicidal thoughts, suicide attempts, and actual suicide, especially during the first weeks of use. Although the link has not been firmly established, the U.S. Federal Drug Administration issued a warning in 2004 about the use of a class of antidepressants known as SSRIs. Although some experts have urged that the use of these antidepressants in children and adolescents be banned completely, current thinking suggests that SSRIs, and fluoxetine, have a role in treating depression in children and adolescents (Satel, 2004; Vedantam, 2004; Kratochvil et al., 2006).

Adolescent Suicide

The rate of adolescent suicide in the United States has tripled in the last 30 years. In fact, one teenage suicide occurs every 90 minutes, for an annual rate of 12.2 suicides per 100,000 adolescents. Moreover, the reported rate may actually understate the true number of suicides; parents and medical personnel are often reluctant to report a death as suicide, preferring to label it an accident. Even with underreporting, suicide is the third most common cause of death in the 15-to-24-year-old age group, after accidents and homicide. It is important to keep in mind, however, that although the rate of suicide for adolescents has risen more than for other age groups, the highest rate of suicide is found in the period of late adulthood (see Figure 13-6; Healy, 2001; Grunbaum et al., 2002; Joe & Marcus, 2003).

In adolescence, the rate of suicide is higher for boys than girls, although girls *attempt* suicide more frequently than boys. Suicide attempts among males are more likely to result in death because of the methods they use: Boys tend to use more violent means, such as guns, while girls are more apt to choose the more-peaceful, yet less-effective, strategy of drug overdose. Some estimates suggest that there are as many as 200 attempted suicides by both sexes for every successful one (Gelman, 1994; Joseph, Reznik, & Mester, 2003).

The reasons behind the increase in adolescent suicide over past decades are unclear. The most obvious explanation is that the stress experienced by teenagers has increased, leading those who are most vulnerable to be more likely to commit suicide (Elkind, 1984). But why should stress have increased only for adolescents? The suicide rate for other segments of the population has remained fairly stable over the same time period. Although we are not yet sure why the rate of adolescent suicide has increased, it is clear that certain factors heighten the risk of suicide. One factor is depression. Depressed teenagers who are experiencing a profound sense of

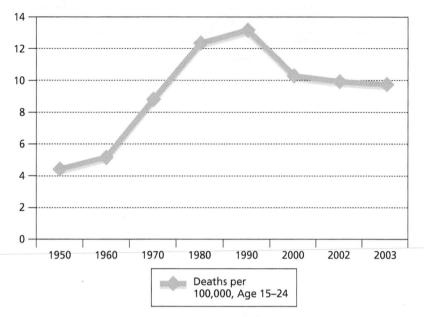

◄ **FIGURE 13-6**
Although the rate of suicide for those between the ages of 15 and 24 has risen more than for other age groups over the past 50 years, the highest rate of suicide is found in late adulthood.

(*Source:* National Center for Health Statistics, United States, 2005.)

hopelessness are at greater risk of committing suicide (although most depressed individuals do not commit suicide). In addition, social inhibition, perfectionism, and a high level of stress and anxiety are related to a greater risk of suicide. The easy availability of guns—which are more prevalent in the United States than in other industrialized nations—also contributes to the suicide rate (Huff, 1999; Goldston, 2003).

In addition to depression, some cases of suicide are associated with family conflicts and relationship or school difficulties. Some stem from a history of abuse and neglect. The rate of suicide among drug and alcohol abusers is also relatively high. As can be seen in Figure 13-7, teens who called a hotline because they were thinking of killing themselves mentioned several other factors as well (Lyon et al., 2000; Bergen, Martin, & Richardson, 2003; Wilcox, Conner, & Caine, 2004).

Some suicides appear to be caused by exposure to the suicide of others. In *cluster suicide*, one suicide leads to attempts by others to kill themselves. For instance, some high schools have experienced a series of suicides following a well-publicized case. As a result, many schools have established crisis intervention teams to counsel students when one student commits suicide (Haas, etal., 2003; Arenson, 2004).

The Warning Signs of Suicide.   Several warning signs should sound an alarm regarding the possibility of suicide. Among them:

- Direct or indirect talk about suicide, such as "I wish I were dead" or "You won't have me to worry about any longer"

- School difficulties, such as missed classes or a decline in grades

- Making arrangements as if preparing for a long trip, such as giving away prized possessions or arranging for the care of a pet

- Writing a will

- Loss of appetite or excessive eating

- General depression, including a change in sleeping patterns, slowness and lethargy, and uncommunicativeness

- Dramatic changes in behavior, such as a shy person suddenly acting outgoing

- Preoccupation with death in music, art, or literature.

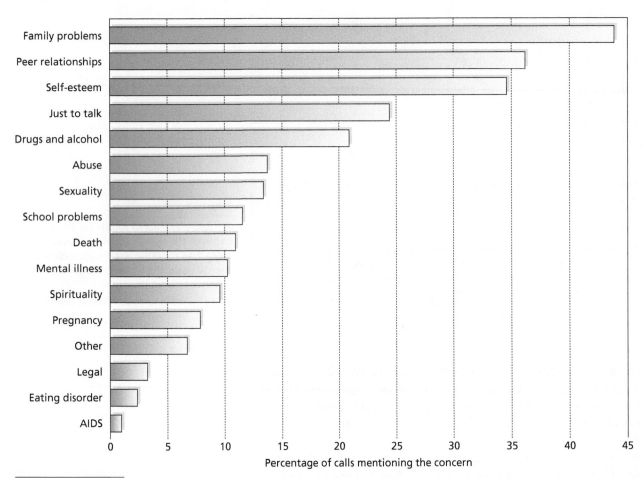

Percentage of calls mentioning the concern

▲ **FIGURE 13-7**

According to one survey of calls to a telephone help line, adolescents contemplating suicide most often mentioned family, peer relationships, and self-esteem as problems in their lives.

(*Source:* Boehm & Campbell, 1995)

If you suspect that an adolescent, or anyone else for that matter, is contemplating suicide, don't stand idly by. Act! Table 13-1 lists several concrete steps for dealing with individuals who you suspect may be suicidal.

Adolescent Abuse: Physical, Sexual, and Psychological

I lived with my Mother, Father and sister in your common middle class house. And although I'd love to say that my experience was not common, it sadly is. I was abused sexually by my father from a young age. I'm not sure when it started but something my Grandmother once told me makes me think I was probably a toddler. I can remember for sure that from 2nd through 6th grade there were weekly and steadily escalating encounters that sometimes involved the whole family and sometimes just me or my sister. They were pretty awful but I'll spare you the details. . . .

Even when we moved to Washington when I was 12 years old and the worst had ended in the way of the sexual abuse and the drugs due to my growing strength of will, we still feared for our lives if my father was upset by something. He had been a gun collector for years and if he stormed off to his room in the heat of the more often occurring arguments we would just hope he wasn't planning to grab a gun. I was actually relieved to be kicked out of the house to live with my Grandparents at the age of 13 for a summer when I showed disrespect over a dented towel rack.

Few problems faced by adolescents are as devastating as abuse. Whether it is physical, sexual, or psychological abuse—or, even worse, some combination of types—such abuse often leads to a lifetime of subsequent difficulties.

TABLE 13-1   Preventing Suicide

If you suspect that a friend, relative, or acquaintance is contemplating suicide, it is critical to act immediately. Despite a common misconception that those who talk about suicide are less likely to actually do it, that's not the case. The situation is serious anytime someone voices suicidal thoughts. Here are some concrete actions you can take in such situations:

- Talk to the person, listen without judging, and give the person an understanding forum in which to try to talk things through.
- Talk specifically about suicidal thoughts, asking such questions as: Do you have a plan? Have you bought a gun? Where is it? Have you stockpiled pills? Where are they? The Public Health Service notes that, "contrary to popular belief, such candor will not give a person dangerous ideas or encourage a suicidal act."
- Evaluate the situation, trying to distinguish between general upset and more serious danger, as when suicide plans *have* been made. If the crisis is acute, *do not leave the person alone*.
- Be supportive, let the person know you care, and try to break down his or her feelings of isolation.
- Take charge of finding help, without concern about invading the person's privacy. Do not try to handle the problem alone; get professional help immediately.
- Make the environment safe, removing from the premises (not just hiding) weapons such as guns, razors, scissors, medication, and other potentially dangerous household items.
- Do not keep suicide talk or threats secret; these are calls for help and require immediate action.
- Do not challenge, dare, or use verbal shock treatment on suicidal persons in an effort to make them realize the errors in their thinking. These can have tragic effects.
- Make a contract with the person, getting a promise or commitment, preferably in writing, not to make any suicidal attempt until you have talked further.
- Don't be overly reassured by a sudden improvement of mood. Such seemingly quick recoveries sometimes reflect the relief of finally deciding to commit suicide or the temporary release of talking to someone, but most likely the underlying problems have not been resolved.

For immediate help with a suicide-related problem, call (800) 784-2433 or (800) 621-4000, national hotlines staffed with trained counselors.

Physical Abuse.   Physical abuse can occur in any household, regardless of economic well-being or the social status of the parents. It is most frequent in families living in stressful environments. Poverty, single parenthood, and higher-than-average levels of marital conflict help create such environments. Stepfathers are more likely to commit abuse against stepchildren than genetic fathers against their own offspring. Child abuse also is more likely when there is a history of violence between spouses (Kitzmann, Gaylord, & Holt, 2003; Litrownik, Newton, & Hunter, 2003; Osofsky, 2003; Evans, 2004).

Why does physical abuse occur? Most parents certainly do not intend to hurt their children. In fact, most parents who abuse their children later express bewilderment and regret about their own behavior.

One reason for child abuse is the vague demarcation between permissible and impermissible forms of physical punishment. With younger children, the line between "spanking" and "beating" is not clear, and spankings begun in anger can escalate easily into abuse. Furthermore, parents who use physical punishment when their children are young may feel that adolescents require even greater degrees of punishment because they are older.

Many times, those who abuse children and adolescents were themselves abused as children. According to the **cycle of violence hypothesis**, the abuse and neglect that children and adolescents suffer predispose them as adults to abuse and neglect their own children (Miller-Perrin & Perrin, 1999; Widom, 2000; Heyman & Slep, 2002).

cycle of violence hypothesis   the theory that the abuse and neglect that children and adolescents suffer predispose them as adults to abuse and neglect their own children.

Transiti⊙ns

Preventing Adolescent Suicide: Dealing with the Crisis in Campus Mental Health

An increasing number of adolescents are starting college with psychological problems, and more students are showing up for treatment who are already on psychiatric medications or who have severe problems. In fact, the increasing difficulty that students are having with stress and psychological problems—coupled with the limited ability of colleges to address the problem effectively—has been called a crisis in campus mental health (Kadison & DiGeronimo, 2004; Gallagher, 2005).

Colleges vary in how well they are adjusting and responding to this crisis. Some have been pressed into hasty action by fear of lawsuits after recent court decisions that held college administrators partly accountable for student suicides. A common response has been to enact policies requiring suicidal students to take a leave of absence—essentially forcing self-destructive students to stop their schooling. Administrators argue that such policies force troubled students to leave the stressful college environment and to get the help they need. They also point out that suicidal students can pose a risk to others as well as to themselves (Rawe & Kingsbury, 2006).

▲ Many campus counseling centers are struggling to meet the mental health needs of students.

This strategy does have some significant disadvantages. Students who fear being forced out of school might resist getting help when they need it, or if they do admit to a problem, may discount the severity of their illness or feign improvement. Such mandatory-leave policies also seem cold and insensitive, creating the appearance that the college cares more about its own well-being than that of its students. Finally, in some cases these policies, ironically, result in lawsuits against colleges rather than preventing them. Some students with psychological disorders who have been dismissed from their colleges have sued for discrimination under the Americans with Disabilities Act.

On the other hand, some colleges have responded to the mental health crisis in ways that seem more promising. For example, a new federal initiative called the Garrett Lee Smith Memorial Act was enacted in 2004 to address the problem of youth suicide. This initiative includes funding to help colleges with specific plans for addressing the suicide problem by improving the mental health services they provide. Different schools have used this funding opportunity in various ways. For example, Arizona State University had a particularly pronounced problem with student suicides, so it focused on improving its program staffing and providing training to employees in identifying students who are at risk of suicide and referring them for help.

The University of Wisconsin–Oshkosh (UWO) wasn't having a problem with increased suicide, but with an epidemic of students contemplating it. UWO recognized that a majority of its students came from blue-collar families who were more likely to view the use of mental health services as stigmatizing; it therefore focused on giving the campus community the knowledge and resources to identify students with problems and persuade them to use the available services, which it also worked to make more accessible. Finally, Blue Mountain Community College (BMCC) in Pendleton, Oregon—a rural community college that had almost no mental health or suicide-prevention resources—experienced its own mental health crisis when a single school year was marred by two suicides. BMCC had more basic work to do to get its own mental health services off the ground—it started by forming partnerships with existing services in the larger community while it worked on developing its own campus-based programs (Whiting & Smulson, 2006).

Many colleges and universities are experiencing growing pains of their own as they struggle to respond to the increasing mental health needs of their mainly adolescent student bodies. As they develop better ways to identify and help students who are struggling with problems, a growing number of young lives can be saved.

- Why might colleges and universities be experiencing an increase in the number of students with psychological problems?

- Is it a good idea for college students who are suicidal to take a break from college? Should colleges mandate such a break?

According to this hypothesis, victims of abuse have learned from their childhood experiences that violence is an appropriate and acceptable form of discipline. Violence may be perpetuated from one generation to another, as each generation learns to behave abusively (and fails to learn the skills needed to solve problems and instill discipline without resorting to physical violence) through its participation in an abusive, violent family (Straus, Sugarman, & Giles-Sims, 1997; Blumenthal, 2000; Ethier, Couture, & Lacharite, 2004).

However, being abused as a child or adolescent does not inevitably lead to abuse of one's own children. In fact, statistics show that only about one third of people who were abused or neglected as children abuse their own children; the remaining two thirds of people abused as children do not turn out to be child abusers. Clearly, suffering abuse as a child is not the full explanation for child abuse in adults (Cicchetti, 1996; Straus & McCord, 1998).

Sexual Abuse. Sexual abuse is surprisingly common during childhood and adolescence. In fact, between 5 and 10% of boys and 20% of girls report having been abused. These figures are probably underestimates, because many, if not most, cases of childhood and adolescent sexual abuse are not reported by the victim (Villarosa, 2003).

In most cases, the abuse is committed by a relative or acquaintance; in only about one quarter of the cases is the abuse carried out by a stranger. The most vulnerable age for being molested is between 7 and 13 years old, and the abusers tend to be about 20 years older than their victims. In most instances, the abuser is a male heterosexual (Finkelhor et al., 2005; Wolfe, 1999).

The short- and longer-term consequences of childhood sexual abuse can be extremely damaging. In terms of initial effects, victims report fear, anxiety, depression, anger, and hostility. Long-term effects may include depression, self-destructive behavior, feelings of isolation, poor self-esteem, and substance abuse. Although they may experience sexual difficulties later in life, the victims are not more likely to become sexual abusers themselves.

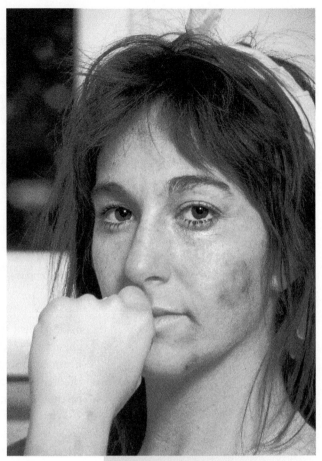

▲ Physical abuse can occur in any family, regardless of the socioeconomic status and social standing of the parents.

Ultimately, the consequences of childhood and adolescent sexual abuse are related to the specific nature of the abuse. Experiences involving fathers, genital contact and penetration, and the use of force are the most damaging. On the other hand, when the sex is consensual and involves brothers and sisters close in age, the consequences may be less negative (Berkowitz, 2000; Hawke, Jainchill, & De Leon, 2000; Berliner & Elliott, 2002).

Psychological Maltreatment. Adolescents may also be the victims of more subtle forms of mistreatment. *Psychological maltreatment* occurs when parents or other caregivers harm their children's behavioral, cognitive, emotional, or physical functioning. It may be the result of, or occur through, either overt behavior or neglect (Hart, Brassard, & Karlson, 1996; Higgins & McCabe, 2003).

For example, abusive parents may belittle or humiliate their children, thereby intimidating and harassing them. Adolescents may be made to feel like disappointments or failures, or they may be constantly reminded that they are a burden to their parents. Parents may tell their children that they wish they had never had children and specifically that they wish that their children had never been born. Adolescents may be threatened with abandonment or even death. They may be forced to seek employment and then to give their earnings to their parents.

In other cases of psychological maltreatment, the abuse takes the form of neglect. Parents may ignore their adolescents or act emotionally unresponsive to them. In such cases, adolescents may be given unrealistic responsibilities or may be left to fend for themselves.

No one is certain how much psychological maltreatment occurs each year, because figures separating psychological maltreatment from other types of abuse are not routinely gathered. Most maltreatment occurs in the privacy of people's homes. Furthermore, psychological

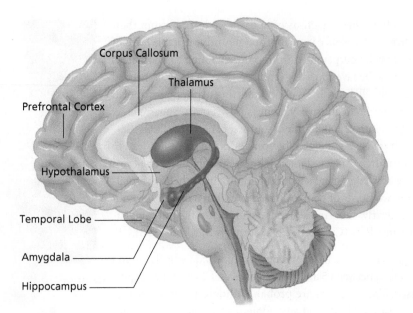

▶ **FIGURE 13-8**

Research has shown that childhood abuse can permanently alter the brain's limbic system, which is comprised of the hippocampus and amygdala.

(*Source: Scientific American*, March 2002, p. 71.)

maltreatment typically causes no physical damage, such as bruises or broken bones, to alert physicians, teachers, and other authorities. Consequently, many cases of psychological maltreatment probably are not identified. However, it is clear that profound neglect that involves children and adolescents who are unsupervised or uncared for is the most frequent form of psychological maltreatment (Hewitt, 1997).

What are the consequences of psychological maltreatment? Some adolescents are sufficiently resilient to survive the abuse and grow into psychologically healthy adults. In many cases, however, lasting damage results. For example, psychological maltreatment has been associated with low self-esteem, lying, misbehavior, and underachievement in school. In extreme cases, it can produce criminal behavior, aggression, and murder. In other instances, adolescents who have been psychologically maltreated become depressed and even commit suicide (Shonk & Cicchetti, 2001; Eigsti & Cicchetti, 2004; Koenig, Cicchetti, & Rogosch, 2004).

One reason that psychological maltreatment—as well as physical abuse—produces so many negative consequences in younger individuals is that the brains of victims undergo permanent changes due to the abuse (see Figure 13-8). For example, maltreatment during childhood and adolescence can lead to reductions in the size of the amygdala and hippocampus in adulthood. Furthermore, the fear and terror produced by abuse may also lead to permanent changes in the brain due to overexcitation of the limbic system, which is involved in the regulation of memory and emotion, leading to antisocial behavior during adulthood (Teicher et al., 2002; Bremner, 2003; Teicher et al., 2003; Navalta et al., 2006).

Adolescent
DIVERSITY Are Gay and Lesbian Adolescents at Greater Risk of Committing Suicide?

G AY AND LESBIAN adolescents are widely believed to be at greater risk of committing suicide. In 1989 the U.S. Department of Health and Human Services sounded an alarm when it reported that gay and lesbian adolescents are two to three times more likely to attempt suicide than are heterosexual adolescents, accounting for as many as 30% of completed suicides each year. A number of studies conducted around that time showed that about one in three gay and lesbian adolescents had attempted suicide (Remafedi, 1999; Kitts, 2005).

Researchers have offered various explanations for the apparent relationship between adolescent sexuality and suicide risk. Some emphasize other risk factors that are associated with homosexuality and also with suicide, such as family problems, dropping out of school, substance abuse, and depression, among others. Other researchers consider homosexuality itself to be a risk factor, perhaps due to gender nonconformity, victimization, or rejection by peers. For example, a Norwegian study controlled for a large number of other known risk factors for suicide and still found that adolescents with same-sex sexual behavior were at greater risk (Remafedi, 2002; Gould et al., 2003; van Wormer & McKinney, 2003; Goodenow, Szalacha, & Westheimer, 2006).

But one psychologist, Ritch Savin-Williams, has called into question the premise that a gay or lesbian identity necessarily increases adolescents' risk of suicide. His research suggests that in many cases the reports of suicide attempts by sexual minority youth are actually fabrications or exaggerations in which no actual suicide attempt was made. Furthermore, many of those who made genuine attempts deliberately chose methods that were unlikely to actually be lethal. Savin-Williams argued that it's more accurate to conclude that a disproportionate number of gay and lesbian adolescents feel enough conflict and distress to report a suicide attempt whether true or not, perhaps as a way to articulate their pain (Savin-Williams, 2001).

Savin-Williams's own research shows that only increased levels of conventional risk factors—and not gay or lesbian identity itself—are associated with suicide risk. He argued that a gay or lesbian identity does, however, produce an added vulnerability that for some sexual minority youth can heighten the effects of conventional risk factors that other youths also face. This may occur, for example, via other people's negative reactions to the youths' sexuality, which can add another element to the youths' stress or result in lost social support. In other words, being gay or lesbian makes some normal stressors harder to deal with for some adolescents (Savin-Williams & Ream, 2003).

But Savin-Williams emphasized that the far more common outcome is that gay and lesbian youth show tremendous resiliency. The wide majority of them never even consider suicide, despite widespread victimization. In fact, most learn to cope very well with stigma, show few ill effects, and say they would not change their sexual orientation if given the opportunity (Savin-Williams, 2001; Savin-Williams & Ream, 2003).

A Final Word

Although we've focused in this chapter on the problems and difficulties that adolescents face, it's critical to keep in mind that the majority of adolescents pass through the period without major problems. Adolescence most typically is a time of growth, development, and advancement, as boys and girls make the transition from childhood to adulthood. Certainly adolescents have their moments of sorrow, fear, anger, and anxiety, but they also experience joy, wonder, and great happiness as they move through this most stimulating period of life.

Review and Apply

Review

1. The most serious internalizing problems that adolescents face include adolescent depression, suicide, and physical or psychological abuse.

2. Only about 3% of adolescents experience major depression, and the problem is found more often among adolescent girls than adolescent boys.

3. Treatment of depression with drugs is controversial, with some psychologists arguing that drugs are the only form of treatment that works, and others arguing that the long-term use of antidepressants by adolescents may have unknown consequences.

4. The incidence of suicide among adolescents is on the rise, with girls making more suicide attempts than boys.

5. Some adolescents are subject to physical, psychological, or sexual abuse, typically perpetrated by relatives or acquaintances.

Apply

1. What ethical responsibility does an adolescent have toward a person who reveals telltale signs of suicidal plans? Does the bond of trust and confidentiality outweigh the responsibility to report dangerous activity?

2. What sort of research study would you conduct to confirm or disprove the cycle of violence hypothesis? Would such a study clearly prove either that there is or isn't a cycle of violence?

EPILOGUE

In this chapter we looked at a number of the typical difficulties that adolescents face, categorizing them as externalizing difficulties and internalizing difficulties. We traced some of the reasons behind these difficulties, discussing theories for their origins.

Then we focused on externalizing difficulties, including especially juvenile delinquency, school violence, substance use, and the prevalence of runaway adolescents and throwaway adolescents. We saw that throwaways in particular have later problems as adults as a result of their being rejected by their families.

We concluded the chapter by looking at internalizing difficulties. We focused on adolescent depression and suicide and discussed physical, sexual, and psychological abuse of adolescents. We noted that this sort of abuse tends to be perpetrated by family members, not strangers.

Before we proceed to the next chapter, return to the description of Matthew Pearlstone, the adolescent from the Prologue who figured that he had his alcoholism under control. Consider the following questions.

1. Did Matthew have an actual problem with alcohol, or did his use of alcohol seem more like normal adolescent experimentation?

2. Do you believe Matthew's assertion that he was in control of his drinking? What is the evidence for and against his claim?

3. Did Matthew seem to be exhibiting any signals of having an alcohol problem?

4. If you had been one of Matthew's friends and were concerned about his drinking, what might you have done to help him?

SUMMARY

REVIEW

● **What are the major types of problems adolescents encounter?** *(p. 416)*

1. Adolescents face internalizing disorders, which are physical and psychological problems that are turned inward, and externalizing disorders, which are displayed as behavioral problems and are turned outward, toward others.

2. Some of the major externalizing problems of adolescence are juvenile delinquency, violence, substance abuse, and running away from home.

3. Externalizing problems during adolescence tend to be comorbid, occurring in groups, a fact that suggests that they are caused by environmental conditions in adolescents' lives.

- **What are some of the underlying causes of the externalizing difficulties of adolescence?** *(p. 420)*

  1. Some adolescents are undersocialized, with personal characteristics that lead to rejection by peers and academic failure, while others are socialized delinquents passing through a fairly normal behavioral phase involving petty crimes that do not continue into adulthood.

  2. Of the two main routes to delinquency, early-onset delinquency is more likely to lead to other problems in later life, while late-onset delinquency typically ends as the individual becomes integrated into society.

  3. An approach called the social control perspective suggests that externalizing problems are caused not by a deviant personality characteristic but by adolescents' difficulties conforming to society's norms.

- **What externalizing problems do adolescents face at school, in their neighborhoods, and at home?** *(p. 422)*

  1. The prevalence and danger of school violence have been overstated by the media; in fact, schools are among the safest environments for adolescents.

  2. The use of addictive drugs—including alcohol, illegal drugs, and tobacco—among adolescents is probably caused by a desire to emulate attractive role models who engage in these practices.

  3. Adolescents who leave home early may be either runaways or throwaways, with throwaways facing a bleaker future than runaways.

- **What are the major internalizing problems of adolescence?** *(p. 431)*

  1. Depression and suicide are among the most common internalizing problems.

  2. Biological factors are often involved in severe, long-term depression, but the main reasons that adolescents become depressed are related to environmental and social changes in adolescents' lives.

  3. Adolescent girls are more prone to depression than adolescent boys, but this may be related to their different ways of dealing with stress.

  4. The reasons for the increase in adolescent suicide in the United States include depression, perfectionism, social inhibition, family conflicts, school problems, and the ready availability of guns.

- **What are the typical kinds of adolescent abuse?** *(p. 436)*

  1. Families living in stressful environments tend to exhibit physical abuse toward their children, and there is evidence of a cycle of violence by which victims of abuse become abusers as adults.

  2. Sexual abuse is common during childhood and adolescence; in most cases the abusive behavior is committed by a relative or acquaintance rather than a stranger.

  3. Psychological maltreatment is a form of abuse that may involve the humiliation or neglect of one's children.

KEY TERMS AND CONCEPTS

internalizing disorders (p. 416)

externalizing disorders (p. 416)

comorbid (p. 417)

undersocialized delinquents (p. 420)

socialized delinquents (p. 421)

addictive drugs (p. 424)

alcoholic (p. 425)

cycle of violence hypothesis (p. 437)

14 Stress, Coping, and Well-Being

CHAPTER OUTLINE

PROLOGUE

A BLOND, SWEET-FACED junior, Katy Haddow very much likes concert choir, an advanced choral music class at Stonewall Jackson High School in Manassas. But she hates having to sing by herself in front of some 75 classmates, many of them strangers. It makes her so nervous, standing there singing while her teacher Ms. Boley assesses her diction, her breathing, her pitch and, often, her ability to sight-sing an unfamiliar song, cold, from looking at the score.

The whole experience raises in Katy's mind the question of whether she should drop concert choir, which, just weeks into her junior year, is turning out to be her most anxiety-producing class. Even IB history, Katy is starting to think, might be less stressful. IB history! Less stressful! Which is saying a lot. IB history, if Katy decides to switch, is going to have two hours of homework a night, plus a major exam at the end of the year. That final exam will, of course, be in addition to the other tests Katy will take this year—the SOLs and the SATs—and in addition to the considerable workload of her other classes, English, Spanish, algebra II and chemistry.

Plus, Katy is already signed up for IB anthropology, which has an even heavier workload and its own end-of-year exam. At Stonewall Jackson, a large, high-performing public high school, the IB, or International Baccalaureate, classes are similar to AP, or Advanced Placement, courses. They are the most advanced, most competitive classes, the classes that may seem to separate the students who are college-bound from the students who are not. . . .

"I feel like if I don't take IB classes, I'll never be anything in life," Katy says. "That's what our teachers are telling us. Our IB coordinator, she will come into our class and tell you to sign up for all the IB classes that you can, girls, or you're not going to make it in college or be anything."

"My problem right now is that I'm feeling like I'm not going to be able to get into a good school; I'm going to end up working at McDonald's," worries Katy. "I break down every day. It's horrible, all of this pressure from school. . . ." (Mundy, 2005, p. W20) ■

th!nk ABOUT THIS

FOR STUDENTS LIKE Katy Haddow, academics is just one of the stressors that she faces. There's also her participation in the track team, with its grueling practices and meets, as well as the many other activities in which she is involved. Then there's her family and her friends, all of whom make additional demands on her time.

Katy's adolescence, like that of most of her peers, is a period in which the world exerts considerable challenges. How effectively she navigates these challenges will have a considerable impact on her well-being, not only during adolescence but throughout later life.

In this chapter we focus on stress, coping, and well-being. We start by looking at stress. We consider the different types of circumstances that produce stress, as well as the short- and long-term costs of stress.

We then examine coping. We consider how adolescents cope with stress most effectively, looking at how social support and hardiness can reduce stress. We also ask why some adolescents are highly resilient, adapting to a considerable number of stressors and yet seeming to do quite well in the face of them.

Finally, we consider well-being in adolescence. We discuss the characteristics of happy adolescents and the degree to which happiness changes, depending on circumstances. We also look at differences in cultural views of subjective well-being. ■

After reading this chapter,

YOU'LL BE ABLE TO ANSWER THESE QUESTIONS:

- **What is stress and what causes it?**
- **How does stress affect adolescents?**
- **How can adolescents learn to cope with stress?**
- **What personal characteristics seem to reduce the effects of stress?**
- **What does it mean to be happy?**

Stress

It was only 10:34 A.M., and already Jennifer Jackson had put in what seemed like a full day. After getting up at 6:30 A.M., she studied a bit for an American History exam scheduled later in the afternoon. She gulped down breakfast as she studied and then headed off to the campus bookstore, where she worked part-time.

Her car was in the shop with some undiagnosed ailment, so she had to take the bus. The bus was late, so Jennifer didn't have time to stop off at the library before work to pick up the reserve book she needed. Making a mental note to try to get the book at lunchtime (although she thought it probably wouldn't be available by then), she sprinted from the bus to the store, arriving a few minutes late. Although her supervisor didn't say anything, she looked irritated as Jennifer explained why she was late. Feeling that she needed to make amends, Jennifer volunteered to sort invoices—a task that she, and everyone else, hated. As she sorted the invoices, she also answered the phone and jumped up to serve a steady stream of customers who were placing special orders. When the phone rang at 10:34 A.M., it was her garage mechanic telling her that the car repair would cost several hundred dollars—a sum she did not have.

If you were to monitor Jennifer Jackson's heart rate and blood pressure, you wouldn't be shocked to find that both were higher than normal. You also wouldn't be surprised if she reported experiencing stress.

Adolescents, like the rest of us, are well acquainted with **stress,** the response to events that threaten or challenge an individual. Everyday life is filled with **stressors,** circumstances that produce threats to one's well-being. And it is not just unpleasant events, such as tests or job demands, that produce stress; even happy circumstances, such as getting prepared for a school dance or winning a leadership post in an election, can produce stress (Brown & McGill, 1989; Lazarus, 1999).

stress the response to events that threaten or challenge an individual.

stressors circumstances that produce threats to one's well-being.

◀ All adolescents experience stress in response to events that threaten or challenge them.

Stress: Reactions to Threat and Challenge

How do particular circumstances become stressful? Stress is the result of a two-step process involving the interpretation of a particular event or set of circumstances in a person's life (see Figure 14-1). The first step is **primary appraisal,** the assessment of an event or circumstance to determine whether its implications are positive, neutral, or negative. If they determine the implications are negative, people appraise the event in terms of how harmful it has been in the past, how threatening it appears to the future, and how likely it is that the challenge can be addressed successfully (Lazarus, 1993, 1999; Folkman & Moskowitz, 2000; Giacobbi et al., 2004).

The next step is secondary appraisal. **Secondary appraisal** is the assessment of whether adolescents feel their coping abilities and resources are adequate to overcome the harm, threat, or

primary appraisal the assessment of an event or circumstance to determine whether its implications are positive, neutral, or negative.

secondary appraisal the assessment of whether adolescents feel their coping abilities and resources are adequate to overcome the harm, threat, or challenge posed by the potential stressor.

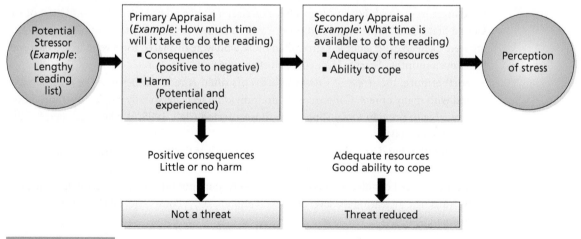

▲ **FIGURE 14-1**

Stress is the result of a two-step process involving a primary appraisal to determine whether the implications of the circumstance are positive or negative, and a secondary appraisal assessing whether adolescents feel their coping abilities are adequate to overcome the harm, threat or challenge posed by the potential stressor.

(*Source*: Adapted from Kaplan, Sallis, & Patterson, 1993, p. 123, based on Lazarus & Folkman, 1984.)

challenge posed by the potential stressor. During this stage, people seek to determine whether their personal resources are sufficient to meet the dangers posed by the situation.

The experience of stress is the outcome of both primary and secondary appraisal. When the potential harm, threat, and challenge produced by circumstances are high, and coping abilities are limited, adolescents experience stress (Mishra & Spreitzer, 1998; Chang, 1998).

For example, consider a high school student who receives a lengthy reading list in her English class that she must complete in the next 3 weeks. First, she engages in primary appraisal, analyzing the implications of the list in terms of the time it will take to do the reading and assessing how threatening the task appears. Next, she engages in secondary appraisal, considering whether she has sufficient time to complete the reading. If the answer is Yes, then the threat is reduced. But if she decides that time will be an issue because she faces numerous other time demands during the same period, her secondary appraisal will result in the perception of stress.

Stressors: What's Pleasure for You is Stress for Me

As the appraisal model suggests, stress is a very personal thing. For some teenagers, bungee-jumping and rock climbing would produce high degrees of stress; for others, these are simply recreational activities that, because of the distractions they present, may ultimately *reduce* stress.

Certain kinds of circumstances, however, produce stress in almost everyone. For instance, taking college admissions tests like the SAT causes stress in almost all students. At a more serious level, adolescents living in areas of the world in which there is war or combat, and who face threats to their lives, experience extreme levels of chronic stress (Betancourt, 2005; Zeidner, 2005; Hampel & Petermann, 2006).

In other cases, specific events or circumstances bring stress. There are three main types: cataclysmic events, personal stressors, and daily hassles.

Cataclysmic Events.   **Cataclysmic events** are strong stressors that occur suddenly and affect many adolescents simultaneously. Disasters such as tornadoes, hurricanes, and floods are examples of cataclysmic events that affect literally hundreds of thousands of individuals at once. Terrorist attacks, too, fall into this category (Polatin et al., 2005).

Although cataclysmic events affect many adolescents—as well as their parents and peers—at the same time, the stress that they produce is often less intense than events that initially are less dramatic. This is because cataclysmic incidents usually have a clear end-point, after which the danger has passed. For instance, after Hurricane Katrina devastated the Gulf Coast of the United States in 2005, teenagers who were able to return to their homes soon after the flooding were likely to experience *less* stress than those who were displaced for several weeks or sometimes even months (Scarpa, Hayden, & Hurley, 2006).

Furthermore, the stress of cataclysmic events often is reduced because the experience is shared with many others. Consequently, no individual feels personally singled out, and others are available to provide social support to those affected (Bell, 1995; Williams, Zinner, & Ellis, 1999; Benight, 2004).

On the other hand, certain cataclysmic events—such as the 9/11 World Trade Center terrorist attacks—produce considerable stress. Terrorist attacks are premeditated, and victims know that future attacks are possible. Furthermore, the government periodically produces heightened terrorist warnings, increasing the level of stress (Graham, 2001; Pomponio, 2002; Murphy, Wismar, & Freeman, 2003).

Personal Stressors.   The second major type of stressor is the **personal stressor,** a major life event with immediate negative consequences. The death of a loved one, the termination of an important relationship, or a major school or job failure might all be considered personal stressors. Although the immediate impact of personal stressors can be profound, with time the consequences often taper off as people learn to adapt. In some cases, however, such as the occurrence

cataclysmic events   strong stressors that occur suddenly and affect many adolescents simultaneously, such as tornadoes, hurricanes, and floods.

personal stressor   a major life event with immediate negative consequences.

of a violent physical assault, people may experience posttraumatic stress disorder (Foa & Riggs, 1995).

People who experience significant personal stressors and cataclysmic events are at risk for posttraumatic stress disorder. **Posttraumatic stress disorder (PTSD)** is a psychological syndrome in which victims of major incidents reexperience the original stress-producing event and associated feelings in flashbacks or dreams.

Symptoms of posttraumatic stress disorder include emotional numbing, sleep difficulties, problems relating to others, alcohol and drug abuse, and—in extreme cases—suicide. For instance, the suicide rate for veterans of the Vietnam War is as much as 25% higher than it is for the general population (Wilson & Keane, 1996; Orr, Metzger, & Pitman, 2002; McKeever & Huff, 2003; Ozer, Best, & Lipsey, 2003).

Adolescents who are the victims of child abuse or rape or of sudden natural disasters or accidents that produce shock, feelings of being overwhelmed, and the sense of helplessness may suffer from the disorder. In addition, 16% of soldiers returning from the Iraq war have symptoms of PTSD (Hoge et al., 2004; Ozer & Weiss, 2004; Schnurr & Cozza, 2004).

Terrorist attacks, too, can produce high levels of PTSD. For example, a tenth of those living in New York City experienced some form of PTSD in the months following the September 11 terrorist attack. The closer someone lived to Ground Zero, the greater the likelihood they had PTSD (see Figure 14-2; Susser, Herman, & Aaron, 2002; Coates, Rosenthan, & Schechter, 2003).

Background Stressors or Daily Hassles.   Finally, there is a third type of stressor, one with which every adolescent is familiar—background stressors or, more informally, daily hassles. **Background stressors** (also known as **daily hassles**) are the small irritants of life that produce minor stress. For instance, an adolescent who fumes while waiting in a slow-moving line at the movies or who is late for school because of a delayed school bus is experiencing a background stressor. In addition, background stressors can be long-term, chronic problems, such as being dissatisfied with one's teachers or being a part of a lingering, unhappy relationship (van Eck, Nicolson, & Berkhof, 1998; Lazarus, 2000; Weinstein et al., 2004).

Although the circumstances that produce daily hassles often are not, by themselves, all that unpleasant, the negative consequences add up and can ultimately produce even more stress for an adolescent than a single, initially more extreme event. In fact, the number of daily hassles faced by an adolescent is associated with psychological symptoms and physiological health problems such as sore throat, flu, and backaches.

Daily hassles have positive counterparts—uplifts. **Uplifts** are those minor positive events that make people feel good, even if only temporarily. Uplifts range from having a pleasant experience with others, to feeling healthy, to having one's parents make one's favorite meal. Uplifts may help to counteract the negative consequences of daily hassles and aid in fending off the stress they cause. In fact, some research suggests that the effects of uplifts may last longer than those of hassles. For example, one study found that although the negative consequences of hassles lasted for one day, uplifts still had lingering effects three days later. (Common daily hassles and uplifts are shown in Figure 14-3 on page 451; Chamberlain & Zika, 1990; Kanner et al., 1981; Roberts, 1995; Ravindran et al., 2002.)

Circumstances that Produce the Greatest Stress.   Although the nature of specific stressors varies from one adolescent to another, several broad principles explain which events are appraised as stressful. Among them (Taylor, 2006):

- *Occurrences that evoke negative emotions are more apt to produce stress than positive occurrences.* For most adolescents, purchasing a dress to wear to the prom—which involves positive emotions—is less stressful than preparing for a test, which is likely to evoke negative emotions (Martin & Dahlen, 2005).

posttraumatic stress disorder (PTSD)   a psychological syndrome in which victims of major incidents reexperience the original stress-producing event and associated feelings in flashbacks or dreams.

background stressors (also known as **daily hassles**):   the small irritants of life that produce minor stress.

uplifts   minor positive events that make people feel good, even if only temporarily.

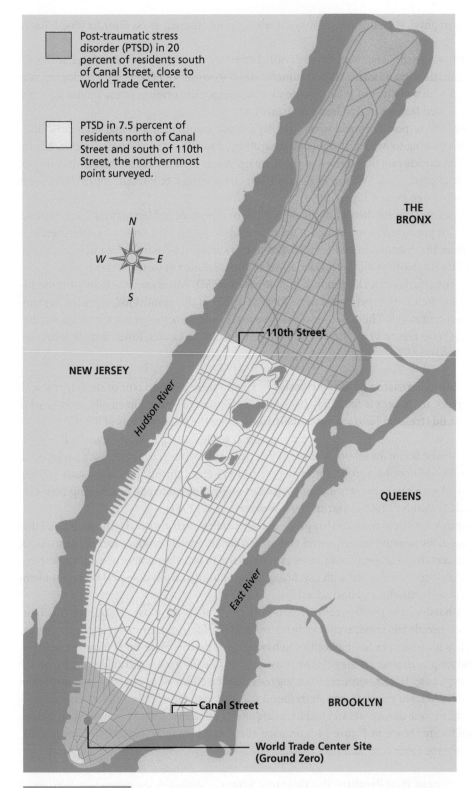

Post-traumatic stress disorder (PTSD) in 20 percent of residents south of Canal Street, close to World Trade Center.

PTSD in 7.5 percent of residents north of Canal Street and south of 110th Street, the northernmost point surveyed.

N
W   E
S

THE BRONX

110th Street

NEW JERSEY

Hudson River

QUEENS

East River

Canal Street

BROOKLYN

World Trade Center Site (Ground Zero)

▲ **FIGURE 14-2**

The rate of posttraumatic stress disorder increased the closer people lived to the World Trade Center during the terrorist attack of September 11, 2001.

(*Source*: Susser, Herman, & Aaron, 2002).

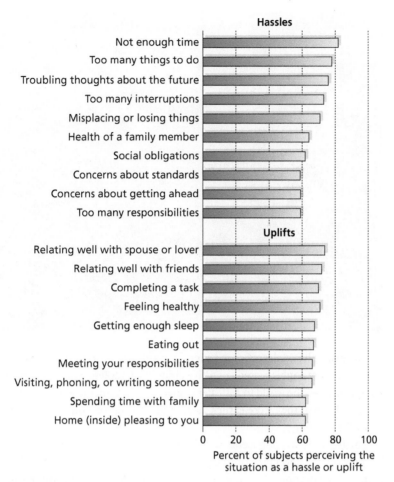

Hassles

- Not enough time
- Too many things to do
- Troubling thoughts about the future
- Too many interruptions
- Misplacing or losing things
- Health of a family member
- Social obligations
- Concerns about standards
- Concerns about getting ahead
- Too many responsibilities

Uplifts

- Relating well with spouse or lover
- Relating well with friends
- Completing a task
- Feeling healthy
- Getting enough sleep
- Eating out
- Meeting your responsibilities
- Visiting, phoning, or writing someone
- Spending time with family
- Home (inside) pleasing to you

0   20   40   60   80   100
Percent of subjects perceiving the
situation as a hassle or uplift

◀ **FIGURE 14-3**

The most common everyday hassles and uplifts.

(*Sources*: Hassles—Chamberlain & Zika, 1990; Uplifts—Kanner et al., 1981.)

- *Events that are uncontrollable or unpredictable are more stressful than those that can be controlled or predicted.* For example, those who live near airports and hear airplane takeoffs and landings at seemingly random intervals report high levels of stress. In comparison, for adolescents who feel they have enough control to stop or influence an unpleasant event, stress is likely to be lower (Miller & Townsend, 2005; Isowa, Ohira, & Murashima, 2006).

- *Circumstances that are unclear and ambiguous typically produce more stress than those that are unambiguous and precise.* If an event is not easily understood, adolescents must struggle to comprehend it, rather than dealing with it directly. For example, an adolescent who faces a complex interpersonal situation may experience considerable stress due to the ambiguous nature of the situation. Similarly, those adolescents who lack clarity in terms of society's expectations for them experience high levels of stress (McDade & Worthman, 2004).

- *Situations in which an adolescent faces multiple tasks that strain resources are more apt to produce stress than those in which adolescents have fewer things to do.* An adolescent with a long to-do list, with many activities that must be accomplished in the same time frame, is a prime candidate for stress.

- *Circumstances involving domains that are central to an adolescent's life produce more stress than those that are more peripheral.* For an adolescent who has been quite successful in the artistic domain and sees art as central to her life, failure at an artistic task is likely to produce a great deal of stress. In contrast, if art is only peripheral to an adolescent, failure at an artistic task will produce considerably less stress.

Stress in Adolescence: Differences from Other Periods of Life. Clearly, a variety of circumstances produce stress in adolescents' lives. In fact, it may be that adolescence is more stressful than other periods of life.

▶ Cataclysmic events like floods, which affect many people simultaneously, may produce less stress than less dramatic stressors because the cataclysmic events may have a clear end point.

For example, adolescence is generally more stressful than childhood. In part, this comes from the more sophisticated cognitive abilities of adolescents, who are able to understand the complexities of the world to a greater degree. In addition, the academic pressures on adolescents are greater than they were earlier, as are the expectations on adolescents to behave in a more adultlike manner.

Furthermore, as adolescents' social worlds become more complex than at earlier stages of life, they encounter new kinds of social stressors. Their relations with their parents and other family members become more intense. In addition, adolescents encounter many new experiences that may trigger a variety of emotions, both positive and negative. Finally, the increase in the production of hormones that we discussed first in Chapter 2 can produce an increase in emotional distress (Susman, Dorn, & Schiefelbein, 2003).

Not only does the experience of stress increase over levels experienced during preadolescent childhood, but it also continues to increase during adolescence. Older adolescents report experiencing more daily stressors than younger ones. In addition, older adolescents say the stressors they experience are more intense than those experienced at a younger age (see Figure 14-4; Jose & Ratcliffe, 2004).

Is adolescence a more stressful time than future adulthood? Certainly some periods of adulthood are every bit as stressful as those experienced by adolescents, particularly during significant transitions. For example, postadolescent adults experience significant stress when they marry, start new jobs, move to new homes, divorce, experience the deaths of those close to them, or otherwise face major life changes.

On the other hand, compared to adults, adolescents experience more emotional mood swings and are in negative emotional states for longer periods of time. They also experience higher highs and lower lows than adults. Adolescents' involvement in romantic activities also can lead to wide mood swings. Furthermore, adolescents feel less in control of events in their lives than do adults. All these characteristics of stress suggest that adolescence is a particularly stressful period (Rosenblum & Lewis, 2006).

Remember, though, that stress is in the eye of the beholder, meaning that people can experience stress at any phase of life if they perceive events as stressful, and not necessarily because the events are inherently stressful themselves. Still, the emotional volatility of adolescents, combined with the significant changes that occur in the physical, cognitive, and social domains, suggest that adolescence is a particularly stressful period of life.

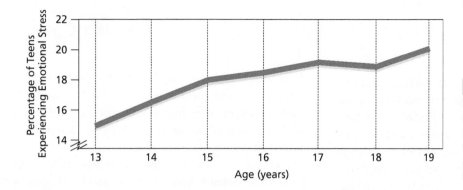

◄ **FIGURE 14-4**

Stress continues to increase during adolescence as teenage students become more concerned about where they will work in the future and at what kind of job.

(*Source:* National Longitudinal Study of Adolescent Health, 2000.)

Gender Differences in Adolescent Stress.   Most research suggests that female adolescents experience greater stress than male adolescents. Compared to males, they not only report experiencing more stressful events, but also perceive having higher stressor intensity. In addition, they say they have more physical symptoms that are the result of stress than boys (Groër, Thomas, & Shoffner, 1992; Baldwin, Harris, & Chambliss, 1997; Jose & Ratcliffe, 2004).

Before we accept these results at face value, however, it is important to consider an alternative interpretation. It is plausible that the actual amount of stress is similar for both male and female adolescents, but what differs is their willingness to report it. Specifically, girls are more self-disclosing than boys, and it may be that girls are more willing to report stress than boys. Because gender role socialization discourages boys from admitting that they may be experiencing negative circumstances that are stressful, the differences in male and female self-reports may mask more similarity than is at first apparent.

However, there is reason to believe that the differences in reported stress between boys and girls is quite real. For one thing, girls experience more concerns about interpersonal issues than boys, and adolescence is a period in which interpersonal connections are particularly volatile. In addition, girls are more likely to be anxious about body image issues than boys, and the significant changes in their bodies can be particularly stressful to adolescent girls. Finally, females are more likely to react to stress by ruminating about their concerns, a thinking style that actually prolongs their stress. In contrast, males are more apt to react to stress by consciously trying to avoid thinking about stressors (Almeida & Kessler, 1998; Mallers, Almeida et al., 2005).

In short, several factors explain why girls experience more stress than boys during adolescence. Moreover, the same pattern continues throughout adulthood.

Socioeconomic Differences in Stress: How Poverty Produces Stress.   Consider the environment in which Cedric Jennings, whose efforts to escape his life of poverty and attend college were chronicled in the book *A Hope in the Unseen*, lives:

Recently, a student was shot dead by a classmate during lunch period outside Frank W. Ballou Senior High. It didn't come as much of a surprise to anyone at the school, in this city's most crime-infested ward. Just during the current school year, one boy was hacked by a student with an ax, a girl was badly wounded in a knife fight with another female student, five fires were set by arsonists, and an unidentified body was dumped next to the parking lot. (Suskind, 1994, p. 1; Suskind, 1999)

For Jennings and other poor adolescents, life overflows with stress. In Jennings's case, not only was there a lack of physical safety, but the crowded, run-down apartment building in which he lived was surrounded by crack dealers. The sound of gunshots was common (Suskind, 1999).

Poverty is the single most troubling social problem that adolescents living in the United States face. Youth living in poverty face circumstances that are at best stressful and at worst deadly. Even adolescents living under less-extreme conditions than Jennings face stressors unknown to those living in families of higher socioeconomic status.

Transiti⊙ns

Does the Stress of Being Bullied in High School Continue into College?

O F THE MANY DIFFERENT events that occur in adolescence that are anxiety provoking, one of the most stressful is being the victim of bullying. Nearly a third of all adolescents have been bullied at some point, and as many as 10% are chronically victimized. Bullying includes aggressive and hurtful acts such as name-calling, rejection, teasing, threats, and physical harm. Given that such experiences provoke negative emotions, are uncontrollable, and directly affect an important domain in adolescents' lives (namely, social development), it's hardly surprising that being bullied is associated with anxiety, depression, and low self-worth, among other negative psychological outcomes (Hawker & Boulton, 2000; Nansel et al., 2001).

Bullying tends to decline in frequency with age, although some victims continue to be bullied throughout later adolescence and even into adulthood, where the workplace replaces the playground as a place of fear and intimidation. To understand the long-term outcomes of bullying, psychologist Matthew Newman and his colleagues explored the psychological effects during later adolescence of being bullied earlier in life. They were specifically interested in how the experience of being bullied in high school continued to affect adolescents after they made the transition to college (Smith, Singer, & Hoel, 2003; Newman, Holden, & Delville, 2005).

University undergraduates provided data on their experiences with bullying in high school and prior to high school as well as on a variety of stress symptoms they were currently experiencing as college students. They found that the prevalence of bullying changed over time as adolescents transitioned into high school. For example, one third of the participants reported being bullied occasionally

during the time before high school, and over another quarter of them reported frequent bullying during that period. But the frequency dropped off in high school, where a quarter of the participants experienced occasional bullying and fewer than 10% were bullied frequently.

Most importantly, the stress that college students currently reported was related to bullying experiences before college. Students who had been bullied more in high school reported more stress symptoms in college; interestingly, even students who had been bullied more *before* high school reported more stress symptoms in college (despite the fact that a wide majority of them reported that the bullying had decreased or stopped during high school).

Clearly, the harmful effects of being bullied during adolescence persist for years, emerging as stress symptoms after the bullied adolescents transition to college. Furthermore, the relationship between being bullied in adolescence and increased stress in college was most pronounced for students who felt the most isolated. Students who were bullied frequently in high school but nevertheless did not feel isolated from others were less likely to continue to be affected into college. This finding underscores the importance of social support as a valuable coping resource.

- Why might being bullied be such a powerfully stressful experience for adolescents?

- Do you think that the greater stress that bullied students feel in college is a direct consequence of being bullied or that it results indirectly from a loss of social support?

For example, poor adolescents live not only in poor households, but in poor neighborhoods as well. Compared to more-affluent adolescents, their home environments are more crowded and noisy, higher levels of parental conflict occur, and parent–adolescent conflict is typically greater. Furthermore, parents in poor households are more likely to employ harsh, punitive disciplinary styles (Lohman, Pittman, & Coley, 2004).

Whereas more affluent adolescents may have Internet access and books and magazines in their homes, poorer ones must use public libraries and computer labs. After-school jobs that poorer adolescents are able to get may be difficult to get to, and they may have to depend on slow, inconvenient public transportation. Virtually every activity is more difficult and time consuming (Compas, 2004).

For members of minority groups, living in poverty is even more stressful, because prejudice and discrimination are additional sources of stress. For example, shopkeepers may treat African-American adolescents with suspicion, and the police may stop and question teenagers primarily on the basis of their race. As a result, members of minority groups are constantly reminded of their minority status and suffer from high levels of stress (Steptoe et al., 2003; Taylor, 2006).

In sum, poverty is associated with stress. The nature of daily stressors is more severe and ultimately more detrimental for poor adolescents than for adolescents living in households of

◀ Adolescents living in poor, crowded neighborhoods may experience substantial stress.

higher socioeconomic status. Ultimately, this higher stress impacts poor adolescents' physical and mental health. There are clear links between poverty and psychological problems in adolescents, with long-term poverty being more damaging than living through temporary periods in which a family sinks into poverty (Grant et al., 2003; Grzywacz et al., 2004; Alemida et al., 2005; Gallo, Smith, & Cox, 2006).

The High Costs of Stress

Stress produces significant costs to adolescents of both a physical and psychological nature. Their immediate physical reactions typically include a rise in heart rate and blood pressure, an increase in skin conductance due to sweating, and the secretion of certain hormones by the adrenal glands. In the short term, these reactions may be helpful in coping with the stressor because they produce a burst of energy that may improve the immediate response to stress. For instance, because of immediate physical reactions to stress, a teenager may be able to outrun a thief who is attempting to steal her iPod (Cacioppo, 1994; Cacioppo et al., 1995).

However, over the long run, the constant wear and tear caused by the physiological arousal that occurs as the body tries to fight off stress produces negative effects. For instance, headaches, backaches, skin rashes, indigestion, chronic fatigue, sleep disturbances, and even the common cold are stress-related illnesses (Kiecolt-Glaser & Glaser, 1991; Cohen, Tyrrell, & Smith 1993; Reid, Patterson, & Snyder, 2002).

Furthermore, ongoing stress can impede the functioning of the **immune system,** the system of organs, glands, and cells that make up the body's defense against disease. In fact, increasing evidence shows conclusively that stress reduces the body's ability to ward off germs, making people more susceptible to disease. For instance, people exposed to stress often experience such common ailments as headaches, backaches, skin rashes, indigestion, and chronic fatigue. Even the common cold is associated with stress (Cohen, 1996; Rice, 2000; Cohen et al., 2003).

Stress may also lead to **psychosomatic disorders,** medical problems caused by the interaction of psychological, emotional, and physical difficulties. For instance, ulcers, asthma, arthritis, and high blood pressure may—although not invariably—be produced or worsened by stress (Lepore, Palsane, & Evans, 1991; Coleman, Friedman, & Burright, 1998).

Stress may also cause more serious, even life-threatening illnesses. According to some research, the greater the number of stressful events an adolescent experiences over the course of

immune system   the system of organs, glands, and cells that make up the body's defense against disease.

psychosomatic disorders   medical problems caused by the interaction of psychological, emotional, and physical difficulties.

a year, the more likely he or she is to have a major illness (see Table 14-1; Holmes & Rahe, 1967; Alverdy, Zabonna, & Wu, 2005).

Before you start calculating whether you are overdue for a major illness, however, keep in mind some important limitations to the research. Not everyone who experiences high stress becomes ill, and the weights given to particular stressors probably vary from one person to the next. Furthermore, there is a kind of circularity to such listings of stressors: Because the research is correlational, it is possible that someone who has a major illness to begin with is more likely to experience some of the stressors on the list. For example, an adolescent may lose a job because of the effects of an illness, rather than develop an illness because of the loss of a job. Still, the list of stressors does provide a way to consider how adolescents react on a physical level to various potentially stressful events in their lives.

Finally, stress can produce reactions that go beyond *internalizing disorders,* the kind of physical and psychological problems that primarily affect oneself, such as depression and anxiety, that we discussed in Chapter 13. Stress can also be at the root of *externalizing disorders,* the problems directed outward, toward others, such as aggression, fighting, destructiveness, and other conduct disorders.

Of course, not everyone reacts to stressors identically. For example, men and women respond in different ways to certain kinds of stressors. In one experiment, when newlyweds engaged in a 30-minute discussion, women responded more strongly on a physiological level than men at points when the actions of the spouse were negative or hostile (Kiecolt-Glaser et al., 1996; Robles & Kiecolt-Glaser, 2003).

Responses to stress also vary across cultures. One of the most extreme examples of this phenomenon is the *Sudden Unexpected Nocturnal Death Syndrome (SUNDS)* that afflicted male Southeast Asian Cambodian Hmong refugees in the United States. In the disorder, apparently healthy males died in their sleep without warning. Victims made gurgling noises, thrashed about in bed, and rapidly died.

Although no clear cause could be found, one explanation suggests that an inherited heart defect put potential victims at risk. When stress was high—due to the pressures of multiple jobs, family arguments, academic concerns, or other factors—extremely vivid unpleasant dreams may have triggered the inherited flaw and led to death. For instance, not long before they died some victims reported dreams foretelling their deaths. Because the Hmong place great credence in their dreams, dreams foretelling death could have produced extremely high levels of stress—leading to the fatal consequence (Adler, 1995; Lane et al., 2005).

Stress and Adolescent Brain Development. Increasing research on the structure and function of the brain helps us to understand how the experience of stress is related to brain development. For example, the prefrontal cortex, the part of the brain responsible for rational, higher-order thinking and control, develops gradually throughout adolescence, as we first discussed in Chapter 2. However, the limbic system, which is the part of the brain related to emotional responses, matures earlier in childhood, and the limbic system's development may be accelerated with the secretion of hormones relating to the start of puberty.

Consequently, there is an asynchrony in development of these two sets of brain functions, with adolescent emotionality ready to be activated earlier than the parts of the brain that control this emotionality. Thus, circumstances may produce strong emotional responses that are difficult to control cognitively, leading to the experience of stress (Nelson et al., 2002; Compas, 2004; Dahl & Spear, 2004).

The General Adaptation Syndrome Model: Charting the Course of Stress. The long-term consequences of stress are illustrated by the General Adaptation Syndrome (GAS) model, a series of stages that show how stress affects the body. The **General Adaptation Syndrome (GAS)** suggests that the physiological response to stress follows a similar three-stage pattern, regardless of the kind of stressor that produces the stress.

General Adaptation Syndrome (GAS) a model that suggests that the physiological response to stress follows a similar three-stage pattern, regardless of the kind of stressor that produces the stress.

TABLE 14-1 Sources of Adolescent Stress

The greater number of stressful events in the life of an adolescent over the course of a year can increase the likelihood of illness. This list offers an estimate of the types and levels of stress faced by adolescents.

Life Change Units (LCUs)	
108	The death of a parent
88	The death of a brother or sister
88	Getting pregnant
78	Getting married
70	Divorce of your parents
63	Death of a close friend
62	Marital separation of your parents
61	Fathering a pregnancy
52	The death of a grandparent
52	Hospitalization of a parent
51	Remarriage of a parent to a stepparent
50	Birth of a brother or sister
50	Being hospitalized for illness or injury
49	Hospitalization of a brother or sister
47	Failing a grade in school
46	Loss of a job by your father or mother
46	Being sent away from home
45	Becoming involved with drugs
43	Start of a new problem between you and your parents
42	Going on the first date of your life
41	Start of a new problem between your parents
41	Move to a new school district
41	Major increase in your parents' income
41	Major decrease in your parents' income
41	Deciding to leave home
40	Getting your first permanent job
39	Outstanding personal achievement (special prize)
39	Breaking up with a boy/girlfriend
39	Being accepted at the college of your choice
36	Being responsible for an automobile accident
35	End of a problem between you and your parents
35	Getting a summer job
35	Change in father's job so he has less time home
35	Being told to break up with a boy/girl-friend
34	Suspension from school
34	Finding a new dating partner
34	A new adult moving into your home
33	Graduating from high school
32	Getting your first driver's license

(continued)

TABLE 14-1 Sources of Adolescent Stress (cont.)	
The greater number of stressful events in the life of an adolescent over the course of a year can increase the likelihood of illness. This list offers an estimate of the types and levels of stress faced by adolescents.	
Life Change Units (LCUs)	
32	Failing to achieve something you really wanted
31	Appearance in a juvenile court
30	Stopping the use of drugs
30	End of a problem between your parents
28	Mother beginning to work outside the home
26	Being told you are very attractive by a friend
25	Becoming an adult member of a church
24	Recognition for excelling in a sport or other activity
22	Finding an adult who really respects you
21	Being invited by a friend to break the law
19	Beginning the first year of senior high school
18	Being invited to join a social organization

*From R. D. Coddington. "Measuring the Stressfulness of a Child's Environment," in J. H. Humphrey, ed., *Stress in Childhood* (New York: AMS Press, 1984).

As can be seen in Figure 14-5, the first stage, *alarm and mobilization,* occurs when adolescents first become aware of a stressor that is affecting them. For example, it might be an upcoming test, a difficult interpersonal situation, or unusual demands from a part-time job. On a biological level, the sympathetic nervous system becomes aroused, helping an adolescent to cope with the stressor by making the body more vigilant and energized and ready to attack the problem.

However, if initial efforts to deal with the stressor are inadequate and the stressor persists, adolescents move into the second stage of response: *resistance.* In this stage, adolescents' bodies and minds act to fight the stressor. For example, a student who faces a stress-producing exam might attempt to resist the stress by putting in long hours of studying, thereby reducing the threat of the exam.

In some cases, though, resistance will be insufficient or will fail altogether. In such cases, adolescents move into the last stage of the GAS, *exhaustion.* During the exhaustion stage, adolescents are unable to adapt to the challenge of the stressor, and negative consequences of stress

▼ FIGURE 14-5

There are three major stages to stress responses according to the general adaptation syndrome (GAS).

(*Source:* Selye, 1976.)

| Stressor | 1. Alarm and mobilization Meeting and resisting stressor. | 2. Resistance Coping with stress and resistance to stressor. | 3. Exhaustion Negative consequences of stress (such as illness) occur when coping is inadequate. |

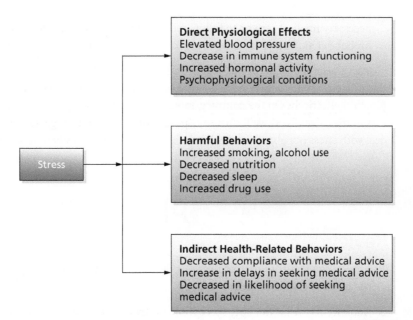

Direct Physiological Effects
Elevated blood pressure
Decrease in immune system functioning
Increased hormonal activity
Psychophysiological conditions

Stress

Harmful Behaviors
Increased smoking, alcohol use
Decreased nutrition
Decreased sleep
Increased drug use

Indirect Health-Related Behaviors
Decreased compliance with medical advice
Increase in delays in seeking medical advice
Decreased in likelihood of seeking
medical advice

◄ **FIGURE 14-6**

Three main types of consequences result from stress: direct physiological effects, harmful behaviors, and indirect health-related behaviors.

(*Source*: Adapted from Baum, 1994).

emerge. For example, adolescents may become physically ill, or they may develop physical symptoms such as the inability to concentrate, or in extreme cases, they may lose touch with reality. In a real sense, people wear out both physically and psychologically, and their physical and psychological reserves are depleted.

Ironically, moving into the exhaustion stage ultimately may be helpful in coping with a stressor. Adolescents who become ill due to stress may have to stay home from school, permitting them to avoid the stressful situation that caused them to get sick in the first place. Consequently, in the short run, stress is reduced.

Although the GAS model has had an enormous impact on the way we understand stress, it has been challenged by stress experts who believe that its assumption that adolescents' biological reactions are similar, regardless of stress, is incorrect. Instead, some researchers believe that biological responses are specific to the nature of stress that is being experienced. For example, responses to novel, extreme stressors may be different from responses to stressors that are more ordinary and anticipated. These criticisms have led to a new approach to stress with the tongue-twisting name of psychoneuroimmunology, as we see next (Lazarus, 2000; Taylor et al., 2000; Gaab et al., 2005).

Psychoneuroimmunology and Stress. Current views of adolescents' reactions to stress have focused on **psychoneuroimmunology,** or **PNI,** the study of the relationship among psychological factors, the immune system, and the brain. PNI has identified three main consequences of stress and its impact on adolescents (see Figure 14-6).

- *Direct physiological effects.* First, stress produces direct physiological consequences. For example, it raises blood pressure, increases the production of hormones, and leads to an overall decline in the efficiency and effectiveness of the body's immune system.

- *Harmful behaviors.* Second, stress produces behavior that may be harmful to an adolescent's health. For example, adolescents under stress may increase their drug or alcohol use, eat more poorly, or sleep less.

- *Indirect health-related behaviors.* Finally, the third consequence of stress is to reduce the general level of health-related behaviors. For example, adolescents may be less willing to obtain

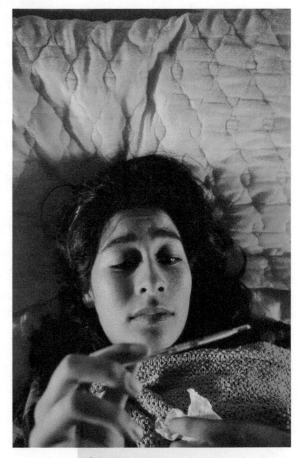

▲ Sustained levels of stress can lead to illness.

psychoneuroimmunology or PNI the study of the relationship among psychological factors, the immune system, and the brain.

necessary medical care or to follow medical advice when they do seek care (Gevirtz, 2000; McCabe et al., 2000; Marsland et al., 2002; Sapolsky, 2003; Broman, 2005).

We've been focusing on the negative consequences of stress. But it is a mistake to believe that adolescents are immersed in a world of stressful circumstances that impair their ability to function effectively. On the contrary, most adolescents deal quite well with the multiple stressors in their lives. Next we'll turn to coping, looking not only at general ways that adolescents deal with stress but also at adolescents who are particularly resilient to stress.

Review and Apply

Review

1. Among the stressors that adolescents face are cataclysmic events, personal stressors, and background stressors (daily hassles).

2. Adolescents are particularly susceptible to stress because of their greater cognitive abilities, the academic and social pressures they face, their bodies' increased production of hormones, and the mood swings that are typical of their age.

3. There are gender and socioeconomic differences in stress because of the different environments that female and poor adolescents encounter daily.

4. The General Adaptation Syndrome Model suggests that responses to stress follow a predictable three-stage pattern of alarm and mobilization, resistance, and in some cases, exhaustion.

5. Psychoneuroimmunology, the study of the relationship among psychological factors, the immune system, and the brain, has identified three main consequences of stress: direct physiological effects, harmful behaviors, and indirect health-related behaviors.

Apply

1. If an adolescent shares the experience of a personal stressor or a daily hassle with others, is it likely to help? Why or why not?

2. Does the higher incidence of stress during adolescence help to explain why friendships are so important during the period? Why is bullying so harmful?

Coping with Stress

Oh my gawd! This stress is killing me! I am on the verge of dying! There is a Chem. test this Thursday and common test is just next week. Guess what? I haven't been revising during the holidays . . . yups! I was SLACKING.

■ ■ ■

I have goals to set . . . Good grades . . . exercises . . . and keeping cool with stress.

■ ■ ■

Thank god this year is ending. The stress level was such a pain . . . , honestly, and I know that I work kinda ok with stress, but not the SAT, AP, kill-myself stress. Whatever. It's done.

Adolescents respond differently to stress. For some, stress produces panic. They may give up quickly, complain about the circumstances in which they find themselves, and generally feel the weight of the world on their shoulders. For others, stress is energizing; they feel motivated to meet the challenges they encounter and overcome them. The difference in reactions depends on adolescents' coping skills.

Coping is the effort to control, reduce, or learn to tolerate the threats that lead to stress. In coping with stress, adolescents are able to manage the demands that are placed on them. It is an ongoing process in which teenagers face demands and constraints that they must repeatedly overcome. Coping, then, is not a one-time response to a one-time challenge, but a pattern of responses that reflect the ongoing and never-ceasing demands of the world in which they live.

Adolescents use a variety of types of coping mechanisms. We'll begin with the distinction between whether they cope by focusing on the situation producing stress or on their emotional reactions to that stress.

Problem-Focused and Emotion-Focused Coping

One central distinction in how adolescents deal with stressful situations is between two alternative coping strategies: problem-focused coping and emotion-focused coping. Some adolescents rely on **problem-focused coping,** in which they attempt to manage a stressful problem or situation by directly changing the situation to make it less stressful. They may try to make the people who generate the stress change their behavior, or they may leave the situation altogether. A student who tries to talk a teacher into extending the due date of a paper, or who decides to drop a stress-inducing class, is using problem-focused coping (Folkman & Lazarus, 1988; Folkman & Moscowitz, 2004).

In contrast, in **emotion-focused coping,** adolescents try to deal with stress by consciously regulating their emotions. For instance, a teenager who is having problems getting along with her boss in her after-school job may tell herself that she should look at the bright side: At least she has a job in the first place.

Does one type of coping work better than the other? It turns out that neither emotion-focused nor problem-focused coping is invariably effective, and that their success may depend on the particular situation. For instance, some kinds of problems are solved best by problem-focused coping, such as dealing with the stress of doing poorly in a course by beginning to study more. In other cases, such as dealing with health problems, it may be that little direct action can be taken, and managing one's emotions is the best strategy (Vitaliano et al., 1990; Yi, Smith, & Vitaliano, 2005).

Furthermore, problem-focused and emotion-focused coping are not mutually exclusive and can often be used together. For instance, an adolescent who loses her job may profitably employ both problem-focused coping ("I'll study the want ads to try to find another job") and emotion-focused coping ("I'll try not to make myself feel worse about this by taking it personally"; Lazarus & Folkman, 1984; Broadstock et al., 1998; Ingledew et al., 1998; Park & Adler, 2003).

Gender differences exist in coping strategies. Females use emotion-focused coping more than males, more often preferring to modify their emotional responses to stress than attempting to deal with its origin. In comparison, males use problem-focused coping more than women, perhaps because they are more apt to inhibit emotionality in general (Matud, 2004; Hampel & Petermann, 2006).

Social Support: Leaning on Others

Adolescents often turn to others in times of distress, and it turns out that social support is an important coping mechanism. **Social support**—assistance and comfort supplied by a network of caring, interested individuals—is a boon to those living under stressful circumstances (Bolger, Zuckerman, & Kessler, 2000; McCabe et al., 2000; Cohen, 2004; Martin & Brantley, 2004).

One way in which the social support of others is valuable in coping with stress is that it provides emotional encouragement. It demonstrates that an adolescent is a valued member of a social network, and it can provide the opportunity for adolescents who are experiencing stress to

coping the effort to control, reduce, or learn to tolerate the threats that lead to stress.

problem-focused coping a coping strategy in which adolescents attempt to manage a stressful problem or situation by directly changing the situation to make it less stressful.

emotion-focused coping a coping strategy in which adolescents try to deal with stress by consciously regulating their emotions.

social support assistance and comfort supplied by a network of caring, interested individuals.

▶ Social support is an important means of coping with stress.

unburden themselves to a sympathetic listener. In addition, other people can provide advice and information about how best to deal with stress (Day & Livingstone, 2003; Lindorff, 2005).

Furthermore, social support can provide concrete help, such as when an adolescent tutors a friend who is struggling academically or gives a friend a ride to her job when her car has broken down (Lepore, Ragan, & Jones, 2000; Natvig, Albrektsen, & Ovamstrom, 2003).

Social support can even offer physiological benefits. For instance, one classic study found that women in the advanced stages of breast cancer who participated in group therapy lived at least 18 months longer than those who did not participate in therapy. Furthermore, the women who participated also experienced less anxiety and pain. The same sorts of benefits occur with adolescents suffering from cancer and other diseases (Spiegel, 1993, 1996; Lockhart, Ray, & Berard, 2003; Spiegel & Giese-Davis, 2003).

In short, social support provides adolescents with an important means of coping with stress. In fact, not only can it diminish psychological distress and provide tangible support, it can also reduce the physiological consequences brought about by stress. For example, first-year college students who experience the greatest degree of loneliness and thus encounter the lowest levels of social support not only feel high levels of stress, but also they are more susceptible to becoming ill. On the other hand, students with the richest network of friends and greatest social support are significantly happier, and they are less susceptible to illness (Pressman et al., 2005).

Defensive Coping

Even if adolescents don't consciously cope with stress, they may unconsciously use defensive coping mechanisms that aid in stress reduction. *Defensive coping* involves the unconscious use of strategies that distort or deny the true nature of a situation. For instance, an adolescent may deny the seriousness of a threat, trivialize a life-threatening illness, or tell himself that academic failure on a series of tests is unimportant.

In one concrete example of defensive coping, California students living in residence halls that are vulnerable to earthquakes say that their susceptibility to future tremors is actually lower than those who reside in safer, earthquake-proof residence halls. The reason: Those living in unsafe dorms deal with the stress by pushing their anxiety into their unconscious and making themselves believe that there is little problem (Lehman & Taylor, 1988; Taylor, 2006).

There's an obvious problem with such defensive coping: It does not deal with the reality of the situation but merely avoids or ignores the problem. By sweeping their stress into their unconscious, adolescents don't deal with the stress-producing situation, which permits it to continue to be a source of stress.

Opening Up: Confronting One's Demons

If defensive coping is often unsuccessful because it avoids dealing with a stressor, is the opposite strategy—confronting a stressor—of benefit? That does seem to be the case.

For example, according to the research of psychologist James Pennebaker, self-disclosure may be good not only for the soul, but also for the mind and the body. Pennebaker and colleagues have found that giving people the opportunity to air their most personal and disturbing experiences, which they typically have kept hidden, produces clear health benefits (Davison & Pennebaker, 1997; Pennebaker, 2004; Petrie et al., 2004).

In a series of experiments, Pennebaker explored the effects of revealing information that people usually keep to themselves. For example, in one study, groups of healthy undergraduates were asked to write over a 4-day period a series of anonymous essays about the most traumatic, emotionally upsetting, and stressful events they had experienced during their lifetimes. One group was told only to describe the events factually; members of a second group were instructed not to write about the facts, but only about their feelings regarding the facts; and a third group wrote about both the facts *and* their feelings concerning the events. There was also a control group that wrote about insignificant topics for the 4-day period.

The nature of participants' confessions had important, long-lasting consequences. Participants who wrote about the emotions connected with past traumatic events, or about combined facts and emotions, initially reported feeling the most upset directly after their participation in the study. However, the long-term outcomes for one of these groups were more positive. Six months after the study, participants who had written about the facts *and* their emotions reported feeling healthier and experiencing fewer illnesses, as well as fewer days of restricted activity due to illness, than participants in the other groups.

In short, although initially upsetting to the participants, the disclosure of traumatic information proved to have lasting benefits. But why should confession be so worthwhile? One reason is that inhibiting or restraining traumatic information requires both a physical and a mental effort. This effort results in heightened stress that ultimately produces physical symptoms and stress-related illness. Conversely, disclosing hidden traumas, even if only during the course of a psychological experiment, provides a temporary respite in the effort required to suppress the information. Ultimately, this results in reduced stress and an enhanced sense of well-being.

BECOMING AN INFORMED CONSUMER OF ADOLESCENT SCIENCE

Reaping the Benefits of Expressive Writing

CONSIDERABLE EVIDENCE exists showing the health benefits of writing about traumatic or emotional experiences. Some of the specific benefits that have been documented include better immune system functioning, lowered blood pressure, improved mood and sense of well-being, fewer trips to the doctor, and even better grades (Pennebaker & Chung, in press). With so much to potentially gain and nothing to lose but a little time and effort, you might want to give expressive writing a try. Pennebaker offered the following specific guidelines for going about it in a way that increases the likelihood of seeing results (Pennebaker & Chung, in press).

- Write about a highly emotional or traumatic experience that has affected you and your life, at least as a starting point. You don't need to restrict yourself to this experience rigidly, but center your writing around it.

- Don't censor yourself—explore your deepest thoughts and emotions. You might tie your topic to your relationships with others, to your past or your future, or to who you have been, who you are now, or who you would like to be.

- Write as long and as frequently as you feel the need, until you get all your thoughts out.

- There are potential benefits to focusing on either the negative or the positive aspects of your emotional experience, as well as to finding the "silver lining." Any of these approaches—or any combination—can be effective; what's most important is that you write whatever it is you want to say.

- Talking about your emotional experience, either to someone else or just into a tape recorder, can be just as beneficial as writing. What matters is the focus on an emotional experience, not the process of writing itself.

- If you want to improve your grades through expressive writing, choose emotional topics related to coming to college.

- It's not necessary (and often isn't a good idea) to let others see what you've written. The benefits occur even when the writing is immediately destroyed.

Hardiness

Coping success also varies as a result of the kind of *coping style* adolescents have, or their general tendency to deal with stress in a particular way. For example, adolescents with a hardy coping style are especially successful in dealing with stress. **Hardiness** is a personality characteristic associated with a lower rate of stress-related illness.

Hardy individuals are take-charge people who revel in life's challenges. They approach stress optimistically, believing that they can understand and modify circumstances that produce stress. They are able to turn stressful events into less-threatening ones (Kobasa et al., 1994; Baumgartner, 2002).

It is not surprising, then, that people who are high in hardiness are more resistant to stress-related illness than those who show less hardiness. Hardy people react to potentially threatening stressors with optimism, feeling that they can respond effectively. By turning threatening situations into challenging ones, they are less apt to experience high levels of stress (Horner, 1998; Maddi, 2006).

Hardiness is composed of three components (Kobasa et al., 1994; Baumgartner, 2002):

- *Commitment.* Commitment is a tendency to throw oneself into whatever one is doing, assuming that one's activities are significant and have important consequences.

- *Challenge.* Hardy adolescents feel that change, rather than stability, is the normal course of life. They anticipate and even welcome change in their lives and perceive challenge as something positive.

- *Control.* Hardy adolescents have a strong sense of control, believing that they have the ability to significantly influence events and circumstances.

Resilience

For adolescents who face the most profound of life's difficulties—such as the death of a loved one or a permanent injury such as a spinal cord injury—a key factor in their reactions is their level of resilience. As we first discussed in Chapter 2, *resilience* is the ability to overcome circumstances that place an adolescent at high risk for psychological or physical damage, such as

hardiness a personality characteristic associated with a lower rate of stress-related illness.

extreme poverty, violent homes, other social ills, or some specific profound adversity (Werner & Smith, 2002; Werner, 2005; O'Leary & Bhaju, 2006).

Resilient individuals are typically easygoing, are good-natured, and have good social and communication skills. They are independent, feeling that they can shape their own fate and are not dependent on others or on luck. In short, they work with what they have and make the best of whatever situation they find themselves in (Staudinger et al., 1999; Luthar, Cicchetti, & Becker, 2000; Trickett, Kurtz, & Pizzigati, 2004).

The most resilient adolescents have a variety of resources to which they can turn under stressful conditions, and the more types of resources available to them, the better able they are to fend off the effects of stress. For example, the most resilient youth have both internal resources, including positive personal characteristics like high intelligence and an optimistic attitude, and external resources, including the social support of friends or teachers (Compas, 2004; Wadsworth et al., 2005).

Resilience is also effective in successfully coping not just with short-term, one-time stressors (such as a sudden death) but with longer-term stressors. For example, resilient adolescents deal with the stress of poverty by using two forms of coping: primary control strategies and secondary control strategies. In *primary control coping strategies*, resilient adolescents cope by using problem-solving strategies and controlling their emotions. In *secondary control coping strategies,* adolescents use acceptance, distract themselves from their situation and cognitively reframe their situation to make it more acceptable to themselves. Secondary control strategies are best in situations in which the stressor cannot be controlled, such as dealing with the divorce of one's parents or the death of one's parent (Grant et al., 2003).

Although both primary and secondary control coping strategies are related to better psychological outcomes, with lower levels of anxiety, depression, and aggression, primary control coping strategies are generally more effective. By dealing directly with stress through primary control strategies, resilient adolescents end up with better psychological adjustment and fewer behavioral problems (Compas, 2004; Connor-Smith & Compas, 2004).

You can get a sense of your own level of resiliency by completing the questionnaire in Table 14-2 on page 466.

▲ Resilient adolescents are able to cope with stress effectively.

Cognitive Approaches to Coping: Thinking Stress Away

I received an F on my first statistics test. I'm really behind now. I'm bound to fail the course. The instructor thinks I'm an idiot. She's probably right—I'm a dummy in all things having to do with math.

Have you ever had thoughts like these, in which you saw the world in such black-and-white—and largely illogical—terms that you felt there was no chance to improve the situation? It's something that many adolescents do, quite consistently.

The reality is that such statements are irrational and illogical. Yet many adolescents hold the implicit assumption that they need to be completely competent and successful all the time, and that when things don't go just the way they want them to, there is little hope of improving the situation.

Such irrational thoughts are self-defeating, but they also suggest a way to deal with stress by replacing dysfunctional statements with ones that can help adolescents better deal with stress. Specifically, by using *cognitive approaches to coping,* adolescents can learn to respond more effectively to stress by systematically asking themselves four questions (Nolen-Hoeksema, 2004):

1. What is the evidence for my thinking?

2. Are there other ways of viewing the situation?

TABLE 14-2	How Resilient Are You?

Rate how much each of the following applies to you on a scale from 1 to 5, with 1 = very little and 5 = very much.

1 2 3 4 5	Curious, ask questions, want to know how things work, experiment.
1 2 3 4 5	Constantly learn from your experience and the experiences of others.
1 2 3 4 5	Need and expect to have things work well for yourself and others. Take good care of yourself.
1 2 3 4 5	Play with new developments, find the humor, laugh at self, chuckle.
1 2 3 4 5	Highly flexible, adapt quickly to change.
1 2 3 4 5	Feel comfortable with paradoxical qualities.
1 2 3 4 5	Anticipate problems and avoid difficulties.
1 2 3 4 5	Develop better self-esteem and self-confidence with the passage of time. Develop a conscious self-concept of professionalism.
1 2 3 4 5	Listen well. Read others, including difficult people, with empathy.
1 2 3 4 5	Think up creative solutions to challenges, invent ways to solve problems. Trust intuition and hunches.
1 2 3 4 5	Manage the emotional side of recovery from trauma; let go of the past.
1 2 3 4 5	Expect tough situations to work out well, keep on going. Help others, bring stability to times of uncertainty and turmoil.
1 2 3 4 5	Find the good in accidents and bad experiences.
1 2 3 4 5	Convert misfortune into good fortune.

Scoring

Add up the numbers you circled, and use the following scale as a rough guide to your level of resilience:

60–70: highly resilient

50–60: above-average resiliency

40–50: average resiliency

30–40: below-average resiliency

below 30: unusually low resiliency

Source: Adapted from Siebert, 1998.

3. What is the worst thing that could happen in this situation?

4. How could I cope if the worst case is true?

For example, suppose an adolescent fails a test, as in the earlier example, and assumes that she is destined to fail the course. First, she should ask herself what evidence there is for this viewpoint. Is it accurate to believe that the performance on that one test will determine her final grade, or are there are other tests and assignments that will be factored into the grade? Second, could the situation be viewed differently—as a wake-up call that more studying is necessary, or that perhaps she should rethink choosing a major that requires statistics?

Third, she might reason that the worst-case scenario is that she will fail the course. But, moving to the next question, she might come to understand that even if this worst-case scenario comes true and she does fail the course, she will have the opportunity to retake the course. Or she could change to a major that doesn't require the statistics course. Yes, it would be embarrassing and inconvenient to fail, but it doesn't mean that she will flunk out of school.

In short, cognitive approaches to coping teach adolescents the skills they need to systematically reframe situations that are producing stress. The basic idea is to identify faulty thoughts and replace them with more realistic ones. By looking more rationally at circumstances that are producing stress, adolescents are able to develop a greater sense of control, thereby lowering stress (Ellis, 1999; Leahy, 2004; Cohen, Gunthert, & Butler, 2006).

Helping Adolescents Deal with Stress: Effective Coping Strategies

Stress is part of all adolescents' lives. However, although the phenomenon is universal, there are no universal formulas for coping with it. This is primarily because stress depends on an individual appraisal of how threatening and challenging particular situations are. Still, several general approaches have proven effective in teaching adolescents how to cope with stress. Among them are the following:

- *Attempt to exert control over the situation.* As we've noted, controllable events produce less stress than those that cannot be controlled. One coping strategy, then, is to try to maintain a sense of control. By attempting to exercise control over a situation, adolescents can induce a sense of mastery over it and reduce the experience of stress (e.g., Taylor et al., 1991; Burger, 1992). For instance, if a paper deadline is looming and causing high stress, it may make sense to negotiate a later due date with the teacher. Not only would such a strategy reduce the immediate stress, but it would also provide more time to do a better job.

- *Reappraise threats as challenges.* If a stressor cannot be controlled, at least it can be appraised in a different, less-threatening manner. The old truism, Every cloud has a silver lining, reflects the reality that adolescents who can discover something positive in otherwise negative situations show less distress and are better able to cope than those who are unable to do so (Salovey et al., 2000; Smith & Lazarus, 2001; Cheng & Cheung, 2005).

- *Seek out social support.* As we've discussed, support from others can provide relief and comfort when we are confronting stress. Consequently, asking for assistance can be a means of reducing stress. Friends, family, and even telephone hotlines staffed by peer counselors can provide significant support. (For help in identifying appropriate hotlines, adolescents can receive a referral from the U.S. Public Health Service, an agency that maintains a "master" toll-free number—800-336-4794—that can provide telephone numbers and addresses of many national groups.)

- *Use relaxation techniques.* If stress produces chronic physiological arousal, it follows that procedures that reduce such arousal might reduce the harmful consequences of physiological wear-and-tear. For instance, it is possible to learn specific relaxation techniques, including transcendental meditation, Zen and yoga, progressive muscle relaxation, and even hypnosis. One procedure that is simple and effective is relaxation training, which includes the basic components of several other techniques (see the *Career Choices* box). What stress expert Herbert Benson calls the "relaxation response" is effective in reducing stress and can be elicited by following the instructions shown in Table 14-3 (Benson, 1993; Benson et al., 1994; Aftanas & Golosheykin, 2005).

▲ Using relaxation techniques such as yoga and Zen can be effective in reducing stress.

The Benefits of Stress

We've been concentrating on the negative outcomes of stress and the ways that adolescents cope with it. However, it's also important to think about some of the benefits of stress in adolescents' lives.

For one thing, stress can be a motivator, leading adolescents to work harder to achieve their goals and to strive to improve themselves. This kind of positive stress, sometimes called *eustress*, can motivate them to seek to better understand their circumstances and what they encounter in their lives. Without stress, they might be content to accept the circumstances in which they

TABLE 14-3   How to Elicit the Relaxation Response

Some general advice on regular practice of the relaxation response:

- Try to find 10 to 20 minutes in your daily routine; before breakfast is a good time.
- Sit comfortably.
- For the period you will practice, try to arrange your life so you won't have distractions. Turn on voicemail.
- Time yourself by glancing periodically at a clock or watch (but don't set an alarm). Commit yourself to a specific length of practice, and try to stick to it.

There are several approaches to eliciting the relaxation response. Here is one standard set of instructions:

Step 1. Pick a focus word or short phrase that's firmly rooted in your personal belief system. For example, a nonreligious individual might choose a neutral word like *one* or *peace* or *love*. A Christian person desiring to use a prayer could pick the opening words of Psalm 23, *The Lord is my shepherd;* a Jewish person could choose *Shalom*.

Step 2. Sit quietly in a comfortable position.

Step 3. Close your eyes.

Step 4. Relax your muscles.

Step 5. Breathe slowly and naturally, repeating your focus word or phrase silently as you exhale.

Step 6. Throughout, assume a passive attitude. Don't worry about how well you're doing. When other thoughts come to mind, simply say to yourself, "Oh, well," and gently return to the repetition.

Step 7. Continue for 10 to 20 minutes. You may open your eyes to check the time, but do not use an alarm. When you finish, sit quietly for a minute or so, at first with your eyes closed and later with your eyes open. Then do not stand for one or two minutes.

Step 8. Practice the technique once or twice a day.

(*Source:* Benson, 1993.)

find themselves. Moreover, stress makes adolescents more alert and vigilant about their surroundings.

Stress can also lead adolescents to reevaluate their goals, making them more realistic, and help them avoid making the same mistake twice. In addition, by learning to cope with stress at lower levels, adolescents learn strategies that can help them deal with larger stressors later in life.

Finally, dealing with stress can lead adolescents to grow in terms of their identity and feelings of self-worth. By coping effectively, they come to see themselves as hardy, resilient individuals who can deal with the challenges that life presents.

Review and Apply

Review

1. Coping with stress involves learning to tolerate the demands that adolescents face. Two main strategies for coping are problem-focused coping and emotion-focused coping.

2. Among the key resources to which adolescents can turn in situations of stress are social support and exercising control over the situation.

CAREER CHOICES

Stress Reduction Counselor

Name: Cindy Kracht Foster

Education: BS, Social Work, Eastern Michigan University; MS, Social Work, Wayne State University; Licensed Clinical Social Worker, LCSW

Position: Stress reduction therapist, founder and program director of the Augusta Stress Reduction Program at St. Joseph's Hospital Wellness Center, Augusta, Georgia

Home: Augusta, Georgia

THE YEARS OF ADOLESCENCE often are a rollercoaster of emotional and physical change. According to stress reduction therapist Cindy Kracht Foster, this volatility makes adolescents particularly sensitive to stress.

"Adolescents face intense physiological responses and hormonal changes, and this combined with rapid growth can greatly contribute to stress. Peer pressures along with other stressors can increase symptoms of asthma, and high blood sugar which puts adolescents more at risk for diabetes," said Foster.

In addition to peer pressure during their teenage years, many adolescents are faced with demands of schools and families. But adolescents are also well equipped to deal with stress, according to Foster.

Foster, who teaches adolescents stress-reduction techniques, begins by teaching breathing awareness as the initial technique for reducing stress.

"The first thing I have the teenager do is deep breathing, using the diaphragm. Breathing is the doorway to controlling the autonomic system and the nervous system responds to it naturally. If you can control your breathing, you can begin to control anxiety and emotions," Foster said.

"Participants learn that the mind interprets changes externally in the environment and also internally within the mind and body," she noted. "The mind will determine when to switch on the fight or flight emergency response."

Foster has noticed that peer pressure can be a positive force when used with stress reduction techniques.

"Another important aspect I have seen is the power of positive peer pressure within groups of teens practicing mediation, biofeedback, and other stress reduction techniques," she said. "Teens become empowered with they see that they can control the numbers on the thermal biofeedback machine based on their breathing and internal self-talk. The group itself seems to generate positive peer pressure when they acknowledge their abilities to each other and support each other in relieving harmful stress reactions and move toward more healthy ways of thinking and doing," Foster added.

Thinking of becoming a stress reduction therapist?

Stress reduction therapists specialize in helping adolescents cope with the stressors in their lives. They may focus on a variety of strategies that may be helpful, ranging from changing physiological reactions to stress to modifying thoughts about situational stressors. They may meet individually with adolescents or in groups, and they work both in medical and educational settings.

Specialists in stress reduction have a variety of backgrounds. Some have doctorates or master's degrees in psychology, counseling, or school psychology. Others may have professional degrees in industrial/organizational psychology or medical degrees.

3. Coping success depends on an adolescent's coping style, one of the most effective of which is a personality characteristic called *hardiness*.

4. Cognitive approaches to coping, which involves mentally reframing the causes of stress, can be helpful in dealing with stress

Apply

1. What developmental characteristics make coping so difficult during adolescence?

2. One explanation for why male adolescents prefer problem-focused coping to emotion-focused coping is because males are more likely to avoid emotionality. What alternative explanation is there? Which do you believe and why?

▲ Focusing on the basis of happiness, positive psychologists seek to understand subjective well-being in adolescents.

Well-Being and Happiness

*A*t 10 AM, I turned *in my final painting to my professor, and he told me he'd given me an A as the final grade, but not to tell people. Wait for the grade report. Hah! I got a A in my painting class! I feel so, so cool. I feel so happy right now.*

■ ■ ■

I've never been happier in my life. He treats me so great and I love it. I never knew that a guy could treat me like he does. It still shocks me the little things he does for me. I have always been very independent and wouldn't let anyone do anything for me, little things or anything like that. Now I guess I have to start. He spoils me and I love it.

What makes for a happy adolescent?

Although philosophers from the time of the Greeks have pondered the broad question of what it means to be happy, until recently surprisingly little attention has been paid to the issue by specialists in adolescence. The primary reason for this lack of attention is that the focus of the field has largely been on the difficulties of adolescence. As we've seen in earlier chapters, from the time of G. Stanley Hall at the beginning of the 20th century, the field has concentrated on the *problems* of adolescence. Spurred on by the early view that adolescence is a period of nearly unceasing upheaval and conflict, researchers and social observers have sought to explain why adolescence is such a difficult and demanding period, focusing on what is wrong with the period rather than what is right.

However, the last decade has seen an increasing number of adolescent specialists begin to focus on the factors that make adolescents experience more positive and constructive emotions and behavior. Led by a focus on *positive psychology,* a new and growing branch of psychology that focuses on well-being and happiness, an increasing number of adolescent specialists are seeking to understand the underpinnings of subjective well-being. **Subjective well-being** refers

subjective well-being adolescents' evaluations of their lives in terms of their thoughts and their emotions.

to adolescents' evaluations of their lives in terms of their thoughts and their emotions. Put another way, subjective well-being is the measure of how happy adolescents are (Oishi & Diener, 2001; Diener, Lucas, & Oishi, 2002; Keyes & Shapiro, 2004).

Making Adolescents Happy: The Characteristics of Happiness

Several characteristics are associated with happiness. One of the most stable associations is between happiness and self-esteem: Happy adolescents usually have higher self-esteem than unhappy ones, viewing themselves (as well as the world) more positively (Mahon & Yarcheski, 2002; Baumeister et al., 2003; Boyd-Wilson, McClure, & Walkey, 2004).

Adolescents who are happy also see themselves as more intelligent and better able to get along with others. Interestingly, it doesn't seem to matter much if the self-esteem is warranted or not; even adolescents who hold positive illusions about themselves and inflated self-views may be happier than those who view themselves and their flaws more realistically (Seginer & Somech, 2000; Taylor et al., 2000).

Happy adolescents also have a stronger sense of control over their lives than those who are less happy. They feel greater responsibility for what happens to themselves, and they expect to have greater control over future events. They also have better control over their emotional responses (Kelley & Stack, 2000; Dickson & MacLeod, 2006).

Optimism is also a key characteristic of happiness. Happy adolescents are more optimistic about their own futures, and they believe that the world is basically a just place. They believe that good things happen to good people and that those who behave badly eventually will be repaid in kind. Because of their optimism, they persevere longer at tasks they are trying to accomplish and ultimately are more likely to accomplish them (Peterson, 2000; Furnham, 2005).

Finally, happier adolescents are generally more outgoing and extraverted. They have a supportive network of close relationships with others and have relatively more friends than those who are less happy (Chang & Furnham, 2002; Fogle, Huebner, & Laughlin, 2002).

Although it is clear that happiness is linked to such characteristics as self-esteem, a sense of control, optimism, and extraversion, it is not clear how these factors are related to one another in a causal sense. For example, does happiness lead to higher self-esteem, or does having higher self-esteem lead to happiness? We can't be sure, so both possibilities are plausible.

The Course of Happiness

Since middle school, Harry Jacobson's dream has been to attend Reed College, his father's alma mater, and a highly selective college in Oregon. To achieve the goal, he worked hard in all his classes, took six Advanced Placement courses, participated in a variety of extra-curricular activities, and studied hard for his SAT exam. In his senior year, he applied to Reed, and one day at the beginning of April, he received news of the result of his long efforts: He was admitted! Harry was ecstatic and felt unbounded happiness. His dream had come true.

Will Harry's extreme happiness last? Probably not, at least according to a growing body of research on the course of happiness. In fact, even if Harry had won millions of dollars in a lottery, he probably wouldn't end up much happier than before. Even people who suffer spinal cord injuries reestablish previous levels of happiness after time has gone by (Diener, Suh, Lucas, & Smith, 1999).

The reason behind this consistency may in part be genetic. Studies of twins suggest that everyone has a *set point* for happiness, a genetically determined characteristic level of mood. Although circumstances can temporarily elevate or depress mood, individuals ultimately return to their general level of happiness (Srivastava, Locke, & Bartol, 2001; Diener & Biswas Diener, 2002; Nissle & Bschor, 2002).

In the twins research, investigators found that identical twins who were raised apart showed little difference in their ratings of their own happiness, even though their circumstances in life varied widely. Salary, marital status, and education were related to happiness to only a minor degree (Lykken & Tellegen, 1996; Kahneman, Diener, & Schwarz, 1998).

Of course, adolescents do vary in their happiness dependent on life events. A death in the family or a school failure will temporarily depress an individual's mood, just as getting into the college of one's choice or starting a new relationship will elevate it. However, the set point theory suggests that both the depression and elevation in mood will be temporary, and that adolescents ultimately return to their general level of happiness (Gilman, 2001; Suldo & Huebner, 2004).

Interestingly, at least by the end of adolescence, most Americans have happiness set points that are relatively high. For instance, surveys show that 3 out of 10 U.S. citizens say they are "very happy," and only 1 in 10 say that they are "not too happy." Most admit to being "pretty happy." Furthermore, there is no difference between men and women in their views of how happy they are, and ethnicity, culture, and geography play only a small role. For instance, African Americans are only slightly less likely than European Americans to rate themselves as "very happy" (Myers & Diener, 1996; Mroczek & Kolarz, 1998; Schkade & Kahneman, 1998; Staudinger, Fleeson, & Baltes, 1999).

Similarly, when people are asked to compare themselves with others—even in comparison to the rich and famous—they tend to rate themselves happier. For example, when asked, "Who of the following people do you think is the happiest?" survey respondents answered "Oprah Winfrey" (23%), "Bill Gates" (7%), "the Pope" (12%), and "yourself" (49%), with 6% saying they didn't know (Black & McCafferty, 1998).

In short, adolescents, and people in general, tend to rate themselves as more happy than sad most of the time. And—according to set point theory—even when bad things happen to them, they are apt to eventually return to their happier state. The downside of this set point view of well-being: That glow adolescents feel following a great accomplishment is also likely to fade, as they eventually return to their characteristic level of happiness (Diener & Seligman, 2004; Nickerson & Nagle, 2004).

▲ Adolescents typically point to the fulfillment of psychological needs—such as participating in volunteer activities—as the basis of their happiness.

The stability of happiness seems to extend across the life span. For example, in one research study, researchers rated old college yearbook photos of women for positive emotional expressions, assuming that positive expressions were related to a general sense of well-being. In order to explore how the women's positive emotional expressions in college related to their later personality development and life outcomes, the researchers also examined personality measures and reports of marriage, family, and career outcomes taken when the women were 21, 27, 43, and 52 years old (Harker & Keltner, 2001).

The results were clear: The women who revealed more positive emotional expression in their yearbook photos tended to express higher degrees of affiliation and competence, personality traits that indicate good interpersonal and cognitive skills. They also reported less negative emotionality and said they experienced decreased negative emotionality over time. Most importantly, they reported fewer psychological and physical problems, better relations with others, and better life satisfaction throughout early and middle adulthood. In short, the positive sense of well-being they communicated through their facial expressions during late adolescence seemed to continue throughout their life spans.

In sum, happiness brings with it a number of advantages. Those who are happy are more sociable, creative, and energetic, and they are more helpful and caring, than those who are unhappy. Ultimately, happy individuals may even live longer. For instance, in one study of a group of Catholic nuns, those who had written the most positive autobiographies when they entered the convent in their early 20s lived on average seven years longer than those who expressed the least positive emotion (Danner, Snowdon, & Friesen, 2001; Lyubomirsky, King, & Diener, 2005).

The Components of Happiness: Fulfillment of Psychological Needs

Think back over the last 7 days of your life. What made you happiest?

During your late adolescence, it probably wasn't money or material objects that brought happiness. Instead, research finds that happiness usually is derived from feelings of independence, competence, self-esteem, or relatedness (Sheldon et al., 2001).

When asked to recall a time when they were happy, college students focus on the satisfaction of psychological needs rather than material needs. Conversely, when they recall times when they were least satisfied, they usually mention incidents in which basic psychological needs were left unfulfilled.

It's interesting to compare these findings, based on research in the United States, with studies conducted in Asian countries. For example, college students in Korea more often associate satisfaction with experiences involving other people, whereas college students in the United States feel satisfaction from experiences relating to the self and self-esteem. Apparently, culture influences which psychological needs are most important in determining happiness (Sheldon et al., 2001).

Adolescent
DIVERSITY   Cultural Differences in Well-Being

How adolescents judge their well-being is dependent at least in part on cultural factors. In fact, some threats to psychological and even physical health vary from one culture to another. For example, only schizophrenia, bipolar disorder, major depression, and anxiety disorder are found in all cultures. Every other psychological disorder is found in only certain cultures (Kleinman, 1996; López & Guarnaccia, 2000; Cohen et al., 1999).

Consider the Western view that dissociate identity disorder, or multiple personalities, represents a severe mental health problem. Labeling the condition a disorder is reasonable only in a culture in which the sense of self is concrete and stable. In some societies, including many cultures in India, the self is based less on internal factors than on external attributes that are relatively independent of the individual. Consequently, when an adolescent shows symptoms of what Westerners would label multiple personalities, the reactions are very different in India. For instance, the cause of the behavior may be assumed to be possession by demons, which is regarded as a malady, or possession by gods—which is not seen as a problem.

Other disorders are found only in certain cultures. For example, *koro* is the sense of panic felt by males in Southeast Asia that the penis is about to retract permanently into the body. There's also a female equivalent: Females fear that their vulva or nipples are about to recede into the body. In Malaya, adolescents may demonstrate *amok*, wild outbursts in which a typically quiet and shy individual severely injures or kills others. And adolescents in rural Japan sometimes are susceptible to *kitsunetsuki*, a belief that they have been possessed by a fox. As a consequence, they show facial expressions that make them look foxlike (Carson, Butcher, & Coleman, 1992; Nolen-Hoeksema, 2004).

Similarly, anorexia nervosa (the disorder in which adolescents develop inaccurate views of their body appearance, become obsessed with their weight, and refuse to eat, sometimes starving in the process) occurs only in cultures that hold the societal standard that slender female bodies are the most desirable. In most of the world, where no such standard exists, anorexia nervosa does not occur. Interestingly, there is no anorexia nervosa in all of Asia, with two exceptions: the upper and upper-middle classes of Japan and Hong Kong, where Western influence tends to be great. In fact, even in Western cultures, anorexia nervosa developed fairly recently. In the 1600s and 1700s it did not occur because the ideal female body in Western cultures at that time was full-figured.

In addition, various cultures have very different definitions of appropriate behavior related to health issues. For instance, in many cultures people routinely undergo procedures that physically alter their bodies. Male circumcision, the removal of the foreskin of the penis, is a practice that has deep cultural and religious roots. Furthermore, in many African cultures a female's clitoris is routinely removed at the beginning of adolescence. This practice, which prevents the experience of sexual pleasure, is seen as enhancing a girl's attractiveness and thereby making her more socially acceptable and marriageable. It is estimated that, worldwide, the operation has been performed on over 100 million girls (French, 1997; Obermeyer, 2001; Lacey, 2002).

In short, cultural views of what is healthy and normal, and what is unhealthy and abnormal, color adolescents' understanding of themselves and others. We cannot fully understand adolescents' sense of well-being and health without taking into account the culture in which they live (Javier, Herron, & Bergman, 1995; Brent & Lewis-Fernandez, 1998).

Review and Apply

Review

1. The view of adolescence as a period of turmoil has impeded the consideration of happiness during adolescence, a gap that positive psychology is seeking to fill.

2. Research on happiness finds that one of the most durable associations is between happiness and self-esteem.

3. Periods of extreme happiness or happiness tend not to last, with adolescents returning to their happiness set point, which is largely determined by genetics.

4. In the United States, happiness primarily depends on the satisfaction of internal needs, but the definition and components of happiness vary across cultures.

Apply

1. If happiness can be predicted from old yearbook pictures, does it make sense to select employees on the basis of those pictures? Why or why not?

2. What accounts for differences in the understanding and experience of happiness across cultures?

EPILOGUE

In this chapter we looked at the related experiences of stress, coping, and happiness. We saw that stress is particularly strong in adolescence and can have serious, long-lasting effects. We discussed ways adolescents find to cope with stress, including approaches based on the problem and approaches based on emotions. We looked at social support and expressiveness as ways to cope, as well as at two personality characteristics—hardiness and resilience—that facilitate coping. Finally, we saw how dealing with stress can help adolescents grow in terms of their identity and self-worth. By coping effectively with stress, they come to see themselves as hardy, resilient individuals who can deal with the challenges that life presents.

Before moving on to the next chapter, consider the following questions.

1. Do you think that Katy might be putting too much pressure on herself to succeed academically? Do you think that she would feel as pressured if she were a boy?

2. In what ways is Katy's stress beneficial to her, and in what ways may it be harmful to her? Does she seem to have much time for fun and friends?

3. What is Katy doing to manage her stress? What else could she be doing? Is there any evidence that her stress is hurting her health?

4. Does Katy seem to be high in hardiness?

SUMMARY

REVIEW

- **What is stress and what causes it?** *(p. 446)*
  1. Stress is the response to events that threaten or challenge us.
  2. Dealing with stress involves a two-step process of primary appraisal focused on the stressor and secondary appraisal focused on the resources available to cope with it.
  3. The main types of stressors are cataclysmic events, personal stressors, and background stressors (also called daily hassles).

- **How does stress affect adolescents?** *(p. 452)*
  4. In general, adolescence is more stressful than earlier periods partly because of adolescents' more sophisticated cognitive abilities and partly because of academic and social pressures that adolescents typically face.
  5. The experience of stress increases throughout adolescence, and adolescents experience more mood swings than adults.
  6. An important cause of stress during adolescence is the different rates at which the brain matures, with development of the rational prefrontal cortex generally trailing that of the emotional limbic system.

- **How can adolescents learn to cope with stress?** *(p. 460)*
  7. Adolescents' responses to stress vary from panic to excitement.
  8. Two main patterns of coping with stress are problem-focused coping, which involves changing the situation, and emotion-focused coping, which involves the regulation of emotions.
  9. Social support and defensive coping are key coping mechanisms.

- **What personal characteristics seem to reduce the effects of stress?** *(p. 464)*
  10. Adolescents develop a general coping style. Hardiness and resilience are personality traits associated with the ability to cope with stress.
  11. Cognitive approaches to coping emphasize rational consideration of the stressor and a careful appraisal of logical ways to cope with it.

- **What does it mean to be happy?** *(p. 470)*
  12. The view that adolescence is a period of stress and turmoil has interfered with the study of adolescent happiness.
  13. Adolescents' happiness is linked to their sense of self-esteem, with those who have high self-esteem and optimism being generally happier than those with low self-esteem.
  14. Happiness fluctuates above and below a fairly stable set point, which has a strong genetic component.
  15. Happiness, at least in the United States, is derived mostly from feelings of independence, competence, self-esteem, or relatedness, but views of happiness vary from culture to culture.

KEY TERMS AND CONCEPTS

stress (p. 446)

stressors (p. 446)

primary appraisal (p. 447)

secondary appraisal (p. 447)

cataclysmic events (p. 448)

personal stressor (p. 448)

posttraumatic stress
disorder (PTSD) (p. 449)

background stressors
(p. 449)

uplifts (p. 449)

immune system (p. 455)

psychosomatic disorders
(p. 455)

general adaptation
syndrome (GAS) (p. 456)

psychoneuroimmunology
or PNI (p. 459)

coping (p. 461)

problem-focused coping
(p. 461)

emotion-focused coping
(p. 461)

social support (p. 461)

hardiness (p. 464)

subjective well-being
(p. 470)

Glossary

Acceleration: An educational approach that allows gifted students to move ahead at their own pace, even if this means skipping to higher grade levels (Ch. 10)

Accommodation: Changes in existing ways of thinking that occur in response to encounters with new stimuli or events (Ch. 3)

Acculturation: The changes and adjustments that occur when groups of different people come into sustained firsthand contact (Ch. 12)

Achievement test: A test designed to determine a person's level of knowledge in a given subject area (Ch. 3)

Addictive drugs: Drugs that produce a biological or psychological dependence in users, leading to increasingly powerful cravings for them (Ch. 13)

Adolescence: The developmental stage that lies between childhood and adulthood (Ch. 1)

Adolescent egocentrism: A state of self-absorption in which the world is viewed from one's own point of view (Ch. 3)

Adolescent growth spurt: A period of very rapid growth in height and weight where males grow 4.1 inches a year and females 3.5 inches a year (Ch. 2)

Adolescent science: A research-based approach to the study of adolescence that evolved from the work of psychologist G. Stanley Hall (Ch. 1)

Agentic professions: Occupations associated with getting things accomplished (Ch. 11)

Alcoholic: Persons with alcohol problems who have learned to depend on alcohol and are unable to control their drinking (Ch. 13)

Ambivalent attachment pattern: A pattern of attachment in which the adolescent displays a combination of positive and negative reactions to their parents. These adolescents received inconsistent treatment as young children (Ch. 6)

Anorexia nervosa: A severe and potentially life-threatening eating disorder in which individuals refuse to eat while denying that their behavior or skeletal appearance is out of the ordinary (Ch. 2)

Aptitude test: A test designed to predict a person's ability in a particular area or line of work (Ch. 3)

Assimilation: The process in which people understand an experience in terms of their current stage of cognitive development and way of thinking (Ch. 3)

Assimilation: The process in which an adolescent begins to identify with the mainstream culture and rejects the minority culture (Ch. 12)

Attachment: The positive emotional bond that develops between a child and particular, special individuals (Ch. 6)

Authoritarian parents: Parents who are controlling, punitive, rigid, cold. Their word is law, and they value strict, unquestioning obedience from their children (Ch. 6)

Authoritative parents: Parents who are firm, setting clear and consistent limits. Although they tend to be relatively strict, like authoritarian parents, they are loving and emotionally supportive (Ch. 6)

Autonomy: The development and expression of independence (Ch. 6)

Avoidant attachment pattern: A pattern of attachment in which the adolescent steers clear of relationships; often the product of distant, aloof caretakers who have ignored or rejected them during their early childhood (Ch. 6)

Background stressors: (also known as daily hassles): The small irritants of life that produce minor stress (Ch. 14)

Behavioral perspective: The approach that suggests that the keys to understanding development are observable behavior and outside stimuli in the environment (Ch. 1)

Bicultural identity: A dual identity in which adolescents maintain their original cultural identities while also integrating themselves into the dominant culture (Ch. 10)

Bioecological approach: The perspective suggesting that different levels of the environment simultaneously influence individuals (Ch. 1)

Blended families: A family consisting of remarried couples with at least one stepchild living with them (Ch. 6)

Bulimia: An eating disorder that primarily afflicts adolescent girls and young women, characterized by binges on large quantities of food followed by purges of the food through vomiting or the use of laxatives (Ch. 2)

Career self-concept: A sense of oneself viewed through the context of work (Ch. 11)

Cataclysmic events: Strong stressors that occur suddenly and affect many adolescents simultaneously, such as tornadoes, hurricanes, and floods (Ch. 14)

Chronological (physical) age: A person's age according to the calendar (Ch. 3)

Cliques (pronounced "kleeks"): Groups of from 2 to 12 people whose members have frequent social interactions with one another (Ch. 7)

Cognitive neuroscience approaches: The approach that examines cognitive development through the lens of brain processes (Ch. 1)

Cognitive perspective: The approach that focuses on the processes that allow people to know, understand, and think about the world (Ch. 1)

Communal professions: Occupations associated with relationships (Ch. 11)

Community service programs: Programs that involve groups that engage in activities meant to improve the social welfare of a town, city, or even the nation (Ch. 7)

Comorbid: A situation in which various difficulties co-occur in the same adolescent (Ch. 13)

Companionate love: The strong affection that we have for those with whom our lives are deeply involved (Ch. 8)

Conformity: A change in behavior or attitudes brought about by a desire to follow the beliefs or standards of others (Ch. 7)

Contextual perspective: The approach that considers the relationship between individuals and their physical, cognitive, personality, and social worlds (Ch. 1)

Contingent self-worth: A concept that is composed of beliefs that one has value and worth that are related to accomplishments in specific, important domains (Ch. 5)

Continuous change: Gradual development in which achievements at one level build on those of previous levels (Ch. 1)

Controversial adolescents: Adolescents who are liked by some and disliked by others (Ch. 7)

Coparenting: The process by which mothers and fathers coordinate their child-rearing practices (Ch. 6)

Coping: The effort to control, reduce, or learn to tolerate the threats that lead to stress (Ch. 14)

Creativity: The combining of responses or ideas in novel ways (Ch. 3)

Cross-sectional research: Research in which adolescents of different ages are compared at the same point in time (Ch. 1)

Crowds: In contrast to cliques, crowds are larger and looser groups, comprising individuals who share particular characteristics but who may not interact with one another (Ch. 7)

Crystallized intelligence: The store of information, skills, and strategies that people have acquired through education and prior experiences and through their previous use of fluid intelligence (Ch. 3)

Cultural assimilation model: An approach in which the goal of education was to assimilate individual cultural identities into a unique, unified American culture (Ch. 10)

Culture: A set of traditions, behaviors, beliefs, values, attitudes, and expectations shared by members of a particular society (Ch. 12)

Cycle of violence hypothesis: The theory that the abuse and neglect that children and adolescents suffer predispose them as adults to abuse and neglect their own children (Ch. 13)

Date rape: Rape in which the rapist is either a date or a romantic acquaintance (Ch. 9)

Dating scripts: Cognitive models of what behavior and expectations are appropriate and inappropriate within the context of a dating relationship (Ch. 8)

Dating: Individual-choice courtship in which boys and girls pair off together as couples in committed relationships—the traditional practices of dating are evolving (Ch. 8)

Decision/commitment component: The component of love that embodies both the initial cognition that one loves another person and the longer-term determination to maintain that love (Ch. 8)

Descriptive self-disclosure: Self-disclosure in which people share *facts* about their lives (Ch. 8)

Discontinuous change: Development that occurs in distinct steps or stages, with each stage bringing about behavior that is assumed to be qualitatively different from behavior at earlier stages (Ch. 1)

Discrimination: The negative (or sometimes positive) actions taken toward members of a particular group because of their membership in the group (Ch. 12)

Divergent thinking: The ability to generate unusual, yet nonetheless appropriate, responses to problems or questions (Ch. 3)

Emotional intelligence: The set of skills that underlie the accurate assessment, evaluation, expression, and regulation of emotions (Ch. 3)

Emotional isolation: Loneliness in which adolescents feel a lack of deep emotional attachment to one specific person (Ch. 8)

Emotional self-regulation: The ability to adjust emotions to a desired state and level of intensity (Ch. 5)

Emotion-focused coping: A coping strategy in which adolescents try to deal with stress by consciously regulating their emotions (Ch. 14)

Emotions: Feelings that have both physiological and cognitive elements and that influence behavior (Ch. 4)

Emotions: Feelings that have both physiological and cognitive elements and that influence behavior (Ch. 5)

Empathy: The understanding of what another individual feels (Ch. 4)

Endocrine system: A chemical communication network that sends messages throughout the body via the bloodstream (Ch. 2)

Enrichment: An alternative approach to acceleration through which students are kept at grade level but are enrolled in special programs and given individual activities to allow greater depth of study on a given topic (Ch. 10)

Ethnic identity: How members of ethnic, racial, and cultural minorities view themselves, both as members of their own group and in terms of their relationships with other groups (Ch. 12)

Evaluative self-disclosure: Self-disclosure that communicates information about personal *feelings* (Ch. 8)

Evolutionary perspective: The approach that seeks to identify behavior that is the result of our genetic inheritance from our ancestors (Ch. 1)

Externalizing disorders: Problems that are directed outward, toward others, and typically are displayed as behavioral problems (Ch. 13)

Fantasy period: According to Ginzberg the period of life when career choices are made—and discarded—without regard to skills, abilities, or available job opportunities (Ch. 11)

Fluid intelligence: The ability to deal with new problems and situations (Ch. 3)

Formal operational stage: The stage at which people develop the ability to think abstractly (Ch. 3)

Friendships: Relationships in which there is a positive, reciprocal relationship between two people (Ch. 8)

Full inclusion: The integration of all students, even those with the most severe disabilities, into regular classes (Ch. 10)

Gender roles: The set of expectations, defined by society, that indicate what is appropriate behavior for males and females (Ch. 12)

Gender schema: A mental framework that organizes information relevant to gender (Ch. 12)

General Adaptation Syndrome (GAS):   A model that suggests that the physiological response to stress follows a similar three-stage pattern, regardless of the kind of stressor that produces the stress (Ch. 14)

Generation gap: A divide between adolescence and other periods of life that supposedly reflects profound differences in behavior, values, attitudes, lifestyle choices, and experiences (Ch. 6)

Gifted and talented: Children who give evidence of high performance capability in areas such as intellectual, creative, artistic, leadership capacity, or specific academic fields (Ch. 10)

Gonadostat: A feedback loop mechanism that regulates the sex hormone concentration in blood through a complicated circuit involving the hypothalamus, pituitary, and gonads in males and ovaries in females (Ch. 2)

Hardiness: A personality characteristic associated with a lower rate of stress-related illness (Ch. 14)

Home schooling: A major educational phenomenon in which students are taught not by teachers in schools, but by their parents in their own homes (Ch. 10)

Hormones: Chemicals that circulate through the blood and affect the functioning or growth of other parts of the body (Ch. 2)

Identification: The process in which children attempt to be similar to their same-sex parent, incorporating the parent's attitudes and values (Ch. 12)

Identity-versus-role-confusion stage: According to Erikson the stage where adolescents seek to understand who they are by narrowing and making choices about their personal, occupational, sexual, and political commitments (Ch. 5)

Imaginary audience: Fictitious observers who pay as much attention to adolescents' behavior as they do themselves (Ch. 3)

Immune system: The system of organs, glands, and cells that make up the body's defense against disease (Ch. 14)

Information processing approaches: The model that seeks to identify the ways individuals take in, use, and store information (Ch. 1)

Integration: The process in which adolescents maintain their own culture while simultaneously seeking to adapt and incorporate the majority culture (Ch. 12)

Intelligence quotient or (IQ):   A score that expresses the ratio between a person's mental and chronological ages (Ch. 3)

Intelligence: The capacity to understand the world, think rationally, and use resources effectively when faced with challenges (Ch. 3)

Internalizing disorders: Physical and psychological problems that are turned inward and primarily affect only the adolescent in question; they include such problems as depression, anxiety, and phobias (Ch. 13)

Intimacy component: The component of love that encompasses feelings of closeness, affection, and connectedness (Ch. 8)

Intimacy: The feeling of emotional closeness and interconnectedness with another person, develops during adolescence because of the cognitive, social, and physical advances that occur during that period (Ch. 8)

Kaufman Assessment Battery for Children, 2nd Edition (KABC-II):   A children's intelligence test permitting unusual flexibility in its administration (Ch. 3)

Lateralization: The dominance of one hemisphere of the brain in specific functions (Ch. 2)

Least restrictive environment: The setting most similar to that of students without special needs (Ch. 10)

Loneliness: The inability to maintain the level of affiliation one desires (Ch. 8)

Longitudinal research: Research in which the behavior of one or more study participants is measured as they age (Ch. 1)

Mainstreaming: An educational approach to special education in which exceptional adolescents are integrated as much as possible into the traditional education system and are provided with a broad range of educational alternatives (Ch. 10)

Marginalization: The process that occurs when adolescents identify neither with their minority culture nor with the majority culture (Ch. 12)

Masturbation: Solitary sexual self-stimulation (Ch. 9)

Maturation: The predetermined unfolding of genetic information (Ch. 1)

Menarche: The onset of menstruation (Ch. 2)

Mental age: The typical intelligence level found for people of a given chronological age (Ch. 3)

Mental retardation: A disability characterized by significant limitations both in intellectual functioning and in adaptive behavior involving conceptual, social, and practical adaptive skills (Ch. 10)

Metacognition: The knowledge that people have about their own thinking processes and their ability to monitor their cognition (Ch. 3)

Mild retardation: Retardation in which IQ scores fall in the range of 50 or 55 to 70 (Ch. 10)

Moderate retardation: Retardation in which IQ scores fall in the range of 35 or 40 to 50 or 55 (Ch. 10)

Modern racism: A subtle form of prejudice in which adolescents appear, on the surface, not to harbor prejudice, while actually holding racist attitudes (Ch. 12)

Moral development: Changes in one's sense of justice and of what is right and wrong and in our behavior related to moral issues (Ch. 4)

Multicultural education: Form of education in which the goal is to help minority students develop competence in the culture of the majority group while maintaining positive group identities that build on their original cultures (Ch. 10)

Myelin: A protective coat of fat and protein that wraps around the axon (Ch. 2)

Neglected adolescents: Adolescents who are neither liked nor disliked (Ch. 7)

Nuclear family: A married couple and their unmarried children living together, considered by most to be the preferred arrangement for families (Ch. 6)

Passion component: The component of love that comprises the motivational drives relating to sex, physical closeness, and romance and is exemplified by intense, physiologically arousing feelings of attraction (Ch. 8)

Passionate (or romantic) love: A state of powerful absorption in someone that includes intense physiological interest and arousal, and caring for another's needs (Ch. 8)

Peer groups: Informal or formal groups composed of individuals of approximately the same age and status (Ch. 7)

Peers: Individuals who are about the same age or level of maturity (Ch. 7)

Permissive parents: Parents who provide lax and inconsistent feedback and require little of their children (Ch. 6)

Personal fables: The view held by some adolescents that what happens to them is unique, exceptional, and shared by no one else (Ch. 3)

Personal stressor: A major life even with immediate negative consequences (Ch. 14)

Personality: The pattern of enduring characteristics that differentiate people—the behaviors that make each adolescent a unique individual (Ch. 4)

Pluralistic society model: The concept in which American society is made up of diverse, coequal cultural groups that should preserve their individual cultural features

Possible selves: Those aspects of the self that relate to the future (Ch. 5)

Posttraumatic stress disorder (PTSD): A psychological syndrome in which victims of major incidents reexperience the original stress-producing even and associated feelings in flashbacks or dreams (Ch. 14)

Practical intelligence: Intelligence that is learned primarily by observing others and modeling their behavior (Ch. 3)

Prejudice: The negative (or positive) evaluations or judgments of members of a group that are based primarily on group membership, and not necessarily on the particular characteristics of individuals (Ch. 12)

Primary appraisal: The assessment of an event or circumstance to determine whether its implications are positive, neutral, or negative (Ch. 14)

Primary orientation model: A situation in which adolescents usually focus their attention mainly either on school or work, but not both (Ch. 11)

Primary sex characteristics: Characteristics that are associated with the development of the organs and structures of the body that directly relate to reproduction (Ch. 2)

Problem-focused coping: A coping strategy in which adolescents attempt to manage a stressful problem or situation by directly changing the situation to make it less stressful (Ch. 14)

Profound retardation: Retardation in which IQ scores fall below 20 or 25 (Ch. 10)

Prosocial behavior: Helping behavior that benefits others (Ch. 4)

Pseudomaturity: A period of adolescent development that involves an unusually early entry into adult roles before an adolescent is ready developmentally to assume them (Ch. 11)

Psychoanalytic theory: The theory proposed by Freud that suggests that unconscious forces act to determine personality and behavior (Ch. 1)

Psychodynamic approach to personality: The approach to the study of development that states behavior is shaped by inner forces and conflicts about which adolescents have little awareness or control (Ch. 4)

Psychodynamic perspective: The approach that states behavior is motivated by inner forces, memories, and conflicts that are generally beyond people's awareness and control (Ch. 1)

Psychoneuroimmunology or PNI: The study of the relationship among psychological factors, the immune system, and the brain (Ch. 14)

Psychosexual development: According to Freud, a series of stages that children pass through in which pleasure, or gratification, is focused on a particular biological function and body part (Ch. 1)

Psychosocial development: The approach that encompasses changes in our interactions with and understandings of one another as well as in our knowledge and understanding of ourselves as members of society (Ch. 1)

Psychosomatic disorders: Medical problems caused by the interaction of psychological, emotional, and physical difficulties (Ch. 14)

Puberty: The period of maturation during which the sexual organs mature (Ch. 2)

Rape: One person forcing another person to submit to sexual activity such as intercourse or oral–genital sex (Ch. 9)

Realistic period: The third and final stage of Ginzberg's three developmental periods in which people explore specific career options either through actual experience on the job or through training for a profession (Ch. 11)

Reciprocal socialization: The process by which at one and the same time parents socialize their children and adolescents, and children and adolescents socialize their parents (Ch. 6)

Reference groups: Groups of people with whom one compares oneself (Ch. 7)

Rejected adolescents: Adolescents who are uniformly disliked (Ch. 7)

Resilience: The ability to overcome circumstances that place adolescents at high risk for psychological or physical damage (Ch. 6)

Rites of passage: Ceremonies or rituals that mark a person's transition from stage of life to another (Ch. 4)

Roles: Behaviors that are associated with and come to be expected of people in a given position (Ch. 4)

Scaffolding: The support for learning and problem solving that encourages independence and growth (Ch. 3)

Scientific method: The process of posing and answering questions using careful, controlled techniques that include systematic, orderly observation and the collection of data (Ch. 1)

Secondary appraisal: The assessment of whether adolescents feel their coping abilities and resources are adequate to overcome the harm, threat, or challenge posed by the potential stressor (Ch. 14)

Secondary sex characteristics: The visible signs of sexual maturity that do not involve the sex organs directly (Ch. 2)

Secular trend: A statistical tendency observed over several generations (Ch. 2)

Secure attachment pattern: A pattern of attachment in which the adolescent is well adjusted, having positive self-esteem and social competence as the result of receiving consistently warm and nurturing care during infancy (Ch. 6)

Self-disclosure: Conversation in which information about the self is exchanged with others (Ch. 8)

Self-esteem: The affective component of self, an individual's general and specific positive and negative self-evaluations (Ch. 5)

Separation: The process in which adolescents identify with the ethnic minority culture to which they belong while rejecting or rebuffing the majority culture (Ch. 12)

Sequential studies: An approach in which researchers examine a number of different age groups at several points in time (Ch. 1)

Severe retardation: Retardation in which IQ scores fall in the range of 20 or 25 to 35 or 40 (Ch. 10)

Sex cleavage: Sex segregation in which boys interact primarily with boys and girls primarily with girls (Ch. 7)

Sexism: Negative attitudes and behavior toward a person that are based on that person's gender (Ch. 12)

Sexual harassment: Unwanted sexual attention, the creation of a hostile or abusive environment, or explicit coercion to engage in unwanted sexual activity (Ch. 9)

Sexually transmitted infection (STI):   An infection that is spread primarily through sexual contact (Ch. 9)

Social comparison: The desire to evaluate one's own behavior, abilities, expertise, and opinions by comparing them to those of others (Ch. 5)

Social identity theory: The theory that adolescents use group membership as a source of pride and self-worth (Ch. 12)

Social isolation: Loneliness in which adolescents suffer from a lack of friends, associates, or relatives (Ch. 8)

Social policy: A national, state, or local governmental response designed to improve the welfare of citizens (Ch. 1)

Social problem solving: The use of strategies for solving social conflicts in ways that are satisfactory both to oneself and to others (Ch. 7)

Social support: Assistance and comfort supplied by a network of caring, interested individuals (Ch. 14)

Socialized delinquents: Adolescents who know and subscribe to the norms of society; they are fairly normal psychologically (Ch. 13)

Sociocultural theory: The approach that emphasizes how cognitive development proceeds as a result of social interactions between members of a culture (Ch. 1)

Stereotype: A set of beliefs and expectations about members of a group that are held simply because of their membership in the group (Ch. 12)

Storm and stress view: Psychologist G. Stanley Hall's theory that adolescence could be characterized in a fundamental way as a period of extraordinary turbulence, filled with mood swings and upheaval (Ch. 1)

Stress: The response to events that threaten or challenge an individual (Ch. 14)

Stressors: Circumstances that produce threats to one's well-being (Ch. 14)

Subjective well-being: Adolescents' evaluations of their lives in terms of their thoughts and their emotions (Ch. 14)

Teacher expectancy effect: The cycle of behavior in which a teacher transmits an expectation about a student and thereby actually brings about the expected behavior (Ch. 10)

Temperaments: Patterns of arousal and emotionality that are consistent and enduring (Ch. 4)

Tentative period: The second stage of Ginzberg's theory, which spans adolescence, in which people begin to think in pragmatic terms about the requirements of various jobs and how their own abilities might fit with those requirements (Ch. 11)

Theory of interpersonal development: Sullivan's theory that focuses on the specific needs that must be resolved to attain growth (Ch. 8)

Traits: Enduring dimensions of personality characteristics along which adolescents differ (Ch. 4)

Triarchic theory of intelligence: The belief that intelligence consists of three aspects of information processing: the componential element, the experiential element, and the contextual element (Ch. 3)

Undersocialized delinquents: Adolescents who are raised with little discipline or with harsh, uncaring parental supervision (Ch. 13)

Uninvolved parents: Parents who show little interest in their children, displaying indifferent, rejecting behavior. In its most extreme form, uninvolved parenting results in *neglect*, a form of child abuse (Ch. 6)

Uplifts: Minor positive events that make people feel good, even if only temporarily (Ch. 14)

Zone of proximal development (ZPD):   According to Vygotsky, the level at which a child can almost, but not fully, comprehend or perform a task without assistance (Ch. 3)

References

AAP Committee on Communications. (1995, June.) Media Violence, *Pediatrics, 95* (6).

AAUW (American Association of University Women). (2001). *Hostile hallways: Bullying, teasing, and sexual harassment in school*. Washington, DC: Author.

Aboud, F. E., & Mendelson, M. J. (1998). Determinants of friendship selection and quality: Developmental perspectives. In W. M. Bukowski, A. F. Newcomb, & W. W. Hartup (Eds.), *The company they keep: Friendship in childhood and adolescence* (pp. 87–112). New York: Cambridge University Press.

Abraham, Y., & Cramer, M. (2006, May 2). Making their statement. *The Boston Globe*, A1.

Abrahams, G., & Ahlbrand, S. (2002). *Boy v. girl? How gender shapes who we are, what we want, and how we get along*. Minneapolis, MN: Free Spirit Publishing, 2002.

Abrams, D., & Hogg, M. A. (Eds.). (1999). *Social identity and social cognition*. Malden, MA: Blackwell.

Abrams, L. S., & Aguilar, J. P. (2005). Negative trends, possible selves, and behavior change: A qualitative study of juvenile offenders in residential treatment. *Qualitative Social Work: Research and Practice, 4*, 175–196.

Ackard, D. M., & Neumark-Sztainer, D. (2002). Date violence and date rape among adolescents: Associations with disordered eating behaviors and psychological health. *Child Abuse and Neglect, 26*, 455–473.

Ackerman, B. P., & Izard, C. E. (2004). Emotion cognition in children and adolescents: Introduction to the special issue. *Journal of Experimental Child Psychology, 89*, 271–275.

Acocella, J. (August 18 & 25, 2003). Little people. *The New Yorker*, 138–143.

Adams, C. R., & Singh, K. (1998). Direct and indirect effects of school learning variables on the academic achievement of African American 10th graders. *Journal of Negro Education 67*, 48–66.

Adams, P. R., & Adams, G. R. (1987). Intervention with runaway youth and their families: Theory and practice. In J. C. Coleman (Ed.), *Working with troubled adolescents: A handbook*. San Diego, CA: Academic Press.

Adams, W. L. (2005, June 16). Practical applications. *Newsweek*. Retrieved from http://www.msnbc. msn. com/id/8214827/site/newsweek/

Adler, S. R. (1995). Refugee stress and folk belief: Hmong sudden deaths. *Social Science & Medicine, 40*, 1623–1629.

Adolphs, R. (2002). Neural systems for recognizing emotion. *Current Opinion in Neurobiology, 12*, 169–177.

Advocates for Youth. (2003). *Science and success: Sex education and other programs that work to prevent teen pregnancy, HIV & sexually transmitted infections*. Washington, DC. Retrieved March 4, 2006 from http://www. advocatesforyouth. org/publications/Science-Success. pdf

Aftanas, L., & Golosheykin, S. (2005). Impact of regular meditation practice on EEG activity at rest and during evoked negative emotions. *International Journal of Neuroscience, 115*, 893–909.

Ainsworth, M. D. S., Blehar, M. C., Waters, E., & Wall, S. (1978). *Patterns of attachment: A psychological study of the strange situation*. Hillsdale, NJ: Erlbaum.

Alasker, F., & Olweus, D. (1992). Stability of global self-evaluations in early adolescence: A cohort longitudinal study. *Journal of Research on Adolescence, 1*, 123–145.

Alderfer, C. (2003). The science and nonscience of psychologists' responses to The Bell Curve. *Professional Psychology: Research & Practice, 34*, 287–293.

Alexander, M. G., Brewer, M. B., & Livingston, R. W. (2005). Putting stereotype content in context: Image theory and interethnic stereotypes. *Personality and Social Psychology Bulletin, 31*, 781–794.

Alfieri, T., Ruble, D. N., & Higgins, E. T. (1996). Gender stereotypes during adolescence: Developmental changes and the transition to junior high school. *Developmental Psychology, 32*, 1129–1137.

Alfonso, V. C., Flanagan, D. P., & Radwan, S. (2005). The impact of the Cattell-Horn-Carroll theory on test development and interpretation of cognitive and academic abilities. In D. P. Flanagan, & P. L. Harrison, (Eds.), *Contemporary intellectual assessment: Theories, tests, and issues*. New York, Guilford Press.

Algozzine, B., & Ysseldyke, J. (2006). *Teaching students with gifts and talents: A practical guide for every teacher*. Thousand Oaks, CA: Sage.

Ali, L., and Scelfo, J. (2002, December 9). Choosing virginity. *Newsweek*, 61–64.

Ali, S. R., McWhirter, E. H., & Chronister, K. M. (2005). Self-efficacy and vocational outcome expectations for adolescents of lower socioeconomic status: A pilot study. *Journal of Career Assessment, 13*, 40–58.

Allen, L. (2004). "Getting off" and "going out": Young people's conceptions of (hetero)sexual relationships. *Culture, Health, & Sexuality, 6*, 463–481.

Allen, M, & Bissell, M. (2004). Safety and stability for foster children: The policy context. *The Future of Children, 14*, 49–74.

Allen, M. (1999, September 19). Help wanted: The not-too-high-Q standard. *New York Times*, p. 3.

Allen, M., Emmers, T., Gebhardt, L., & Giery, M. A. (1995). Exposure to pornography and acceptance of rape myths. *Journal of Communication, 45*, 88–97.

Alley, T. R., & Hicks, C. M. (2005). Peer attitudes towards adolescent participants in male- and female-oriented sports. *Adolescence, 40*, 273–280.

Allison, B., & Schultz, J. (2001). Interpersonal identity formation during early adolescence. *Adolescence, 36*, 509–523.

Almeida, D. M., & Kessler, R. C. (1998). Everyday stressors and gender differences in daily distress. *Journal of Personality and Social Psychology, 75*, 670–680.

Almeida, D. M., Neupert, S. D., Banks, S. R., & Serido, J. (2005). Do daily stress processes account for socioeconomic health disparities? *The Journals of Gerontology: Series B: Psychological Sciences and Social Sciences, 60B*, 34–39.

Alverdy, J., Zaborina, O., & Wu, L. (2005). The impact of stress and nutrition on bacterial-host interactions at the intestinal epithelial surface. *Current Opinion in Clinical Nutrition and Metabolic Care, 8*, 205–209.

Amato, P., & Booth, A. (1997). *A generation at risk*. Cambridge, MA: Harvard University Press.

American Association of University Women. (1992). *How schools shortchange women: The AAUW report*. Washington, DC: Author.

American College Testing Program. (2001). *National Dropout Rates*. Iowa City, Iowa: American College Testing Program.

American Heart Association. (2005). *Top ten ways to help children develop healthy habits*. Dallas, TX: American Heart Association.

Andersen, S. L., & Navalta, C. P. (2004). Altering the course of neurodevelopment: A framework for understanding the enduring effects of psychotropic drugs. *Journal of Developmental Neuroscience, 22*, Special Issue: Developmental aspects of addiction, 423–440.

Anderson, C. A. (2004). An update on the effects of playing violent video games. *Journal of Adolescence, 27*, 113–122.

Anderson, C. A., Berkowitz, L., Donnerstein, E., Huesmann, L. R., Johnson, J. D., Linz, D., et al. (2003). The influence of media violence on youth. *Psychological Science in the Public Interest, 4*, 81–110.

Anderson, C. A., Funk, Jeanne, B., Griffiths, M. D. (2004). Contemporary issues in adolescent video game playing: brief overview and introduction to the special issue. *Journal of Adolescence, 27*, 1–3.

Anderson, C. A., Carnagey, N. L., & Eubanks, J. (2003). Exposure to violent media: The effects of songs with violent lyrics on aggressive thoughts and feelings. *Journal of Personality and Social Psychology, 84*, 960–971.

Anderson, C. A., & Dill, K. E. (2000). Video games and aggressive thoughts, feelings, and behavior in the laboratory and in life. *Journal of Personality and Social Psychology, 78*, 772–790.

Anderson, D. R., Huston, A. C., Schmitt, K. L., Linebarger, D. L., & Wright, J. C. (2001). Early childhood television viewing and adolescent behavior: The recontact study. *Monographs of the Society for Research in Child Development, 66*, vii–147.

Anderson, K. B., Cooper, H., & Okamura, L. (1997). Individual differences and attitudes toward rape: A meta-analytic review. *Personality and Social Psychology Bulletin, 23*, 295–315.

Anderson, K. J., & Smith, G. (2005). Students' preconceptions of professors: Benefits and barriers according to ethnicity and gender. *Hispanic Journal of Behavioral Science, 27*, 184–201.

Anderson, N. B., & Nickerson, K. J. (2005). Genes, race, and psychology in the genome era. An introduction. *American Psychologist, 60*, 5–8.

Anderson, R. W. (2002). Youth and information technology. In J. T. Mortimer & R. W. Larson (Eds.), *The changing adolescent experience: Societal trends and the transition to adulthood* (pp. 175–207). New York: Cambridge University Press.

Anderson, R. W., Plomp, T., Law, N., & Quale, A (Eds.), (2003). *Cross National Policies and Practices on Information and Communication Technology in Education.* Greenwich, CT: Information Age Publishing.

Andersson, L. (1998). Loneliness research and interventions: A review of the literature. *Aging & Mental Health, 2*, 264–274.

Andrews, J., & Boyle, J. S. (2003). African American adolescents' experiences with unplanned pregnancy and elective abortion. *Health Care for Women International, 24*, 414–433.

Angier, N. (2000, August 22). Do races differ? Not really, genes show. *New York Times*, pp. S1, S6.

Anthony, J. L., Lonigan, C. J., Hooe, E. S., & Phillips, B. M. (2002). An affect-based, hierarchical model of temperament and its relations with internalizing symptomatology. *Journal of Clinical Child and Adolescent Psychology, 31*, 480–490.

APA Reproductive Choice Working Group. (2000). *Reproductive choice and abortion: A resource packet.* Washington, DC: American Psychological Association.

Apter, A., Galatzer, A., Beth-Halachmi, N., & Laron, Z. (1981). Self-image in adolescents with delayed puberty and growth retardation. *Journal of Youth and Adolescence, 10*, 501–505.

Aquilino, W. (2005). Impact of family structure on parental attitudes toward the economic support of adult children over the transition to adulthood. *Journal of Family Issues, 26*, 143–167.

Aratani, L. (2006, March 12). Vo-Tech as a door to college evolving programs draw on strong backs, strong minds. *Washington Post*, C11.

Arbona, C. (2005). Promoting the career development and academic achievement of at-risk youth: College access programs. In S. D. Brown & R. W. Lent (Eds), *Career development and counseling: Putting theory and research to work* (pp. 525–550). Hoboken, NJ: Wiley.

Archer, S. L., & Waterman, A. S. (1994). Adolescent identity development: Contextual perspectives. In C. B. Fisher & R. M. Lerner (Eds.), *Applied developmental psychology.* New York: McGraw-Hill.

Archibald, F. F., Bartholomew, K., & Marx, R. (1995). Loneliness in early adolescence: A test of the cognitive discrepancy model of loneliness. *Personality & Social Psychology Bulletin, 21*, 296–301.

Arcus, D. (2001). Inhibited and uninhibited children: Biology in the social context. In T. D. Wachs, & G. A. Kohnstamm, (Eds.), *Temperament in context.* Mahwah, NJ: Lawrence Erlbaum Associates.

Arenson, K. W. (2004, December 4). Worried colleges step up efforts over suicide. *The New York Times*, pg. A1.

Aries, P. (1962). *Centuries of childhood.* New York: Knopf.

Arnett, J. J. (1995). Adolescents' uses of media for self-socialization. *Journal of Youth and Adolescence, 24*, 519–534.

Arnett, J. J. (2000). Emerging adulthood: A theory of development from the late teens through the 20s. *American Psychologist, 55*, 469–480.

Arnett, J. J. (2004). *Emerging adulthood: The winding road from late teens through the twenties.* Cambridge: Oxford University Press.

Arnett, J. J., & Tanner, J. L. (Eds.). (2006). *Emerging adults in America: Coming of age in the 21st century.* Washington, DC: American Psychological Association.

Aron, A., Fisher, H., Mashek, D., Strong, G., Haifant, L., & Brown, L. L. (2005). Reward, motivation, and emotion systems associated with early-stage intense romantic love. *Journal of Neurophysiology, 94*, 327–337.

Aronson, E. (2000). *Nobody left to hate: Teaching compassion after Columbine.* New York: Freeman.

Aronson, J., & Steele, C. M. (2005). Stereotypes and the fragility of academic competence, motivation, and self-concept. In A. J. Elliot & C. S. Dweck, (Eds.), *Handbook of competence and motivation* (pp. 436–456). New York: Guilford.

Arredondo, P., Avilés, R. M. D., Zalaquett, C. P., Grazioso, M. D., Bordes, V., Hita, L., et al. (2006). The psychohistorical approach in family counseling with Mestizo/Latino Immigrants: A continuum and synergy of worldviews. *Family Journal: Counseling and Therapy for Couples and Families, 14*, 13–27.

Asher, S. R., & Paquette, J. A. (2003). Loneliness and peer relations in childhood. *Current Directions in Psychological Science, 12*, 75–78.

Asher, S. R., Parker, J. G., & Walker, D. L. (1998). Distinguishing friendship from acceptance: Implications for intervention and assessment. In W. M. Bukowski, A. F. Newcomb, & W. W. Hartup (Eds.), *The company they keep: Friendship in childhood and adolescence* (pp. 366–405). New York: Cambridge University Press.

Asher, S. R., Rose, A. J. & Gabriel, S. W. (2001). Peer rejection in everyday life. In M. Leary (Ed.), *Interpersonal rejection* (pp. 105–142). New York: Oxford University Press.

Ask Beth. (1988, October 28). Questioning identity is normal. *Boston Globe*, p. 52. Retrieved January 9, 2006, from NewsBank/America's Newspapers.

Aspinwall, L. G. & Taylor, S. E. (1992). Modeling cognitive adaptation: A longitudinal investigation of the impact of individual differences and coping on college adjustment and performance. *Journal of Personality & Social Psychology, 63*, 989–1003.

Aspinwall, O. G., & Taylor, S. E. (1993). Effects of social comparison direction, threat, and self-esteem on affect, evaluation, and expected success. *Journal of Personality and Social Psychology, 64*, 708–722.

Astbury-Ward, E. (2002). From Kama Sutra to dot. com: The history, myths and management of premature ejaculation. *Sexual and Relationship Therapy, 17*, 367–380.

Attie, I., & Brooks-Gunn, J. (1989). The development of eating problems in adolescent girls: A longitudinal study. *Developmental Psychology, 25*, 70–79.

Averill, J. (1994). *The nature of emotion: Fundamental questions.* New York: Oxford University Press.

Aviezer, O., Sagi, A., & Resnick, G. (2002). School competence in young adolescence: Links to early attachment relationships beyond concurrent self-perceived competence and representations of relationships. *International Journal of Behavioral Development, 26*, 397–409.

Azziz, R., Farah, L. A., Moran, C., Knochenhauer, E. S., Potter, H. D., & Boots, L. R. (2004). Early adrenarche in normal prepubertal girls: A prospective longitudinal study. *Journal of Pediatric Endocrinology Metabolism, 17*, 1231–1237.

Bachman, J. G., Safron, D. J., Sy, S. R., & Schulenberg, J. E. (2003). Wishing to work: New perspectives on how adolescents' part-time work intensity is linked to educational disengagement, substance use, and other problem behaviours. *International Journal of Behavioral Development, 27*, 301–315.

Baer, J. (1993). *Creativity and divergent thinking: A task-specific approach.* Hillsdale, NJ: Erlbaum.

Baird, A., John, R., & Hayslip, Jr., B. (2000). Custodial grandparenting among African Americans: A focus group perspective. In B. Hayslip, Jr. & R. Goldberg-Glen, (Eds.). *Grandparents raising grandchildren: Theoretical, empirical, and clinical perspectives.* New York: Springer.

Baker, T., Brandon, T., & Chassin, L. (2004). Motivational influences on cigarette smoking. *Annual Review of Psychology, 55*, 463–491.

Baldwin, D. R., Harris, S. M., & Chambliss, L. N. (1997). Stress and illness in adolescence: Issues of race and gender. *Adolescence, 32*, 839–853.

Baldwin, S. A., & Hoffman, J. (2002). The dynamics of self-esteem: A growth-curve analysis. *Journal of Youth and Adolescence, 31*, 101–113.

Bamshad, M. J., & Olson, S. E. (2003, December). Does race exist? *Scientific American*, 78–85.

Bamshad, M. J., et al. (2003). Human population genetic structure and inference of group membership. *American Journal of Human Genetics, 72*, 578–589.

Bandura, A. (1977). *Social learning theory.* Englewood Cliffs, NJ: Prentice Hall.

Bandura, A. (1991). Social cognitive theory of moral thought and action. In W. M. Kurtines & J. L. Gewirtz (Eds.), *Handbook of moral behavior and development.* Hillsdale, NJ: Erlbaum.

Bandura, A. (1994). Social cognitive theory of mass communication. In J. Bryant & D. Zillmann (Eds.), *Media effects: Advances in theory and research. LEA's communication series.* Hillsdale, NJ: Erlbaum.

Bandura, A. (2002). Social cognitive theory in cultural context. *Applied Psychology: An International Review, Special Issue, 51*, 269–290.

Banerji, S. (2006). George Mason's SAT-optional admissions policy could boost diversity. *Diverse Issues in Higher Education, 23*, 12.

Banich, M. T., & Nicholas, C. D. (1998). Integration of processing between the hemispheres in word recognition. In M. Beeman & C. Chiarello (Eds.), *Right hemisphere language comprehension: Perspectives from cognitive neuroscience* (pp. 349–371). Mahwah, NJ: Erlbaum.

Barber, B. K., & Olsen, J. A. (2004). Assessing the transitions to middle and high school. *Journal of Adolescent Research, 19,* 3–30.

Barber, B. K., Stolz, H. E., Olsen, J. A. (2005). Parental support, psychological control, and behavioral control: Assessing relevance across time, culture, and method. *Monographs of the Society for Research in Child Development, 70* (Serial No. 282).

Barber, B. L., Eccles, J. S., & Stone, M. R. (2001). What ever happened to the jock, the brain, and the princess? Young adult pathways linked to adolescent activity involvement and social identity. *Journal of Adolescent Research, 16,* 429–455.

Barker, V., Giles, H., & Noels, K. (2001). The English-only movement: A communication analysis of changing perceptions of language vitality. *Journal of Communication, 51,* 3–37.

Barnow, S., Schultz, G., Lucht, M., Ulrich, I., Preuss, U., & Freyberger, H. J. (2004). Do alcohol expectancies and peer delinquency/substance use mediate the relationship between impulsivity and drinking behaviour in adolescence? *Alcohol and Alcoholism, 39,* 213–219.

Baron-Cohen, S. (2003). *The essential difference: Men, women and the extreme male brain.* London: Allen Lane/Penguin.

Baron-Cohen, S. (2005). Testing the extreme male brain (EMB) theory of autism: Let the data speak for themselves. *Cognitive Neuropsychiatry, 10,* 77–81.

Barrera, M., Jr., Hageman, D. N., & Gonzales, N. A. (2004). Revisiting Hispanic adolescents' resilience to the effects of parental problem drinking and life stress. *American Journal of Community Psychology, 34,* 83–94.

Barron, F. (1990). *Creativity and psychological health: Origins of personal vitality and creative freedom.* Buffalo, NY: Creative Education Foundation.

Barry, C. M., & Wentzel, K. R. (2006). Friend influence on prosocial behavior: The role of motivational factors and friendship characteristics. *Developmental Psychology, 42,* 153–163.

Bartecchi, C. E., MacKenzie, T. D., & Schrier, R. W. (1995, May). The global tobacco epidemic. *Scientific American,* 44–51.

Bartholow, B. D., & Anderson, C. A. (2002). Effects of violent video games on aggressive behavior: Potential sex differences. *Journal of Experimental Social Psychology, 38,* 283–290.

Bass, S., Shields, M. K., Behrman, R. E. (2004). Children, families, and foster care: Analysis and recommendations. *The Future of Children, 14,* 5–30.

Bauman, K. J. (2001, March 29–31). *Home schooling in the United States: Trends and characteristics (Working Paper No. 53).* Paper presented at the annual meeting of the Population Association of American, Washington, DC.

Baumeister, R. F. (1998). The self. In D. T. Gilbert & S. T. Fiske (Eds.) et al., *The handbook of social psychology,* 4th edition. Boston, MA: McGraw-Hill Companies, Inc.

Baumeister, R. F. (Ed.). (1993). *Self-esteem: The puzzle of low self-regard.* New York: Plenum.

Baumeister, R. F. Twenge, J. M., & Nuss, C. K. (2002). Effects of social exclusion on cognitive processes: Anticipated aloneness reduces intelligent thought. *Journal of Personality and Social Psychology, 83,* 817–827.

Baumeister, R. F., Bushman, B. J., & Campbell, W. K. (2000). Self-esteem, narcissism, and aggressions: Does violence result from low self-esteem or from threatened egotism? *Current Directions in Psychological Science, 9,* 26–29.

Baumeister, R. F., Campbell, J. D., Krueger, J. I., & Vohs, K. D. (2003). Does high self-esteem cause better performance, interpersonal success, happiness, or healthier lifestyles? *Psychological Science in the Public Interest, 4,* 1–44.

Baumeister, R. F., Campbell, J. D., Kreueger, J. I., & Vohs, K. D. (2005, January). Exploding the self-esteem myth. *Scientific American,* pp. 84–91.

Baumgartner, F. (2002). The effect of hardiness in the choice of coping strategies in stressful situations. *Studia Psychologica, 44,* 69–75.

Baumrind, D. (1971). Current patterns of parental authority. *Developmental Psychology Monographs, 4* (1, pt. 2).

Baumrind, D. (1980). New directions in socialization research. *Psychological Bulletin, 35,* 639–652.

Baydar, N., & Brooks-Gunn, J. (1998). Profiles of grandmothers who help care for their grandchildren in the United States. *Family Relations, 47,* 385–393.

Beal, C. R. (1994). *Boys and girls: The development of gender roles.* New York: McGraw-Hill.

Bearman, P. S, & Bruckner, H. (2001). Promising the future: Virginity pledges and first intercourse. *American Journal of Sociology, 106,* 859–912.

Bearman, Peter, & Bruckner, H. (2004). *Study on teenage virginity pledge.* Paper presented at meeting of the National STD Prevention Conference, Phildadelphia, PA.

Beck, L., & Feldman, R. S. (1990). Enhancing children's decoding of facial expression. *Journal of Nonverbal Behavior, 13,* 269–277.

Beckman, M. (2004, July 30). Neuroscience: crime, culpability, and the adolescent brain. *Science, 305,* 596–599.

Beekhoven, S., & Dekkers, H. (2005). Early school leaving in the lower vocational track: Triangulation of qualitative and quantitative data. *Adolescence, 40,* 197–213.

Begley, S. (1998, December 28). Into the gene pool: Ethical aspects of genetic research. *Newsweek,* p. 68.

Belcher, J. R. (2003). Stepparenting: Creating and recreating families in America today. *Journal of Nervous & Mental Disease, 191,* 837–838.

Bell, A., & Weinberg, M. S. (1978). *Homosexuality: A study of diversities among men and women.* New York: Simon & Schuster.

Bell, R., Matthews, S. R., Lassister, L., & Leverett, K. (2002). Validity of the Wonderlic Personnel Test as a measure of fluid or crystallized intelligence: Implications for career assessment. *North American Journal of Psychology, 4,* 113–120.

Belluck, P. (2000, October 18). New advice for parents: Saying `That's great!' may not be. *The New York Times,* A14.

Belmont, J. M. (1995). Discussion: A view from the empiricist's window. Special Issue: Lev S. Vygotsky and contemporary educational psychology. *Educational Psychologist, 30,* 99–102.

Bem, S. L. (1998). *An unconventional family.* New Haven, CT: Yale University Press.

Ben-Ari, A. T. (1995). Coming out: A dialectic of intimacy and privacy. *Families in Society, 76,* 306–314.

Benbow, C. P., Lubinski, D., & Hyde, J. S. (1997). Mathematics: Is biology the cause of gender differences in performance? In M. R. Walsh (Ed.), *Women men & gender: Ongoing debates* (pp. 271–287). New Haven, CT: Yale University Press.

Bendixen, M., Endresen, I. M., & Olweus, D. (2003). Variety and frequency scales of antisocial involvement: Which one is better? *Legal and Criminological Psychology, 8,* 135–150.

Benight, C. C. (2004). Collective efficacy following a series of natural disasters. *Stress and Coping: An International Journal, 17,* 401–420.

Benin, M., & Robinson, L. B. (1997). Marital happiness across the family life cycle: A longitudinal analysis. Paper presented at the annual meeting of the American Sociological Association (ASA).

Bennett, S., and Assefi, N. (2005). School-based teenage pregnancy prevention programs: A systematic review of randomized controlled trials. *Journal of Adolescent Health, 36,* 72–81.

Benson, H. (1993). The relaxation response. In D. Goleman & J. Guerin (Eds.), *Mind-body medicine: How to use your mind for better health.* Yonkers, NY: Consumer Reports Publications.

Benson, H., Corliss, J., & Cowley, G. (2004, September 27). Brain check. *Newsweek,* 45–48.

Benson, H., Kornhaber, A., Kornhaber, C., LeChanu, M. N., Zattermeister, P. C., Meyers, P. et al. (1994). Increases in positive psychological characteristics with a new relaxation-response curriculum in high school students. *Journal of Research and Development in Education, 27,* 226–231.

Berenbaum, S. A. (1999). Effects of early androgens on sex-typed activities and interests in adolescents with congenital adrenal hyperplasia. *Hormonal Behavior, 35,* 102–110.

Berenbaum, S. A., & Bailey, J. M. (2003). Effects on gender identity of prenatal androgens and genital appearance: Evidence from girls with congenital adrenal hyperplasia. *Journal of Clinical Endocrinology and Metabolism, 88,* 1102–1106.

Berenbaum, S. A., & Snyder, E. (1995). Early hormonal influences on childhood sex-typed activity and playmate preferences: Implications for the development of sexual orientation. Special Issue: Sexual orientation and human development. *Developmental Psychology, 31,* 31–42.

Berenson, P. (2005). *Understand and treat alcoholism.* New York: Basic Books.

Berg, J. H., & Archer, R. L. (1982). Responses to self-disclosure and interaction goals. *Journal of Experimental Social Psychology, 18*, 501–512.

Bergen, H., Martin, G., & Richardson, A. (2003). Sexual abuse and suicidal behavior: A model constructed from a large community sample of adolescents. *Journal of the American Academy of Child & Adolescent Psychiatry, 42*, 1301–1309.

Berkowitz, C. D. (2000). The long-term medical consequences of sexual abuse. In R. M. Reece, *Treatment of child abuse: Common ground for mental health, medical, and legal practitioners.* Baltimore, MD: Johns Hopkins University Press.

Berliner, L,, & Elliott, D. M. (2002). Sexual abuse of children. In J. E. B. Myers, L. Berliner, J Briere, C. T. Hendrix, & C. Jenny, *The APSAC handbook on child maltreatment (2nd ed.).* Thousand Oaks, CA: Sage Publications.

Bernburg, J. G., & Thorlindsson, T. (2005). Violent values, conduct norms, and youth aggression: A multilevel study in Iceland. *Sociological Quarterly, 46*, 457–478.

Berndt, T. J. (1999). Friends' influence on students' adjustment to school. *Educational Psychologist, 34*, 15–28.

Berndt, T. J. (2004). Children's friendships: Shifts over a half-century in perspectives on their development and their effects. *Merrill-Palmer Quarterly, 50*, (3), *Special issue: The Maturing of the Human Developmental Sciences: Appraising Past, Present, and Prospective Agendas*, 206–223.

Berndt, T. J., & Perry, T. B. (1986). Children's perceptions of friendships as supportive relationships. *Developmental Psychology, 22*, 640–648.

Berndt, T. J. (1981). Relations between social cognition, nonsocial cognition, and social behavior: The case of friendship. In J. Flavell & L. Ross (Eds.), *Social cognitive development: Frontiers and possible futures* (pp. 176–200). Cambridge, England: Cambridge University Press.

Bernstein, N. (2004, March 7). Behind fall in pregnancy, a new teenage culture of restraint. *The New York Times, 1*, 20.

Bernstein, N. (2006, April 26). Student's prize is a trip into immigration limbo. *The New York Times*, A1.

Berrick, J. D. (1998). When children cannot remain home: Foster family care and kinship care. *Future of Children, 8*, 72–87.

Bersamin, M. M., Walker, S., Fisher, D. A., & Grube, J. W. (2006). Correlates of oral sex and vaginal intercourse in early and middle adolescence. *Journal of Research on Adolescence, 16*, 59–68.

Berscheid, E., & Walster, E. (1974). Physical attractiveness. In G. Lindzey & E. Aronson (Eds.), *Handbook of social psychology* (3rd ed.). New York: Random House.

Bertelsen, A., & Flanagan, C. A. (2005). Political and civic development. In C. B. Fisher & R. M. Lerner (Eds.), *Encyclopedia of applied developmental science* (pp. 1168–1171). Thousand Oaks, CA: Sage.

Best, D. L. (2004). Gender roles in childhood and adolescence. In U. P. Gielen & J. Roopnarine (Eds.), *Childhood and adolescence: Cross-cultural perspectives and applications* (pp. 199–228). Westport, CT: Praeger Publishers/Greenwood Publishing Group.

Betancourt, H., & Lopez, S. R. (1993). The study of culture, ethnicity, and race in American psychology. *American Psychologist, 48*, 1586–1596.

Betancourt, T. S., (2005). Stressors, supports and the social ecology of displacement: Psychosocial dimensions of an emergency education program for Chechen adolescents displaced in Ingushetia, Russia. *Culture, Medicine and Psychiatry, 29*, 309–340.

Beyers, W., Goossens, L., Vansant, I., & Moors, E. (2003). Structural model of autonomy in middle and late adolescence: Connectedness, separation, detachment, and agency. *Journal of Youth and Adolescence, 32*, 351–365.

Bialystok, E., McBride-Chang, C., & Luk, G. (2005). Bilingualism, language proficiency, and learning to read in two writing systems. *Journal of Educational Psychology, 97*, 580.

Biddle, B. J. (2001). *Social class, poverty, and education.* London: Falmer Press.

Bierman, L. B. (2003). *Peer rejection: Developmental processes and intervention strategies.* New York: Guilford Press.

Biernat, M, Vescio, T. K., & Theno, S. A. (1996). Values and prejudice: Toward understanding the impact of American values on outgroup attitudes. In C. Seligman, J. M. Olson, & M. P. Zanna, *The psychology of values: The Ontario symposium, Vol. 8.* Hillsdale, NJ: Lawrence Erlbaum Associates, Inc.

Bigelow, B. J., Tesson, G., & Lewko, J. (1999). The contextual influences of sibling and dating relations on adolescents' personal relations and their close friends, dating partners, and parents: The Sullivan-Piaget-Hartup hypothesis considered. In J. A. McClellan & M. J. V. Pugh (Eds.), *The role of peer groups in adolescent social identity: Exploring the importance of stability and change* (pp. 71–86). San Francisco: Jossey-Bass.

Bingham, C. R., & Crocket, L. J. (1996). Longitudinal adjustment patterns of boys and girls experiencing early, middle, and late sexual intercourse. *Developmental Psychology, 32*, 647–658.

Birndorf, S., Ryan, S. Auinger, P., & Aten, M. (2005). High self-esteem among adolescents: Longitudinal trends, sex differences, and protective factors. *Journal of Adolescent Health, 37*, 194–201.

Bishop, J. A., & Inderbitzen, H. M. (1995). Peer acceptance and friendship: An investigation of their relation to self-esteem. *Journal of Early Adolescence, 15*, 476–489.

Bjorklund, D. F., & Ellis, B. (2005). Evolutionary psychology and child development: An emerging synthesis. In B. J. Ellis, *Origins of the social mind: Evolutionary psychology and child development.* New York: Guilford Press.

Black, K. (2002). Associations between adolescent-mother and adolescent-best friend interactions. *Adolescence, 37*, 235–253.

Blank, M., & White, S. J. (1999). Activating the zone of proximal development in school: Obstacles and solutions. In P. Llyod, & C. Fernyhough (Eds.), *Lev Vygotsky: Critical assessments: The zone of proximal development, Vol. III.* New York: Routledge.

Blasi, H., & Bjorklund, D. F. (2003). Evolutionary developmental psychology: A new tool for better understanding human ontogeny. *Human Development, 46*, 259–281.

Blum, R., & Rinehart, P. (2000). *Reducing the risk: Connections that make a difference in the lives of youth.* Minneapolis: Division of General Pediatrics and Adolescent Health, University of Minnesota.

Blumenthal, S. (2000). Developmental aspects of violence and the institutional response. *Criminal Behaviour & Mental Health, 10*, 185–198.

Blustein, D. L, & Palladino, D. E. (1991). Self and identity in late adolescence: A theoretical and empirical integration. *Journal of Adolescent Research, 6*, 437–453.

Blyth, D. A., Hill, J. P., & Thiel, K. S. (1982). Early adolescents' significant others: Grade and gender differences in perceived relationships with familial and nonfamilial adults and young people. *Journal of Youth and Adolescence, 11*, 425–450.

Bochner, S. (1996). The learning strategies of bilingual versus monolingual students. *British Journal of Educational Psychology, 66*, 83–93.

Bogenschneider, K., Wu, M. -Y., Raffaelli, M., & Tsay, J. C. (1998). Parent influences on adolescent peer orientation and substance use: The interface of parenting practices and values. *Child Development, 69*, 1672–1688.

Bolger, N., Zuckerman, A., & Kessler, R. C. (2000). Invisible support and adjustment to stress. *Journal of Personality and Social Psychology, 79*, 953–961.

Bonds, D. D., Gondoli, D. M., Sturge-Apple, M. L., & Salem, L. N. (2002). Parenting stress as a mediator of the relation between parenting support and optimal parenting. *Parenting: Science and Practice, 2*, 409–435

Boonstra, H. (2002). Teen pregnancy: Trends and lessons learned. *The Guttmacher Report on Public Policy, 5*, 27–35.

Borders, A., Earleywine, M., & Huey, S. J. (2004). Predicting problem behaviors with multiple expectancies: Expanding expectancy-value theory. *Adolescence, 39*, 539–550.

Borland, M. V., & Howsen, R. M. (2004). An examination f the effect of elementary school size on student academic achievement. *International Review of Education, 49*, 463–474.

Bornstein, M. H., & Lamb, M. E. (Eds.). (2005). *Developmental science.* Mahwah, NJ: Lawrence Erlbaum Associates.

Bosma, H. A., & Koops, W. (2004). Social cognition in adolescence: A tribute to Sandy (A. E.) Jackson (1937–2003). *European Journal of Developmental Psychology, 14*, Special issue: Social cognition in adolescence: It's developmental significance, 281–288.

Bosman, J. (2005, October 13). Putting the gym back in gym class. *The New York Times*, Sec G., p. 10.

Botvin, G. J., Epstein, J. A., Schinke, S. P., & Diaz, T. (1994). Predictors of cigarette smoking among inner-city minority youth. *Journal of Developmental and Behavioral Pediatrics, 15,* 67–73.

Boul, L. A. (2003). Men's health and middle age. *Evolution & Gender, 5,* 5–22

Bourne, V. & Todd, B. (2004). When left means right: An explanation of the left cradling bias in terms of right hemisphere specializations. *Developmental Science, 7,* 19–24.

Bourque, L. M. (2005). Leave no standardized test behind. In R. P. Phelps, *Defending standardized testing.* Mahwah, NJ: Lawrence Erlbaum Associates.

Bowen, D. J., Kahl, K., Mann, S. L., & Peterson, A. V. (1991). Descriptions of early triers. *Addictive Behaviors, 16,* 95–101.

Bowen, N. K., & Bowen, G. L. (1999). Effects of crime and violence in neighborhoods and schools on the school behavior and performance of adolescents. *Journal of Adolescent Research, 14,* 319–342.

Bowlby, J. (1951). Maternal care and mental health. *Bulletin of the World Health Organization, 3,* 355–534.

Boyd, G. M., Howard, J., & Zucker, R. A. (Eds.) (1995). *Alcohol problems among adolescents: Current directions in prevention research.* Hillsdale, NJ: Erlbaum.

Boyd-Wilson, B. M., McClure, J., & Walkey, F. H. (2004). Are wellbeing and illusory perceptions linked? The answer may be yes, but. . . *Australian Journal of Psychology, 56,* 1–9.

Bradford, K., Barber, B. K., Olsen, J. A., Maughan, S. L, Erickson, L. D., Ward, D., et al. (2004). A multi-national study of interparental conflict, parenting, and adolescent functioning: South Africa, Bangladesh, China, India, Bosnia, Germany, Palestine, Colombia, and the United States. *Marriage & Family Review, 35, Special issue: Parenting Styles in Diverse Perspectives,* 107–137.

Bradley, E. (2005, June 19). Grand Theft Auto; Lawsuit claims "Grand Theft Auto" trained teen to kill. *60 Minutes.*

Bradley, M. J. (2004). *Yes, your parents are crazy: A teen survival handbook.* Gig Harbor, WA: Harbor Press.

Branscombe, N. R., Ellemers, N., & Spears, R. (1999). The context and content of social identity threat. In N. Ellemers, R. Spears, & B. Doosje, *Social identity: Context commitment, content.* Oxford, England: Blackwell Science.

Brehm, S. S. (1992). *Intimate relationships* (2nd ed.). New York: McGraw-Hill.

Brehm, S. S., & Brehm, J. W. (1981). *Psychological reactance.* New York: Academic Press.

Bremner, J. D. (2003). Long-term effects of childhood abuse on brain and neurobiology. *Child and Adolescent Psychiatric Clinics of North America, 12,* 271–292.

Brendgen, M., Wanner, B., Morin, A. J. S., & Vitaro, F. (2005). Relations with parents and with peers, temperament, and trajectories of depressed mood during early adolescence. *Journal of Abnormal Child Psychology, 33,* 579–594.

Brendt, T. J. (2004). Children's friendships: Shifts over a half-century in perspectives on their development and their effects. *Merrill-Palmer Quarterly, 50, Special issue: The Maturing of the Human Developmental Sciences: Appraising Past, Present, and Prospective Agendas,* 206–223.

Brockman, D. D. (2003). *From Late Adolescence to Young Adulthood.* Madison, CT: International Universities Press, 2003

Brodsky, S. L. (2004). Ingratiation. In S. L. Brodsky, *Coping with cross-examination and other pathways to effective testimony.* Washington, DC: American Psychological Association.

Broman, C. L. (2005). Stress, Race and Substance Use in College. *College Student Journal, 39,* 340–352.

Bronfenbrenner, U. (1989). Ecological systems theory. In R. Vasta (Ed.), *Six theories of child development.* Greenwich, CT: JAI Press.

Bronfenbrenner, U. (2000). Ecological theory. In A. Kazdin (Ed.), *Encyclopedia of psychology.* Washington, DC, and New York: American Psychological Association/Oxford University Press.

Brook, U., & Tepper, I. (1997). High school students' attitudes and knowledge of food consumption and body image: Implications for school-based education. *Patient Education & Counseling, 30,* 282–288.

Brooks, R. B. (1994). Children at risk: Fostering resilience and hope. *American Journal of Orthopsychiatry, 64,* 545–553.

Brooks-Gunn, J., & Paikoff, R. (1997). Sexuality and developmental transitions during adolescence. In J. Schulenberg, J. L. Maggs, & K. Hurrelman (Eds.), *Health risks and developmental transitions during adolescence* (pp. 190–220). New York: Cambridge University Press.

Brooks-Gunn, J., & Reiter, E. (1990). The role of pubertal processes. In S. S. Feldman & G. R. Elliott (Eds.), *At the threshold: The developing adolescent.* Cambridge, MA: Harvard University Press.

Brooks-Gunn, J., & Warren, M. P. (1989). Biological contributions to affective expression in young adolescent girls. *Child Development, 60,* 372–385.

Brooks-Gunn, J., Klebanov, P. K., & Duncan, G. J. (1996). Ethnic differences in children's intelligence test scores: Role of economic deprivation, home environment, and maternal characteristics. *Child Development, 67,* 396–408.

Brown, A. L., & Ferrara, R. A. (1999). Diagnosing zones of proximal development. In P. Lloyd, & C. Fernyhough (Eds.), *Lev Vygotsky: Critical assessments: The zone of proximal development, Vol. III.* New York: Routledge.

Brown, B. (1990). Peer groups. In S. Feldman & G. Elliott (Eds.), *At the threshold: The developing adolescent.* Cambridge, MA: Harvard University Press.

Brown, B. (2004). Adolescents' relationship with peers. In R. M. Lerner, & L. Steinberg, *Handbook of Adolescent Psychology, 2ⁿᵈ Edition.* New York: John Wiley & Sons.

Brown, B. B. (1999). "You're going out with who?": Peer group influences on adolescent romantic relationships. In W. Furman, B. B. Brown, & C. Feiring, (Eds.), *The development of romantic relationships in adolescence* (pp. 291–329). New York: Cambridge University Press.

Brown, B. B., & Klute, C. (2006), Friendships, cliques, and crowds. In G. R. Adams & M. D. (Eds.), Berzonsky, *Blackwell handbook of adolescence* (pp. 330–348). Malden, MA: Blackwell Publishing.

Brown, B. B., Eicher, S. A., & Petrie, S. (1986). The importance of peer group ("crowd") affiliation in adolescence. *Journal of Adolescence, 9,* 73–96.

Brown, B. B., Lohr, M. J., & Trujillo, C. M. (1990). Multiple crowds and multiple lifestyles: Adolescents' perceptions of peer group characteristics. In R. E. Muuss, (Ed.), *Adolescent behavior and society: A book of readings.* New York: Random House.

Brown, E. C., Catalano, R. F., Fleming, C. B., Haggerty, K. P., Abbott, R. D., Cortes, R. R., et al. (2005). Mediator effects in the social development model: An examination of constituent theories. *Criminal Behaviour and Mental Health, 15,* 221–235.

Brown, J. D. (2002). Mass media influences on sexuality. *Journal of Sex Research, 39,* 42–45.

Brown, J. D., & McGill, K. L. (1989). The cost of good fortune: When positive life events produce negative health consequences. *Journal of Personality and Social Psychology, 57,* 1103–1110.

Brown, J. D., & Dutton, K. A. (1995). Truth and consequences: the costs and benefits of accurate self-knowledge. *Personality and Social Psychology Bulletin, 21,* 1288–1296.

Brown, L. M., Bradley, M. M., & Lang, P. J. (2006). Affective reactions to pictures of ingroup and outgroup members. *Biological Psychology, 71,* 303–311.

Browne, B. A. (1998). Gender stereotypes in advertising on children's television in the 1990s: A cross-national analysis. *Journal of Advertising, 27,* 83–96.

Buchanan, C. M., Eccles, J. S., & Becker, J. B. (1992). Are adolescents the victims of raging hormones? Evidence for activational effects of hormones on moods and behavior at adolescence. *Psychological Bulletin, 111,* 62–107.

Buchanan, C. M., Maccoby, E. E., & Dornbusch, S. M. (1996). *Adolescents after divorce.* Cambridge, MA: Harvard University Press.

Buchanan, C., Maccoby, E., & Dornbusch, S. (1991). Caught between parents: Adolescents' experience in divorced homes. *Child Development, 62,* 1008–1029.

Buckley, M., Storino, M., & Saarni, C. (2003). Promoting emotional competence in children and adolescents: Implications for school psychologists. *School Psychology Quarterly, 18,* 177–191.

Budris, J. (1998, April 26). Raising their children's children. *Boston Globe 55–Plus,* pp. 8–9, 14–15.

Buhrmester, D. (1996), Need fulfillment, interpersonal competence, and the developmental contexts of early adolescent friendship. In W. Bukowski, A. Newcomb, & W. Hartup (Eds.), *The company they keep: Friendship in childhood and adolescence* (pp. 158–185) New York: Cambridge University Press.

Buhrmester, D. (2001, April) *Romantic development: Does age at which romantic involvement start to matter?* Paper presented at the meeting of the Society for Research in Child Development, Minneapolis, MN.

Bukowski, W. M. (2003). Peer relationships. In M. H. Bornstein, L. Davidson, C. L. M. Keyes, & K. A. Moore (Eds.), *Well-being: Positive development across the life course* (pp. 221–234). Mahwah, NJ: Lawrence Erlbaum Associates.

Bukowski, W. M., Sippola, L. K., & Newcomb, A. F. (2000). Variations in patterns of attraction to same- and other-sex peers during early adolescence. *Developmental Psychology, 36,* 147–154.

Bulmahn, G., & Krakel, M. (2002). Overeducated workers as an insurance device. *Labour, 16,* 383–402.

Bumpus, M. F., Crouter, A. C., & McHale, S. M. (2001). Parental autonomy granting during adolescence: Exploring gender differences in context. *Developmental Psychology, 37,* 163–173.

Burager, J. M. (1992). Desire for control and academic performance. *Canadian Journal of Behavioural Science Revue canadienne des Sciences du comportement, 24,* Apr 1992. Special issue: The psychology of control. pp. 147–155.

Burleson, K., Leach, C. W., & Harrington, D. M. (2005). Upward social comparison and self-concept: Inspiration and inferiority among art students in an advanced programme. *British Journal of Social Psychology, 44,* 109–123.

Burnett, P. C., Pillay, H., & Dart, B. C. (2003). The influences of conceptions of learning and learner self-concept on high school students' approaches to learning. *School Psychology International, 24,* 54–66.

Burns, E. (2003). *A handbook for supplementary aids and services: A best practice and IDEA guide "to enable children with disabilities to be educated with nondisabled children to the maximum extent appropriate.* Springfield, IL: Charles C Thomas Publisher.

Burton, L., & Jarrett, R. (2000). In the mix, yet on the margins: The place of families in urban neighborhood and child development research. *Journal of Marriage and the Family, 62,* 1114–1135.

Bushman, B. J. (1993). Human aggression while under the influence of alcohol and other drugs: An integrative research review. *Current Directions in Psychological Science, 2,* 148–152.

Bushman, B. J., & Anderson, C. A. (2002). Violent video games and hostile expectations: A test of the General Aggression Model. *Personality and Social Psychology Bulletin, 28,* 1679–1689.

Buss, D. (2003). *Evolutionary psychology.* Boston: Allyn & Bacon.

Bussey, K. (1992). Lying and truthfulness: Children's definition, standards, and evaluative reactions. *Child Development, 63,* 1236–1250.

Butters, J. (2005). Promoting healthy choices: The importance of differentiating between ordinary and high risk cannabis use among high-school students. *Substance Use and Misuse, 40,* 845–855.

Byra, M. (2004). Applying a task progression to the reciprocal style of teaching. *Journal of Physical Education, Recreation & Dance, 75,* 42–47.

Byrne, B. (2000). Relationships between anxiety, fear, self-esteem, and coping strategies in adolescence. *Adolescence, 35,* 201–215.

Cafri, G., Thompson, J. K., Ricciardelli, L., McCabe, M., Smolak, L., & Yesalis, C. (2005). Pursuit of the muscular ideal: Physical and psychological consequences and putative risk factors. *Clinical Psychology Review, 25,* 215–239.

Cai, Y., Reeve., J. M., & Robinson, D. T. (2002). Home schooling and teaching style: Comparing the motivating styles of home school and public school teachers. *Journal of Educational Psychology, 94,* 372–380.

Caino, S., Kelmansky, D., Lejarraga, H., & Adamo, P. (2004). Short-term growth at adolescence in healthy girls. *Annals of Human Biology, 31,* 182–195.

Caldera, Y. M., & Sciaraffa, M. A. (1998). Parent-toddler play with feminine toys: Are all dolls the same? *Sex Roles, 39,* 657–668.

Callahan, C. M., & Kyburg, R. M. (2005). Talented and gifted youth. In D. L. DuBois & M. J. Karcher, *Handbook of youth mentoring.* Thousand Oaks, CA: Sage Publications.

Calvert, S. L., Kotler, J. A., Zehnder, S. & Shockey, E. (2003). Gender stereotyping in children's reports about educational and informational television programs. *Media Psychology, 5,* 139–162.

Cameron, J. L. (2004). Interrelationships between hormones, behavior, and affect during adolescence: Complex relationships exist between reproductive hormones, stress-related hormones, and the activity of neural systems that regulate behavioral affect. Comments on part III. *Annuals of the New York Academy of Sciecnes, 1021,* 134–142.

Cami, J., & Farré, M., (2003). Drug addiction. *New England Journal of Medicine, 349,* 975–986.

Cantor, N., Pittman, T. S., & Jones, E. E. (1982). Choice and attitude attributions: The influence of constraint information on attributions across levels of generality. *Social Cognition, 1,* 1–20.

Capaldi, D. M., & Shortt, J. W. (2006). Understanding conduct problems in adolescence from a lifespan perspective. In G. R. Adams & M. D. Berzonsky (Eds.), *Blackwell handbook of adolescence* (pp. 470–493). Malden, MA: Blackwell Publishing.

Capaldi, D. M., Stoolmiller, M., Clark, S., & Owen, L. D. (2002). Heterosexual risk behaviors in at-risk young men from early adolescence to young adulthood: Prevalence, prediction, and association with STD contraction. *Developmental Psychology, 38,* 394–406.

Cardman, M. (2004). Rising GPAs, course loads a mystery to researchers. *Education Daily, 37,* 1–3.

Carlo, G., Eisenberg, N., Troyer, D., Switzer, G., & Speer, A. L. (1991). The altruistic personality: In what contexts is it apparent? *Journal of Personality and Social Psychology, 61,* 450–458.

Carlo, G., Fabes, R. A., Laible, D., & Kupanoff, K. (1999). Early adolescence and prosocial/moral behavior II: The role of social and contextual influences. *Journal of Early Adolescence, 19,* Special issue: Prosocial and moral development in early adolescence, Part II, 133–147.

Carnegie Council on Adolescent Development. (1995). *Great transitions: Preparing adolescents for a new century.* New York: Carnegie Foundation.

Carnegie Task Force on Meeting the Needs of Young Children. (1994). *Starting points: Meeting the needs of our youngest children.* New York: Carnegie Corporation.

Carpendale, J. I. M. (2000). Kohlberg and Piaget on stages and moral reasoning. *Developmental Review, 20,* 181–205.

Carpenter, D. M., H., Flowers, N., & Mertens, S. B. (2004). High expectations for every student. *Middle School Journal, 35,* 64.

Carpenter, S. (2000, October). Human Genome Project director says psychologists will play a critical role in the initiative's success. *Monitor on Psychology,* 14–15.

Carpenter, S. (2001). Sleep deprivation may be undermining teen health. *APA Monitor, 32,* 42–45.

Carrel, A. L., Clark, R. R., Peterson, S. E., Nemeth, B. A., Sullivan, J., & Allen, D. B. (2005). Improvement of fitness, body composition, and insulin sensitivity in overweight children in a school-based exercise program: A randomized, controlled study. *Archives of Pediatric Adolescent Medicine, 159,* 963–968.

Carsakadon, M. A. (Ed.). (2002). *Adolescent sleep patterns: Biological, social, and psychological influences.* New York: Cambridge University Press.

Carter, C., & Weaver, C. K. (2003). *Violence and the Media.* Buckingham/Philadelphia, PA: Open University Press.

Case, R. (1991). Stages in the development of the young child's first sense of self. *Developmental Review, 11,* 210–230.

Case, R., & Okamoto, Y. (1996). The role of central conceptual structures in the development of children's thought. *Monographs of the Society for Research in Child Development, 61,* v–265.

Cashman, H. R. (2005). Identities at play: Language preference and group membership in bilingual talk in interaction. *Journal of Pragmatics, 37, Special issue: Conversational Code-Switching,* 301–315.

Caskey, C. (2005). Snooze factor: Educators are starting to hear the ticking of sleepy teens' body clocks. *Sacramento Bee,* J1.

Castañeda, D., & Burns-Glover, A. (2004). Gender, sexuality, and intimate relationships. In M. A. Paludi (Ed.), *Praeger guide to the psychology of gender* (pp. 69–92). Westport, CT: Praeger Publishers/Greenwood Publishing Group.

Catell, R. B. (1967). *The scientific analysis of personality.* Chicago: Aldine.

Catell, R. B. (1987). *Intelligence: Its structure, growth, and action.* Amsterdam: North-Holland.

Cath, S., & Shopper, M. (2001). *Stepparenting: Creating and recreating families in America today.* Hillsdale, NJ: Analytic Press, Inc.

Caughy, M. O., & Franzini, L. (2005). Neighborhood correlates of cultural differences in perceived effectiveness of parental disciplinary tactics. *Science and Practice, 5,* 119–151.

Centers for Disease Control and Prevention. (1998). *Youth risk behavior surveillance—United States, 1997.* Atlanta: Author.

Centers for Disease Control and Prevention. (2004). *Youth risk behavior surveillance—United States, 2004.* Atlanta: Centers for Disease Control.

Centers for Disease Control and Prevention. (2005a). *The Surgeon General's report for kids about smoking.* Retrieved June 15, 2006, from http://www. cdc. gov/tobacco/sgr/sgr4kids/realdeal. htm

Centers for Disease Control and Prevention. (2005b). *Tips for youth: Facts you should know.* Retrieved June 15, 2006, from http://www. cdc. gov/tobacco/tips_4_youth/facts. htm

Centers for Disease Control and Prevention. (2005c). *What you(th) should know about tobacco.* Retrieved June 15, 2006, from http://www. cdc.gov/tobacco/educational_materials/KIDTIPS4sm2.pdf

Chadha, N., & Misra, G. (2004). Patterns of prosocial reasoning in Indian children. *Psychology and Developing Societies, 16,* 159–186.

Chaiken, M. R. (2000). Violent neighborhoods, violent kids. *Juvenile Justice Bulletin,* March, 2000. *Office of Juvenile Justice and Delinquency Prevention.* Washington, DC.

Chaiklin, S. (2003). The zone of proximal development in Vygotsky's analysis of learning and instruction. In A. Kozulin and B. Gindis (Eds.), *Vygotsky's educational theory in cultural context.* New York: Cambridge University Press.

Chamberlain, K., & Zika, S. (1990). The minor events approach to stress: Support for the use of daily hassles. *British Journal of Psychology, 81,* 469–481.

Chan, E. (2006). Teacher experiences of culture in the curriculum. *Journal of Curriculum Studies, 38,* 161.

Chanal, J. P., Marsh, H. W., & Sarazin, P. G. (2005). Big-fish-little-pond effects on gymnastics self-concept: Social comparison processes in a physical setting. *Journal of Sport & Exercise Psychology, 27,* 53–70.

Chang, E. C. (1998). Hope, problem-solving ability, and coping in a college student population: Some implications for theory and practice. *Journal of Clinical Psychology, 54,* 953–962.

Chao, R. K. (1994). Beyond parental control and authoritarian parenting style: Understanding Chinese parenting through the cultural notion of training. *Child Development, 65,* 1111–1119.

Chatterji, M. (2004). Evidence on "What works": An argument for extended-term mixed-method (ETMM) evaluation designs. *Educational Researcher, 33,* 3–14.

Chen, H. (2006). Digitization of the experience sampling method: Transformation, implementation, and assessment. *Social Science Computer Review, 24,* 106–118.

Chen, J., & Gardner, H. (2005). Assessment based on multiple-intelligences theory. In D. P. Flanagan, & P. L. Harrison, (Eds.), *Contemporary intellectual assessment: Theories, tests, and issues.* New York, Guilford Press.

Chen, K., & Kandel, D. (2002). Relationship between extent of cocaine use and dependence among adolescents and adults in the United States. *Drug and Alcohol Dependence, 68,* 65–85.

Chen, X., Liu, M., Rubin, K. H., Cen, G., Gao, X., & Li, D. (2002). Sociability and prosocial orientation as predictors of youth adjustment: A seven-year longitudinal study in a Chinese sample. *International Journal of Behavioral Development, 26,* 128–136.

Chen, X., Rubin, K. H., & Li, Z. (1995). Social functioning and adjustment in Chinese children: A longitudinal study. *Developmental Psychology, 31,* 531–539

Chen-Yu, J. H., & Seock, Y-K. (2002). Adolescents' clothing purchase motivations, information sources, and store selection criteria: A comparison of male/female and impulse/nonimpulse shoppers. *Family & Consumer Sciences Research Journal, 31,* 50–77.

Cheng, C., & Cheung, M. W. L. (2005). Cognitive processes underlying coping flexibility: differentiation and integration. *Journal of Personality, 73,* 859–886.

Cheng, H., & Furnham, A. (2002). Personality, peer relations, and self-confidence as predictors of happiness and loneliness. *Journal of Adolescence, 25,* 327–339.

Cherney, I., Kelly-Vance, L., & Glover, K. (2003). The effects of stereotyped toys and gender on play assessment in children aged 18–47 months. *Educational Psychology, 23,* 95–105.

ChildStats. (2005). *America's children: Key national indicators of children's well-being 2005.* Washington, DC: Federal Interagency Forum on Child and Family Statistics.

Chua, H. F., Leu, J., & Nisbett, R. E. (2005). Culture and diverging views of social events. *Personality and Social Psychology Bulletin, 31,* 925–934.

Chun, J., & Springer, D. W. (2005). Correlates of depression among runaway adolescents in Korea. *Child Abuse & Neglect, 29,* 1433–1438.

Cicchetti, D. (1996). Child maltreatment: Implications for developmental theory and research. *Human Development, 39,* 18–39.

Cicchetti, D., & Toth, S. L. (1998). The development of depression in children and adolescents. *American Psychologist, 53,* 221–241.

Cillessen, A. H., Jiang, X. L., West, T. V., & Laszkowski, D. K. (2005). Predictors of dyadic friendship quality in adolescence. *International Journal of Behavioral Development, 29,* 165–172.

Ciricelli, V. G. (1995). *Sibling relationships across the life span.* New York: Plenum.

Claes, M., Lacourse, E., & Bouchard, C. (2003). Parental practices in late adolescence, a comparison of three countries: Canada, France and Italy. *Journal of Adolescence, 26,* 387–399.

Clark, M. (1989). Friendships and peer relations of Black adolescents. In L. Reginald (Ed.), *Black adolescents* (pp. 175–204). Berkeley, CA: Cobb & Henry.

Clarke, G. N., Hawkins, W., Murphy, M., & Sheeber, L. B. (1995). Targeted prevention of unipolar depressive disorder in an at-risk sample of high school adolescents: A randomized trial of group cognitive intervention. *Journal of the American Academy of Child & Adolescent Psychiatry, 34,* 312–321.

Clarke-Stewart, A., & Friedman, S. (1987). *Child development: Infancy through adolescence.* New York: Wiley.

Clary, E. G., & Snyder, M. (2002). Community involvement: Opportunities and challenges in socializing adults to participate in society. *Journal of Social Issues, 58,* 581–591.

Clay, D., Vignoles, V. L., & Dittmar, H. (2005). Body image and self-esteem among adolescent girls: Testing the influence of sociocultural factors. *Journal of Research on Adolescence, 15,* 451–477.

Cleveland, H. H. (2003). The influence of female and male risk on the occurrence of sexual intercourse within adolescent relationships. *Journal of Research on Adolescence, 13,* 81–112.

Clinton, A. M., & Anderson, L. R. (1999). Social and emotional loneliness: Gender differences and relationships with self-monitoring and perceived control. *Journal of Black Psychology, 25,* 61–77.

Coates, S. W., Rosenthan, J. L., & Schechter D. S. (Eds.). (2003). *September 11: Trauma and human bonds (Relational Perspectives Book Series Volume 23).* Hillsdale, NJ: The Analytic Press.

Cobb, L. T. (2006, April 8). A young blade. *Daily Hampshire Gazette,* pp. C9–C10.

Cohen, D. (1996). Law, social policy, and violence: The impact of regional cultures. *Journal of Personality and Social Psychology, 70,* 961–978.

Cohen, L. H., Gunthert, K. C., & Butler, A. C. (2006). Stress, coping, and outcome in cognitive therapy. In R. R. Bootzin & P. E. McKnight (Eds.), *Strengthening research methodology: Psychological measurement and evaluation* (pp. 63–74). Washington, DC: American Psychological Association.

Cohen, L., and Cashon, C. (2003). Infant perception and cognition. In R. Lerner and M. Easterbrooks (Eds.), *Handbook of psychology: Developmental psychology,* Vol. 6 (pp. 267–291). New York: Wiley.

Cohen, P., Slomkowski, C., & Robins, L. N. (Eds.). (1999). *Historical and geographical influences on psychopathology.* Mahwah, NJ: Erlbaum.

Cohen, S. (2004, November). Social relationships and health. *American Psychologist,* 676–684.

Cohen, S., Doyle, W. J., Turner, R., Alper, C. M., & Skoner, D. P. (2003). Sociability and susceptibility to the common cold. *Psychological Science, 14,* 389–395.

Cohen, S., Tyrrell, D. A., & Smith, A. P. (1993). Negative life events, perceived stress, negative affect, and susceptibility of the common cold. *Journal of Personality and Social Psychology, 64,* 131–140.

Coie, J. D. (2004). The impact of negative social experiences on the development of antisocial behavior. In J. B. Kupersmidt & K. A. Dodge (Eds.), *Children's peer relations: From development to intervention.* Washington, DC: American Psychological Association.

Cokley, K. (2003). What do we know about the motivation of African American students? Challenging the "anti-intellectual" myth. *Harvard Educational Review, 73,* 524–558.

Colby, A., & Damon, W. (1987). Listening to a different voice: A review of Gilligan's in a different voice. In M. R. Walsh (Ed.), *The psychology of women.* New Haven, CT: Yale University Press.

Colby, A., & Kohlberg, L. (1987). *The measurement of moral adjudgment* (Vols. 1–2). New York: Cambridge University Press.

Cole, D. A., Maxwell, S. E., Martin, J. M., Peeke, L. G., Seroczynski, A. D., Tram, J. M., Joffman, K. B., Ruiz, M. D., Jacquez, F., & Maschman, T. (2001). The development of multiple domains of child and adolescent self-concept: A cohort sequential longitudinal design. *Child Development, 72,* 1723–1746.

Coleman, C. A., Friedman, A. G., & Burright, R. G. (1998). The relationship of daily stress and health-related behaviors to adolescents' cholesterol levels. *Adolescence, 33,* 447–460.

Coles, R., & Stokes, G. (1985). *Sex and the American teenager.* New York: Harper & Row.

College Board (2005). 2001 *College Bound Seniors Are the Largest, Most Diverse Group in History.* NY: College Board.

Collett, B. R., Gimpel, G. A., Greenson, J. N., & Gunderson, T. L. (2001). Assessment of discipline styles among parents of preschool through school-age children. *Journal of Psychopathology and Behavioral Assessment, 23,* 163–170.

Collin, C. (2006). Spatial-frequency thresholds for object categorization at basic and subordinate levels. *Perception, 35,* 41–52. Retrieved May 27, 2007, from PsychINFO database.

Collins, A., & van Dulmen, M. (2006). Friendships and romance in emerging adulthood: Assessing distinctiveness in close relationships. In J. J. Arnett & J. L. Tanner (Eds.), *Emerging adults in America: Coming of age in the 21st century* (pp. 219–234). Washington, DC: American Psychological Association.

Collins, W. A. (1990). Parent-child relationships in the transition to adolescence. Continuity and change in interaction. In G. R. Adams, T. Gullotta, & R. Montemayor, *From childhood to adolescence: A transitional period?* Thousand Oaks, CA: Sage Publications.

Collins, W. A. (2003). More than a myth: The developmental significance of romantic relationships during adolescence. *Journal of Research on Adolescents, 13,* 1–24.

Collins, W. A., & Laursen, B. (2004). Changing relationships, changing youth: Interpersonal contexts of adolescent development. *Journal of Early Adolescence, Special issue: Memorial Issue: Adolescence: The Legacy of Hershel and Ellen Thornburg, 24,* 55–62.

Collins, W. A., & Laursen, B. (2004). Parent-adolescent relationships and influences. In R. Lerner & L. Steinberg (Eds.), *Handbook of adolescent psychology* (2nd ed., pp. 000) New York: Wiley.

Collins, W. A., & Repinski, D. J. (1994). Relationships during adolescence: Continuity and change in interpersonal perspective. In R. Montemayor, G. R. Adams, & T. P. Gullota (Eds.), *Advances in adolescent development: An annual book series; Vol. 6* (pp. 7–36). Thousand Oaks, CA: Sage Publications.

Colvin, C. R., & Block, J. (1994). Do positive illusions foster mental health? An examination of the Taylor and Brown formulation. *Psychological Bulletin, 116,* 3–20.

Colvin, C. R., Block, J., & Funder, D. C. (1995). Overly positive self-evaluations and personality: Negative implications for mental health. *Journal of Personality and Social Psychology, 68,* 1152–1162.

Compas, B. E. (2004). Processes of risk and resilience during adolescence: Linking contexts and individuals. In R. M. Lerner & L. Steinberg (Eds.), *Handbook of adolescent psychology* (2nd ed.) New York: Wiley.

Compton, R., & Weissman, D. (2002). Hemispheric asymmetries in global-local perception: Effects of individual differences in neuroticism. *Laterality, 7,* 333–350.

Comstock, G., & Scharrer, E. (1999). *Television: What's on, who's watching, and what it means.* San Diego, CA: Academic Press.

Condit, V. (1990). Anorexia nervosa: Levels of causation. *Human Nature, 1,* 391–413.

Conduct Problems Prevention Research Group. (2004a). The effects of the Fast Track Program on serious problem outcomes at the end of elementary school. *Journal of Clinical Child and Adolescent Psychology, 33,* 650–661.

Conduct Problems Prevention Research Group. (2004b). The Fast Track experiment: Translating the developmental model into a prevention design. In J. B. Kupersmidt & K. A. Dodge (Eds.), *Children's peer relations: From development to intervention.* Washington, DC: American Psychological Association.

Conger, K. J., Rueter, M. A., & Conger, R. D. (2000). The role of economic pressure in the lives of parents and their adolescents: The Family Stress Model. In L. J. Crockett & R. K. Silbereisen (Eds.), *Negotiating adolescence in times of social change.* New York: Cambridge University Press.

Conger, R. D., & Lorenz, F. O. (2005). Predicting change in adolescent adjustment from change in marital problems. *Developmental Psychology, 41,* 812–823.

Conger, R. D., Jewsbury Conger, K., Matthews, L. S., & Elder, G. H., Jr. (1999). Pathways of economic influence on adolescent adjustment. *American Journal of Community Psychology, 27, Special issue: Prevention science, part 1,* 519–541.

Connolly, J., Craig, W., Goldberg, A., & Pepler, D. (1999). Conceptions of cross-sex friendships and romantic relationships in early adolescence. *Journal of Youth and Adolescence, 28,* 481–494.

Connor-Smith, J. K., & Compas, B. E. (2004). Coping as a moderator of relations between reactivity to interpersonal stress, health status, and internalizing problems. *Cognitive Therapy and Research, 28,* 347–368.

Cook, W. L. (2001). Interpersonal influence in family systems: A social relations model analysis. *Child Development, 72,* 1179–1197.

Cook, W. L. (2005). The SRM approach to family assessment: An introduction and case example. *European Journal of Psychological Assessment, 21,* 216–225.

Coontz, S. (2006). Romance and sex in adolescence and emerging adulthood. In A. C. Crouter & A. Booth (Eds.), *Romance and sex in adolescence and emerging adulthood: Risks and opportunities.* Mahwah, NJ: Erlbaum.

Cooper, A., & Sportolari, L. (1997). Romance in cyberspace: Understanding online attraction. *Journal of Sex Education & Therapy, 22,* 7–14.

Cooper, C. R. (1994). Cultural perspectives on continuity and change in adolescents' relationships. In R. Montemayor, G. R. Adams, & T. P. Gullotta (Eds), *Personal relationships during adolescence. Series Title: Advances in adolescent development: An annual book series; Vol. 6.* Thousand Oaks, CA: Sage.

Cooper, C. R., and Cooper, R. G. (1992). Links Between Adolescents' Relationships with Their Parents and Peers: Models, Evidence, and Mechanisms. In R. D. Parke and G. W. Ladd (eds.). *Family-Peer Relationships: Modes of Linkages.* Mahwah, NJ: Lawrence Erlbaum.

Cooper, C. R., Coll, C. T., Thorne, B., & Orellana, M. (2005). Beyond demographic categories: How immigration, ethnicity, and "race" matter for children's identities and pathways through school. In C. R. Cooper, C. T. Coll, T. W. Bartko, H. Davis, & C. Chatman (Eds.), *Developmental pathways through middle childhood: Rethinking contexts and diversity as resources.* Mahwah, NJ: Erlbaum.

Cooper, J., & Mackie, D. (1986). Video games and aggression in children. *Journal of Applied Social Psychology, 16,* 726–744.

Cooperative Institutional Research Program. (1990). *The American freshman: National norms for fall 1990.* Los Angeles: American Council on Education.

Corballis, P. (2003). Visuospatial processing and the right-hemisphere interpreter. *Brain & Cognition, 53,* 171–176.

Corenblum, B., & Meissner, C. A. (2006). Recognition of faces of ingroup and outgroup children and adults. *Journal of Experimental Child Psychology, 93,* 187–206.

Cossman, J. S. (2004). Parent's heterosexism and children's attitudes toward people with AIDS. *Sociological Spectrum, 24,* 319–339.

Costa, F. M., Jessor, R., & Turbin, M. S. (2005). The role of social contexts in adolescence: Context protection and context risk in the United States and China. *Applied Developmental Science, 9,* 67–85.

Costa, P. T., Jr., McCrae, R. R., & Siegler, I. C. (1999). Continuity and change over the adult life cycle: Personality and personality disorders. In C. R. Cloninger (Ed.), *Personality and psychopathology* (pp. 000). Washington, DC: American Psychiatric Association.

Costigan, A. T., Crocco, M. S., & Zumwalt, K. K. (2004). *Learning to teach in an age of accountability.* Mahwah, NJ: Lawrence Erlbaum Associates.

Cotman, C. W., & Berchtold, N. C. (2002). Exercise: A behavioral intervention to enhance brain health and plasticity. *Trends in Neurscience, 25,* 295–301.

Couzin, J. (2004, July 23). Volatile chemistry: Children and antidepressants. *Science, 305,* 468–470.

Cowan, P. A., Bradburn, I., & Cowan, C. P. (2005). Parents' working models of attachment: The intergenerational context of parenting and children's adaptation to school. In P. A. Cowan, C. P. Cowarn, J. C. Ablow, V. K. Johnson, & J. R. Measelle (Eds.), *The family context of parenting in children's adaptation to elementary school.* Mahwah, NJ: Erlbaum.

Côté, J. (2005). Editor's introduction. *Identity, 5,* 95–96.

Côté, J. E. (2005). *The postmodern critique of developmental perspectives.* Mahwah, NJ: Lawrence Erlbaum.

Craske, M. G. (2003). *Origins of phobias and anxiety disorders: Why more women than men?* Kidlington, Oxon, England: Elsevier.

Crawford, D., Houts, R., & Huston, T. (2002). Compatiability, leisure, and satisfaction in marital relationships. *Journal of Marriage & Family, 64,* 433–449.

Crawford, M., & Kaufman, M. R. (2006). Sex differences versus social processes in the construction of gender. In K. Dindia & D. J. Canary (Eds.), *Sex differences and similarities in communication* (2nd ed.). Mahwah, NJ: Erlbaum.

Crawford, M., & Unger, R. (2004). *Women and gender: A feminist psychology* (4th ed.). New York: McGraw-Hill.

Creighton, S., & Miller, R. (2003). Unprotected sexual intercourse in teenagers—causes and consequences. *Journal of Research and Social Health, 123,* 7–8.

Critser, G. (2003). *Fat land: How Americans became the fattest people in the world.* Boston: Houghton Mifflin.

Crocker, J., & Knight, K. M. (2005). Contingenices of self-worth. *Current Directions in Psychological Science, 14,* 200–203.

Crocker, J., & Park, L. E. (2004). The costly pursuit of self-esteem. *Psychological Bulletin, 150,* 392–414.

Crockett, L. J., & Crouter, A. C. (Eds.). (1995). Pathways through adolescence: Individual development in relation to social contexts. Hillsdale, NJ: Lawrence Erlbaum.

Crockett, L. J., Raffaelli, M., & Moilanen, K. (2006). Adolescent sexuality: Behavior and meaning. In G. R. Adams & M. D. Berzonsky (Eds.), *Blackwell handbook of adolescence.* Malden, MA: Blackwell Publishing.

Croizet, J., Després, G., Gauzins, M., Huguet, P., Leyens, J., & Méot, A. (2004). Stereotype threat undermines intellectual performance by triggering a disruptive mental load. *Personality and Social Psychology Bulletin, 30,* 721–731.

Croninger, R. G., & Lee, V. E. (2001). Social capital and dropping out of high school: Benefits to at-risk students of teachers' support and guidance. *Teachers College Record, 103,* 548–581.

Cross, W. (1995). The psychology of nigrescence: Revising the Cross model. In J. Ponterotto, J. Casas, L. Suzuki, & C. Alexander (Eds.), *Handbook of multicultural counseling.* Thousand Oaks, CA: Sage.

Crosscope-Happel, C., Hutchins, D. E., Getz, H. G., & Hayes, G. L. (2000). Male anorexia nervosa: A new focus. *Journal of Mental Health Counseling, 22,* 365–370.

Crouter, A. C., & Booth, A. (Eds.). (2006). *Romance and sex in adolescence and emerging adulthood.* Mahwah, NJ: Erlbaum.

Crowther, M., & Rodriguez, R. (2003). A stress and coping model of custodial grandparenting among African Americans. In B. Hayslip and J. Patrick (Eds.), *Working with custodial grandparents.* New York: Springer Publishing.

Crutchley, A. (2003). Bilingualism in development: language, literacy and cognition. *Child Language Teaching & Therapy, 19,* 365–367.

Crystal, D. S., Chen, C., Fuligni, A. J., & Stevenson, H. W. (1994). Psychological maladjustment and academic achievement: A cross-cultural study of Japanese, Chinese, and American high school students. *Child Development, 65,* 738–753.

Csikszentmihalyi, M. (1997). *Creativity: Flow and the psychology of discovery and invention.* New York: Basic-Books/Mastermind Series.

Csikszentmihaliyi, M., & Larson, R. (1984). *Being adolescent.* New York: Basic Books.

Csikszentmihalyi, M., & Larson, R. (1992) Validity and reliability of the Experience Sampling Method. In M. W. deVries (Ed.), *The experience of psychopathology: Investigating mental disorders in their natural settings* (pp. 000). New York: Cambridge University Press.

Cubbin, C., Santelli, J., Brindis, C. D., & Braveman, P. (2005). Neighborhood context and sexual behaviors among adolescents: findings from the national longitudinal study of adolescent health. *Perpsective on Sexual Reproductive Health, 37,* 125–134.

Curtis, W. J., & Cicchetti, D. (2003). Moving research on resilience into the 21st century: Theoretical and methodological considerations in examining the biological contributors to resilience. *Development and Psychopathology, 15,* 126–131.

Cvijanovich, N. Z., Cook, L. J., Mann, N. C., & Dean, J. M. (2001). A population-based study of crashes involving 16- and 17-year-old drivers: The potential benefit of graduated driver licensing restrictions. *Pediatrics, 107,* 632–637.

Daddis, C., & Smetana, J. (2005). Middle-class African American families' expectations for adolescents' behavioural autonomy. *International Journal of Behavioral Development, 29,* 371–381.

Dahl, R. E. (2004). Adolescent brain development: A period of vulnerabilities and opportunities. In R. E. Dahl, & L. P. Spear (Eds.), *Adolescent brain development: Vulnerabilities and opportunities.* New York: New York Academy of Sciences.

Dailard, C. (2001). Sex education: Politicians, parents, teachers and teens. *The Guttmacher Report on Public Policy* (Alan Guttmacher Institute), 4, 1–4. Retrieved March 4, 2006, from http://www.guttmacher. org/pubs/tgr/04/1/gr040109. pdf

Dainton, M. (1993). The myths and misconceptions of the step-mother identity. *Family Relations, 42,* 93–98.

Daly, T., & Feldman, R. S. (1994). *Benefits of social integration for typical preschool children.* Unpublished manuscript.

Damon, W. (1997), *The youth charter: How communities can work together to raise standards for all our children.* New York: Free Press.

Daniels, H. (Ed.). (1996). *An introduction to Vygotsky.* New York: Routledge.

Danish, S. J., Taylor, T. E., & Fazio, R. J. (2006). Enhancing adolescent development through sports and leisure. In G. R. Adams & M. D. Berzonsky (Eds.), *Blackwell handbook of adolescence.* Malden, MA: Blackwell Publishing.

Danner, D. D., Snowden, D. A., & Friesen, W. V. (2001). Positive emotions in early life and longevity: Findings from the nun study. *Journal of Personality and Social Psychology, 80,* 804–813.

Darroch, J. E., Singh, S., & Frost, J. J. (2001). Differences in teenage pregnancy rates among five developed countries: The roles of sexual activity and contraceptive use. *Family Planning Perspectives, 33,* 244–250.

Dasen, P. R. (2000). Rapid social change and the turmoil of adolescence: A cross-cultural perspective. *World Psychology, 7,* 114–122.

Dasen, P. R., & Mishra, R. C. (2002). Cross-cultural views on human development in the third millennium. In W. W. Hartup & R. K. Silbereisen, *Growing points in developmental science: An introduction.* Philadelphia, PA: Psychology Press.

Davidson, J. K., Darling, C. A., & Norton, L. (1995). Religiosity and the sexuality of women: Sexual behavior and sexual satisfaction revisited. *Journal of Sex Research, 32,* 235–243.

Davies, P. G., Spencer, S. J., & Steele, C. M. (2005). Clearing the air: Identity safety moderates the effects of stereotype threat on women's leadership aspirations. Journal of Personality & Social Psychology, 88, 276–287.

Davies, P. T., Harold, G. T., Goeke-Morey, M. C., & Cummings, E. M. (2002). Child emotional security and interparental conflict. *Monographs of the Society for Research in Child Development, 67.*

Davis, A. (2003). *Your divorce, your dollars: Financial planning before, during, and after divorce.* Bellingham, WA: Self-Counsel Press.

Davis, J. A. (2004). *Don't take it personally: A parent's guide to surviving adolescence.* Boulder, CO: Break Inn Books.

Davison, G. C. (2005). Issues and nonissues in the gay-affirmative treatment of patients who are gay, lesbian, or bisexual. Clinical Psychology: Science & Practice, 12, 25–28.

Davison, K. K., Susman, E. J., & Birch, L. L. (2003). Percent body fat at age 5 predicts earlier pubertal development among girls at age 9. *Pediatrics, 111,* 815–821.

Davison, K. P. & Pennebaker, J. W. (1997). Virtual naratives: Illness representations in online support groups. In K. J. Petrie, & J. A. Weinman, *Perceptions of health and illness: Current research and applications.* Amsterdam, Netherlands: Harwood Academic Publishers.

Dawson, D. (1991). Family structure and children's health and well-being: Data from the 1998 National Health Interview Survey on child health. *Journal of Marriage and the Family, 53,* 573–584.

Day, A. L., & Livingstone, H. A. (2003). Gender differences in perceptions of stressors and utilization of social support among university students. *Canadian Journal of Behavioural Science, 35,* 73–83.

Day, R. D., & Lamb, M. E. (Eds.). (2004). *Conceptualizing and measuring father involvement.* Mahwah, NJ: Erlbaum.

DeAngelis, T. (2005). Stepfamily success depends on ingredients. *Monitor on Psychology,* 58–60.

de Bruyn, E. H. (2005). Role strain, engagement and academic achievement in early adolescence. *Educational Studies, 31,* 15–27.

de Minzi, M. C. R., & Sacchi, C. (2004). Adolescent loneliness assessment. *Adolescence, 39,* 701–709.

Deardorff, J., Gonzales, N. A., & Sandler, I. N. (2003). Control beliefs as a mediator of the relation between stress and depressive symptoms among inner-city adolescents. *Journal of Abnormal Child Psychology, 31,* 205–217.

DeBaryshe, B. D., Patterson, G. R., & Capaldi, D. M. (1993). A performance model for academic achievement in early adolescent boys. *Developmental Psychology, 29,* 795–804.

Delaney, C. H. (1995). Rites of passage in adolescence. *Adolescence, 30,* 891–897.

Denizet-Lewis, B. (2004, May 30). Friends, friends with benefits, and the benefits of the local mall. *New York Times Magazine,* 30.

Dennis, J. G. (2004). *Homeschooling high school: Planning ahead for college admission.* Cambridge, MA: Emerald Press.

Desoete, A., Roeyers, H., & De Clercq, A. (2003). Can offline metacognition enhance mathematical problem solving? *Journal of Educational Psychology, 95,* 188–200.

de St. Aubin, E., McAdams, D. P., & Kim, T. C. (Eds.), (2004). *The generative society: Caring for future generations.* Washington, DC: American Psychological Association.

Devin-Sheehan, L., Feldman, R. S., & Allen, V. L. (1976). Research on children tutoring children: A critical review. *Review of Educational Research, 46,* 355–385.

Diamond, L. (2003a). Love matters: Romantic relationships among sexual-minority adolescents. In P. Florsheim (Ed.), *Adolescent romantic relations and sexual behavior: Theory, research, and practical implications.* Mahwah, NJ: Lawrence Erlbaum Associates.

Diamond, L. (2003b). Was it a phase? Young women's relinquishment of lesbian/bisexual identities over a 5-year period. *Journal of Personality & Social Psychology, 84,* 352–364.

Diamond, L. M., & Dubé, E. M. (2002). Friendship and attachment among heterosexual and sexual-minority youths: Does the gender of your friend matter? *Journal of Youth and Adolescence, 31,* 155–166.

Diamond, L. M., Savin-Williams, R. C., & Dubé, E. M. (1999). Sex, dating, passionate friendships, and romance: Intimate peer relations among lesbian, gay, and bisexual adolescents. In W. Furman, B. B. Brown, & C. Feiring, (Eds.), *The development of romantic relationships in adolescence.* New York: Cambridge University Press.

Dickson, J. M., & MacLeod, A. K. (2006). Dysphoric adolescents' causal explanations and expectancies for approach and avoidance goals. *Journal of Adolescence, 29,* 177–191.

Diekman, A. B., Eagly, A. H., Mladinic, A., & Ferreira, M. C. (2005). Dynamic stereotypes about women and men in Latin America and the United States. *Journal of Cross-Cultural Psychology, 36,* 209–226.

Diener, E., & Biswas-Diener, R. (2002). Will money increase subjective well-being? *Social Indicators Research, 57,* 119–169.

Diener, E., & Seligman, M. E. P. (2004). Beyond money: Toward an economy of well-being. *Psychological Science in the Public Interest, 5,* 1–31.

Diener, E., Lucas, R. E., & Oishi, S. (2002). Subjective well-being: The science of happiness and life satisfaction. In C. R. Snyder & S. J. Lopez (Eds.), *Handbook of positive psychology* (pp. 463–73). London: Oxford University Press.

Dingfelder, S. F. (2005, December). The kids are all right. *Monitor on Psychology,* 66–68.

Dion, K. L., & Dion, K. K. (1988). Romantic love: Individual and cultural perspectives. In R. J. Sternberg & M. L. Barnes (Eds.), *The psychology of love.* New Haven, CT: Yale University Press.

Dishion, T. J., & Dodge, K. A. (2005). Peer contagion in interventions for children and adolescents: Moving towards an understanding of the ecology and dynamics of change. *Journal of Abnormal Child Psychology, 33,* 395–400.

Dishion, T. J., & Patterson, G. R. (2006). The development and ecology of antisocial behavior in children and adolescents. In D. Cicchetti, & D. J. Cohen (Eds.), *Developmental psychopathology, Vol 3: Risk, disorder, and adaptation* (2nd ed.). Hoboken, NJ: Wiley.

Dishion, T. J., Haas, E., & Poulin, F. (1999). The peer influence paradox: Friendship quality and deviancy training within mail adolescent friendships. *Merrill-Palmer Quarterly, 45,* 88–101.

Dishion, T. J., Nelson, S. E., & Bullock, B. M. (2004). Premature adolescent autonomy: Parent disengagement and deviant peer process in the amplification of problem behaviour. *Journal of* Adolescence, *27, Special issue: Families, peers and contexts as multiple determinants of adolescent problem behavior,* 515–530.

Dluzen, D. E. (2005). Estrogen, testosterone, and gender differences. *Endocrine, 27,* 259–267.

Dodge, K. A., & Coie, J. D. (1987). Social information-processing factors in reactive and proactive aggression in children's peer groups. *Journal of Personality and Social Psychology, 53,* 1146–1158.

Dodge, K. A., & Crick, N. R. (1990). Social information-processing bases of aggressive behavior in children. *Personality and Social Psychology Bulletin, 16,* 8–22.

Dodge, K. A., & Price, J. M. (1994). On the relation between social information processing and socially competent behavior in early school-aged children. *Child Development, 65,* 1385–1397.

Dodgson, P. G. & Wood, J. V. (1998). Self-esteem and the cognitive accessibility of strengths and weaknesses after failure. *Journal of Personality & Social Psychology, 75,* 178–197.

Dolan, R. J. (2002, November 8). Emotion, cognition, and behavior. *Science, 298,* 1191–1194.

Dolgin, K., & Minowa, N. (1997). Gender differences in self-presentation: A comparison of the roles of flatteringness and intimacy in self-disclosure to friends. *Sex Roles, 36,* 371–380.

Donnellan, M. B., Trzesniewski, K. H., Robins, R. W., Moffitt, T. E., & Caspi, A. (2005). Low self-esteem is related to aggression, antisocial behavior, and delinquency. *Psychological Science, 16,* 328–335.

Donnelly, B. W., & Voydanoff, P. (1996). Parenting versus placing for adoption: Consequences for adolescent mothers. *Family Relations: Journal of Applied Family & Child Studies, 45,* 427–434.

Donnerstein, E., & Malamuth, N. (1997). Pornography: Its consequences on the observer. In Schlesinger, L. B. and Revitch, E. (Eds.) *Sexual dynamics of antisocial behavior.* Pp. 30–49.

Donovan, P. (1995). *Politics of blame—family planning and the poor.* New York: Alan Guttmacher Institute.

Dorn, L. D., & Rotenstein, D. (2004). Early puberty in girls: The case of premature adrenarche. *Women's Health Issues, 14,* 177–183.

Dorn, L., Susman, E., & Ponirakis, A. (2003). Pubertal timing and adolescent adjustment and behavior: Conclusions vary by rater. *Journal of Youth & Adolescence, 32,* 157–167.

Dornbusch, S. M., Carlsmith, J., Bushwall, S., Ritter, P. L., Leiderman, P., Hastorf, A., et al. (1985). Single parents, extended households, and the control of adolescents. *Child Development, 56,* 326–341.

Douvan, E., & Adelson, J. (1966). *The adolescent experience.* New York: Wiley.

Dovidio, J. F., & Gaertner, S. L. (1986). *Prejudice, discrimination, and racism.* San Diego, CA: Academic Press.

Dovidio, J. F., & Gaertner, S. L. (1991). Changes in the expression and assessment of racial prejudice. In J. J. Knopke, R. J. Norrell, & R. W. Rogers, *Opening doors: Perspectives on race relations in contemporary America.* University, AL: The University of Alabama Press.

Dovidio, J. F., Glick, P., & Rudman, L. A. (2005). *On the nature of prejudice: Fifty years after.* Malden, MA: Blackwell Publishing.

Dowling, N., Smith, D., & Thomas, T. (2005). Electronic gaming machines: Are they the 'crack-cocaine' of gambling? *Addiction, 100,* 33–45.

Doyle, A. B., Brendgen, M., Markiewicz, D., & Kamkar, K. (2003). Family relationships as moderators of the association between romantic relationships and adjustment in early adolescence. *Journal of Early Adolescence, 23,* 316–340.

Drummond, P., and Quah, S. (2001). The effect of expressing anger on cardiovascular reactivity and facial blood flow in Chinese and Caucasians. *Psychophysiology, 38,* 190–196.

DuBois, D. L., & Hirsch, B. J. (1990). School and neighborhood friendship patterns of Blacks and Whites in early adolescence. *Child Development, 61,* 524–536.

DuBois, D. L., & Hirsch, B. J. (1993). School/nonschool friendship patterns in early adolescence. *Journal of Early Adolescence, 13,* 102–122.

DuBois, D. L., Lockerd, E. M., Reach, K., & Parra, G. R. (2003). Effective strategies for esteem-enhancement: What do young adolescents have to say? *Journal of Early Adolescence, 23,* 405–434.

Duck, S. (1986). *Human relationships: An introduction to social psychology.* Thousand Oaks, CA: Sage Publications.

Duck, S. (1988). *Handbook of personal relationships: Theory, research and interventions.* Oxford, England: John Wiley & Sons.

Duckworth, A. L., & Seligman, M. E. P. (2005). Self-discipline outdoes IQ in predicting academic performance of adolescents. *Psychological Science, 16,* 939–944.

Dugan, E., & Kivett, V. R. (1994). The importance of emotional and social isolation to loneliness among very old rural adults. *Gerontologist, 34,* 340–346.

Dukes, R., & Martinez, R. (1994). The impact of gender on self-esteem among adolescents. *Adolescence, 29,* 105–115.

Dunger, D. B., Ahmed, M., & Ong, K. K. (2005). Effects of obesity on growth and puberty. *Best Practices Research in Clinical Endocrinology Metabolism, 19,* 375–390.

Dunham, R. M., Kidwell, J. S., & Wilson, S. M. (1986). Rites of passage at adolescence: A ritual process paradigm. *Journal of Adolescent Research, 1,* 139–153.

Dunn, W., & Pitts, S. (1993). Heinz dilemma? Let the subject choose. *Psychological Reports, 73,* 1399–1402.

Dunphy, D. (1963). The social structure of urban adolescent peer groups. *Sociometry, 26,* 230–246.

Dyk, P. H., & Adams, G. R. (1990). Identity and intimacy: An initial investigation of three theoretical models using cross-lag panel correlations. *Journal of Youth and Adolescence, 19,* 91–110.

Eagly, A. H., & Crowley, M. (1986). Gender and helping behavior: A meta-analytic review of the social psychological literature. *Psychological Bulletin, 100,* 283–308.

Eagly, A. H., & Steffen, V. J. (1986). Gender and aggressive behavior: A meta-analytic review of the social psychological literature. *Psychological Bulletin, 100,* 309–330.

Eagly, A. H., Beall, A. E., & Sternberg, R. J. (Eds.). (2004). *The psychology of gender* (2nd ed.). New York: Guilford Press.

Eaton, M. J. & Dembo, M. H. (1997). Differences in the motivational beliefs of Asian American and non-Asian students. Journal of Educational Psychology, 89, 433–440.

Eccles, J., Templeton, J., and Barber, B. (2003). Adolescence and emerging adulthood: The critical passage ways to adulthood. In M. Bornstein & L. Davidson (Eds.), *Well-being: Positive development across the life course.* Mahwah, NJ: Lawrence Erlbaum Associates.

Ecenbarger, W. (1993, April 1). America's new merchants of death. *The Reader's Digest,* 50.

Eckes, T., Trautner, H. M., & Behrendt, R. (2005). Gender subgroups and intergroup perception: Adolescents' views of own-gender and other-gender groups. *Journal of Social Psychology, 145,* 85–111.

Eder, D. (1985). The cycle of popularity: Interpersonal relations among female adolescents. *Sociology of Education, 58,* 154–165.

Eder, D., & Kinney, D. A. (1995): The effect of middle school extracurricular activities on adolescents popularity and peer status. *Youth & Society, 26,* 298–324.

Edwards, S. (2005). Constructivism does not only happen in the individual: Sociocultural theory and early childhood education. *Early Child Development & Care, 17,* 37–47.

Eigsti, I., & Cicchetti, D. (2004). The impact of child maltreatment on expressive syntax at 60 months. *Developmental Science, 7,* 88–102.

Eisenberg, N., & Morris, A. (2004). Moral cognitions and prosocial responding in adolescence. In R. Lerner & L. Steinberg (Eds.), *Handbook of adolescent psychology.* New York: Wiley.

Eisenberg, N., Spinrad, T. L, & Smith, C. L. (2004). Emotion-related regulation: Its conceptualization, relations to social functioning, and socialization. In P. Philippot & R. S. Feldman (Eds.), *The regulation of emotion.* Mahwah, NJ: Erlbaum.

Eisenberg, N., & Valiente, C. (2002). Parenting and children's prosocial and moral development. In M. Bornstein (Ed), *Handbook of parenting: Vol. 5: Practical issues in parenting.* Mahwah, NJ: Lawrence Erlbaum Associates.

Eisenberg, N., Valiente, C., & Champion, C. (1999). Empathy-related responding: Moral, social, and socialization correlates. In A. G. Miller, *Social psychology of good and evil.* New York: Guilford Press.

Eisenberg, N., Zhour, Q., & Koller, S. (2001). Brazilian adolescents' prosocial moral judgment and behavior: Relations to sympathy, perspective taking, gender-role orientation, and demographic characteristics. *Child Development, 72,* 518–534

Eley, T. C., Lichtenstein, P., & Moffitt, T. E. (2003). A longitudinal behavioral genetic analysis of the etiology of aggressive and nonaggressive antisocial behavior. *Development and Psychopathology, 15,* 383–402.

Eley, T., Liang, H., & Plomin, R. (2004). Parental familial vulnerability, family environment, and their interactions as predictors of depressive symptoms in adolescents. *Child & Adolescent Social Work Journal, 21,* 298–306.

Elias, M. J. (2001). Middle school transition: It's harder than you think: Making the transition to middle school successful. *Middle Matters,* 1–2.

Elkind, D. (1985). Egocentrism redux. *Developmental Review, 5,* 218–226.

Elkind, D. (1996). Inhelder and Piaget on adolescence and adulthood: A postmodern appraisal. *Psychological Science, 7,* 216–220.

Elkins, I. J., King, S. M., & McGue, M. (2006). Personality traits and the development of nicotine, alcohol, and illicit drug disorders: prospective links from adolescence to young adulthood. *Journal of Abnormal Psychology, 115,* 26–39.

Ellis, A. (1999). Early theories and practices of rational emotive behavior therapy and how they have been augmented and revised during the last three decades. *Journal of Rational-Emotive & Cognitive Behavior Therapy, 17,* 69–93.

Else-Quest, N. M., Hyde, J. S., & DeLamater, J. D. (2005). Context counts: Long-term sequelae of premarital intercourse or abstinence. Journal of Sex Research, 42, 102–112.

Employment Policies Institute. (2000). *Correcting part-time misconceptions.* Washington, DC: Author.

Emslie, G. J., Rush, A. J., Weinberg, W. A., Kowatch, R. A., Hughes, C. W., Carmody, T., & Rintelmann, J. A. (1997). Double-blind, randomized, placebo-controlled trial of fluoxetine in children and adolescents with depression. *Archives of General Psychiatry, 54,* 1031–1037.

Englund, M. M., Levy, A. K., Hyson, D. M., & Sroufe, L. A. (2000). Adolescent social competence: Effectiveness in a group setting. *Child Development, 71,* 1049–1060.

Ennett, S. T., & Bauman, K. E. (1996). Adolescent social networks: School, demographic, and longitudinal considerations. *Journal of Adolescent Research, 11,* 194–215.

Epperson, S. E. (1988, September 16). Studies link subtle sex bias in schools with women's behavior in the workplace. Wall Street Journal, p. 19.

Erikson, E. H. (1963). *Childhood and society.* New York: Norton.

Eriksson, A. L., Suuriniemi, M., Mahonen, A., Cheng, S., & Ohlsson, C. (2005). The COMT val158met polymorphism is associated with early pubertal development, height and cortical bone mass in girls. *Pediatric Research, 58,* 71–77.

Eshel, Y., & Kurman, J. (1994). Availability, similarity, and gender as determinants of adolescent peer acceptance. *Journal of Applied Social Psychology, 24,* 1944–1964.

Ester, B. (2003). Gender schemas: Configuration and activation processes. *Canadian Journal of Behavioural Science, 35,* 176–184.

Ethier, K. A., Kershaw, T. S., Lewis J. B., Milan, S., Niccolai, L. M., & Ickovics, J. R. (2006). Self-esteem, emotional distress and sexual behavior among adolescent females: Inter-relationships and temporal effects. *Journal of Adolescent Health, 38,* 268–274.

Ethier, K., & Deaux, K. (1990). Hispanics in ivy: Assessing identity and perceived threat. *Sex Roles, 22,* 427–440.

Ethier, L., Couture, G., & Lacharite, C. (2004). Risk factors associated with the chronicity of high potential for child abuse and neglect. *Journal of Family Violence, 19,* 13–24.

Evans, C. (2004a). Exploring the relationship between cognitive style and teaching style. *Educational Psychology, 24,* 509–515.

Evans, G. (2004b). The environment of childhood poverty. *American Psychologist, 59,* 77–92.

Everett, S. A., Warren, C. W., Santelli, J. S., Kann, L., Collins, J. L., & Kolbe, L. J. (2000). Use of birth control pills, condoms, and withdrawal among U.S. high school students. *Journal of Adolescent Health, 27,* 112–118.

Fabrikant, G (1996), "Murdoch bets heavily on a global vision: media magnate seeks to own and broadcast every form of programming", *The New York Times,* pp. D1.

Farrar, K., Kunkel, D., Biely, E., Eyal, K., Fandrich, R., & Donnerstein, E. (2003). Sexual messages during prime-time programming. *Sexuality & Culture: An Interdisciplinary Quarterly, 7,* 7–37.

Fazio, R. H., Jackson, J. R., & Dunton, B. C. (1995). Variability in automatic activation as an unobstrusive measure of racial attitudes: A bona fide pipeline? *Journal of Personality and Social Psychology, 69,* 1013–1027.

Featherstone, D., Cundick, B., & Jensen, L. (1992). Differences in school behavior and achievement between children from intact, reconstituted, and single-parent families. *Adolescence, 27*, 1–12.

Feinberg, E., Swartz, K., Zaslavsky, A., Gardner, J., & Klein, W. D. (2001). Family income and crowd out among children enrolled in Massachusetts Children's Medical Security Plan. *Health Services Research, 36*, 45–63.

Feingold, A. (1992). Gender differences in mate selection preferences: A test of the parental investment model. *Psychological Bulletin, 112*, 125–139.

Feldman, R. S. (2006). P. O. W. E. R. *Learning: Strategies for Success in College and Life.* (3rd ed.) New York: McGraw-Hill.

Feldman, R. S., Coats, E. J., & Schwartzberg, S. (1994). *Case studies and critical thinking about psychology.* New York: McGraw-Hill.

Feldman, R. S., Forrest, J. A., & Happ, B. R. (2002.) Self-presentation and verbal deception: Do self-presenters lie more? *Basic and Applied Social Psychology, 24*, 163–170.

Feldman, R. S., Tomasian, J., & Coats, E. J. (1999a) Adolescents' social competence and nonverbal deception abilities: Adolescents with higher social skills are better liars. *Journal of Nonverbal Behavior, 23*, 237–249.

Feldman, R. S., Tomasian, J. C., & Coats, E. J. (1999b). Nonverbal deception abilities and adolescents' social competence: Adolescents with higher social skills are better liars. *Journal of Nonverbal Behavior, 23*, 237–249.

Feldman, S. S., & Rosenthal, D. A. (1991). Age expectations of behavioural autonomy in Hong Kong, Australian and American youth: The influence of family variables and adolescents' values. *International Journal of Psychology, 26*, 1–23.

Feldman, S. S., & Wood, D. N. (1994). Parents' expectations for preadolescent sons' behavioral autonomy: A longitudinal study of correlates and outcomes. *Journal of Research on Adolescence, 4*, 45–70.

Felner, R. D. (2005). Poverty in childhood and adolescence: A transactional-ecological approach to understanding and enhancing resilience in contexts of disadvantage and developmental risk. In S. Goldstein & R. B. Brooks (Eds.), *Handbook of resilience in children.* New York: Kluwer Academic/Plenum Publishers.

Ferri, B. A., & Connor, D. J., (2005). Tools of exclusion: Race, disability, and (re)segregated education. *Teachers College Record, 107*, 453–475.

Fetterman, D. M. (2005). Empowerment evaluation: From the digital divide to academic distsress. In D. Fetterman & A. Wandersman, *Empowerment evaluation principles in practice.* New York: Guilford Press.

Field, M. (2003). Self-esteem and school spirit: A winning combination. *Momentum, 33*, 11.

Field, T. M., Harding, J., Yando, R., Gonzalez, K., Lasko, D., Bendell, D., et al. (1998). Feelings and attitudes of gifted students. *Adolescence, 39*, 331–342.

Fields, J., & Casper, L. M. (2001). *American families and living arrangements, March 2000.* Current Population Report P20-537. U. S. Census Bureau: Washington, DC.

Fields-Meyer, T. (1999). Gifted children. *People Magazine*, 61–65.

Finke, R. A. (1995). Creative insight and preinventive forms. In R. J. Sternberg & J. E. Davidson (Eds.), *The nature of insight.* Cambridge, MA: MIT Press.

Finkelhor, D., Ormrod, R., & Turner, H. (2005). The victimization of children and youth: a comprehensive, national survey. *Child Maltreatment, 10*, 5–25.

Finken, L. L. (2005). The role of consultants in adolescents' decision making: A focus on abortion decisions. In J. E. Jacobs & P. A. Klaczynski (Eds.), *The development of judgment and decision making in children and adolescents.* Mahwah, NJ: Erlbaum.

Firestone, R. W., & Firestone, L. A. (2006). Factors that affect an individual's sexuality. In R. W. Firestone, L. A. Firestone, & J. Catlett (Eds.), *Sex and love in intimate relationships.* Washington, DC: American Psychological Association.

Firestone, R. W., Firestone, L. A., & Catlett, J. (2006). Men, women, and sexual stereotypes. In R. W. Firestone, L. A. Firestone, & J. Catlett (Eds.), *Sex and love in intimate relationships.* Washington, DC: American Psychological Association, 2006.

Fish, J. M. (Ed.). (2001). *Race and intelligence: Separating science from myth.* Mahwah, NJ: Erlbaum.

Fiske, A. P., Kitayama, S., Markus, H. R., & Nisbett, R. E. (1998). The cultural matrix of social psychology. In D. T. Gilbert & S. T. Fiske (Eds.) et al., *The handbook of social psychology*, 4th edition. Boston, MA: McGraw-Hill Companies, Inc.

Fiske, S. T. (2001). Effects of power on bias: Power explains and maintains individual, group, and societal disparities. In A. Y. Lee-Chai & J. A. Bargh (Eds.), *Multiple perspectives on the causes of corruption.* New York: Psychology Press.

Fiske, S. T., Cuddy, A. J., & Glick, P. (2002). A model of (often mixed) stereotype content: Competence and warmth respectively follow from perceived status and competition. *Journal of Personality and Social Psychology, 82*, 878–902.

Flammer, A., & Schaffner, B. (2003). Adolescent leisure across European nations In S. Verma & R. W. Larson (Eds.), *Examining adolescent leisure time across cultures: Developmental opportunities and risks: New directions for child and adolescent development, No. 99.* New York: Jossey-Bass.

Flanagan, C. A. (2004) Volunteerism, leadership, political socialization, and civic engagement. In R. M. Lerner & L. Steinberg (Eds.), *Handbook of adolescent psychology* (2nd ed.), New York: Wiley.

Flanagan, C. A., & Van Horn, B. (2003). Youth civic development: A logical next step in community youth development. In J. G. Keith (Ed.), *Community youth development: programs, policies, practices.* Thousand Oaks, CA: Sage.

Flanagan, C. A., Gill, S., & Gallay, L. S. (2005). Social participation and social trust in adolescence: The importance of heterogeneous encounters. In A. M. Omoto (Ed.), *Processes of community change and social action.* Mahwah, NJ: Erlbaum.

Fletcher, A. C., Darling, N. E., Steinberg, L., & Dornbusch, S. M. (1995). The company they keep: Relation of adolescents' adjustment and behavior to their friends' perceptions of authoritative parenting in the social network. *Developmental Psychology, 31*, 300–310.

Flewelling, R., & Bauman, K. (1990). Family structure as a predictor of initial substance use and sexual intercourse in early adolescence. *Journal of Marriage and the Family, 52*, 171–181.

Flor, D. L., & Knap, N. F. (2001). Transmission and transaction: Predicting adolescents' internalization of parental religious values. *Journal of Family Psychology, 15*, 627–645.

Florsheim, P. (Ed.). (2003). *Adolescent romantic relations and sexual behavior: Theory, research, and practical implications.* Mahwah, NJ: Erlbaum.

Flouri, E. (2005). *Fathering and child outcomes.* New York: Wiley.

Flouri, E., & Buchanan, A. (2003). The role of father involvement and mother involvement in adolescents' psychological well-being. *British Journal of Social Work, 33*, 399–406.

Floyd, R. G. (2005). Information-processing approaches to interpretation of contemporary intellectual assessment instruments. In D. P. Flanagan, & P. L. Harrison, (Eds.), *Contemporary intellectual assessment: Theories, tests, and issues.* New York, Guilford Press.

Foa, E. B., & Riggs, D. S. (1995). Posttraumatic stress disorder following assault: Theoretical considerations and empirical findings. *Current Directions in Psychological Science, 4*, 61–65.

Fogel, A., Today, S., & Kawai, M. (1988). Mother infant face-to-face interaction in Japan and the United States: A laboratory comparison using 3-month-old infants. *Developmental Psychology, 24*, 398–406.

Fogle, L. M., Huebner, E. S., & Laughlin, J. E. (2002). The relationship between temperament and life satisfaction in early adolescence: Cognitive and behavioral mediation models. *Journal of Happiness Studies, 3*, 373–392.

Folkman, S., & Lazarus, R. S. (1988). Coping as a mediator of emotion. *Journal of Personality and Social Psychology, 54*, 466–475.

Folkman, S., & Moskowitz, J. T. (2000). Stress, positive emotion, and coping. *Current Directions in Psychological Science, 9*, 115–118.

Folkman, S., & Moskowitz, J. T. (2004). Coping: Pitfalls and promise. *Annual Review of Psychology, 55*, 745–774.

Food and Drug Administration. (2003). *Birth control guide.* Retrieved April 1, 2006, from http://www. fda. gov/fdac/features/1997/babyguide2.pdf

Ford, V. E. (2003). Coming out as Lesbian or gay: A potential precipitant of crisis in adolescence. *Journal of Human Behavior in the Social Environment, 8*, 93–110.

Fordham, C., & Ogbu, J (1986). Black students' school success: Coping with the burden of "acting white." *Urban Review, 18*, 176–206.

Formoso, D., Gonzales, N. A., & Aiken, L. S. (2000). Family conflict and children's internalizing and externalizing behavior: Protective factors. *American Journal of Community Psychology, 28, Special issue: Minority Issues in Prevention*, 175–199.

Fouad, N. A., & Byars-Winston, A. M. (2005). Cultural context of career choice: Meta-analysis of race/ethnicity differences. *Career Development Quarterly, 53*, 223–233.

Franck, I., & Brownstone, D. (1991). *The parent's desk reference.* New York: Prentice Hall.

Frank, M. G., Ekman, P., & Friesen, W. V. (1997). Behavioral markers and recognizability of the smile of enjoyment. In P. Ekman & E. L. Rosenberg (Eds.), *What the face reveals: Basic and applied studies of spontaneous expression using the Facial Action Coding System (FACS). Series in affective science.* New York: Oxford University Press.

Frankel, T. (2006, May 15). Brainy student sang praises of alcohol, then it killed him. *St. Louis Post-Dispatch*, p. A1.

Frankenberger, K. D. (2000). Adolescent egocentrism: A comparison among adolescents and adults. *Journal of Adolescence*, 23, 343–354.

Frankenberger, K. D. (2004). Adolescent egocentrism, risk perceptions, and sensation seeking among smoking and nonsmoking youth. *Journal of Adolescent Research*, 19, 576–590.

Franko, D., and Striegel-Moore, R. (2002). The role of body dissatisfaction as a risk factor for depression in adolescent girls: Are the differences Black and White? *Journal of Psychosomatic Research*, 53, 975–983.

Franzoi, S. L., Davis, M. H., & Vasquez-Suson, K. A. (1994). Two social worlds: Social correlates and stability of adolescent status groups. *Journal of Personality and Social Psychology*, 67, 462–473.

Fredericks, J. A., & Eccles, J. S. (2006). Is extracurricular participation associated with beneficial outcomes? Concurrent and longitudinal relations. *Developmental Psychology*, 42, 698–713.

Fredriksen, K., Rhodes, J., Reddy, R., & Way, N. (2004). Sleepless in Chicago: Tracking the effects of adolescent sleep loss during the middle school years. *Child Development*, 75, 84–95.

Freeman, R. (1990, December 17). A victim's anguish: Raped on Campus, Casey Letvin. People Magazine, 91–95.

Freeman, S. C. (1993). Donald Super: A perspective on career development. *Journal of Career Development*, 19, 255–264.

French, H. W. (1997, February 2). Africa's culture war: Old customs, new values. *The New York Times*, 1E, 4E.

French, S., Seidman, E., Allen, L., and Aber, J. (2000). Racial/ethnic identity, congruence with the social context, and the transition to high school. *Journal of Adolescent Research*, 15, 587–602.

French, S., Seidman, E., Allen, L., and Aber, J. (2006). The development of ethnic identity during adolescence. *Developmental Psychology*, 42, 1–10.

Freud, S. (1922/1959). Group psychology and the analysis of the ego. London: Hogarth.

Frick, P. J., Cornell, A. H., Bodin, S. D., Dane, H. A., Barry, C. T., & Loney, B. R. (2003). Callous-unemotional traits and developmental pathways to severe conduct problems. *Developmental Psychology*, 39, 246–260.

Friedlander, M. (1999). Ethnic identity development of internationally adopted children and adolescents: Implications for family therapists. *Journal of Marital and Family Therapy*, 25, 43–60.

Frisch, M. J., Herzog, D. B., & Franko, D. L. (2006). Residential treatment for eating disorders. *International Journal of Eating Disorders*, 39, 434–442.

Fryer, R. G. (2005, Winter). "Acting white." *Education Next*, 53–59.

Fuchs, I., Eisenberg, N., Hertz-Lazarowitz, R., & Sharabany, R. (1986). Kibbutz, Israeli city and American children's moral reasoning about prosocial moral conflicts. *Merrill-Palmer Quarterly*, 32, 37–50.

Fuligni, A. J. (1998). Authority, autonomy, and parent-adolescent conflict and cohesion: A study of adolescents from Mexican, Chinese, Filipino, and European backgrounds. *Developmental Psychology*, 34, 782–792.

Fuligni, A. J. (2005). Commentary: Convergence and divergence in the developmental contexts of immigrants to the United States. In K. W. Schaie & G. H. Elder, Jr. (Eds.), *Historical influences on lives & aging.* New York: Springer Publishing.

Fuligni, A. J., & Zhang, W. (2004). Attitudes toward family obligation among adolescents in contemporary urban and rural China. *Child Development*, 75, 180–192.

Fuligni, A. J., Tseng, V., & Lam, M. (1999). Attitudes toward family obligations among American adolescents with Asian, Latin American, and European backgrounds. *Child Development*, 70, 1030–1044.

Fuligni, A. J., Witkow, M., & Garcia, C. (2005). Ethnic identity and the academic adjustment of adolescents from Mexican, Chinese, and European backgrounds. *Developmental Psychology*, 41, 799–811.

Fuligni, A., & Yoshikawa, H. (2003). Socioeconomic resources, parenting, and child development among immigrant families. In M. Bornstein & R. Bradley (Eds.), *Socioeconomic status, parenting, and child development.* Mahwah, NJ: Lawrence Erlbaum Associates.

Funk, J. B. (2005). Children's exposure to violent video games and desensitization to violence. *Child and Adolescent Psychiatric Clinics of North American*, 14, 387–404.

Furman, W., & Buhrmester, D. (1992). Age and sex differences in perceptions of networks of personal relationships. *Child Development*, 63, 103–115.

Furman, W., & Hand L. S. (2006). The slippery nature of romantic relationships: Issues in definition and differentiation. In A. C. Crouter & A. Booth (Eds.), *Romance and sex in adolescence and emerging adulthood: Risks and opportunities.* Mahwah, NJ: Erlbaum.

Furman, W., & Shaffer, L. (2003). The role of romantic relationships in adolescent development. In P. Florsheim (Ed.), *Adolescent romantic relations and sexual behavior: Theory, research, and practical implications* (pp. 000). Mahwah, NJ: Erlbaum.

Furman, W., Shaffer, L. H. (2006). The slippery nature of romantic relationships: Issues in definition and differentiation. In A. C. Crouter & A. Booth, *Romance and sex in adolescence and emerging adulthood: Risks and opportunities.* Mahwah, NJ: Lawrence Erlbaum Associates.

Furman, W., Wehner, E. A. (1998). Adolescent romantic relationships: A developmental perspective. In S. Shulman & W. A. Collins (Eds.), *Romantic relationships in adolescence: Developmental perspectives.* San Francisco: Jossey-Bass.

Furnham, A. (2005). The justice motive in adolescence and young people: Origins and consequences. *Social Justice Research*, 18, 203–210.

Gaab, J., Rohleder, N., & Heitz, V. (2005). Stress-induced changes in LPS-induced pro-inflammatory cytokine production in chronic fatigue syndrome. *Psychoneuroendocrinology*, 30, 188–198.

Gable, S., & Lutz, S. (2000). Household, parent, and child contributions to childhood obesity. *Family Relations: Interdisciplinary Journal of Applied Family Studies*, 49, 293–300.

Gaertner, S. L. & Dovidiio, J. F. (1986). The aversive form of racism. In J. F. Dovidio & S. L. Gaertner, *Prejudice, discrimination, and racism.* San Diego, CA: Academic Press.

Gagnon, G. H. (1977). *Human sexualities.* Glenview, IL: Scott, Foresman.

Galambos, N. L., Barker, T. T., & Tilton-Weaver, L. C. (2003). Who gets caught at maturity gap? A study of pseudomature, immature and mature adolescents. *International Journal of Behavioral Development*, 27, 253–263.

Galambos, N., Leadbeater, B., and Barker, E. (2004). Gender differences in and risk factors for depression in adolescence: A 4-year longitudinal study. *International Journal of Behavioral Development*, 28, 16–25.

Gallagher, J. J. (1994). Teaching and learning: New models. Annual Review of Psychology, 45, 171–195.

Gallagher, R. (2005). *National survey of counseling center directors 2005.* Alexandria, VA: International Association of Counseling Services.

Gallo, L. C., Smith, T. W., & Cox, A. M. (2006). Socioeconomic status, psychosocial processes, and perceived health: An interpersonal perspective. *Annals of Behavioral Medicine*, 31, 109–119.

Gangestad, S. W., Simpson, J. A., Cousins, A. J., Garver-Apgar, C. E., & Christensen, P. N. (2004). Women's preferences for male behavioral displays change across the menstrual cycle. *Psychological Science*, 15, 203–207.

Garcia, D. M., Reser, A. H., Amo, R. B., Redersdorff, S., & Branscombe, N. R. (2005). Perceivers' responses to ingroup and out-group members who blame a negative outcome on discrimination. *Personality and Social Psychology Bulleting*, 31, 769–780.

Gardner, H. (2000). *Intelligence reframed: Multiple intelligences for the 21st century.* New York: Basic Books.

Gardner, H. (2003). Three distinct meanings of intelligence. In R. Sternberg and J. Lautrey (Eds.), *Models of intelligence: International perspectives.* Washington, DC: American Psychological Association.

Gardner, M., & Steinberg, L. (2005). Peer influence on risk taking, risk preference, and risky decision making in adolescence and adulthood: An experimental Study. *Developmental Psychology*, 41, 625–635.

Garland, J. E. (2004). Facing the evidence: antidepressant treatment in children and adolescents. *Canadian Medical Association Journal*, 17, 489–491.

Garnett, S. P., Hogler, W., Blades, B., Baur, L. A., Peat, J., Lee, J., & Cowell, C. T. (2004). Relation between hormones and body composition, including bone, in prepubertal children. *American Journal of Clinical Nutrition*, 80, 966–972.

Gauvain, M. (1998). Cognitive development in social and cultural context. *Current Directions in Psychological Science, 7*, 188–194.

Gauze, C., Bukowski, W. M., Aquan-Assee, J., & Sippola, L. K. (1996). Interactions between family environment and friendship and associations with self-perceived well-being during adolescence. *Child Development, 67*, 2201–2216.

Gavin, L. A., Furman, W. (1996). Adolescent girls' relationships with mothers and best friends. *Child Development, 67*, 375–386.

Gazzaniga, M. S. (2005). *Cognitive neurosciences.* Cambridge, MA: MIT Press.

Ge, X., Kim, I. J., Brody, G. H., Conger, R. D., Simons, R. L., Gibbons, F. X., & Cutrona, C. E. (2003). It's about timing and change: Pubertal transition effects on symptoms of major depression among African American youths. *Developmental Psychology, 39*, 430–439.

Geary, D. C. (1998). *Male, female: The evolution of human sex differences.* Washington, DC: APA Books.

Gehring, T. M., Wentzel, K. R., Feldman, S. S., & Munson, J. (1990). Conflict in families of adolescents: The impact on cohesion and power structures. *Journal of Family Psychology, 3*, 290–309.

Geierstanger, S. P., & Amaral, G. (2005). *School-based health centers and academic performance: What is the intersection?* April 2004 Meeting Proceedings. White Paper. Washington, DC: National Assembly on School-Based Health Care.

Geierstanger, S. P., Amaral, G., Mansour, M., & Walters, S. R. (2004). School-based health centers and academic performance: Existing research, challenges and recommendations. *Journal of School Health, 74*, 347–352.

Gelman, D. (1994, April 18). The mystery of suicide. *Newsweek*, 44–49.

Gershoff, E. (2002). Corporal punishment by parents and associated child behaviors and experiences: A meta-analytic and theoretical review. *Psychological Bulletin, 128*, 539–579.

Gershon, A., Gowen, L. K., Compian, L., & Hayward, C. (2004). Gender-stereotyped imagined dates and weight concerns in sixth-grade girls. *Sex Roles, 50*, 515–523.

Gevirtz, R. (2000). The physiology of stress. In D. T. Kenny, J. G. Carlson, J. F. McGuigan, & J. L. Sheppard, *Stress and health: Research and clinical applications.* Amsterdam, Netherlands: Harwood Academic Publishers.

Gewertz, C. (2005, April 6). Training focuses on teachers' expectations. Education Week, 24, 1, 2.

Giacobbi, P. R., Jr., Lynn, T. K. Wetherington, J. M., Jenkins, J., Bodendorf, M., & Langley, B. (2004). Stress and coping during the transition to university for first-year female athletes. *Sports Psychologist, 18*, 1–20.

Giammattei, J., Blix, G., Marshak, H. H., Wollitzer, A. O., & Petitt, D. J. (2003). Television watching and soft drink consumption: Associations with obesity in 11-to-13-year-old schoolchildren. *Archives of Pediatric Adolescence, 157*, 882–886.

Gibbs, J. C. (2003). *Moral development and reality: Beyond the theories of Kohlberg and Huffman.* Thousand Oaks, CA: Sage.

Giedd, J. N. (2004). Structural magnetic resonance imaging of the adolescent brain. In R. E. Dahl, & L. P. Spear, Adolescent brain development: Vulnerabilities and opportunities. New York: New York Academy of Sciences.

Gilbert, D. T., Miller, A. G., & Ross, L. (1998). Speeding with Ned: A personal view of the correspondence bias. In J. M. Darley, J. Cooper et al. (Eds.), *Attribution and social interaction: The legacy of Edward E. Jones.* Washington, DC: American Psychological Association.

Gilbert, D. T., McNulty, S. E., Giuliano, T. A., & Benson, J. E. (1992). Blurry words and fuzzy deeds: The attribution of obscure behavior. *Journal of Personality and Social Psychology, 62*, 18–25.

Gilbert, S. (2004, March 16). New clues to women veiled in black. *The New York Times*, D1.

Giles-Sims, J., & Lockhart, C. (2005). Culturally shaped patterns of disciplining children. *Journal of Family Issues, 26*, 196–218.

Gilligan, C. (1982). *In a different voice: Psychological theory and women's development.* Cambridge, MA: Harvard University Press.

Gilligan, C. (1987). Adolescent development reconsidered. In C. E. Irwin (Ed.), *Adolescent social behavior and health.* San Francisco: Jossey-Bass.

Gilligan, C. (2004). Recovering psyche: Reflections on life-history and history. *Annual of Psychoanalysis, 32*, 131–147.

Gilligan, C., Brown, L. M., & Rogers, A. G. (1990). Psyche embedded: A place for body, relationships, and culture in personality theory. In A. I. Rabin, & R. A. Zucker (Eds.) *Studying persons and lives.* New York: Springer.

Gilligan, C., Lyons, N. P., & Hammer, T. J. (Eds.). (1990). *Making connections.* Cambridge, MA: Harvard University Press.

Gilligan, C., Ward, J. V., & Taylor, J. M. (Eds.). (1988). *Mapping the moral domain: A contribution of women's thinking to psychological theory and education.* Cambridge, MA: Harvard University Press.

Gilman, R. (2001). The relationship between life satisfaction, social interest, and frequency of extracurricular activities among adolescent students. *Journal of Youth and Adolescence, 30*, 749–767.

Ginzberg, E. (1972). Toward a theory of occupational choice: A restatement. *Vocational Guidance Quarterly, 12*, 10–14.

Giordana, S. (2005). *Understanding eating disorders: Conceptual and ethical issues in the treatment of anorexia (Issues in Biomedical Ethics).* New York: Oxford University Press.

Giordano, P. C., Cernkovich, S. A., Groat, H. T., Pugh, M. D., & Swinford, S. P. (1998). The quality of adolescent friendships: Long term effects? *Journal of Health and Social Behavior, 39*, 55–71.

Giordano, P. C., Manning, W. D., & Longmore, M. A. (2006). Adolescent romantic relationships: An emerging portrait of their nature and developmental significance. In A. C. Crouter & A. Booth (Ed.), *Romance and sex in adolescence and emerging adulthood: Risks and opportunities.* Mahwah, NJ: Erlbaum.

Giordano, P., Manning, W., and Longmore, M. (2005). The romantic relationships of African-American and white adolescents. *Sociological Quarterly, 46*, 545–568.

Gleick, E., Reed, S., & Schindehette, S. (1994, October 24) The baby trap. *People Weekly, 42*, 38–55.

Glenn, N., & Marquardt, E. (2001). *Hooking up, hanging out, and looking for Mr. Right: College women on dating and mating today.* New York: Institute for American Values.

Glick, P., Fiske, S. T., & Miadinic, A. (2000). Beyond prejudice as simple antipathy: Hostile and benevolent sexism across cultures. *Journal of Personality and Social Psychology, 79*, 763–775.

Glick, P., Zion, C., & Nelson, C. (1988). What mediates sex discrimination in hiring decisions? Journal of Personality and Social Psychology, 55, 178–186.

Goldberg, C. J., Fogarty, E. E., Moore, D. P., & Dowling, F. E. (1997). Scoliosis and developmental theory: Adolescent idiopathic scoliosis. *Spine, 22*, 2228–2237.

Goldfield, G. S., Blouin, A. G., & Woodside, D. B. (2006). Body image, binge eating, and bulimia nervosa in male bodybuilders. *Canadian Journal of Psychiatry, 61*, 160–168.

Goldsmith, S. K., Pellmar, T. C., Kleinman, A. M., & Bunney, W. E. (2002). *Reducing suicide: A national imperative.* Washington, DC: The National Academies Press.

Goldstein, I. (2000, August). Male sexual circuitry. Scientific American, 283, 70–75.

Goldston, D. B. (2003). *Measuring suicidal behavior and risk in children and adolescents.* Washington, DC: American Psychological Association.

Golombok, S., & Tasker, F. (1996). Do parents influence the sexual orientation of their children? Findings from a longitudinal study of lesbian families. *Developmental Psychology, 32*, 3–11.

Golombok, S., Golding, J., Perry, B., Burston, A., Murray, C., Mooney-Somers, J., & Stevens, M. (2003). Children with lesbian parents: A community study. *Developmental Psychology, 39*, 20–33.

Gong, R. (2005). The essence of critical thinking. *Journal of Developmental Education, 28*, 40–41.

González, C., & Gándara, P. (2005). Why we like to call ourselves Latinas. *Journal of Hispanic Higher Education, 4*, 392–398.

Goode, E. (2004, February 3). Stronger warning is urged on antidepressants for teenagers. *The New York Times*, A12.

Goodenow, C., Szalacha, L., & Westheimer, K. (2006). School support groups, other school factors, and the safety of sexual minority adolescents. *Psychology in the Schools, 43*, 573–589.

Goodheart, C. D. (2006). An integrated view of girls' and women's health: Psychology, physiology, and society. In J. Worell & C. D. Goodheart (Eds.), *Handbook of girls' and women's psychological health: Gender and well-being across the lifespan.* New York: Oxford University Press.

Gosserand, R. H., & Diefendorff, J. M. (2005). Emotional display rules and emotional labor: The moderating role of commitment. *Journal of Applied Psychology, 90*, Special issue: Special Section: Theoretical Models and Conceptual Analyses—Second Installment, 1256–1264.

Goswami, U. (1998). *Cognition in children.* Philadelphia: Psychology Press.

Gottfredson, G. D., & Holland, J. L. (1990). A longitudinal test of the influence of congruence: Job satisfaction, competency utilization, and counterproductive behavior. *Journal of Counseling Psychology, 37,* 389–398.

Gottlieb, D. A. (2004). Acquisition with partial and continuous reinforcement in pigeon autoshaping. *Learning and Behavior, 32,* 321–334.

Gottman, J. M., & Parker, J. G. (1986). *Conversations of friends: Speculations on affective development.* New York: Cambridge University Press.

Gottsch, M. L., Cunningham, M. J., Smith, J. T., Popa, S. M., Acohido, B. V., Crowley, et al. (2004). A role for kisspeptins in the regulation of gonadotropin secretion in the mouse. *Endocrinology, 145,* 4073–4077.

Gould, M., Greenberg, T., Velting, D., & Shaffer, D. (2003). Youth suicide risk and preventive interventions: A review of the past 10 years. *Journal of the American Academy of Child & Adolescent Psychiatry, 42,* 386–405.

Gowaty, P. A. (2003). Power asymmetries between the sexes, mate preferences, and components of fitness. In C. B. Travis (Ed.), *Evolution, gender, and rape* (pp. 61–86). Cambridge, MA: MIT Press.

Gowen, A. (2006, May 12). 2,800 prom gowns from a single thread; New Orleans students salute Beltsville teen who restored their hope. *The Washington Post,* A01.

Graber, J. A. (2004). Internalizing problems during adolescence. In R. M. Lerner & L. Steinberg (Eds.), *Handbook of adolescent psychology* (2nd ed.) New York: Wiley.

Graham, E. (1995, February 9). Leah: Life is all sweetness and insecurity. *Wall Street Journal,* p. B1.

Graham, S. (2001, November 12). *9/11: The psychological aftermath.* Scientific American website: www. sciam. com/explorations/2001/111201anxiety/index. html

Granic, I., & Patterson, G. R. (2006). Toward a comprehensive model of antisocial development: A dynamic systems approach. *Psychological Review, 113,* 101–131.

Granic, I., Dishion, T. J., & Hollenstein, T. (2005). The family ecology of adolescence. In G. R. Adams & M. D. Berzonsky (Eds.), *Blackwell handbook of adolescence.* Oxford, England: Blackwell.

Granic, I., Hollenstein, T., & Dishion, T. J. (2003). Longitudinal analysis of flexibility and reorganization in early adolescence: A dynamic systems study of family interactions. *Developmental Psychology, 39,* 606–617.

Grant, K. E., Compas, B. E., Stuhlmacher, A. F., Thurm, A. E., McMahon, S. D., & Halpert, J. A. (2003). Stressors and child and adolescent psychopathology: Moving from markers to mechanisms of risk. *Psychological Bulletin, 129,* 447–466.

Grantham, T., & Ford, D. (2003). Beyond self-concept and self-esteem: Racial identity and gifted African American students. *High School Journal, 87,* 18–29.

Gratch, G., & Schatz, J. A. (1987). Cognitive development: The relevance of Piaget's infancy books. In J. D. Osofsky (Ed.), *Handbook of infant development* (2nd ed.). New York: Wiley.

Grattan, M. P., De Vos, E. S., Levy, J., & McClintock, M. K. (1992). Asymmetric action in the human newborn: Sex differences in patterns of organization. *Child Development, 63,* 273–289.

Gray, M. R., & Steinberg. L. (1999). Adolescent romance and the parent–child relationship: A contextual perspective. In W. Furman, B. B. Brown, & C. Feiring (Eds.), *The development of romantic relationships in adolescence,* (pp. 235–265). New York: Cambridge University Press.

Gray-Little, B., & Hafdahl, A. R. (2000). Factors influencing racial comparisons of self-esteem: A quantitative review. *Psychological Bulletin, 126,* 26–54.

Green, A. S., Rafaeli, E., Bolger, N. Shrout, P. E., & Reis, H. T. (2006). Paper or plastic? Data equivalence in paper and electronic diaries. *Psychological Methods, 11,* 87–105.

Greenberg, S. H., & Kuchment, A. (2006, January 9). The "Familymoon." *Newsweek,* 44–46.

Greene, B. A., & DeBacker, T. K. (2004). Gender and orientations toward the future: Links to motivation. *Educational Psychology Review, 16,* 91–120.

Greene, D. A., Naughton, G. A., Briody, J. N., Kemp, A., & Woodhead, H. (2005). Assessment of bone strength at differentially-loaded skeletal regions in adolescence middle-distance runners. *Medicine & Science in Sports & Exercise, 37,* Supplement S89, 88–97.

Greene, J. P., & Winters, M. A. (2006). *Leaving boys behind: Public high school graduation rates.* Civic Report 48. New York: Manhattan Institute for Policy Research.

Greene, K., Krcmar, M., & Rubin, D. (2002). Elaboration in processing adolescent health messages: The impact of egocentrism and sensation seeking on message processing. *Journal of Communication, 52,* 812–831.

Greene, K., Krcmar, M., Walters, L. H., Rubin, D. L., & Hale, J. L. (2000). Targeting adolescent risk-taking behaviors: The contribution of egocentrism and sensation-seeking. *Journal of Adolescence, 23,* 439–461.

Greene, S., Anderson, E., & Hetherington, E. (2003). Risk and resilience after divorce. In F. Walsh (Ed.), *Normal family processes: Growing diversity and complexity.* New York: Guilford.

Greenfield, P. M. (2004). Inadvertent exposure to pornography on the Internet: Implications of peer-to-peer file-sharing networks for child development and families. *Journal of Applied Developmental Psychology, 25,* Special issue: Developing Children, Developing Media: Research from Television to the Internet from the Children's Digital Media Center: A Special Issue Dedicated to the Memory of Rodney R. Cocking, 741–750.

Greenway, C. (2002). The process, pitfalls, and benefits of implementing a reciprocal teaching intervention to improve the reading comprehension of a group of year 6 pupils. *Educational Psychology in Practice, 18,* 113–137.

Greydanus, D. F., Patel, D. R., & Rimsza, M. F. (2001). Contraception in the adolescent: An update. *Pediatrics, 107,* 562–573.

Grieshaber, S. (1998). Constructing the gendered infant. In N. Yelland, *Gender in early childhood.* Florence, KY: Taylor & Frances/Routledge.

Griffiths, M. (1997). Video games and clinical practice: Issues, uses and treatments. *British Journal of Clinical Psychology, 36,* 639–641.

Groër, M., Thomas, S., & Shoffner, D. (1992). Adolescent stress and coping: A longitudinal study. *Research in Nursing and Health, 15,* 209–217.

Grolnick, W. S. (2003). *The psychology of parental control: How well-meant parenting backfires.* Mahwah, NJ: Erlbaum.

Grolnick, W. S., Kurowski, C. O., & Dunlap, K. G. (2000). Parental resources and the transition to junior high. *Journal of Research on Adolescence, 10,* 465–488.

Grossmann, K. E., Grossmann, K., & Waters, E. (Eds.) (2005). *Attachment from infancy to adulthood: The major longitudinal studies.* New York: Guilford Press.

Grotevant, H. D., & Cooper, C. R. (1998). Individuality and connectedness in adolescent development: Review and prospects for research on identity, relationships, and context. In E. E. A. Skoe & A. L. von der Lippe (Eds.), *Personality development in adolescence: A cross national and life span perspective.* New York: Taylor & Frances/Routledge.

Grunbaum, J. A., Kann, L., Kinchen, S. A., Williams, B., Ross, J. G., Lowry, R., & Kolbe, L. (2002). *Youth risk behavior surveillance—United States, 2001.* Atlanta, GA: Centers for Disease Control.

Grunbaum, J., Lowry, R., & Kann, L. (2001). Prevalence of health-related behaviors among alternative high school students as compared with students attending regular high schools. *Journal of Adolescent Health, 29,* 337–343.

Grusec, J. E., & Kuczynski, L. E. (Eds.). (1997). *Parenting and children's internalization of values: A handbook of contemporary theory.* New York: Wiley.

Grzywacz, J. G., Almeida, D. M., Neupert, S. D., & Ettner, S. L. (2004). Socioeconomic status and health: A micro-level analysis of exposure and vulnerability to daily stressors. *Journal of Health and Social Behavior, 45,* 1–16.

Guinote, A., & Fiske, S. T. (2003). Being in the outgroup territory increases stereotypic perceptions of outgroups: Situational sources of category activation. *Group Processes & Intergroup Relations, 6,* 323–331.

Gullotta, T. P. (2006). Leaving home: The runaway and the forgotten throwaway. In G. R. Adams & M. D. Berzonsky (Eds.), *Blackwell handbook of adolescence.* Malden, MA: Blackwell Publishing.

Gullotta, T. P., Adams, G. R., & Markstrom, C. A. (2000). *The adolescent experience* (4th ed.). San Diego, CA: Academic Press.

Gump, L. S., Baker, R. C., & Roll, S. (2000). Cultural and gender differences in moral judgment: A study of Mexican Americans and Anglo Americans. *Hispanic Journal of Behavioral Sciences, 22,* 78–93.

Gunnoe, M. L., & Hetherington, E. M. (2004). Stepchildren's perceptions of noncustodial mothers and noncustodial fathers: Differences in socioemotional involvement and associations with adolescent adjustment problems. *Journal of Family Psychology, 18,* 555–563.

Gur, R. C., Gur, R. E., Obrist, W. D., Hungerbuhler, J. P., Younkin, D., Rosen, A. D., et al. (1982). Sex and handedness differences in cerebral blood flow during rest and cognitive activity. *Science, 217,* 659–661.

Gurin, P., Nagda, B. A., Lopez, G. E. (2004). The benefits of diversity in education for democratic citizenship. Journal of Social Issues, 60, 17–34.

Guterl, F. (2002, November 11). What Freud got right. *Newsweek*, 50–51.

Gutman, L. M., McLoyd, V. C., & Tokoyawa, T. (2005). Financial strain, neighborhood stress, parenting behaviors, and adolescent adjustment in urban African American families. *Journal of Research on Adolescence, 15*, 425–449.

Guttmacher Institute. (2006). *Minors' access to contraceptive services*. Washington, DC: Guttmacher Institute.

Guttmann, J., & Rosenberg, M. (2003). Emotional intimacy and children's adjustment: A comparison between single-parent divorced and intact families. *Educational Psychology, 23*, 457–472.

Haas, A. P., Hendin, H., & Mann, J. J. (2003). Suicide in college students. *American Behavioral Scientist, 46*, Special Issue: *Suicide in Youth*, 1224–1240.

Haberstick, B. C., Young, S. E., & Hewitt, J. K. (2005). Contributions of genes and environments to stability and change in externalizing and internalizing problems during elementary and middle school. *Behavioral Genetics, 35*, 381–396.

Halberstadt, A. G., Grotjohn, D. K., Johnson, C. A., & Furth, M. S. (1992). Children's abilities and strategies in managing the facial display of affect. *Journal of Nonverbal Behavior, 16*, 215–230.

Hall, A. S., & Torres, I. (2002). Partnerships in preventing adolescent stress: Increasing self-esteem, coping, and support through effective counseling. *Journal of Mental Health Counseling, 24*, 97–109.

Hall, G. S. (1916). *Adolescence*. New York: Appleton. (Original work published 1904)

Hall, N., & Sham, S. (1998). *Language brokering by Chinese children*. Paper presented at the Annual Conference of the British Educational Research Association, Dublin. Retrieved February 5, 2006, from http://www. esri. mmu. ac. uk/resprojects/brokering/BERA_1998_copy. doc

Halpern, C. T., Joyner, K., Udery, J. R., & Suchindran, C. (2000). Smart teens don't have sex (or kiss much either). *Journal of Adolescent Health, 26*, 213–225.

Halpern, D. F. (1998). Teaching critical thinking for transfer across domains. *American Psychologist, 53*, 449–455.

Hamilton, A. (2006, June 5). When foster teens find a home. *Time*, 58–63.

Hamilton, D., & Oswalt, S. (1998). A lesson to enhance student self-esteem. *The Education Digest, 64*, 35–39.

Hamilton, M., & Yee, J. (1990). Rape knowledge and propensity to rape. Journal of Research in Personality, 24, 111–122.

Hamilton, S. F., & Hamilton, M. A. (2004). *The youth development handbook: Coming of age in American communities*. Thousand Oaks, CA: Sage.

Hammer, H., Kinkelhor, D., Sedlak, A. J., & Porcellini, L. E. (2004). *National estimates of missing children: Selected trends, 1988–1999*. Washington, DC: U. S. Department of Justice.

Hampel, P., & Petermann, F. (2006), Perceived stress, coping, and adjustment in adolescents. *Journal of Adolescent Health, 38*, 409–415.

Hancox, R. J., Milne, B. J., & Poulton, R. (2004). Association between child and adolescent television viewing and health: A longitudinal birth cohort study. *Lancet, 364*, 257–262.

Haney, C., & Zimbardo, P. (1998). The past and future of U. S. prison policy: Twenty-five years after the Stanford Prison Experiment. *American Psychologist, 53*, 709–727.

Haney, C., Banks, C., & Zimbardo, P. (1973). Interpersonal dynamics in a simulated prison. *International Journal of Criminology and Penology, 1*, 69–97.

Hankin, B. L., & Abramson, L. Y. (2001). Development of gender differences in depression: An elaborated cognitive vulnerability–transactional stress theory. *Psychological Bulletin, 127*, 773–796.

Hardcastle, M. (2003). *Things you oughta know about breakups*. Retrieved March 16, 2006 from http://teenadvice. about. com/library/bl10thingsbreakingup. htm

Harrell, J. S., Bangdiwala, S. I., Deng, S., Webb, J. P., & Bradley, C. (1998). Smoking initiation in youth: The roles of gender, race, socioeconomics, and developmental status. *Journal of Adolescent Health, 23*, 271–279.

Harris, C. M. (2004). Personality and sexual orientation. College Student Journal, 38, 207–211.

Harris, C. R., & Alvarado, N. (2005). Facial expressions, smile types, and self-report during humour, tickle, and pain. *Cognition & Emotion, 19*, 655–669.

Hart, C. H., Yang, C., Nelson, D. A., Jin, S., Bazarskaya, N., & Nelson, L. (1998). Peer contact patterns, parenting practices, and preschoolers' social competence in China, Russia, and the United States. In P. Slee & K. Rigby (Eds.), *Peer relations amongst children: Current issues and future directions*. London: Routledge.

Hart, D., & Atkins, R. (2002). Civic competence in urban youth. *Applied Developmental Science, 6*, 227–236.

Hart, D., Burock, D., & London, B. (2003). Prosocial tendencies, antisocial behavior, and moral development. In A. Slater & G. Bremner (Eds.), *An introduction to developmental psychology*. Malden, MA: Blackwell Publishers.

Hart, D., Hofmann, V., Edelstein, W., & Keller, M. (1997). The relation of childhood personality types to adolescent behavior and development: A longitudinal study of Icelandic children. *Developmental Psychology, 33*, 195–205.

Hart, S. N., Brassard, M. R., & Karlson, H. (1996). Psychological maltreatment. In J. N. Briere, L. Berliner, J. Bulkley, C. Jenny, & T. Reid (Eds.). (1996). *The APSAC handbook on child maltreatment*. Thousand Oaks, CA: Sage.

Hart, T. A., & Heimberg, R. G. (2005). Social anxiety as a risk factor for unprotected intercourse among gay and bisexual male youth. *AIDS Behavior, 9*, 505–512.

Harter, S. (1990a). Identity and self-development. In S. Feldman & G. Elliott (Eds.), *At the threshold: The developing adolescent*. Cambridge, MA: Harvard University Press.

Harter, S. (1990b). Issues in the assessment of self-concept of children and adolescents. In A. LaGreca (Ed.), *Through the eyes of a child*. Boston: Allyn & Bacon.

Harter, S. (1998). The effects of child abuse on the self-system. *Journal of Aggression, Maltreatment, and Trauma, 2*, 147–169.

Harter, S. (1999). *The construction of the self*. New York: Guilford Press.

Harter, S. (2001). *The construction of the self: A developmental perspective*. New York: Guilford Press.

Harter, S. (2003). The development of self-representations during childhood and adolescence. In M. R. Leary & J. P. Tangney (Eds.), *Handbook of self and identity*. New York: Guilford Press.

Harter, S. (2006). Developmental and individual difference perspectives on self-esteem. In D. K. Mroczek & T. D. Little (Eds.), *Handbook of personality development*. Mahwah, NJ: Erlbaum.

Harter, S., & Whitesell, N. R. (2003). Beyond the debate: Why some adolescents report stable self-worth over time and situation, whereas others report changes in self-worth. *Journal of Personality, 71*, 1027–1058.

Harter, S., Whitesell, N. R., & Junkin, L. J. (1998). Similarities and differences in domain-specific and global self-evaluations of learning-disabled, behaviorally disordered, and normally achieving adolescents. *American Educational Research Journal, 35*, 653–680.

Hartup, W. W. (1993). Adolescents and their friends. In B. Laursen (Ed.), *Close friendships in adolescence: New directions for child development*. San Francisco: Jossey-Bass.

Harvey, J. H., & Fine, M. A. (2004). *Children of divorce: Stories of loss and growth*. Mahwah, NJ: Lawrence Erlbaum Associates.

Harway, M., & Nutt, R. (2006). Women and giving. In J. Worell & C. D. Goodheart (Eds.), *Handbook of girls' and women's psychological health: Gender and well-being across the lifespan*. New York: Oxford University Press.

Harwood, R. L., Schoelmerich, A., Ventura-Cook, E., Schulze, P. A., & Wilson, S. P. (1996). Culture and class influences on Anglo and Puerto Rican mothers' beliefs regarding long-term socialization goals and child behavior. *Child Development, 67*, 2446–2461.

Hasher, L., & Zacks, R. T. (1984). Automatic processing of fundamental information: The case of frequency of occurrence. *American Psychologist, 39*, 1372–1388.

Hatfield, E. (1988). Passionate and companionate love. In R. J. Sternberg, & M. L. Barnes, *The psychology of love*. New Haven, CT: Yale University Press.

Hatfield, E., & Rapson, R. L. (1993). Historical and cross-cultural perspectives on passionate love and sexual desire. *Annual Review of Sex Research, 4*, 67–97.

Hatfield, E., & Rapson, R. L. (2002). Passionate love and sexual desire: Cultural and historical perspectives. In A. Vangelisti, H. T. Reis, & M. A. Fitzpatrick (Eds.), *Stability and change in relationships*. New York: Cambridge University Press.

Havighurst, R. J. (1972). *Developmental tasks and education*. New York: David McKay.

Haviv, S., & Leman, P. (2002). Moral decision-making in real life: Factors affecting moral orientation and behavior justification. *Journal of Moral Education, 31*, 121–140.

Hawke, J. M., Jainchill, N., & De Leon, G. (2000). The prevalence of sexual abuse and its impact on the onset of drug use among adolescents in therapeutic community drug treatment. *Journal of Child & Adolescent Substance Abuse, 9,* 35–49.

Hawker, D., & Boulton, M. (2000). Twenty years' research on peer victimization and psychsocial maladjustment: A meta-analytic review of cross-sectional studies. *Journal of Child Psychology and Psychiatry, 41,* 441–455.

Hawley, P. H. (2003). Prosocial and coercive configurations of resource control in early adolescence: A case for the well-adapted Machiavellian. *Merrill-Palmer Quarterly, 4, Special issue: Aggression and Adaptive Functioning: The bright side to bad behavior,* 279–309.

Hays, R. B., (1985). A longitudinal study of friendship development. *Journal of Personality and Social Psychology, 48,* 909–924.

Head, D. (2005). Young people, sex and the media: The facts of life? *Journal of Family Studies, 11,* 326–327.

Healy, P. (2001, March 3). Data on suicides set off alarm. *Boston Globe,* B1.

Heatherton, T. F., & Polivy, J. (1991). Development and validation of a scale for measuring state self-esteem. *Journal of Personality and Social Psychology, 60,* 895–910.

Heller, S. (2005). *Freud A to Z.* New York: Wiley.

Herdt, G. H. (Ed.). (1998). *Rituals of manhood: Male initiation in Papua New Guinea.* Somerset, NJ: Transaction Books.

Herdt, G., & McClintock, M. (2000). The magical age of 10. *Archives of Sexual Behavior, 29,* 587–606.

Herek, G. (2000). The psychology of sexual prejudice. *Current Directions in Psychological Science, 9,* 19–22.

Herrnstein, R. J., & Murray, C. (1994). *The Bell Curve: Intelligence and class structure in American life.* New York: Free Press.

Hetheringon, E. M., Stanley-Hagan, M., & Anderson, E. (1989). Marital transitions: A child's perspective. *American Psychologist, 44,* 303–312.

Hetherington, E. M., & Clingempeel, W. (1992). Coping with marital transitions: A family systems perspective. *Monographs of the Society for Research in Child Development, 57,* (2–3, Serial No. 227).

Hetherington, E. M., & Kelly, J. (2002). *For better or worse: Divorce reconsidered.* New York: Norton.

Hetherington, E., & Elmore, A. (2003). Risk and resilience in children coping with their parents' divorce and remarriage. In S. Luthar (Ed), *Resilience and vulnerability: Adaptation in the context of childhood adversities.* New York: Cambridge University Press.

Hewitt, B. (1997, December 15). A day in the life. *People Magazine,* 49–58.

Hewstone, M. (2003). Intergroup contact: Panacea for prejudice? *Psychologist, 16,* 352–355.

Heyman, R., & Slep, A. M. (2002). Do child abuse and interparental violence lead to adulthood family violence? *Journal of Marriage & Family, 64,* 864–870.

Higgins, D., & McCabe, M. (2003). Maltreatment and family dysfunction in childhood and the subsequent adjustment of children and adults. *Journal of Family Violence, 18,* 107–120.

Highley, J. R., Esiri, M. M., McDonald, B., Cortina-Borja, M., Herron, B. M., & Crow, T. J. (1999). The size and fibre composition of the corpus callosum with respect to gender and schizophrenia: A post-mortem study. *Brain, 122,* 99–110.

Hightower, J. R. R. (2005). Women and depression. In A. Barnes *Handbook of women, psychology, and the law.* New York: John Wiley & Sons.

Hillier, L., & Harrision, L. (2004). Homophobia and the production of shame: Young people and same sex attraction. *Culture, Health, & Sexuality, 6,* 79–94.

Hines, M., & Kaufman, F. R. (1994). Androgen and the development of human sex-typical behavior: Rough-and-tumble play and sex of preferred playmates in children with congenital adrenal hyperplasi (CAH*). Child Development, 65,* 1042–1053.

Hines, M., Golombok, S., Rust, J., Johnston, K. J., & Golding, J. (2002). Testosterone during pregnancy and gender role behavior of preschool children: A longitudinal, population study. *Child Development, 73,* 1678–1687.

Hirschi, T. (2004). Self-control and crime. In R. F. Baumeister & K. D. Vohs (Eds.), *Handbook of self-regulation: Research, theory, and applications.* New York: Guilford Press.

Hiser, E., & Kobayashi, J. (2003). Hemisphere lateralization differences: A cross-cultural study of Japanese and American students in Japan. *Journal of Asian Pacific Communication, 13,* 197–229.

Hocutt, A. M. (1996). Effectiveness of special education: Is placement the critical factor? The Future of Children, 6, 77–102.

Hoek, H. W., (2006). Incidence, prevalence and mortality of anorexia nervosa and other eating disorders. *Current Opinions in Psychiatry, 19,* 389–394.

Hoffman, M. L. (1991). Is empathy altruistic? *Psychological Inquiry, 2,* 131–133.

Hoffman, M. L. (2001). Toward a comprehensive empathy-based theory of prosocial moral development. In A. C. Bohart & D. J. Stipek (Eds.), *Constructive & destructive behavior: Implications for family, school, & society.* Washington, DC: American Psychological Association.

Hoge, C. W., Castro, C. A., Messer, S. C., McGurk, D., Cotting, D. I., & Koffman, R. L. (2004). Combat duty in Iraq and Afghanistan, mental health problems and barriers to care. *New England Journal of Medicine, 351,* 13–22.

Holden, G. W., & Miller, P. C. (1999). Enduring and different: A meta-analysis of the similarity in parents' child rearing. *Psychological Bulletin, 125,* 223–254.

Holland, J. L. (1973). *Making vocational choices: A theory of careers.* Englewood Cliffs, NJ: Prentice Hall.

Holland, J. L. (1987). Current status of Holland's theory of careers: Another perspective. *Career Development Quarterly, 36,* 24–30.

Hollman, F. W., Mulder, T. J., & Kallan, J. E. (2000). *Methodology and assumptions for the population projections of the United States: 1999 to 2100.* Washington, DC: U. S. Census Bureau.

Holmbeck, G., & Hill, J. P. (1988). Storm and stress beliefs about adolescence: Prevalence, self-reported antecedents, and effects of an undergraduate course. *Journal of Youth and Adolescence, 17,* 285–306.

Holmes, T. H., & Rahe, R. H. (1967). The Social Readjustment Scale. *Journal of Psychosomatic Research, 11,* 257–261.

Hong, E., Milgram, R. M., & Gorsky, H. (1995). Original thinking as a predictor of creative performance in young children. *Roeper Review, 18,* 147–149.

Hoppe, M. J., Graham, L., Wilsdon, A., Wells, E. A., Nahom, D., & Morrison, D. M. (2004). Teens speak out about HIV/AIDS: focus group discussions about risk and decision-making. *Journal of Adolescent Health, 35,* 27–35.

Hoppe-Graff, S., & Kim, H. (2005). Understanding rights and duties in different cultures and contexts: Observations from German and Korean adolescents. In N. J. Finkel & F. M. Moghaddam (Eds.), *The psychology of rights and duties: Empirical contributions and normative commentaires.* Washington, DC: American Psychological Association.

Hoptman, M. J., & Davidson, R. J. (1994). How and why do the two cerebral hemispheres interact? *Psychological Bulletin, 116,* 195–219.

Horner, K. L. (1998). Individuality in vulnerability: Influences on physical health. *Journal of Health Psychology, 3,* 71–85.

House, J. S. (2002). Understanding Social Factors and Inequalities in Health: 20th Century Progress and 21st Century Prospects. *Journal of Health and Social Behavior, 43,* 125–142.

Howe, M. J. (1997). *IQ in question: The truth about intelligence.* London: Sage.

Howe, M. J. (2004). Some insights of geniuses into the causes of exceptional achievement. In L. V. Shavinina & M. Ferrari, Beyond knowledge: Extracognitive aspects of developing high ability. Mahwah, NJ: Lawrence Erlbaum Associates.

Howe, N., & Ross, H. S. (1990). Socialization, perspective-taking, and the sibling relationship. *Developmental Psychology, 26,* 160–165.

Hrubes, D., Feldman, R. S. & Tyler, J. M. (2004). Emotion-focused deception: The role of deception in the regulation of emotion. In P. Philippot, & R. S. Feldman, *The regulation of emotion.* Mahwah, NJ: Lawrence Erlbaum Associates.

Hsu, B., Koing, A., Kessler, C., Knapke, K., et al. (1994). Gender differences in sexual fantasy and behavior in a college population: A ten-year replication. *Journal of Sex and Marital Therapy, 20,* 103–118.

Huddleston, J., and Ge, X. (2003). Boys at puberty: Psychosocial implications. In C. Hayward (Ed.), *Gender differences at puberty.* New York: Cambridge University Press.

Huesmann, L. R., Moise-Titus, J., & Podolski, C. L. (2003). Longitudinal relations between children's exposure to TV violence and their aggressive and violent behavior in young adulthood: 1977–1992. *Developmental Psychology, 39,* 201–221.

Huff, C. O. (1999). Source, recency, and degree of stress in adolescence and suicide ideation. *Adolescence, 34,* 81–89.

Huget, J. (2002, June 12). Teen's invention catches liars infrared-handedly. *The Washington Post,* C16.

Hughes, J. O., & Sandler, B. R. (1987). *"Friends" raping friends. Could it happen to you?* Washington, DC: Association of American Colleges, Project on the Status and Education of Women.

Hunt, M. (1974). Sexual behaviors in the 1970s. New York: Dell.

Hunter, J., & Mallon, G. P. (2000). Lesbian, gay, and bisexual adolescent development: Dancing with your feet tied together. In B. Greene, & G. L. Croom, (Eds.). Education, research, and practice in lesbian, gay, bisexual, and transgendered psychology: A resource manual, Vol. 5. Thousand Oaks, CA: Sage.

Huston, A. (Ed.). (1991). Children in poverty: Child development and public policy. Cambridge, England: Cambridge University Press.

Huston, A. C., Donnerstein, F, Fairchild, H., & Feshbach, N. D. (1992). *Big world, small screen: The role of television in American society.* Lincoln, NB: University of Nebraska Press.

Hutchinson, A., Whitman, R., and Abeare, C. (2003). The unification of mind: Integration of hemispheric semantic processing. *Brain & Language, 87,* 361–368.

Hutton, P. H. (2004). *Phillippe Aries and the politics of French cultural history.* Amherst, MA: University of Massachusetts Press.

Hyde, J. S. (2005). The gender similarities hypothesis. *American Psychologist, 60,* 581–592.

Hyde, J. S., & DeLamater, J. D. (2003). Understanding human sexuality. (8th ed.). New York: McGraw-Hill.

Iervolino, A. C., Hines, M., Golombok, S. E., Rust, J., & Plomin, R. (2005). Genetic and environmental influences on sex-typed behavior during the preschool years. *Child Development, 76,* 826–840.

Iglesias, J., Eriksson, J., Grize, F., Tomassini, M., & Villa, A. E. (2005). Dynamics of pruning in simulated large-scale spiking neural networks. *Biosystems, 79,* 11–20.

Iglowstein, I., Jenni, O. G., & Molinari, L., & Largo, R. H. (2003). Sleep duration from infancy to adolescence: Reference values and generational trends. *Pediatrics, 111,* 302–307.

Ingledew, D. K., Markland, D., & Medley, A. R. (1998). Exercise motives and stages of change. *Journal of Health Psychology, 3,* 477–489.

Irwin, E. G. (1993). A focused overview of anorexia nervosa and bulimia: Etiological issues. *Archives of Psychiatric Nursing, 7,* 342–346.

Isaacs, S. L., & Schroeder, S. A. (2004). Class—the ignored determinant of the nation's health. *New England Journal of Medicine, 351,* 1137–1142.

Isay, R. A. (1990). Being homosexual: Gay men and their development. New York: Avon.

Isowa, T., Ohira, H., & Murashima, S. (2006). Immune, endocrine and cardiovascular responses to controllable and uncontrollable acute stress. *Biological Psychology, 71,* 202–213.

Ito, Y. (2001). Development of gender identity in female adolescents: Self-esteem and degree of satisfaction with their physique. *Japanese Journal of Educational Psychology, 49,* 458–468.

Jaccard, J., & Dodge, T. (2002). Parent-adolescent communication about sex and birth control: A conceptual framework. In S. S. Feldman & D. A. Rosenthal (Eds.), *Talking sexuality: Parent-adolescent communication.* San Francisco: Jossey-Bass.

Jaccard, J., Dodge, T., & Dittus, P. (2003). Do adolescents want to avoid pregnancy? Attitudes toward pregnancy as predictors of pregnancy. *Journal of Adolescent Health, 33,* 79–83.

Jackson, A. W. (1997). Middle grade school state policy initiative. *Phi Delta Kappan, 78,* 527.

Jackson, T. L. (Ed.). (1996). *Acquaintance rape: Assessment, treatment, and prevention.* Sarasota, FL: Professional Resource Press/Professional Resource Exchange.

Jacobi, C., Hayward, C., de Zwaan, M., Kraemer, H. C., & Agras, W. S. (2004). Coming to terms with risk factors for eating disorders: Application of risk terminology and suggestions for a general taxonomy. *Psychological Bulletin, 130,* 19–65.

Jacobs, J. E., & Klaczynski, P. A. (2002). The development of judgment and decision making during childhood and adolescence. *Current Directions in Psychological Science, 11,* 145–149.

Jacobs, J. E., & Potenza, M. (1991). The use of judgment heuristics to make social and object decisions: A developmental perspective. *Child Development, 62,* 166–178.

Jacobson, J. W., Foxx, R. M., & Mulick, J. A. (Eds.) (2001). Controversial therapies for developmental disabilities: Fad, fashion and science in professional practice. Mahwah, N. J. : Lawrence Erlbaum Associates.

Jacques, H., & Mash, E. (2004). A test of the tripartite model of anxiety and depression in elementary and high school boys and girls. *Journal of Abnormal Child Psychology, 32,* 13–25.

Jahoda, G. (1980). Theoretical and systematic approaches in mass-cultural psychology. In H. C. Triandis & W. W. Lambert (Eds.), *Handbook of cross-cultural psychology* (Vol. 1). Needham Heights, MA: Allyn & Bacon.

Janssens, J. M. A. M., & Dekovic, M. (1997). Child rearing, prosocial moral reasoning, and prosocial behavior. *International Journal of Behavioral Development, 20,* 509–527.

Jarvela, S., & Hakkinen, P. (2005). How to make collaborative learning more successful with innovative technology. *Educational Technology, 45,* 34.

Jehlen, A., & Winans, D. (2005). No child left behind – Myth or Truth? NEA Today, 23, 32–34.

Jenkins, J. E. (1996). The influence of peer affiliation and student activities on adolescent drug involvement. *Adolescence, 31,* 297–306.

Jennings, M. K., & Stoker, L. (2001). *Generations and civic engagement: A longitudinal multiple-generation analysis.* Paper delivered at the 2001 American Political Science Association Convention, San Francisco, CA, p. 22.

Jennings, M. K., & Stoker, L. (2002, June). *Generational change, life cycle processes and social capital.* Paper presented at the Conference Citizenship on Trial: Interdisciplinary Perspectives on the Political Socialization of Adolescents, McGill University, Montreal, Canada

Jensen, L. A., Arnett, J. J., Feldman, S. S., & Cauffman, E. (2002). It's wrong, but everybody does it: Academic dishonesty among high school and college students. *Contemporary Educational Psychology, 27,* 2009–228.

Jepsen, D. A., & Sheu, H-B. (2003). General job satisfaction from a developmental perspective: Exploring choice-job matches at two career stages. *Career Development Quarterly, 52,* 162–179.

Jepsen, D. A., & Sheu, H-B. (2003). General job satisfaction from a developmental perspective: Explaining choice-job matches as two career stages. *Development Quarterly, 52,* 162–179.

Jessor, R., Donovan, J. E., & Costa, F. (1996). Personality, perceived life chances, and adolescent behavior. In K. Hurrelman, & S. F. Hawthorne, *Social problems and social contexts in adolescence: Perspectives across boundaries.* Hawthorne, NY: Aldine de Gruyter.

Jeynes, H. (2005). Effects of parental involvement and family structure on the academic achievement of adolescents. *Marriage and Family Review, 37,* 99–116.

Jiao, S., Ji, G., & Jing, Q. (1996). Cognitive development of chines urban only children and children with siblings. *Child Development, 67,* 387–395.

Joe, S., & Marcus, S. (2003). Datapoints: Trends by race and gender in suicide attempts among U. S. adolescents, 1991–2001. *Psychiatric Services, 54,* 454.

Johnson, A. M., Wadsworth, J., Wellings, K., & Bradshaw, S. (1992). Sexual lifestyles and HIV risk. Nature, 360, 410–412.

Johnson, C. D., & Stokes, G. S. (2002). The meaning, development, and career outcomes of breadth of vocational interests. *Journal of Vocational Behavior, 61,* 327–347.

Johnson, D. J., Jaeger, E., Randolph, S. M., Cauce, A. M., Ward, J., National Institute of Child Health and Human Development: Early Child care Research Network. (2003). Studying the effects of early child care experiences on the development of children of color in the United States: Toward a more inclusive research agenda. *Child Development, 74,* 1227–1244.

Johnson, J., Cohen, P., Smailes, E. M., Kasen, S., & Brook, J. S. (2002, March 29). Television viewing and aggressive behavior during adolescence and adulthood. *Science, 295,* 2468–2471.

Johnson, M. H. (1998). The neural basis of cognitive development. In D. Kuhn & R. S. Siegler (Eds.), *Handbook of child psychology: Vol. 2. Cognition, perception, and language* (5th ed.). New York: Wiley.

Johnson, N. G., Roberts, M. C., & Worell, J. (Eds.). (1999). *Beyond appearance: A new look at adolescent girls.* Washington, DC: American Psychological Association.

Johnston, L. D., Bachman, J. G., & O'Malley, P. M. (2006). *Monitoring the Future study.* Lansing: University of Michigan.

Jones, A. (2005, September 18). Students linking with students: Facebook site gives college students chance to meet, share interests. *The Palm Beach Post*, E1.

Jones, C., & Trickett, E. (2005). Immigrant adolescents behaving as culture brokers: A study of families from the former Soviet Union. *Journal of Social Psychology, 145*, 405–427.

Jones, J. C., & Barlow, D. H. (1990). Self-reported frequency of sexual urges, fantasies, and masturbatory fantasies in heterosexual males and females. *Archives of Sexual Behavior, 19*, 269–279.

Jones, M. C. (1965). Psychological correlates of somatic development. *Child Development, 36*, 899–911.

Jones, R. G., & Jones, E. E. (1964). Optimum conformity as an ingratiation tactic. *Journal of Personality, 32*, 436–458.

Jones, R. K., Darroch, J. E., & Henshaw, S. K. (2002). Patterns in the socioeconomic characteristics of women obtaining abortions in 2000–2001. *Perspectives on Sexual and Reproductive Health, 34*, 27–35.

Jones-Harden, B. (2004). Safety and stability for foster children: A developmental perspective. *The Future of Children, 14*, 31–48.

Jose, P. E., & Ratcliffe, V., (2004). Stressor frequency and perceived intensity as predictors of internalizing symptoms: Gender and age differences in adolescence. *New Zealand Journal of Psychology, 33*, 145–154.

Joseph, H., Reznik, I., & Mester, R. (2003). Suicidal behavior of adolescent girls: Profile and meaning. *Israel Journal of Psychiatry & Related Sciences, 40*, 209–219.

Joseph, R. (1999). Environmental influences on neural plasticity, the limbic system, emotional development and attachment: A review. *Child Psychiatry & Human Development, 29*, 189–208.

Jost, J. T., & Hamilton, D. L. (2005). Stereotypes in our culture. In J. F. Dovidio, P. Click, & L. A. Rudman (Eds.), *On the nature of prejudice: Fifty years after Allport.* Malden, MA: Blackwell Publishing.

Judd, C. M., & Park, B. (2005). Group differences and stereotype accuracy. In J. F. Dovidio, P. Click, & L. A. Rudman (Eds.), *On the nature of prejudice: Fifty years after Allport.* Malden, MA: Blackwell Publishing.

Judd, C. M., Park, B., Yzerbyt, V., Gordijn, E. H., & Muller, D. (2005). Attributions of intergroup bias and outgroup homogeneity to ingroup and outgroup others. *European Journal of Social Psychology, 35*, 677–704.

Judd, C. M., Ryan, C. S., & Park, B. (1991). Accuracy in the judgment of in-group and out-group variability. *Journal of Personality and Social Psychology, 6*, 366–379.

Juvonen, J., Le, V. -N., Kaganoff, T., Augustine, C. H., & Constant, L. (2004). *Focus on the wonder years: Challenges facing the American middle school.* Santa Monica, CA: Rand Corporation.

Kadison, R., & DiGeronimo, T. (2004). *College of the overwhelmed: The campus mental health crisis and what to do about it.* San Francisco: Jossey-Bass.

Kagan, J., & Snidman, N. (1991). Infant predictors of inhibited and uninhibited profiles. *Psychological Science, 2*, 40–44.

Kagan, J., Arcus, D., & Snidman, N. (1993). The idea of temperament: Where do we go from here? In R. Plomin, & G. E. McClearn (Eds.), *Nature, nurture, and psychology.* Washington, DC: American Psychological Association.

Kahneman, D., Diener, E., & Schwarz, N. (1998). *Well-being: The foundations of hedonic psychology.* New York: Russell Sage Foundation.

Kail, R. V. (2003). Information processing and memory. In M. H. Bornstein & L. Davidson, *Well-being: Positive development across the life course.* Mahwah, NJ: Lawrence Erlbaum Associates.

Kail, R. V. (2004). Cognitive development includes global and domain-specific processes. *Merrill-Palmer Quarterly, 50*, Special Issue: 50th Anniversary Issue: Part II, The maturing of the human development sciences: Appraising past, present, and prospective agendas, 445–455.

Kaiser Family Foundation. (2001). *Generation Rx. com: How young people use the Internet for health information.* Menlo Park, CA: Kaiser Family Foundation.

Kalick, S. M., Zebrowitz, L. A., Langlois, J. H., & Johnson, R. M. (1998). Does human facial attractiveness honestly advertise health? Longitudinal data on an evolutionary question. *Psychological Science, 9*, 8–13

Kaltiala-Heino, R., Kosunen, E., & Rimpela, M. (2003). Pubertal timing, sexual behavior and self-reported depression in middle adolescence. *Journal of Adolescence, 26*, 531–545.

Kantrowitz, B. A., & Springen, K. (2003, September 22). Why sleep matters. *Newsweek, 142*, 75–77.

Kao, G. (2000). Psychological well-being and educational achievement among immigrant youth. In D. J. Hernandez (Ed.), *Children of immigrants: Health, adjustment, and public assistance.* Washington, D. C. : National Academy Press.

Kao, G., & Vaquera, E. (2006). The salience of racial and ethnic identification in friendship choices among Hispanic adolescents. *Hispanic Journal of Behavioral Sciences, 28*, 23–47.

Karlins, M., Coffman, T. L., & Walters, G. (1969). On the fading of social stereotypes: Studies in three generations of college students. *Journal of Personality and Social Psychology, 13*, 1–16.

Karlsen, S., Nazroo, J. Y., McKenzie, K., Bhui, K., & Weich, S. (2005). Racism, psychosis and common mental disorder among ethnic minority groups in England. *Psychological Medicine, 29*, 1–9

Karpov, Y. V., & Haywood, H. C. (1998). Two ways to elaborate Vygotsky's concept of mediation: Implications for instruction. *American Psychologist, 53*, 27–36.

Kaslow, N. J., & Celano, M. P. (1995). The family therapies. In A. S. Gurman, & S. B. Messer (Eds.), *Essential psychotherapies: Theory and practice.* New York: Guilford Press.

Katrowitz, B., & Springen, K. (2005, May 16.) A peaceful adolescence. *Newsweek International Edition*, pp. 50–52.

Katz, I., & Hass, R. G. (1988). Racial ambivalence and American value conflict: Correlational and priming studies of dual cognitive structures. *Journal of Personality and Social Psychology, 55*, 893–905.

Kaufman, J. C., & Baer, J. (2005). *Creativity across domains: Faces of the muse.* Mahwah, NJ: Erlbaum.

Kaufman, J. C., Kaufman, A. S., Kaufman-Singer, J., & Kaufman, N. L. (2005). The Kaufman Assessment Battery for Children – Second Edition and the Kaufman Adolescent and Adult Intelligence Test. In D. P. Flanagan, & P. L. Harrison, (Eds.), *Contemporary intellectual assessment: Theories, tests, and issues.* New York, Guilford Press.

Kaufmann, D., Gesten, E., Santa Lucia, R. C., Salcedo, O., Rendina-Gobioff, G., & Gadd, R. (2000). The relationship between parenting style and children's adjustment: The parents' perspective. *Journal of Child & Family Studies, 9*, 231–245.

Kavale, K. A., & Forness, S. R. (2000). History, rhetoric, and reality: Analysis of the inclusion debate. *Remedial and Special Education, 21*, 279–296.

Kawai, Y., (2005). Stereotyping Asian Americans: The dialectic of the model minority and the yellow peril. *Howard Journal of Communications, 16*, 109–130.

Kaye, W. H., Devlin, B., Barbarich, N., Bulik, C. M., Thornton, L., Badanu, S. A., Fichter, M. M., Halmi, K. A., Kaplan, A. S., Strober, M., Woodside, D. B., Bergen, A. W., Crow, S., Mitchell, J., Rotondo, A., Mauri, M., Cassano, G., Keel, P., Plotnicov, K., Pollice, C., Klump, K. L., Lilenfeld, L. R., Ganjei, J. K., Quadflieg, N., Berrettini, W. H., & Kaye, W. H. (2004). Genetic analysis of bulimia nervosa: Methods and sample description. *Journal of Eating Disorders, 35*, 556–570.

Keating, D. P. (1990). Adolescent thinking. In S. S. Feldman & G. R. Elliott (Eds.), *At the threshhold: The developing adolescent.* Cambridge, MA: Harvard University Press.

Kecskes, I., & Papp, T. (2000). Foreign language and mother tongue. Mahwah, NJ: Erlbaum.

Keel, P. K., Leon, G. R., & Fulkerson, J. A. (2000). Vulnerability to eating disorders in childhood and adolescence. In R. E. Ingram & J. M. Price, (Eds.) *Vulnerability to psychopathology: Risk across the life span.* New York: Guilford Press.

Keith, V., & Finlay, B. (1988). The impact of parental divorce on children's educational attainment, marital timing, and likelihood of divorce. *Journal of Marriage and the Family, 50*, 797–809.

Kelley, T. M., & Stack, S. A. (2000). Thought recognition, locus of control, and adolescent well-being. *Adolescence, 35*, 531–550.

Kelly, G. (2001). *Sexuality today: A human perspective* (7th ed.). New York: McGraw-Hill.

Kempler, D., Van Lancker, D., Marchman, V., & Bates, E. (1999). Idiom comprehension in children and adults with unilateral brain damage. *Developmental Neuropsychology, 15*, 327–349.

Kennedy, P. (2002). Learning cultures and learning styles: Myth-understandings about adult (Hong Kong) Chinese learners. *International Journal of Lifelong Education, 21*, 430.

Kessels, U. (2005). Fitting into the stereotype: How gender-stereotyped perceptions of prototypic peers relate to liking for school subjects. *European Journal of Psychology of Education, 20, Special issue: Societal values and school motivation. Students' goals in different life domains,* 309–323.

Keyes, C. L., & Shapiro, A. D. (2004). Social well-being in the United States: A descriptive epidemiology. In O. G. Brim and C. D. Ryff (Eds.), *How healthy are we? A national study of well-being at midlife.* Chicago: University of Chicago Press.

Kidwell, J. S., Dunyam, R. M., Bacho, R. A., Pastorino, E., & Portes, P. R. (1995). Adolescent identity exploration: A test of Erikson's theory of transitional crisis. *Adolescence, 30,* 785–793.

Kiecolt-Glaser, J. K., & Glaser, R. (1991). Stress and immune function in humans. In R. Ader, D. L. Felton, & N. Cohen (Eds.), *Psychoneuroimmunology* (2nd ed.). San Diego, CA: Academic Press.

Kiecolt-Glaser, J. K., Newton, T., & Cacioppo, J. T. (1996). Marital conflict and endocrine function: Are men really more physiologically affected than women? *Journal of Consulting and Clinical Psychology, 64,* 324–332.

Kiehl, S. (1998, August 12). Living a lesson in friendship as college roommate, teen will be disabled friend's attendant. *The Boston Globe,* C1.

Kiesner, J. M. & Pastore, M. (2005). Differences in the relations between antisocial behavior and peer acceptance across contexts and across adolescence. *Child Development, 76,* 1278–1293.

Kiesner, J., Kerr, M., & Stattin, H. (2004). Very important persons in adolescence: Going beyond ink-school, single friendships in the study of peer homophily. *Journal of Adolescence, 27, Special issue: Families, peers and contexts as multiple determinants of adolescent problem behavior,* 545–560.

Killen, M., & Hart, D. (Eds.). (1995). *Morality in everyday life: Developmental perspectives.* New York: Cambridge University Press.

Killeya-Jones, L. A. (2005). Identity structure, role discrepancy and psychological adjustment in male college student-athletes. *Journal of Sport Behavior, 28,* 167–185.

Killgore, W. D., & Yurgelun-Todd, D. A. (2004). Sex-related developmental differences in the lateralized activation of the prefrontal cortex and amygdala during perception of facial affect. *Perception and Motor Skills, 99,* 371–391.

Kim, E. (2005). Korean American parental control: Acceptance or rejection? *Ethos, 33,* 347–366.

Kim, J., & Cicchetti, D. (2003). Social self-efficacy and behavior problems in maltreated children. *Journal of Clinical Child & Adolescent Psychology, 32,* 106–117.

Kim, M. T., Han, H. -R., Shin, H. S., Kim, K. B., & Lee, H. B. (2005). Factors associated with depression experience of immigrant populations: A study of Korean immigrants. *Archives of Psychiatric Nursing, 19,* 217–225.

Kimm, S. Y., Glynn, N. W., Kriska, A. M., Barton, B. A., Kronsberg, S. S., Daniels, S. R., Crawford, P. B., Sabry, Z. I., & Liu, K. (2002). Decline in physical activity in black girls and white girls during adolescence. *New England Journal of Medicine, 347,* 709–715.

King, J. E. (2005). Academic success and financial decisions: Helping students make crucial choices. In R. S. Feldman (Ed.), *Improving the first year of college: Research and practice.* Mahwah, NJ: Erlbaum.

King, K. (2003). Racism or sexism? Attributional ambiguity and simultaneous memberships in multiple oppressed groups. *Journal of Applied Social Psychology, 33,* 223–247.

King, T., & Bannon, E. (2002). *At what cost? The price that working students pay for a college education.* Washington, DC: The State PIRG's Higher Education Project.

Kinney, D. A. (1993). From nerds to normals: The recovery of identity among adolescents from middle school to high school. *Sociology of Education, 66,* 21–40.

Kinney, D. A. (1999) From "Headbangers" to "Hippies": Delineating adolescents' active attempts to form an alternative peer culture. In J. McLellan & M. J. Pugh (Eds.), *The role of peer group stability and change in adolescent social identity: New Directions for child and adolescent development.* No. 84. San Francisco: Jossey-Bass.

Kinsey, A. C., Pomeroy, W. B., & Martin, C. E. (1948). Sexual behavior in the human male. Philadelphia: Saunders.

Kirby, D., Baumler, E., Coyle, K., Basen-Engquist, K., Parcel, G., Harrist, R., & et al. (2004). The "Safer Choices" intervention: Its impact on the sexual behaviors of different subgroups of high school students. *Journal of Adolescent Health, 35,* 442–452.

Kitchener, R. F. (1996). The nature of the social for Piaget and Vygotsky. *Human Development, 39,* 243–249.

Kitts, R. (2005). Gay adolescents and suicide: Understanding the association. *Adolescence, 40,* 621–628.

Kitzmann, K., Gaylord, N., and Holt, A. (2003). Child witnesses to domestic violence: A meta-analytic review. *Journal of Consulting & Clinical Psychology, 71,* 339–352.

Klaczynski, P. A. (2004). A dual-process model of adolescent development: Implications for decision making, reasoning, and identity. In R. V. Kail (Ed.), *Advances in child development and behavior, Vol. 32.* San Diego, CA: Elsevier Academic Press.

Klaczynski, P. A., Fauth, M. M., & Swanger, A. (1998). Adolescent identity: Rational vs. experiential processing, formal operations, and critical thinking beliefs. *Journal of Youth and Adolescence, 27,* 185–208.

Kleinman, A. (1996). How is culture important for DSM-IV? In J. E Mezzich, A. Kleinman, H. Fabrega, Jr., & D. L. Parron (Eds.), *Culture and psychiatric diagnosis: A DSM-IV perspective.* Washington, DC: American Psychiatric Press.

Klingner, J., & Artiles, A. J. (2006). English language learners struggling to learn to read: Emergent scholarship on linguistic differences and learning disabilities. *Journal of Learning Disabilities, 39,* 386–389.

Knafo, A., & Schwartz, S. H. (2003). Parenting and accuracy of perception of parental values by adolescents. *Child Development, 73,* 595–611.

Knecht, S., Deppe, M., Draeger, B., Bobe, L., Lohmann, H., Ringelstein, E. B., & Henningsen, H. (2000). Language lateralization in healthy right-handers. *Brain, 123,* 74–81.

Knight, G. P., Jonson, L. G., Carlo, G., & Eisenberg, N. (1994). A multiplicative model of the dispositional antecedents of a prosocial behavior: Predicting more the people more of the time. *Journal of Personality and Social Psychology, 66,* 178–183.

Knowles, J. (2005). Birth control choices for teens. Retrieved April 1, 2006, from http://www. planned parenthood.   org/pp2/portal/files/portal/medical info/birthcontrol/pub-bc-choices-teens. xml

Knox, D., Zusman, M. E., Buffington, C., & Hemphill, G. (2000). Interracial dating attitudes among college students. *College Student Journal, 34, Special issue: Social studies instruction,* 69–71.

Knox, D., Zusman, M. E., Kaluzny, M., & Cooper, C. (2000). College student recovery from a broken heart. *College Student Journal, 34,* 322–324.

Kobasa, S. C. O., Maddi, S. R., Puccetti, M. C., & Zola, M. A. (1994). Effectiveness of hardiness, exercise and social support as resources against illness. In A. Steptoe & J. Wardle (Eds.), *Psychosocial processes and health: A reader* (pp. 000). Cambridge, England: Cambridge University Press.

Kodl, M., & Mermelstein, R. (2004). Beyond modeling: Parenting practices, parental smoking history, and adolescent cigarette smoking. *Addictive Behaviors, 29,* 17–32.

Koechlin, E., Basso, G., Pietrini, P., Panzer, S., & Grafman, J. (1999, May 13). The role of the anterior prefrontal cortex in human cognition. *Nature, 399,* 148–151

Koenig, A., Cicchetti, D., & Rogosch, F. (2004). Moral development: The association between maltreatment and young children's prosocial behaviors and moral transgressions. *Social Development, 13,* 97–106.

Kogan, S. M. (2004). Disclosing unwanted sexual experiences: Results from a national sample of adolescent women. *Child Abuse & Neglect, 28*(2), 147–165.

Kohlberg, L. (1984). *The psychology of moral development: Essays on moral development* (Vol. 2). San Francisco: Harper & Row.

Kohn, M. (1977). *Class and conformity* (2nd ed.). Chicago: University of Chicago Press.

Koivisto, M., & Revonsuo, A. (2003). Object recognition in the cerebral hemispheres as revealed by visual field experiments. *Laterality: Asymmetries of Body, Brain & Cognition, 8,* 135–153.

Korobov, N. (2004). Inoculating against prejudice: A Discursive approach to homophobia and sexism in adolescent male talk. *Psychology of Men & Masculinity, 5,* 178–189.

Kosic, A., (2004). Acculturation strategies, coping process and acculturative stress. *Scandinavian Journal of Psychology, 45,* 269–278.

Koss, M. P., Goodman, L. A., Browne, A., Fitzgerald, L. F., Keita, G. P., & Russo, N. F. (1993). No safe haven: Violence against women, at home, at work, and in the community. Final report of the American Psychological Association Women's Programs Office Task Force on Violence Against Women. Washington, DC: American Psychological Association.

Kozulin, A., (2004). Vygotsky's theory in the classroom: Introduction. *European Journal of Psychology of Education, 19,* 3–7.

Kramer, L., & Koval, A. K. (2005). Sibling relationship quality from birth to adolescence: The enduring contributions of friends. *Journal of Family Psychology, 19,* Special issue: *Sibling relationship contributions to individual and family well-being,* 503–511.

Kratochvil, C. J., Vitiello, B., Walkup, J., Emslie, G., Waslick, B. D., Weller, E. B., et al. (2006). Selective serotonin reuptake inhibitors in pediatric depression: Is the balance between benefits and risks favorable? *Journal of Child and Adolescent Psychopharmacology, 16,* 11–24.

Krein, S. (1986). Growing up in a single parent family: The effect on education and earnings of young men. *Family Relations: Journal of Applied Family & Child Studies, 35,* 161–168.

Kroger, J. (2006). Identity development during adolescence. In G. R. Adams & M. D. Berzonsky (Eds.), *Blackwell handbook of adolescence.* Malden, MA: Blackwell Publishing.

Krueger, R. F., Caspi, A., & Moffitt, T. E. (2000). Epidemiological personology: The unifying role of personality in population-based research on problem behaviors. *Journal of Personality, 68,* Special issue: *Personality processes and problem behavior,* 967–998.

Krueger, R. F., Caspi, A., Moffitt, T. E., & Silva, P. A. (1998). The structure and stability of common mental disorders (DSM-III-R): A longitudinal-epidemiological study. *Journal of Abnormal Psychology, 107,* 216–227.

Kuhn, D. (2000). Metacognitive development. *Current Directions in Psychological Science, 9,* 178–181.

Kuhn, D. (2006) Do cognitive changes accompany developments in the adolescent brain? *Perspectives on Psychological Science, 1,* 59–67.

Kulis, S., Marsiglia, F. F., & Hurdle, D. (2003). Gender identity, ethnicity, acculturation, and drug use: Exploring differences among adolescents in the Southwest. *Journal of Community Psychology, 31,* 167–188.

Kunkel, D., Wilcox, B. L., Cantor, J., Palmer, E., Linn, S., & Dowrick, P. (2004, February 20). *Report of the APA task force on advertising and children.* Washington, DC: American Psychological Association.

Kupersmidt, J. B., Dodge, K. A. (Eds.). (2004). *Children's peer relations: From development to intervention.* Washington, DC: American Psychological Association.

Kurcinka, M. S. (2006). *Sleepless in America: Is your child misbehaving or missing sleep?* New York: HarperCollins.

Kurdek, L. A., & Sinclair, R. J. (2000). Psychological, family, and peer predictors of academic outcomes in first-through fifth-grade children. *Journal of Educational Psychology, 92,* 449–457.

Kurdek, L. A., Fine, M. A., & Sinclair, R. J. (1995). School adjustment in sixth graders: Parenting transitions, family climate, and peer norm effects. *Child Development, 66,* 430–445.

Kurtines, W. M., & Gewirtz, J. L. (1987). *Moral development through social interaction.* New York: Wiley.

Kuther, T. L. (2000). Moral reasoning, perceived competence, and adolescent engagement in risky activity. *Journal of Adolescence, 23,* 599–604.

Kuther, T. L., & Higgins-D'Alessandro, A. (2000). Bridging the gap between moral reasoning and adolescent engagement in risky behavior. *Journal of Adolescence, 23,* 409–422.

Kuther, T. L., & Higgins-D'Alessandro, A. (2003). Attitudinal and normative predictors of alcohol use by older adolescents and young adults. *Journal of Drug Education, 33,* 71–90.

Kwan, V. S. Y., Bond, M. H., Singelis, T. M. (1997). Pancultural explanations for life satisfaction: Adding relationship harmony to self-esteem. *Journal of Personality & Social Psychology, 73,* 1038–1051.

Labouvie-Vief, G. (1986). Modes of knowledge and the organization of development. In M. L. Commons, L. Kohlberg, F. Richards, & J. Sinnott (Eds.), *Beyond formal operations: Vol. 3. Models and methods in the study of adult and adolescent thought.* New York: Praeger.

Labouvie-Vief, G., & Diehl, M. (2000). Cognitive complexity and cognitive-affective integration: Related or separate domains of adult development? *Psychology & Aging, 15,* 490–504.

Lacey, M. (2002, January 6). In Kenyan family, ritual for girls still divides. *The New York Times,* 6.

Laird, R. D., Pettit, G. S., Dodge, K. A., & Bates, J. E. (2005). Peer relationship antecedents of delinquent behavior in late adolescence: Is there evidence of demographic group differences in developmental processes? *Development and Psychopathology, 17,* 127–144.

Lam, S. -F., Chiu, C. -Y., Lau, I. Y., Chan, W. -M., & Yim, P. (2006). Managing intergroup attitudes among Hong Kong adolescents: Effects of social category inclusiveness and time pressure. *Asian Journal of Social Psychology, 9,* 1–11.

Lambert, W. E., & Peal, E. (1972). The relation of bilingualism to intelligence. In A. S. Dil (Ed.), Language, psychology, and culture (3rd ed.). New York: Wiley.

Lamm, H., & Wiesmann, U. (1997). Subjective attributes of attraction: How people characterize their liking, their love, and their being in love. *Personal Relationships, 4,* 271–284.

Landsheer, H. A., Maassen, G. H., Bisschop, P., & Adema, L. (1998). Can higher grades result in fewer friends? A reexamination of the relation between academic and social competence. *Adolescence, 33,* 185–191.

Lane, R. D., Laukes, C., Marcus, F. I., Chesney, M. A., Sechrest, L., Gear, K., et al. (2005). Psychological stress preceding idiopathic ventricular fibrillation. *Psychosomatic Medicine, 67,* 359–365.

Langford, P. E. (1995). *Approaches to the development of moral reasoning.* Hillsdale, NJ: Erlbaum.

Lantz, P. M., House, J. S., Mero, R. P., & Williams. D. R. (2005). Stress, life events, and socioeconomic disparities in health: results from the Americans' changing lives study. *Journal of Health & Social Behavior, 46,* 274–288.

Larsen, R. J., & Buss, D. M. (2005). Personality assessment, measurement, and research design. In R. J. Larsen & D. M. Buss (Eds.), *Personality psychology: Domains of knowledge about human nature* (2nd ed.). Boston: McGraw-Hill.

Larson, R. (1991). Daily companionship in late childhood and early adolescence: Changing developmental contexts. *Child Development, 62,* 284–300.

Larson, R. W., & Richards, M. (1994). *Divergent realities: The emotional lives of mothers, father, and adolescents.* New York: Basic Books.

Larson, R. W., & Richards, M. H. (1991). Daily companionship in late childhood and early adolescence: Changing developmental contexts. *Child Development, 62,* 284–300.

Larson, R. W., & Verma, S. (1999). How children and adolescents spend time across the world: Work, play, and developmental opportunities. *Psychological Bulletin, 125,* 701–736.

Larson, R. W., Richards, M. H., Moneta, G., Holmbeck, G., & Duckett, E. (1996). Changes in adolescents' daily interactions with their families from ages 10 to 18: Disengagement and transformation. *Developmental Psychology, 32,* 744–754.

Larson, R. W., Richards, M. H., Sims, B., & Dworkin, J. (2001). How urban African American young adolescents spend their time: Time budgets for locations, activities, and companionship. *American Journal of Community Psychology, 29,* 565–597.

Larson, R., & Lampman-Petraitis, C. (1989). Daily emotional states as reported by children and adolescents. *Child Development, 60,* 1250–1260.

Lash, H. (2006, March 2) Study: Dropout rates decline when voc ed is included. *Education Daily, 39,* 3.

Lattibeaudiere, V. H. (2000). An exploratory study of the transition and adjustment of former home-schooled students to college life. Dissertation Abstracts International Section A: Humanities & Social Sciences, 61, p. 2211.

Lau, S., & Kwok, L. K. (2000). Relationship of family environment to adolescents' depression and self-concept. *Social Behavior & Personality, 28,* 41–50.

Lauer, T. (2005). Teaching critical-thinking skills using course content material. *Journal of College Science Teaching, 34,* 34–38.

Laumann, E. O., Gagnon, J. H., Michael, R. T., & Michaels, S. (1994). *The social organization of sexuality: Sexual practices in the United States (1994).* Chicago: University of Chicago Press.

Laurenceau, J-P., Barrett, L. F., & Pietromonaco, P. R. (1998). Intimacy as an interpersonal process: The importance of self-disclosure, partner disclosure, and perceived partner responsiveness in interpersonal exchanges. *Journal of Personality and Social Psychology, 74,* 1238–1251.

Lauricella, T. (2001, November). The education of a home schooler. Smart Money, 115–121.

Laursen, B. (1993). The perceived impact of conflict on adolescent relationships. *Merrill-Palmer Quarterly, 39,* 535–550.

Laursen, B. (1995). Conflict and social interaction in adolescent relationships. *Journal of Research on Adolescence, 5,* 55–70.

Laursen, B., & Collins. W. A. (2004). Parent-child communication during adolescence. In A. L. Vangelisti (Ed.), *Handbook of family communication.* Mahwah, NJ: Erlbaum.

Laursen, B., Finkelstein, B. D., & Townsend Betts, N. (2001). A developmental meta-analysis of peer conflict resolution. *Developmental Review, 21,* 423–449.

Laursen, B., Hartup, W. W., & Koplas, A. L. (1996). Toward understanding peer conflict. *Merrill-Palmer Quarterly, 42,* 76–102.

Lavellee, K. L., Bierman, K. L., & Nix, R. L. (2005). The impact of first-grade "friendship group" experiences on child social outcomes in the Fast Track Program. *Journal of Abnormal Child Psychology, 33,* 307–324.

Lawlor, D. A., O'Callaghan, M. J., Mamun, A. A., Williams, G. M., Bor, W., & Najman, J. M. (2005), Socioeconomic position, cognitive function, and clustering of cardiovascular risk factors in adolescence: Findings from the Mater University study of pregnancy and its outcomes. *Psychosomatic Medicine, 67,* 862–868

Lazarus, R. S. (2000). *Stress and emotion: A new synthesis.* New York: Springer Publishing Co.

Lazarus, R. S. (2000). Toward better research on stress and coping. *American Psychologist, 55,* 665–673.

Lazarus, R. S., & Folkman, S. (1984). *Stress, appraisal, and coping.* New York: Springer.

Leahy, R. L. (2004). *Contemporary cognitive therapy: Theory, research, and practice.* New York: Guilford Press.

Leaper, C. (2002). Parenting girls and boys. In M. Bornstein (Ed.), *Handbook of parenting: Vol. 1: Children and parenting, 2nd ed.* Mahwah, NJ: Lawrence Erlbaum Associates.

Leary, W. E. (1996, November 20). U. S. rate of sexual diseases highest in developed world. New York Times, p. C1.

Lee, M. E., Matsumoto, D., Kobayashi, M., Krupp, D., Maniatis, E. F., & Roberts, W. (1992). Cultural influences on nonverbal behavior in applied settings. In R. S. Feldman (Ed.), *Applications of nonverbal behavioral theories and research.* Hillsdale, NJ: Erlbaum.

Lee, V. E., & Burkam, D. T. (2003). Dropping out of high school: The role of school organization and structure. *American Educational Research Journal, 40,* 353–393.

Lehman, D. R., & Nisbett, R. E. (1990). A longitudinal study of the effects of undergraduate training on reasoning. *Developmental Psychology, 26,* 952–960.

Lemonick, M. D. (2000, October 30). Teens before their time. *Time, 67,* 68–74.

Leonard, C. M., Lombardino, L. J., Mercado, L. R., Browd, S. R., Breier, J. I., & Agee, O. F. (1996). Cerebral asymmetry and cognitive development in children: A magnetic resonance imaging study. *Psychological Science, 7,* 89–95.

Lepore, S. J., Palsane, M. N., & Evans, G. W. (1991). Daily hassles and chronic strains: A hierarchy of stressors? *Social Science and Medicine, 33,* 1029–1036.

Lepore, S. J., Ragan, J. D., & Jones, S. (2000). Talking facilitates cognitive-emotional processes of adaptation to an acute stressor. *Journal of Personality and Social Psychology, 78,* 499–508.

Lepper, R. (2006, March 2). Home-school includes hands-on work. *The San Diego Union-Tribune,* NC-8.

Lerner, R. M., Theokas, C., & Jelicic, H. (2005). Youth as active agents in their own positive development: A developmental systems perspective. In W. Greve, K. Rothermund, & D. Wentura, *Adaptive self: Personal continuity and intentional self-development.* Ashland, OH: Hogrefe & Huber Publishers.

Leung, K. (2005). Special issue: Cross-cultural variations in distributive justice perception. *Journal of Cross-Cultural Psychology, 36,* 6–8.

Leung, S. A., Ivey, D., & Suzuki, L. (1994). Factors affecting the career aspirations of Asian Americans. *Journal of Counseling & Development, 72,* 404–410.

LeVay, S., & Valente, S. M. (2003). Human Sexuality. Sunderland, MA: Sinauer Associates.

Leve, L. D., Kim, H. K., & Pears, K. C. (2005). Childhood temperament and family environment as predictors of internalizing and externalizing trajectories from ages 5 to 17. *Journal of Abnormal Child Psychology, 33,* 505–520.

Levenson, R., Ekman, P., Heider, K. & Friesen, W. (1992). Emotion and autonomic nervous system activity in the Minangkabau of West Sumatra. *Journal of Personality and Social Psychology, 62,* 972–988.

Lever, N., Sander, M. A., Lombardo, S., Randall, C., Axelrod, J., Rubenstein, M. & Weist, M. D. (2004). A dropout prevention program for high-risk inner-city youth. *Behavior Modification, 28, Special issue: Expanded School Mental Health: Exploring Program Details and Developing the Research Base,* 513–527.

Levine, J. M., & Moreland, R. L. (2002). Group reactions to loyalty and disloyalty. In S. R. Thye & E. J. Lawler (Eds.), *Group cohesion, trust and solidarity.* New York: Elsevier Science/JAI Press.

LeVine, R. A. (1972). *Ethnocentrism: Theories of conflict, ethnic attitudes, and group behavior.* Oxford, England: John Wiley & Sons.

Lewin, T. (1995, May 11). Women are becoming equal providers: Half of working women bring home half the household income. *The New York Times,* A14.

Lewis, D. M., & Haug, C. A. (2005). Aligning policy and methodology to achieve consistent across-grade performance standards. Applied Measurements in Education, 18, 11–34.

Li, S. (2003). Biocultural orchestration of developmental plasticity across levels: The interplay of biology and culture in shaping the mind and behavior across the life span. *Psychological Bulletin, 129,* 171–194.

Licari, L., Nemer, L., & Tamburlini, G. (2005). *Children's health and the environment.* Geneva, Switzerland: UNESCO.

Lindorff, M. (2005). Determinants of received social support: Who gives what to managers? *Journal of Social and Personal Relationships, 22,* 323–337.

Lines, P. M. (2001). Home schooling. Eric Digest, EDO-EA-01–08, 1–4.

Linn, M. C. (1997, September 19). Finding patterns in international assessments. Science, 277, 1743.

Linville, P. W., & Fischer, G. W. (1999). Group variability and covariation: Effects on intergroup judgment and behavior. In C. Sedikides, J. Schopler, & C. A. Insko, *Intergroup cognition and intergroup behavior.* Mahwah, NJ: Lawrence Erlbaum Associates Publishers.

Linville, P. W., Fischer, G. W., & Yoon, C. (1996). Perceived covariation among the features of ingroup and outgroup members: The outgroup covariation effect. *Journal of Personality and Social Psychology, 70,* 421–436.

Lippa, R. A. (2003). Are 2D:4D finger-length rations related to sexual orientation? Yes for men, no for women. Journal of Personality and Social Psychology, 85, 179–188.

Lips, H. M. (2003). The gender pay gap: Concrete indicator of women's progress toward equality. *Analyses of Social Issues and Public Policy (ASAP), 3,* 87–109.

Litrownik, A., Newton, R., & Hunter, W. (2003). Exposure to family violence in young at-risk children: A longitudinal look at the effects of victimization and witnessed physical and psychological aggression. *Journal of Family Violence, 18,* 59–73.

Little, T. D., & Lopez, D. F. (1997). Regularities in the development of children's causality beliefs about school performance across six sociocultural contexts. Developmental Psychology, 33, 165–175.

Little, T., Miyashita, T., & Karasawa, M. (2003). The links among action-control beliefs, intellective skill, and school performance in Japanese, U. S., and German school children. International Journal of Behavioral Development, 27, 41–48.

Livson, N., & Peskin, H. (1980). Perspectives on adolescence from longitudinal research. In J. Adelson (Ed.), *Handbook of adolescent psychology.* New York: Wiley.

Lobel, T. E., Bar-David, E., Gruber, R., Lau, S., & Bar-Tal, Y. (2000). Gender schema and social judgments: A developmental study of children from Hong Kong. *Sex Roles, 43,* 19–42.

Locher, P. Unger, G., Sociedade, P., & Wahl, J. (1993). At first glance: Accessibility of the physical attractiveness stereotype. *Sex Roles, 28,* 729–743

Locke, T. F., & Newcomb, M. (2004). Child maltreatment, parent alcohol- and drug-related problems, polydrug problems, and parenting practices: A test of gender differences and four theoretical perspectives. *Journal of Family Psychology, 18,* 120–134.

Lockhart, I. A., & Berard, R. M. F. (2001). Psychological vulnerability and resilience to emotional distress: A focus group study of adolescent cancer patients. *International Journal of Adolescent Medicine and Health, 13,* 221–229.

Loeber, R., Lacourse, E., & Homish, D. (2005). Homicide, violence, and developmental trajectories. In R. E. Tremblay, W. W. Hartup, & J. Archer (Eds.), *Developmental origins of aggression* (pp. 202–219). New York: Guilford Press.

Lohman, B. J., Pittman, L. D., & Coley, R. L. (2004). Welfare history, sanctions, and developmental outcomes among low-income children and youth. *Social Service Review, 78,* 41–73.

Lonigan, C. J., Phillips, B. M., & Hooe, E. S. (2003). Relations of positive and negative affectivity to anxiety and depression in children: Evidence from a latent variable longitudinal study. *Journal of Consulting and Clinical Psychology, 71,* 465–481.

López, S. R., & Guarnaccia, P. J. J. (2000). Cultural psychopathology: Uncovering the social world of mental illness. *Annual Review of Psychology, 51,* 571–598.

Lounsbury, J. W., Hutchens, T., & Loveland, J. M. (2005). An investigation of big five personality traits and career decidedness among early and middle adolescents. *Journal of Career Assessment, 13,* 25–39.

Low, K. S. D., Yoon, M., Roberts, B. W., & Rounds, J. (2005). The stability of vocational interests from early adolescence to middle adulthood: A quantitative review of longitudinal studies. *Psychological Bulletin, 131,* 713–737.

Lu, X. (2001). Bicultural identity development and Chinese community formation: An ethnographic study of Chinese schools in Chicago. Howard Journal of Communications, 12, 203–220.

Lubinski, D. (2004). Introduction to the special section on cognitive abilities: 100 years after Spearman's (1904) "'General Intelligence,' objectively determined and measured." Journal of Personality and Social Psychology, 86, 96–111.

Lubinski, D., & Benbow, C. P. (2001). Choosing excellence. American Psychologist, 56, 76–77.

Lucas, S. R., & Berends, M. (2002). Sociodemographic diversity, correlated achievement, and de facto tracking. Sociology of Education, 75, 328–349.

Luna, B., Garver, K. E., Urban, T. A., Lazar, N. A., & Sweeney, J. A. (2004). Maturation of cognitive processes from late childhood to adulthood. Child Development, 75, 1357–1372.

Luria, R., & Meiran, N. (2005). Increased control demand results in serial processing: Evidence from dual-task performance. Psychological Science, 16, 833–840.

Luster, T., & McAdoo, H. P. (1994). Factors related to the achievement and adjustment of young African American children. Child Development, 65, 1080–1094.

Luster, T., & Okagaki, L. (Ed.). (2005). Parenting: An ecological perspective (2nd ed.). Mahwah, NJ: Erlbaum.

Luthar, S. S., Cicchetti, D., & Becker, B. (2000). The construct of resilience: A critical evaluation and guidelines for future work. Child Development, 71, 543–562.

Lykken, D., & Tellegen, A. (1996). Happiness is a stochastic phenomenon. Psychological Science, 7, 181–185.

Lyman, D. R., Milich, R., Zimmerman, R., Novak, S. P., Logan, T. K., Martin, C., Leudefeld, M. C., & Clayton, R. (1999). Project DARE: No effects at 10-year follow-up. Journal of Consulting and Clinical Psychology, 67, 590–593.

Lynam, D. R. (1996). Early identification of chronic offenders: Who is the fledgling psychopath? Psychological Bulletin, 120, 209–234.

Lynam, D. R., Caspi, A., Moffitt, T. E., Raine, A., Loeber, R., & Stouthamer-Loeber, M. (2005). Adolescent psychopathy and the big five: Results from two samples. Journal of Abnormal Child Psychology, 33, 431–443.

Lyon, M. E., Benoit, M., O'Donnell, R. M., Getson, P. R., Silber, T., & Walsh, T. (2000). Assessing African American adolescents' risk for suicide attempts: Attachment theory. Adolescence, 35, 121–134.

Lyubomirsky, S., King, L., & Diener, E. (2005). The benefits of frequent positive affect: Does happiness lead to success? Psychological Bulletin, 131, 803–855.

Maassen, G. H., & Landsheer, J. A. (2000). Peer-perceived social competence and academic achievement of low-level educated young adolescents. Social Behavior and Personality, 28, 29–39.

Maccoby, E. E., & Martin, J. A. (1983). Socialization in the context of the family: Parent-child interaction. In W. Damon, and R. M. Lerner, (Eds). Handbook of Child Psychology. New York: John Wiley & Sons.

Maddi, S. R. (2006). Hardiness: The courage to be resilient. In J. C. Thomas, D. L. Segal, & M. Hersen (Eds.), Comprehensive handbook of personality and psychopathology, Vol. 1: Personality and everyday functioning. Hoboken, NJ: Wiley.

Mael, F. A. (1998). Single-sex and coeducational schooling: Relationships to socioemotional and academic development. Review of Education Research, 68, 101–129.

Mahon, N. E., & Yarcheski, A. (2002). Alternative theories of happiness in early adolescence. Clinical Nursing Research, 11, 306–323.

Mahoney, E. R. (1983). Human sexuality. New York: McGraw-Hill.

Malamuth, N. M. (1998). A multidimensional approach to sexual aggressing: Combining measures of past behavior and present likelihood. New York Academy of Sciences, 528, 723–731.

Malamuth, N. M., Addison, T., & Koss, M. (2000). Pornography and sexual aggression: Are there reliable effects and can we understand them? Annual Review of Sex Research, 11, 26–91.

Malamuth, N. M., Huppin, M., & Paul, B. (2005). Sexual Coercion. In D. M. Buss (Ed.), The handbook of evolutionary psychology. Hoboken, NJ: Wiley.

Mallan, K., & Pearce, S. (Eds.) (2003). Youth cultures: Texts, images, and identities. Westport, CT: Praeger Publishers.

Maller, S. (2003). Best practices in detecting bias in nonverbal tests. In R. McCallum (Ed.), Handbook of nonverbal assessment. New York: Kluwer Academic/Plenum Publishers.

Mallers, M. H., Almeida, D. M., & Neupert, S. D. (205). Women's daily physical health symptoms and stressful experiences across adulthood. Psychology & Health, 20, 389–403.

Mangweth, B., Hausmann, A., and Walch, T. (2004). Body fat perception in eating-disordered men. International Journal of Eating Disorders, 35, 102–108.

Manlove, J., Romano-Papillo, A., and Ikramullah, E. (2004). Not yet: Programs to delay first sex among teens. Washington, DC: National Campaign to Prevent Teen Pregnancy. Retrieved March 4, 2006, from http://www.teenpregnancy. org/works/pdf/NotYet. pdf.

Manlove, J., Terry-Humen, E., Romano Papillo, A., Franzetta, K., Williams, S., & Ryan, S. (2002). Preventing teenage pregnancy, childbearing, and sexually transmitted diseases: What the research shows. Washington, DC: Child Trends. Retrieved March 4, 2006, from http:/ /www. childtrends. org/Files/K1Brief. pdf

Mann, L. (1980). Cross-cultural studies in small groups. In H. C. Triandis & R. W. Brislin (Eds.), Handbook of Cross-Cultural Psychology. Vol. 5. Boston: Allyn & Bacon.

Mannes, M., Roehlkepartain, E., & Benson, P. L. (2005). Unleashing the power of community to strengthen the well-being of children, youth, and families: An asset-building approach. Child Welfare, 84, Special issue: Community Building and 21st-century Child Welfare, 233–250.

Manzo, K. K. (2003, May 21). Work partly accomplished, benefactors exit middle grades. Education Week, 22, 11.

March, J. S., Klee, B. J., & Kremer, C. M. E. (2006). Treatment benefit and the risk of suicidality in multicenter, randomized, controlled trials of sertraline in children and adolescents. Journal of Child and Adolescent Psychopharmacology, 16, 91–102.

Marcia, J. E. (1980). Identity in adolescence. In J. Adelson (Ed.), Handbook of adolescent psychology. New York: Wiley.

Markus, H. R., & Kitayama, S. (1991). Culture and the self: Implications for cognition, emotion, and motivation. Psychological Review, 98, 224–253.

Marsh, H. W., & Ayotte, V. (2003). Do multiple dimensions of self-concept become more differentiated with age? The differential distinctiveness hypothesis. Journal of Educational Psychology, 95, 687–706.

Marsh, H. W., & Perry, C. (2005). Self-concept contributes to winning gold medals: Causal ordering of self-concept and elite swimming performance. Journal of Sport & Exercise Psychology, 27, 71–91.

Marsh, H., & Hau, K. (2004). Explaining paradoxical relations between academic self-concepts and achievements: Cross-cultural generalizability of the internal/external frame of reference predictions across 26 countries. Journal of Educational Psychology, 96, 56–67.

Marsh, H. W. (1986). Global self-esteem: its relation to specific facets of self-concept and their importance. Journal of Personality and Social Psychology, 51, 1224–1236.

Marsland, A. L., Bachen, E. A., & Cohen, S. (2002). Stress, immune reactivity and susceptibility to infectious disease. Physiology & Behavior, 77, Special issue: The Pittsburgh special issue. pp. 711–716.

Martin, C. L. (2000). Cognitive theories of gender development. In T. Eckes & H. M. Trautner, (Eds.), et al. The developmental social psychology of gender. Mahwah, NJ: Erlbaum.

Martin, C. L., & Ruble, D. (2004). Children's search for gender cues: Cognitive perspectives on gender development. Current Directions in Psychological Science, 13, 67–70.

Martin, P. D., & Brantley, P. J. (2004). Stress, coping, and social support in health and behavior. In J. M. Raczynski & L. C. Leviton (Eds.), Handbook of clinical health psychology: Volume 2. Disorders of behavior and health. Washington, DC: American Psychological Association.

Martin, R. C., & Dahlen, E. R. (2005). Cognitive emotion regulation in the prediction of depression, anxiety, stress, and anger. Personality and Individual Differences, 39, 1249–1260.

Martinez, R. O., & Dukes, R. L. (1997). The effects of ethnic identity, ethnicity, and gender on adolescent well-being. Journal of Youth and Adolescence, 26, 503–516.

Masling, J. M., & Bornstein, R. F. (Eds.). (1996). Psychoanalytic perspectives on developmental psychology. Washington, DC: American Psychological Association.

Matlin, M. (2003). From menarche to menopause: Misconceptions about women's reproductive lives. Psychology Science, 45, 10–122.

Matsumoto, A. (1999). Sexual differentiation of the brain. Boca Raton, FL: CRC Press.

Matsumoto, D. (1990). Cultural similarities and differences in display rules. *Motivation and Emotion, 14*, 195–214.

Matsumoto, D. (2004). Culture and emotion. *Journal of Cross-Cultural Psychology, 35*, 118–119.

Matsumoto, D., & Yoo, S. H. (2005). Culture and applied nonverbal communication. In R. E. Riggio & R. S. Feldman (Eds.), *Applications of nonverbal communication.* Mahwah, NJ: Lawrence Erlbaum Associates.

Matsumoto, D., Yoo, S. H., & Petrova, G. (2005). Development and validation of a measure of display rule knowledge: The display rule assessment inventory. *Emotion, 5*, 23–40.

Matsushima, R., & Shiomi, K. (2001). The effect of hesitancy toward and the motivation for self-disclosure on loneliness among Japanese junior high school students. *Social Behavior and Personality, 29*, 661–670.

Matsushima, R., & Shiomi, K. (2002). Self-disclosure and friendship in junior high school students. *Social Behavior & Personality: An International Journal, 30*, 515–526.

Matud, M. P. (2004). Gender differences in stress and coping styles. *Personality and Individual Differences, 37*, 1401–1415.

Matusov, E., & Hayes, R. (2000). Sociocultural critique of Piaget and Vygotsky. *New Ideas in Psychology, 18*, 215–239.

Matute-Bianchi, E. (1986). Ethnic identities and patterns of school success and failure among Mexican-descent and Japanese-American students in a California high school: An ethnographic analysis. *American Journal of Education, 95*, 233–255.

Maughan, B. (2001). Conduct disorder in context. In J. Hill & B. Maughan (Eds.), *Conduct disorders in childhood and adolescence.* New York: Cambridge University Press.

Maurer, M., Brackett, M., & Plain, F. (2004). *Emotional literacy in the middle school.* Port Chester, NY: National Professional Resources.

Mayer, J. D., Salovey, P., & Caruso, D. R. (2004). Emotional intelligence: Theory, findings, and implications. *Psychological Inquiry, 15*, 197–215.

McAuliffe, S. P., & Knowlton, B. J. (2001). Hemispheric differences in object identification. *Brain & Cognition., 45*, 119–128.

McBride, C. K., Paikoff, R. L., & Holmbeck, G. N. (2003). Individual and familial influences on the onset of sexual intercourse among urban African American adolescents. *Journal of Consulting and Clinical Psychology, 71*, 159–167.

McCabe, P. M., Schneiderman, N., Field, T., & Wellens, A. R. (Eds.). (2000). *Stress, coping, and cardiovascular disease.* Mahwah, NJ: Erlbaum.

McClelland, D. C. (1993). Intelligence is not the best predictor of job performance. *Current Directions in Psychological Research, 2*, 5–8.

McConahay, J. B. (1986). Modern racism, ambivalence, and the Modern Racism Scale. In J. F. Dovidio & S. L. Gaertner, *Prejudice, discrimination, and racism.* San Diego, CA: Academic Press.

McConahay, J. B., Hardee, B. B., & Batts, V. (1981). Has racism declined in America? It depends on who is asking and what is asked. *Journal of Conflict Resolution, 25.*

McCrae R. R., Terracciano A., and 78 Members of the Personality Profiles of Cultures Project. (2005). Universal features of personality traits from the observer's perspective: Data from 50 cultures. *Journal of Personality and Social Psychology, 88*, 547–561.

McCrae, R. R., Costa, P. T., Jr., Ostendorf, F., Angleitner, A., Hebíková, M., Avia, M. D., Sanz, J., Sánchez-Bernardos, M. L., Kusdil, M. E., Woodfield, R., Saunders, P. R., & Smith, P. B. (2000). Nature over nurture: Temperament, personality, and life span development. *Journal of Personality and Social Psychology, 78*, 173–186.

McDade, T. W., & Worthman, C. M. (2004). Socialization ambiguity in Samoan adolescents: A model for human development and stress in the context of culture change. *Journal of Research on Adolescence, 14*, 49–72.

McDonald, L. & Stuart-Hamilton, I. (2003). Egocentrism in older adults: Piaget's three mountains task revisited. *Educational Gerontology, 29*, 417–425.

McGrew, K. S. (2005). The Cattell-Horn-Carroll theory of cognitive abilities: Past, present, and future. In D. P. Flanagan, & P. L. Harrison, (Eds.), *Contemporary intellectual assessment: Theories, tests, and issues.* New York, Guilford Press.

McHale, J. P., & Kuersten-Hogan, R. (2004a). Introduction: The dynamics of raising children together. *Journal of Adult Development, 11, Special issue: Coparenting,* 163–164.

McHale, J. P., Kuersten-Hogan, R., & Rao, N. (2004b). Growing points for coparenting theory and research. *Journal of Adult Development, 11*, 135–141.

McIntosh, H., Metz, E., & Youniss, J. (2005). Community service and identity formation in adolescents. In J. L. Mahoney, R. W. Larson, & J. S. Eccles (Eds.), *Organized activities as contexts of development: Extracurricular activities, after-school and community programs.* Mahwah, NJ: Erlbaum.

McKeever, V. M., & Huff, M. E. (2003). A diathesis-stress model of posttraumatic stress disorder: Ecological, biological, and residual stress pathways. *Review of General Psychology, 7*, 237–250.

McKenzie, R. B. (1997). Orphanage alumni: How they have done and how they evaluate their experience. *Child & Youth Care Forum, 26*, 87–111.

McLoyd, V. C., Cauce, A. M., Takeuchi, D., & Wilson, L. (2000). Marital processes and parental socialization in families of color: a decade review of research. *Journal of Marriage and Family, 62*, 1070–1093.

McMahon, S. D., & Washburn, J. J. (2003). "Violence Prevention: An Evaluation of Program Effects with Urban African-American Students." *Journal of Primary Prevention, 24*, 43–62.

McMahon, S. I., & Goatley, V. J. (1995). Fifth graders helping peers discuss texts in student-led groups. *Journal of Educational Research, 89*, 23–34.

McNelles, L. R., & Connolly, J. A. (1999). Intimacy between adolescent friends: Age and gender differences in intimate affect and intimate behaviors. *Journal of Research on Adolescence, 9*, 143–159.

McPherson, M., Smith-Lovin, L., & Cook, J. M. (2001). Birds of a feather: Homophily in social networks. *Annual Review of Sociology, 27*, 415–444.

McWhirter, D. P., Sanders, S., & Reinisch, J. M. (1990). Homosexuality, heterosexuality: Concepts of sexual orientation. New York: Oxford University Press.

Mead, M. (1935). *Sex and temperament in three primitive societies.* New York: William Morrow.

Mead, M. (1942). Environment and education, a symposium held in connection with the fiftieth anniversary celebration of the Univeristy of Chicago. Chicago: University of Chicago Press.

Mednick, S. A. (1963). Research creativity in psychology graduate students. *Journal of Consulting Psychology, 27*, 265–266.

Meece, J. L., & Kurtz-Costes, B. (2001). Introduction: The schooling of ethnic minority children and youth. Educational Psychologist, 36, 1–7.

Meeus, W. (1996). Studies on identity development in adolescence: An overview of research and some new data. *Journal of Youth and Adolescence, 25*, 569–598.

Meeus, W. (2003). Parental and peer support, identity development and psychological well-being in adolescence. *Psychology: The Journal of the Hellenic Psychological Society, 10*, 192–201.

Mendelsohn, J. (2003, November 7–9). What we know about sex. *USA Weekend*, 6–9.

Mercer, J. R. (1973). *Labeling the mentally retarded.* Berkeley: University of California Press.

Merten, D. (1997). The meaning of meanness: Popularity, competition nnd conflict among junior high school girls. *Sociology of Education, 70*, 175–191.

Messer, S. B., & McWilliams, N. (2003). The impact of Sigmund Freud and the interpretation of dreams. In R. J. Sternberg (Ed.), *The anatomy of impact: What makes the great works of psychology great* (pp. 71–88). Washington, DC: American Psychological Association.

Meyer, D. E., Kieras, D. E. Lauber, E., Schumacher, E. H., Glass, J., Zurbriggen, E., et al. (2002). Adaptive executive control: Flexible multiple-task performance without pervasive immutable response-selection bottlenecks. In T. A. Polk & C. M. Seifert (Eds.), *Cognitive modeling.* Cambridge, MA: MIT Press.

Meyer-Bahlburg, H. F. L., Ehrhardt, A. A., Rosen, L. R., Gruen, R. S., Veridiano, N. P., Vann, F. H., & Neuwalder, H. F. (1995). Prenatal estrogens and the development of homosexual orientation. Developmental Psychology, 31, 12–21.

Miao, X., and Wang, W. (2003). A century of Chinese developmental psychology. *International Journal of Psychology, 38*, 258–273.

Michael, B. J., Gaulin, S., & Agyei, Y. (1994). Effects of gender and sexual orientation on evolutionarily relevant aspects of human mating psychology. Journal of Personality and Social Psychology, 66, 1081–1093.

Michael, R. T., Gagnon, J. H., Laumann, E. O., & Kolata, G. (1994). Sex in America: A definitive survey. Boston: Little, Brown.

Mikulincer, M., & Shaver, P. R. (2005). Attachment security, compassion, and altruism. *Current Directions in Psychological Science, 14,* 34–38.

Mikulincer, M., Dolev, T., & Shaver, P. (2004). Attachment-related strategies during thought suppression: Ironic rebounds and vulnerable self-representations. *Journal of Personality and Social Psychology, 87,* 940–956.

Miller, B. C., & Coyl, D. D. (2000). Adolescent pregnancy and childbearing in relation to infant adoption in the United States. *Adoption Quarterly, 4,* 3–25

Miller, B. C., Benson, B., & Galbraith, K. A. (2001). Family relationships and adolescent pregnancy risk: A research synthesis. *Developmental Review, 21,* 1–38.

Miller, D. B., & Townsend, A. (2005). Urban hassles as chronic stressors and adolescent mental health: The Urban Hassles Index. *Brief Treatment and Crisis Intervention, 5,* 85–94.

Miller, E. M., (1998). Evidence from opposite-sex twins for the effects of prenatal sex hormones. In L. Ellis, & L. Ebertz (Eds.), *Males, females, and behavior: Toward biological understanding.* Westport, CT: Praeger Publishers/Greenwood Publishing Group.

Miller, J. G . (1997). Culture and self: Uncovering the cultural grounding of psychological theory. In J. G. Snodgrass and R. L. Thompson (Eds.), The self across psychology: Self-recognition, self-awareness, and the self concept. *Annals of the New York Academy of Sciences, Vol. 818.* New York: New York Academy of Sciences.

Miller, J. G. & Bersoff, D. M. (1994). Cultural influences on the moral status of reciprocity and the discounting of endogenous motivation. Special Issue: The self and the collective. *Personality and Social Psychology Bulletin, 20,* 592–602.

Miller, K. J., & Mizes, J. S. (Eds.). (2000). *Comparative treatments for eating disorders.* New York: Springer.

Miller-Lewis, L., Wade, T., & Lee, C. (2006). Psychosocial risk factors for pregnancy risk-taking in young women in emerging adulthood: Evidence from the Australian Longitudinal Study on Women's Health. Australian Journal of Psychology, 58, 17–30

Miller-Perrin, C. L., & Perrin, R. D. (1999). *Child maltreatment: An introduction.* Thousand Oaks, CA: Sage.

Mills, J. S., Polivy, J., Herman, C. P., & Tiggermann, M. (2002). Effects of exposure to thin media images: Evidence of self-enhancement among restrained eaters. Personality and Social Psychology Bulletin, 28, 1687–1699.

Millsted, R., & Frith, H. (2003). Being large-breasted: Women negotiating embodiment. *Women's Studies International Forum, 26,* 455–465.

Mimura, K., Kimoto, T., & Okada, M. (2003). Synapse efficiency diverges due to synaptic pruning following overgrowth. *Phys Rev E Stat Nonlinear Soft Matter Physics, 68,* 124–131.

Miner, M. H., & Munns, R. (2005). Isolation and normlessness: Attitudinal comparisons of adolescent sex offenders, juvenile offenders, and nondelinquents. *International Journal of Offender Therapy and Comparative Criminology, 49,* 491–504.

Minorities in Higher Education. (1995). Annual status report on minorities in higher education. Washington, DC: Author.

Minuchin, P. (2002). Looking toward the horizon: Present and future in the study of family systems. In J. P. McHale & W. S. Grolnick (Eds.), *Retrospect and prospect in the psychological study of families.* Mahwah, NJ: Erlbaum.

Mischel, W. (2004). Toward an integrative science of the person. *Annual Review of Psychology, 55,* 1–22.

Mishra, A. K., & Spreitzer, G. M. (2001). Explaining how survivors respond to downsizing: The roles of trust, empowerment, justice, and work redesign. *Academy of Management Review, 23,* 567–588.

Miyamoto, R. H., Hishinuma, E. S., Nishimura, S. T., Nahulu, L. B., Andrade, N. N., & Goebert, D. A. (2000). Variation in self-esteem among adolescents in an Asian/Pacific-Islander sample. *Personality & Individual Differences, 29,* 13–25.

Modell, J., & Goodman, M. (1990). Historical perspecftives. In S. S. Feldman & G. R. Elliott, *At the threshold: The developing adolescent.* Cambridge, MA: Harvard University Press.

Moghaddam, F. M., Taylor, D. M., & Wright, S. C. (1993). *Social psychology in cross-cultural perspective.* New York: Freeman.

Mok, T. A. (1998). Getting the message: Media images and stereotypes and their effect on Asian Americans. *Cultural Diversity & Mental Health, 4,* 185–202.

Monitoring the Future Study. (2005). *National results on the adolescent drug use: Overview of key findings, 2005.* Bethesda, MD: National Institute on Drug Abuse.

Monk, C. S., Grillon, C., Baas, J. M. P., McClure, E. B., Nelson, E. E., Zarahn, E. et al. (2003). A neuroimaging method for the study of threat in adolescents. *Developmental Psychobiology, 43,* 359–366.

Montemayor, R. (1983). Parents and adolescents in conflict: All families some of the time and some families most of the time. *Journal of Early Adolescence, 3,* 83–103.

Montgomery, M. J. (2005). Psychosocial intimacy and identity: From early adolescence to emerging adulthood. *Journal of Adolescent Research, 20,* 346–374.

Montgomery, M. J., & Sorell, G. T. (1998). Love and dating experience in early and middle adolescence: Grade and gender comparisons. *Journal of Adolescence, 21,* 677–689.

Moores, D. F. (2004). No child left behind: The good, the bad, and the ugly. American Annals of the Deaf, 148, 347–348.

Moretti, M. M., & Higgins, E. T. (1990). Relating self-discrepancy to self-esteem: The contribution of discrepancy beyond actual-self ratings. *Journal of Experimental and Social Psychology, 26,* 101–123.

Morrison, L., & L'Heureux, J. (2001). Suicide and gay/lesbian/bisexual youth: Implications for clinicians. *Journal of Adolescence, 24,* 39–49.

Mortimer, J. T. (2003). *Working and growing up in America.* Cambridge, MA: Harvard University Press.

Mosher, C. E., & Danoff-Burg, S. (2005). Agentic and communal personality traits: Relations to attitudes toward sex and sexual experiences. *Sex Roles: A Journal of Research, 22,* 343–355.

Mosher, D. L., & Anderson, R. D. (1986). Macho personality, sexual aggression, and reactions to guided imagery of realistic rape. Journal of Research in Personality, 20, 77–94.

Mosher, W. D., et al. (2004). *Use of contraception and use of family planning services in the United States: 1982–2002, Advance data from vital and health statistics, No. 350.* Washington, DC: National Center for Health Statistics.

Mossakowski, K. N. (2003). Coping with perceived discrimination: Does ethnic identity protect mental health? *Journal of Health and Social Behavior, 44, Special issue: Race, Ethnicity and Mental Health,* 318–331.

Mouttapa, M., Huang, T. T. -K., Shakib, S., Sussman, S., & Unger, J. B. (2003). Authority-related conformity as a protective factor against adolescent health risk behaviors. *Journal of Adolescent Health, 33,* 320–321.

Muehlenhard, C. L., & Hollbaugh, L. C. (1988). Do women sometimes say no when they mean yes? The prevalence and correlates of women's token resistance to sex. Journal of Personality and Social Psychology, 54, 872–879.

Mueller, D., & Cooper, P. (1986). Children of single parent families: How they fare as young adults. *Family Relations: Journal of Applied Family & Child Studies, 35,* 169–176.

Mullis, R. L., Mullis, A. R., & Gerwels, D. (1998). Stability of vocational interests among high school students. *Adolescence, 33,* 699–707.

Mundy, L. (2005, October 23). High anxiety: Today's teen girls get more A's and go to college more often than ever before. But there's a price: stomach-clenching, sleep-stealing stress. *The Washington Post,* W20.

Munsch, J., & Blyth, D. A., (1993). An analysis of the functional nature of adolescents' supportive relationships. *Journal of Early Adolescence, 13,* 132–153.

Munsey, C. (2006, June). Emerging adults: The in-between age. *Monitor on Psychology,* 68–70.

Munzar, P., Cami, J., & Farré, M. (2003). Mechanisms of Drug Addiction. *New England Journal of Medicine, 349,* 2365–2365.

Murdock, T. B., & Bolch, M. B. (2005). Risk and protective factors for poor school adjustment in lesbian, gay, and bisexual (LGB) high school youth: Variable and person-centered analyses. Psychology in the Schools, 42, 159–172.

Murdock, T. B., Hale, N. M., & Weber, M. J. (2001). Predictors of cheating among early adolescents: Academic and social motivations. *Contemporary Educational Psychology, 26,* 96–115.

Muris, P., Meesters, C., van de Blom, W., & Mayer, B. (2005). Biological, psychological, and sociocultural correlates of body change strategies and eating problems in adolescent boys and girls. *Eating Behavior, 6,* 11–22.

Murphy, B., & Eisenberg, N. (2002). An integrative examination of peer conflict: Children's reported goals, emotions, and behaviors. *Social Development, 11,* 534–557.

Murphy, R. T., Wismar, K., & Freeman, K. (2003). Stress symptoms among African-American college students after the September 11, 2001 terrorist attacks. *Journal of Nervous and Mental Disease, 191*, 108–114.

Murray, B. (1996, July). Getting children off the couch and onto the field. APA Monitor, 42–43.

Nadal, K. (2004). Filipino American identity development model. *Journal of Multicultural Counseling & Development, 32*, 45–62.

Naik, G. (2004, March 10). Unlikely way to cut hospital costs: Comfort the dying. The Wall Street Journal, A1, A12.

Nansel, T. R., Overpeck, M., Pilla, R. S., Ruan, W. J., Simons-Morton, B., & Scheidt, P. (2001). Bullying behaviors among US youth: Prevalence and association with psychosocial adjustment. *Journal of the American Medical Association, 285*, 2094.

Nathanson, A., Wilson, B., & McGee, J. (2002). Counteracting the effects of female stereotypes on television via active mediation. *Journal of Communication, 52*, 922–937.

National Adoption Information Clearinghouse. (1994). *Transracial and transcultural adoption.* Retrieved January 24, 2006, from http://naic. acf.hhs. gov/pubs/f_trans. pdf

National Center for Children in Poverty (2006). *Basic facts about low-income children in the United States.* New York: National Center for Children in Poverty.

National Center for Education Statistics. (2001). *Time spent on homework and on the job (Indicator No. 21).* Retrieved from http://nces.ed.gov/programs/coe/2001/ section3/indicator21. asp

National Center for Educational Statistics (2003). Public High School Dropouts and Completers From the Common Core of Data: School Year 2000–01 Statistical Analysis Report. Washington, DC: NCES.

National Center for Health Statistics. (2001). Births to teenagers in the United States, 1940–2000. *National Vital Statistics Report, 49*, No. 10. Washington, DC: Author

National Center for Health Statistics. (2005). *Health United States, 2005 with adolescent health chartbook.* Hyattsville, MD.

National Middle School Association (NMSA). (2002). *Supporting students in their transition to middle school—A position paper jointly adopted by the National Middle School Association and the National Association of Elementary School Principals.* Westerville, OH: National Middle School Association.

National Sleep Foundation (2006). Children, obesity, and sleep. http://www. sleepfoundation.org

National Sleep Foundation. (2002, March). *2002 Sleep in America poll.* Washington, DC: Author.

National Sleep Foundation. (2006). *2006 Sleep in America Poll.* Washington, DC: National Sleep Foundation.

Natvig, G. K., Albrektsen, G., & Ovarnstrom, U. (2003). Methods of teaching and class participation in relation to perceived social support and stress: Modifiable factors for improving health and well-being among students. *Educational Psychology, 23*, 261–274.

Navalta, C. P., Polcari, A., Webster, D. M., Boghossian, A., & Teicher, M. H. (2006). Effects of childhood sexual abuse on neuropsychological and cognitive function in college women. *Journal of Neuropsychiatry & Clinical Neurosciences, 18*, 45–53.

NCPYP (National Campaign to Prevent Youth Pregnancy). (2003). 14 and younger: The sexual behavior of young adolescents. Washington, DC.

Needle, R., Su, S., & Doherty, W. (1990). Divorce, remarriage, and adolescent substance use: A prospective longitudinal study. *Journal of Marriage and the Family, 52*, 157–169.

Neiderhiser, J. M., Reiss, D., Hetherington, E. M., & Plomin, R. (1999). Relationships between parenting and adolescent adjustment over time: Genetic and environmental contributions. *Developmental Psychology, 35*, 680–692.

Nell, V. (2002). Why young men drive dangerously: Implications for injury prevention. *Current Directions in Psychological Science, 11*, 75–79.

Nelson, C. A., Bloom, F. E., Cameron, J. L., Amaral, D., Dahl, R. E., & Pine, D. (2002). An integrative, multidisciplinary approach to the study of brain-behavior relations in the context of typical and atypical development. *Development and Psychopathology, 14*, 499–520.

Nelson, E. E., McClure, E. B., Monk, C. S., Zarahn, E., Leibenluft, E., Pine, D. S., et al. (2003). Developmental differences in neuronal engagement during implicit encoding of emotional faces: An event-related fMRI study. *Journal of Child Psychology and Psychiatry, 44*, 1015–1024.

Nelson, L., Badger, S., & Wu, B. (2004). The influence of culture in emerging adulthood: Perspectives of Chinese college students. *International Journal of Behavioral Development, 28*, 26–36.

Nelson, T. O. (1994). Metacognition. In V. S. Ramachandran (Ed.), *Encyclopedia of human behavior* (Vol. 3). San Diego: Academic Press.

Nelson, T., & Wechsler, H. (2003). School spirits: Alcohol and collegiate sports fans. *Addictive Behaviors, 28*, 1–11.

Nemours Foundation. (2004). *Dealing with divorce.* Retrieved January 23, 2006, from http://kidshealth.org/ teen/your_mind/families/divorce. html

Newcomb, M. D. (1996). Pseudomaturity among adolescents: Construct validation, sex differences, and associations in adulthood. *Journal of Drug Issues, 26*, 477–504.

Newcomb, T. M. (1961). *The acquaintance process.* Oxford, England: Holt, Rinehart & Winston.

Newman, M., Holden, G., and Delville, Y. (2005). Isolation and the stress of being bullied. *Journal of Adolescence, 28*, 343–357.

Nicholas, S. L., & Good, T. L. (2004). *America's teenagers—myths and realities: Media images, schooling, and the social costs of careless indifference.* Mahwah, NJ: Erlbaum.

Nickerson, A. B., & Nagle, R. J. (2004). The influence of parent and peer attachments on life satisfaction in middle childhood and early adolescence. *Social Indicators Research, 66*, 35–60.

Nickman, S., Rosenfeld, A., & Fine, P. (2005). Children in adoptive families: Overview and update. *Journal of the American Academy of Child & Adolescent Psychiatry, 44*, 987–995.

Niemann, Y. F., Jennings, L, & Rozell, R. M. (1994). Use of free responses and cluster analysis to determine stereotypes of eight groups. *Personality and Social Psychology Bulletin, 20*, 379–390.

Nieto, S. (2005). Public Education in the Twentieth Century and Beyond: High Hopes, Broken Promises, and an Uncertain Future. Harvard Educational Review, 75, 43–65.

Nikitaras, N., & Ntoumanis, N. (2003). Criteria of personal, boys', and girls' popularity as ranked by Greek adolescents. *Perceptual and Motor Skills, 97*, 281–288.

Nisbett, R. (1994, October 31). Blue genes. *New Republic, 211*, 15.

Nishino, J., & Larson, R. (2003). Japanese adolescents' free time. In S. Verma & R. W. Larson (Eds.). *Examining adolescent leisure time across cultures: Developmental opportunities and risks: New directions for child and adolescent development, No. 99.* New York: Jossey-Bass.

Nissinen, M. J., Heliovaara, M. M., Seitsamo, J. T., Kononen, M. H., Hurmerinta, K. A., & Poussa, M. S. (2000). Development of trunk asymmetry in a cohort of children ages 11 to 22 years. *Spine, 255*, 70–74.

Nissle, S., & Bschor, T. (2002). Winning the jackpot and depression: Money cannot buy happiness. *International Journal of Psychiatry in Clinical Practice, 6*, 183–186.

Niu, W., & Sternberg, R. J. (2003). Societal and school influences on student creativity: The case of China. *Psychology in the Schools. Special Issue: Psychoeducational and psychosocial functioning of Chinese children, 40*, 103–114.

Noack, P., & Buhl, H. M. (2004). Relations with parents and friends during adolescence and early adulthood. *Marriage & Family Review, 36*, 31–51.

Noack, P., & Buhl, H. M. (2005). Relations with parents and friends during adolescence and early adulthood. In G. W. Peterson, S. K. Steinmetz, & S. M. Wilson (Eds.), *Parent-youth relations: Cultural and cross-cultural perspectives.* New York: Haworth Press.

Nockels, R., & Oakeshott, P. (1999). Awareness among young women of sexually transmitted Chlamydia infection. Family Practice, 16, 94.

Nolen-Hoeksema, S. (2003). *Women who think too much: How to break free of overthinking and reclaim your life.* New York: Henry Holt.

Noom, M. J., Dekovic, M., & Meeus, W. (1999). Autonomy, attachment and psychosocial adjustment during adolescence: A double-edged sword? *Journal of Adolescence, 22*, 771–783.

Noom, M. J., Dekovic, M., & Meeus, W. (2001). Conceptual analysis and measurement of adolescent autonomy. *Journal of Youth and Adolescence, 30*, 577–595.

O'Donohue, W. (Ed.). (1997). *Sexual harassment: Theory, research, and treatment.* Boston: Allyn & Bacon.

O'Leary, V. E., & Bhaju, J. (2006). Resilience and empowerment. Oxford series in clinical psychology. In J. Worell & C. D. Goodheart (Eds.), *Handbook of girls' and women's psychological health: Gender and well-being across the lifespan* (pp. 000) New York: Oxford University Press.

O'Sullivan, L. F., & Brooks-Gunn, J. (2005). The timing of changes in girls' sexual cognitions and behaviors in early adolescence: A prospective, cohort study. *Journal of Adolescent Health, 37,* 211–219.

O'Toole, M. E. (2000). *The school shooter: A threat assessment perspective.* Washington, DC: Federal Bureau of Investigation.

Oatley, K., & Jenkins, J. M. (1996). *Understanding Emotions.* New York: Blackwell Publishing.

Obermeyer, C. M. (2001, May 18). Complexities of a controversial practice. *Science, 292,* 1305–1304.

Ochsner, K. N., & Gross, J. J. (2005). The cognitive control of emotion. *Trends in Cognitive Sciences, 9,* 242–249.

Offer, D., & Schonert-Reichl, K. A. (1992). Debunking the myths of adolescence: Findings from recent research. *Journal of the American Academy of Child & Adolescent Psychiatry, 31, Special issue: Special article: Adolescence: Findings from recent research,* 1003–1014.

Offer, D., Ostrov, E., Howard, K. I., & Atkinson, R. (1988). *The teenage world: Adolescents' self-image in ten countries.* New York: Plenum Medical Books/Plenum Press.

Ogbu, J. (1992). Understanding cultural diversity and learning. *Educational Researcher, 21,* 5–14.

Ogbu, J. U. (1988). Black education: A cultural-ecological perspective. In H. P. McAdoo (Ed.), *Black families.* Beverly Hills, CA: Sage.

Oishi, S., & Diener, E. (2001). Goals, culture, and subjective well-being. *Personality and Social Psychology Bulletin, 27,* 1674–1682.

Olivardia, R., & Pope, H. (2002). Body image disturbance in childhood and adolescence. In D. Castle & K. Phillips (Eds.), *Disorders of body image.* Petersfield, England: Wrightson Biomedical Publishing.

Oliver, M. B., & Hyde, J. S. (1993). Gender differences in sexuality: A meta-analysis. Psychological Bulletin, 114, 29–51.

Olson, D. H., & DeFrain, J. (2006). *Marriages & families: Intimacy, diversity, and strengths* (5th ed.). Boston: McGraw-Hill.

Olson, J. M., Roese, N. J., & Zanna, M. P. (1996). Expectancies. In E. T. Higgins & A. W. Kruglanski (Eds.), *Social psychology: Handbook of basic principles.* New York: Guilford Press.

Olson, S. (2003). *Mapping human history: genes, race, and our common origins.* New York: Mariner Books.

Olsson, C. A., Bond, L., Burns, J. M., Vella-Brodrick, D. A., & Sawyer, S. M. (2003). Adolescent resilience: A concept analysis. *Journal of Adolescence, 26,* 1–11.

Oman, R., Vesely, S., & Aspy, C. (2005). Youth assets, aggression, and delinquency within the context of family structure. *American Journal of Health Behavior, 29,* 557–568.

Omoto, A. M., & Malsch, A. M. (2005). Psychological sense of community: Conceptual issues and connections to volunteerism-related activism. In A. M. Omoto (Ed.), *Processes of community change and social action.* Mahwah, NJ: Erlbaum.

Oppenheimer, D. M. (2004). Spontaneous discounting of availability in frequency judgment tasks. *Psychological Science, 15,* 100–105.

Organization for Economic Cooperation and Development. (1998). Education at a glance: OECD indicators, 2001. Paris: Author.

Organization for Economic Cooperation and Development. (2001). Education at a glance: OECD indicators, 2001. Paris: Author.

Organization for Economic Cooperation and Development. (2005). Education at a glance: OECD indicators, 2001. Paris: Author.

Orr, S. P., Metzger, L. J., & Pitman, R. K. (2002). Psychophysiology of post-traumatic stress disorder. *Psychiatric Clinics of North America: Special Issue: Recent advances in the study of biological alterations in post-traumatic stress disorders, 25,* 271–293.

Osofsky, J. (2003). Prevalence of children's exposure to domestic violence and child maltreatment: Implications for prevention and intervention. *Clinical Child & Family Psychology Review, 6,* 161–170.

Oyserman, D., & Fryberg, S. (2006). The possible selves of diverse adolescents: Content and function across gender, race and national origin. In C. Dunkel and J. Kerpelman, *Possible selves: Theory, research and applications.* Hauppage, NY: Nova Science Publishers.

Oyserman, D., Kemmelmeier, M., Fryberg, S., Brosh, H., & Hart-Johnson, T. (2003). Racial ethnic self-schemas. *Social Psychology Quarterly, 66,* 333–347.

Ozawa, M., & Yoon, H. (2003). Economic impact of marital disruption on children. *Children & Youth Services Review, 25,* 611–632.

Ozer, E. J., & Weiss, D. S. (2004). Who develops posstraumatic stress disorder? *Current Directions in Psychological Science, 13,* 169–172.

Ozer, E. J., Best, S. R., & Lipsey, T. L. (2003). Predictors of posttraumatic stress disorder and symptoms in adults: A meta-analysis. *Psychological Bulletin, 129,* 52–73.

Ozer, E., Macdonald, T., & Irwin, C., Jr. (2002). Adolescent health: Implications projections for the new millennium. In J. Mortimer & R. Larson (Eds.), *The changing adolescent experience: Societal trends and the transition to adulthood.* New York: Cambridge University Press.

Paikoff, R. L., & Brooks-Gunn, J. (1990). Physiological processes: What role do they play during the transition to adolescence? In R. Montemayor, G. R. Adams, & T. P. Gulotta (Eds.), *From childhood to adolescence: A transitional period?* Newbury Park, CA: Sage.

Paikoff, R. S., & Brooks-Gunn, J. (1991). Do parent-child relationships change during puberty? *Psychological Bulletin, 110,* 47–66.

Paludi, M. A. (Ed.). (1996). *Sexual harassment on college campuses: Abusing the Ivory Power.* Albany: State University of New York Press.

Papps, F., Walker, M., Trimboli, A., & Trimboli, C. (1995). Parental discipline in Anglo, Greek, Lebanese, and Vietnamese cultures. *Journal of Cross-Cultural Psychology, 26,* 49–64.

Park, C. L., & Adler, N. E. (2003). Coping style as a predictor of health and well-being across the first year of medical school. *Health Psychology, 22,* 627–631.

Parke, R. D. (2004). Fathers, families, and the future: A plethora of plausible predictions. *Merrill-Palmer Quarterly, 50,* 456–470.

Parke, R. D., Dennis, J., Flyr, M. L., Morris, K. L., Leidy, M. S., & Schofield, T. J. (2005). Fathers: Cultural and ecological perspectives. In T. Luster & L. Okagaki (Eds), *Parenting: An ecological perspective* (pp. 000) Mahwah, NJ: Erlbaum.

Parke, R. D., & Buriel, R. (1998). Socialization in the family: Ethnic and ecological perspectives. *N W. Damon & N. Eisnberg, Social, emotional and personality development. Vol. 3. Handbook of child psychology.* New York: Wiley.

Parker, S. T. (2005). Piaget's legacy in cognitive constructivism, niche construction, and phenotype development and evolution. In S. T. Parker & J. Langer, *Biology and knowledge revisited: From neurogenesis to psychogenesis.* Mahwah, NJ: Lawrence Erlbaum Associates.

Pascoe, C. (2005). "Dude, you're a fag": Adolescent masculinity and the fag discourse. *Sexualities, 8,* 329–346.

Passow, A. H. (1996). Acceleration over the years. In C. P. Benbow & D. J. Lubinski (Eds.), *Intellectual talent: Psychometric and social issues.* Baltimore: Johns Hopkins University Press.

Pate, R. R., Trost, S. G., Levin, S., & Dowda, M. (2000) Sports participation and health-related behaviors among U. S. youth. *Archives of Pediatric and Adolescent Medicine, 154,* 904–911.

Patterson, C. (2003). Children of lesbian and gay parents. In L. Garnets, & D. Kimmel (Eds.), *Psychological perspectives on lesbian, gay, and bisexual experiences,* 2nd ed. New York: Columbia University Press.

Patterson, C. J. (2002). Lesbian and gay parenthood. In M. Bornstein (Ed.), *Handbook of parenting.* Mahwah, NJ: Erlbaum.

Patterson, C. J. (1995). Families of the baby boom: Parents' division of labor and children's adjustment. *Special Issue: Sexual orientation and human development. Developmental Psychology, 31,* 115–123.

Patterson, C., & Friel, L. V. (2000). Sexual orientation and fertility. In G. R. Bentley & N. Mascie-Taylor (Eds.) *Infertility in the modern world: Biosocial perspectives.* Cambridge, England: Cambridge University Press.

Patterson, G. R., & Fisher, P. A. (2002). Recent developments in our understanding of parenting: Bidirectional effects, causal models, and the search for parsimony. In M. H. Bornstein (Ed.), *Handbook of parenting* (2nd ed.). Mahwah, NJ: Erlbaum.

Patterson, G. R., DeBaryshe, B. D., & Ramsey, E. (1989). A developmental perspective on antisocial behavior. *American Psychologist, 44,* 329–335.

Patton, W., & Creed, P. A. (2001). Developmental issues in career maturity and career decision status. *Career Development Quarterly, 15,* 88–96.

Paunonen, S. V. (2003). Big five factors of personality and replicated predictions of behavior. *Journal of Personality and Social Psychology, 84,* 411–422.

Pavis, S., Cunningham-Burley, S., & Amos, A. (1997). Alcohol consumption and young people: Exploring meaning and social context. *Health Education Research, 12,* 311–322.

Paxton, S. J., Schutz, H. K., Wertheim, E. H., & Muir, S. L. (1999). Friendship clique and peer influences on body image concerns, dietary restraint, extreme weight-loss behaviors, and binge eating in adolescent girls. *Journal of Abnormal Psychology, 108*, 255–266.

Pedlow, R., Sanson, A., Prior, M., & Oberklaid, F. (1993). Stability of maternally reported temperament from infancy to 8 years. *Developmental Psychology, 29*, 998–1007.

Peets, K., & Kikas, E. (2006). Aggressive strategies and victimization during adolescence: Grade and gender differences, and cross-informant agreement. *Aggressive Behavior, 32*, 68–79.

Pelham, B. W., & Swann, W. B., Jr. (1989). From self-conceptions to self-worth: The sources and structure of self-esteem. *Journal of Personality and Social Psychology, 57*, 672–680.

Pennebaker, J. W. (2004). Theories, therapies, and taxpayers: On the complexities of the expressive writing paradigm. *Clinical Psychology: Science and Practice, 11*, 138–142.

Pennebaker, J. W., & Chung, C. K. (in press). Expressive writing, emotional upheavals, and health. In H. Friedman and R. Silver (Eds.), *Handbook of health psychology*. New York: Oxford University Press.

Pennebaker, J. W., Zech, E., & Rimé, B. (2001). Disclosing and sharing emotion: Psychological, social and health consequences. In M. S. Stroebe, R. O. Hansson, W. Stroebe, & H. Schut (Eds.), *Handbook of bereavement research: Consequences, coping, and care* (pp. 517–544). Washington, DC: American Psychological Association.

Peplau, L. A. (2003). Human sexuality: How do men and women differ? *Current Directions in Psychological Science, 12*, 37–40.

Pepler, D. J., Madsen, K. C., Webster, C. & Levene, K. S. (2005). *The development and treatment of girlhood aggression*. Mahwah, NJ: Erlbaum.

Perlmann, J., & Waters, M. (Eds.). (2002). *The new race question: How the census counts multiracial individuals*. New York: Russell Sage Foundation.

Perozzi, J. A., & Sanchez, M. C. (1992). The effect of instruction in L1 on receptive acquisition of L2 for bilingual children with language delay. Language, Speech, and Hearing Services in Schools, 23, 348–352.

Perrine, N., E., & Aloise-Young, P. A. (2004). The role of self-monitoring in adolescents' susceptibility to passive peer pressure. *Personality and Individual Differences, 37*, 1701–1716.

Perry, H. (1982). *Psychiatrist of America. The life of Harry Stack Sullivan*, Cambridge, MA: Harvard University Press.

Perry, T., Steele, C., & Hilliar, A., III. (2003). Promoting high achievement among African-American students. Boston: Beacon Press.

Petersen, A. C. (1988, September). Those gangly years. *Psychology Today*, 28–34.

Petersen, A. C. (2000). A longitudinal investigation of adolescents' changing perceptions of pubertal timing. *Developmental Psychology, 36*, 37–43.

Peterson, D. M., Marcia, J. E., & Carpendale, J. I. M. (2004). Identity: Does thinking make it so? In C. Lightfoot, C. Lalonde, & M. Chandler, *Changing conceptions of psychological life*. Mahwah, NJ: Lawrence Erlbaum Associates.

Petit, G., & Dodge, K. A. (2003). Violent children: Bridging development, intervention, and public policy. *Developmental Psychology, Special Issues: Violent Children, 39*, 187–188.

Petrie, K., Fontanilla, I., Thomas, M. G., Booth, R. J., & Pennebaker, J. W. (2004). Effect of written emotional expression on immune function in patients with human immunodeficiency virus infection: A randomized trial. *Psychosomatic Medicine, 66*, 272–275.

Pettigrew, T. F. (1989). The nature of modern racism in the United States. *Revue Internationale de Psychologie Sociale, 2*, 291–303.

Pettijohn, T. F. (2004). Playboy playmate curves: Changes in facial and body feature preferences across social and economic conditions. Personality and Social Psychology Bulletin, 30, 1186–1197.

Pettit, G. S., Bates, J. E., & Dodge, K. A. (1997). Supportive parenting, ecological context, and children's adjustment: A 7-year longitudinal study. *Child Development, 68*, 908–923.

Pfeifer, J. E., & Ogloff, J. R. (1991). Ambiguity and guilt determinations: A modern racism perspective. *Journal of Applied Social Psychology, 21*, 1713–1725.

Pfeiffer, S. I., & Stocking, V. B. (2000). Vulnerabilities of academically gifted students. Special Services in the Schools, 16, 83–93.

Phelps, R. P. (2005). Defending standardized testing. Mahwah, NJ: Lawrence Erlbaum Associates.

Philippot, P., & Feldman, R. S. (2004). *The regulation of emotion*. Mahwah, NJ: Erlbaum.

Phillips, D. A., Voran, M., Kisker, E., Howes, C., & Whitebook, M. (1994). Child care for children in poverty: Opportunity or inequity? Child Development, 65, 472–492.

Phinney, J. S. (1990). Ethnic identity in adolescents and adults: Review of research. *Psychological Bulletin, 108*, 499–514.

Phinney, J. S. (2003). Ethic identity and acculturation. In K. M. Chun, P. Organista, & G. Marin (Eds.), *Acculturation: Advances in theory, measurement, and applied research*. Washington, DC: American Psychological Association.

Phinney, J. S. (2005). Ethnic identity in late modern times: A response to Rattansi and Phoenix. *Identity, 5*, 187–194.

Phinney, J. S. (2006). Ethnic identity exploration in emerging adulthood. In J. J. Arnett & J. L. Tanner (Eds.), *Emerging adults in America: Coming of age in the 21st century*(pp. 000). Washington, DC: American Psychological Association.

Phinney, J. S., Ferguson, D. L., & Tate, J. D. (1997). Intergroup attitudes among ethnic minority adolescents: A causal model. *Child Development, 68*, 955–969.

Phinney, J. S., Lochner, B., & Murphy, R. (1990). Ethnic identity development and psychological adjustment in adolescence. In A. Stiffman & L. Davis (Eds.), *Advances in adolescent mental health: Vol. 5. Ethnic issues*. Greenwich, CT: JAI Press.

Piaget, J. (1932). *The moral judgment of the child*. New York: Harcourt, Brace & World.

Piaget, J. (1952). *The origins of intelligence in children*. New York: International Universities Press.

Piaget, J. (1962). *Play, dreams and imitation in childhood*. New York: Norton.

Piaget, J. (1983). Piaget's theory. In W. Kessen (Ed.) & P. H. Mussen (Series Ed.), *Handbook of child psychology: Vol 1. History, theory, and methods*. New York: Wiley.

Piaget, J., & Inhelder, B. (1958). *The growth of logical thinking from childhood to adolescence* (A. Parsons & S. Seagrin, Trans.). New York: Basic Books.

Pierce, K. (1993). Socialization of teenage girls through teen-magazine fiction: The making of a new woman or an old lady? *Sex Roles, 29*, 59–68.

Pillsworth, E. G., Haselton, M. G., & Buss, D. M. (2004). Ovulatory shifts in female sexual desire. *Journal of Sex Research, 41*, 55–65.

Pinsof, W. E., & Lebow, J. L. (Eds.). (2005). *Family psychology: The art of the science*. New York: Oxford University Press.

Plomin, R., & McClearn, G. E. (Eds.) (1993). *Nature, nurture and psychology*. Washington, DC: American Psychological Association.

Plummer, D. (2001). The quest for modern manhood: Masculine stereotypes, peer culture and the social significance of homophobia. *Journal of Adolescence, 24*, 15–23.

Polatin, P. B., Young, M., Mayer, M., & Gatchel, R. (2005). Bioterrorism, stress, and pain: The importance of an anticipatory community preparedness intervention. *Journal of Psychosomatic Research, 58*, 311–316.

Policy and Program Studies Service. (2004). *National assessment of vocational education: Final report to Congress*. Washington, DC: U. S. Department of Education.

Pollak, S., Holt, L., & Wismer Fries, A. (2004). Hemispheric asymmetries in children's perception of nonlinguistic human affective sounds. *Developmental Science, 7*, 10–18.

Pomponio, A. T. (2002). *Psychological consequences of terrorism*. New York: Wiley.

Pong, S. -L., Hao, L., & Gardner, E. (2005). The roles of parenting styles and social capital in the school performance of immigrant Asian and Hispanic adolescents. *Social Science Quarterly, 86*, 928–950.

Ponterotto, J. G., Gretchen, D., & Utsey, S. O. (2003). The multigroup ethnic identity measure (MEIM): Psychometric review and further validity testing. *Educational and Psychological Measurement, 63*, 502–515.

Ponton, L. E. (1999, May 10). Their dark romance with risk. *Newsweek*, 55–58.

Ponton, L. E. (2001). The sex lives of teenagers: Revealing the secret world of adolescent boys and girls. New York: Penguin Putnam.

Poole, M. S., Hollingshead, A. B., McGrath, J. E., Moreland, R. L., & Rohrbaugh, J. (2004). Interdisciplinary perspectives on small groups. *Small Group Research, 35*, 3–16

Porzelius, L. K., Dinsmore, B. D., & Staffelbach, D. (2001). Eating disorders. In M. Hersen & V. B. Van Hasselt, (Eds.). *Advanced abnormal psychology* (2nd ed.). New York: Kluwer Academic/Plenum Publishers.

Prater, L. (2002). African American families: Equal partners in general and special education. In F. Obiakor & A. Ford (Eds.), Creating successful learning environments for African American learners with exceptionalities. Thousand Oaks, CA: Corwin Press, Inc.

Pratt, H., Phillips, E., & Greydanus, D. (2003). Eating disorders in the adolescent population: Future directions. *Journal of Adolescent Research, 18*, 297–317.

Pratt, M. W., & Fiese, B. H. (Eds.) (2004). *Family stories and the life course: Across time and generations.* Mahwah, NJ: Erlbaum.

President's Council on Physical Fitness and Sports. (2003). *Fitness fundamentals: Guidelines for personal exercise programs.* Washington, DC: President's Council on Physical Fitness and Sports.

Pressley, M. & Schneider, W. (1997). *Introduction to memory development during childhood and adolescence.* Mahwah, NJ: Erlbaum.

Pressman, S. D., Cohen, S., Miller, G. E., Barkin, A., Rabin, B. S., & Treanor, J. J. (2005). Loneliness, social network size, and immune response to influenza vaccination in college freshman. *Health Psychology, 24*, 297–306.

Prinstein, M. J., Borelli, J. L., Cheah, C. S. L., Simon, V. A., & Aikins, J. W. (2005). Adolescent girls' interpersonal vulnerability to depressive symptoms: A longitudinal examination of reassurance-seeking and peer relationships. *Journal of Abnormal Psychology, 11*, 676–688.

Probert, B. (2005). "I just couldn't fit in": Gender and unequal outcomes in academic careers. *Gender, Work & Organization, 12*, 50–72.

Puig, M. (2002). The adultification of refugee children: Implications for cross-cultural social work practice. *Journal of Human Behavior in the Social Environment, 5*, 85–95.

Puntambekar, S., & Hübscher, R. (2005). Tools for saffolding students in a complex learning environment: What have we gained and what have we missed? *Educational Psychologist, 40*, 1–12.

Purvis, A. (2001, June 24). The global epidemic. Time, 32–35.

Pyryt, M. C., & Mendaglio, S. (1994). The multidimensional self-concept: A comparison of gifted and average-ability adolescents. *Journal for the Education of the Gifted, 17*, 299–305.

Quinn, M. (1990, January 29). Don't aim that pack at us. *Time,* 60.

Quintana, S. (2004). Race, ethnicity, and culture in child development. *Child Development, 75*, v–vi.

Raeburn, P. (2004, October 1). Too immature for the death penalty? *The New York Times Magazine*, 26–29.

Raffaelli, M. (1997). Young adolescents' conflicts with siblings and friends. *Journal of Youth and Adolescence, 26*, 539–558.

Raffaelli, M. (2005). Adolescent dating experiences described by Latino college students. *Journal of Adolescence, 28*, 559–572

Raffaelli, M., & Crockett, L. J. (2003). Sexual risk taking in adolescence: The role of self-regulation and attraction to risk. Developmental Psychology, 39, 1036–1046.

Raffaelli, M., & Ontai, L. L. (2001). "She's 16 years old and there's boys calling over to the house": An exploratory study of sexual socialization in Latino families. *Culture, Health & Sexuality, 3*, 295–310.

Rahman, Q., & Wilson, G. (2003). Born gay? The psychobiology of human sexual orientation. Personality & Individual Differences, 34, 1337–1382.

Ramachandran, N. (2006, April 8). Working life. *U. S. News & World Report.*

Ramsey, P. G., & Myers, L. C. (1990). Salience of race in young children's cognitive, affective, and behavioral responses to social environments. *Journal of Applied Developmental Psychology, 11*, 49–67.

Randahl, G. J. (1991). A typological analysis of the relations between measured vocational interests and abilities. *Journal of Vocational Behavior, 38*, 333–350.

Rankin, J., Lane, D., & Gibbons, F. (2004). Adolescent self-consciousness: Longitudinal age changes and gender differences in two cohorts. *Journal of Research on Adolescence, 14*, 1–21.

Rasheed, S. A., McWhirter, & Chronister, K. M. (2005). Self-efficacy and vocational outcome expectations for adolescents of lower socioeconomic status: A Pilot study. *Journal of Career Assessment, 13*, 40–58.

Ravindran, A. V., Matheson, K., Griffiths, J., Merali, Z., & Anisman, H. (2002). Stress, coping, uplifts, and quality of life in subtypes of depression: A conceptual framework and emerging data. *Journal of Affective Disorders, 71*, 121–130.

Rawe, J., & Kingsbury, K. (2006, May 22). When colleges go on suicide watch. *Time*, 162, 167.

Ready, D. D., Lee, V. E., & Welner, K. G. (2004). Educational equity and school structure: School size, overcrowding, and schools-within-schools. *Teachers College Record, 106*, 1989–2014.

Reddy, L. A., & Pfeiffer, S. I. (1997). Effectiveness of treatment of foster care with children and adolescents: A review of outcome studies. *Journal of the American Academy of Child & Adolescent Psychiatry, 36*, 381–588.

Reese-Weber, M., & Kahn, J. H. (2005). Familial predictors of sibling and romantic-partner conflict resolution: Comparing late adolescents from intact and divorced families. *Journal of* Adolescence, *28*, 479–493.

Reid, J. B., Patterson, G. R., & Snyder, J. (2002). *Antisocial behavior in children and adolescents: A developmental analysis and model for intervention.* Washington, DC: American Psychological Association.

Reid, M., Miller, W., & Kerr, B. (2004). Sex-based glass ceilings in U. S. state-level bureaucracies, 1987–1997. *Administration & Society, 36*, 377–405.

Reifman, A. (2000). Revisiting *The Bell Curve. Psycoloquy, 11*, 99.

Reinders, H., & Youniss, J. (2006). School-based required community service and civic development in adolescents. *Applied Developmental Science, 10*, 2–12.

Reiner, W. G., & Gearhart, J. P. (2004). Discordant sexual identity in some genetic males with cloacal exstrophy assigned to female sex at birth. *The New England Journal of Medicine, 350,* 333–341.

Reis, H. T., Collins, W. A., & Berscheid, E. (2000). The relationship context of human behavior and development. *Psychological Bulletin, 126,* 844–872.

Reis, S., & Renzulli, J. (2004). Current research on the social and emotional development of gifted and talented students: good news and future possibilities. Psychology in the Schools, 41, 119–130.

Reisberg, D. (2001). *Cognition* (2nd ed.). New York: Norton.

Remafedi, G. (1999). Sexual orientation and youth suicide. *Journal of the American Medical Association, 282,* 1291–1292.

Remafedi, G. (2002). Suicidality in a venue-based sample of young men who have sex with men. *Journal of Adolescent Health, 31,* 305–310.

Remafedi, G., French, S., & Story, M. (1998). The relationship between suicide risk and sexual orientation: Results of a population-based study. *American Journal of Public Health, 88,* 57–60.

Remer, T., Boye, K. R., Hartmann, M. F., & Wudy, S. A. (2005). Urinary markers of adrenarche: Reference values in healthy subjects, aged 3–18 years. *Clinical Endocrinology Metabolism, 90,* 2015–2021.

Renk, K., Liljequist, L., Simpson, J. E., & Phares, V. (2005). Gender and age differences in the topics of parent-adolescent conflict. *Family Journal: Counseling and Therapy for Couples and Families, 13*, 139–149.

Renold, E. (2002). Presumed innocence: (Hetero)sexual, heterosexist and homophobic harassment among primary school girls and boys. *Childhood: A Global Journal of Child Research, 8*, 415–434.

Reschly, D. J. (1996). Identification and assessment of students with disabilities. *Future of Children, 6*, 40–53.

Resnick, H., Acierno, R., Kilpatrick, D. G., & Holmes, M., (2005). Description of an early intervention to prevent substance abuse and psychopathology in recent rape victims. *Behavior Modification, 29*, 156–188.

Resnick, M. D., Bearman, P., Blum, R., Bauman, K., Harris, K., Jones, J., et al. (1997). Protecting adolescents from harm: Findings from the National Longitudinal Study of Adolescent Health. *Journal of the American Medical Association, 278*, 823–832.

Resnick, M. D., Blum, R. W., Bose, J., & Smith M. (1990). Characteristics of unmarried adolescent mothers: Determinants of child rearing versus adoption. *American Journal of Orthopsychiatry, 60*, 577–584.

Reyna, V. F. (1997). Conceptions of memory development with implications for reasoning and decision making. In R. Vasta (Ed.), *Annals of child development: A research annual* (Vol. 12, pp. 87–118). London: Jessica Kingsley Publishers.

Ricciardelli, L. A., & McCabe, M. P. (2004). A biopsychosocial model of disordered eating and the pursuit of muscularity in adolescent boys. *Psychological Bulletin, 130*, 179–205.

Rice, V. H. (Ed.). (2000). *Handbook of stress, coping and health*. Thousand Oaks, CA: Sage.

Richard, J. F., & Schneider, B. H., (2005). Assessing friendship motivation during preadolescence and early adolescence. *Journal of Early Adolescence, 25*, 367–385.

Richards, H. D., Bear, G. G., Stewart, A. L., & Norman, A. D. (1992). Moral reasoning and classroom conduct: Evidence of a curvilinear relationship. *Merrill-Palmer Quarterly, 38*, 176–190.

Richards, J. M., & Gross, J. J. (2000). Emotion regulation and memory: The cognitive consequence of keeping one's cool. *Journal of Personality and Social Psychology, 79*, 410–424.

Richards, J. M., Butler, E. A., & Gross, J. J. (2003). Emotion regulation in romantic relationships: The cognitive consequences of concealing feelings. *Journal of Social and Personal Relationships, 20*, 599–620.

Richards, M. P. M. (1996). The childhood environment and the development of sexuality. In C. J. K. Henry & S. J. Ulijaszek (Eds.), *Long-term consequences of early environment: Growth, development and the lifespan developmental perspective*. Cambridge, England: Cambridge University Press.

Richards, M. H., Crowe, P. A., Larson, R., & Swarr, A. (1998). Developmental patterns and gender differences in the experience of peer companionship during adolescence. *Child Development, 69*, 154–163.

Richards, R., Kinney, D. K., Benet, M., & Merzel, A. P. C. (1990). Assessing everyday creativity: Characteristics of the lifetime creativity scales and validation with three large samples. *Journal of Personality and Social Psychology, 54*, 476–485.

Richmond, M. K., Stocker, C. M., & Rienks, S. L. (2005). Longitudinal associations between sibling relationship quality, parental differential treatment, and children's adjustment. *Journal of Family Psychology, 19*, 550–559.

Richtel, M. (2006, April 11). The long-distance journey of a fast-food order. *New York Times*, A1, C4.

Richter, L. M. (2006, June 30). Studying adolescence. *Science, 312*, 1902–1905.

Rickel, A. U., & Becker, E. (1997). *Keeping children from harm's way: How national policy affects psychological development*. Washington, DC: American Psychological Association.

Rickert, V. J., & Weimann, C. M. (1998). Date rape among adolescents and young adults. *Journal of Pediatric Adolescent Gynecology, 11*, 167–175.

Rideout, V. J., Vandewater, E. A., & Wartella, E. A. (2003). *Zero to Six: Electronic media in the lives of infants, toddlers and preschoolers*. Menlo Park, CA: Henry J. Kaiser Foundation.

Rideout, V., Roberts, D. F., & Foehr, U. G. (2005). *Generation M: Median in the lives of 8 to 18 year olds*. Menlo Park, CA: The Henry J. Kaiser Family Foundation.

Ridgeway, C. L., Diekema, D., & Johnson, C. (1995). Legitimacy, compliance, and gender in peer groups. *Social Psychology, Quarterly, 58*, 298–311.

Riley, L. D., & Bowen, C. (2005). The sandwich generation: Challenges and coping strategies of multigenerational families. *Family Journal: Counseling and Therapy for Couples and Families, 13*, 52–58.

Rinaldi, C. (2002). Social conflict abilities of children identified as sociable, aggressive, and isolated: Developmental implications for children at-risk for impaired peer relations. *Developmental Disabilities Bulletin, 30*, 77–94.

Ringwalt, C. L., Greene, J. M., & Robertson, M. J. (1998). Familial backgrounds and risk behaviors of youth with thrownaway experiences. *Journal of Adolescence, 21*, 241–252.

Ritzen, E. M. (2003). Early puberty: What is normal and when is treatment indicated? *Hormone Research, 60*, Supplement, 31–34.

Rivers, I. (2004). Recollections of bullying at school and their long-term implications for lesbians, gay men, and bisexuals. *Crisis, 25*, 169–175

Robb, A., & Dadson, M. (2002). Eating disorders in males. *Child & Adolescent Psychiatric Clinics of North America, 11*, 399–418.

Robbins, J. M., & Krueger, J. I. (2005). Social projection to ingroups and outgroups: A review and meta-analysis. *Personality and Social Psychology Review, 9*, 32–47.

Robbins, S. B., Lauver, K., Le, H., Davis, D., Langley, R., & Carlstrom, A. (2004). Do psychosocial and study skill factors predict college outcomes? A meta-analysis. *Psychological Bulletin, 130*, 261–288.

Roberts, D. F., & Foehr, U. (2003). *Kids and media in America: Patterns of use at the millennium*. New York: Cambridge University Press.

Roberts, D. F., Henriksen, L., & Foehr, U. G. (2004). Adolescents and media. In R. M. Lerner & L. Steinberg (Eds.), *Handbook of adolescent psychology* (2nd ed.) New York: John Wiley & Sons.

Roberts, R. E., Phinney, J. S., Masse, L. C., Chen, Y. R., Roberts, C. R., & Romero, A. (1999). The structure of ethnic identity of young adolescents from diverse ethnocultural groups. *Journal of Early Adolescence, 19*, 301–322.

Roberts, S. M. (1995). Applicability of the goodness-of-fit hypothesis to coping with daily hassles. *Psychological Reports, 77*, 943–954.

Robertson, P. (2001). *The power of the land: Identity, ethnicity, and class among the Oglala Lakota* (Native Americans: Interdisciplinary Perspectives). New York: Routledge.

Robins, R. W., & Trzesniewski, K. H. (2005). Self-esteem development across the lifespan. *Current Directions in Psychological Science, 14*, 158–162.

Robins, R. W., Trzesniewski, K. H., Tracy, J. L., Gosling, S. D., & Potter, J. (2002). Global self-esteem across the life span. *Psychology and Aging, 17*, 423–434.

Robinson, N. M., Zigler, E., & Gallagher, J. J. (2000). Two tails of the normal curve: Similarities and differences in the study of mental retardation and giftedness. *American Psychologist, 55*, 1413–1421.

Robinson, W. P., & Gillibrand, E. (2004, May 14). Single-sex teaching and achievement in science. International Journal of Science Education, 26, 659.

Robles, T. F., & Kiecolt-Glaser, J. K. (2003). The physiology of marriage: Pathways to health. *Physiology & Behavior, 79*, 409–416.

Roche, T. (2000, November 13). The crisis of foster care. *Time*, 74–82.

Rodrigues, C. A. (2005). Culture as a determinant of the importance level business students place on ten teaching/learning techniques: A survey of university students. *The Journal of Management Development, 24*, 608–622.

Roeser, R. W., Eccles, J. S., & Sameroff, A. J. (2000). School as a context of early adolescents' academic and social-emotional development: A summary of research findings. *Elementary School Journal, 100*, 443–471.

Rogoff, B. (1995). *Observing sociocultural activity on three planes: Participatory appropriation, guided participation, and apprenticeship*. New York: Cambridge University Press.

Rogoff, B., & Chavajay, P. (1995). What's become of research on the cultural basis of cognitive development? *American Psychologist, 50*, 859–877.

Rogol, A. D., Roemmich, J. N., & Clark, P. A. (2002). Growth at puberty. *Journal of Adolescent Health, 31*, 192–200.

Roisman, G. L., Collins, W. A., & Sroufe, L. A., (2005). Predictors of young adults' representations of and behavior in their current romantic relationship: Prospective tests of the prototype hypothesis. *Attachment & Human Development, 7*, 105–121.

Romaine, S. (1994). *Bilingualism* (2nd ed.). London: Blackwell.

Romero, A. J., & Roberts, R. E. (2003). The impact of multiple dimensions of ethnic identity on discrimination and adolescents' self-esteem. *Journal of Applied Social Psychology, 33*, 2288–2305.

Rönkä, A., & Pulkkinen, L. (1995). Accumulation of problems in social functioning in young adulthood: A developmental approach. *Journal of Personality and Social Psychology, 69*, 381–391.

Rose, A. J., & Asher, S. R. (1999). Children's goals and strategies in response to conflicts within a friendship. *Developmental Psychology, 35*, 69–79.

Rose, R. J., Viken, R. J., Dick, D. M., Bates, J. E., Pulkkinen, L., & Kaprio, J. (2003). It *does* take a village: Nonfamilial environments and children's behavior. *Psychological Science, 14*, 273–278.

Rose, S. (2000). Heterosexism and the study of women's romantic and friend relationships. *Journal of Social Issues, 56*, 315–328.

Rose, S., & Frieze, I. H. (1993). Young singles' contemporary dating scripts. *Sex Roles, 28*, 499–509.

Rosen, V. M., Caplan, L., Sheesley, L., Rodriguez, R., & Grafman, J. (2003). An examination of daily activities and their scripts across the adult lifespan. *Behavior Research Methods, Instruments & Computers, 35*, 32–48.

Rosenblum, G. (2006, February 11). The state of the DATE; Hanging out. hooking up. Friends with benefits. Today's teens are experiencing a whole new world when it comes to love, sex and commitment. Or are they?, *Minneapolis Star Tribune*, 1E.

Rosenblum, G. D., & Lewis, M. (2003). Emotional development in adolescence. In G. Adams & M. Berzonskyu (Eds.), *Blackwell handbook of adolescence* (pp. 000). Malden, MA: Blackwell.

Rosenthal, D., & Hansen, J. (1980). Comparison of adolescents' perceptions and behaviors in single- and two-parent families. *Journal of Youth and Adolescence, 9,* 407–417.

Rosenthal, R. (2002). The Pygmalion effect and its mediating mechanisms. In J. Aronson, Improving academic achievement: Impact of psychological factors on education. San Diego: Academic Press.

Rosenthal, R. (2006). Applying psychological research on interpersonal expectations and covert communication in classrooms, clinics, corporations, and courtrooms. In S. I. Donaldson, D. E. Berger, & K. Pezdek, *Applied psychology: New frontiers and rewarding careers.* Mahwah, NJ: Lawrence Erlbaum Associates.

Rosenthal, R., & Jacobson, L. (1968). Pygmalion in the classroom: Teacher expectation and pupils' intellectual development. New York: Holt, Rinehart & Winston.

Rosselló, J., & Bernal, G. (1999). The efficacy of cognitive-behavioral and interpersonal treatments for depression in Puerto Rican adolescents. *Journal of Consulting and Clinical Psychology, 67,* 734–745.

Rossier J., Dahourou D., & McCrae R. R. (2005). Structural and mean level analyses of the five-factor model and locus of control: Further evidence from Africa. *Journal of Cross-Cultural Psychology* 36: 227–246.

Rothbaum, F., Pott, M., Azuma, H., Miyake, K., & Weisz, J. (2000). The development of close relationships in Japan and the United States: Paths of symbiotic harmony and generative tension. *Child Development, 71,* 1121–1142.

Rothblum, E. D., (1990). Women and weight: Fad and fiction. Journal of Psychology, 124, 5–24.

Rotheram-Borus, M., & Langabeer, K. (2001). Developmental trajectories of gay, lesbian, and bisexual youths. In A. D'Augelli & C. Patterson (Eds.), *Lesbian, gay, and bisexual identities and youth: Psychological perspectives* (pp. 97–128). New York: Oxford University Press.

Rotigel, J. V. (2003). Understanding the young gifted child: Guidelines for parents, families, and educators. Early Childhood Education Journal, 30, 209–214.

Rowe, R., Maughan, B., Worthman, C. M., Costello, E. J., & Angold, A. (2004). Testosterone, antisocial behavior, and social dominance in boys: Pubertal development and biosocial interaction. *Biological Psychiatry, 55,* 546–552.

Rubin, K. H. (1998). Social and emotional development from a cultural perspective. *Developmental Psychology, 34,* 611–615.

Rubinstein, J. S., Meyer, D. E., & Evans, J. E. (2001). Executive control of cognitive processes in task switching. *Journal of Experimental Psychology: Human Perception and Performance, 27,* 763–797.

Runco, M. A., & Sakamoto, S. O. (1993). Reaching creatively gifted students through their learning styles. In R. M. Milgram, R. S. Dunn, & G. E. Price (Eds.), *Teaching and counseling gifted and talented adolescents: An international learning style perspective.* Westport, CT: Praeger Publishers/Greenwood Publishing Group.

Russell, S., & Consolacion, T. (2003). Adolescent romance and emotional health in the United States: Beyond binaries. Journal of Clinical Child & Adolescent Psychology, 32, 499–508.

Russell, S., & Joyner, K. (2001). Adolescent sexual orientation and suicide risk: Evidence from a national study. *American Journal of Public Health, 91,* 1276–1281.

Rust, J., Golombok, S., Hines, M., Johnston, K., & Golding, J.; ALSPAC Study Team. (2000). The role of brothers and sisters in the gender development of preschool children. *Journal of Experimental Child Psychology, 77,* 292–303.

Rutter, M. (2003). Commentary: Causal processes leading to antisocial behavior. *Developmental Psychology, 39,* 372–378.

Ryan, C., & Rivers, I. (2003). Lesbian, gay, bisexual and transgender youth: victimization and its correlates in the USA and UK. Culture, Health & Sexuality, 5, 103–119.

Ryan, K. E., & Ryan, A. M. (2005). Psychological process underlying stereotype threat and standardized math test performance. Educational Psychologist, 40, 53–63.

Ryan, R. M., & Deci, E. L. (2004). Autonomy is no illusion: Self-determination theory and the empirical study of authenticity, awareness and will. In J. Greenberg, S. L. Koole, & T. Pyszczynski (Eds.) *Handbook of experimental existential psychology.* New York: Academic Press.

Rycek, R. F., Stuhr, S. L., McDermott, J., Benker, J., & Swartz, M. D. (1998). Adolescent egocentrism and cognitive functioning during late adolescence. *Adolescence, 33,* 745–749.

Saarni, C. (2002). *The development of emotional competence.* New York: Guilford Press.

Sadker, D., & Sadker, M. (2005). Teachers, schools, and society. NY: McGraw-Hill.

Sadker, M., & Sadker, D. (1994). Failing at fairness: How American's schools cheat girls. New York: Scribners.

Safron, D., Schulenberg, J., & Bachman, J. G. (2001). Part-time work and hurried adolescence: The links among work intensity, social activities, health behaviors, and substance use. *Journal of Health and Social Behavior, 42,* 425–449.

Salber, E. J., Freeman, H. E., & Abelin, T. (1968). Needed research on smoking: Lessons from the Newton study. In E. F. Borgatta & R. R. Evans (Eds.), *Smoking, health, and behavior.* Chicago: Aldine.

Salmivalli, C., Ojanen, T., Haanpää, J., & Peets, K. (2005). "I'm OK but you're not" and other peer-relational schemas: Explaining individual differences in children's social goals. *Developmental Psychology, 41,* 363–375.

Salovey, P., Rothman, A. J., & Rodin, J. (1998). Health Behavior. In D. T. Gilbert & S. T. Fiske (Eds.) et al., *The handbook of social psychology,* 4th edition. Boston, MA: McGraw-Hill Companies, Inc.

Salovey, P., Rothman, A. J., Detweiler, J. B., & Steward, W. T. (2000). Emotional states and physical health. *American Psychologist, 55,* 110–121.

Samuels, C. A. (2005). Special educators discuss NCLB effect at national meeting. Education Week, 24, 12.

Sanborn, C. F., & Jankowski, C. M. (1994). Physiologic considerations for women in sport. *Clinical Sports Medicine, 13,* 315–327.

Sandoval, J., Frisby, C. L., Geisinger, K. F., Scheuneman, J. D., & Grenier, J. R. (Eds.). (1998). *Test interpretation and diversity: Achieving equity in assessment.* Washington, DC: APA Books.

Sanoff, A. P., & Minerbrook, S. (1993, April 19). Race on campus. *U. S. News & World Report,* 52–64.

Santelli, J., Ott., M., Lyon, M., Rogers, J., Summers, D., & Schleifer, R. (2006). Abstinence and abstinence-only education: A review of U. S. policies and programs. *Journal of Adolescent Health, 38,* 72–81.

Sapolsky, R. M. (2003). Altering behavior with gene transfer in the limbic system. *Physiology & Behavior, 79,* 479–486.

Saslow, E. (2005, August 22). High schools address the cruelest cut; Pressure to make team forces new methods upon imperfect process. *The Washington Post,* A01.

Satel, S. (2004, May 25). Antidepressants: Two countries, two views. *The New York Times,* H2.

Saunders, J., Davis, L., & Williams, T. (2004). Gender differences in self-perceptions and academic outcomes: A study of African American high school students. Journal of Youth & Adolescence, 33, 81–90.

Savin-Williams, R. C. (1990). *Gay and lesbian youth: Expressions of identity.* Washington, DC: Hemisphere.

Savin-Williams, R. C. (1998). ". . . and then I became gay." Young men's stories. New York: Routledge.

Savin-Williams, R. C. (2001). Suicide attempts among sexual-minority youths: Population and measurement issues. *Journal of Consulting and Clinical Psychology, 69,* 983–991.

Savin-Williams, R. C. (2003). Are adolescent same-sex romantic relationships on our radar screen? In P. Florsheim (Ed.), *Adolescent romantic relations and sexual behavior: Theory, research, and practical implications.* Mahwah, NJ: Erlbaum.

Savin-Williams, R. C., & Berndt, T. J. (1990). Friendship and peer relations. In S. Feldman & G. Elliott (Eds.), *At the threshold: The developing adolescent.* Cambridge, MA: Harvard University Press.

Savin-Williams, R. C., & Cohen, K. M. (2004). Homoerotic development during childhood and adolescence. *Child and Adolescent Psychiatric Clinics of North America, 13,* 529–549.

Savin-Williams, R. C., & Demo, D. (1983). Situational and transituational determinants of adolescent self-feelings. *Journal of Personality and Social Psychology, 44,* 824–833.

Savin-Williams, R. C., & Diamond, L. M. (2004). Sex. In R. M. Lerner & L. Steinberg (Eds.), *Handbook of adolescent psychology* (2nd ed., New York: Wiley).

Savin-Williams, R., & Ream, G. (2003a). Sex variations in the disclosure to parents of same-sex attractions. *Journal of Family Psychology, 17,* 429–438.

Savin-Williams, R., & Ream, G. (2003b). Suicide attempts among sexual-minority male youth. *Journal of Clinical Child and Adolescent Psychology, 32,* 509–522.

Sawrikar, P., & Hunt, C. J. (2005). The relationship between mental health, cultural identity and cultural values in non-English Speaking Background (NESB) Australian adolescents. *Behaviour Change, 22,* 97–113.

Sax, et al (2004). *The American Freshman: National Norms for Fall 2004.* Los Angeles: Higher Education Research Institute, UCLA.

Sax, L. (2005, March 2). The promise and peril of single-sex public education. *Education Week, 24*, 48–51.

Sayer, L. C., Gauthier, A. H., & Furstenberg, F. F., Jr. (2004). Educational differences in parents' time with children: Cross-national variations. *Journal of Marriage and Family, 66*, 1152–1169.

Sbarra, D. (2006). Predicting the onset of emotional recovery following nonmarital relationship dissolution: Survival analyses of sadness and anger. *Personality and Social Psychology Bulletin, 32*, 298–312.

Sbarra, D., & Emery, R. (2005). The emotional sequelae of nonmarital relationship dissolution: Analysis of change and intraindividual variability over time. *Personal Relationships, 12*, 213–232.

Scarpa, A., Haden, S. C., & Hurley, J. (2006). Community violence victimization and symptoms of posttraumatic stress disorder: The moderating effects of coping and social support. *Journal of Interpersonal Violence, 21*, 446–469.

Schaefer, R. T. (2005). *Sociology.* New York: McGraw-Hill.

Schemo, D. J. (2001, December 5). U. S. students prove middling on 32-nation test. *The New York Times*, A21.

Schemo, D. J. (2004, March 2). Schools, facing tight budgets, leave gifted programs behind. *The New York Times*, A1, A18.

Scherer, K. (1994). Evidence for both universality and cultural specificity of emotion elicitation. In J. Averill, *The nature of emotion: Fundamental questions.* New York: Oxford University Press.

Schlegel, A., & Barry, H., III. (1991). *Adolescence: An anthropological inquiry.* New York: Free Press.

Schmitt, E. (2001, March 13). For 7 million people in census, one race category isn't enough. *The New York Times*, A1, A14.

Schneider, B. A., Atkinson, L., & Tardif, C. (2001). Child–parent attachment and children's peer relations: A quantitative review. *Developmental Psychology, 37*, 86–100.

Schneider, B. H., Woodburn, S., del Pilar Soteras del Toro, M., & Udvari, S. J. (2005). Cultural and gender differences in the implications of competition for early adolescent friendship. *Merrill-Palmer Quarterly, 51*, 163–191.

Schneider, B., & Stevenson, D. (2000). *The ambitious generation: America's teenagers motivated but directionless,* New Haven, CT: Yale University Press.

Schnurr, P. P., & Cozza, S. J. (Eds.). (2004). *Iraq war clinician guide* (2nd ed.) Washington, DC: National Center for Post-Traumatic Stress Disorder.

Schultz, N. R., Jr., & Moore, D. (1984). Loneliness: Correlates, attributions, and coping among older adults. *Personality and Social Psychology Bulletin, 10* 67–77.

Schutz, H., Paxton, S., & Wertheim, E. (2002). Investigation of body comparison among adolescent girls. *Journal of Applied Social Psychology, 32*, 1906–1937.

Schwartz, C. E., Wright, C. L., Shin, L. M., Kagan, J. & Rauch, S. L. (2003, June 20). Inhibited and uninhibited infants "grown up": Adult amygdalar response to novelty. *Science, 300*, 1952–1953.

Schwartz, I. M. (1999). Sexual activity prior to coital interaction: A comparison between males and females. *Archives of Sexual Behavior, 28*, 63–69.

Schwartz, K. D., Bukowski, W. M., & Aoki, W. T., (2006). Mentors, friends and gurus: Peer and nonparent influences on spiritual development. In E. C. Roehkleparatain, P. E. King, L. Wagener, & P. L. Bensen (Eds.), *The handbook of spiritual development in childhood and adolescence.* Thousand Oaks, CA: Sage Publications.

Schwartz, P. (2006). What elicits romance, passion, and attachment, and how do they affect our lives throughout the life cycle? In A. C. Crouter & A. Booth (Eds.), *Romance and sex in adolescence and emerging adulthood: Risks and opportunities.* Mahwah, NJ: Erlbaum.

Schwartz, S. J., Montgomery, M. J., & Briones, E. (2006). The role of identity in acculturation among immigrant people: Theoretical propositions, empirical questions, and applied recommendations. *Human Development, 49*, 1–30.

Scott, D. (1998). Rites of passage in adolescent development: A reapprecation. *Child and Youth Care Forum, 27*, 317–335.

Scrimsher, S., & Tudge, J. (2003). The teaching/learning relationship in the first years of school: Some revolutionary implications of Vygotsky's theory. *Early Education and Development, Special Issue, 14*, 293–312.

Sears, R. R. (1977). Sources of life satisfaction of the Terman gifted men. *American Psychologist, 32*, 119–129.

Sedikides, C., Gaertner, L., & Toguchi, Y. (2003). Pancultural self-enhancement. *Journal of Personality and Social Psychology, 84*, 60–79.

Segal, B. M., & Stewart, J. C. (1996). Substance use and abuse in adolescence: An overview. *Child Psychiatry & Human Development, 26*, 193–210.

Segall, M. H., Dasen, P. R., Berry, J. W., & Poortinga, Y. H. (1990). *Human behavior in global perspective.* Boston: Allyn & Bacon.

Seginer, R., & Somech, A. (2000). In the eyes of the beholder: How adolescents, teachers and school counselors construct adolescent images. *Social Psychology of Education, 4*, 139–157.

Seidman, S. N., & Rieder, R. O. (1994). A review of sexual behavior in the United States. *American Journal of Psychiatry, 151*, 330–341.

Seiffge-Krenke, I., & Beyers, W. (2005). Coping trajectories from adolescence to young adulthood: Links to attachment state of mind. *Journal of Research on Adolescence, 15*, 561–582.

Serbin, L. A., Poulin-Dubois, D., Colburne, K. A., Sen, M. G., & Eichstedt, J. A. (2001). Gender stereotyping in infancy: Visual preferences for and knowledge of gender-stereotyped toys in the second year. *International Journal of Behavioral Development, 25*, 7–15.

Servin, A., Nordenström, A., Larsson, A., & Bohlin, G. (2003). Prenatal androgens and gender-typed behavior: A study of girls with mild and severe forms of congenital adrenal hyperplasia. *Developmental Psychology, 39*, 440–450.

Sesser, S. (1993, September 13). Opium war redux. *The New Yorker*, 78–89.

Shafer, R. G. (1990, March 12). An anguished father recounts the battle he lost—Trying to rescue a teenage son from drugs. *People Weekly*, 81–83.

Shanahan, M. J., & Flaherty, B. P. (2001). Biobehavioral developments, perception, and action dynamic patterns of time use in adolescence. *Child Development, 72*, 385–401.

Sharma, B., & Sharma, N. (2004). Emotional competence in children: A qualitative analysis. *Psychological Studies, 49*, 124–127.

Sharp, D. (1997, March 14). Your kids' education is at stake. *USA Weekend*, pp. 4–6.

Shaw, P., Greenstein, D., Lerch, J., Clasen, L., Lenroot, R., Gogtay, N., et al. (2006, March 30). Intellectual ability and cortical development in children and adolescents. *Nature, 440*, 676–679.

Shea, J. D. (1985). Studies of cognitive development in Papua New Guinea. *International Journal of Psychology, 20*, 33–61.

Shealy, C. N. (1995). From Boys Town to Oliver Twist: Separating fact from fiction in welfare reform and out-of-home placement of children and youth. *American Psychologist, 50*, 565–580.

Shepard, B. (2004). In search of self: A qualitative study of the life-career development of rural young women. *Canadian Journal of Counselling, 38*, 75–90.

Shepard, B., & Marshall, A. (1999). Possible selves mapping: Life-career exploration with young adolescents. *Canadian Journal of Counselling, 33* 37–54

Shi, L., & Stevens, G. D. (2005). Disparities in access to care and satisfaction among U. S. children: The roles of race/ethnicity and poverty status. *Public Health Reports, 120*, 431–441.

Shih, M., & Sanchez, D. T. (2005). Perspectives and research on the positive and negative implications of having multiple racial identities. *Psychological Bulletin, 131*, 569–591.

Shirk, S., Burwell, R., & Harter, S. (2003). Strategies to modify low self-esteem in adolescents. In M. A. Reinecke, F. M. Dattilio, & A. Freeman (Eds.), *Cognitive therapy with children and adolescents: A casebook for clinical practice* (2nd ed.) New York: Guilford Press.

Shonk, S. M., & Cicchetti, D. (2001). Maltreatment, competency deficits, and risk for academic and behavioral maladjustment. *Developmental Psychology, 37*, 3–17.

Shrauger, J., S. (1975). Responses to evaluation as a function of initial self-perceptions. *Psychological Bulletin, 82*, 581–596.

Shrum, W., Cheek, N., Jr., & Hunter, S. M. (1988). Friendship in school: Gender and racial homophily. *Sociology of Education, 61*, 227–239.

Shulman, S. (2003). Conflict and negotiation in adolescent romantic relationships. In P. Florsheim (Ed.), *Adolescent romantic relations and sexual behavior: Theory, research, and practical implications.* Mahwah, NJ: Lawrence Erlbaum Associates.

Shulman, S., & Ben-Artzi, E. (2003). Age-related differences in the transition from adolescence to adulthood and links with family relationships. *Journal of Adult Development, 10*, 217–226.

Shulman, S., & Laursen, B. (2002). Adolescent perceptions of conflict in interdependent and disengaged friendships. *Journal of Research on Adolescence, 12,* 353–372.

Shultz, S. K., Scherman, A., & Marshall, L. J. (2000). Evaluation of a university-based date rape prevention program: Effect on attitudes and behavior related to rape. *Journal of College Student Development, 41,* 193–201

Shurkin, J. N. (1992). Terman's kids: The groundbreaking study of how the gifted grow up. Boston: Little, Brown.

Shweder, R. A., Much N. C., & Mahapatra, M. (1997). The "big three" of morality (autonomy, community, divinity) and the "big three" explanations of suffering. In A. M. Brandt & P. Rozin (Eds.), *Morality and health.* New York Taylor & Frances/Routledge.

Siegler, R. S. (1994). Cognitive variability: A key to understanding cognitive development. *Current Directions in Psychological Science, 3,* 1–5.

Siegler, R. S. (1998). *Children's thinking* (3rd ed.). Upper Saddle River, NJ: Prentice Hall.

Silbereisen, R., Peterson, A., Albrecht, H., & Krache, B. (1989). Maturational timing and the development of problem behavior: Longitudinal studies in adolescence. *Journal of Early Adolescence, 9,* 247.

Silk, J. S., Morris, A. S., Kanaya, T., & Steinberg, L. (2003). Psychological control and autonomy granting: Opposite ends of a continuum or distinct constructs? *Journal of Research on Adolescence, 13,* 113–128.

Silverman, J. (2001, August 1). Dating violence against adolescent girls linked with teen pregnancy, suicide attempts, and other health risk behaviors. *Journal of the American Medical Association, 286,* 15–20.

Silverthorn, P., & Frick, P. J. (1999). Developmental pathways to antisocial behavior: The delayed-onset pathway in girls. *Developmental and Psychopathology, 11,* 101–126.

Simmons, R., & Blyth, D. (1987). *Moving into adolescence.* Hawthorne, NY: Aldine de Gruyter.

Simonton, D. K. (1997). Creative productivity: A predictive and explanatory model of career trajectories and landmarks. *Psychological Review, 104,* 66–89.

Simonton, D. K., (2003). Scientific creativity as stochastic behavior: The integration of product, person, and process perspectives. *Psychological Bulletin, 129,* 475–494.

Simpkins, S. D., Fredricks, J. A., Davis-Kean, P. E., & Eccles J. S. (2006). Healthy mind, healthy habits: The influence of activity involvement in middle childhood. In A. C. Huston & M. N. Ripke (Eds.), *Developmental contexts in middle childhood: Bridges to adolescence and adulthood: Cambridge studies in social and emotional development.* New York: Cambridge University Press.

Sin, Y. W., Kim, D. J., Ha, T. H., Park, H. J., Moon, W. J., Chung, E. C., et al. (2005). Sex differences in the human corpus callosum: Diffusion tensor imaging study. *Neuroreport, 31,* 795–798.

Singh, J. (2000). The readability of HIV/AIDS education materials. *AIDS Education and Prevention, 12,* 214–224.

Slater, M., Henry, K., & Swaim, R. (2003). Violent media content and aggressiveness in adolescents: A downward spiral model. *Communication Research, 30,* 713–736.

Slavin, R. E. (1995). Enhancing intergroup relations in schools: Cooperative learning and other strategies. In W. D. Hawley & A. W. Jackson (Eds.), *Toward a common destiny: Improving race and ethnic relations in America.* San Francisco: Jossey-Bass.

Smeeding, T. M. (1995). An interdisciplinary model and data requirements for studying poor children. In P. Chase-Lansdale, & J. Brooks-Gunn *Escape from poverty: What makes a difference for children?* New York: Cambridge University Press.

Smetana, J. G. (2005). Adolescent-parent conflict: Resistance and subversion as developmental process. In L. Nucci, *Conflict, contradiction, and contrarian elements in moral development and education.* Mahwah, NJ: Lawrence Erlbaum Associates.

Smetana, J. G., & Daddis, C. (2002). Domain-specific antecedents of parental psychological control and monitoring: The role of parenting beliefs and practices. *Child Development, 73,* 563–580.

Smetana, J. G., & Gaines, C. (1999). Adolescent-parent conflict in middle-class African American families. *Child Development, 70,* 1447–1463.

Smetana, J. G., & Turiel, E. (2006). Moral development during adolescence. In G. Adams & M. Berzonsky (Eds.), *Blackwell handbook of adolescence.* Malden, MA: Blackwell.

Smith, C. A., & Lazarus, R. S. (2001). Appraisal components, core relational themes, and the emotions. In W. G. Parrott (Ed.), *Emotions in social psychology: Essential readings* (pp. 94–114). Philadelphia: Psychology Press.

Smith, P. B., Buzi, R. S., & Weinman, M. L. (2001). Mental health problems and symptoms among male adolescents attending a teen health clinic. *Adolescence, 36,* 323–332.

Smith, P. K., Singer, M., & Hoel, H. (2003). Victimization in the school and the workplace: Are there any links? *British Journal of Psychology, 94,* 175–188.

Smith, P., & Drew, L. (2002). Grandparenthood. In M. Bornstein (Ed.), *Handbook of parenting: Vol. 3: Being and becoming a parent* (2nd ed. ; pp. 141–172). Mahwah, NJ: Lawrence Erlbaum Associates.

Smith, R. A., & Weber, A. L. (2005). Applying social psychology in everyday life. In F. W. Schneider, J. A. Gruman, & L. M. Coutts (Eds.), *Applied social psychology: Understanding and addressing social and practical problems.* Thousand Oaks, CA: Sage.

Smokowski, P. R., Mann, E. A., Reynolds, A. J., & Fraser, M. W. (2004). Childhood risk and protective factors and late adolescent adjustment in inner city minority youth. *Children and Youth Services Review, 26,* 63–91.

Smuts, A. B., & Hagen, J. W. (1985). History of the family and of child development: Introduction to Part 1. *Monographs of the Society for Research in Child Development, 50* (4–5, Serial No. 211).

Snarey, J. R. (1995). In a communitarian voice: The sociological expansion of Kohlbergian theory, research, and practice. In W. M. Kurtines & J. L. Gerwirtz (Eds.), *Moral development: An introduction.* Boston: Allyn & Bacon.

Snyder, H., & Sickmund, M. (2006). *Juvenile offenders and victims: 2006 national report.* Washington, DC: U. S. Department of Justice, Office of Justice Programs, Office of Juvenile and Delinquency Prevention.

Snyder, J., Cramer, A., & Frank, J. (2005). The contributions of ineffective discipline and parental hostile attributions of child misbehavior to the development of conduct problems at home and school. *Developmental Psychology, 41,* 30–41.

Snyder, M., & Clary, E. G. (2004). Volunteerism and the generative society. In E. de St. Aubin, D. P. McAdams, & T. -C. Kim (Eds.), *The generative society: Caring for future generations.* Washington, DC: American Psychological Association.

Snyder, M., & Omoto, A. M. (2001). Basic research and practical problems: Volunteerism and the psychology of individual and collective action. In W. Wosinska, R. B. Cialdini, D. W. Barrett, & J. Reykowski (Eds.), *The practice of social influence in multiple cultures.* Mahwah, NJ: Erblaum.

Snyder, M., Clary, E. G., & Stukas, A. A. (2000). The functional approach to volunteerism. In G. R. Maio & J. M. Olson (Eds.), *Why we evaluate: Functions of attitudes.* Mahwah, NJ: Erlbaum.

Soto, J. A., Levenson, R. W., & Ebling, R. (2005). Cultures of moderation and expression: Emotional experience, behavior, and physiology in Chinese Americans and Mexican Americans. *Emotion, 5,* 154–165.

Southern Poverty Law Center. (1999). *Responding to hate at school: A guide for teachers, counselors, and administrators.* Retrieved May 20, 2006, from http://www. tolerance. org/pdf/rthas. pdf

Southern Poverty Law Center. (2005). *Ten ways to fight hate on campus: A response guide for collegiate communities.* Retrieved May 20, 2006, from http: //www. tolerance. org/pdf/ten_ways. pdf

Sowell E. R., Peterson, B. S., Thompson, P. M., Welcome, S. E., Henkenius, A. L., & Toga, A. W. (2003). Mapping cortical change across the human life span. *Nature Neuroscience, 6,* 309–315.

Sowell, E. R., Thompson, P. M., Tessner, K. D., & Toga, A. W. (2001). Mapping continued brain growth and gray matter density reduction in dorsal frontal cortex: Inverse relationships during postadolescent brain maturation. *Journal of Neuroscience, 21,* 8819–8829.

Spear, L. P. (2002). The adolescent brain and the college drinker: Biological basis of propensity to use and misuse alcohol. *Journal of Studies on Alcohol, Special Issue: College drinking, what it is, and what to do about it: Review of the state of the science, Suppl. 14,* 71–81.

Spearman, C. (1927). *The abilities of man.* London: Macmillan.

Spencer, J. (2001). How to battle school violence. *MSNBC News.* Retrieved from http://www. msnbc. com/news/

Spencer, M. B. (1991). Identity, minority development of. In R. M. Lerner, A. C. Petersen, & J. Brooks-Gunn (Eds.), *Encyclopedia of adolescence* (Vol. 1). New York: Garland.

Spencer, M. B. (2005). Crafting identities and accessing opportunities post-Brown. *American Psychologist, 60,* 821–830.

Spencer, M. B., & Dornbusch, S. M. (1990). Challenges in studying minority youth. In S. Feldman & G. Elliott (Eds.), *At the threshold: The developing adolescent*. Cambridge, MA: Harvard University Press.

Spiegel, D. (1993). Social support: How friends, family, and groups can help. In D. Goleman & J. Gurin (Eds.), *Mind-body medicine*. Yonkers, NY: Consumer Reports Books.

Spiegel, D. (1996). Dissociative disorders. In R. E. Hales & S. C. Yudofsky, (Eds.), *The American Psychiatric Press synopsis of psychiatry*. Washington, DC: American Psychiatric Press.

Spiegel, D., & Giese-Davis, J. (2003). Depression and cancer: Mechanisms and disease progression. *Biological Psychiatry, 54*, 269–282.

Spiegel, D., Bloom, J. R., Kraemer, H. C., & Gottheil, E. (1989, October 14). Effect of psychosocial treatment on survival of patients with metastatic breast cancer. *Lancet, 2*, 888–891.

Spira, A., Bajos, N., Bejin, A., Beltzer, N. (1992). AIDS and sexual behavior in France. Nature, 360, 407–409.

Sprecher, S., Felmlee, D., Metts, S., Fehr, B., & Vanni, D. (1998). Factors associated with distress following the breakup of a close relationship. *Journal of Social and Personal Relationships, 15*, 791–809.

Springer, S. P., & Deutsch, G. (1989). *Left brain, right brain* (3rd ed.). New York: Freeman.

Srivastava, A., Locke, E. A., & Bartol, K. M. (2001). Money and subjective well-being: It's not the money, it's the motives. *Journal of Personality and Social Psychology, 80*, 959–971.

Sroufe, L. A., Egeland, B., Carlson, E., & Collins, W. A. (2005). Placing early attachment experiences in developmental context: The Minnesota Longitudinal Study. In K. E. Grossmann, K. Grossmann, & E. Watters (Eds.), *Attachment from infancy to adulthood: The major longitudinal studies*. New York: Guilford Press.

Stacy, A. W., Sussman, S., Dent, C. W., Burton, D., et al. (1992). Moderators of peer social influence in adolescent smoking. *Personality & Social Psychology Bulletin, 18*, 163–172.

Staff, J., Mortimer, J. T., & Uggen, C. (2004). Work and leisure in adolescence. In R. M. Lerner & L. Steinberg (Eds.), *Handbook of adolescent psychology* (2nd ed.) NY: Wiley.

Stambor, Z. (2005, December). Can teaching troubled teens social problem-solving keep them out of trouble? *Monitor on Psychology*, 90–91.

Staudenmeier, J. J., Jr. (1999). Children and computers. *Journal of the American Academy of Child and Adolescent Psychiatry, 38*, 5.

Staudinger, U. M., Fleeson, W., & Baltes, P. B. (1999). Predictors of subjective physical health and global well-being: Similarities and differences between the United States and Germany. *Journal of Personality and Social Psychology, 76*, 305–319.

Stedman, L. C. (1997). International achievement differences: An assessment of a new perspective. Educational Researcher, 26, 4–15.

Steele, C. M. (1997). A threat in the air: How stereotypes shape intellectual identity and performance. American Psychologist, 52, 613–629.

Stein, J. H., & Reiser, L. W. (1994). A study of white middle-class adolescent boys' responses to "semenarche" (the first ejaculation). *Journal of Youth and Adolescence, 23*, 373–384.

Steinberg, G., & Hall, B. (2000). *Inside transracial adoption*. New York: Perspective Press.

Steinberg, L. (1993). *Adolescence*. New York: McGraw-Hill.

Steinberg, L. D. (1990). Autonomy, conflict, and harmony in the family relationship. In S. S. Feldman & G. R. Elliott (Eds.), *At the threshold: The developing adolescent*. Cambridge, MA: Harvard University Press.

Steinberg, L. D. (2001). We know some things: Adolescent-parent relationships in retrospect and prospect. *Journal of Research on Adolescence, 11*, 1–19.

Steinberg, L. D., & Avenevoli, S. (1998). Disengagement from school and problem behavior in adolescence: A developmental-contextual analysis of the influences of family and part-time work. In R. Jessor (Ed.), *New perspectives on adolescent risk behavior*. New York: Cambridge University Press.

Steinberg, L. D., & Cauffman, E. (1995). The impact of employment on adolescent development. In R. Vasta, *Annals of child development: A research annual, Vol. 11*. Philadelphia: Jessica Kingsley Publishers.

Steinberg, L. D., & Cauffman, E. (1996). Maturity of judgment in adolescence: Psychosocial factors in adolescent decision making. *Law and Human Behavior, 20*, 249–272.

Steinberg, L. D., & Silk, J. S. (2002). Parenting adolescents. In M. M. Bornstein (Ed.), *Handbook of parenting: Vol. 1: Children and parenting* (2nd ed., pp. 000). Mahwah, NJ: Erlbaum.

Steinberg, L. D., & Steinberg, W. (1994). *Crossing paths: How your child's adolescence triggers your own crisis*. New York: Simon & Schuster.

Steinberg, L. D., Fegley, S., & Dornbusch, S. M. (1003). Negative impact of part-time work on adolescent adjustment: Evidence from a longitudinal study. *Developmental Psychology, 29*, 171–180.

Steinberg, L. D., Greenberger, E., Garduque, L., & McAuliffe, S. (1982). High school students in the labor force: Some costs and benefits to schooling and learning. *Educational Evaluation and Policy Analysis, 4*, 363–372.

Steinberg, L., Dornbusch, S. M., & Brown, B. B. (1992). Ethnic differences in adolescent achievement: An ecological perspective. *American Psychologist, 47*, 723–729.

Steinberg, L. D., & Scott, S. S. (2003). Less guilty by reason of adolescence: Developmental immaturity, diminished responsibility, and the juvenile death penalty. *American Psychologist, 58*, 1009–1018.

Steinberg, L., Lamborn, S. D., Darling, N., Mounts, N. S., & Dornbusch, S. M. (1994). Over-time changes in adjustment and competence among adolescents from authoritative, authoritarian, indulgent, and neglectful families. *Child Development, 65*, 754–770.

Steinbrook, R. (2004). Disparities in health care—from politics to policy. *New England Journal of Medicine, 350*, 1486–1488.

Steptoe, A., Kunz-Ebrecht, S., Owen, N., Feldman, P. J., Willesem, G., & Kirschbaum, C. (2003). Socioeconomic status and stress-related biological responses over the working day. *Psychosomatic Medicine, 65*, 461–470.

Sternberg, R. (2003). A broad view of intelligence: The theory of successful intelligence. *Consulting Psychology Journal: Practice & Research, 55*, 139–154.

Sternberg, R. J. (1985). *Beyond IQ: A triarchic theory of human intelligence*. New York: Cambridge University Press.

Sternberg, R. J. (1986). Triangular theory of love. *Psychological Review, 93*, 119–135.

Sternberg, R. J. (1990). *Metaphors of mind: Conceptions of the nature of intelligence*. Cambridge, England: Cambridge University Press.

Sternberg, R. J. (1991). Theory-based testing of intellectual abilities: Rationale for the Sternberg triarchic abilities test. In H. A. H. Rowe (Ed.), *Intelligence: Reconceptualization and measurement*. Hillsdale, NJ: Erlbaum.

Sternberg, R. J. (1998). *Cupid's arrow: The course of love through time*. New York: Cambridge University Press.

Sternberg, R. J. (2001). What is the common thread of creativity? Its dialectical relation to intelligence and wisdom. *American Psychologist, 56*, 360–362.

Sternberg, R. J. (2004). A triangular theory of love. In H. T. Reis & C. E. Rusbult (Eds.), *Close relationships: Key readings*. Philadelphia: Taylor & Francis.

Sternberg, R. J. (2005). The triarchic theory of successful intelligence. In D. P. Flanagan, & P. L. Harrison, (Eds.), *Contemporary intellectual assessment: Theories, tests, and issues*. New York, Guilford Press.

Sternberg, R. J., & Grigorenko, E. L. (Eds.). (1997). *Intelligence, heredity, and environment*. New York: Cambridge University Press.

Sternberg, R. J., & Grigorenko, E. L. (Eds.). (2002). *The general factor of intelligence: How general is it?* Mahwah, NJ: Lawrence Erlbaum.

Sternberg, R. J., & O'Hara, L. A. (2000). Intelligence and creativity. In R. Sternberg, (Ed.), *Handbook of intelligence*. New York: Cambridge University Press.

Sternberg, R. J., & Wagner, R. K. (1986). *Practical intelligence*. New York: Cambridge University Press.

Sternberg, R. J., Conway, B. E., Ketron, J. L., & Bernstein, M. (1981). Peoples' conceptions of intelligence. *Journal of Personality and Social Psychology, 41*, 37–55.

Sternberg, R. J., Wagner, R. K., Williams, W. M., & Horvath, J. A. (1997). Testing common sense. In D. Russ-Eft, H. Preskill, & C. Sleezer (Eds.), *Human resource development review: Research and implications* (pp. 102–132). Thousand Oaks, CA: Sage.

Stevenson, H. W., Chen, C., & Lee, S. Y. (1992). A comparison of the parent–child relationship in Japan and the United States. In L. L. Roopnarine & D. B. Carter (Eds.), Parent-child socialization in diverse cultures. Norwood, NJ: Ablex.

Stevenson, J. L. & Wright, P. S. (1999). Group Dynamics. *Activities, Adaptation & Aging, 23* (3), 139–173.

Stewart, D. E. (Ed.). (2005). *Menopause: A mental health practitioner's guide.* Washington, DC: American Psychiatric Publishing.

Stice, E., & Shaw, H. (2004). Eating disorder prevention programs: A meta-analytic review. *Psychological Bulletin, 130,* 206–227.

Stice, E., Presnell, K., & Bearman, K. (2001). Relation of early menarche to depression, eating disorders, substance abuse, and comorbid psychopathology among adolescent girls. *Developmental Psychology, 37,* 608–619.

Stipek, D., Hakuta, K. (2007). Strategies to ensure that no child starts from behind. In J. L. Aber, S. J. Bishop-Josef, S. M. Jones, K. T. McLean, & D. A. Phillips (Eds.), *Child development and social policy*: Knowledge for action. Washington, DC: American Psychological Association.

Stolberg, S. G. (1998, April 3). Rise in smoking by young Blacks erodes a success story in health. *The New York Times,* A1.

Stone, C. (2003). Counselors as advocates for gay, lesbian, and bisexual youth: A call for equity and action. Journal of Multicultural Counseling & Development, 31, 143–155.

Stormshak, E. A., Bierman, K. L., Bruschi, C., Dodge, K. A., & Coie, J. D. (1999). The relation between behavior problems and peer preference in different classroom contexts. *Child Development, 70,* 169–182.

Strauch, B. (1997, August 10). Use of antidepression medicine for young patients has soared. *The New York Times,* A1, A24.

Straus, M. A., & McCord, J. (1998). Do physically punished children become violent adults? In S. Nolen-Hoeksema (Ed.), *Clashing views on abnormal psychology: A Taking Sides custom reader* (pp. 130–155). Guilford, CT: Dushkin/McGraw-Hill.

Straus, M. A., Sugarman, D. B., & Giles-Sims, J. (1997). Spanking by parents and subsequent antisocial behavior of children. *Archives of Pediatrics and Adolescent Medicine, 151,* 761–767.

Stroebe, K., Lodewijkx, H. F. M., & Spears, R. (2005). Do unto others as they do unto you: Reciprocity and social identification as determinants of ingroup favoritism. *Personality and Social Psychology Bulletin, 31,* 831–845.

Stroh, L, K., Langlands, C. L., & Simpson, P. A. (2004). Shattering the glass ceiling in the new millennium. In M. S. Stockdale & F. J. Crosby, *Psychology and management of workplace diversity.* Malden, MA: Blackwell Publishers.

Strouse, D. L. (1999). Adolescent crowd orientations: A social and temporal analysis. In J. A. McLellan & M. J. V. Pugh (Eds.), *The role of peer groups in adolescent social identity: Exploring the importance of stability and change.* San Francisco: Jossey-Bass.

Stukas, A. A., & Dunlap, M. R. (2002). Community involvement: Theoretical approaches and educational initiatives. *Journal of Social Issues, 58,* 411–427.

Stukas, A., Snyder, M., & Clary, G. (1999). The effects of "mandatory volunteerism" on intentions to volunteer. *Psychological Science, 10,* 59–64.

Sue, S., & Chu, J. Y. (2003). The mental health of ethnic minority groups: Challenges posed by the supplement to the Surgeon General's report on mental health. *Culture, Medicine and Psychiatry, 27,* 447–465.

Sugarman, S. (1988). *Piaget's construction of the child's reality.* Cambridge, England: Cambridge University Press.

Suitor, J. J., & Reavis, R. (1995). Football, fast cars, and cheerleading: Adolescent gender norms, 1978-1989. *Adolescence, 30,* 265–272.

Suitor, J. J., Minyard, S. A., & Carter, R. S. (2001). 'Did you see what I saw?' Gender differences in perceptions of avenues to prestige among adolescents. *Sociological Inquiry, 71,* 437–454.

Suldo, S. M., & Huebner, E. S. (2004). Does life satisfaction moderate the effects of stressful life events on psychopathological behavior during adolescence? *School Psychology Quarterly, 19,* 93–105.

Sullivan, H. S. (1953). *The interpersonal theory of psychiatry,* New York: Norton.

Suls, J., & Wills, T. A. (Eds.). (1991). *Social comparison: Contemporary theory and research.* Hillsdale, NJ: Erlbaum.

Summers, J., Schallert, D., & Ritter, P. (2003). The role of social comparison in students' perceptions of ability: An enriched view of academic motivation in middle school students. *Contemporary Educational Psychology, 28,* 510–523.

Sung, B. L. (1985). Bicultural conflicts in Chinese immigrant children. *Journal of Comparative Family Studies, 16,* 255–270.

Super, D. E. (1990). A life-span, life-space approach to career development. In D. Brown & L. Brooks (Eds.), *Career choice and development.* (2nd ed.) San Francisco: Jossey-Bass.

Suskind, R. (1994, September 24). Class struggle: Poor, black, and smart. *New York Times,* p. A1.

Suskind, R. (1999). *A hope in the unseen: An American odyssey from the inner city to the Ivy League.* New York: Broadway Books.

Susman, E. J., & Rogol, A. (2004). Puberty and psychological development. In R. Lerner & L. Steinberg (Eds.), *Handbook of adolescent psychology* (2nd ed.) New York: Wiley.

Susman, E. J., Dorn, L. D., & Schiefelbein, V. L. (2003). Puberty, sexuality, and health. In R. M. Lerner, M. A. Easterbrooks, & J. Mistry (Eds.), *Handbook of psychology: Developmental psychology, Vol. 6.* Hoboken, NJ: Wiley.

Susser, E. S., Herman, D. B., & Aaron, B. (2002, August). Combating the terror of terrorism. *Scientific American,* pp. 70–77.

Sutton, M. J., Brown, J. D., Wilson, K. M., & Klein, J. D. (2002). Shaking the tree of knowledge: Where adolescents learn about sexuality and contraception. In J. D. Brown, J. R. Steele, & K. Walsh-Childers (Eds). *Sexual teens, sexual media: Investigating media's influence on adolescent sexuality.* Mahwah, NJ: Erlbaum.

Suzuki, L., & Aronson, J. (2005). The cultural malleability of intelligence and its impact on the racial/ethnic hierarchy. Psychology, Public Policy, and Law, 11, 320–327.

Swain, J. (2004). Is placement in the least restrictive environment a restricted debate? PsycCRITIQUES, p. 23–30.

Swanson, D. P., Spencer, M. B., Harpalani, V., Dupree, D., Noll, E., Ginzburg, S., & Seaton, G. (2003). Psychosocial development in racially and ethnically diverse youth: Conceptual and methodological challenges in the 21st century. *Development and Psychopathology, 15,* 743–771.

Swanson, H., Saez, L., & Gerber, M. (2004). Literacy and cognitive functioning in bilingual and nonbilingual children at or not at risk for reading disabilities. Journal of Educational Psychology, 96, 3–18.

Swiatek, M. (2002). Social coping among gifted elementary school students. Journal for the Education of the Gifted, 26, 65–86.

Sy, S. R., & Schulenberg, J. E. (2005). Parent beliefs and children's achievement trajectories during the transition to school in Asian American and European American families. *International Journal of Behavioral Development, 29,* 505–515.

Tajfel, H., & Turner, J. (2001). An integrative theory of intergroup conflict. In M. A., Hogg & D. Abrams (Eds.), *Intergroup relations: Essential readings.* New York: Psychology Press.

Tajfel, H., & Turner, J. (2004). The social identity theory of intergroup behavior. In J. T. Jost & J. Sidanius (Eds.), *Political psychology: Key readings.* New York: Psychology Press.

Takanishi, R., Hamburg, D. A., & Jacobs, K. (Eds.). (1997). *Preparing adolescents for the twenty-first century: Challenges facing Europe and the United States.* New York: Cambridge University Press.

Tamis-LeMonda, C. S., & Cabrera, N. (Eds). (2002). *Handbook of father involvement: Multidisciplinary perspectives.* Mahwah NJ: Erlbaum.

Tangmunkongvorakul, A., Kane, R., & Wellings, K. (2005). Gender double standards in young people attending sexual health services in Northern Thailand. *Culture, Health & Sexuality, 7,* 361–373.

Tangney, J., & Dearing, R. (2002). Gender differences in morality. In R. Bornstein & J. Masling (Eds.), *The psychodynamics of gender and gender role.* Washington, DC: American Psychological Association.

Taniguchi, H., & Ura, M. (2005). Support reciprocity and depression among children. In S. P. Shohov (Ed.), *Advances in psychology research, Vol. 33.* Hauppauge, NY: Nova Science Publishers.

Tanner, J. (1972). Sequence, tempo, and individual variation in growth and development of boys and girls aged twelve to sixteen. In J. Kagan & R. Coles (Eds.), *Twelve to sixteen: Early adolescence.* New York: Norton.

Tappan, M. B. (1997). Language, culture and moral development: A Vygotskian perspective. *Developmental Review, 17,* 199–212.

Tartamella, L., Herscher, E., & Woolston, C. (2005). *Generation extra large: Rescuing our children fro the epidemic of obesity.* New York: Basic Books.

Tatum, B. D. (2003). *"Why are all the black kids sitting together in the cafeteria?": A psychologist explains the development of racial identity.* New York: Basic Books.

Taylor, D. M. (2002). *The quest for identity: From minority groups to Generation Xers*. Westport, CT: Praeger Publishers/Greenwood Publishing.

Taylor, S. (2006). *Health psychology* (6th ed.). New York: McGraw-Hill.

Taylor, S. E. (1991). *Health psychology* (2nd ed.). New York: McGraw-Hill.

Taylor, S. E., & Brown, J. D. (1988). Illusion and well-being: A social psychological perspective on mental health. *Psychological Bulletin, 103,* 193–210.

Taylor, S. E., Kemeny, M. E., Reed, G. M., Bower, J. E., & Gruenewald, T. L. (2000). Psychological resources, positive illusions, and health. *American Psychologist, 55,* 99–109.

Taylor, S., Peplau, L., & Sears, D. (2006). *Social Psychology* (12th ed.). Upper Saddle River, NJ: Prentice Hall.

Taylor, S. E., & Brown, J. D. (1994). Positive illusions and well-being revisited: Separating fact from fiction. *Psychological Bulletin, 116,* 21–27.

Teicher, M. H., Anderson, S. L., Polcari, A., Anderson, C. M., & Navalta, C. P. (2002). Developmental neurobiology of childhood stress and trauma. *Psychiatric Clinics of North America, 25,* 397–426.

Teicher, M. H., Anderson, S. L., Polcari, A., Anderson, C. M., Navalta, C. P., & Kim, D. M. (2003). The neurobiological consequences of early stress and childhood maltreatment. *Neuroscience and Biobehavioral Review, 27,* 33–44.

Tellegen, A., Lykken, D. T., Bouchard, T. J., Jr., Wilcox, K. J., Segal, N. L., & Rich, S. (1988). Personality similarity in twins reared apart and together. *Journal of Personality and Social Psychology, 54,* 1031–1039.

Terman, D. L., Larner, M. B., Stevenson, C. S., & Behrman, R. E. (1996). Special education for students with disabilities: Analysis and recommendations. *The Future of Children, 6,* 4–24.

Terman, L. M., & Oden, M. H. (1959). The gifted group at mid-life: Thirty-five years follow-up of the superior child. Stanford, CA: Stanford University Press.

Thanasiu, P. L. (2004). Childhood sexuality: Discerning healthy from abnormal sexual behaviors. *Journal of Mental Health Counseling, 26,* 309–319.

Thao, P. (2005) Cultural variation within southeast Asian American families. In C. L. Frisby & C. R. Reynolds (Eds.), *Comprehensive handbook of multicultural school psychology*. Hoboken, NJ: Wiley.

Tharp, R. G. (1989). Psychocultural variables and constants: Effects on teaching and learning in schools: Special issue: Children and their development: Knowledge base, research agenda, and social policy application. *American Psychologist, 44,* 349–359.

The Endocrine Society (2001, March 1). *The Endocrine Society and Lawson Wilkins Pediatric Endocrine Society call for further research to define precocious puberty*. Bethesda, MD: The Endocrine Society.

The Guttmacher Institute. (2002). *Teen pregnancy: Trends and lessons learned*. The Guttmacher Report on Public Policy. Washington, DC: The Guttmacher Institute.

Thomas, A., Chess, S., & Birch, H. G. (1968). *Temperament and behavior disorders in children*. New York: New York University Press.

Thomas, N., Cohen, P., Johnson, J. G., Sneed, J. R. & Brook, J. S. (2004). The course and psychosocial correlates of personality disorder symptoms in adolescence: Erikson's developmental theory revisited. *Journal of Youth and Adolescence, 33,* 373–387.

Thompson, R. A., & Nelson, C. A. (2001, January). Developmental science and the media: Early Brain Development. *American Psychologist,* 5–15.

Thompson, S. J., Safyer, A. J., & Pollio, D. E. (2001). Differences and predictors of family reunification among subgroups of runaway youths using shelter services. *Social Work Research, 25,* 163–172.

Thompson, S. J., Zittel-Palamara, K. M., & Maccio, E. (2004). Runaway youth utilizing crisis shelter services: Predictors of presenting problems. *Child & Youth Care Forum, 33,* 387–404.

Thornberry, T. P., & Krohn, M. D. (1997). Peers, drug use, and delinquency. In D. M. Stoff, J. Breiling, & J. D. Maser (Eds.), *Handbook of antisocial behavior*. New York: Wiley.

Thornburgh, N. (2006, April 17). Dropout nation. *Time,* 31–40.

Thurlow, C. (2001a). Naming the "outsider within": Homophobic pejoratives and the verbal abuse of lesbian, gay and bisexual high-school pupils. *Journal of Adolescence, 24,* 25–38.

Thurlow, C. (2001b). The usual suspects? A comparative investigation of crowds and social-type labelling among young British teenagers. *Journal of Youth Studies, 4,* 319–334.

Thurlow, M. L., Lazarus, S. S., & Thompson, S. J. (2005). State policies on assessment participation and accommodations for students with disabilities. Journal of Special Education, 38, 232–240.

Tillery, B. (1974). *Problem solving techniques*. Retrieved from http://www. dushkin. com/online/study/problem-solving. mhtml

Tinsley, B., Lees, N., & Sumartojo, E. (2004). Child and adolescent HIV risk: Familial and cultural perspectives. Journal of Family Psychology, 18, 208–224.

Toch, T. (1995, January 2). Kids and marijuana: The glamour is back. *U. S. News & World Report,* 12.

Toga, A. W., & Thompson, P. M. (2003). Temporal dynamics of brain anatomy. *Annual Review of Biomedical Engineering, 5,* 119–145.

Tolstedt, B. E., & Stokes, J. P. (1984). Self-disclosure, intimacy, and the depenetration process. *Journal of Personality and Social Psychology, 46,* 84–90.

Toner, M. A., & Heaven, P. C. L. (2005). Peer-social attributional predictors of socio-emotional adjustment in early adolescence: A two-year longitudinal study. *Personality and Individual Differences, 38,* 579–590.

Tornstam, L. (1992). Loneliness in marriage. *Journal of Social and Personal Relationships, 9,* 197–217.

Torstveit, M. K., & Sundgot-Borgen, J. (2005). Participation in leanness sports but not training volume is associated with menstrual dysfunction: A national survey of 1276 elite athletes and controls. *British Journal of Sports Medicine, 39,* 141–147.

Townsend, T. (2005, December 28). Jewish teens explain their faith. *St. Louis Post-Dispatch,* p. C1. Retrieved May 17, 2006 from LexisNexis Academic.

Trautner, H. M., Ruble, D. N., Cyphers, L., Kirsten, B., Behrendt, R., & Hartmann, P. (2005). Rigidity and flexibility of gender stereotypes in childhood: Develpmental or differential? *Infant and Child Development, 14,* 365–381.

Treasure, J., & Tiller, J. (1993). The aetiology of eating disorders: Its biological basis. *International Review of Psychiatry, 5,* 23–31.

Tremblay, G., Tremblay, R. E., & Saucier, J. -F. (2004). The development of parent-child relationship perceptions in boys from childhood to adolescence: A comparison between disruptive and non-disruptive boys. *Child & Adolescent Social Work Journal, 21,* 407–426.

Trickett, P. K., Kurtz, D. A., & Pizzigati, K. (2004). Resilient outcomes in abused and neglected children: Bases for strength-based intervention and prevention policies. In K. I. Maton & C. J. Schellenbach, (Eds.), *Investing in children, youth, families and communities: Strength-based research and policy*. Washington, DC: American Psychological Association.

Tropp, L. (2003). The psychological impact of prejudice: Implications for intergroup contact. *Group Processes & Intergroup Relations, 6,* 131–149.

Trost, S. G., Saunders, R., & Ward D. S. (2002) Determinants of physical activity in middle school children. *American Journal of Health Behavior, 26,* 95–102.

Trzesniewski, K., Donnellan, M., & Robins, R. (2003). Stability of self-esteem across the life span. *Journal of Personality and Social Psychology, 84,* 205–220.

Tsai, J., & Levenson, R. (1997). Cultural influences on emotional responding: Chinese American and European American dating couples during interpersonal conflict. *Journal of Cross-Cultural Psychology, 28,* 600–625.

Tsai, J., Chentsova-Dutton, Y., Freire-Bebeau, L., & Przymus, D. (2002). Emotional expression and physiology in European Americans and Hmong Americans. *Emotion, 2,* 380–397.

Tsai, J., Levenson, R., & Carstensen, L. (2000). Autonomic, expressive, and subjective responses to emotional films in older and younger Chinese American and European American adults. *Psychology and Aging, 15,* 684–693.

Tseung, C. N., & Schott, G. (2004). The quality of sibling relationship during late adolescence: Are there links with other significant relationships? *Psychological Studies, 49,* 20–30.

Tsunoda, T. (1985). *The Japanese brain: Uniqueness and universality*. Tokyo: Taishukan.

Tsunokai, G. T. (2005). Beyond the lenses of the "model" minority myth: A descriptive portrait of Asian gang members. *Journal of Gang Research, 12,* 37–58.

Tung, Y. C., Lee, J. S., Tsai, W. Y., & Hsiao, P. H. (2004). Physiological changes of adrenal androgens in childhood. *Journal of the Formosa Medical Association, 103,* 921–924.

Tur-Kaspa, H., Weisel, A., & Segev, L. (1998). Attributions for feelings of loneliness of students with learning disabilities. *Learning Disabilities Research & Practice, 13,* 89–94.

Turiel, E. (2006). Thought, emotions, and social interactional processes in moral development. In M. Killen & J. G. Smetana (Ed.), *Handbook of moral development*. Mahwah, NJ: Erlbaum.

Turkheimer, E., Haley, A., Waldreon, M., D'Onofrio, B., & Gottesman, I. I. (2003). Socioeconomic status modifies heritability of IQ in young children. *Psychological Science, 14*, 623–628.

Turkington, C. (1987). The world of Mindie. Psychology Today, 23–26.

Turner, S. L., & Lapan, R. T. (2005). Promoting career development and aspirations in school-age youth. In S. D. Brown & R. W. Lent (Eds.), Career *development and counseling: Putting theory and research to work*. Hoboken, NJ: Wiley.

Turner-Bowker, D. M. (1996). Gender stereotyped descriptors in children's picture books: Does "Curious Jane" exist in the literature? *Sex Roles, 35*, 461–488.

TV Week. (2006). Listings. Chicago: Crain Communications.

Twenge, J. M. (2006). *Generation Me: Why today's young Americans are more confident, assertive, entitled—and more miserable than ever before*. New York: Basic Books.

Twenge, J. M., & Crocker, J. (2002). Race and self-esteem: Meta-analyses comparing whites, blacks, Hispanics, Asians, and American Indians and comment on Gray-Little and Hafdahl (2000). *Psychological Bulletin, 128*, 371–408.

Tyler, J. M., Feldman, R. S., & Reichert, A. (2006) The price of deceptive behavior: Disliking and lying to people who lie to us. *Journal of Experimental Social Psychology, 42*, 69–77.

Tyler, J. M., & Feldman, R. S. (2005). Deflecting threat to one's image: Dissembling personal information as a self-presentation strategy. *Basic and Applied Social Psychology, 27*, 371–378.

Tyre, P. (2006, January 30.) The trouble with boys. *Newsweek*, 44–52.

U. S. Bureau of the Census. (2000). Current population reports. Washington, DC: U. S. Government Printing Office.

U. S. Bureau of the Census. (2002). *Statistical abstract of the United States (122nd ed.)*. Washington, DC: U. S. Government Printing Office.

U. S. Census Bureau (2000). The condition of education. *Current Population Surveys, October 2000*. Washington, DC: U. S. Census Bureau.

U. S. Census Bureau. (1998). Poverty by educational attainment. Washington, DC: U. S. Census Bureau.

U. S. Census Bureau. (2003). *Population reports*. Washington, DC: GPO.

U. S. Department of Health and Human Services. (1989). *Report of the Secretary's Task Force on Youth Suicide: Vol. 3. Prevention and interventions in youth suicide*. Rockville, MD: U. S. Department of Health and Human Services.

U. S. Department of Health and Human Services. (1996). *You can quit smoking consumer guide*. Retrieved June 15, 2006, from http://www.cdc.gov/tobacco/quit/smconsumr.pdf

U. S. Department of Health and Human Services. (2001). *The Surgeon General's call to action to prevent and decrease overweight and obesity*. Rockville, MD: U. S. Government Printing Office.

U. S. Secret Service. (2002). *The final report and findings of the safe school initiative: Implications for the prevention of school attacks in the United States*. Washington, DC: National Threat Assessment Center.

Umaña-Taylor, A. J., Bhanot, R., & Shin, N. (2006). Ethnic identity formation during adolescence: The critical role of families. *Journal of Family Issues, 27*, 390–414.

Umana-Tayler, A. J., Diversi, M., & Fine, M. A. (2002). Ethnic identity and self-esteem of Latino adolescents: Distinctions among the Latino populations. Journal of Adolescent Research, 17, 303–327.

UNESCO. (2005). *International Health*. Geneva, Switzerland: World Health Statistics.

Ungar, J. B., Molina, G. B., & Teran, L. (2000). Perceived consequences of teenage childbearing among adolescent girls in an urban sample. *Journal of Adolescent Health, 26*, 205–212.

Unger, J. B., Gallaher, P., Shakib, S., Ritt-Olson, A., Palmer, R. H., & Johnson, C. A. (2002). The AHIMSA Acculturation Scale: A new measure of acculturation for adolescents in a multicultural society. *Journal of Early Adolescence, 22*, 225–251.

Unger, J. W. (2006). A review of a culture approach to discourse. *Language in Society, 35*, 617–620.

Unger, R. K. (Ed.) (2001). *Handbook of the psychology of women and gender*. New York: Wiley.

Unger, R., & Crawford, M. (1992). *Women and gender: A feminist psychology* (2nd ed.). New York: McGraw-Hill.

Upchurch, D. M., Levy-Storms, L., Sucoff, C. A., & Aneshensel, C. S. (1998). Gender and ethnic differences in the timing of first sexual intercourse. *Family Planning Perspectives, 30*, 27–36.

Updegraff, K. A., Helms, H. M., McHale, S. M., Crouter, A. C., Thayer, S. M., & Sales, L. H. (2004). Who's the boss? Patterns of perceived control in adolescents' friendships. *Journal of Youth & Adolescence, 33*, 403–420.

Updegraff, K. A., McHale, S. M., Crouter, A. C., & Kupanoff, K. (2001). Parents' involvement in adolescents' peer relationships: A comparison of mothers' and fathers' roles. *Journal of Marriage & the Family, 63*, 655–668.

Urberg, K. A., Degirmencioglu, S. M., & Pilgrim, C. (1997). Close friend and group influence on adolescent cigarette smoking and alcohol use. *Developmental Psychology, 33*, 834–844.

Urberg, K. A., Degirmencioglu, S. M., Tolson, J. M., & Halliday-Scher, K. (1995). The structure of adolescent peer networks. *Developmental Psychology, 31*, 540–547.

Urberg, K. A., Degirmencioglu, S. M., Tolson, J. M., & Halliday-Scher, K. (2000). Adolescent social crowds: Measurement and relationship to friendships. *Journal of Adolescent Research, 15*, 427–445.

Urberg, K., Luo, Q., & Pilgrim, C. (2003). A two-stage model of peer influence in adolescent substance use: Individual and relationship-specific differences in susceptibility to influence. *Addictive Behaviors, 28*, 1243–1256.

U.S. Bureau of the Census. (2002). *Statistical Abstract of the United States, 2002*. Washington, D. C.

Van Der Veer, R., & Valsiner, J. (1993). *Understanding Vygotsky*. Oxford, England: Blackwell.

Van der Veer, R., & Valsiner, J. (Eds.). (1994). *The Vygotsky reader*. Cambridge, MA: Blackwell.

van Eck, M., Nicolson, N. A., & Berkhof, J. (1998). Effects of stressful daily events on mood states: Relationship to global perceived stress. *Journal of Personality and Social Psychology, 75*, 1572–1585.

Van Schoiack-Edstrom, L., Frey, K. S., & Beland, K. (2002). "Changing Adolescents' Attitues About Relational and Physical Aggression. " *School Psychology Review, 31*, 201–216.

Van Tassel-Baska, J., Olszewski-Kubilius, P., & Kulieke, M. (1994). A study of self-concept and social support in advantaged and disadvantaged seventh and eighth grade gifted students. *Roeper Review, 16*, 186–191.

van Wormer, K., & McKinney, R. (2003). What schools can do to help gay/lesbian/bisexual youth: A harm reduction approach. *Adolescence, 38*, 409–420.

VandeBerg, L. R., & Streckfuss, D. (1992). Prime-time televiosn's portrayal of women and the world of work: A demographic profile. *Journal of Broadcasting & Electronic Media, 36* 195–208.

Vargas, A. (2005, October 23). In living colors. *Washington Post*, W28.

Vartanian, L. R. (2000). Revisiting the imaginary audience and personal fable constructs of adolescent egocentrism: A conceptual review. *Adolescence, 35*, 639–661.

Vaughn, L. A., & Weary, G. (2002). Roles of the availability of explanations, feelings of ease, and dysphoria in judgments about the future. *Journal of Social and Clinical Psychology, 21*, 686–704.

Vedantam, S. (2004, April 23). Antidepressants called unsafe for children: Four medications singled out in analysis of many studies. *The Washington Post*, A03.

Veenman, S., Denessen, E., van den Akker, A., & van der Rijt, A. (2005). Effects of a cooperative learning program on the elaborations of students during help seeking and help giving. *American Educational Research Journal, 42*, 115–152.

Veldhuis, J. D., Roemmich, J. N., Richmond, E. J., Rogol, A. D., Lovejoy, J. C., Sheffield-Moore, M., et al. (2005). Endocrine control of body composition in infancy, childhood, and puberty. *Endocrinology Review, 26*, 114–146.

Verkuyten, M. (2003). Positive and negative self-esteem among ethnic minority early adolescents: Social and cultural sources and threats. *Journal of Youth & Adolescence, 32*, 267–277.

Verma, S., & Larson, R. W. (Eds.). (2003). *Examining adolescent leisure time across cultures: Developmental opportunities and risks: New directions for child and adolescent development, No. 99*. New York: Jossey-Bass.

Viadero, D. (2005, November 16), Minority students' popularity found to fall as grades rise. *Education Week, 25*, 14.

Villarosa, L. (2003, December 23). More teenagers say no to sex, and experts are sure why. *The New York Times*, D6.

Vitaliano, P. P., Maiuro, R. D., Russo, J., & Katon, W. (1990). Coping profiles associated with psychiatric, physical health, work, and family problems. *Health Psychology, 9,* 348–376

Vitaro, F., & Pelletier, D. (1991). Assessment of children's social problem-solving skills in hypothetical and actual conflict situations. *Journal of Abnormal Child Psychology, 19,* 505–518.

Vizmanos, B. & Marti-Henneberg, C. (2000). Puberty begins with a characteristic subcutaneous body fat mass in each sex. *European Journal of Clinical Nutrition, 54,* 203–206.

Vogel, G. (2005, July 22). A powerful first KiSS-1. *Science, 309,* 551–552.

Vohs, K. D., & Heatherton, T. (2004). Ego threats elicits different social comparison process among high and low self-esteem people: Implications for interpersonal perceptions. *Social Cognition, 22,* 168–191.

Von Salisch, M., & Vogelgesang, J. (2005). Anger regulation among friends: Assessment and development from childhood to adolescence. *Journal of Social and Personal Relationships, 22,* 837–855.

Vondracek, F. W., & Porfeli, E. J. (2006). The world of work and careers. In G. R. Adams, & M. D. Berzonsky (Eds.), *Blackwell handbook of adolescence.* Malden, MA: Blackwell Publishing.

Vyas, S. (2004). Exploring bicultural identities of Asian high school students through the analytic window of a literature club. *Journal of Adolescent & Adult Literacy, 48,* 12–18.

Vygotsky, L. S. (1926/1997). *Educational psychology.* Delray Beach, FL: St. Lucie Press.

Vygotsky, L. S. (1978). *Mind in society: The development of higher mental processes* (M. Cole, Ed.). Cambridge, MA: Harvard University Press. (Original works published 1930–1935)

Wachs, T. D. (1996). Known and potential processes underlying developmental trajectories in childhood and adolescence. *Developmental Psychology, 32,* 796–801.

Wadsworth, M. E., Raviv, T., Compas, B. E., & Connor-Smith, J. K. (2005). Parent and adolescent responses to poverty-related stress: Tests of mediated and moderated coping models. *Journal of Child and Family Studies, 14,* 283–298.

Wagner, M., Schuetze, Y., & Lang, F. R. (1999). Social relationships in old age. In P. B. Baltes & K. U. Mayer (Eds.), *The Berlin aging study: Aging from 70 to 100.* New York: Cambridge University Press.

Wagner, R. K., & Sternberg, R. J. (1991). *Tacit knowledge inventory.* San Antonio, TX: The Psychological Corporation.

Wahlstrom, K. L., Davison, M. L., Choi, J., & Ross, J. N. (2001, August). *School start time study: Executive summary.* Minneapolis: University of Minnesota, Center for Applied Research and Educational Improvement.

Wainright, J. L., Russell, S. T., & Patterson, C. J. (2004). Psychosocial adjustment, school outcomes, and romantic relationships of adolescents with same-sex parents. *Child Development, 75,* 1886–1898.

Waite, S. J., Bromfield, C., & McShane, S. (2005). Successful for whom? A methodology to evaluate and inform inclusive activity in schools. European Journal of Special Needs Education, 20, 71–88.

Walcott, D., Pratt, H., & Patel, D. (2003). Adolescents and eating disorders: Gender, racial, ethnic, sociocultural, and socioeconomic issues. *Journal of Adolescent Research, 18,* 223–243.

Walker, E. F., Sabuwalla, Z., & Huot, R. (2004). Pubertal neuromaturation, stress sensitivity, and psychopathology. *Developmental Psychopathology, 16,* 807–24.

Wallis, C. (2006, March 27). The multitasking generation. *Time,* 48–55.

Wang, Q., Nicholson, P. H., Suuriniemi, M., Lyytikainen, A., Helkala, E., Alen, M., et al. (2004). Relationship of sex hormones to bone geometric properties and mineral density in early pubertal girls. *Journal of Clinical Endocrinology Metabolism, 89,* 1698–1703.

Wang, S., and Tamis-LeMonda, C. (2003). Do child-rearing values in Taiwan and the United States reflect cultural values of collectivism and individualism? *Journal of Cross-Cultural Psychology, 34,* 629–642.

Wang, S., Baillargeon, R., & Paterson, S. (2005). Detecting continuity violations in infancy: A new account and new evidence from covering and tube events. *Cognition, 95,* 129–173.

Ward, L. M., & Friedman, K. (2006). Using TV as a guide: Associations between television viewing and adolescents' sexual attitudes and behavior. *Journal of Research on Adolescence, 16,* 133–156.

Waring, E. M., Schaefer, B., & Fry, R. (1994). The influence of therapeutic self-disclosure on perceived marital intimacy. *Journal of Sex & Marital Therapy, 20,* 135–146.

Warren J. R. (2002). Reconsidering the relationship between student employment and academic outcomes: A new theory and better data. *Youth & Society, 33,* 366–370.

Warren, J. R., & Lee, J. C. (2003). The impact of adolescent employment on high school dropout: Differences by individual and labor-market characteristics. *Social Science Research, 32,* 98–128

Warren, J. R., Lee, J. C., & Cataldi, E. F. (2004). Teenage employment and high school completion. In D. Conley & K. Albright, eds., *After the bell – Family background, public policy, and educational success.* London: Routledge.

Warwick, P., & Maloch, B. (2003). Scaffolding speech and writing in the primary classroom: A consideration of work with literature and science pupil groups in the USA and UK. *Reading: Literacy & Language, 37,* 54–63.

Wasserman, J. D., & Tulsky, D. S. (2005). The history of intelligence assessment. In D. P. Flanagan, & P. L. Harrison; (Eds.), *Contemporary intellectual assessment: Theories, tests, and issues.* New York, Guilford Press.

Waters, E., Hamilton, C. E., & Weinfield, N. S. (2000). The stability of attachment security from infancy to adolescence and early adulthood: General introduction. *Child Development, 71,* 678–683.

Watkins, D., Dong, Q., & Xia, Y. (1997). Age and gender differences in the self-esteem of Chinese children. *Journal of Social Psychology, 137,* 374–379.

Way, N. (2004). Intimacy, desire, and distrust in the friendships of adolescent boys. In N. Way & J. Y. Chu (Eds.), *Adolescent boys: Exploring diverse cultures of boyhood.* New York: New York University Press.

Webb, L. D. (2005). *The history of American education: A great American experiment.* Upper Saddle River, NJ: Prentice Hall.

Webb, R. M., Lubinski, D., & Benbow, C. P. (2002). Mathematically facile adolescents with math/science aspirations: New perspectives on their educational and vocational development. Journal of Educational Psychology, 94, 785–794.

Webber, M. P., Carpiniello, K. E., Oruwariye, T., Lo, Y., Burton, W. B., & Appel, D. K. (2003). Burden of asthma in inner-city elementary schoolchildren. *Archives of Pediatric Adolescent Medicine, 157,* 125–129.

Weber, R., Ritterfeld, U., & Mathiak, K. (2006). Does playing violent video games induce aggression? Empirical evidence of a functional magnetic resonance imaging study. *Media Psychology, 8,* 39–60.

Webster, R. A., Hunter, M., & Keats, J. A. (1994). Peer and parental influences on adolescents' substance use: A path analysis. *International Journal of the Addictions, 29,* 647–657.

Wechsler, D. (1975). Intelligence defined and undefined. *American Psychologist, 30,* 135–139.

Weichold, K., Silbereisen, R., & Schmitt-Rodermund, E. (2003). Short-term and long-term consequences of early versus late physical maturation in adolescents. In C. Hayward (Ed.), *Gender differences at puberty.* New York: Cambridge University Press.

Weinberg, R., Waldman, I., van Dulman, M., & Scarr, S. (2004). The Minnesota transracial adoption study: Parent reports of psychosocial adjustment at late adolescence. *Adoption Quarterly, 8,* 27–44.

Weinberger, D. R. (2001, March 10). A brain too young for good judgment. *The New York Times,* p. D1.

Weiner, K. (2004). Bringing social and emotional skills to the classroom: Applying new theory, practice, and research in emotional development. *Proceedings from the Association for University and College Counseling Center Directors Conference.* Retrieved January 7, 2006, from http://www. aucccd. org/conference/2004Proceedings. htm

Weinstein, M., Glei, D. A., Yamazaki, A., & Ming-Cheng, C. (2004). The role of intergenerational relations in the association between life stressors and depressive symptoms. *Research on Aging, 26,* 511–530.

Weinstock, H., Berman, S., & Cates, W., Jr. (2004). Sexually transmitted diseases among American youth: Incidence and prevalence estimates, 2000. Perspectives on Sexual and Reproductive Health, 36, 182–191.

Weiss, M. R., Ebbeck, V., & Horn. T. S. (1997). Children's self-perceptions and sources of physical competence information: A cluster analysis. *Journal of Sport and Exercise Psychology, 19,* 52–70.

Weiss, R. (2003, September 2). Genes' sway over IQ may vary with class. *The Washington Post,* A1.

Weisz, A., & Black, B. (2002). Gender and moral reasoning: African American youth respond to dating dilemmas. *Journal of Human Behavior in the Social Environment, 5,* 35–52.

Weitzman, E., Nelson, T., & Wechsler, H. (2003). Taking up binge drinking in college: The influences of person, social group, and environment. *Journal of Adolescent Health, 32,* 26–35.

Welsh, D. P., Grello, C. M., & Harper, M. S. (2003). When love hurts: Depression and adolescent romantic relationships. In P. Florsheim (Eds.), *Adolescent romantic relations and sexual behavior: Theory, research, and practical implications.* Mahwah, NJ: Lawrence Erlbaum Associates.

Wentzel, K. R., & Feldman, S. S. (1996). Relations of cohesion and power in family dyads to social and emotional adjustment during early adolescence. *Journal of Research on Adolescence, 6,* 225–244.

Wentzel, K. R., Barry, C. M., & Caldwell, K. A. (2004). Friendships in middle school: Influences on motivation and school adjustment. *Journal of Educational Psychology, 96,* 195–203.

Werner, E. E. (1995). Resilience in development. *Current Directions in Psychological Science, 4,* 81–85.

Werner, E. E. (2005). Resilience research: Past, present, and future. In R. D. Peters, B. Leadbeater, & R. J. McMahon (Eds.), *Resilience in children, families, and communities: Linking context to practice and policy.* New York: Kluwer Academic/Plenum Publishers.

Werner, E. E., & Smith, R. S. (2002). Journeys from childhood to midlife: Risk, resilience and recovery. *Journal of Developmental and Behavioral Pediatrics, 23,* 456.

Wertsch, J. V. (1999). The zone of proximal development: Some conceptual issues. In P. Lloyd & C. Fernyhough (Eds.), *Lev Vygotsky: Critical assessments,* Vol. 3: *The zone of proximal development.* New York: Routledge.

Wertsch, J. V., & Tulviste, P. (1992). L. S. Vygotsky and contemporary developmental psychology. *Developmental Psychology, 28,* 548–557.

West, S. L., & O'Neal, K. K. (2004). Project D. A. R. E. outcome effectiveness revisited. *American Journal of Public Health, 94,* 1027–1029.

Westen, D. (2000). Psychoanalysis: Theories. In A. E. Kazdin (Ed.), *Encyclopedia of psychology, Vol. 6* (pp. 000). Washington, DC: American Psychological Association.

Westerhausen, R., Kreuder, F., Sequeira Sdos, S., Walter, C., Woerner, W., Wittling, R. A., Schweiger, E., Wittling, W. (2004). Effects of handedness and gender on macro- and microstructure of the corpus callosum and its subregions: a combined high-resolution and diffusion-tensor MRI study. *Brain Research and Cognitive Brain Research, 21,* 418–426.

Wethington, E., Kessler, R. C., & Pixley, J. E. (2004). Turning points in adulthood. In O. Brim, C. D. Ryff, & R. C. Kessler (Eds.), *How healthy are we?: A national study of well-being at midlife.* Chicago: University of Chicago Press.

Whalen, J. & Begley, S. (2005, March 30). In England, girls are closing the gap with boys in math. The Wall Street Journal, A1.

Wheeler, G. (1998, March 13). The wake-up call we dare not ignore. Science, 279, 1611.

Whitaker, R. C., Wright, J. A., Pepe, M. S., Seidel, K. D., & Dietz, W. H. (1997). September 25). Predicting obesity in young adulthood from childhood and parental obesity. *The New England Journal of Medicine, 337,* 869–873.

Whitbeck, L. B., & Hoyt, D. R. (1994). Social prestige and assortive mating: A comparison of students from 1956 and 1988. *Journal of Social and Personal Relationships, 11,* 137–145.

Whitbeck, L. B., Hoyt, D. R., Yoder, K. A., Cauce, A. M., & Paradise, M. (2001). Deviant behavior and victimization among homeless and runaway adolescents. *Journal of Interpersonal Violence, 16,* 1175–1204.

Whitbourne, S. K. (2001). Stability and change in adult personality: Contributions of process-oriented perspectives. *Psychological Inquiry, 12,* 101–103.

Whitbourne, S. K., Zuschlag, M. K., Elliot, L. B., & Waterman, A. S. (1992). Psychosocial development in adulthood: A 22-year sequential study. *Journal of Personality and Social Psychology, 63,* 260–271.

White, J. W., & Humphrey, J. A. (1990). A theoretical model of sexual assault: An empirical test. Paper presented at the Annual Meeting of the Southeastern Psychological Association (36th, Atlanta, GA, April 4–7, 1990).

Whiting, B, M., & Whiting, J. W. (1975). *Children of six countries: A psychological analysis.* Cambridge, MA: Harvard University Press.

Whiting, B. B., & Edwards, C. P. (1988). *Children of different worlds: The foundation of social behavior.* Cambridge, MA: Harvard University Press.

Whiting, M., and Smulson, J. (2006). Small grants with big promise. *Monitor on Psychology, 37,* 90.

Whitley, B. E. (1998). Factors associated with cheating among college students: A Review. *Research in Higher Education, 39,* 235–274.

Wichstrom, L., & Hegna, K. (2003). Sexual orientation and suicide attempt: A longitudinal study of the general Norwegian adolescent population. *Journal of Abnormal Psychology, 112,* 144–151.

Wickelgren, W. A. (1999). Webs, cell assemblies, and chunking in neural nets: Introduction. *Canadian Journal of Experimental Psychology, 53,* 118–131.

Widom, C. S. (2000). Motivation and mechanisms in the "cycle of violence." In D. J. Hansen (Ed.), *Nebraska Symposium on Motivation Vol. 46, 1998: Motivation and child maltreatment* (Current theory and research in motivation series). Lincoln: University of Nebraska Press.

Wiederman, M. W. (2005). The gendered nature of sexual scripts. *Family Journal: Counseling and Therapy for Couples and Families, 13,* 496–502.

Wigfield, A., & Eccles, J. S. (2002). Students' motivation during the middle school years. In J. Aronson (Ed.), *Improving academic achievement: Impact of psychological factors on education.* San Diego, CA: Academic Press.

Wilcox, H. C., Conner, K. R., & Caine, E. D. (2004). Association of alcohol and drug use disorders and completed suicide: An empirical review of cohort studies. *Drug & Alcohol Dependence, 76,* Special Issue: Drug Abuse and Suicidal Behavior, s11–s19.

Wiley, M. O., & Baden, A. L. (2005). Birth parents in adoption: Research, practice, and counseling psychology. *Counseling Psychologist, 33,* 13–50.

Wilkins, D. (2006). *American Indian politics and the American political system* (2nd ed.) (The Spectrum Series, Race and Ethnicity in National and Global Politics). New York: Rowman.

Williams, J. E., & Best, D. L. (1990). *Sex and psyche: Gender and self viewed cross-culturally.* Thousand Oaks, CA: Sage Publications.

Williams, J. M., & Currie, C. (2000). Self-esteem and physical development in early adolescence: Pubertal timing and body image. *Journal of Early Adolescence, 20,* 129–149.

Williams, M. B., Zinner, E. S., & Ellis, R. R. (2004). The connection between grief and trauma: An overview. In E. S. Zinner, & M. B. Williams, *When a community weeps: Case studies in group survivorship.* Philadelphia, PA: Brunner/Mazel.

Williamson, R., & Johnston, J. H. (1999). Challenging orthodoxy: An emerging agenda for middle level reform. *Middle School Journal, 12,* 10–17.

Wills, T. A., & DePaulo, B. M. (1991).) Interpersonal analysis of the help-seeking process. In C. R. Snyder & D. R. Forsyth (Eds.), *Handbook of social and clinical psychology: The health perspective.* New York: Pergamon Press.

Wills, T., Resko, J., & Ainette, M. (2004). Smoking onset in adolescence: A person-centered analysis with time-varying predictors. *Health Psychology, 23,* 158–167.

Wilson, B. J., Smith, S. L., Potter, W. J., Kunkel, D., Linz, D., Colvin, C. M., & Donnerstein, E. (2002). Violence in children's television programming: Assessing the risks. *Journal of Communication, 52,* 5–35.

Wilson, J. P., & Keane, T. M. (Eds.). (1996). *Assessing psychological trauma and PTSD.* New York: Guilford Press.

Wilson, R. (2004, December 3). Where the elite teach, it's still a man's world. Chronicle of Higher Education, 51, A8.

Windle, M. (1994). A study of friendship characteristics and problem behaviors among middle adolescents. *Child Development, 65,* 1764–1777.

Wingert, P., & Katrowitz, B. (2002, October 7). Young and depressed. *Newsweek,* 53–61.

Winner, E. (1997). Gifted children: Myths and realities. NY: BasicBooks.

Winsler, A. (2003). Introduction to special issue: Vygotskian perspectives in early childhood education. *Early Education and Development, Special Issue, 14,* 253–269.

Winstead, B. A., & Sanchez, J. (2005). Gender and Psychopathology. In J. E. Maddux, & B. A. Winstead, *Psychopathology: Foundations for a contemporary understanding.* Mahwah, NJ: Lawrence Erlbaum Associates.

Winters, K. C., Stinchfield, R. D., & Botzet, A. (2005). Pathways fo youth gambling problem severity. *Psychology of Addictive Behaviors, 19,* 104–107.

Witelson, S. (1989, March). *Sex differences.* Paper presented at the annual meeting of the New York Academy of Science, New York.

Witt, S. D. (1997). Parental influence on children's socialization to gender roles. *Adolescence, 32,* 253–259.

Wolfe, D. A. *Child abuse: Implications for children development and psychopathology (2nd ed.).* Thousand Oaks, CA: Sage Publications, Inc, 1999. xii, 140 pp.

Women's Bureau, U. S. Department of Labor. (2002). *Women's Bureau frequently asked questions.* Retrieved from http://www. dol. gov/wb/faq38.htm

Wonderlic. (2003, February 9). *Wonderlic Personnel Test.* Available on the World Wide Web at http://www. wonderlic. com/products/product.asp?prod_id=4

Wong, F., & Halgin, R. (2006). The "model minority": Bane or blessing for Asian Americans? *Journal of Multicultural Counseling and Development, 34,* 38–49.

Woody, J. D., Russel, R., & D'Souza, H. J. (2000). Adolescent non-coital sexual activity: Comparisons of virgins and non-virgins. *Journal of Sex Education & Therapy, 25,* 261–268

Worrell, F., Szarko, J., & Gabelko, N. (2001). Multi-year persistence of nontraditional students in an academic talent development program. Journal of Secondary Gifted Education, 12, 80–89.

Wright, J. C., Huston, A. C., Truglio, R., Fitch, M., Smith, E., & Piemyat, S. (1995). Occupational portrayals on television: Children's role schemata, career aspirations, and perceptions of reality. *Child Development, 66,* 1706–1718.

Wright, S. C., & Taylor, D. M. (1995). Identity and the language of the classroom: Investigation of the impact of heritage versus second language instruction on personal and collective self-esteem. Journal of Educational Psychology, 87, 241–252.

Wu, P., Robinson, C., & Yang, C. (2002). Similarities and differences in mothers' parenting of preschoolers in China and the United States. *International Journal of Behavioral Development, 26,* 481–491.

Wyer, R. (2004). The cognitive organization and use of general knowledge. In J. Jost & M. Banaji (Eds.) *Perspectivism in social psychology: The yin and yang of scientific progress.* Washington, DC: American Psychological Association.

Xiaohe, X., & Whyte, M. K. (1990). Love matches and arranged marriages: A Chinese replication. *Journal of Marriage and the Family, 52,* 709–722.

Yamaguchi, K., & Kandel, D. (1987). Drug use and other determinants of premarital pregnancy and its outcome: A dynamic analysis of competing life events. *Journal of Marriage & the Family, 49,* 257–270.

Yamaguchi, S., Gelfand, M., Ohashi, M. M., & Zemba, Y. (2005). The cultural psychology of control: Illusions of personal versus collective control in the United States and Japan. *Journal of Cross-Cultural Psychology, 36,* 750–761.

Yang, R., & Blodgett, B. (2000). Effects of race and adolescent decision-making on status attainment and self-esteem. *Journal of Ethnic & Cultural Diversity in Social Work, 9,* 135–153.

Yasui, M., Dorham, C., L., & Dishion, T. J. (2004). Ethnic identity and psychological adjustment: A validity analysis for European American and African American adolescents. *Journal of Adolescent Research, 19,* 807–825.

Yecke, C. P. (2005). *Mayhem in the middle.* Washington, DC: Thomas B. Fordham Institute.

Yelland, G. W., Pollard, J., & Mercuri, A. (1993). The metalinguistic benefits of limited contact with a second language. Applied Psycholinguistics, 14, 423–444.

Yi, J. P., Smith, R. E., & Vitaliano, P. P. (2005). Stress-resilience, illness, and coping: A person-focused investigation of young women athletes. *Journal of Behavioral Medicine, 28,* 257–265.

Young, E. A., & Altemus, M. (2004). Puberty, ovarian steroids, and stress. *Annals of the New York Academy of Sciences, 1021,* 124–33.

Young, H., & Ferguson, L. (1979). Developmental changes through adolescence in the spontaneous nomination of reference groups as a function of decision context. *Journal of Youth and Adolescence, 8,* 239–252.

Youniss, J., & Haynie, D. L. (1992). Friendship in adolescence. *Journal of Developmental and Behavioral Pediatrics, 13,* 59–66.

Youniss, J., Bales, S., & Christmas-Best, V. (2002). Youth civic engagement in the twenty-first century. *Journal of Research on Adolescence, 12,* 121–148.

Youniss, J., McClellan, J. A., & Yates, M. (1997). What we know about engendering civic identity. *American Behavioral Scientist, 40,* 620–631.

Yuill, N., & Perner, J. (1988). Intentionality and knowledge in children's judgments of actor's responsibility and recipient's emotional reaction. *Developmental Psychology, 24,* 358–365.

Zahn-Waxler, C., Klimes-Dougan, B., & Slattery, M. J. (2000). Internalizing problems of childhood and adolescence: Prospects, pitfalls, and progress in understanding the development of anxiety and depression. *Development and Psychopathology, 12,* 443–466.

Zauszniewski, J. A., & Martin, M. H. (1999). Developmental task achievement and learned resourcefulness in healthy older adults. *Archives of Psychiatric Nursing, 13,* 41–47.

Zehr, M. A. (2006, February 1). Advocates note need to polish "bilingual" pitch. *Education Week, 25,* 12.

Zeidner, M. (2005). Contextual and personal predictors of adaptive outcomes under terror attack: The case of Israeli adolescents. *Journal of Youth and Adolescence, 34,* 459–470.

Zeidner, M., Matthews, G., & Roberts, R. D. (2004). Emotional intelligence in the workplace: A critical review. *Applied Psychology: An International Review, 53,* 371–399.

Zettergren, P. (2004). School adjustment in adolescence for previously rejected, average and popular children. *British Journal of Educational Psychology, 73,* 207–221.

Zhang, Y., Proenca, R., Maffel, M., Barone, M., Leopold, L., & Friedman, J. M. (1994). Positional cloning of the mouse obese gene and its human homologue. *Nature, 372,* 425–432.

Zhe, C., & Siegler, R. S. (2000). Across the Great Divide: Bridging the gap between understanding of toddlers' and older children's thinking. *Monographs of the Society for Research in Child Development, 65,* 2, Serial No. 261.

Zhou, M., & Kim, S. S. (2006). Community forces, social capital, and educational achievement: The case of supplementary education in the Chinese and Korean immigrant communities. *Harvard Educational Review, 76,* 1–29.

Zhu, J., & Weiss, L. (2005). The Wechsler Scales. In D. P. Flanagan, & P. L. Harrison, (Eds.), *Contemporary intellectual assessment: Theories, tests, and issues.* New York, Guilford Press.

Zigler, E. F., & Gilman, E. (1998). The legacy of Jean Piaget. In G. A. Kimble & M. Wertheimer (Eds.), *Portraits of pioneers in psychology* (Vol. 3). Washington, DC: American Psychological Association.

Zillman, D. (2000). Influence of unrestrained access to erotica on adolescents' and young adults' dispositions toward sexuality. *Journal of Adolescent Health, 27,* 41–44.

Zillman, D., & Weaver, J. B., III (1999). Effects of prolonged exposure to gratuitous media violence on provoked and unprovoked hostile behavior. *Journal of Applied Social Psychology, 29,* 145–165.

Zimbardo, P. G. (1973). On the ethics of intervention in human psychological research: With special reference to the Stanford prison experiment. *Cognition, 2,* 243–256.

Zimmer-Gembeck, M. J., & Collins, W. A. (2005). Autonomy development during adolescence. In G. R. Adams & M. D. Berzonsky (Eds.), *Blackwell handbook of adolescence* (pp. 000). Oxford, England: Blackwell.

Zimmer-Gembeck, M. J., Geiger, T. C., & Crick, N. R. (2005). Relational and physical aggression, prosocial behavior, and peer relations: Gender moderation and bidirectional associations. *Journal of Early Adolescence, 25,* 421–452.

Zirkel, S., & Cantor, N. (2004). 50 years after Brown v. Board of Education: The promise and challenge of multicultural education. Journal of Social Issues, 60, 1–15.

Zisman, P., & Wilson, V. (1992). Table hopping in the cafeteria: An exploration of "racial" integration in early adolescent social groups. *Anthropology & Education Quarterly, 23,* 199–220.

Zurbriggen, E. L. (2000). Social motives and cognitive power-sex associations: Predictors of aggressive sexual behavior. *Journal of Personality and Social Psychology, 78,* 559–581.

Zweig, J. M., Lindberg, L. D., & McGinley, K. A. (2001). Adolescent health risk profiles: The co-occurrence of health risks among females and males. *Journal of Youth and Adolescence, 30,* 707–728.

Zwiers, J. (2004). *Developing academic thinking skills in Grades 6-12: A handbook of multiple intelligence activities.* Newark, DE: International Reading Association.

Credits

(1999, May 13). The role of the anterior prefrontal cortex in human cognition. Nature, 339, 148–51; page 356: Photo Researchers, Inc. (Gusto); page 358: NewsCom (LA119/Rockstar Games/Zuma Press); page 359: (left and right) Photo by Courtesy Rockstar Games/ZUMA Press. © Copyright 2004 by Rockstar Games; page 364: Getty Images Inc.—Hulton Archive Photos; page 365: Radius Images/Alamy; page 368: Juice Images/Alamy; page 375: Corbis Royalty Free (Scott Barrow).

CHAPTER 12

Page 382: AP Wide World Photos (Traverse City Réord-Eagle, Meegan M. Reid); page 383: Corbis/SABA Press Photos, Inc. (Mark Peterson); page 386: (top) The Image Works (Lee Snider), (bottom) Samuel Borges/Fotolia; page 391: Francesca Yorke © Dorling Kindersley; page 394: The Image Works (Dick Blume/Syracuse Newspapers); page 397: Getty Images Inc.— Stone Allstock; page 400: AP Wide World Photos (Mark Humphrey); page 404: Erick Skydive; page 407: Seventeen Magazine.

CHAPTER 13

Page 414: AP Wide World Photos; page 415: Adam Gault/Getty Images/Digital Vision; page 417: Martin Novak/Shutterstock.com; page 421: Ardelean Andreea/Shutterstock.com; page 425: Kevin Sullivan, The Orange County Register/ZUMA Press/Alamy; page 428: © Russell Gordon/DanitaDelimont.com; page 432: The Image Works (John Powell/ Topham); page 438: Alamy Images (GIPhotoStock); page 439: PhotoEdit Inc. (Bill Aron).

CHAPTER 14

Page 444: PhotoEdit Inc. (Michelle D. Bridwell); page 445: Axel Bernstorff/Cultura Creative (RF)/Alamy; page 447: PhotoEdit Inc. (Myrleen Ferguson Cate); page 450: Image by © MAPS.com/Corbis; page 452: AP Wide World Photos (David J. Phillip); page 455: PhotoEdit Inc. (Peter Byron); page 459: Getty Images, Inc.—Photodisc (SW Productions); page 462: Bonnie Kamin/PhotoEdit; 465: Christopher Nuzzaco/Fotolia; page 467: DenisNata/Fotolia; page 469: Cindy Kracht Foster, LCSW, ACSW; page 470: Ken Karp/PH Photo; page 472: Pearson Education/PH College (Laima Druskis).

Index

A

Aaron, B., 449, 450
Abeare, C., 45
Abelin, T., 428
Abortion, 295
Abraham, Y., 396
Abrahams, G., 404
Abrams, D., 400
Abrams, L. S., 145
Abramson, L. Y., 433
Abstinence, 284, 298, 302
Abstract modeling, 132
Academic performance
    and popularity, 237
    and work, 365–367
Acceleration, 337
Accommodation, 72
Acculturation, 385–388
Achieved ethnic identity, 388
Achievement tests, 97–98
Ackard, D. M., 305
Ackerman, B. P., 166
Acocella, J., 12, 113
ACT, 97
Activity level, 122
Adams, C. R., 323
Adams, G. R., 250, 430
Adams, M., 82
Adams, P. R., 430
Adams, W. L., 69
Addictive drugs, 424
Adelson, J., 262
Adler, S. R., 456, 461
Adolescence
    and cohort membership, 29–30
    decision making during, 103–104
    defined, 5–6
    and developmental change, 30
    field in the 20th century, 12–13
    future of, 31–32
    growth during, 49–50
    health and wellness, 55–64
    improving health, 62–64
    measuring change in, 14–15
    and moral development, 125–140
    and nature *vs.* nurture development,
        30–31
    and the scientific method, 13
    sleep and, 61–62
    and social policy, 31
    social transitions of, 112–118
    study of, 12

today, 9–10
today's perspective, 15–26
topical areas of, 6–7, 8
transitions and tasks of, 27–29
truths and myths, 24–26
Adolescence (Hall), 12, 27
Adolescent cliques, 222–224
Adolescent egocentrism, 100
Adolescent growth spurt, 49–50
Adolescent science, 13
Adolphs, R., 167
Adrenarche, 41–42
African-Americans, 393–394
    and computer use, 362
    earnings, 376
    and higher education, 339, 340
    high school dropouts, 332
    and informal adoption, 297
    and leisure activities, 351
    and masturbation, 281
    and multigenerational families, 201
    and parallel crowds, 225
    and popularity, 237
    and relationship intimacy, 263
    and self-esteem, 161
    and sense of family, 202–203
    and single-parent homes, 198
    and smoking, 426
    and special education, 334
    and teenage pregnancy, 290
    time with peers, 213
    upward mobility, 378
    view of success, 325
Aftanas, L., 467
Age-graded influences, 29
Age grading, 215–216
Agentic professions, 375, 376
Age segregation, 215–216
Aggressive, 234
Aggressive-withdrawn, 234
Aguilar, J. P., 145
Ahlbrand, S., 404
Ahmed, M., 42
AIDS, 300–302
Aiken, L. S., 192
Ainette, M., 427
Ainsworth, M., 184
Alarm and mobilization, 458
Alaskan natives, and higher education,
    339
Alasker, F., 158
Albrektsen, G., 462

Alcoholics, 425
Alderfer, 96
Alexander, M. G., 400
Alfieri, T., 404
Alfonso, V. C., 90
Algozzine, B., 337
Ali, L., 277
Ali, S. R., 374
Allen, L., 270
Allen, M., 94, 206, 360
Alley, T. R., 404
Allison, B., 149
Almeida, D. M., 453, 455
Altemus, M., 41
Alvarado, N., 169
Alverdy, J., 456
Amaral, G., 63
Amato, P., 199
Ambivalent attachment pattern, 185
American Academy of Pediatrics, 25
American Association on Mental
    Retardation (AAMR), 333
American Medical Association, 25
American Psychological Association, 25, 113
Amok, 474
Amos, A., 425
Anal stage, 16
Analytical learning style, 81–82
Andersen, S. L., 433
Anderson, C. A., 305, 355, 356, 357, 358, 360,
    362
Anderson, J., 82
Anderson, K. B., 305
Anderson, K. J., 403
Anderson, L. R., 259
Andersson, L., 259
Andrews, J., 295
Androgens, 39, 279
Angier, N., 8
Anorexia nervosa, 58–61
Anthony, J. L., 419
Apter, A., 54
Aptitude tests, 97–98
Aratani, L., 368, 369
Arbona, C., 378
Archer, R. L., 254
Archer, S. L., 149
Archibald, F. F., 259
Arcus, D., 122
Arenson, K. W., 435
Ariès, P., 12, 112, 113
Aristotle, 12, 113

525